# The Mis-Education
# of the Negro

CARTER GODWIN WOODSON

---

**THE MIS-EDUCATION OF THE NEGRO**
by Carter Godwin Woodson

Published by Tribeca Books

ISBN 978-1612930206
Printed in the United States of America

Cover Design by SoHo Books
Cover Photo © Margot Petrowski / dreamstime.

# CONTENTS

# FOREWORD

---

THE thoughts brought together in this volume have been expressed in recent addresses and articles written by the author. From time to time persons deeply interested in the point of view therein presented have requested that these comments on education be made available in book form. To supply this demand this volume is given to the public. In the preparation of the volume the author has not followed in detail the productions upon which most of the book is based. The aim is to set forth only the thought developed in passing from the one to the other. The language in some cases, then, is entirely new; and the work is not a collection of essays. In this way repetition has been avoided except to emphasize the thesis which the author sustains.

Carter Godwin Woodson *Washington, D. C.*

*January, 1933.*

---

# PREFACE

---

HEREIN are recorded not opinions but the reflections of one who for forty years has participated in the education of the black, brown, yellow and white races in both hemispheres and in tropical and temperate regions. Such experience, too, has been with students in all grades from the kindergarten to the university. The author, moreover, has traveled around the world to observe not only modern school systems in various countries but to study the special systems set up by private agencies and governments to educate the natives in their colonies and dependencies. Some of these observations, too, have been checked against more recent studies on a later tour.

Discussing herein the mistakes made in the education of the Negro, the writer frankly admits that he has committed some of these errors himself. In several chapters, moreover, he specifically points out wherein he himself has strayed from the path of wisdom. This book, then, is not intended as a broadside against any particular person or class, but it is given as a corrective for methods which have not produced satisfactory results.

The author does not support the once popular view that in matters of education Negroes are rightfully subjected to the will of others on the presumption that these poor people are not large taxpayers and must be content with charitable contributions to their uplift. The author takes the position that the consumer pays the tax, and as such every individual of the social order should be given unlimited opportunity make the most of himself. Such opportunity, too, should not be determined from without by

3

forces set to direct the proscribed element in a way to redound solely to the good of others but should be determined by the make-up of the Negro himself and by what his environment requires of him.

This new program of uplift, the author contends, should not be decided upon by the trial and error method in the application of devices used in dealing with others in a different situation and at another epoch. Only by careful study of the Negro himself and the life which he is forced to lead can we arrive at the proper procedure in this crisis. The mere imparting of information is not education. Above all things, the effort must result in making a man think and do for himself just as the Jews have done in spite of universal persecution.

In thus estimating the results obtained from the so-called education of the Negro the author does not go to the census figures to show the progress of the race. It may be of no importance to the race to be able to boast today of many times as many "educated" members as it had in 1865. If they are of the wrong kind the increase in numbers will be a disadvantage rather than an advantage. The only question which concerns us here is whether these "educated" persons are actually equipped to face the ordeal before them or unconsciously contribute to their own undoing by perpetuating the regime of the oppressor.

Herein, however, lies no argument for the oft-heard contention that education for the white man should mean one thing and for the Negro a different thing. The element of race does not enter here. It is merely a matter of exercising common sense in approaching people through their environment in order to deal with conditions as they are rather than as you would like to see them or imagine that they are. There may be a difference in method of attack, but the principle remains the same.

"Highly educated" Negroes denounce persons who advocate for the Negro a sort of education different in some respects from that now given the white man. Negroes who have been so long inconvenienced and denied opportunities for development are naturally afraid of anything that sounds like discrimination. They are anxious to have everything the white man has even if it is harmful. The possibility of originality in the Negro, therefore, is discounted one hundred per cent to maintain a nominal equality. If the Whites decide to take up Mormonism the Negroes must follow their lead. If the Whites neglect such a study, then the Negroes must do likewise.

The author, however, does not have such an attitude. He considers the educational system as it has developed both in Europe and America an

4

antiquated process which does not hit the mark even in the case of the needs of the white man himself. If the white man wants to hold on to it, let him do so; but the Negro, so far as he is able, should develop and carry out a program of his own.

The so-called modern education, with all its defects, however, does others so much more good than it does the Negro, because it has been worked out in conformity to the needs of those who have enslaved and oppressed weaker peoples. For example, the philosophy and ethics resulting from our educational system have justified slavery, peonage, segregation, and lynching. The oppressor has the right to exploit, to handicap, and to kill the oppressed. Negroes daily educated in the tenets of such a religion of the strong have accepted the status of the weak as divinely ordained, and during the last three generations of their nominal freedom they have done practically nothing to change it. Their pouting and resolutions indulged in by a few of the race have been of little avail. No systematic effort toward change has been possible, for, taught the same economics, history, philosophy, literature and religion which have established the present code of morals, the Negro's mind has been brought under the control of his oppressor. The problem of holding the Negro down, therefore, is easily solved. When you control a man's thinking you do not have to worry about his actions. You do not have to tell him not to stand here or go yonder. He will find his "proper place" and will stay in it. You do not need to send him to the back door. He will go without being told. In fact, if there is no back door, he will cut one for his special benefit. His education makes it necessary.

The same educational process which inspires and stimulates the oppressor with the thought that he is everything and has accomplished everything worth while, depresses and crushes at the same time the spark of genius in the Negro by making him feel that his race does not amount to much and never will measure up to the standards of other peoples. The Negro thus educated is a hopeless liability of the race.

The difficulty is that the "educated Negro" is compelled to live and move among his own people whom he has been taught to despise. As a rule, therefore, the "educated Negro" prefers to buy his food from a white grocer because he has been taught that the Negro is not clean. It does not matter how often a Negro washes his hands, then, he cannot clean them, and it does not matter how often a white man uses his hands he cannot soil them. The educated Negro, moreover, is disinclined to take part in Negro business, because he has been taught in economics that Negroes cannot operate in this particular sphere. The "educated Negro" gets less and less pleasure out of the Negro church, not on account of its primitiveness and increasing corruption, but because of his preference for the seats of "righteousness" controlled by his oppressor. This has been his education, and nothing else can be expected of him.

If the "educated Negro" could go off and be white he might be happy, but only a mulatto now and then can do this. The large majority of this class, then, must go through life denouncing white people because they are trying to run away from the Blacks and decrying the Blacks because they are not white.

---

# CHAPTER 1
## The Seat on the Trouble

---

THE "educated Negroes" have the attitude of contempt toward their own people because in their own as well as in their mixed schools Negroes are taught to admire the Hebrew, the Greek, the Latin and the Teuton and to despise the African. Of the hundreds of Negro high schools recently examined by an expert in the United States Bureau of Education only eighteen offer a course taking up the history of the Negro, and in most of the Negro colleges and universities where the Negro is thought of, the race is studied only as a problem or dismissed as of little consequence. For example, an officer of a Negro university, thinking that an additional course on the Negro should be given there, called upon a Negro Doctor of Philosophy of the faculty to offer such work. He promptly informed the officer that he knew nothing about the Negro. He did not go to school to waste his time that way. He went to be educated in a system which dismisses the Negro as a nonentity.

At a Negro summer school two years ago, a white instructor gave a course on the Negro, using for his text a work which teaches that whites are superior to the Blacks. When asked by one of the students why he used such a textbook the instructor replied that he wanted them to get that point of view. Even schools for Negroes, then, are places where they must be convinced of their inferiority.

The thought of the inferiority of the Negro is drilled into him in almost every class he enters and in almost every book he studies. If he happens to leave school after he masters the fundamentals, before he finishes high school or reaches college, he will naturally escape some of this bias and may recover in time to be of service to his people.

Practically all of the successful Negroes in this country are of the un-educated type or of that of Negroes who have had no formal education at all. The large majority of the Negroes who have put on the finishing touches of our best colleges are all but worthless in the development of their people. If after leaving school they have the opportunity to give out to Negroes what traducers of the race would like to have it learn such persons may thereby earn a living at teaching or preaching what they have been taught but they never become a constructive force in the development of the race. The so-called school, then, becomes a questionable factor in the life of this despised people.

As another has well said, to handicap a student by teaching him that his black face is a curse and that his struggle to change his condition is hopeless is the worst sort of lynching. It kills one's aspirations and dooms him to vagabondage and crime. It is strange, then, that the friends of truth and the promoters of freedom have not risen up against the present propaganda in the schools and crushed it. This crusade is much more important than the anti-lynching movement, because there would be no lynching if it did not start in the schoolroom. Why not exploit, enslave, or exterminate a class that everybody is taught to regard as inferior?

To be more explicit we may go to the seat of the trouble. Our most widely known scholars have been trained in universities outside of the South. Northern and Western institutions, however, have had no time to deal with matters which concern the Negro especially. They must direct their attention to the problems of the majority of their constituents, and too often they have stimulated their prejudices by referring to the Negro as unworthy of consideration. Most of what these universities have offered as language, mathematics, and science may have served a good purpose, but much of what they have taught as economics, history, literature, religion and philosophy is propaganda and cant that involved a waste of time and misdirected the Negroes thus trained.

And even in the certitude of science or mathematics it has been unfortunate that the approach to the Negro has been borrowed from a "foreign" method. For example, the teaching of arithmetic in the fifth grade in a backward county in Mississippi should mean one thing in the Negro school and a decidedly different thing in the white school. The Negro children, as a rule, come from the homes of tenants and peons who have to migrate annually from plantation to plantation, looking for light which they have never seen. The children from the homes of white planters and merchants live permanently in the midst of calculations, family budgets, and the like, which enable them sometimes to learn more by contact than the Negro can acquire in school. Instead of teaching such Negro children less arithmetic, they should be taught much more of it than the white children, for the latter attend a graded school consolidated by free transportation when the Negroes go to one-room rented hovels to be taught without equipment and by incompetent teachers educated scarcely beyond the eighth grade.

In schools of theology Negroes are taught the interpretation of the Bible worked out by those who have justified segregation and winked at the economic debasement of the Negro sometimes almost to the point of starvation. Deriving their sense of right from this teaching, graduates of such schools can have no message to grip the people whom they have been ill trained to serve. Most of such mis-educated ministers, therefore, preach to benches while illiterate Negro preachers do the best they can in supplying the spiritual needs of the masses.

In the schools of business administration Negroes are trained exclusively in the psychology and economics of Wall Street and are, therefore, made to despise the opportunities to run ice wagons, push banana carts, and sell peanuts among their own people. Foreigners, who have not studied economics but have studied Negroes, take up this business and grow rich.

In schools of journalism Negroes are being taught how to edit such metropolitan dailies as the Chicago Tribune and the New York Times, which would hardly hire a Negro as a janitor; and when these graduates come to the Negro weeklies for employment they are not prepared to function in such establishments, which, to be successful, must be built upon accurate knowledge of the psychology and philosophy of the Negro

When a Negro has finished his education in our schools, then, he has been equipped to begin the life of an Americanized or Europeanized white man, but before he steps from the threshold of his alma mater he is told by his teachers that he must go back to his own people from whom he has been estranged by a vision of ideals which in his disillusionment he will realize that he cannot attain. He goes forth to play his part in life, but he must be both social and bisocial at the same time. While he is a part of the body politic, he is in addition to this a member of a particular race to which he must restrict himself in all matters social. While serving his country he must serve within a special group. While being a good American, he must above all things be a "good Negro"; and to perform this definite function he must learn to stay in a "Negro's place."

For the arduous task of serving a race thus handicapped, however, the Negro graduate has had little or no training at all. The people whom he has been ordered to serve have been belittled by his teachers to the extent that he can hardly find delight in undertaking what his education has led him to think is impossible. Considering his race as blank in achievement, then, he sets out to stimulate their imitation of others The performance is kept up a while; but, like any other effort at meaningless imitation, it results in failure.

Facing this undesirable result, the highly educated Negro often grows sour. He becomes too pessimistic to be a constructive force and usually develops into a chronic fault-finder or a complainant at the bar of public opinion. Often when he sees that the fault lies at the door of the white oppressor whom he is afraid to attack, he turns upon the pioneering Negro who is at work doing the best he can to extricate himself from an uncomfortable predicament.

In this effort to imitate, however, these "educated people" are sincere. They hope to make the Negro conform quickly to the standard of the Whites and thus remove the pretext for the barriers between the races. They do not realize, however, that even if the Negroes do successfully imitate the Whites, nothing new has thereby been accomplished. You simply have a larger number of persons doing what others have been doing. The unusual gifts of the race have not thereby been developed, and an unwilling world, therefore, continues to wonder what the Negro is good for.

These "educated" people, however, decry any such thing as race consciousness; and in some respects they are right. They do not like to hear such expressions as "Negro literature," "Negro poetry," "African art," or "thinking black"; and, roughly speaking, we must concede that such things do not exist. These things did not figure in the courses which they pursued in school, and why should they? "Aren't we all Americans? Then, whatever is American is as much the heritage of the Negro as of any other group in this country."

The "highly educated" contend, moreover, that when the Negro emphasizes these things he invites racial discrimination by recognizing such differentness of the races. The thought that the Negro is one thing and the white man another is the stock-in-trade argument of the Caucasian to justify segregation. Why, then, should the Negro blame the white man for doing what he himself does?

These "highly educated" Negroes, however, fail to see that it is not the Negro who takes this position. The white man forces him to it, and to extricate himself therefrom the Negro leader must so deal with the situation as to develop in the segregated group the power with which they can elevate themselves.

The differentness of races, moreover, is no evidence of superiority or of inferiority. This merely indicates that each race has certain gifts which the others do not possess. It is by the development of these gifts that every race must justify its right to exist.

---

# CHAPTER 2
## How We Missed The Mark

---

How we have arrived at the present state of affairs can be understood only by studying the forces effective in the development of Negro education since it was systematically undertaken immediately after Emancipation. To point out merely the defects as they appear today will be of little benefit to the present and future generations. These things must be viewed in their historic setting. The conditions of today have been determined by what has taken place in the past, and in a careful study of this history we may see more clearly the great theatre of events in which the Negro has played a part. We may understand better what his rôle has been and how well he has functioned in it.

The idea of educating the Negroes after the Civil War was largely a prompting of philanthropy. Their white neighbors failed to assume this responsibility. These black people had been liberated as a result of a sectional conflict out of which their former owners had emerged as victims. From this class, then, the freedmen could not expect much sympathy or cooperation in the effort to prepare themselves to figure as citizens of a modern republic.

From functionaries of the United States Government itself and from those who participated in the conquest of the secessionists early came the plan of teaching these freedmen the simple duties of life as worked out by the Freedmen's Bureau and philanthropic agencies. When systematized this effort became a program for the organization of churches and schools and the direction of them along lines which had been considered most conducive to the progress of people otherwise circumstanced. Here and there some variation was made in this program in view of the fact that the status of the freedmen in no way paralleled that of their friends and teachers, but such thought was not general. When the Negroes in some way would learn to perform the duties which other elements of the population had prepared themselves to discharge they would be duly qualified, it was believed, to function as citizens of the country. Inasmuch as most Negroes lived in the agricultural South, moreover, and only a few of them at first acquired small farms there was little in their life which any one of thought could not have easily understood. The poverty which afflicted them for a generation after Emancipation held them down to the lowest order of society, nominally free but economically enslaved. The participation of the freedmen in government for a few years during the period known as the Reconstruction had little bearing on their situation except that they did join with the uneducated poor Whites in bringing about certain much-desired social reforms, especially in giving the South its first plan of democratic education in providing for a school system at public expense.

Neither this inadequately supported school system nor the struggling higher institutions of a classical order established about the same time, however, connected the Negroes very closely with life as it was. These institutions were concerned rather with life as they hoped to make it. When the Negro found himself deprived of influence in politics, therefore, and at the same time unprepared to participate in the higher functions in the industrial development which this country began to undergo, it soon became evident to him that he was losing ground in the basic things of life. He was spending his time studying about the things which had been or might be, but he was learning little to help him to do better the tasks at hand. Since the Negroes believed that the causes of this untoward condition lay without the race, migration was attempted, and emigration to Africa was again urged. At this psychological moment came the wave of industrial education which swept the country by storm. The educational authorities in the cities and States throughout the Black Belt began to change the course of study to make the training of the Negro conform to this policy.

The missionary teachers from the North in defense of their idea of more liberal training, however, fearlessly attacked this new educational policy; and the Negroes participating in the same dispute arrayed themselves respectively on one side or the other. For a generation thereafter the quarrel as to whether the Negro should be given a classical or a practical education was the dominant topic in Negro schools and churches throughout the United States. Labor was the most important thing of life, it was argued; practical education counted in reaching that end; and the Negro worker must be taught to solve this problem of efficiency before directing attention to other things.

Others more narrow-minded than the advocates of industrial education, seized upon the idea, feeling that, although the Negro must have some semblance of education, it would be a fine stroke to be able to make a distinction between the training given the Negro and that provided for the Whites. Inasmuch as the industrial educational idea rapidly gained ground, too, many Negroes for political purposes began to espouse it; and schools and colleges hoping thereby to obtain money worked out accordingly makeshift provisions for such instruction, although they could not satisfactorily offer it. A few real industrial schools actually equipped themselves for this work and turned out a number of graduates with such preparation.

Unfortunately, however, the affair developed into a sort of battle of words, for in spite of all they said and did the majority of the Negroes, those who did make some effort to obtain an education, did not actually receive either the industrial or the classical education. Negroes attended industrial schools, took such training as was prescribed, and received their diplomas; but few of them developed adequate efficiency to be able to do what they were supposedly trained to do. The schools in which they were educated could not provide for all the experience with machinery which white apprentices trained in factories had. Such industrial education as these Negroes received, then, was merely to master a technique already discarded in progressive centres; and even in less complicated operations of industry these schools had no such facilities as to parallel the numerous processes of factories conducted on the plan of the division of labor. Except what value such training might have in the development of the mind by making practical applications of mathematics and science, then, it was a failure.

The majority of Negro graduates of industrial schools, therefore, have gone into other avenues, and too often into those for which they have had no preparation whatever. Some few who actually prepared for the industrial sphere by self-improvement likewise sought other occupations for the reason that Negroes were generally barred from higher pursuits by trades unions; and, being unable to develop captains of industry to increase the demand for persons in these lines, the Negroes have not opened up many such opportunities for themselves.

During these years, too, the schools for the classical education for Negroes have not done any better. They have proceeded on the basis that every ambitious person needs a liberal education when as a matter of fact this does not necessarily follow. The Negro trained in the advanced phases of literature, philosophy, and politics has been unable to develop far in using his knowledge because of having to function in the lower spheres of the social order. Advanced knowledge of science, mathematics and languages, moreover, has not been much more useful except for mental discipline because of the dearth of opportunity to apply such knowledge among people who were largely common laborers in towns or peons on the plantations. The extent to which such higher education has been successful in leading the Negro to think, which above all is the chief purpose of education, has merely made him more of a malcontent when he can sense the drift of things and appreciate the impossibility of success in visioning conditions as they really are.

It is very clear, therefore, that we do not have in the life of the Negro today a large number of persons who have been benefited by either of the systems about which we have quarreled so long. The number of Negro mechanics and artisans have comparatively declined during the last two generations. The Negroes do not proportionately represent as many skilled laborers as they did before the Civil War. If the practical education which the Negroes received helped to improve the situation so that it is today no worse than what it is, certainly it did not solve the problem as was expected of it.

On the other hand, in spite of much classical education of the Negroes we do not find in the race a large supply of thinkers and philosophers. One excuse is that scholarship among Negroes has been vitiated by the necessity for all of them to combat segregation and fight to retain standing ground in the struggle of the races. Comparatively few American Negroes have produced creditable literature, and still fewer have made any large contribution to philosophy or science. They have not risen to the heights of black men farther removed from the influences of slavery and segregation. For this reason we do not find among American Negroes a Pushkin, a Gomez, a Geoffrey, a Captein or a Dumas. Even men like Roland Hayes and Henry O. Tanner have risen to the higher levels by getting out of this country to relieve themselves of our stifling traditions and to recover from their education.

---

# CHAPTER 3
## How We Drifted Away From The Truth

---

How, then, did the education of the Negro take such a trend? The people who maintained schools for the education of certain Negroes before the Civil War were certainly sincere; and so were the missionary workers who went South to enlighten the freedmen after the results of that conflict had given the Negroes a new status. These earnest workers, however, had more enthusiasm than knowledge. They did not understand the task before them. This undertaking, too, was more of an effort toward social uplift than actual education. Their aim was to transform the Negroes, not to develop them. The freedmen who were to be enlightened were given little thought, for the best friends of the race, ill-taught themselves, followed the traditional curricula of the times which did not take the Negro into consideration except to condemn or pity him.
In geography the races were described in conformity with the program of the usual propaganda to engender in Whites a race hate of the Negro, and in the Negroes contempt for themselves. A poet of distinction was selected to illustrate the physical features of the white race, a bedecked chief of a group those of the red a proud warrior the brown, a prince the yellow, and a savage with a ring in his nose the black The Negro, of course, stood at the foot of the social ladder.

The description of the various parts of the world was worked out according to the same Plan. The parts inhabited by the Caucasian were treated in detail. Less attention was given to the yellow people, still less to the red, very little to the brown, and practically none to the black race. Those people who are far removed from the physical characteristics of the

Caucasians or who do not materially assist them in the domination or exploitation of others were not mentioned except to be belittled or decried.

From the teaching of science the Negro was likewise eliminated. The beginnings of science in various parts of the Orient were mentioned, but the Africans' early advancement in this field was omitted. Students were not told that ancient Africans of the interior knew sufficient science to concoct poisons for arrowheads, to mix durable colors for paintings, to extract metals from nature and refine them for development in the industrial arts. Very little was said about the chemistry in the method of Egyptian embalming which was the product of the mixed breeds of Northern Africa, now known in the modern world as "colored people."

In the study of language in school pupils were made to scoff at the Negro dialect as some peculiar possession of the Negro which they should despise rather than directed to study the background of this language as a broken-down African tongue—in short to understand their own linguistic history, which is certainly more important for them than the study of French Phonetics or Historical Spanish Grammar. To the African language as such no attention was given except in case of the preparation of traders, missionaries and public functionaries to exploit the natives. This number of persons thus trained, of course, constituted a small fraction hardly deserving attention.

From literature the African was excluded altogether. He was not supposed to have expressed any thought worth knowing. The philosophy in the African proverbs and in the rich folklore of that continent was ignored to give preference to that developed on the distant shores of the Mediterranean. Most missionary teachers of the freedmen, like most men of our time, had never read the interesting books of travel in Africa, and had never heard of the Tarikh Es-Soudan.

In the teaching of fine arts these instructors usually started with Greece by showing how that art was influenced from without, but they omitted the African influence which scientists now regard as significant and dominant in early Hellas. They failed to teach the student the Mediterranean Melting Pot with the Negroes from Africa bringing their wares, their ideas and their blood therein to influence the history of Greece, Carthage, and Rome. Making desire father to the thought, our teachers either ignored these influences or endeavored to belittle them by working out theories to the contrary.

The bias did not stop at this point, for it invaded the teaching of the professions. Negro law students were told that they belonged to the most criminal element in the country; and an effort was made to justify the procedure in the seats of injustice where law was interpreted as being one thing for the white man and a different thing for the Negro. In constitutional law the spinelessness of the United States Supreme Court in permitting the judicial nullification of the Fourteenth and Fifteenth Amendments was and still is boldly upheld in our few law schools.

In medical schools Negroes were likewise convinced of their inferiority in being reminded of their rôle as germ carriers. The prevalence of syphilis and tuberculosis among Negroes was especially emphasized without showing that these maladies are more deadly among the Negroes for the reason that they are Caucasian diseases; and since these plagues are new to Negroes, these sufferers have not had time to develop against them the immunity which time has permitted in the Caucasian. Other diseases to which Negroes easily fall prey were mentioned to point out the race as an undesirable element when this condition was due to the Negroes' economic and social status. Little emphasis was placed upon the immunity of the Negro from diseases like yellow fever and influenza which are so disastrous to Whites. Yet, the Whites were not considered inferior because of this differential resistance to these plagues.

In history, of course, the Negro had no place in this curriculum. He was pictured as a human being of the lower order, unable to subject passion to reason, and therefore useful only when made the hewer of wood and the drawer of water for others. No thought was given to the history of Africa except so far as it had been a field of exploitation for the Caucasian. You might study the history as it was offered in our system from the elementary school throughout the university, and you would never hear Africa mentioned except in the negative. You would never thereby learn that Africans first domesticated the sheep, goat, and cow, developed the idea of trial by jury, produced the first stringed instruments, and gave the world its greatest boon in the discovery of iron. You would never know that prior to the Mohammedan invasion about 1000 A.D. these natives in the heart of Africa had developed powerful kingdoms which were later organized as the Songhay Empire on the order of that of the Romans and boasting of similar grandeur.

Unlike other people, then, the Negro, according to this point of view, was an exception to the natural plan of things, and he had no such mission as that of an outstanding contribution to culture. The status of the Negro, then, was justly fixed as that of an inferior. Teachers of Negroes in their first schools after Emancipation did not proclaim any such doctrine, but the content of their curricula justified these inferences.

An observer from outside of the situation naturally inquires why the Negroes, many of whom serve their race as teachers, have not changed this program. These teachers, however, are powerless. Negroes have no control over their education and have little voice in their other affairs pertaining thereto. In a few cases Negroes have been chosen as members of public boards of education, and some have been appointed members of private boards, but these Negroes are always such a small minority that they do not figure in the final working out of the educational program. The education of the Negroes, then, the most important thing in the uplift of the Negroes, is almost entirely in the hands of those who have enslaved them and now segregate them.

With "mis-educated Negroes" in control themselves, however, it is doubtful that the system would be very much different from what it is or that it would rapidly undergo change. The Negroes thus placed in charge would be the products of the same system and would show no more conception of the task at hand than do the Whites who have educated them and shaped their minds as they would have them function. Negro educators of today may have more sympathy and interest in the race than the Whites now exploiting Negro institutions as educators, but the former have no more vision than their competitors. Taught from books of the same bias, trained by Caucasians of the same prejudices or by Negroes of enslaved minds, one generation of Negro teachers after another have served for no higher purpose than to do what they are told to do. In other words, a Negro teacher instructing Negro children is in many respects a white teacher thus engaged, for the program in each case is about the same.

There can be no reasonable objection to the Negro's doing what the white man tells him to do, if the white man tells him to do what is right; but right is purely relative. The present system under the control of the whites trains the Negro to be white and at the same time convinces him of the impropriety or the impossibility of his becoming white. It compels the Negro to become a good Negro for the performance of which his education is ill-suited. For the white man's exploitation of the Negro through economic restriction and segregation the present system is sound and will doubtless continue until this gives place to the saner policy of actual interracial cooperation—not the present farce of racial manipulation in which the Negro is a figurehead. History does not furnish a case of the elevation of a people by ignoring the thought and aspiration of the people thus served.

This is slightly dangerous ground here, however, for the Negro's mind has been all but perfectly enslaved in that he has been trained to think what is desired of him. The "highly educated" Negroes do not like to hear anything uttered against this procedure because they make their living in this way, and they feel that they must defend the system. Few mis-educated Negroes ever act otherwise; and, if they so express themselves, they are easily crushed by the large majority to the contrary so that the procession may move on without interruption.

The result, then, is that the Negroes thus mis-educated are of no service to themselves and none to the white man. The white man does not need the Negroes' professional, commercial or industrial assistance; and as a result of the multiplication of mechanical appliances he no longer needs them in drudgery or menial service. The "highly educated" Negroes, moreover, do not need the Negro professional or commercial classes because Negroes have been taught that Whites can serve them more efficiently in these spheres. Reduced, then, to teaching and preaching, the Negroes will have no outlet but to go down a blind alley, if the sort of education which they are now receiving is to enable them to find the way out of their present difficulties.

---

# CHAPTER 4
## Education Under Outside Control

---

"IN the new program of educating the Negro what would become of the white teachers of the race?" some one recently inquired. This is a simple question requiring only a brief answer. The remaining few Christian workers who went South not so long after the Civil War and established schools and churches to lay the foundation on which we should now be building more wisely than we do, we would honor as a martyred throng. Anathema be upon him who would utter a word derogatory to the record of these heroes and heroines! We would pay high tribute also to unselfish Southerners like Hay-good, Curry, Ruffner, Northern, and Vance, and to white men of our time, who believe that the only way to elevate people is to help them to help themselves.

The unfortunate successors of the Northern missionary teachers of Negroes, however, have thoroughly demonstrated that they have no useful function in the life of the Negro. They have not the spirit of their predecessors and do not measure up to the requirements of educators desired in accredited colleges. If Negro institutions are to be as efficient as those for the Whites in the South the same high standard for the educators to direct them should be maintained. Negro schools cannot go forward with such a load of inefficiency and especially when the white presidents of these institutions are often less scholarly than Negroes who have to serve under them.

By law and custom the white presidents and teachers of Negro schools are prevented from participating freely in the life of the Negro. They occupy, therefore, a most uncomfortable dual position. When the author once taught in a school with a mixed faculty the white women connected with the institution would bow to him in patronizing fashion when on the campus, but elsewhere they did not see him. A white president of one Negro school never entertains a Negro in his home, preferring to shift such guests to the students' dining-room. Another white president of a Negro college maintains on the campus a guest cottage which Negroes can enter only as servants. Still another such functionary does not allow students to enter his home through the front door. Negroes trained under such conditions without protest become downright cowards, and in life will continue as slaves in spite of their nominal emancipation.

"What different method of approach or what sort of appeal would one make to the Negro child that cannot be made just as well by a white teacher?" some one asked not long ago. To be frank we must concede that there is no particular body of facts that Negro teachers can impart to children of their own race that may not be just as easily presented by persons of another race if they have the same attitude as Negro teachers; but in most cases tradition, race hate, segregation, and terrorism make such a thing impossible. The only thing to do in this case, then, is to deal with the situation as it is.

Yet we should not take the position that a qualified white person should not teach in a Negro school. For certain work which temporarily some Whites may be able to do better than the Negroes there can be no objection to such service, but if the Negro is to be forced to live in the ghetto he can more easily develop out of it under his own leadership than under that which is super-imposed. The Negro will never be able to show all of his originality as long as his efforts are directed from without by those who socially proscribe him. Such "friends" will unconsciously keep him in the ghetto.

Herein, however, the emphasis is not upon the necessity for separate systems but upon the need for common sense schools and teachers who understand and continue in sympathy with those whom they instruct. Those who take the position to the contrary have the idea that education is merely a process of imparting information. One who can give out these things or devise an easy plan for so doing, then, is an educator. In a sense this is true, but it accounts for most of the troubles of the Negro. Real education means to inspire people to live more abundantly, to learn to begin with life as they find it and make it better, but the instruction so far given Negroes in colleges and universities has worked to the contrary. In most cases such graduates have merely increased the number of malcontents who offer no program for changing the undesirable conditions about which they complain. One should rely upon protest only when it is supported by a constructive program.

Unfortunately Negroes who think as the author does and dare express themselves are branded as opponents of interracial cooperation. As a matter of fact, however, such Negroes are the real workers in carrying out a program of interracial effort. Cooperation implies equality of the participants in the particular task at hand. On the contrary, however, the usual way now is for the Whites to work out their plans behind closed doors, have them approved by a few Negroes serving nominally on a board, and then employ a White or mixed staff to carry out their program. This is not interracial cooperation. It is merely the ancient idea of calling upon the "inferior" to carry out the orders of the "superior." To express it in post-classic language, as did Jessie O. Thomas, "The Negroes do the `coing' and the Whites the `operating.'"

This unsound attitude of the "friends" of the Negro is due to the persistence of the mediaeval idea of controlling underprivileged classes. Behind closed doors these "friends" say you need to be careful in advancing Negroes to commanding positions unless it can be determined beforehand that they will do what they are told to do. You can never tell when some Negroes will break out and embarrass their "friends." After being advanced to positions of influence some of them have been known to run amuck and advocate social equality or demand for their race the privileges of democracy when they should restrict themselves to education and religious development.

It is often said, too, that the time is not ripe for Negroes to take over the administration of their institutions, for they do not have the contacts for raising money; but what becomes of this argument when we remember what Booker T. Washington did for Tuskegee and observe what R. R. Moton and John Hope are doing today? As the first Negro president of Howard University Mordecai W. Johnson has raised more money for that institution among philanthropists than all of its former presidents combined. Furthermore, if, after three generations the Negro colleges have not produced men qualified to administer their affairs, such an admission is an eloquent argument that they have failed ingloriously and should be immediately closed.

Recently some one asked me how I connect my criticism of the higher education of the Negroes with new developments in this sphere and especially with the four universities in the South which are to be made possible by the millions obtained from governments, boards, and philanthropists. I believe that the establishment of these four centres of learning at Washington, Atlanta, Nashville, and New Orleans can be so carried out as to mark an epoch in the development of the Negro race. On the other hand, there is just as much possibility for a colossal failure of the whole scheme. If these institutions are to be the replica of universities like Harvard, Yale, Columbia and Chicago, if the men who are to administer them and teach in them are to be the products of roll-top desk theorists who have never touched the life of the Negro, the money thus invested will be just as profitably spent if it is used to buy peanuts to throw at the animals in a circus.

Some of the thought behind the new educational movement is to provide in the South for educating the Negroes who are now crowding Northern universities, especially the medical schools, many of which will not admit Negroes because of the racial friction in hospital practice. In the rush merely to make special provisions for these "undesirable students," however, the institutions which are to train them may be established on false ideas and make the same blunders of the smaller institutions which have preceded them. It will hardly help a poisoned patient to give him a large dose of poison.

In higher institutions for Negroes, organized along lines required for people differently circumstanced, some few may profit by being further grounded in the fundamentals, others may become more adept in the exploitation of their people, and a smaller number may cross the divide and join the Whites in useful service; but the large majority of the products of such institutions will increase rather than diminish the load which the masses have had to carry ever since their emancipation. Such ill-prepared workers will have no foundation upon which to build. The education of any people should begin with the people themselves, but Negroes thus trained have been dreaming about the ancients of Europe and about those who have tried to imitate them.

In a course at Harvard, for example, students were required to find out whether Pericles was justly charged with trying to supplant the worship of Jupiter with that of Juno. Since that time Negroes thus engaged have learned that they would have been much better prepared for work among the Negroes in the Black Belt if they had spent that time learning why John Jasper of "sun-do-move" fame joined with Joshua in contending that the planet stood still "in the middle of the line while he fought the battle the second time."

Talking the other day with one of the men now giving the millions to build the four Negro universities in the South, however, I find that he is of the opinion that accredited institutions can be established in mushroom fashion with theorists out of touch with the people. In other words, you can go almost anywhere and build a three million dollar plant, place in charge a white man to do what you want accomplished, and in a short while he can secure or have trained to order the men necessary to make a university. "We want here," he will say, "a man who has his Master's degree in English. Send me another who has his Doctor's degree in sociology, and I can use one more in physics."

Now, experience has shown that men of this type may "fill in," but a university cannot be established with such raw recruits. The author once had some experience in trying to man a college in this fashion, and the result was a story that would make an interesting headline for the newspapers. When Dr. William Bainey Harper was establishing the University of Chicago he called to the headship of the various departments only men who had distinguished themselves in the creative world. Some had advanced degrees, and some had not. Several of them had never done any formal graduate work at all. All of them, however, were men whose thought was moving the world. It may be argued that the Negroes have no such men and must have them trained, but such a thing cannot be forced as we are now doing it. It would be much better to stimulate the development of the more progressive teachers of old than experiment with novices produced by the degradation of higher education.

The degradation of the doctorate especially dawned upon the author the other day more clearly than ever when a friend of his rushed into his office saying, "I have been trying to see you for several days. I have just failed to get a job for which I had been working, and I am told that I cannot expect a promotion until I get my `darkter's 'gree.'" That is what he called it. He could not even pronounce the words, but he is determined to have his "darkter's 'gree" to get the job in sight.

This shameful status of higher education is due in a large measure to low standards of institutions with a tendency toward the diplomamill procedure. To get a job or to hold one you go in and stay until they "grind" you out a "darkter's 'gree." And you do not have to worry any further. The assumption is that almost any school will be glad to have you thereafter, and you will receive a large salary.

Investigation has shown, however, that men who have the doctorate not only lose touch with the common people, but they do not do as much creative work as those of less formal education. After having this honor conferred upon them, these so-called scholars often rest on their oars. Few persons have thought of the seriousness of such inertia among men who are put in the lead of things because of meeting statutory requirements of frontier universities which are not on the frontier.

The General Education Board and the Julius Rosenwald Fund have a policy which may be a partial solution of the undeveloped Negro college instructor's problem. These foundations are giving Negro teachers scholarships to improve themselves for work in the sphere in which they are now laboring in the South. These boards, as a rule, do not send one to school to work for the Doctor's degree. If they find a man of experience and good judgment, showing possibilities for growth, they will provide for him to study a year or more to refresh his mind with whatever there is new in his field. Experience has shown that teachers thus helped have later done much better work than Doctors of Philosophy made to order. The Northern universities, moreover, cannot do graduate work for Negroes along certain lines when they are concentrating on the educational needs of people otherwise circumstanced. The graduate school for Negroes studying chemistry is with George W. Carver at Tuskegee. At least a hundred youths should wait daily upon the words of this scientist to be able to pass on to the generations unborn his great knowledge of agricultural chemistry. Negroes desiring to specialize in agriculture should do it with workers like T. M. Campbell and B. F. Hubert among the Negro farmers of the South.

In education itself the situation is the same. Neither Columbia nor Chicago can give an advanced course in Negro rural education, for their work in education is based primarily upon what they know of the educational needs of the Whites. Such work for Negroes must be done under the direction of the trail blazers who are building school houses and reconstructing the educational program of those in the backwoods. Leaders of this type can supply the foundation upon which a university of realistic education may be established.

We offer no argument here against earning advanced degrees, but these should come as honors conferred for training crowned with scholastic distinction, not to enable a man to increase his salary or find a better paying position. The schools which are now directing attention exclusively to these external marks of learning will not contribute much to the uplift of the Negro.

In Cleveland not long ago the author found at the Western Reserve University something unusually encouraging. A native of Mississippi, a white man trained in a Northern university and now serving as a professor in one, has under him in sociology a Negro student from Georgia. For his dissertation this Negro is collecting the sayings of his people in every-day life — their morning greetings, their remarks about the weather, their comments on things which happen around them, their reactions to things which strike them as unusual, and their efforts to interpret life as the panorama passes before them. This white Mississippian and black Georgian are on the right way to understand the Negro and, if they do not fall out about social equality, they will serve the Negro much better than those who are trying to find out whether Henry VIII lusted more after Anne Boleyn than after Catherine of Aragon or whether Elizabeth was justly styled as more untruthful than Philip II of Spain.

---

# CHAPTER 5
## The Failure To Learn To Make A Living

---

THE greatest indictment of such education as Negroes have received, however, is that they have thereby learned little as to making a living, the first essential in civilization. Rural Negroes have always known something about agriculture, and in a country where land is abundant they have been able to make some sort of living on the soil even though they have not always employed scientific methods of farming. In industry where the competition is keener, however, what the Negro has learned in school has had little bearing on the situation, as pointed out above. In business the rôle of education as a factor in the uplift of the Negro has been still less significant. The Negroes of today are unable to employ one another, and the Whites are inclined to call on Negroes only when workers of their own race have been taken care of. For the solution of this problem the "mis-educated" Negro has offered no remedy whatever.

What Negroes are now being taught does not bring their minds into harmony with life as they must face it. When a Negro student works his way through college by polishing shoes he does not think of making a special study of the science underlying the production and distribution of leather and its products that he may some day figure in this sphere. The Negro boy sent to college by a mechanic seldom dreams of learning mechanical engineering to build upon the foundation his father has laid, that in years to come he may figure as a contractor or a consulting engineer. The Negro girl who goes to college hardly wants to return to her mother if she is a washerwoman, but this girl should come back with sufficient knowledge of physics and chemistry and business administration to use her mother's work as a nucleus for a modern steam laundry. A white professor of a university recently resigned his position to become rich by running a laundry for Negroes in a Southern city. A Negro college instructor would have considered such a suggestion an insult. The so-called education of Negro college graduates leads them to throw away opportunities which they have and to go in quest of those which they do not find.

In the case of the white youth in this country, they can choose their courses more at random and still succeed because of numerous opportunities offered by their people, but even they show so much more wisdom than do Negroes. For example, a year or two after the author left Harvard he found out West a schoolmate who was studying wool. "How did you happen to go into this sort of thing?" the author inquired. His people, the former replied, had had some experience in wool, and in college he prepared for this work. On the contrary, the author studied Aristotle, Plato, Marsiglio of Padua, and Pascasius Rathbertus when he was in college. His friend who studied wool, however, is now independently rich and has sufficient leisure to enjoy the cultural side of life which his knowledge of the science underlying his business developed, but the author has to make his living by begging for a struggling cause.

An observer recently saw at the market near his office a striking example of this inefficiency of our system. He often goes over there at noon to buy a bit of fruit and to talk with a young woman who successfully conducts a fruit stand there in cooperation with her mother. Some years ago he tried to teach her in high school; but her memory was poor, and she could not understand what he was trying to do. She stayed a few weeks, smiling at the others who toiled, and finally left to assist her mother in business. She learned from her mother, however, how to make a living and be happy.

This observer was reminded of this young woman soon thereafter when there came to visit him a friend who succeeded in mastering everything taught in high school at that time and later distinguished himself in college. This highly educated man brought with him a complaint against life. Having had extreme difficulty in finding an opportunity to do what he is trained to do, he has thought several times of committing suicide. A friend encouraged this despondent man to go ahead and do it. The sooner the better. The food and air which he is now consuming may then go to keep alive some one who is in touch with life and able to grapple with its problems. This man has been educated away from the fruit stand.

This friend had been trying to convince this misfit of the unusual opportunities for the Negroes in business, but he reprimanded his adviser for urging him to take up such a task when most Negroes thus engaged have been failures.

"If we invest our money in some enterprise of our own," said he, "those in charge will misuse or misappropriate it. I have learned from my study of economics that we had just as well keep on throwing it away." Upon investigation, however, it was discovered that this complainant and most others like him have never invested anything in any of the Negro enterprises, although they have tried to make a living by exploiting them. But they feel a bit guilty on this account, and when they have some apparent ground for fault-finding they try to satisfy their conscience which all but condemns them for their suicidal course of getting all they can out of the race while giving nothing back to it.

Gossiping and scandal-mongering Negroes, of course, come to their assistance. Mis-educated by the oppressors of the race, such Negroes expect the Negro business man to fail anyway. They seize, then, upon unfavorable reports, exaggerate the situation, and circulate falsehoods throughout the world to their own undoing. You read such headlines as GREATEST NEGRO BUSINESS FAILS, NEGRO BANK ROBBED BY ITS OFFICERS, and THE TWILIGHT OF NEGRO BUSINESS. The mis-educated Negroes, then, stand by saying:

"I told you so. Negroes cannot run business. My professors pointed that out to me years ago when I studied economics in college; and I never intend to put any of my money in any Negro enterprise." Yet, investigation shows that in proportion to the amount of capital invested Negro enterprises manifest about as much strength as businesses of others similarly situated. Negro business men have made mistakes, and they are still making them; but the weak link in the chain is that they are not properly supported and do not always grow strong enough to pass through a crisis. The Negro business man, then, has not failed so much as he has failed to get support of Negroes who should be mentally developed sufficiently to see the wisdom of supporting such enterprises. Now the "highly educated" Negroes who have studied economics at Harvard, Yale, Columbia, and Chicago, will say that the Negro cannot succeed in business because their professors who have never had a moment's experience in this sphere have written accordingly. The Whites, they say, have the control of the natural resources and so monopolize the production of raw materials as to eliminate the competition of the Negro. Apparently this is true. All things being equal from the point of view of the oppressor, he sees that the Negro cannot meet the test.

The impatient, "highly educated" Negroes, therefore, say that since under the present system of capitalism the Negro has no chance to toil upward in the economic sphere, the only hope for bettering his condition in this respect is through socialism, the overthrow of the present economic régime, and the inauguration of popular control of resources and agencies which are now being operated for personal gain. This thought is gaining ground among Negroes in this country, and it is rapidly sweeping them into the ranks of what are commonly known as "Communists."

There can be no objection to this radical change, if it brings with it some unselfish genius to do the task better than it is now being done under the present régime of competition. Russia so far has failed to do well this particular thing under a proletarian dictatorship in an agricultural country. But whether this millennium comes or not, the capitalistic system is so strongly intrenched at present that the radicals must struggle many years to overthrow it; and if the Negro has to wait until that time to try to improve his condition he will be starved out so soon that he will not he here to tell the story. The Negro, therefore, like all other oppressed people, must learn to do the so-called "impossible."

The "uneducated" Negro business man, however, is actually at work doing the very thing which the "mis-educated" Negro has been taught to believe cannot be done. This much-handicapped Negro business man could do better if he had some assistance, but our schools are turning out men who do as much to impede the progress of the Negro in business as they do to help him. The trouble is that they do not think for themselves. If the "highly educated" Negro would forget most of the untried theories taught him in school, if he could see through the propaganda which has been instilled into his mind under the pretext of education, if he would fall in love with his own people and begin to sacrifice for their uplift — if the "highly educated" Negro would do these things, he could solve some of the problems now confronting the race.

During recent years we have heard much of education in business administration departments in Negro colleges; but if they be judged by the products turned out by these departments they are not worth a "continental." The teachers in this field are not prepared to do the work, and the trustees of our institutions are spending their time with trifles instead of addressing themselves to the study of a situation which threatens the Negro with economic extermination.

Recently the author saw the need for a change of attitude when a young woman came almost directly to his office after her graduation from a business school to seek employment.

After hearing her story he finally told her that he would give her a trial at fifteen dollars a week.

"Fifteen dollars a week!" she cried, "I cannot live on that, sir."

"I do not see why you cannot," he replied. "You have lived for some time already, and you say that you have never had permanent employment, and you have none at all now."

"But a woman has to dress and to pay board," said she; "and how can she do it on such a pittance?"

The amount offered was small, but it was a great deal more than she is worth at present. In fact, during the first six or nine months of her connection with some enterprise it will be of more service to her than she will be to the firm. Coming out of school without experience, she will be a drag on a business until she learns to discharge some definite function in it. Instead of requiring the firm to pay her she should pay it for training her. Negro business today, then, finds the "mis-educated employees" its heaviest burden. Thousands of graduates of white business schools spend years in establishments in undergoing apprenticeship without pay and rejoice to have the opportunity thus to learn how to do things.

The schools in which Negroes are now being trained, however, do not give our young people this point of view. They may occasionally learn the elements of stenography and accounting, but they do not learn how to apply what they have studied. The training which they undergo gives a false conception of life when they believe that the business world owes them a position of leadership. They have the idea of business training that we used to have of teaching when it was thought that we could teach anything we had studied.

Graduates of our business schools lack the courage to throw themselves upon their resources and work for a commission. The large majority of them want to be sure of receiving a certain amount at the end of the week or month. They do not seem to realize that the great strides in business have been made by paying men according to what they do. Persons with such false impressions of life are not good representatives of schools of business administration.

Not long ago a firm of Washington, D. C., appealed to the graduates of several of our colleges and offered them an inviting proposition on the commission basis, but only five of the hundreds appealed to responded and only two of the five gave satisfaction. Another would have succeeded, but he was not honest in handling money because he had learned to purloin the treasury of the athletic organization while in college. All of the others, however, were anxious to serve somewhere in an office for a small wage a week.

Recently one of the large insurance companies selected for special training in this line fifteen college graduates of our accredited institutions and financed their special training in insurance. Only one of the number, however, rendered efficient service in this field. They all abandoned the effort after a few days' trial and accepted work in hotels and with the Pullman Company, or they went into teaching or something else with a fixed stipend until they could enter upon the practice of professions. The thought of the immediate reward, shortsightedness, and the lack of vision and courage to struggle and win the fight made them failures to begin with. They are unwilling to throw aside their coats and collars and do the groundwork of Negro business and thus make opportunities for themselves instead of begging others for a chance.

The educated Negro from the point of view of commerce and industry, then, shows no mental power to understand the situation which he finds. He has apparently read his race out of that sphere, and with the exception of what the illiterate Negroes can do blindly the field is left wide open for foreign exploitation. Foreigners see this opportunity as soon as they reach our shores and begin to manufacture and sell to Negroes especially such things as caps, neckties, and housedresses which may be produced at a small cost and under ordinary circumstances. The main problem with the Negro in this field, however, is salesmanship; that is where he is weak.

It is unfortunate, too, that the educated Negro does not understand or is unwilling to start small enterprises which make the larger ones possible. If he cannot proceed according to the methods of the gigantic corporations about which he reads in books, he does not know how to take hold of things and organize the communities of the poor along lines of small businesses. Such training is necessary, for the large majority of Negroes conducting enterprises have not learned business methods and do not understand the possibilities of the field in which they operate. Most of them in the beginning had had no experience, and started out with such knowledge as they could acquire by observing some one's business from the outside. One of them, for example, had waited on a white business club in passing the members a box of cigars or bringing a pitcher of water. When they began to discuss business, however, he had to leave the room. About the only time he could see them in action was when they were at play, indulging in extravagances which the Negro learned to take up before he could afford them.

Negro businesses thus handicapped, therefore, have not developed stability and the capacity for growth. Practically all worth while Negro businesses which were flourishing in 1900 are not existing today. How did this happen? Well, Negro business men have too much to do. They have not time to read the business literature and study the market upon which they depend, and they may not be sufficiently trained to do these things. They are usually operating in the dark or by the hit-or-miss method. They cannot secure intelligent guidance because the schools are not turning out men properly trained to take up Negro business as it is to develop and make it what it ought to be rather than find fault with it. Too often when the founder dies, then, the business dies with him; or it goes to pieces soon after he passes away, for nobody has come into sufficiently close contact with him to learn the secret of his success in spite of his handicaps.

The business among Negroes, too, continues individualistic in spite of advice to the contrary. The founder does not take kindly to the cooperative plan, and such business education as we now give the youth does not make their suggestions to this effect convincing. If the founder happens to be unusually successful, too, the business may outgrow his knowledge, and becoming too unwieldy in his hands, may go to pieces by errors of judgment; or because of mismanagement it may go into the hands of Whites who are usually called in at the last hour to do what they call refinancing but what really means the actual taking over of the business from the Negroes. The Negroes, then, finally withdraw their patronage because they realize that it is no longer an enterprise of the race, and the chapter is closed.

All of the failures of the Negro business, however, are not due to troubles from without. Often the Negro business man lacks common sense. The Negro in business, for example, too easily becomes a social "lion." He sometimes plunges into the leadership in local matters. He becomes popular in restricted circles, and men of less magnetism grow jealous of his inroads.

He learns how richer men of other races waste money. He builds a finer home than anybody else in the community, and in his social program he does not provide for much contact with the very people upon whom he must depend for patronage. He has the finest car, the most expensive dress, the best summer home, and so far outdistances his competitors in society that they often set to work in child-like fashion to bring him down to their level.

---

# CHAPTER 6
## The Educated Negro Leaves the Masses

---

One of the most striking evidences of the failure of higher education among Negroes is their estrangement from the masses, the very people upon whom they must eventually count for carrying out a program of progress. Of this the Negro churches supply the most striking illustration. The large majority of Negro communicants still belong to these churches, but the more education the Negroes undergo the less comfort they seem to find in these evangelical groups. These churches do not measure up to the standard set by the university preachers of the Northern centers of learning. Most Negroes returning as finished products from such institutions, then, are forever lost to the popular Negro churches. The unchurched of this class do not become members of such congregations, and those who have thus connected themselves remain chiefly for political or personal reasons and tend to become communicants in name only.

The Negro church, however, although not a shadow of what it ought to be, is the great asset of the race. It is a part of the capital that the race must invest to make its future. The Negro church, has taken the lead in education in the schools of the race, it has supplied a forum for the thought of the "highly educated" Negro, it has originated a large portion of the business controlled by Negroes, and in many cases it has made it possible for Negro professional men to exist. It is unfortunate, then, that these classes do not do more to develop the institution. In thus neglecting it they are throwing away what they have, to obtain something which they think they need. In many respects, then, the Negro church during recent generations has become corrupt. It could be improved, but those Negroes who can help the institution have deserted it to exploiters, grafters, and libertines. The "highly educated" Negroes have turned away from the people in the churches, and the gap between the masses and the "talented tenth" is rapidly widening.

Of this many examples may be cited. When the author recently attended in Washington, D. C., one of the popular Negro churches with a membership of several thousand he saw a striking case in evidence. While sitting there he thought of what a power this group could become under the honest leadership of intelligent men and women. Social uplift, business, public welfare—all have their possibilities there if a score or more of our "highly educated" Negroes would work with these people at that center. Looking carefully throughout the audience for such persons, however, he recognized only two college graduates, Kelly Miller and himself; but the former had come to receive from the church a donation to the Community Chest, and the author had come according to appointment to make an appeal in behalf of Miss Nannie H. Burroughs' school. Neither one had manifested any interest in that particular church. This is the way most of them receive attention from our "talented tenth."

Some "highly educated" Negroes say that they have not lost their interest in religion, that they have gone into churches with a more intellectual atmosphere in keeping with their new thoughts and aspirations. And then there is a sort of contagious fever which takes away from the churches of their youth others of less formal education. Talking with a friend from Alabama, the other day, the author found out that after her father had died and she had moved to Washington she forsook the Baptist church in which he had been a prominent worker and joined a ritualistic church which is more fashionable.

Such a change of faith is all right in a sense, for no sensible person today would dare to make an argument in favor of any particular religion. Religion is but religion, if the people live up to the faith they profess. What is said here with respect to the popular churches of Negroes, which happen to be chiefly Methodist and Baptist, would hold also if they were mainly Catholic and Episcopal, provided the large majority of Negroes belonged to those churches. The point here is that the ritualistic churches into which these Negroes have gone do not touch the masses, and they show no promising future for racial development. Such institutions are controlled by those who offer the Negroes only limited opportunity and then sometimes on the condition that they be segregated in the court of the gentiles outside of the temple of Jehovah.

How an "educated Negro" can thus leave the church of his people and accept such Jim Crowism has always been a puzzle. He cannot be a thinking man. It may be a sort of slave psychology which causes this preference for the leadership of the oppressor. The excuse sometimes given for seeking such religious leadership is that the Negro evangelical churches are "fogy," but a thinking man would rather be behind the times and have his self-respect than compromise his manhood by accepting segregation. They say that in some of the Negro churches bishoprics are actually bought, but it is better for the Negro to belong to a church where one can secure a bishopric by purchase than be a member of one which would deny the promotion on account of color.

With respect to developing the masses, then, the Negro race has lost ground in recent years. In 1880 when the Negroes had begun to make themselves felt in teaching, the attitude of the leaders was different from what it is today. At that time men went off to school to prepare themselves for the uplift of a downtrodden people. In our time too many Negroes go to school to memorize certain facts to pass examinations for jobs. After they obtain these positions they pay little attention to humanity. This attitude of the "educated Negro" toward the masses results partly from the general trend of all persons toward selfishness, but it works more disastrously among the Negroes than among the Whites because the lower classes of the latter have had so much more opportunity.

For some time the author has been making a special study of the Negroes in the City of Washington to compare their condition of today with that of the past. Now although the "highly educated" Negroes of the District of Columbia have multiplied and apparently are in better circumstances than ever, the masses show almost as much backwardness as they did in 1880.

Sometimes you find as many as two or three store-front churches in a single block where Negroes indulge in heathen-like practices which could hardly be equaled in the jungle. The Negroes in Africa have not descended to such depths. Although born and brought up in the Black Belt of the South the author never saw such idolatrous tendencies as he has seen under the dome of the Capitol.

Such conditions show that the undeveloped Negro has been abandoned by those who should help him. The educated white man, said an observer recently, differs from the "educated Negro" who so readily forsakes the belated element of his race. When a white man sees persons of his own race trending downward to a level of disgrace he does not rest until he works out some plan to lift such unfortunates to higher ground; but the Negro forgets the delinquents of his race and goes his way to feather his own nest, as he has done in leaving the masses in the popular churches.

This is sad indeed, for the Negro church is the only institution the race controls. With the exception of the feeble efforts of a few all but starved-out institutions, the education of the Negroes is controlled by the other element; and save the dramatization of practical education by Booker T. Washington, Negroes have not influenced the system at all in America. In business, the lack of capital, credit, and experience has prevented large undertakings to accumulate the wealth necessary for the ease and comfort essential to higher culture.

In the church, however, the Negro has had sufficient freedom to develop this institution in his own way; but he has failed to do so. His religion is merely a loan from the Whites who have enslaved and segregated the Negroes; and the organization, though largely an independent Negro institution is dominated by the thought of the oppressors of the race. The "educated" Negro minister is so trained as to drift away from the masses and the illiterate preachers into whose hands the people inevitably fall are unable to develop a doctrine and procedure of their own. The dominant thought is to make use of the dogma of the Whites as means to an end. Whether the system is what it should be or not it serves the purpose.

In chameleon-like fashion the Negro has taken up almost everything religious which has come along instead of thinking for himself. The English split off from the Catholics because Henry VIII had difficulty in getting sanction from the Church to satisfy his lust for amorous women, and Negroes went with this ilk, singing "God save the King." Others later said the thing necessary is baptism by immersion; and the Negroes joined them as Baptists.

Another circle of promoters next said we must have a new method of doing things and we shall call ourselves Methodists; and the Negroes, then, embraced that faith. The Methodists and Baptists split up further on account of the custom of holding slaves; and the Negroes arrayed themselves on the respective sides. The religious agitators divided still more on questions beyond human power to understand; and the Negroes started out in similar fashion to imitate them. For example, thirty of the two hundred and thirteen religious bodies reported in 1926 were exclusively Negro, while thirty which were primarily white denominations had one or more Negro churches among their number. In other words, Negroes have gone into practically all sects established by the Whites; and, in addition to these, they have established thirty of their own to give the system further complication and subdivision. The situation in these churches is aggravated, too, by having too many ministers and about five times as many supervisory officials as a church embracing all Negro communicants would actually need. All of the Negro Methodists in the world, if united, would not need more than twelve bishops, and these would have time to direct the affairs of both Methodists and Baptists in a united church. There is no need for three or four bishops, each teaching the same faith and practice while duplicating the work of the other in the same area merely because a long time ago somebody following the ignorant oppressors of the race in these churches committed the sin of dissension and strife. For all of this unnecessary expense impoverished Negroes have to pay.

The "theology" of "foreigners," too, is the important factor in this disunion of churches and the burden which they impose on an unenlightened people. Theologians have been the "bane of bliss and source of woe." While bringing the joy of conquest to their own camp they have confused the world with disputes which have divided the church and stimulated division and subdivision to the extent that it no longer functions as a Christian agency for the uplift of all men.

To begin with, theology is of pagan origin Albert Magnus and Thomas Aquinas worked out the first system of it by applying to religious discussion the logic of Aristotle, a pagan philosopher, who believed neither in the creation of the world nor the immortality of the soul. At best it was degenerate learning, based upon the theory that knowledge is gained by the mind working upon itself rather than upon matter or through sense perception. The world was, therefore, confused with the discussion of absurdities as it is today by those of prominent churchmen. By their peculiar "reasoning," too, theologians have sanctioned most of the ills of the ages. They justified the Inquisition, serfdom, and slavery. Theologians of our time defend segregation and the annihilation of one race by the other. They have drifted away from righteousness into an effort to make wrong seem to be right.

While we must hold the Negroes responsible for following these ignorant theorists, we should not charge to their account the origination of this nonsense with which they have confused thoughtless people. As said above, the Negro has been so busy doing what he is told to do that he has not stopped long enough to think about the meaning of these things. He

43

has borrowed the ideas of his traducers instead of delving into things and working out some thought of his own.

Some Negro leaders of these religious factions know better, but they hold their following by keeping the people divided, in emphasizing non-essentials the insignificance of which the average man may not appreciate. The "highly educated" Negroes who know better than to follow these unprincipled men have abandoned these popular churches.

While serving as the avenue of the oppressor's propaganda, the Negro church, although doing some good, has prevented the union of diverse elements and has kept the race too weak to overcome foes who have purposely taught Negroes how to quarrel and fight about trifles until their enemies can overcome them. This is the keynote to the control of the so-called inferior races by the self-styled superior. The one thinks and plans while the other in excited fashion seizes upon and destroys his brother with whom he should cooperate.

---

# CHAPTER 7
## Dissension and Weakness

---

In recent years the churches in enlightened centers have devoted less attention to dissension than formerly, but in the rural districts and small cities they have not changed much; and neither in urban communities nor in the country has any one succeeded in bringing these churches together to work for their general welfare. The militant sects are still fighting one another, and in addition to this the members of these sects are contending among themselves. The spirit of Christ cannot dwell in such an atmosphere.

Recent experiences show that these dissensions are about as rank as ever. For example, a rural community, in which an observer spent three weeks a year ago, has no church at all, although eight or ten families live there. No church can thrive among them because, with one or two exceptions, each family represents a different denomination, and the sectarian bias is so pronounced that one will not accept the procedure of the other. Each one loves his fellow man if he thinks as he does; but if his fellow man does not, he hates and shuns him.

In another rural community where the same observer recently spent two weeks he found a small and poorly attended Methodist church. Worshiping there one Sunday morning, he counted only four persons who lived in the community. Others might have come, for there was no other church for them in that place; but this particular church was not of their faith, and their number was too small to justify the establishment of one to their liking. The support given the unfortunate pastor there is so meager that he can hardly afford to come to them once a month, and consequently these peasants are practically without spiritual leadership. People who are so directed as to develop such an attitude are handicapped for life.

Someone recently inquired as to why the religious schools do not teach the people how to tolerate differences of opinion and to cooperate for the common good. This, however, is the thing which these institutions have refused to do. Religious schools have been established, but they are considered necessary to supply workers for denominational outposts and to keep alive the sectarian bias by which the Baptists hope to outstrip the Methodists or the latter the former. No teacher in one of these schools has advanced a single thought which has become a working principle in Christendom, and not one of these centers is worthy of the name of a school of theology. If one would bring together all of the teachers in such schools and carefully sift them he would not find in the whole group a sufficient number qualified to conduct one accredited school of religion. The large majority of them are engaged in imparting to the youth worn-out theories of the ignorant oppressor.

This lack of qualified teachers in Negro schools of theology, however, is not altogether the fault of the teachers themselves. It is due largely to the system to which they belong. Their schools of "theology" are impoverished by their unnecessary multiplication, and consequently the instructors are either poorly paid or not compensated at all. Many of them have to farm, conduct enterprises, or pastor churches to make a living while trying to teach. Often, then, only the inefficient can be retained under such circumstances. Yet those who see how they have failed because of these things nevertheless object to the unification of the churches as taught by Jesus of Nazareth, whom they have all but ceased to follow because of their sectarian bias obtained from thumb-worn books of misguided Americans and Europeans.

Recently an observer saw a result of this in the sermon of a Negro college graduate, trying to preach to a church of the masses. He referred to all the great men in the history of a certain country to show how religious they were, whether they were or not. When he undertook to establish the Christian character of Napoleon, however, several felt like leaving the place in disgust. The climax of the service was a prayer by another "miseducated" Negro who devoted most of the time to thanking God for Cicero and Demosthenes. Here, then, was a case of the religion of the pagan handed down by the enslaver and segregationist to the Negro.

Returning from the table where he had placed his offering in a church on a Sunday morning not long thereafter, this observer saw another striking example of this failure to hit the mark. He stopped to inquire of his friend, Jim Minor, as to why he had not responded to the appeal for a collection.

"What!" said Jim, "I ain't givin' that man nothing. That man ain't fed me this morning, and I ain't feedin' him."

This was Jim's reaction to a "scholarly" sermon entitled "The Humiliation of the Incarnation."

During the discourse, too, the minister had had much to say about John Knox Orthodox, and another of the communicants bowing at that shrine inquired of the observer later as to who this John Knox Orthodox was and where he lived. The observer could not answer all of the inquiries thus evoked, but he tried to explain the best he could that the speaker had "studied" history and theology.

This was the effect this sermon had on an earnest congregation. The minister had attended a school of theology but had merely memorized words and phrases, which meant little to him and nothing to those who heard his discourse. The school in which he had been trained followed the traditional course for ministers, devoting most of the time to dead languages and dead issues. He had given attention to polytheism, monotheism, and the doctrine of the Trinity. He had studied also the philosophical basis of the Caucasian dogma, the elements of that theology, and the schism by which fanatics made religion a football and multiplied wars only to moisten the soil of

Europe with the blood of unoffending men.

This minister had given no attention to the religious background of the Negroes to whom he was trying to preach. He knew nothing of their spiritual endowment and their religious experience as influenced by their traditions and environment in which the religion of the Negro has developed and expressed itself. He did not seem to know anything about their present situation. These honest people, therefore, knew nothing additional when he had finished his discourse. As one communicant pointed out, their wants had not been supplied, and they wondered where they might go to hear a word which had some bearing upon the life which they had to live.

Not long ago when the author was in Virginia he inquired about a man who was once a popular preacher in that state. He is here, they said, but he is not preaching now. He went off to school, and when he came back the people could not understand what he was talking about. Then he began to find fault with the people because they would not come to church. He called them fogy, because they did not appreciate his new style of preaching and the things he talked about. The church went down to nothing, and he finally left it and took up farming.

In a rural community, then, a preacher of this type must fail unless he can organize separately members of the popular Methodist and Baptist churches who go into the ritualistic churches or establish certain "refined" Methodist or Baptist churches catering to the "talented tenth." For lack of adequate numbers, however, such churches often fail to develop sufficient force to do very much for themselves or for anybody else. On Sunday morning, then, their pastors have to talk to the benches. While these truncated churches go higher in their own atmosphere of selfsatisfaction the mentally undeveloped are left to sink lower because of the lack of contact with the better trained. If the latter exercised a little more judgment, they would be able to influence these people for good by gradually introducing advanced ideas.

Because our "highly educated" people do not do this, large numbers of Negroes drift into churches led by the "uneducated" ministers who can scarcely read and write. These preachers do not know much of what is found in school books and can hardly make use of a library in working out a sermon; but they understand the people with whom they deal, and they make such use of the human laboratory that sometimes they become experts in solving vexing problems and meeting social needs. They would be much better preachers if they could have attended a school devoted to the development of the mind rather than to cramming it with extraneous matters which have no bearing on the task which lies before them. Unfortunately, however, very few of such schools of religion now exist.

For lack of intelligent guidance, then, the Negro church often fulfills a mission to the contrary of that for which it was established. Because the Negro church is such a free field and it is controlled largely by the Negroes themselves, it seems that practically all the incompetents and undesirables who have been barred from other walks of life by race prejudice and economic difficulties have rushed into the ministry for the exploitation of the people. Honest ministers who are trying to do their duty, then, find their task made difficult by these men who stoop to practically everything conceivable. Almost anybody of the lowest type may get into the Negro ministry. The Methodists claim that they have strict regulations to prevent this, but their net draws in proportionately as many undesirables as one finds among the Baptists.

As an evidence of the depths to which the institution has gone a resident of Cincinnati recently reported a case of its exploitation by a railroad man who lost his job and later all his earnings in a game in a den of vice in that city. To refinance himself he took an old black frock coat and a Bible and went into the heart of Tennessee, where he conducted at various points a series of distracted, protracted meetings which netted him two hundred and ninety-nine converts to the faith and four hundred dollars in cash. He was enabled thereby to return to the game in Cincinnati and he is still in the lead. Other such cases are frequently reported.

The large majority of Negro preachers of today, then, are doing nothing more than to keep up the mediaeval hell-fire scare which the Whites have long since abandoned to emphasize the humanitarian trend in religion through systematized education. The young people of the Negro race could be held in the church by some such program, but the Negro's Christianity does not conceive of social uplift as a duty of the church; and consequently Negro children have not been adequately trained in religious matters to be equal to the social demands upon them. Turning their back on medievalism, then, these untrained youth think nothing of taking up moon-shining, gambling, and racketeering as occupations; and they find great joy in smoking, drinking, and fornication as diversions. They cannot accept the old ideas, and they do not understand the new.

What the Negro church is, however, has been determined largely by what the white man has taught the race by precept and example. We must remember that the Negroes learned their religion from the early white Methodists and Baptists who evangelized the slaves and the poor Whites when they were barred from proselytizing the aristocracy. The American white people themselves taught Negroes to specialize unduly in the "Praise the Lord," "Hallelujah" worship. In the West Indies among the Anglicans and among the Latin people Negroes do not show such emotionalism. They are cold and conservative.

Some of the American Whites, moreover, are just as far behind in this respect as are the Negroes who have had less opportunity to learn better. While in Miami, Florida, not long ago the author found in two interracial "Holiness Churches" that the following was a third or fourth White. The Whites joined whole-heartedly with the Negroes in their "holy rolling" and some of them seemed to be "rollers not holy."

A few months ago in Huntington, West Virginia, where the author was being entertained by friends, the party was disturbed throughout the evening by the most insane outbursts of white worshippers in a "Church of God" across the street. There they daily indulged in such whooping and screaming in "unknown tongues" that the Negroes have had to report them to the police as a nuisance. The author has made a careful study of the Negro church, but he has never known Negroes to do anything to surpass the performance of those heathen.

The American Negroes' ideas of morality, too, were borrowed from their owners. The Negroes could not be expected to raise a higher standard than their aristocratic governing class that teemed with sin and vice. This corrupt state of things did not easily pass away. The Negroes have never seen any striking examples among the Whites to help them in matters of religion. Even during the colonial period the Whites claimed that their ministers sent to the colonies by the Anglican Church, the progenitor of the Protestant Episcopal Church in America, were a degenerate class that exploited the people for money to waste it in racing horses and drinking liquor. Some of these ministers were known to have illicit relations with women and, therefore, winked at the sins of the officers of their churches, who sold their own offspring by slave women.

Although the author was born ten years after the Civil War the morals and religion of that régime continued even into his time. Many of the rich or well-to-do white men belonging to the churches in Buckingham County, Virginia, indulged in polygamy. They raised one family by a white woman and another by a colored or poor white woman. Both the owner of the largest slate quarry and the proprietor of the largest factory in that county lived in this fashion. One was an outstanding Episcopalian and the other a distinguished Catholic.

One day the foreman of the factory, a polygamous deacon of the local white Baptist Church, called the workmen together at noon for a short memorial service in honor of Parson Taylor, for almost half a century the pastor of the large white Baptist church in that section. The foreman made some remarks on the life of the distinguished minister, and then all sang "Shall We Meet Beyond the River?" But "to save his life" the author could not restrain himself from wondering all that time whether the foreman's white wife or colored paramour would greet him on the other side, and what a conflict there would be if they happened to get into an old-fashioned hairpulling.

In spite of his libertine connections, however, this foreman believed that he was a Christian, and when he died his eulogist commended his soul to God.

Some years later when the author was serving his six years' apprenticeship in the West Virginia coal mines he found at Nutallburg a very faithful vestryman of the white Episcopal Church at that point. He was one of the most devout from the point of view of his co-workers. Yet, privately, this man boasted of having participated in that most brutal lynching of the four Negroes who thus met their doom at the hands of an angry mob in Clifton Forge, Virginia, in 1892.

It is very clear, then, that if Negroes got their conception of religion from slaveholders, libertines, and murderers, there may be something wrong about it, and it would not hurt to investigate it. It has been said that the Negroes do not connect morals with religion. The historian would like to know what race or nation does such a thing. Certainly the Whites with whom the Negroes have come into contact have not done so.

---

# CHAPTER 8
# Professional Education Discouraged

---

In the training for professions other than the ministry and teaching the Negro has not had full sway. Any extensive comment on professional education by the Negro, then, must be mainly negative. We have not had sufficient professional schools upon which we can base an estimate of what the Negro educator can do in this sphere. If mistakes have been made in mis-educating the Negro professionally it must be charged not so much to the account of the Negroes themselves as to that of their friends who have performed this task. We are dealing here, then, mainly with information obtained from the study of Negroes who have been professionally trained by Whites in their own schools and in mixed institutions.

The largest numbers of Negroes in professions other than the ministry or education are physicians, dentists, pharmacists, lawyers and actors. The numbers in these and other lines have not adequately increased because of the economic status of the Negroes and probably because of a false conception of the role of the professional man in the community and its relation to him.

The people whom the Negro professional men have volunteered to serve have not always given them sufficient support to develop that standing and solidarity which will make their position professional and influential. Most Whites in contact with Negroes, always the teachers of their brethren in black, both by precept and practice, have treated the professions as aristocratic spheres to which Negroes should not aspire. We have had, then, a much smaller number than those who under different circumstances would have dared to cross the line; and those that did so were starved out by the Whites who would not treat them as a professional class. This made it impracticable for Negroes to employ them in spheres in which they could not function efficiently. For example, because of a law that a man could not be admitted to the bar in Delaware without practicing a year under some lawyer in the state (and no white lawyer would grant a Negro such an opportunity until a few years ago) it was only recently that a Negro was admitted there.

Negroes, then, learned from their oppressors to say to their children that there were certain spheres into which they should not go because they would have no chance therein for development. In a number of places young men were discouraged and frightened away from certain professions by the poor showing made by those trying to function in them. Few had the courage to face this ordeal; and some professional schools in institutions for Negroes were closed about thirty or forty years ago, partly on this account.

This was especially true of the law schools, closed during the wave of legislation against the Negro, at the very time the largest possible number of Negroes needed to know the law for the protection of their civil and political rights. In other words, the thing which the patient needed most to pass the crisis was taken from him that he might more easily die. This one act among many others is an outstanding monument to the stupidity or malevolence of those in charge of Negro schools, and it serves as a striking demonstration of the mis-education of the race.

Almost any observer remembers distinctly the hard trials of the Negro lawyers. A striking example of their difficulties was supplied by the case of the first to be permanently established in Huntington, West Virginia. The author had entrusted to him the matter of correcting an error in the transfer of some property purchased from one of the most popular white attorneys in the state. For six months this simple transaction was delayed, and the Negro lawyer could not induce the white attorney to act. The author finally went to the office himself to complain of the delay.

The white attorney frankly declared that he had not taken up the matter because he did not care to treat with a Negro attorney; but he would deal with the author, who happened to be at that time the teacher of a Negro school, and was, therefore, in his place.

At one time the Negroes in medicine and correlated fields were regarded in the same light They had difficulty in making their own people believe that they could cure a complaint, fill a tooth, or compound a prescription. The Whites said that they could not do it; and, of course, if the Whites said so, it was true, so far as most Negroes were concerned. In those fields, however, actual demonstrations to the contrary have convinced a sufficient number of both Negroes and Whites that such an attitude toward these classes is false, but there are many Negroes who still follow those early teachings, especially the "highly educated" who in school have been given the "scientific" reasons for it. It is a most remarkable process that while in one department of a university a Negro may be studying for a profession, in another department of the same university he is being shown how the Negro professional man cannot succeed. Some of the "highly educated," then, give their practice to those who are often inferior to the Negroes whom they thus pass by. Although there has been an increase in these particular spheres, however, the professions among Negroes, with the exception of teaching and preaching, are still undermanned.

In the same way the Negro was once discouraged and dissuaded from taking up designing, drafting, architecture, engineering and chemistry. The Whites, they were told, will not employ you and your people cannot provide such opportunities. The thought of pioneering or of developing the Negro to the extent that he might figure in this sphere did not dawn on those monitors of the Negroes preparing for their life's work. This tradition is still a heavy load in Negro education, and it forces many Negroes out of spheres in which they might function into those for which they may not have any aptitude.

In music, dramatics and correlated arts, too, the Negro has been unfortunately misled. Because the Negro is gifted as a singer and can render more successfully than others the music of his own people, he has been told that he does not need training. Scores of those who have undertaken to function in this sphere without adequate education, then, have developed only to a certain point beyond which they have not had ability to go. We cannot easily estimate how popular Negro musicians and their music might have become had they been taught to the contrary.

Of these, several instances may be cited. A distinguished man, talking recently as a member of a large Episcopal church, which maintains a Negro mission, mentioned his objection to the budget of fifteen hundred dollars a year for music for these segregated communicants. Inasmuch as the Negroes were naturally gifted in music he did not believe that any expensive training or direction was required. The small number of Negro colleges and universities which undertake the training of the Negro in music is further evidence of the belief that the Negro is all but perfect in this field and should direct his attention to the traditional curricula.

55

The same misunderstanding with respect to the Negro in dramatics is also evident. We have long had the belief that the Negro is a natural actor who does not require any stimulus for further development. In this assertion is the idea that because the Negro is good at dancing, joking, minstrelsy and the like he is "in his place" when "cutting a shine" and does not need to be trained to function in the higher sphere of dramatics. Thus misled, large numbers of Negroes ambitious for the stage have not bloomed forth into great possibilities. Too many of them have finally ended with roles in questionable cafés, cabarets, and night clubs of America and Europe; and instead of increasing the prestige of the Negro they have brought the race into disgrace.

We scarcely realize what a poor showing we make in dramatics in spite of our natural aptitude in this sphere. Only about a half dozen Negro actors have achieved greatness, but we have more actors and showmen than any other professionals except teachers and ministers. Where are these thousands of men and women in the histrionic sphere? What do we hear of them? What have they achieved? Their record shows that only a few measure up to the standard of the modern stage. Most of these would-be artists have no preparation for the tasks undertaken.

A careful study of the Negro in dramatics shows that only those who have actually taken the time to train themselves as they should be have finally endured. Their salvation has been to realize that adequate training is the surest way to attain artistic maturity. And those few who have thus understood the situation clearly demonstrate our ineptitude in the failure to educate the Negroes along the lines in which they could have admirably succeeded. Some of our schools have for some time undertaken this work as imitators of institutions dealing with persons otherwise circumstanced. Desirable results, therefore, have not followed, and the Negro on the stage is still mainly the product of the trial and error method.

Several other reasons may be given for the failure of a larger number of Negro actors to reach a higher level. In the first place, they have been recognized by the white man only in parely plantation comedy and minstrelsy, and because of the large number entering the field it has failed to offer a bright future for many of such aspirants. Repeatedly told by the white man that he could not function as an actor in a different sphere, the American Negro has all but ceased to attempt anything else. The successful career of Ira Aldridge in Shakespeare was forgotten until recently recalled by the dramatic success of Paul Robeson in Othello. The large majority of Negroes have settled down, then, to contentment as ordinary clowns and comedians. They have not had the courage or they have not learned how to break over the unnatural barriers and occupy higher ground.

The Negro author is no exception to the traditional rule. He writes, but the white man is supposed to know more about everything than the Negro. So who wants a book written by a Negro about one? As a rule, not even a Negro himself, for if he is really "educated," he must show that he has the appreciation for the best in literature. The Negro author, then, can neither find a publisher nor a reader; and his story remains untold. The Negro editors and reporters were once treated the same way, but thanks to the uneducated printers who founded most of our newspapers which have succeeded, these men of vision have made it possible for the "educated" Negroes to make a living in this sphere in proportion as they recover from their education and learn to deal with the Negro as he is and where he is.

---

## CHAPTER 9
## Political Education Neglected

---

Some time ago when Congressman Oscar De Priest was distributing by thousands copies of the Constitution of the United States certain wiseacres were disposed to make fun of it. What purpose would such an act serve? These critics, however, probably did not know that thousands and thousands of Negro children in this country are not permitted to use school books in which are printed the Declaration of Independence or the Constitution of the United States. Thomas Jefferson and James Madison are mentioned in their history as figures in politics rather than as expounders of liberty and freedom. These youths are not permitted to learn that Jefferson believed that government should derive its power from the consent of the governed.

Not long ago a measure was introduced in a certain State Legislature to have the Constitution of the United States thus printed in school histories, but when the bill was about to pass it was killed by someone who made the point that it would never do to have Negroes study the Constitution of the United States. If the Negroes were granted the opportunity to peruse this document, they might learn to contend for the rights therein guaranteed; and no Negro teacher who gives attention to such matters of the government is tolerated in those backward districts.

The teaching of government or the lack of such instruction, then, must be made to conform to the policy of "keeping the Negro in his place."

In like manner, the teaching of history in the Negro area has had its political significance.

Starting out after the Civil War, the opponents of freedom and social justice decided to work out a program which would enslave the Negroes' mind inasmuch as the freedom of the body had to be conceded. It was well understood that if by the teaching the history of the white man could be further assured of his superiority and the Negro could be made to feel that he had always been a failure, and that the subjection of his will to some other race is necessary, then, he would still be a slave.

If you can control a man's thinking you do not have to worry about his action. When you determine what a man shall think you do not have to concern yourself about what he will do. If you make a man feel that he is inferior, you do not have to compel him to accept an inferior status, for he will seek it himself. If you make a man think that he is justly an outcast, you do not have to order him to the back door. He will go without being told; and if there is no back door, his very nature will demand one.

This program, so popular immediately after the Civil War, was not new, but after this upheaval, its execution received a new stimulus. Histories written elsewhere for the former slave area were discarded, and new treatments of local and national history in conformity with the recrudescent propaganda were produced to give Whites and Blacks the biased point of view of the development of the nation and the relations of the races. Special treatments of the Reconstruction period were produced in apparently scientific form by propagandists who went into the first graduate schools of the East to learn modern historiography about half a century ago. Having the stamp of science, the thought of these polemics was accepted in all seats of learning. These rewriters of history fearlessly contended that slavery was a benevolent institution; the masters loved their slaves and treated them humanely; the abolitionists meddled with the institution which the masters eventually would have modified; the Civil War brought about by "fanatics" like William Lloyd Garrison and John Brown was unnecessary; it was a mistake to make the Negro a citizen, for he merely became worse off by incurring the displeasure of the master class that will never tolerate him as an equal; and the Negro must live in this country in a state of recognized inferiority.

Some of these theories may seem foolish, but historians even in the North have been won to this point of view. They ignore the recent works of Miss Elizabeth Donnan, Mrs. H. T. Catterall, and Dr. Frederic Bancroft, who have spent years investigating slavery and slave-trading. These are scientific productions with the stamp of the best scholarship in America, treatises produced from such genuine documents as the court records of the slaveholding section itself, and these authors have rendered the public a valuable service in removing the whitewash which pseudo-historians have been giving to slavery and slaveholders for more than a century.

In the preparation of Negroes, many of whom teach in the South, these biased Northern historians even convert them to such a faith. A few years ago the author happened to listen to a conversation of Negro lawyers in one of our Southern cities, in which they unanimously conceded practically every contention set forth in this program of propaganda. They denounced, therefore, all reconstructionists who advocated equality and justice for all. These Negroes had the biased point of view of the rewriters like Claude Bowers and had never been directed to the real history of that drama as set forth by A. A. Taylor, Francis B. Simkins and Robert H. Woodly of the new Southern school of thought.

These Negro critics were especially hard on Negroes of our day who engage in agitation for actual democracy. Negroes themselves in certain parts join with the Whites, then, in keeping out of the schools teachers who may be bold enough to teach the truth as it is. They usually say the races here are getting along amicably now, and we do not want these peaceful relations disturbed by the teaching of new political thought.

What they mean to say with respect to the peaceful relation of the races, then, is that the Negroes have been terrorized to the extent that they are afraid even to discuss political matters publicly.

There must be no exposition of the principles of government in the schools, and this must not be done in public among Negroes with a view to stimulating political activity. Negroes engaged in other spheres in such communities finally come to the point of accepting silence on these matters as a fixed policy. Knowing that action to the contrary means mob rule which may destroy the peace and property of the community, they constitute themselves a sort of a vigilant committee to direct their fellows accordingly.

A few years ago a rather youthful looking high school principal in one of the large cities was unceremoniously dismissed because he said jocosely to the president of the board of education, in reply to his remark about his youthful bearing, "I am old enough to vote." "Horrors!" said the infuriated official. "Put him out. We brought him here to teach these Negroes how to work, and here he is thinking about voting," A few prominent Negroes of the place muttered a little, but they did nothing effective to correct this injustice.

In certain parts, therefore, the Negroes under such terrorism have ceased to think of political matters as their sphere. Where such things come into the teaching in more advanced work they are presented as matters of concern to a particular element rather than as functions in which all citizens may participate. The result is that Negroes grow up without knowledge of political matters which should concern all elements. To prevent the Negroes from learning too much about these things the Whites in the schools are sometimes neglected also, but the latter have the opportunity to learn by contact, close observation, and actual participation in the affairs of government.

Negroes in certain parts, then, have all but abandoned voting even at points where it might be allowed. In some cases not as many as two thousand Negroes vote in a whole state. By special legislation providing for literacy tests and the payment of taxes their number of voters has been reduced to a negligible quantity, and the few who can thus function do not do so because they are often counted out when they have the deciding vote.

The tests established for the restriction of suffrage were not intended to stimulate political education but to eliminate the Negro vote by subterfuge. Negroes presenting themselves for registration are asked to do the all but impossible thing of expounding parts of the Constitution which have baffled high courts; but Whites are asked simple questions which almost any illiterate man can answer. In this way the Negroes, however intelligent, are turned down; and all ignorant Whites are permitted to vote. These laws, then, have retarded rather than stimulated the political education of both races. Such knowledge is apparently useless for Negroes and unnecessary for the Whites, for the Negroes do not immediately profit by having it and the Whites may function as citizens without it.

The effect of such a one-sided system is decidedly bad. One does not realize it until he talks with men and women of these districts, who because of the denial of these privileges have lost interest in political matters. A book agent working in the plantation area of Mississippi tested the knowledge of Negroes of these matters by asking them questions about the local and State government. He discovered that they knew practically nothing in this sphere. It was difficult to find any who knew who was president of the United States. One meets teachers, physicians, and ministers who do not know the ordinary operations of courts, the functions of the counsel, jury or judge, unless such knowledge has come by the bitter experience of having been imposed upon by some tribunal of injustice. Some of the "educated" Negroes do not pay attention to such important matters as "the assessment of property and the collection of taxes, and they do not inform themselves as to how these things are worked out. An influential Negro in the South, then, is one who has nothing to do or say about politics and advises others to follow the same course.

The elimination of the Negro from politics, then, has been most unfortunate. The Whites may have profited thereby temporarily, but they showed very little foresight. How the Whites can expect to make of the Negroes better citizens by leading them to think that they should have no part in the government of this country is a mystery. To keep a man above vagabondage and crime he needs among other things the stimulus of patriotism, but how can a man be patriotic when the effect of his education is to the contrary?

What little chance the Negro has to learn by participation in politics in most parts of the South is unfortunately restricted now to corruption. The usual stir about electing delegates to the National Republican Convention from the Southern States and the customary combat the Negroes have with Lily-white corruptionists are about all the political matters which claim their attention in the Lower South. Neither the White nor the Black faction, as a rule, makes any effort to restore suffrage to Negroes.

The objective is merely the control of delegates and Federal patronage for the financial considerations involved. To do this they resort to numerous contests culminating in closing hotels and bolting doors for secret meetings. Since this is the only activity in which Negroes can participate they have learned to look upon it as honorable. Large numbers of Negroes become excited over the contest and give much publicity to it on the rostrum and in the press as a matter of great importance. The methods of these corruptionists of both races, however, should be condemned as a disgrace to the state and nation.

Instead of doing something to get rid of this ilk, however, we find the "highly educated" Negroes trying to plunge also into the mire. One of the most discouraging aspects in Negro life recently observed was that of a presidential campaign. Prominent Negroes connected with three of our leading institutions of learning temporarily abandoned their work to round up Negro votes for one of the candidates. The objective, of course, was to control the few ordinary jobs which are allotted to Negro politicians for their campaign services. When the successful candidate had been inaugurated, however, he carefully ignored them in the make-up of the personnel of his administration and treated Negroes in general with contempt. When you think of the fact that the Negroes who are being thus used are supposedly the most reputable Negro leaders and our most highly educated men you have to wonder whether the Negro has made any progress since Emancipation. The only consolation one can get out of it is that they may not represent the whole race.

In the North the Negroes have a better chance to acquire knowledge of political matters of the simple kind, but the bosses do not think it is advisable to enlighten them thoroughly. Negroes in parts are employed in campaigns, but they are not supposed to discuss such issues of the day as free trade, tariff for protection, the World Court, and the League of Nations. These Negro workers are supposed to tell their people how one politician seeking office has appointed more Negro messengers or charwomen in the service than the other or how the grandfather of the candidate stood with Lincoln and Grant through their ordeal and thus brought the race into its own. Another important task of these Negroes thus employed is also to abuse the opposing party, showing how hostile it has been to the Negro while the highly favorable party was doing so much for the race.

The course of these bosses has been interesting. At first the white man used the Negro leader by giving him a drink occasionally. The next step was to give him sufficient money to set up drinks in the name of the white candidate. When drinking at the expense of the candidate became too common the politicians fell back on the distribution of funds in small amounts. When this finally proved to be insufficient, however, the politicians had to go a bit further and provide Jim Crow jobs in certain backrooms with the understanding that the functions of the so-called office would be merely nominal and the incumbents would have no close contact with white people. In this stage the Negroes find themselves today.

The undesirable aspect of the affair is that the Negro in spite of the changes from one method of approach to that of another is never brought into the inner circle of the party with which he is affiliated. He is always kept on the outside and is used as a means to an end. To obtain the meager consideration which he receives the Negro must work clandestinely through the back door. It has been unnecessary for the white man to change this procedure, for until recent years he has generally found it possible to satisfy the majority of Negroes with the few political positions earmarked as "Negro jobs" and to crush those who clamor for more recognition.

It is unfortunate, too, that such a large number of Negroes do not know any better than to stake their whole fortune on politics. History does not show that any race, especially a minority group, has ever solved an important problem by relying altogether on one thing, certainly not by parking its political strength on one side of the fence because of empty promises. There are Negroes who know better, but such thinkers are kept in the background by the traducers of the race to prevent the enlightenment of the masses. The misleading politicians are the only persons through whom the traducers act with respect to the Negro, and there are always a sufficient number of mentally undeveloped voters who will supply them a large following.

Even the few Negroes who are elected to office are often similarly uninformed and show a lack of vision. They have given little attention to the weighty problems of the nation; and in the legislative bodies to which they are elected; they restrict themselves as a rule to matters of special concern to the Negroes themselves, such as lynching, segregation and disfranchisement, which they have well learned by experience. This indicates a step backwards, for the Negroes who sat in Congress and in the State Legislatures during the Reconstruction worked for the enactment of measures of concern to all elements of the population regardless of color.

Historians have not yet forgot what those Negro statesmen did in advocating public education, internal improvements, labor arbitration, the tariff, and the merchant marine.

---

# CHAPTER 10
## The Loss Of Vision

---

History shows, then, that as a result of these unusual forces in the education of the Negro he easily learns to follow the line of least resistance rather than battle against odds for what real history has shown to be the right course. A mind that remains in the present atmosphere never undergoes sufficient development to experience what is commonly known as thinking. No Negro thus submerged in the ghetto, then, will have a clear conception of the present status of the race or sufficient foresight to plan for the future; and he drifts so far toward compromise that he loses moral courage. The education of the Negro, then, becomes a perfect device for control from without. Those who purposely promote it have every reason to rejoice, and Negroes themselves exultingly champion the cause of the oppressor.

A comparison of the record of the spokesmen of the race today with that of those of the eighteenth century shows a moral surrender. During the prolonged struggle between the French and English in America the Negroes held the balance of power at several strategic points and used it accordingly; today the Negro finds himself inconsequential because he can be parked on one side of the fence. The same balance of power was evident also during the American Revolution when Negro soldiers insisted on serving side by side with others; today many Negroes are content as menials in the army. At that time Negroes preached to mixed congregations; today we find Negroes busy separating them. The eighteenth-century Negro resented any such thing as social distinctions; today Negroes are saying that they do not want social equality. Negroes of that epoch said with the ancient poet, "I am a man and deem nothing that relates to man a matter of indifference to me"; today, however, the average Negro says, "Now, I am a colored man, and you white folks must settle that matter among yourselves."

At a still later date the American Negro showed more courage than he does today with all of his so-called enlightenment. When the free Negroes were advised a hundred years ago to go to Africa they replied that they would never separate themselves from the slave population of this country as they were brethren by the "ties of consanguinity, of suffering, and of wrong." Today, however, the Negro in the North turns up his nose at the crude migrant from the South who brings to the North the race problem, but along with it more thrift and actual progress than the Northern Negro ever dreamed of.

When, again in 1816, free Negroes like Richard Allen, James Forten, and Robert Purvis, were referred to as a foreign element whose social status might not be secure in this country, instead of permitting the colonist to shove them aside as criminals to be deported to a distant shore, they replied in no uncertain terms that this soil in America which gave them birth is their only true home. "Here their fathers fought, bled, and died for this country and here they intended to stay."

Today when such things come up you find Negroes appearing upon the scene to see how much pay they can obtain to assist in the proposed undoing of the race.

Further emphasizing this thought of resistance a few years later, Nathaniel Paul, a Baptist preacher of Albany, informed the colonist that the free Negroes would not permit their traducers to formulate a program for the race. You may go ahead with your plan to deport this element in order to make slavery secure, he warned; but the free Negroes will never immigrate to Africa.

"We shall stay here and fight until the foul monster is crushed. Slavery must go."

"Did I believe it would always continue," said he, "and that man to the end of time would be permitted with impunity to usurp the same undue authority over his fellow, I would disavow any allegiance or obligation I was under to my fellow creatures, or any submission that I owed to the laws of my country! I would deny the superintending power of divine Providence in the affairs of this life; I would ridicule the religion of the Savior of the world, and treat as the worst of men the ministers of the everlasting gospel; I would consider my Bible as a book of false and delusive fables, and commit it to the flames; nay, I would still go farther; I would at once confess myself an atheist, and deny the existence of a holy God."

And these Negroes of a century ago stood their ground and fought the pro-slavery deportationist to a standstill, for with the exception of a few pioneers the emigrants to Liberia were largely slaves manumitted on the condition that they would settle in Africa. These freedmen, then, could have no ideals but those of the slave-holding section from which they were sent. They established, therefore, a slavocracy in Liberia. If Liberia has failed, then, it is no evidence of the failure of the Negro in government. It is merely evidence of the failure of slavery.

The Negroes attacking Jim-Crowism almost a century ago fearlessly questioned the constitutionality of such a provision. Speaking through Charles Lenox Remond of that day, they said, "There is a distinction between social and civil rights. We all claim the privilege of selecting our society and associations, but, in civil rights, one man has not the prerogative to define rights for another. These [race] distinctions react in all their wickedness—to say nothing of their concocted and systematized odiousness and absurdity—upon those who are illiberal and mean enough to practice them."

In our day, however, we find some "highly educated" Negroes approving such Jim Crowism. For example, not many years ago an outstanding Baptist preacher, dabbling in politics in West Virginia, suggested to the Whites that they enact a Jim Crow car law in that State, and we had difficulty in crushing that sentiment. A few years thereafter the author heard one of our bishops say that we should not object to such separation, for we want to be by ourselves. When this distinguished churchman died the traducers of the Negro lauded him to the skies; and thoughtless members of the race, thinking that he deserved it, joined in the loud acclaim.

In this way, the large majority of "educated" Negroes in the United States have accepted segregation, and have become its fearless champions. Their filled but undeveloped minds do not enable them to understand that, although an opiate furnishes temporary relief, it does not remove the cause of the pain. In this case we have yielded on principle to satisfy the mob, but have not yet found an ultimate solution of the problem at hand. In our so-called democracy we are accustomed to give the majority what they want rather than educate them to understand what is best for them. We do not show the Negro how to overcome segregation, but we teach him how to accept it as final and just.

Numerous results from this policy may be cited. The white laboring man refuses to work with Negroes because of the false tradition that the Negro is an inferior, and at the same time the Negro for the same reason becomes content with menial service and drudgery. The politician excludes the Negro from the councils of his party and from the government because he has been taught that such is necessary to maintain the supremacy of his race; the Negro, trained in the same school of thought, accepts this as final and contends for such meager consideration as the bosses may begrudgingly grant him. An irate resident in an exclusive district protests against an invasion by Negroes because he has learned that these poverty-stricken people are carriers of disease and agents of crime; the Negroes, believing that such is the truth, remain content in the ghetto. The irrational parent forces the separation of the races in some schools because his child must occupy a seat next to a pupil of "tainted" African blood; the educated Negro accepts this as inevitable and welcomes the makeshift for his people. Children of Negroes are excluded from the playgrounds because of the assertion that they will contaminate those of the Whites; the Negroes yielding, settle down to a policy of having their children grow up in neglected fashion in the most undesirable part of the city. The Negro is forced to ride in a Jim Crow car to stamp upon him more easily the badge of his "inferiority"; the "educated Negro" accepts it as settled and abandons the fight against this social proscription.

And thus goes segregation which is the most far-reaching development in the history of the Negro since the enslavement of the race. In fact, it is a sequel of slavery. It has been made possible by our system of mis-educating innocent people who did not know what was happening.

It is so subtle that men have participated in promoting it without knowing what they were doing.

There are a few defenders of segregation who are doubtless sincere. Although nominally free they have never been sufficiently enlightened to see the matter other than as slaves. One can cite cases of Negroes who opposed emancipation and denounced the abolitionists. A few who became free re-enslaved themselves. A still larger number made no effort to become free because they did not want to disconnect themselves from their masters, and their kind still object to full freedom.

Ever since the Civil War when Negroes were first given a chance to participate in the management of their affairs they have been inconsistent and compromising. They have tried to gain one thing on one day by insisting on equality for all, while at the same time endeavoring to gain another point the next day by segregation. At one moment Negroes fight for the principle of democracy, and at the very next moment they barter it away for some temporary advantage. You cannot have a thing and dispose of it at the same time.

For example, the Negro political leaders of the Reconstruction period clamored for suffrage and the right of holding office, serving in the militia, and sitting on the jury; but few of them wanted white and colored children to attend the same school. When expressing themselves on education most of them took the position of segregationists; and Charles Sumner in his fight for the civil rights of the Negro had to eliminate mixed schools from his program not only because many Whites objected but also because the Negroes themselves did not seem to want them. All of these leaders might not have been looking for jobs in those days; but as nominal freemen, who were still slaves, they did not feel comfortable in the presence of their former masters.

These timorous men were very much like some Negroes who were employed near the author's home in Virginia by a Northern farmer, who had moved into the State after the Civil War. When breakfast time came the first morning he called them in to eat at the table with his family. These actual slaves, however, immediately lost their appetite. One finally called the employer aside and settled the matter in another way. He said:

"Now boss, you ain't used to de rules ob dis country. We just can't sit at de table wid wite folks. We been use ter eating a cake er bread out yonder 'tween de plow handles. Les us go out dar."

The system, therefore, has extended from one thing to another until the Negroes today find themselves hedged in by the color bar almost every way they turn; and, set off by themselves, the Negroes cannot learn from the example of others with whom they might come into contact. In the ghetto, too, they are not permitted to construct and carry out a program of their own. These segregating institutions interfere with the development of self-help among Negroes, for often Negroes fail to raise money to establish institutions which they might control, but they readily contribute large sums for institutions which segregate persons of African blood.

Denied participation in the higher things of life, the "educated" Negro himself joins, too, with illdesigning persons to handicap his people by systematized exploitation. Feeling that the case of the Negro is hopeless, the "educated" Negro decides upon the course of personally profiting by whatever he can do in using these people as a means to an end. He grins in their faces while "extracting money" from them, hut his heart shows no fond attachment to their despised cause.

With a little larger income than they receive he can make himself somewhat comfortable in the ghetto; and he forgets those who have no way of escape.

Some of these "educated" classes join with unprincipled real estate men in keeping Negroes out of desirable parts of the city and confining them to unsanitary sections. Such persons help the profiteer to collect from Negroes thus cornered a larger rental than that exacted from Whites for the same property. In similar fashion a Negro minister sometimes goes into a community where the races are moving along amicably together in their churches and rents a shack or an old empty store to start a separate church for "our people," not to supply any practical need but to exploit those who have never learned to think. Professional men, too, walking in their footsteps, impose also upon the poor innocent Negroes who do not know when they are being treated properly and when they are not, but high fees may be obtained from them inasmuch as they cannot always go to others for service.

Settling in a community with mixed schools, the educated Negro often advocates their separation that his daughter may secure a position in the system. The Negro politician is accustomed to corner the Negro vote, by opening a separate office from which he may bargain with the chieftains of the machine for the highest price available. When paid off by some position, which is not very lofty, this office-holder accepts such employment with the understanding that he will be set off by himself as if he were destructive of the rest of mankind.

In the present crisis, however, the "highly educated" Negroes find very little to exploit, and in their untoward condition they have no program of finding a way out. They see numerous instances of Negroes losing their jobs in white establishments. In fact, these things occur daily.

Janitors who have been giving satisfaction are abruptly told that they will no longer be needed.

Negro waiters in hotels are being informed that their places will go to white workers. Negro truck drivers are ordered to step down and let the needy of the other race go up. We hear so much of this that we wonder what the outcome will be.

In this readjustment, of course, when there are fewer opportunities left for those who cannot or do not have the opportunity to operate machines the Negroes will naturally be turned out of their positions by their employers who think first of their own race. In the ultimate passing of the depression, however, Negroes will not be much better off when some of the Whites now displacing them will rise to higher levels. In the economic order of tomorrow there will be little use for the factotum or scullion. Man will not need such personal attention when he can buy a machine to serve him more efficiently. The menial Negroes, the aggregate of parasites whom the "highly educated" Negro has exploited, will not be needed on tomorrow. What, then, will become of "our highly educated" Negroes who have no initiative?

We have appealed to the talented tenth for a remedy, but they have nothing to offer. Their minds have never functioned in this all-important sphere. The "educated" Negro shows no evidence of vision. He should see a new picture. The Negroes are facing the alternative of rising in the sphere of production to supply their proportion of the manufacturers and merchants or of going down to the graves of paupers. The Negro must now do for himself or die out as the world undergoes readjustment. If the Whites are to continue for some time in doing drudgery to the exclusion of Negroes, the latter must find another way out. Nothing forces this upon one more dramatically than when he learns that white women in Montgomery, Alabama, are coming to the back door of Negro homes asking for their washing. If the Whites have reached this extremity, and they must be taken care of first, what will be left for the Negroes?

At this moment, then, the Negroes must begin to do the very thing which they have been taught that they cannot do. They still have some money, and they have needs to supply. They must begin immediately to pool their earnings and organize industries to participate in supplying social and economic demands. If the Negroes are to remain forever removed from the producing atmosphere, and the present discrimination continues, there will be nothing left for them to do.

There is no reason for lack of confidence because of the recent failure of Negro enterprises, although the "highly educated" Negroes assert the contrary. This lack of confidence is the cause of the failure of these enterprises. If the Negroes had manifested enough confidence in them and had properly supported them, they would have been strong enough to stand the test in the crisis.

Negro banks, as a rule, have failed because the people, taught that their own pioneers in business cannot function in this sphere, withdrew their deposits. An individual cannot live after you extract the blood from his veins. The strongest bank in the United States will last only so long as

73

the people will have sufficient confidence in it to keep their money there. In fact, the confidence of the people is worth more than money.

The lack of confidence of the Negro in himself and in his possibilities is what has kept him down. His mis-education has been a perfect success in this respect. Yet it is not necessary for the Negro to have more confidence in his own workers than in others. If the Negro would be as fair to his own as he has been to others, this would be all that is necessary to give him a new lease on life and start the trend upward.

Here we find that the Negro has failed to recover from his slavish habit of berating his own and worshipping others as perfect beings. No progress has been made in this respect because the more "education" the Negro gets the worse off he is. He has just had so much longer to learn to decry and despise himself. The race looking to this educated class for a solution of its problems does not find any remedy; and, on the contrary, sees itself further and further away from those things to which it has aspired. By forgetting the schoolroom for the time being and relying upon an awakening of the masses through adult education we can do much to give the Negro a new point of view with respect to economic enterprise and group cooperation. The average Negro has not been sufficiently mis-educated to become hopeless.

Our minds must become sufficiently developed to use segregation to kill segregation, and thus bring to pass that ancient and yet modern prophecy, "The wrath of man shall praise thee." If the Negro in the ghetto must eternally be fed by the hand that pushes him into the ghetto, he will never become strong enough to get out of the ghetto. This assumption of Negro leadership in the ghetto, then, must not be confined to matters of religion, education, and social uplift; it must deal with such fundamental forces in life as make these things possible. If the Negro area, however, is to continue as a district supported wholly from without, the inept dwellers therein will merit and will receive only the contempt of those who may occasionally catch glimpses of them in their plight.

As Frederick Douglass said in 1852, "It is vain that we talk of being men, if we do not the work of men. We must become valuable to society in other departments of industry than those servile ones from which we are rapidly being excluded. We must show that we can do as well as they.

When we can build as well as live in houses; when we can make as well as wear shoes; when we can produce as well as consume wheat, corn and rye—then we shall become valuable to society.

"Society," continued Douglass, "is a hard-hearted affair. With it the helpless may expect no higher dignity than that of paupers. The individual must lay society under obligation to him or society will honor him only as a stranger and sojourner."

---

## CHAPTER 11
## The Need For Service Rather Than Leadership

---

In this untoward situation the Negro finds himself at the close of the third generation from Emancipation. He has been educated in the sense that persons directed a certain way are more easily controlled, or as Ovid remarked, "In time the bull is brought to bear the yoke." The Negro in this state continues as a child. He is restricted in his sphere to small things, and with these he becomes satisfied. His ambition does not rise any higher than to plunge into the competition with his fellows for these trifles. At the same time those who have given the race such false ideals are busy in the higher spheres from which Negroes by their mis-education and racial guidance have been disbarred.

Examples of this failure of the mis-educated Negro to have high ideals may be cited. The author has known numerous cases of Negro lawyers, physicians and business men who, while attending local Sunday schools, churches, and lodges, have fallen out about trifles like a resolution or the chairmanship of a committee, which so embittered them as to make themselves enemies for life and stumbling blocks preventing any such thing as organization or community cooperation.

It is a common on occurrence to see a Negro well situated as a minister or teacher aspiring to a political appointment which temporarily pays little more than what he is receiving and offers no distinction except that of being earmarked as a Jim Crow job set aside for some Negro who has served well the purposes of the bosses as a ward heeler in a campaign. Negroes who have begun promising business enterprises sometimes abandon them temporarily for the same sort of empty honor. In this way they have been known to hamper their business by incurring the displeasure of ambitious politicians who might otherwise patronize them.

Negroes of this point of view have developed in that part of the country where it is thought that the most distinguished persons in the community are those who hold and exploit the local offices or those who are further honored with positions in the state and nation. While this may apply in the case of their oppressors the few positions allotted the Negroes are magnified beyond all reasonable bounds. This comes as a natural result, however, for the "education" of the Negro requires it. The ambitious mis-educated Negro in the struggle for the little things allotted by others prevents any achievement of the people in matters more constructive. Potentially the colored people are strong although they are actually weak.

This much-ado-about-nothing renders impossible cooperation, the most essential thing in the development of a people. The ambitious of this class do more to keep the race in a state of turmoil and to prevent it from serious community effort than all the other elements combined.

The one has a job that the other wants; or the one is a leader of a successful faction, and the other is struggling to supplant him. Everything in the community, then, must yield ground to this puerile contest.

In one city of a few thousand Negroes there is no chance for community cooperation because of the antagonism of the Methodist and Baptist preachers in charge of the two largest churches. The one is determined to dictate the appointment of the teaching corps and the social welfare workers; the other is persistently struggling to undo everything accomplished by his opponent.

The one is up today and the other in ascendency tomorrow. Several efforts have been made to start business enterprises there, but none has succeeded because one faction tears down what the other builds up.

In another city the cleavage is along political lines. Preachers are there, but a lawyer and a dentist plunging into politics have dispossessed the clergy of the stage. The leader of one faction is so bitterly opposed to the other that he even warns strangers against going to the home of his adversary. To present a sane proposition to the community through one of these leaders means local warfare rather than an effort to work together for the common good. Consequently, although there are thousands of Negroes living together in one quarter they have no business enterprises of worth. The selfish struggle for personal aggrandizement, which has not yet brought either faction more than an appointment on the police force or a clerkship in one of the city offices, thus blocks the social and economic progress of thousands of unoffending people.

In another state the ambition of the highly educated Negro is restricted to becoming principals of the high schools. The neglected state school has not developed sufficiently to become attractive.

The warring area, then, is in the cities. In one of them, where several Negroes own considerable wealth which, if pooled and properly used, would produce all but wonderful results, the petty strife has been most disastrous. Little thought is given to social uplift, and economic effort is crushed by factional wrangling. Before the author had been in one of the towns an hour a stalwart of one faction sounded him on becoming a candidate for the position held by the principal of the high school. A few minutes thereafter another approached him for advice as to how "to get him out."

The high cost of this childishness to the community can be estimated only by taking into consideration the fact that this strife is all but endless. If it were a matter that developed now and then only to be forgotten by people directing their attention thereafter to more important things, it would not do much harm; but this confusion continues for years. Sometimes it grips a community for a whole generation, vitiating the entire life of the people.

In spite of the meager rewards, however, the idea of leadership looms high in the Negro mind. It always develops thus among oppressed people. The oppressor must have some dealing with the despised group, and rather than have contact with individuals he approaches the masses through his own spokesman. The term itself connotes a backward condition. In its strides upward a race shuffles off its leaders because they originate outside of the group. They constitute a load that sinks the oppressed in the mire of trials and tribulations.

Leadership is usually superimposed for the purpose of "directing the course of the ostracized group along sane lines." This was accomplished during the days of slavery by restricting the assembly of Negroes to certain times and places and compelling them to meet in the presence of a stipulated number of the "wisest and discreetist men of the community." These supervisors of the conduct of Negroes would prevent them from learning the truth which might make them "unruly" or ambitious to become free.

After the Negroes became free the same end was reached by employing a Negro or some white man to spy upon and report behind closed doors on a plan to enslave the Negroes' minds. In case that actual employment as a spy seemed too bold, the person to be used as such an instrument took up some sort of enterprise which the oppressors of the race warmly supported to give him the desired influence in the community. This "racial racketeer" might be a politician, minister, teacher, director of a community center, or head of a "social uplift agency." As long as he did certain things and expressed the popular opinion on questions he lacked nothing, and those who followed him found their way apparently better paid as the years went by. His leadership, then, was recognized and the ultimate undoing of the Negroes in the community was assured.

Such leadership, too, has continued into our day and it goes from bad to worse. The very service which this racial toady renders hardens him to the extent that he loses his soul. He becomes equal to any task the oppressor may impose upon him, and at the same time he becomes artful enough to press his case convincingly before the thoughtless multitude. What is right is sacrificed because everything that is right is not expedient; and what is expedient soon becomes unnecessary.

Recently a citizen, observing how we have been thus betrayed, suggested that there be called a national meeting to take steps for a program of development of the race from within under "a new leadership." Such a movement can be made to mean something, and then it can degenerate into an assembly of abuse and vituperation followed by the usual whereas-therefore-be-itresolved effort which has never meant anything in the awakening and the development of an oppressed people.

The Negroes, however, will not advance far if they continue to waste their energy abusing those who misdirect and exploit them. The exploiters of the race are not so much at fault as the race itself. If Negroes persist in permitting themselves to be handled in this fashion they will always find someone at hand to impose upon them. The matter is one which rests largely with the Negroes themselves. The race will free itself from exploiters just as soon as it decides to do so.

No one else can accomplish this task for the race. It must plan and do for itself.

Checking up on what they do, Negroes often find themselves giving money and moral support to various persons and institutions which influence the course of the race in the wrong way. They do not often ask themselves whether the support thus given will rebound in the long run to the good of the people with whom they are identified. They do not inquire whether the assistance thus given offers temporary relief but eventually results in irreparable loss. So many Negroes often do themselves harm when they actually believe that they are doing good. Under their present teachers they cannot easily learn to do any better, for such training as we undergo does not open our eyes sufficiently for us to see far ahead of us.

If the Negro could abandon the idea of leadership and instead stimulate a larger number of the race to take up definite tasks and sacrifice their time and energy in doing these things efficiently the race might accomplish something. The race needs workers, not leaders. Such workers will solve the problems which race leaders talk about and raise money to enable them to talk more and more about. When you hear a man talking, then, always inquire as to what he is doing or what he has done for humanity. Oratory and resolutions do not avail much. If they did, the Negro race would be in a paradise on earth. It may be well to repeat here the saying that old men talk of what they have done, young men of what they are doing, and fools of what they expect to do.

The Negro race has a rather large share of the last mentioned class.

If we can finally succeed in translating the idea of leadership into that of service, we may soon find it possible to lift the Negro to a higher level. Under leadership we have come into the ghetto; by service within the ranks we may work our way out of it. Under leadership we have been constrained to do the biddings of others; by service we may work out a program in the light of our own circumstances. Under leadership we have become poverty-stricken; by service we may teach the masses how to earn a living honestly. Under leadership we have been made to despise our own possibilities and to develop into parasites; by service we may prove sufficient unto the task of self-development and contribute our part to modern culture.

---

## CHAPTER 12
## Hirelings In The Places Of Public Servants

---

If the highly educated Negroes have not learned better the simple lessons of life one cannot expect the laboring classes to conduct themselves differently. In the large number of cases the employers of Negroes in common labor, in which most of them are now engaged, assert that there is no hope for advancement of Negroes in their employ because Negroes will not work under foremen of their own color. In other words, the average Negro has not yet developed to the point that one is willing to take orders from another of his own race.

While it is true that such an answer is often given as a mere excuse for not placing Negroes in responsible positions when it can be done without any particular trouble, the investigation among Negroes themselves reveals numerous facts to prove that there is more truth than falsehood in this statement. Hundreds of employees of African blood frankly say that they will not work under a Negro. One is afraid that the other may prosper more than he does and be recognized accordingly.

Some of these instances are interesting. A head of one of the Government departments, in which Negro women are employed to do unskilled labor, reports that he placed in charge of the group of these workers an intelligent colored woman who seemed to have all of the necessary qualifications which he had found in other women thus employed. Those working under her, however, refused to obey instructions; kept the place in turmoil and soon destroyed the morale of the whole force. As soon as he placed a white woman in charge, however, order was reestablished on the premises, and everything moved along smoothly.

Another employer conducting a wholesale business placed a Negro foreman in charge of others of his race to function as one of the important departments of the establishment. The Negroes working under him, who had formerly taken orders without question from the white foreman, soon undertook to take liberties with the promoted Negro and to ignore his orders. Knowing that the Negro foreman was well qualified, however, and being personally interested in him, the employer instead of doing what so many others under such circumstances had done, dismissed those who refused to cooperate and supplied the vacancies with others until an efficient working force could thus be obtained. Only a few employers, however, have had such patience and have manifested such interest in the advancement of the Negro. As a rule they merely dispose of Negro foremen with the excuse that one Negro will not take orders from another.

This refusal of Negroes to take orders from one another is due largely to the fact that slaveholders taught their bondmen that they were as good as or better than any others and, therefore, should not be subjected to any member of their race. If they were to be subordinated to someone it should be to the white man of superior culture and social position. This keeps the whole race on a lower level, restricted to the atmosphere of trifles which do not concern their traducers. The greater things of life which can be attained only by wise leadership, then, they have no way to accomplish.

The strong have always used this as a means of dealing with the so-called weaker races of the world. The Caucasian arrays the one against the other so that they may never combine their forces and thus deprive their so-called superiors of control over them, which they could easily do if organized. One white man was thus able to maintain himself on a plantation where there were thirty or forty slaves because the Negroes were mis-educated in such a way as to keep them divided into distinct factions. In petty strife their power would be lost in the process of attrition.

Today we find the same thing in Africa where this end is reached by embittering one group against another; and it worked the same way in India until recently when it began to break down under the masterful leadership of Mahatma Gandhi.

The Negroes of the United States have followed leadership slavishly but sometimes unfortunately that of those leaders who are selected for them by the traducers of the race. The enemies of the race, for example, will find a Negro willing to do certain things they desire to have accomplished and will finance him and give him sufficient publicity to get before the world, for the few favors which he may dispense among his followers as a result of his influence and economic position will bring to him the adequate number of Negroes for the constituency which he desires.

Negroes, however, sometimes choose their own leaders but unfortunately they are too often of the wrong kind. Negroes do not readily follow persons with constructive programs. Almost any sort of exciting appeal or trivial matter presented to them may receive immediate attention and temporarily at least liberal support. When the bubble collapses, of course, these same followers will begin to decry Negro leadership and call these misrepresentatives of the group rascals and scoundrels. Inasmuch as they have failed to exercise foresight, however, those who have deceived them should not be blamed so much as those who have liberally supported these impostors. Yet the fault here is not inherently in the Negro but in what he has been taught.

The Negroes' point of view, therefore, must be changed before they can construct a program which will bring them out of the wilderness. For example, no good can be expected from one of our teachers who said that she had to give up her class in Sunday school to accept an extra job of waiting on table at that hour because she had bought a twenty-four-hundred-dollar coat and her husband had purchased an expensive car. Such a teacher has no message for the Negro child. Her example would tend to drag the youth downward, and the very thought of having such a person in the schoolroom is most depressing.

We must feel equally discouraged when we see a minister driving up to his church on Sunday morning in a Cadillac. He does not come to feed the multitude spiritually. He comes to fleece the flock. The appeal he makes is usually emotional. While the people are feeling happy the expensive machine is granted, and the prolonged vacation to use it is easily financed. Thus the thoughtless drift backward toward slavery.

When you see a physician drive to one's door in his Pierce Arrow, you cannot get the impression he has come to treat the patient for a complaint. He has come to treat him for a dollar. Such physicians, as a rule know less and less medicine as the years go by, although they make much money by learning human psychology and using it for personal gain. With leeches of this type feeding upon an all but impoverished people and giving them nothing back there can be no hope for advancement.

No people can go forward when the majority of those who should know better have chosen to go backward, but this is exactly what most of our misleaders do. Not being learned in the history and background of the race, they figure out that there is no hope for the masses; and they decide, then, that the best thing they can do is to exploit these people for all they can and use the accumulations selfishly. Such persons have no vision and therefore perish at their own hands.

It is an injustice to the Negro, however, to mis-educate him and suffer his manners to be corrupted from infancy unto old age and then blame him for making the mistakes which such guidance necessitates. "People who have been restricted and held down naturally condescend to the lower levels of delinquency. When education has been entirely neglected or improperly managed we see the worst passions ruling with uncontrolled and incessant sway. Good sense degenerates into craft, anger wrangles into malignity, restraint which is thought most solitary comes too late, and the most judicial admonitions are urged in vain."

Philosophers have long conceded, however, that every man has two educations: "that which is given to him, and the other that which he gives himself. Of the two kinds the latter is by far the more desirable. Indeed all that is most worthy in man he must work out and conquer for himself.

It is that which constitutes our real and best nourishment. What we are merely taught seldom nourishes the mind like that which we teach ourselves."

The same eternal principle applies to a race forced to live apart from others as a separate and distinct group. Inasmuch as the education of the Negro has come from without we can clearly see that he has received only a part of the development which he should have undergone or he has developed negatively. The Negro lacks mental power, which cannot be expected from ill-fed brains.

This naturally brings up a serious question. The people on the outside, who are directing the race from afar, will take this condition of affairs as evidence that the Negro is not prepared for leadership. What they ought to say is that they have not prepared the Negro to assume the responsibility of his own uplift. Instead of doing this, however, they play up this result of their own failure as an argument for imposing upon the Negro race the guidance of others from without.

As to whether or not a white man should be a leader of the Negroes may be dismissed as a silly question. What has the color to do with it? Such a worker may be white, brown, yellow, or red, if he is heart and soul with the people whom he would serve. It just happens, however, that most white men now in control of Negro institutions are not of this required type. Practically all of those with whom I have talked and communicated believe in imposing some sort of disability upon Negroes. Some object to the freedom of intermarriage as a substitute for concubinage, scoff at the idea of the enfranchisement of the Negroes, approve their segregation, and justify the economic exploitation of the race. Now if these are the persons to elevate the Negroes, to what point do they expect to lift them, and what will the Negroes be when they get there?

With this same thought in mind a white director of Negroes recently said to the author:

"I realize that I have no useful function in my present position as a president of a Negro institution. I do not approve of their aspirations to many things. I cannot accept the students in my house as I would white students because it might lead to an interracial romance. Marrying is such a difficult problem at the best that I should not like to see one of my children make a failure in life by marrying a Negro."

"In other words," continued he, "we live in two different worlds. While I am among them I cannot become a part of them. How then can I help them under these circumstances?"

I am acquainted with another white educator at the head of a Negro institution, who will not address a colored girl as Miss, and to avoid the use of a title in speaking to women of the race he addresses them as his kin. One of them was sharp enough to reply to him thus when he accosted her as auntie:

"Oh, I am so glad that I have found my lost relatives at last. My mother often told me that I had some distinguished kin, and just to think that you are my nephew makes me feel glad."

Another such exploiter in charge of a Negro college never wears his hat on the campus. His confidential explanation is that he might have to lift it when he meets a Negro woman. Of course, that would never do. "White supremacy" would be lost in the Negro school.

As we realize more and more that education is not merely imparting information which is expected to produce certain results, we see very clearly the inconsistency of the position of white persons as executives of Negro institutions. These misfits belong to the very group working out the segregation of the Negro, and they come into these institutions mainly to earn a living. They make no particular contribution to the development of education, for they are not scholarly enough to influence educational theory; and they are so far out of sympathy with the Negro that they cannot make any contribution to educational practice. These "foreigners" are not bringing to such institutions large sums of money which the Negroes cannot obtain, for the institutions now directed by Negroes are receiving larger appropriations than those under the management of Whites.

Our so-called thinkers, however, seldom see the inevitable results of this unsound policy. Not long ago when the author wrote the textbook entitled Negro Makers of History it was adversely criticized by a Negro who said that the book should have had as an illustration the cut of the white man who established a certain Negro college. The author had to explain that the book was to give an account of what the Negro has done, not of what has been done for him.

The school referred to, moreover, was in no sense a Negro school. It had very few Negro teachers and only one Negro trustee. The policy of the school was determined altogether by others without giving the Negro credit for having a thought on education. In other words, it was merely a school which Negroes were permitted to attend. If they picked up here and there something to help them, well and good; if not, may God help them!

It is all right to have a white man as the head of a Negro college or to have a red man at the head of a yellow one, if in each case the incumbent has taken out his naturalization papers and has identified himself as one of the group which he is trying to serve. It seems that the white educators of this day are unwilling to do this, and for that reason they can never contribute to the actual development of the Negro from within. You cannot serve people by giving them orders as to what to do. The real servant of the people must live among them, think with them, feel for them, and die for them.

The white worker in Negro institutions, too, can never be successful without manifesting some faith in the people with whom he has cast his lot. His efforts must not be merely an attempt to stimulate their imitation of things in a foreign sphere. He must study his community sufficiently to discover the things which have a trend in the proper direction that he may stimulate such forces and thus help the community to do better the good things which it may be capable of doing and at the same time may be interested in doing. If these people are to be brought the ideas of "foreigners," and must be miraculously transformed into something else before anything can be made of them, such effort will be a fruitless task like most of the so-called education and uplift of the Negroes in America.

The Negro, in spite of his confinement to the ghetto, has some opportunities to develop his special capacities if they are properly studied and understood. The real servant of the people, then, will give more attention to those to be served than to the use that somebody may want to make of them. He will be more concerned with what he can do to increase the ease, comfort, and happiness of the Negro than with how the Negro may be used to contribute to the ease, comfort, and happiness of others.

The servant of the people, unlike the leader, is not on a high horse elevated above the people and trying to carry them to some designated point to which he would like to go for his own advantage. The servant of the people is down among them, living as they live, doing what they do and enjoying what they enjoy. He may be a little better informed than some other members of the group; it may be that he has had some experience that they have not had, but in spite of this advantage he should have more humility than those whom he serves, for we are told that "Whosoever is greatest among you, let him be your servant."

---

# CHAPTER 13
# Understand The Negro

---

"We do not offer here any course in Negro history, Negro literature, or race relations," recently said a professor of a Negro college. "We study the Negro along with other people."

"An excellent idea," the interviewer replied. "No one should expect you to do any more than this, but how do you-do it when the Negro is not mentioned in your textbooks except to be condemned? Do you, a teacher in a Negro school, also condemn the race in the same fashion as the writers of your textbooks of history and literature?"

"No," said he, "we bring the Negro in here and there."

"How often does 'here and there' connote?"

"Well, you know," said he, "Negroes have not done much; and what they have accomplished may be briefly covered by referring to the achievements of a few men and women.

"Why do you emphasize the special study of the Negro?" said he further. "Why is it necessary to give the race special attention in the press, on the rostrum, or in the schoolroom? This idea of projecting the Negro into the foreground does the race much harm by singing continually of his woes and problems and thus alienating the public which desires to give its attention to other things."

It is true that many Negroes do not desire to hear anything about their race, and few Whites of today will listen to the story of woe. With most of them the race question has been settled. The Negro has been assigned to the lowest drudgery as the sphere in which the masses must toil to make a living; and socially and politically the race has been generally proscribed.

Inasmuch as the traducers of the race have "settled" the matter in this fashion, they naturally oppose any effort to change this status.

Many Negro professional men who are making a living attending to the affairs of these laborers and servants in their mentally undeveloped state and many teachers, who in conservative fashion are instructing their children to maintain the status quo ante bellum, also oppose any movement to upset this arrangement. They are getting paid for their efforts, why should they try innovations? The gods have so decreed it. Human beings cannot change it. Why be foolish?

A Negro with sufficient thought to construct a program of his own is undesirable, and the educational systems of this country generally refuse to work through such Negroes in promoting their cause. The program for the uplift of the Negroes in this country must be handed over to an executive force like orders from the throne, and they must carry it out without question or get out of line and let the procession go on. Although the Negro is being daily forced more and more by segregation into a world peculiarly his own, his unusually perplexing status is given little or no thought, and he is not considered capable of thinking for himself.

The chief difficulty with the education of the Negro is that it has been largely imitation resulting in the enslavement of his mind. Somebody outside of the race has desired to try out on Negroes some experiment which interested him and his coworkers; and Negroes, being objects of charity, have received them cordially and have done what they required. In fact, the keynote in the education of the Negro has been to do what he is told to do. Any Negro who has learned to do this is well prepared to function in the American social order as others would have him.

Looking over the courses of study of the public schools, one finds little to show that the Negro figures in these curricula. In supplementary matter a good deed of some Negro is occasionally referred to, but oftener the race is mentioned only to be held up to ridicule. With the exception of a few places like Atlantic City, Atlanta, Tulsa, St. Louis, Birmingham, Knoxville, and the states of Louisiana and North Carolina no effort is made to study the Negro in the public schools as they do the Latin, the Teuton, or the Mongolian. Several mis-educated Negroes themselves contend that the study of the Negro by children would bring before them the race problem prematurely and, therefore, urge that the study of the race be deferred until they reach advanced work in the college or university. These misguided teachers ignore the fact that the race question is being brought before Black and white children daily in their homes, in the streets, through the press and on the rostrum. How, then, can the school ignore the duty of teaching the truth while these other agencies are playing up falsehood?

The experience of college instructors shows that racial attitudes of the youth are not easily changed after they reach adolescence. Although students of this advanced stage are shown the fallacy of race superiority and the folly of social distinctions, they nevertheless continue to do the illogical thing of still looking upon these despised groups as less worthy than themselves and persist in treating them accordingly. Teachers of elementary and secondary schools giving attention to this interracial problem have succeeded in softening and changing the attitude of children whose judgment has not been so hopelessly warped by the general attitude of the communities in which they have been brought up.

In approaching this problem in this fashion to counteract the one-sided education of youth the thinking people of this country have no desire to upset the curricula of the schools or to force the Negro as such into public discussion; but, if the Negro is to be elevated he must be educated in the sense of being developed from what he is, and the public must be so enlightened as to think of the Negro as a man. Furthermore, no one can be thoroughly educated until he learns as much about the Negro as he knows about other people.

Upon examining the recent catalogues of the leading Negro colleges, one finds that invariably they give courses in ancient, mediaeval, and modern Europe, but they do not give such courses in ancient, mediaeval, and modern Africa. Yet Africa, according to recent discoveries, has contributed about as much to the progress of mankind as Europe has, and the early civilization of the Mediterranean world was decidedly influenced by Africa.

Negro colleges offer courses bearing on the European colonists prior to their coming to America, their settlement on these shores, and their development here toward independence. Why are they not equally generous with the Negroes in treating their status in Africa prior to enslavement, their first transplantation to the West Indies, the Latinization of certain Negroes in contradistinction to the development of others under the influence of the Teuton, and the effort of the race toward self-expression?

A further examination of their curricula shows, too, that invariably these Negro colleges offer courses in Greek philosophy and in that of modern European thought, but they direct no attention to the philosophy of the African. Negroes of Africa have and always have had their own ideas about the nature of the universe, time, and space, about appearance and reality, and about freedom and necessity. The effort of the Negro to interpret man's relation to the universe shows just as much intelligence as we find in the philosophy of the Greeks. There were many Africans who were just as wise as Socrates.

Again, one observes in some of these catalogues numerous courses in art but no well defined course in Negro or African art which early influenced that of the Greeks. Thinkers are now saying that the early culture of the Mediterranean was chiefly African. Most of these colleges do not even direct special attention to Negro music in which the Negro has made his outstanding contribution in America. The unreasonable attitude is that because the Whites do not have these things in their schools the Negroes must not have them in theirs. The Catholics and Jews, therefore, are wrong in establishing special schools to teach their principles of religion, and the Germans in America are unwise in having their children taught their mother tongue.

Such has been the education of Negroes. They have been taught facts of history, but have never learned to think. Their conception is that you go to school to find out what other people have done, and then you go out in life to imitate them. What they have done can be done by others, they contend; and they are right. They are wrong; however, in failing to realize that what others have done, we may not need to do. If we are to do identically the same thing from generation to generation, we would not make any progress. If we are to duplicate from century to century the same feats, the world will grow tired of such a monotonous performance.

In this particular respect "Negro education" is a failure, and disastrously so, because in its present predicament the race is especially in need of vision and invention to give humanity something new. The world does not want and will never have the heroes and heroines of the past. What this age needs is an enlightened youth not to undertake the tasks like theirs but to imbibe the spirit of these great men and answer the present call of duty with equal nobleness of soul.

Not only do the needs of generations vary, but the individuals themselves are not duplicates the one of the other; and being different in this respect, their only hope to function efficiently in society is to know themselves and the generation which they are to serve. The chief value in studying the records of others is to become better acquainted with oneself and with one's possibilities to live and to do in the present age. As long as Negroes continue to restrict themselves to doing what was necessary a hundred or a thousand years ago, they must naturally expect to be left out of the great scheme of things as they concern men of today.

The most inviting field for discovery and invention, then, is the Negro himself, but he does not realize it. Frederika Bremer, when reflecting upon her visit to America about 1850, gave this country a new thought in saying to Americans, "The romance of your history is the fate of the Negro." In this very thought lies unusual possibilities for the historian, the economist, the artist, and the philosopher. Why should the Negro writer seek a theme abroad when he has the greatest of all at home?

The bondage of the Negro brought captive from Africa is one of the greatest dramas in history, and the writer who merely sees in that ordeal something to approve or condemn fails to understand the evolution of the human race. Negroes now studying dramatics go into our schools to reproduce Shakespeare, but mentally developed members of this race would see the possibilities of a greater drama in the tragedy of the man of color. Negroes graduating from conservatories of music dislike the singing of our folk songs. For some reason such misguided persons think that they can improve on the productions of the foreign drama or render the music of other people better than they can themselves.

A knowledge of real history would lead one to think that slavery was one of the significant developments which, although evil in themselves, may redound sometimes to the advantage of the oppressed rather than to that of the oppressor. Someone has said that the music of Poland was inspired by incidents of a struggle against the despots invading and partitioning their prostrate land. The Greeks never had an art until the country was overrun by hostile Orientals. Someone then began to immortalize in song the sons who went forth to fight for the native land. Another carved in marble the thought evoked by the example of the Greek youth who blocked the mountain pass with his body or who bared his breast to the javelin to defend the liberty of his country. These things we call art.

In our own country the other elements of the population, being secure in their position, have never faced such a crisis; and the Europeans, after whose pattern American life is fashioned, have not recently had such experience. White Americans, then, have produced no art at all, and that of Europe has reached the point of stagnation. Negroes who are imitating Whites, then, are engaged in a most unprofitable performance. Why not interpret themselves anew to the world?

If we had a few thinkers we could expect great achievements on tomorrow. Some Negro with unusual insight would write an epic of bondage and freedom which would take its place with those of Homer and Virgil. Some Negro with esthetic appreciation would construct from collected fragments of Negro music a grand opera that would move humanity to repentance.

Some Negro of philosophic penetration would find a solace for the modern world in the soul of the Negro, and then men would be men because they are men.

The Negro in his present plight, however, does not see possibilities until it is too late He exercises much "hindsight," and for that reason he loses ground in the hotly contested battles of life. The Negro as a rule waits until a thing happens before he tries to avert it. He is too much like a man whom the author once saw knocked down in a physical combat. Instead of dodging the blow when it was being dealt he arose from his prostration dodging it.

For example, the author has just received a letter from a lady in Pittsburgh complaining that the librarian in one of its schools insists upon reading to the children "a great deal of literature containing such words as `nigger,' `blackie,' `Little Black Sambo,' etc." This lady, therefore, would like to place in that school some books by Negro authors. This is a commendable effort, but it comes a little late; we hope not too late.

For centuries such literature has been circulated among the children of the modern world; and they have, therefore, come to regard the Negro as inferior. Now that some of our similarly miseducated Negroes are seeing how they have been deceived they are awakening to address themselves to a long neglected work. They should have been thinking about this generations ago, for they have a tremendous task before them today in dispelling this error and counteracting the results of such bias in our literature.

There has just come, too, from a friend of humanity in Edinburgh, Scotland, a direful account of the increase in race prejudice in those parts. Sailors who had frequented the stronghold of race prejudice in South Africa undertook recently to prevent Negro men from socializing with Scotch women at a dance; and certain professors of the University of Edinburgh with the same attitude show so much of it in their teaching that this friend entreats us to send them informing books on the Negro. We are doing it.

Here again, however, the effort to uproot error and popularize the truth comes rather late. The Negro since freedom has gone along grinning, whooping, and "cutting capers" while the white man has applied himself to the task of defining the status of the Negro and compelling him to accept it as thus settled forever. While the Negro has been idle, propaganda has gone far ahead of history. Unfortunately, too, Negro "scholars" have assisted in the production of literature which gives this point of view.

---

# CHAPTER 14
# The New Program

---

It seems only a reasonable proposition, then, that, if under the present system which produced our leadership in religion, politics, and business we have gone backward toward serfdom or have at least been kept from advancing to real freedom, it is high time to develop another sort of leadership with a different educational system. In the first place, we must bear in mind that the Negro has never been educated. He has merely been informed about other things which he has not been permitted to do. The Negroes have been shoved out of the regular schools through the rear door into the obscurity of the backyard and told to imitate others whom they see from afar, or they have been permitted in some places to come into the public schools to see how others educate themselves. The program for the uplift of the Negro in this country must be based upon a scientific study of the Negro from within to develop in him the power to do for himself what his oppressors will never do to elevate him to the level of others.

Being without actual education, we have very few persons prepared to help the Negroes whom they have set out to lead. These persons are not all dishonest men and women. Many of them are sincere, and believe that they are doing the race some great good in thus holding it backward.

They must be awakened and shown the error of their ways.

We have very few teachers because most of those with whom we are afflicted know nothing about the children whom they teach or about their parents who influence the pupils more than the teachers themselves. When a boy comes to school without knowing his lesson he should be studied instead of being punished. The boy who does well in the beginning of the year and lags behind near the end of the term should not always be censured or ridiculed. As a rule, such children are not responsible for their failures. Their parents and their social status account mainly for these shortcomings. The Negro teacher, then, must treat the disease rather than its symptoms.

But can you expect teachers to revolutionize the social order for the good of the community?

Indeed we must expect this very thing. The educational system of a country is worthless unless it accomplishes this task. Men of scholarship and consequently of prophetic insight must show us the right way and lead us into the light which shines brighter and brighter.

In the church where we have much freedom and independence we must get rid of preachers who are not prepared to help the people whom they exploit. The public must refuse to support men of this type. Ministers who are the creations of the old educational system must be awakened, and if this is impossible they must be dethroned. Those who keep the people in ignorance and play upon their emotions must be exiled. The people have never been taught what religion is, for most of the preachers find it easier to stimulate the superstition which develops in the unenlightened mind. Religion in such hands, then, becomes something with which you take advantage of weak people. Why try to enlighten the people in such, matters when superstition serves just as well for exploitation?

The ministers with the confidence of the people must above all things understand the people themselves. They must find out the past of their parishioners, whether they were brought up in Georgia, Alabama or Texas, whether they are housed under desirable circumstances, what they do to make a living, what they do with their earnings, how they react to the world about them, how they spend their leisure, or how they function along with other elements of the social order.

In our schools, and especially in schools of religion, attention should be given to the study of the Negro as he developed during the antebellum period by showing to what extent that remote culture was determined by ideas which the Negro brought with him from Africa. To take it for granted that the ante-bellum Negro was an ignoramus or that the native brought from Africa had not a valuable culture merely because some prejudiced writers have said so does not show the attitude of scholarship, and Negro students who direct their courses accordingly will never be able to grapple with the social problems presented today by the Negro church.

The preachers of today must learn to do as well as those of old. Richard Allen so interpreted Christianity anew to his master that he was converted, and so did Henry Evans and George Bentley for other Whites in North Carolina and Tennessee. Instead of accepting and trying to carry out the theories which the exploiters of humanity have brought them for a religious program the Negroes should forget their differences and in the strength of a united church bring out a new interpretation of Christ to this unwilling world. Following the religious teachings of their traducers, the Negroes do not show any more common sense than a people would in permitting criminals to enact the laws and establish the procedure of the courts by which they are to be tried.

Negro preachers, too, must be educated to their people rather than away from them. This, of course, requires a new type of religious school. To provide for such training the Negro church must get rid of its burdensome supervisory force. If the number of bishops of the various Negro Methodist churches were reduced to about twelve or fifteen, as they should be, the amount of a hundred thousand dollars or more now being paid to support the unnecessary number could be used to maintain properly at least one accredited college; and what is now being raised here and there to support various struggling but starving institutions kept alive by ambitious bishops and preachers could be saved to the people. With this money diverted to a more practical use the race would be able to establish some other things which would serve as assets rather than as liabilities.

We say liabilities, for practically all of our denominational schools which are bleeding the people for the inadequate support which they receive are still unable to do accredited work. There are so many of them that the one impoverishes the other. Outstanding men of the church, therefore, have to acquire their advanced education by attending other schools in the beginning or by taking additional training elsewhere after learning all our denominational schools can offer. This is a loss of ground which should be regained if the church is to go forward.

By proper unification and organization the Negro churches might support one or two much needed universities of their own. With the present arrangement of two or three in the same area and sometimes as many in one city there is no chance for emerging from the trying povertystricken state. And even if these institutions could do well what they undertake they do not supply all educational needs. To qualify for certification in the professions Negroes must go to other schools, where, although they acquire the fundamentals, they learn much about their "inferiority" to discourage them in their struggle upward.

We should not close any accredited Negro colleges or universities, but we should reconstruct the whole system. We should not eliminate many of the courses now being offered, but we should secure men of vision to give them from the point of view of the people to be served. We should not spend less money for the higher education of the Negro, but should redefine higher education as preparation to think and work out a program to serve the lowly rather than to live as an aristocrat.

Such subjects of certitude as mathematics, of course, would continue and so would most of the work in practical languages and science. In theology, literature, social science, and education, however, radical reconstruction is necessary. The old worn-out theories as to man's relation to God and his fellowman, the system of thought which has permitted one man to exploit, oppress, and exterminate another and still be regarded as righteous must be discarded for the new thought of men as brethren and the idea of God as the lover of all mankind.

After Negro students have mastered the fundamentals of English, the principles of composition, and the leading facts in the development of its literature, they should not spend all of their time in advanced work on Shakespeare, Chaucer and Anglo-Saxon. They should direct their attention also to the folklore of the African, to the philosophy in his proverbs, to the development of the Negro in the use of modern language, and to the works of Negro writers.

The leading facts of the history of the world should be studied by all, but of what advantage is it to the Negro student of history to devote all of his time to courses bearing on such despots as Alexander the Great, Caesar, and Napoleon, or to the record of those nations whose outstanding achievement has been rapine, plunder, and murder for world power? Why not study the African background from the point of view of anthropology and history, and then take up sociology as it concerns the Negro peasant or proletarian who is suffering from sufficient ills to supply laboratory work for the most advanced students of the social order? Why not take up economics as reflected by the Negroes of today and work out some remedy for their lack of capital, the absence of cooperative enterprise, and the short life of their establishments. Institutions like Harvard, Yale and Columbia are not going to do these things, and educators influenced by them to the extent that they become blind to the Negro will never serve the race efficiently.

To educate the Negro we must find out exactly what his background is, what he is today, what his possibilities are, and how to begin with him as he is and make him a better individual of the kind that he is. Instead of cramming the Negro's mind with what others have shown that they can do, we should develop his latent powers that he may perform in society a part of which others are not capable.

During his life the author has seen striking examples of how people should and should not be taught. Some of these are worth relating. Probably the most interesting was that of missionary work in China. In 1903 the author crossed the Pacific Ocean with twenty-six missionaries who were going to take the Orient by storm. One Todd, from North Carolina, was orating and preaching almost every day to stimulate his coworkers to go boldly to the task before them. Dr. De Forest, long a missionary to Japan, informed them that the work required more than enthusiasm; that they could not rush into the homes of the natives saying, "Peace be to this house." for it might turn out the other way and give somebody the opportunity to say, "Peace be to his ashes."

Dr. De Forest explained to them how he chose a decidedly different course, preferring first to study the history, the language, the manners and the customs of the people to approach them intelligently; and not until he had been in the country four years did he undertake to exhort, but after that time he had had great success and had been invited to preach before the Mikado himself. Now Todd did not take this advice, and he had not been in China five months before he and his wife had been poisoned by their native cook who had become incensed at the way they interfered with the institutions of his people.

Another striking illustration was the education of the Filipinos. Not long after the close of the Spanish-American War the United States Government started out to educate the Filipinos over night. Numbers of "highly trained" Americans were carried there to do the work they entered upon their task by teaching the Filipinos just as they had taught American children who were otherwise circumstanced. The result was failure. Men trained at institutions like Harvard, Yale, Columbia, and Chicago could not reach these people and had to be dismissed from the service.

Some of these "scholarly" Americans had to be maintained by the subscription of friends until they could be returned to this country on Government transportation.

In the meantime, however, there came along an insurance man, who went to the Philippines to engage in business. He had never taught at all, and he had never studied authorities like Bagley, Judd, and Thorndike; but he understood people seeing that others had failed; he went into the work himself. He filled the schoolroom with thousands of objects from the pupil's environment.

In the beginning he did not use books very much, because those supplied were not adapted to the needs of the children. He talked about the objects around them. Everything was presented objectively. When he took up the habits of the snake he brought the reptile to the school for demonstration. When he taught the crocodile he had one there. In teaching the Filipinos music he did not sing "Come shake the Apple-Tree." They had never seen such an object. He taught them to sing "Come shake the Lomboy Tree," something which they had actually done. In reading he did not concentrate on the story of how George Washington always told the truth. They had never heard of him and could not have appreciated that myth if someone had told them about it.

This real educator taught them about their own hero, José Rizal, who gave his life as a martyr for the freedom of his country. By and by they got rid of most books based on the life of American people and worked out an entirely new series dealing with the life of Filipinos. The result, then, was that this man and others who saw the situation as he did succeeded, and the work of the public schools in the Philippines is today the outstanding achievement of the Americans in that country.

We do not mean to suggest here, however, that any people should ignore the record of the progress of other races. We would not advocate any such unwise course. We say, hold on to the real facts of history as they are, but complete such knowledge by studying also the history of races and nations which have been purposely ignored. We should not underrate the achievements of Mesopotamia, Greece, and Rome; but we should give equally as much attention to the internal African kingdoms, the Songhay empire, and Ethiopia, which through Egypt decidedly influenced the civilization of the Mediterranean world. We would not ignore the rise of Christianity and the development of the Church; but we would at the same time give honorable mention to the persons of African blood who figured in these achievements, and who today are endeavoring to carry out the principles of Jesus long since repudiated by most so-called Christians. We would not underestimate the achievements of the captains of industry who in the commercial expansion of the modern world have produced the wealth necessary to ease and comfort; but we would give credit to the Negro who so largely supplied the demand for labor by which these things have been accomplished.

In our own particular history we would not dim one bit the luster of any star in our firmament.

We would not learn less of George Washington, "First in War, First in Peace and First in the Hearts of his Countrymen"; but we would learn something also of the three thousand Negro soldiers of the American Revolution who helped to make this "Father of our Country" possible.

We would not neglect to appreciate the unusual contribution of Thomas Jefferson to freedom and democracy; but we would invite attention also to two of his outstanding contemporaries, Phyllis Wheatley, the writer of interesting verse, and Benjamin Banneker, the mathematician, astronomer, and advocate of a world peace plan set forth in 1793 with the vital principles of Woodrow Wilson's League of Nations. We would in no way detract from the fame of Perry on Lake Erie or Jackson at New Orleans in the second struggle with England; but we would remember the gallant Black men who assisted in winning these memorable victories on land and sea. We would not cease to pay tribute to Abraham Lincoln as the "Savior of the Country"; but we would ascribe praise also to the one hundred and seventy-eight thousand Negroes who had to be mustered into the service of the Union before it could be preserved, and who by their heroism demonstrated that they were entitled to freedom and citizenship.

---

# CHAPTER 15
# Vocational Guidance

---

But how can the Negro in this new system learn to make a living, the most important task to which all people must give attention? In view of the Negro's economic plight most of the schools are now worked up over what is called "vocational guidance" in an effort to answer this very question. To what, however, are they to guide their Negro students? Most Negroes now employed are going down blind alleys, and unfortunately some schools seem to do no more than to stimulate their going in that direction.

This may seem to be a rash statement, but a study of our educational system shows that our schools are daily teaching Negroes what they can never apply in life or what is no longer profitable because of the revolution of industry by the multiplication of mechanical appliances.

For example, some of our schools are still teaching individual garment making which offers no future today except in catering to the privileged and rich classes. Some of these institutions still offer instruction in shoemaking when the technique developed under their handicaps makes impossible competition with that of the modern factory based upon the invention of a Negro, Jan Matzeliger.

These facts have been known for generations, but some of these institutions apparently change not. Education, like religion, is conservative. It makes haste slowly only, and sometimes not at all. Do not change the present order of thinking and doing, many say, for you disturb too many things long since regarded as ideal. The dead past, according to this view, must be the main factor in determining the future. We should learn from the living past, but let the dead past remain dead.

A survey of employment of the Negroes in this country shows a most undesirable situation the education of the masses has not enabled them to advance very far in making a living and has not developed in the Negro the power to change this condition. It is revealed that in many establishments the Negro when a young man starts as a janitor or porter and dies in old age in the same position. Tradition fixes his status as such, and both races feel satisfied.

When this janitor or porter dies the dailies headline the passing of this Negro who knew his place and rendered satisfactory service in it. "Distinguished" white men, for whom he ran errands and cleaned cuspidors, volunteer as honorary pall-bearers and follow his remains to the final resting place. Thoughtless Negro editors, instead of expressing their regret that such a life of usefulness was not rewarded by promotion, take up the refrain as some great honor bestowed upon the race.

Among people thus satisfied in the lower pursuits of life and sending their children to school to memorize theories which they never see applied, there can be no such thing as vocational guidance. Such an effort implies an objective; and in the present plight of economic dependence there is no occupation for which the Negro may prepare himself with the assurance that he will find employment. Opportunities which he has today may be taken from him tomorrow; and schools changing their curricula in hit-and-miss fashion may soon find themselves on the wrong track just as they have been for generations.

Negroes do not need someone to guide them to what persons of another race have developed.

They must be taught to think and develop something for themselves. It is most pathetic to see Negroes begging others for a chance as we have been doing recently. "Do not force us into starvation." we said. "Let us come into your stores and factories and do a part of what you are doing to profit by our trade." The Negro as a slave developed this fatal sort of dependency; and, restricted mainly to menial service and drudgery during nominal freedom, he has not grown out of it. Now the Negro is facing the ordeal of either learning to do for himself or to die out gradually in the bread line in the ghetto.

If the schools really mean to take a part in necessary uplift they must first supply themselves with teachers. Unfortunately we have very few such workers. The large majority of persons supposedly teaching Negroes never carry to the schoolroom any thought as to improving their condition. From the point of view of these so-called teachers they have done their duty when in automaton fashion they impart in the schoolroom the particular facts which they wrote out in the examination when they "qualified" for their respective positions. Most of them are satisfied with receiving their pay and spending it for the toys and gewgaws of life.

For example, the author is well acquainted with a Negro of this type, who is now serving as the head of one of the largest schools in the United States. From the point of view of our present system he is well educated. He holds advanced degrees from one of the leading institutions of the world; and he is known to be well informed on all the educational theories developed from the time of Socrates down to the day of Dewey. Yet this "educator" says repeatedly that in his daily operations he never has anything to do with Negroes because they are impossible. He says that he never buys anything from a Negro store, and he would not dare to put a penny in a Negro bank.

From such teachers large numbers of Negroes learn this fateful lesson. For example, not long ago a committee of Negroes in a large city went to the owner of a chain store in their neighborhood and requested that he put a Negro manager in charge. This man replied that he doubted that the Negroes themselves wanted such a thing. The Negroes urging him to make the change assured him that they were unanimously in favor of it. The manager, however, asked them to be fair enough with his firm and themselves to investigate before pressing the matter any further. They did so and discovered that one hundred thirty-seven Negro families in that neighborhood seriously objected to buying from Negroes and using articles handled by them. These Negroes, then, had to do the groundwork of uprooting the inferiority idea which had resulted from their mis-education.

To what, then, can a Negro while despising the enterprise of his fellows guide the youth of his race; and where do you figure out that the youth thus guided will be by 1950? The Whites are daily informing Negroes that they need not come to them for opportunities. Can the Negro youth, mis-educated by persons who depreciate their efforts, learn to make, opportunities for themselves? This is the real problem which the Negroes must solve; and he who is not interested in it and makes no effort to solve it is worthless in the present struggle.

Our advanced teachers, like "most highly educated" Negroes, pay little attention to the things about them except when the shoe begins to pinch on one or the other side. Unless they happen to become naked they never think of the production of cotton or wool; unless they get hungry they never give any thought to the output of wheat or corn; unless their friends lose their jobs they never inquire about the outlook for coal or steel, or how these things affect the children whom they are trying to teach. In other words, they live in a world, but they are not of it. How can such persons guide the youth without knowing how these things affect the Negro community?

The Negro community, in a sense, is composed of those around you, but it functions in a different way. You cannot see it by merely looking out of the windows of the schoolroom. This community requires scientific investigation. While persons of African blood are compelled to sustain closer relation to their own people than to other elements in society, they are otherwise influenced socially and economically. The Negro community suffers for lack of delimitation because of the various ramifications of life in the United States. For example, there may be a Negro grocer in the neighborhood, but the Negro chauffeur for a rich man down town and the washerwoman for an aristocratic family in "quality row" will be more than apt to buy their food and clothing at the larger establishment with which their employers have connections, although they may be insulted there. Negroes of the District of Columbia have millions of dollars deposited in banks down town, where Negro women are not allowed in the ladies' rest rooms.

Right in the heart of the highly educated Negro section of Washington, too, is a restaurant catering through the front door exclusively to the white business men, who must live in the Negroes' section to supply them with the necessities of life, and catering at the same time through the back door to numbers of Negroes who pile into that dingy room to purchase whatever may be thrown at them. Yet less than two blocks away are several Negroes running cafés where they can be served for the same amount and under desirable circumstances. Negroes who do this, we say, do not have the proper attitude toward life and its problems, and for that reason we do not take up time with them. They do not belong to our community. The traducers of the race, however, are guiding these people the wrong way. Why do not the "educated" Negroes change their course by identifying themselves with the masses?

For similar reasons the Negro professional man may not always have a beautiful home and a fine car. His plight to the contrary may result from action like that of a poor man who recently knocked on the author's door about midnight to use his telephone to call the ambulance of the Casualty Hospital to take immediate charge of his sick wife. Although living nearer to the Freedmen's Hospital, where more sympathetic consideration would have been given this patient, he preferred to take her to the other hospital where she would have to be carried through the back yard and placed in a room over a stable. He worked there, however; and because of long association with his traducers and the sort of treatment that they have meted out to him he was willing to entrust to their hands the very delicate matter of the health of his wife. This was a part of his community.

Large numbers of Negroes live in such a community. You say that such an atmosphere is not congenial and you will not lose time with these people who are thus satisfied, but the exploiting preacher, the unprincipled politician, the notorious gambler, and the agent of vice are all there purposely misleading these people who have not as yet shaken from their minds the shackles of slavery. What is going to become of them? What is going to become of you?

We avoid them because we find enjoyment among others; but they are developing their own community. Their teacher lives in another community which may or may not be growing. Will his community so expand as to include theirs? If not, their community may encroach upon his. It is a sort of social dualism. What will the end be? The teacher will help to answer this question.

Such guidance, however, must not be restricted to the so-called common people. So many Negroes now engaged in business have no knowledge of its possibilities and limitations. Most of them are as unwise as a Negro business man who came to Washington recently in a tenthousand dollar car representing a firm with only one hundred thousand dollars invested. It is only a matter of time before his firm will be no more. He started out destroying his business at the very source. While Negroes are thus spending their means and themselves in riotous living the foreigners come to dwell among them in modest circumstances long enough to get rich and to join those who close in on these unfortunates economically until all the hopes for their redemption are lost.

If the Negroes of this country are to escape starvation and rise out of poverty unto comfort and ease, they must change their way of thinking and living. Never did the author see a more striking demonstration of such a necessity than recently when a young man came to him looking for a job. He was well bedecked with jewelry and fine clothes, and while he was in the office he smoked almost enough cigars to pay one's board for that day. A man of this type in a povertystricken group must suffer and die.

A young woman recently displaced in a position from which she received considerable income for a number of years approached the author not long ago to help her solve the problem of making a living. He could not feel very sympathetic toward her, however, for she had on a coat which cost enough to maintain one comfortably for at least two years. While talking with him, moreover, she was so busy telling him about what she wanted that she had little time to inform him as to what she can do to supply her needs.

A man whom the author knows is decidedly handicapped by having lost a lucrative position. He must now work for a little more than half of what he has been accustomed to earn. With his former stipend he was able to maintain two or three girls in addition to his wife, and he drank the best of bootleg stuff available. In now trying to do all of these things on a small wage he finds himself following a most tortuous course to make his ends meet, and he suffers within as well as without.

This undesirable attitude toward life results from the fact that the Negro has learned from others how to spend money much more rapidly than he has learned how to earn it. During these days, therefore, it will be very wise for Negroes to concentrate on the wise use of money and the evil results from the misuse of it. In large cities like Washington, Baltimore, Philadelphia, New York, and Chicago they earn millions and millions every year and throw these vast sums immediately away for trifles which undermine their health, vitiate their morals, and contribute to the undoing of generations of Negroes unborn.

This enlightenment as to economic possibilities in the Negro community must not only include instruction as to how enterprises can be made possible but how they should be apportioned among the various parts of the Negro community. Such knowledge is especially necessary in the case of Negroes because of the fatal tendency toward imitation not only of the white man but the imitation of others in his own group. For example, a Negro starts a restaurant on a corner and does well. Another Negro, observing this prosperity, thinks that he can do just as well by opening a similar establishment next door. The inevitable result is that by dividing the trade between himself and his forerunner he makes it impossible for either one to secure sufficient patronage to continue in business.

In undertakings of great importance this same undesirable tendency toward duplication of effort is also apparent. It has been a common thing to find two or three banks in a Negro community, each one struggling for an existence in competing for the patronage of the small group of people, all of whom would hardly be able to support one such financial institution. These banks continue their unprofitable competition and never think of merging until some crisis forces them to the point that they have to do so or go into bankruptcy. The Negro community, then, never has a strong financial institution with sufficient resources to stimulate the efforts of the business men who otherwise might succeed.

The same shortsightedness has been evident in, the case of the insurance companies organized by Negroes. One was established here and then another followed there in imitation of the first. We have been accustomed to boast that the Negroes have about fifty insurance companies in this country, marking the corners of the streets of the cities with large signs displaying what they are doing for the race. Instead of boasting of such unwise expansion we should have received such information with sorrow, for what the race actually needs is to merge all of the insurance companies now supported by Negroes and make one good one. Such a step away from duplication would be a long stride toward our much needed awakening, and it would certainly give us prestige in the business world.

This imitation and duplication are decidedly disastrous to economic enterprise as we can daily observe. A few days ago a young man in the East lamented the fact that after investing his life's earnings in the drug business and making every effort to stimulate the enterprise, he has failed.

Someone took occasion, thereupon, to remind him that men have grown rich, as a rule, not by doing what thousands of others are doing but by undertaking something new. If instead of going into the retail dispensing of drugs, he had conceived and carried out the idea of the chain-drug store, he would have become an independently rich man.

There is always a chance to do this because the large majority of people do not think and, therefore, leave the field wide open for those who have something new with which to please the public. Negroes even found this possible during the days of slavery when the race supposedly had no chance at all.

About a hundred years ago Thomas Day, a North Carolina Negro, realized that the rough furniture of the people in his community did not meet the requirements of those of modern taste.

He, therefore, worked out a style of ornate and beautiful furniture which attracted the attention of the most aristocratic people of the state and built up for himself a most successful business.

Persons in that state are still talking about the Day furniture, and not long ago it became the subject of a magazine article. If North Carolina would turn out, more Negroes of this type today, instead of the rather large number who are going to teach and preach, some of its present economic problems might thereby be solved.

During these same years another Negro was showing himself to be equally ingenious. This was Henry Boyd. After buying himself in Kentucky, he went to Cincinnati to start life as a free man.

There he encountered so much prejudice against Negro labor that he could not find employment at his trade of cabinetmaking. A new thought came to him, however; and in this way he solved his own problem.

Boyd became convinced that people had been sleeping long enough on straw ticks and wooden slats, and he invented the corded bed, the most comfortable bed prior to the use of springs which brought still more ease. Boyd's corded bed became popular throughout the Ohio and Mississippi Valleys, and he built up a profitable trade which required the employment of twenty-five white and Black artisans. Other enterprising Negro business men like Boyd gave the Negro element of Cincinnati more of an aspect of progress before the Civil War than it has today. Has the Negro less chance today than he had a century ago?

For about thirty years the author knew an old Negro lady at Gordonsville, Virginia, who gave the world something new in frying chicken. She discovered the art of doing this thing in the way that others could not, and she made a good living selling her exceptionally prepared chicken and fried puffs at the windows of the cars when the trains stopped at the station. Well-to-do men and women of both races would leave the Pullman train with its modern diner attached and go out and supply themselves and their friends with this old lady's tastefully made up lunches.

Another woman of color living in Columbia, Missouri, recently gave the world another new idea.

She had learned cooking, especially baking, but saw no exceptional opportunity in the usual application of the trade. After studying her situation and the environment in which she had to live, she hit upon the scheme of popularizing her savory sweet potato biscuits, beaten whiter than all others by an invention of her own; and the people of both races made a well-beaten path to her home to enjoy these delicious biscuits. In this way she has made herself and her relatives independent.

This is the way fortunes are made, but Negroes, who are conscientiously doing their best to rise in the economic sphere, do not follow the noble examples of those who had less opportunity than we have today. We spend much time in slavish imitation, but our white friends strike out along new lines. Almost all of the large fortunes in America have been made in this way.

John D. Rockefeller did not set out in life to imitate Vanderbilt. Rockefeller saw his opportunity in developing the oil industry. Carnegie had better sense than to imitate Rockefeller, for that task was already well done, and he consolidated the steel interests. Henry Ford knew better than to take up what Carnegie had exploited, for there appeared a still larger possibility for industrial achievement in giving the world the facility of cheap transportation in the low-priced car.

While such guidance as the Negro needs will concern itself first with material things, however, it must not stop with these as ends in themselves. In the acquisition of these we lay the foundation for the greater things of the spirit. A poor man properly directed can write a more beautiful poem than one who is surfeited. The man in the hovel composes a more charming song than the one in the palace. The painter in the ghetto gets an inspiration for a more striking portrait than his landlord can appreciate. The ill-fed sculptor lives more abundantly than the millionaire who purchases the expression of his thought in marble and bronze. For the Negro, then, the door of opportunity is wide open. Let him prepare himself to enter this field where competition is no handicap. In such a sphere he may learn to lead the world, while keeping pace with it in the development of the material things of life.

---

## CHAPTER 16
## The New Type Of Professional Man Required

---

Negroes should study for the professions for all sane reasons that members of another race should go into these lines of endeavor and also on account of the particular call to serve the lowly of their race. In the case of the law we should cease to make exceptions because of the possibilities for failure resulting from prejudice against the Negro lawyer and the lack of Negro business enterprises to require his services Negroes must become like English gentlemen who study the law of the land, not because they intend to practice the profession, but because every gentleman should know the law. In the interpretation of the law by the courts, too, all the rights of the Negroes in this country are involved, and a larger number of us must qualify for this important service. We may have too many lawyers of the wrong kind, but we have not our share of the right kind.

The Negro lawyer has tended to follow in the footsteps of the average white practitioner and has not developed the power which he could acquire if he knew more about the people whom he should serve and the problems they have to confront. These things are not law in themselves, but they determine largely whether or not the Negro will practice law and the success he will share in the profession. The failure to give attention to these things has often meant the downfall of many a Negro lawyer.

There are, moreover, certain aspects of law to which the white man would hardly address himself but to which the Negro should direct special attention. Of unusual importance to the Negro is the necessity for understanding the misrepresentations in criminal records of Negroes, and race distinctions in the laws of modern nations. These matters require a systematic study of the principles of law and legal procedure and, in addition thereto, further study of legal problems as they meet the Negro lawyer in the life which he must live. This offers the Negro law school an unusual opportunity.

Because our lawyers do not give attention to these problems they often fail in a crisis. They are interested in the race and want to defend its cause. The case, however, requires not only the unselfish spirit they sometimes manifest but much more understanding of the legal principles, involved. Nothing illustrates this better than the failure of one of our attorneys to measure up in the case brought up to the United States Supreme Court from Oklahoma to test the validity of the exclusion of Negroes from Pullman cars. The same criticism may be made of the segregation case of the District of Columbia brought before this highest tribunal by another Negro attorney.

In both of these cases the lawyers started wrong and therefore ended wrong. They lacked the knowledge to present their cases properly to the court.

Our lawyers must learn that the judges are not attorneys themselves, for they have to decide on the merits of what is presented to them. It is not the business of the judges to amend their pleadings or decide their cases according to their good intentions. Certainly such generosity cannot be expected from prejudiced courts which are looking for every loophole possible to escape from a frank decision on the rights of Negroes guaranteed by the constitution. These matters require advanced study and painstaking research; but our lawyers, as a rule, are not interested in this sort of mental exercise.

The Negro medical schools have had a much better opportunity than the few Negro law schools which have functioned in the professional preparation of Negroes. On account of the racial contact required of white physicians who are sometimes unwilling to sustain this relation to Negroes the Negro physicians and dentists have a better chance among their people than the Negro lawyers; and the demand for the services of the former assures a larger income than Negro lawyers are accustomed to earn. But in spite of this better opportunity Negro medical institutions and their graduates have done little more than others to solve the peculiar problems confronting the Negro race Too many Negroes go into medicine and dentistry merely for selfish purposes, hoping thereby to increase their income and spend it in joyous living. They have the ambition to own fine automobiles, to dress handsomely, and to figure conspicuously in society.

The practice of these professions among poor Negroes yields these results. Why not be a physician or dentist then?

Too many of our physicians are like the one whom the author recently visited in New York City.

"When I heard you coming up the stairs," said he, "I began to feel glad, for I was sure that you were another patient from whom I might extract at least two dollars for a prescription."

Yet one would wonder how that physician could prosper in his profession, for he had no special equipment for the practice of any kind of advanced phases of medicine. About all he could do was to look at the patient's tongue, feel his pulse, ask him a few questions, write a prescription and collect the fee. The apparatus required for the modern treatment of serious maladies he did not have and seemed to have no ambition to possess.

The Negroes of today are very much in need of physicians who in their professional work will live up to what they are taught in school, and will build upon their foundation by both experience and further training. In his segregated position in the ghetto the Negro health problem presents more difficulties than that of the Whites who are otherwise circumstanced. The longevity of the Negro depends in part upon the supply of Negro physicians and nurses who will address themselves unselfishly to the solution of this particular problem. Since the Negroes are forced into undesirable situations and compelled to inhabit germ-infested districts, they cannot escape ultimate extermination if our physicians do not help them to work out a community health program which will provide for the Negroes some way to survive.

Negro medical schools and their graduates must do more preaching of the necessity for improving conditions which determine health and eradicate disease. A large number of physicians and nurses must be trained, and new opportunities for them to practice must be found This can be done by turning out better products from these schools and the extension of hospitals among Negroes who have been so long neglected In this campaign, however, the Negro physicians must supply the leadership, and others must join with them in these efforts.

From medical schools, too, we must have Negroes with a program of medical research. Today the world is inclined to give attention to the health of the Negro since unsanitary conditions of the race will mean the loss of health among the Whites. Philanthropists, however, hardly know how to proceed or which way to go because they have so long neglected the Negroes that they do not know how to provide wisely for them; and the Negro physicians themselves have failed to give adequate attention to these conditions. Negro medical students have not directed sufficient attention to the ante-bellum background of the Negro who, still under that influence, indulges in superstitious and religious practices which impede the progress of medicine among them. One would be surprised to know the extent to which primitive medicine is practiced Among American Negroes today. Often in the rural districts they seldom see a physician. The midwife and the herb doctor there control the situation.

The greatest problem now awaiting solution is the investigation of the differential resistance of races to disease. What are the diseases of which Negroes are more susceptible than Whites? What are the diseases of which the Whites are more susceptible than Negroes? The Negro escapes yellow fever and influenza, but the white man dies. The white man withstands syphilis and tuberculosis fairly well, but the Negro afflicted with these maladies easily succumbs. These questions offer an inviting field of research for Negro medical students.

While we hear much about medicine, law and the like their importance must not be unduly emphasized. Certainly men should not crowd into these spheres to make money, but all professions among Negroes except those of teaching and preaching are undermanned. All Negroes in professions constitute less than two and a half per cent of those over ten years of age who are gainfully employed. At the same time the Whites find certain of their professions overcrowded, and some of their practitioners could not exist without the patronage of Negroes.

Negroes, too, should undergo systematic training for those professions in which they have shown special aptitude as in the arts. They must not wait for the Americans to approve their plunging into unknown spheres. The world is not circumscribed by the United States, and the Negro must become a pioneer in making use of a larger portion of the universe. If the people here do recognize the Negro in these spheres let him seek a hearing in the liberal circles of Europe. If he has any art Europeans will appreciate it and assure him success in forbidden fields In Europe, it should be noted, the Negro artist is not wanted as a mere imitator Europeans will recognize him in the role of an enlightened artist portraying the life of his people. As an English abolitionist said more than a century ago, "The portrait of the Negro has seldom been drawn but by the pencil of his oppressor and the Negro has sat for it in the distorted attitude of slavery." A new method of approach, however, is now possible. There has been an awakening in Europe to the realization of the significance of African culture, and circles there want to see that life depicted by the Negro who can view it from within. There is a philosophy in it that the world must understand. From its contemplation may come a new social program herein lay the opportunity of the Negro artist as a world reformer? Will he see it and live or continue the mere imitation of others and die?

---

# CHAPTER 17
## Higher Strivings In The Service Of The Country

---

Another factor the Negro needs is a new figure in politics, one who will not concern himself so much with what others can do for him as with what he can do for himself. He will know sufficient about the system of government not to carry his trouble to the federal functionaries and thus confess himself a failure in the community in which he lives. He will know that his freedom from peonage and lynching will be determined by the extent that he can develop into a worthy citizen and impress himself upon his community.

The New Negro in politics will not be so unwise as to join the ignorant delegations from conferences and convention which stage annual pilgrimages to the White House to complain to the President because they have socially and economically failed to measure up to demands of self-preservation.

The New Negro in politics will understand clearly that in the final analysis federal functionaries cannot do anything about these matters within the police powers of the states, and he will not put himself in the position of being received with coldness and treated with contempt as these ignorant misleaders of the Negro race have been from time immemorial. The New Negro in politics, then, will appeal to his own and to such friends of other races in his locality as believe in social justice. If he does something for himself others will do more for him.

The increasing vigor of the race, then, will not be frittered away in partisan strife in the interest of the oppressors of the race. It ought not to be possible for the political bosses to induce almost any Negro in the community to abandon his permanent employment to assist them and their ilk in carrying out some program for the selfish purposes of the ones engineering the scheme. It ought not to be possible for the politicians to distribute funds at the rate of fifty or a hundred dollars a head among the outstanding ministers and use them and their congregations in vicious partisan strife. It is most shameful that some ministers resort to religion as a camouflage to gain influence in the churches only to use such power for selfish political purpose.

The Negro should endeavor to be a figure in politics, not a tool for the politicians. This higher role can be played not by parking all of the votes of a race on one side of the fence as both Blacks and Whites have done in the South, but by independent action. The Negro should not censure the Republican Party for forgetting him and he should not blame the Democratic Party for opposing him. Neither can the South blame anyone but itself for its isolation in national politics. Any people who will vote the same way for three generations without thereby obtaining results ought to be ignored and disfranchised.

As a minority element the Negro should not knock at the door of any particular political party; he should appeal to the Negroes themselves and from them should come harmony and concerted action for a new advance to that larger freedom of men. The Negro should use his vote rather than give it away to reward the dead for some favors done in the distant past. He should clamor not for the few offices earmarked as Negro jobs but for the recognition of these despised persons as men according to the provision of the Constitution of the United States.

The few state and national offices formerly set aside for Negroes have paled into insignificance when compared with the many highly lucrative positions now occupied by Negroes as a result of their development in other spheres. Sometimes a Negro prominent in education, business or professional life can earn more in a few months than the most successful politicians can earn in years. These political jobs, moreover, have diminished in recent years because the increase of race prejudice, which this policy has doubtless aided, supplies the political leaders with an excuse for not granting their Negro coworkers anything additional.

The New Negro in politics must learn something that the old "ward-heelers" have never been able to realize, namely, not only that the few offices allotted Negroes are insignificant but that even if the Negro received a proportionate share of the spoils, the race cannot hope to solve any serious problem by the changing fortunes of politics. Real politics, the science of government, is deeply rooted in the economic foundation of the social order. To figure greatly in politics the Negro must be a great figure in politics. A class of people slightly lifted above poverty, therefore, can never have much influence in political circles. The Negro must develop character and worth to make him a desirable everywhere so that he will not have to knock at the doors of political parties but will have them thrown open to him.

The New Negro in politics must not ask the party for money, he must not hire himself for a pittance to swing voters in line. He must contribute to the campaign of the party pleasing him, rather than draw upon it for an allowance to drive the wolf from the door during the three months of the political canvass. It will be considered a stroke of good fortune that a Negro of such influence and character has aligned himself with a party, and this fact will speak eloquently for the element to which he belongs.

The New Negro in politics, moreover, must not be a politician. He must be a man. He must try to give the world something rather than extract something from it. The world, as he should see it, does not owe him anything, certainly not a political office; and he should not try solely to secure one, and thus waste valuable years which might be devoted to the development of something of an enduring value. If he goes into office, it should be as a sacrifice, because his valuable time is equired elsewhere. If he is needed by his country in a civil position, he may respond to the call as a matter of duty, for his usefulness is otherwise assured. From such a Negro, then, we may expect sound advice, intelligent guidance, and constructive effort fort the good of all elements of our population.

When such Negroes go into office you will not find them specializing in things which peculiarly concern the Negroes, offering merely anti-lynching bills and measures for pensioning the freedmen. The New Negro in politics will see his opportunity not in thus restricting himself but in visioning the whole social and economic order with his race as a part of it. In thus working for the benefit of all as prompted by his liberal mindedness the New Negro will do much more to bring the elements together for common good than he will be able to do in prating only of the ills of his particular corner and extending his hand for a douceur.

In suggesting herein the rise of the New Negro in politics the author does not have in mind the so-called radical Negroes who have read and misunderstood Karl Marx and his disciples and would solve the political as well as the economic problems of the race by an immediate application of these principles. History shows that although large numbers of people have actually tried to realize such pleasant dreams, they have in the final analysis come back to a social program based on competition.

If no one is to enjoy the fruits of his exceptional labor any more than the individual who is not prepared to render such extraordinary service, not one of a thousand will be sufficiently humanitarian to bestir himself to achieve much of importance, and force applied in this case to stimulate such action has always broken down. If the excited Whites who are bringing to the Negroes such strange doctrines are insane enough to believe them, the Negroes themselves should learn to think before it is too late History shows that it does not matter who is in power or what revolutionary forces take over the government, those who have not learned to do for themselves and have to depend solely on others never obtain any more rights or privileges in the end than they had in the beginning. Even if the expected social upheaval comes, the Negro will be better prepared to take care of himself in the subsequent reconstruction if he develops the power to ascend to a position higher up after the radically democratic people will have recovered from their revelry in an impossible Utopia.

To say that the Negro cannot develop sufficiently in the business world to measure arms with present-day capitalists is to deny actual facts, refute history, and discredit the Negro as a capable competitor in the economic battle of life. No man knows what he can do until he tries. The Negro race has never tried to do very much for itself. The race has great possibilities. Properly awakened, the Negro can do the so-called impossible in the business world and thus help to govern rather than merely be governed.

In the failure to see this and the advocacy of the destruction of the whole economic order to right social wrong we see again the tendency of the Negro to look to some force from without to do for him what he must learn to do for himself. The Negro needs to become radical, and the race will never amount to anything until it does become so, but this radicalism should come from within. The Negro will be very foolish to resort to extreme measures in behalf of foreign movements before he learns to suffer and die to right his own wrongs. There is no movement in the world-working especially for the Negro. He must learn to do this for himself or be exterminated just as the American Indian has faced his doom in the setting sun.

Why should the Negro wait for someone from without to urge him to self-assertion when he sees himself robbed by his employer, defrauded by his merchant, and hushed up by government agents of injustice? Why wait for a spur to action when he finds his manhood insulted, his women outraged, and his fellowmen lynched for amusement? The Negroes have always had sufficient reason for being radical, and it looks silly to see them taking up the cause of others who pretend that they are interested in the Negro when they merely mean to use the race as a means to an end. When the desired purpose of these so-called friendly groups will have been served, they will have no further use for the Negro and will drop him just as the Republican machine has done.

The radicals bring forward, too, the argument that the Negro, being of a minority group, will always be overpowered by others From the point of view of the selfish elements this may be true, and certainly it has worked thus for some time; but things do not always turn out according to mathematical calculations. In fact, the significant developments in history have never been thus determined. Only the temporary and the trivial can be thus forecast. The human factor is always difficult for the materialist to evaluate and the prophecies of the alarmist are often upset why should we expect less in the case of the Negro?

---

# CHAPTER 18
## The Study Of The Negro

---

The facts drawn from an experience of more than twenty years enable us to make certain deductions with respect to the study of the Negro. Only one Negro out of every ten thousand is interested in the effort to set forth what his race has thought and felt and attempted and accomplished that it may not become a negligible factor in the thought of the world By traditions and education, however, the large majority of Negroes have become interested in the history and status of other races, and they spend millions annually to promote such knowledge. Along with this sum, of course, should be considered the large amount paid for devices in trying not to be Negroes.

The chief reason why so many give such a little attention to the background of the Negro is the belief that this study is unimportant. They consider as history only such deeds as those of Mussolini who after building up an efficient war machine with the aid of other Europeans would now use it to murder unarmed and defenseless Africans who have restricted themselves exclusively to attending to their own business. If Mussolini succeeds in crushing Abyssinia he will be recorded in "history" among the Caesars, and volumes written in praise of the conqueror will find their way to the homes and libraries of thousands of mis-educated Negroes. The oppressor has always indoctrinated the weak with this interpretation of the crimes of the strong.

The war lords have done good only accidentally or incidentally while seeking to do evil. The movements which have ameliorated the condition of humanity and stimulated progress have been inaugurated by men of thought in lifting their fellows out of drudgery unto ease and comfort, out of selfishness unto altruism. The Negro may well rejoice that his hands, unlike those of his oppressors, are not stained with so much blood extracted by brute force. Real history is not the record of the successes and disappointments, the vices, the follies, and the quarrels of those who engage in contention for power.

The Association for the Study of Negro Life and History is projected on the fact that there is nothing in the past of the Negro more shameful than what is found in the past of other races The Negro is as human as the other members of the family of mankind. The Negro, like others, has been up at times; and at times he has been down. With the domestication of animals, the discovery of iron, the development of stringed instruments, an advancement in fine art, and the inauguration of trial by jury to his credit, the Negro stands just as high as others in contributing to the progress of the world.

The oppressor, however, raises his voice to the contrary. He teaches the Negro that he has no worth-while past, that his race has done nothing significant since the beginning of time, and that there is no evidence that he will ever achieve anything great. The education of the Negro then must be carefully directed lest the race may waste time trying to do the impossible. Lead the Negro to believe this and thus control his thinking. If you can thereby determine what he will think, you will not need to worry about what he will do. You will not have to tell him to go to the back door. He will go without being told; and if there is no back door he will have one cut for his special benefit.

If you teach the Negro that he has accomplished as much good as any other race he will aspire to equality and justice without regard to race such an effort would upset the program of the oppressor in Africa and America. Play up before the Negro, then, his crimes and shortcomings.

Let him learn to admire the Hebrew, the Greek, the Latin and the Teuton. Lead the Negro to detest the man of African blood—to hate himself. The oppressor then may conquer exploit, oppress and even annihilate the Negro by segregation without fear or trembling. With the truth hidden there will be little expression of thought to the contrary.

The American Negro has taken over an abundance of information which others have made accessible to the oppressed, but he has not yet learned to think and plan for himself as others do for themselves. Well might this race be referred to as the most docile and tractable people on earth. This merely means that when the oppressors once start the large majority of the race in the direction of serving the purposes of their traducers, the task becomes so easy in the years following that they have little trouble with the masses thus controlled. It is a most satisfactory system, and it has become so popular that European nations of foresight are sending some of their brightest minds to the United States to observe the Negro in "inaction" in order to learn how to deal likewise with Negroes in their colonies. What the Negro in America has become satisfied with will be accepted as the measure of what should be allotted him elsewhere. Certain Europeans consider the "solution of the race problem in the United States" one of our great achievements.

The mis-educated Negro joins the opposition with the objection that the study of the Negro keeps alive questions which should be forgotten. The Negro should cease to remember that he was once held a slave, that he has been oppressed, and even that he is a Negro. The traducer, however, keeps before the public such aspects of this history as will justify the present oppression of the race. It would seem, then, that the Negro should emphasize at the same time the favorable aspects to justify action in his behalf. One cannot blame the Negro for not desiring to be reminded of being the sort of creature that the oppressor has represented the Negro to be; but this very attitude shows ignorance of the past and a slavish dependence upon the enemy to serve those whom he would destroy. The Negro can be made proud of his past only by approaching it scientifically himself and giving his own story to the world. What others have written about the Negro during the last three centuries has been mainly for the purpose of bringing him where he is today and holding him there.

The method employed by the Association for the Study of Negro Life and History, however, is not spectacular propaganda or fire-eating agitation. Nothing can be accomplished in such fashion. "Whom the gods would destroy they first make mad." The Negro, whether in Africa or America, must be directed toward a serious examination of the fundamentals of education, religion, literature, and philosophy as they have been expounded to him. He must be sufficiently enlightened to determine for himself whether these forces have come into his life to bless him or to bless his oppressor. After learning the facts in the case the Negro must develop the power of execution to deal with these matters as do people of vision. Problems of great importance cannot be worked out in a day. Questions of great moment must be met with far-reaching plans.

The Association for the Study of Negro Life and History is teaching the Negro to exercise foresight rather than "hindsight." Liberia must not wait until she is offered to Germany before realizing that she has few friends in

Europe. Abyssinia must not wait until she is invaded by Italy before she prepares for self-defense. A scientific study of the past of modern nations would show these selfish tendencies as inevitable results from their policies in dealing with those whom they have professed to elevate. For example, much of Africa has been conquered and subjugated to save souls how expensive has been the Negro's salvation! One of the strong arguments for slavery was that it brought the Negro into the light of salvation. And yet the Negro today is all but lost.

The Association for the Study of Negro Life and History, however, has no special brand for the solution of the race problem except to learn to think. No general program of uplift for the Negroes in all parts of the world will be any more successful than such a procedure would be in the case of members of other races under different circumstances. What will help a Negro in Alabama may prove harmful to one in Maine.

The African Negro may find his progress retarded by applying "methods used for the elevation of the Negro in America." A thinking man, however, learns to deal wisely with conditions as he finds them rather than to take orders from someone who knows nothing about his status and cares less. At present the Negro, both in Africa and America, is being turned first here and there experimentally by so-called friends who in the final analysis assist the Negro merely in remaining in the dark.

In the furtherance of the program of taking up these matters dispassionately the Association had made available an outline for the systematic study of the Negro as he has touched the life of others and as others have functioned in their relation to him, The African Background Outlined:

A Handbook. This book is written from the point of view of history, literature, art, education, religion and economic imperialism. In seventeen chapters as Part I of the work a brief summary of the past in Africa is presented; and courses on "The Negro in Africa," "The Negro in the European Mind," "The Negro in America," "The Negro in Literature," "The Negro in Art," "The Education of the Negro," "The Religious Development of the Negro," and "Economic Imperialism," follow as Part II with ample bibliographical comment for every heading and subhead of these outlines. This facilitates the task of clubs, young peoples' societies, and special classes organized where the oppressors of the race and the Negroes co-operating with them are determined that the history and status of the Negro shall not be made a part of the curricula.

In this outline there is no animus, nothing to engender race hate. The Association does not bring out such publications. The aim of this organization is to set forth facts in scientific form, for facts properly set forth will tell their own story. No advantage can be gained by merely inflaming the Negro's mind against his traducers. In a manner they deserve to be congratulated for taking care of their own interests so well. The Negro needs to become angry with himself because he has not handled his own affairs wisely. In other words, the Negro must learn from others how to take care of himself in this trying ordeal. He must not remain content with taking over what others set aside for him and then come in the guise of friends to subject even that limited information to further misinterpretation.

---

# APPENDIX

---

## MUCH ADO ABOUT A NAME

A participant who recently attended an historical meeting desired to take up the question as to what the race should be called. Africans, Negroes, colored people, or what? This is a matter of much concern to him because he hopes thereby to solve the race problem. If others will agree to call Negroes Nordics, he thinks, he will reach the desired end by taking a short cut.

This may sound all but insane, but there are a good many "highly educated" Negroes who believe that such can be accomplished by this shift in terminology; and they have spent time and energy in trying to effect a change. Many of this class suffer mentally because of the frequent use of "offensive expressions" in addressing Negroes. When dealing with them, then, one has to be very careful. For this reason our friends in other races have to seek guidance in approaching us. For example, Lady Simon, the wife of Sir John Simon of the British Cabinet, has recently asked an American Negro what his people prefer to be called, and later in England she took up the same matter with another member of this race. Being an advocate of freedom, she has written considerably to advance its cause. She would not like to use in her works, then, an expression which may hurt some one's feelings.

Although a student of social problems, this learned woman cannot fathom this peculiar psychology. Americans, too, must confess the difficulty of understanding it, unless it is that the "highly educated Negro mind" tends to concern itself with trifles rather than with the great problems of life. We have known Negroes to ask for a separate YMCA. or YWCA., a separate church or a separate school, and then object to calling the institution colored or Negro. These segregationists have compromised on principle, but they are unwilling to acknowledge their crime against justice. The name, they believe, will save them from the disgrace.

It does not matter so much what the thing is called as what the thing is. The Negro would not cease to be what he is by calling him something else; but, if he will struggle and make something of himself and contribute to modern culture, the world will learn to look upon him as an American rather than as one of an undeveloped element of the population.

The word Negro or Black is used in referring to this particular element because most persons of native African descent approach this color. The term does not imply that every Negro is black; and the word White does not mean that every white man is actually white. Negroes may be colored, but many Caucasians are scientifically classified as colored. We are not all Africans, moreover, because many of us were not born in Africa; and we are not all Afro-Americans, because few of us are natives of Africa transplanted to America.

There is nothing to be gained by running away from the name. The names of practically all races and nations at times have connoted insignificance and low social status. Angles and Saxons, once the slaves of Romans, experienced this; and even the name of the Greek for a while meant no more than this to these conquerors of the world. The people who bore these names, however, have made them grand and illustrious. The Negro must learn to do the same.

It is strange, too, that while the Negro feels ashamed of his name, persons abroad do not usually think of it in this sense. One does find in Europe a number of West Indian and American Negroes of some Caucasian blood, who do not want to be known as Negroes. As a rule, however, a European of African Negro blood feels proud of this racial heritage and delights to be referred to as such. The writer saw a striking case of this in London in the granddaughter of a Zulu chief. She is so far removed from the African type that one could easily mistake her for a Spaniard; and yet she thinks only for her African connection and gets her inspiration mainly from the story of her people beyond the Pillars of Hercules.

The writer was agreeably surprised a few days later, too, when he met a prominent Parisian with the same attitude. He has produced several volumes in which he champions the cause of the Negro because he has in his veins the same blood. A well-to-do European woman, the daughter of a Dutchman and an African mother, is similarly enthusiastic over her Negro blood. The first thing she mentioned in conversing with the writer was that Black mother. This young woman expressed the regret that she did not have more of that color that she, too, might say, as do members of certain groups of Africa: "I am Black and comely. I am Black and beautiful. I am beautifully Black."

These people surprise you when you think of the attitude of many American Negroes on this question. These race-conscious people can think, but it is seldom that the American Negro indulges in such an exercise. He has permitted other people to determine for him the attitude that he has toward his own people. This means the enslavement of his mind and eventually the enslavement of his body.

Some Europeans rather regard the word Negro as romantic. Going now along the streets of Paris, one will see advertised such places as "l'Elan Noir," and the "Café au Nègre de Toulouse." In one of these cases the writer was especially attracted by the "Choppe du Nègre" end took dinner there one day. The cuisine was excellent, the music rendered by the orchestra was charming, and a jolly crowd came to enjoy themselves. However, he was the only "Nègre" there.

Walking along a street in Geneva not long ago, the writer's attention was attracted to something of the sort, which is still more significant. It was a wholesale coffee house called "A La Case de l'Oncle Tom." He entered and asked: "Why did you give this store such a name?" The proprietress laughed and explained that her grandfather, François Prudhom, who had read "Uncle Tom's Cabin" and had been deeply impressed thereby, selected this name for the store when he established it in 1866.

## THE VALUE OF COLOR

Not long ago the writer saw on a street ear one of the prettiest women in the world. She was a perfectly Black woman becomingly dressed in suitable gray and modest adornments which harmonized with her color. She was naturally a commanding figure without any effort to please others, for her bearing was such that she would not fail to attract attention. He could not restrain myself from gazing at her; and, looking around to see whether others were similarly concerned, he found the Whites in the car admiring her also, even to the point of commenting among themselves.

This woman's common sense, manifested in knowing how to dress, had made her color an asset rather than a liability. The writer easily recalled, then, that group in Africa that feels unusually proud of being Black. We are told that they are so anxious to be Black that if they find one of the group with a tendency to depart the least from this color they go to the heart of nature and extract from it its darkest dye and paint therewith that native's face that he may continue perfectly Black.

Here in America, however, we are ashamed of being Black. So many of us who are actually black powder our faces and make ourselves blue. In so doing we become all but hideous by the slavish aping of those around us in keeping with our custom of imitation. We fail to take ourselves for what we are actually worth, and do not make the most of ourselves.

We show lack of taste in the selection of our dress. We long for what others wear whether it harmonizes with our color or not they have given particular attention to design with respect to their race and have written books to this effect. Thinking, however, that the Negro is not supposed to wear anything but what the poor may pick up, the artists have not thought seriously of him. Both teachers and students of nearby schools thus concerned, then, repeatedly appeal to us for help in the study of design with respect to the Negro, but we have nothing scientific to offer them. We have no staff of artists who can function in this sphere.

To be able to supply this need requires the most painstaking effort to understand colors and color schemes. It is a very difficult task because of the variation of color within the race. Sometimes in one family of ten you will hardly find two of the same shade. To dress them all alike may be economical, but the world thereby misses that much of beauty. The Negro mother, then, needs to be the real artist, and the schools now training the youth to be the parents of tomorrow should give as much attention to these things esthetic as they do to language, literature or mathematics.

In neglecting to know himself better from this point of view, then, the Negro is making a costly mistake. He should be deeply concerned with the esthetic possibilities of his situation. In this socalled Negro race we have the prettiest people in the world, when they dress in harmony with the many shades and colors with which we are so richly endowed. Why do we so away from home to find what we already have on hand?

Recently one saw in Washington a demonstration of the value of color when the Masonic conclave staged a tremendous parade in this national city. The Whites were attracted to the upstanding, outstanding Negroes so becomingly bedecked in costumes of the Orient. This, however, was accidental. The color of the Negroes happened to be Oriental, and the colors of this order were originally worked out to suit the people of those parts.

The dead white of the Caucasian does not harmonize with such garb. Why, then should the Negro worry about what others wear?

Carrying the imitation of others to an extreme today, we do not find ourselves far in advance of the oppressed antebellum Negroes, who, unable to dress themselves, had to take whatever others threw at them. We make a most hideous spectacle, then, when we are on dress parade in our social atmosphere. So many of us clad in unbecoming colors often look like decorated pet horses turned loose for an hour or so of freedom.

Appreciating the value of color, the artists in European cities are trying to change their hue to that of the colored people. They can understand how inexpressive the dead white is, and they are trying to make use of what we are seeking to conceal. The models in their shops are purposely colored to display to good effect the beautiful costumes which require color. Some of these Europeans frankly tell Negroes how they envy them for their color.

One is not surprised, then, to find European cafés and hotels employing American or African Negroes to supply this color which the Europeans lack. Pictures of such Black men are sometimes displayed to great effect. That of Josephine Baker adorns the windows of large stores in Paris. Here in America, too, we observe that art centers are likewise getting away from the dead white to enjoy the richness of color.

The writer felt somewhat encouraged recently when he talked with a Washington lady who runs "The Pandora," a unique establishment devoted to design. Upon inquiring about her progress in the effort to teach colored people how to wear what becomes them, she reported considerable success. Sometimes customers insist on purchasing unbecoming attire, but usually she has shown them the un-wisdom of so doing, and most of them now take her advice.

In this way this enterprising woman is not only conducting a pioneer business, but she is rendering a social service. She has not had any special training in this work, but on her initiative she is building upon what she has learned by studying the Negroes in her community. Others of us may do likewise, if we try to help the Negro rather than exploit him.

CPSIA information can be obtained at www.ICGtesting.com
Printed in the USA
BVOW05s1126270115

385152BV00001B/23/P

SOCIOLOGY

AND

EVERYDAY LIFE

*edited by*
**Marcello Truzzi**

*University of Michigan*

# SOCIOLOGY
# AND
# EVERYDAY LIFE

PRENTICE-HALL, INC., *Englewood Cliffs, New Jersey*

**Prentice-Hall Sociology Series**   Neil J. Smelser, *Editor*

© 1968 by PRENTICE-HALL, INC., *Englewood Cliffs, New Jersey*

Library of Congress Catalog Card No.: 68-24429

Current printing (*last number*):
10   9   8   7   6   5   4   3

*Printed in the United States of America*

Cover design by Pat Truzzi

PRENTICE-HALL INTERNATIONAL, INC., *London*
PRENTICE-HALL OF AUSTRALIA, PTY. LTD., *Sydney*
PRENTICE-HALL OF CANADA, LTD., *Toronto*
PRENTICE-HALL OF INDIA PRIVATE LTD., *New Delhi*
PRENTICE-HALL OF JAPAN, INC., *Tokyo*

# Contents

SOCIOLOGY

AND

EVERYDAY LIFE

# Introduction

*Marcello Truzzi*

Examination of the variety of anthologies prepared for introductory courses in sociology quickly reveals two general problems for the beginning student: (1) Most such collections consist of the major writings of professional sociologists for other professional sociologists, thereby presuming a conceptual knowledge of the theoretical and methodological issues in the field, a knowledge often not possessed by beginning students; and (2) most of the articles in these anthologies deal with substantive areas that have little natural attraction for the student, especially the one not majoring in sociology. It is hoped that this volume will largely avoid these two problems. This is attempted through a presentation of articles dealing with areas that, it is hoped, students will perceive as highly concrete fields of intrinsic substantive interest.

In most cases, the basic methods of the sociological perspective can be communicated through a variety of applications. Therefore, why not use those applications that might hold a high interest and curiosity value for the student? The method of content analysis, after all, can be demonstrated on a popular magazine like *Playboy* or *Mad* as well as it can be done through studies of, for example, Texas newspapers from 1945–1946. The effects of industrialization can be exemplified by changes in the American circus, or the bicycle, as well as in the factory or underdeveloped country. Emile Durkheim's method of analysis has been applied to rape as well as to suicide; and his analysis of religion has also been applied to an investigation of the collective representation known as Santa Claus.

In the title *Sociology and Everyday Life,* we use the term "everyday life" not so much as it refers to the commonplace or usual, but, rather, with its connotation of both the *mundane* and the *salient*.[1] Although we have concentrated on the sociology *of* everyday life, we have also tried to augment this collection with studies of the esoteric and curious corners of the social world. Thus, the volume is intended primarily as a motivational adjunct to introductory courses in sociology. It is not intended to replace the special and classic statements that the individual instructor may wish to place before the student; it is intended, however, to supplement and complement such studies. The main purpose of this anthology is to make the sociological discipline more *alive,* more *real,* and more *immediate* to the student. And this is attempted through an appeal to his natural curiosity about the immediate

---

[1] In his book *The Social Meanings of Suicide* (Princeton, N. J.: Princeton University Press, 1967), Jack D. Douglas draws an interesting distinction between what he terms "everyday" and "anyday" phenomena, the latter being those that a person can encounter at almost any time and any place within the normally expected boundaries of everyday discourse, insofar as the persons involved are intimate enough to allow. Much of what we term "everyday" phenomena in this volume might better be termed "anyday," since such events do not in fact occur for the social actor each day, regularly.

world of the commonplace (his every-day life) and his interest in the exotic and offbeat aspects of social life. It is hoped that by thus "concretizing" his early experiences with the sociological literature, the student will extend this positive experience to an interest in the more abstract and analytical concerns that are most central to the discipline. I can only state that my experiences in offering these readings to my own students have shown them to be effective toward these goals.

Finally, a word might be added about the general orientation of this volume. Although all the sciences perform (to some degree) the four functions of providing *description, prediction, explanation,* and *control*,[2] much

current sociology has centered its concerns largely about the latter three functions; description has thus been generally left in the hands of the ethnographic branch of anthropology. In the rush to pattern itself after the science of physics, rather than biology or one of the other less analytic natural sciences, sociology has generally relegated its descriptive function to a secondary position. Upset by certain atheoretical excesses of some members of the early Chicago School of Sociology,[3] who concentrated heavily on urban ethnography, many sociologists swung in the opposite direction, focusing solely on a search for general uniformities (i.e., nomothetic laws) that transcend the individual case. Today, however, some sociologists are much less confident that adequate data for theory construction have been collected. Some have been concerned with the obsolescence of much previously collected data, seeing it as no longer representative of our times and the altered social system; others, however, have been concerned with the lack of data in what have emerged as theoretically critical areas. Thus, in many quarters of sociology, we are seeing a reconsideration of and return to more specialized data gathering. This is especially true in the area of deviance,[4] and among those sociol-

---

[2] As used here, *description* consists of statements made about the observed presence or absence of specified variables in a given time and place. (Thus, "*x* was followed by *y*.") Prediction consists of a statement of description in which one or more of the variables is not currently observed, its presence or absence to be validated at some future time; in some cases, a variable is "predicted" to have been present at some past time and place. (Thus, "Where *x* is or was present, we expect to find *y*.") *Explanation* consists of subsuming statements about the relation between specific variables under a more general, class level proposition. (Thus, "Particular event *x* leading to event *y* is a specific case illustrating the more general lawlike statement, *X* leads to *Y*.") Note that explanation automatically gives prediction, but a statement of prediction is not necessarily explanatory: a prediction may be merely actuarial, e.g., we know approximately how many people will have traffic accidents next Memorial Day, but we don't claim to know exactly why. This form of scientific explanation is usually called the "covering-law" model of explanation (see footnote 13 for further discussion). *Control* refers to the making of statements about the use of the above to manipulate nature. (Thus, "If *x* is brought about, *y* will be forthcoming.") Note that no evaluation is made of what *should* be brought about,

merely that certain manipulations will result in certain effects.

[3] For the best portrait of this period, see Robert E. L. Faris, *Chicago Sociology, 1930–1932* (San Francisco, Cal.: Chandler Publishing Co., 1967). Typical feeling about such excesses is expressed in the joke often cited during this period, in which a sociologist is defined as a man who needs a $100,-000 grant to find the local whorehouse.

[4] E.g., Donald W. Ball, "An Abortion Clinic Ethnography," *Social Problems*, XIV (1967), 293–301. For similar material, see the appendix.

ogists interested in the underlying grounds of everyday life.[5]

With reference to this fear of a premature moratorium on data collection, many sociologists today have suggested that such a closed-minded approach—especially to man's everyday phenomenal world of experience —may have already misdirected our social theory, away from valuable insights into the true nature of the fruitful social variables that must be found in order to construct any ultimate, lawlike statements in sociology.[6]

In addition to such questions pertaining to the best program or route for obtaining systematic knowledge of the social order, there seems to be a much more basic question concerning the goals of sociology as a science. For, to the functions of description, prediction, explanation and control— which are present to some degree in all the sciences—many sociologists would like to add what is often termed subjective understanding (*verstehen*). In fact, numerous sociologists consider this added function to constitute a major difference between the social and natural sciences. By *subjective understanding* we mean a special insight into the social situation, taken from the perspective of the actors through an empathic process by the investigator.[7] It is this sympathetic understanding of the role of the social actor that numerous sociologists have seen as a critical part of sociology.

Severyn T. Bruyn has recently argued that there are two major research approaches in sociology.[8] On the one hand, he places the naturalistic position of Durkheim, who saw social facts as "things" to be taken by the sociologist as basically no different from the objects of any other natural science.[9] At the other end of the spectrum, Bruyn puts the position of Florian Znaniecki, who made a distinction between *natural* and *cultural* facts. The approach to the latter involves what Znaniecki called the *humanistic coefficient*, the perspective of the social actor.[10]

Adopting a variety of forms, most sociologists today have taken a somewhat intermediary position, the grounds for which were laid out by Max Weber, whose empirical-analytical position in regard to his study of social typologies (similar to that of Durkheim) incorporated a humanistic position on the importance of subjective understanding (similar to that of Znaniecki).[11]

---

[5] E.g., Harold Garfinkel, "Studies of the Routine Grounds of Everyday Activity," *Social Problems*, XI (1964), 225–50; and Severyn T. Bruyn, "The Participant Observer and Phenomenologist" (Paper presented at the Annual Meeting of the American Sociological Association, Miami, Fla., 1966).

[6] E.g., Harold Garfinkel, *Studies in Ethnomethodology* (Englewood Cliffs, N. J.: Prentice-Hall, Inc., 1967); and Jack D. Douglas, *The Social Meaning of Suicide.*

[7] Cf. Theodore Abel, "The Operation Called *Verstehen*," in *Readings in the Philosophy of Science*, H. Feigl and M. Brod-

beck, eds. (New York: Appleton-Century-Crofts, 1953), pp. 677–87.

[8] Severyn T. Bruyn, *The Human Perspective in Sociology: The Methodology of Participant Observation* (Englewood Cliffs, N. J.: Prentice-Hall, Inc., 1966), pp. 2–9.

[9] Cf. Emile Durkheim, *The Rules of Sociological Method* (8th ed.), trans. S. A. Solovay and J. H. Mueller; G. E. G. Catlin, ed. (New York: The Free Press, 1950), pp. xliii–liii.

[10] Cf. Florian Znaniecki, *The Method of Sociology* (New York: Holt, Rinehart & Winston, Inc., 1934), pp. 44–45; and *Cultural Sciences: Their Origin and Development* (Urbana, Ill.: University of Illinois Press, 1963), pp. 131–42.

[11] Cf. Max Weber, trans., ed. E. Shils and H. A. Finch, *The Methodology of the Social Sciences* (New York: The Free Press, 1949).

The dispute over the role of subjective understanding in sociology is still raging within the discipline, and no attempt will be made to resolve this complex issue here. But one thing seems clear: Whether or not sociology must incorporate subjective understanding as an essential criterion for validation (a viewpoint this writer does not share),[12] or even as an essential part of its method of investigation (an issue far more controversial), the fact remains that subjective understanding plays important roles for many sociologists. The heuristic value of subjective understanding—the degree to which it helps us to learn and discover the nature of social reality—seems undeniable, given the many great sociologists who have found it so useful; but there is also the greater value of personal satisfaction psychologically gained by the holder of the insight through subjective understanding. For, to many sociologists, a major subjective insight into the social world (even if rather thinly supported by the validating measures of empirical research) may be perceived as more valuable than a trivial or truistic fact upheld by a mountain of researches. In fact, it might be argued

that this search for insights into social life is a primary motive for a majority of persons who choose to enter professional sociology.[13] Therefore—sophisticated methodological questions about the proper role of subjective insight aside—the search for such insight is an important part of the daily quest of most sociologists. And it is this quality of insight that most beginning students find to be a major attraction of sociology.

This anthology consists mainly of papers emphasizing description and subjective understanding. However, balance has been sought, and it is hoped that the other major functions of science are not slighted. In many ways, then, the articles represent a highly personal selection; their inclusion depended not only on the usual critical evaluation of their methodological purity (such as would be made by any editor of an anthology for introductory sociology courses), but also, in many cases, on a rating of their ability to transmit a feeling of subjective understanding and insight to the reader. I can only hope that the reader enjoys reading these articles for the first time as much as I did.

---

H. H. Gerth and C. Wright Mills noted this inconsistency on Weber's part in their edited collection of translations, *From Max Weber: Essays in Sociology* (New York: Oxford University Press, Inc., 1958), p. 57.

[12] For two excellent brief discussions surrounding this issue, cf. Ernest Nagel, *The Structure of Science: Problems in the Logic of Scientific Explanation* (New York: Harcourt, Brace & World, Inc., 1961), pp. 480–85; and Richard Rudner, *Philosophy of Social Science* (Englewood Cliffs, N. J.: Prentice-Hall, Inc., 1966), pp. 71–73.

[13] It should be borne in mind that personal satisfaction with answers to the question "Why?"—what we might term "psychological explanation"—is not to be confused with "scientific explanation," whereby we refer primarily to a deductive model in which particular events are "explained" as being specific cases subsumed under more general or universal propositions. Cf. R. B. Braithwaite, *Scientific Explanation* (New York: Harper & Brothers, 1953); and Carl G. Hempel and Paul Oppenheim, "The Logic of Explanation," in *Readings in the Philosophy of Science*, Feigl and Brodbeck, eds., pp. 319–53.

PART I

Sociology
and
Everyday Life

# Life as Theater:
# Some Notes
# on the Dramaturgic Approach
# to Social Reality *

*Sheldon L. Messinger* with *Harold Sampson* and *Robert D. Towne* †

In *The Presentation of Self in Everyday Life*,[1] Erving Goffman has pointed out that the study of social establishments as relatively closed systems has been undertaken in four mutually relevant and sometimes overlapping perspectives or analytic contexts. First, there is the *technical* approach, which consists of an appraisal of the system of activity in terms of its efficiency or inefficiency in attaining predefined group goals. Second, there is the *political* approach, which consists of a study of the power relations among the social actors, i.e., the social controls, the positive and negative sanctions, in force. Third, there is the *structural* approach, which is an examination in terms of the relations between various status divisions (both horizontal and vertical) among and between the social groupings. Fourth, there is the *cultural* approach, wherein the norms and values of the social system are examined. And fifth, Goffman argues, is the *dramaturgic* approach, wherein social interaction is likened (not as a true analogy, but as a scaffold for insight) to a theatrical production or play-in-progress consisting of individual and team performances in a complex patterning of intersecting roles and settings. It is with this last general orientation—one adopted by several authors appearing in this volume—that the following paper deals.

EDITOR

---

The aim of this paper is to raise some questions about the uses of the "dramaturgic approach"[2] to social experience, a mode of analysis finding increasing use in social-psychological circles. In particular, we wish to inquire into and comment upon the nature of the actor's[3] perspective in

* Reprinted from *Sociometry*, XXV (1962), 98–110, by permission of the authors and the American Sociological Association. Footnotes renumbered.

† We should like to thank Aaron Cicourel, Fred Davis, and Leo F. Schnore for critical comment on earlier versions of this paper. We are indebted to several unpublished papers by Harold Garfinkel for a number of the views expressed. And we owe a special debt to Erving Goffman, for his patience in the face of "constructive criticism."

[1] (Garden City, N. Y.: Doubleday Anchor Books, 1959), pp. 239–42.

[2] This phrase is used by Erving Goffman in (4). Reference (6) is a revised and enlarged edition of the same work. Our criticism, as well as appreciation, of the "dramaturgic approach" are directed primarily at Goffman's work as its foremost exponent.

[3] When used in an unqualified way, we intend the term "actor" to refer to that

everyday life, as this is sometimes assumed to appear to the dramaturgic
analyst.

To this end, we shall describe a
perspective on the world and the self
within it, a perspective that renders
life a kind of "theater" in which a
"show" is "staged." Someone viewing
self and world from within this perspective will be said to be "on." In
order to show the incompatibility of
this perspective with the view that
persons in everyday life seem to consider "natural," we shall present some
observations by and about mental patients taken from a recently completed
study.[4] Finally, we shall suggest that
the perspective of persons who are
"on" is akin or identical to the view
seemingly attributed by the dramaturgic analyst to his subjects, that is,
to persons plying their routine rounds
of daily activities. We shall hold that
this seeming attribution is a misreading of dramaturgic analysis, although
it is a misreading against which the
dramaturgic analyst has not sufficiently guarded.

# I

A reported comment by Sammy
Davis, Jr. first suggested our usage of
the term "to be on." Remarking on
the hazards of fame, he said, "As soon
as I go out the front door of my

house in the morning, I'm on, Daddy,
I'm on." [5] And further, "But when
I'm with the group I can relax. We
trust each other" (12). Drawing on
his experience in the theater, Davis
seems to be saying that there are
times when, although "off-stage," he
feels "on-stage." He contrasts this perspective on self and other with another associated with "relaxation" and
"trust."

Seeing that someone who has been
"on-stage" may find the same experience in everyday life, we can appreciate that those who have never
crossed the boards may attain the
same perspective, even though they
may have no consistent name for it.
Thus Bernard Wolfe tells us that, seldom out of sight of a white audience,
"Negroes in our culture spend most
of their lives 'on'. . . . Every Negro is
to some extent a performer." At other
times, "relaxing among themselves,"
Negroes will "mock the 'type' personalities they are obliged to assume
when they're 'on'" (11, p. 202). We
may expect, perhaps, that the members of any oppressed group will have
similar experiences.

But there seems no reason to confine these experiences to the oppressed. It would seem that adolescents at graduation ceremonies, as
well as buying drinks at bars, and
clerks taken for store owners, as well
as those mistaken for customers, share
with Norman Mailer's "hip" the need
to "come on strong" (8). And we can
see that a person may be rendered
"on" when he has no prior reason to
believe that this will be his fate. Thus,
the plight of one "put on" by joking
if sadistic friends, and the person sud-

"Anybody" whose "action" is the subject of
the dramaturgic analyst's analytic efforts.
"Anybody" need not be a stage actor.

[4] The study was carried out by the California Department of Mental Hygiene and
partially supported by Grant 3M-9124 from
the National Institute of Mental Health.
The study, carried out by the authors and
others, consisted in observing and frequently interviewing the members of 17
families in which the wife was hospitalized
for "schizophrenia." A description of the
study group and of study procedures may
be found in (10).

[5] The context of his remarks is Davis' discussion of a group of intimates of which he
is a member—known as the "Clan" by some,
the "Rat Pack" by others—and the relations
between this group and the "public."

denly made aware of a *gaffe* by an-other's inability to be tactful (3, 5).

All of these situations point up the fact that under some circumstances in everyday life the actor becomes, is, or is made *aware* of an actual or potential discrepancy between his "real" and his "projected" selves, be-tween his "self" and his "character." [6] He may greet this sensed discrepancy with joy or anxiety; presumably he usually finds himself somewhere be-tween these affective poles. However this may be, insofar as he *consciously* orients himself to narrow, sustain, or widen this discrepancy and thereby achieves a sense of "playing a role" or "managing a character," he is "on" in the sense intended here. It may be inferred that it is during such periods, if his projection is a joint enterprise, that the actor *experiences* the con-straints of "dramaturgic loyalty," "dis-cipline," and "circumspection" (6, pp. 212–228); although, as we shall try to make clear later, it may *not* be in-ferred that when the actor fails to experience these constraints they have ceased to operate. It is at these other times, however, when the actor is not "on," that we shall refer to his per-spective as "natural." At these other times persons tell us that their con-duct appears to them as "spontane-ous."

## II

We may be better able to appre-ciate the difference between being "on" and being "natural"—and the dif-ference this difference makes—if we turn to the experiences of a class of persons who must cope with it for a

relatively long period of time. Enter-tainers would seem to be such a class, as Davis' statement suggests. Davis' statement also suggests, however, that a relatively well supported hiatus ex-ists for entertainers between occasions of being "on" and "natural." There are those before whom one is "on," like the "public," and those with whom one is "natural," like the "group." These worlds may on occa-sion touch or even overlap, but pre-sumably the boundaries usually re-main clear.[7] What we seek is a class of persons who have difficulty creat-ing or sustaining such a hiatus. For them, presumably, the incompatibil-ities of being "on" and being "nat-ural," should such incompatibilities exist, will be magnified. Mental pa-tients are such a class of persons.

There can be little doubt but that mental patients are in a situation pro-ductive of being "on." Bereft of mem-bership in the group of reasonable men, they are forced to address the task of restoring their "character," of becoming "sane persons" again. It does not take mental patients long to discover that, as they lost their "san-ity" in the eyes of others through what they did and said, so may they regain it. Under these conditions, we might expect mental patients to be "on" without reserve, that for them, truly,

[7] Jonathan Winters, an entertainer, pro-vides us with an example of the breakdown of these boundaries. Of a period in his life when he experienced a "crack-up" he says, "I was 'on' all the time, always playing the part—in parks, restaurants, whenever [*sic*] I went—and I couldn't get 'off.' Well, I got 'off.' I look around now and think how much I have to be thankful for. And there's no use throwing myself on the floor because once in a while something bugs me" (13, p. 32). Stories about stage actors who carry their "parts" home, as well as audience members who take "character" for "reality," are common, if the events they point to infrequent.

[6] Perhaps the best description of the vari-ety of these situations is found in Goffman (5).

life becomes a theater.[8] There is some truth in this: mental patients are "on" at times and feel under pressure to be "on" even more often. But, given their motives to be "on" and the pressure they are under, it is perhaps more remarkable that mental patients cannot sustain this perspective without experiencing severe anxiety and discomfort. From this, as from other experiences of mental patients, we may learn something of importance about everyday life.[9]

We can get at this experience by considering more closely some aspects of the perspective of being "on." Let us consider that, when one is "on," activities come to be regarded as "performances," other persons as an "audience," and the world around as a series of "scenes" and "props." Let us also consider how this view conflicts with what mental patients consider "natural."

Like others who are "on," the mental patient comes to regard his own activities as potential "performances," as potential means of creating and sustaining a "character" for the benefit of others. At times, he uses them this way. Unlike some who are "on," however, the mental patient faces a dilemma. The "show" he experiences himself as "staging" concerns a fundamental matter, a matter that, as he sees it, should not and should not need to be "staged"; namely, his "normality." This is not only an aspect of self that he wants others to again take

for granted. This he might indeed accomplish through a judicious "performance." More important, "normality" is an aspect of self the mental patient *himself* profoundly desires to take for granted again. And regarding his activities as "performances" interferes with this crucial aim.

Thus, a patient may enact a "normal character," succeed in "taking in" the audience, and retrospectively discover that he has, in the process, left himself more unconvinced than ever about the "reality" of his "normality."

Mr. Yale [10] told the interviewer that a nurse had remarked to him that his wife was much "improved." As a mark of "improvement" the nurse cited the fact that Mrs. Yale was playing "Scrabble" (a word game) a great deal. The next day, after some hesitance about confidentiality, Mrs. Yale confided to the interviewer that she and her friends had recently taken to playing "Scrabble" as a means of impressing the staff with their ability to think clearly and be sociable. During the balance of the interview, Mrs. Yale expressed a great deal of concern over whether she was "really" better or had merely misled personnel.

Or, anticipating this sort of conflict, a patient may pointedly avoid "performing."

Mrs. White said that, if she decided to, she could easily get out of the hospital: she realized that she had come to learn what one was "supposed to say and do" to accomplish this. However, she added, *to do these things was to deny one's "own self"* and what "one felt."

Finally, what the patient has been saying and doing may be defined by

[8] Goffman has something like this in mind when he remarks that the mental patient "can learn, at least for a time, to practice before all groups the amoral arts of shamelessness" (7, "The Moral Career of the Mental Patient," p. 169).

[9] The whole remarkable series of papers by Goffman on mental patients and their keepers provides an example of what we may learn about everyday life from them (7).

[10] This, as the other patients' and relatives' names we have used, is fictitious. We have, however, consistently used the same names for identical patients and relatives throughout the several papers we have published or are publishing.

an authoritative other *as* "performing," thereby provoking the conflict.

Mrs. Quinn said that when Dr. X suggested that she was "painting the picture too rosy," she realized that she had been trying to impress hospital staff just to get out of the hospital, and this frightened her.

We are led to see, then, that the mental patient is not satisfied to *appear* "normal," he strives to *be* "normal." Paradoxically, this means, in part, that he wants to "appear normal" to *himself*. Striving to "appear normal" for others—"putting on a show of normality"—interferes with this objective.

It may also be noted that the mental patient addresses others as a potential "audience." The hospital, self-defined as a place of "observation," is obviously conducive to this effect. Others, the patient learns, are "witnesses" of as well as "participants" in his activities. With this a matter of awareness—and, moreover, assumed by the patient to be a matter of awareness for the other—it becomes difficult for a patient to have a relationship in which the impression the other receives of his "illness" or lack of it is not relevant.

During hospitalization patients tend to construe all situations as, potentially, "test" situations in which their "sanity" is being assessed. Thus, many patients make a particular point of knowing the day, month, year, and season, anticipating that "requests for information" will in fact be "orientation examinations." And others, not appreciating how seldom hospital personnel have a chance to become familiar with "the record," consider what are in fact requests for information (like, "how many children do you have?") as further tests. The perspective, in a few cases, tends to become omnipresent: thus, Mrs. Karr believed throughout her hospitalization that several of the "patients" were "spies" who collected information for the hospital and were only feigning illness. And, of course, there is little reason to believe that regarding others as an "audience" ends with release from the hospital. So for a time during the post-hospital period several patients responded to the greeting "How are you?" by launching a description of their mental health or by inquiring into the interviewers' motives for asking such a "question." Information received from patients' relatives suggests that this kind of response was not confined to the interview situation.

These kinds of responses suggest that, within his perspective, the patient consciously follows a kind of "script" in which his primary appearance is that of a "suspect person." In part, it is the others who have these "suspicions" and the patient must disabuse them of these. This is to be accomplished by "watching" one's own "reactions" and by fitting them to the model of a "normal person," also included in the "script." As well, the patient attempts to restrict the actions of others toward him to those which may appropriately be directed to a "normal person."

But, again, the patient's appearance before others is only part of a weighty problem. Not only must he fashion a "normal character" for others and attempt to induce them to provide the social conditions under which he can carry this off, he must do these things while remaining the most critical "audience" of his own "show." Viewing his own activities from "inside," the mental patient finds that he must work with "reactions" which *he* perceives as contrived and controlled. And for him, as for his other "audiences," a critical aspect of "normality" is that "reactions" are just that: they appear "spontaneous." More is at stake, then, than "putting on" a creditable "performance" for an "audience"; indeed, doing so would seem to undermine the most important "show" of all.

Finally, let us note that the mental patient tends to view things as potential "props." That is, "things," including persons and places ("scenes"), tend to be appreciated directly for the information they potentially and actually convey about the self, for their communicative value in creating, sustaining, or disrupting a "character."

Thus some patients, as well as some sociologists, recognize that the limited expressive materials afforded by the hospital insure that many activities will almost certainly "look crazy." And patients feel under constant pressure to remain aware of the communicative value of their own affective expressions.

Mrs. Vick said, "Life is a pretense. I have to pretend every day that I'm here. That I'm gay and happy in order to stay out of the isolation ward. So I laugh and pretend to be gay."

Other persons, too, may be regarded as "props" to be maneuvered in the interests of the "show" at hand. Thus patients frequently demand that relatives visibly express affection and need for them on the ward. Such expressions were correctly perceived by patients as important to personnel in establishing the patients' "return to normality."

The problem with this view of "things" is that the patient reinforces his own uncertainty as to what is "real" and what is "mere appearance." Thus, the effort to appear "gay" seems to make patients wonder if all "gayness" isn't "mere appearance"; and

prearrangements with relatives seem to make patients more uncertain about just what their relatives "really" feel toward them, as well as how they "really" feel toward their relatives. Indeed, this seems to be the core problem with being "on" in regard to fundamental matters: not only can the patient no longer trust others but, most devastating of all, he can no longer trust himself. He is, for a while, anxiously uncertain as to whether the "normal character" he projects *is* his "self." And the more he appears to himself as "acting"—the more single-mindedly he strives for "effect"—the more uncertain he seems to become.

The foregoing may be summarized in this way. The mental patient is under pressure to experience the world, with his self at its center, in a "technical" way. Like the stage actor contemplating the cloak-over-self he will don for his audience, so the mental patient comes to address his own character. Instead of a "natural" phenomenon, flowing from and reflecting the self, the mental patient's character comes to appear to him as a "constructed object," [11] as a "function" of manipulated activities and contrived scenes, of the assessments of an audience and the standards they invoke, and of the nature and availability of props.[12] The connection between self and character becomes a questionable, undependable matter. Or, to use another figure, this connection becomes a matter of wit and stagecraft, of the contingencies of "staging a show." An intrinsic link is shattered.

[11] Harold Garfinkel has used this term—and "assembled object"—in a similar way, but in another connection, in his unpublished work.
[12] Compare Goffman's view of the "self" in (6), especially pp. 252–253, in (2), "The Moral Career . . . ," pp. 168–169, and in (3), p. 271.

## III

We have said that, for a while, the mental patient is "on." It remains to note that this perspective bears a remarkable resemblance to the perspective that the dramaturgic analyst seems to attribute to the individual in everyday life, whatever the mental status of the latter. Thus, the dramaturgic analyst conceives the individual as a "performer" whose activities function to create the "appearance" of a "self"—a "character"—for an "audience." In the process of maintaining or changing his "character" for others, the individual manipulates things as "props." Others are related to the individual in terms of their "parts" in putting a "show" together, of witnessing it, of sustaining it, or of disrupting it. Places become "scenes" which are fitted or unfitted for the creation of "character" at hand. The outcome of interest to the analyst is the "effective" creation of a "character" which by "taking in" the "audience" or failing to do so, will permit the individual to continue a rewarding line of activity or to avoid an unrewarding one, or which will result in his being "discredited." Finally, the dramaturgic analyst seems to make mental patients of us all, for he conceives the individual as "staging" *fundamental* qualities: aspects of self taken for granted *with* intimate others.[13]

This vision of the world is for a time, as we have tried to show, a core aspect of the mental patient's perspective. Finding himself in the eyes of others either a doubtful person or a thoroughly discredited one, he may consciously undertake to fashion an image of "normality." Insofar as this is the case, he will "act" with full awareness; he will see himself as "acting"; he will be "on."

Now we must ask, is the dramaturgic analyst asserting that individuals are "on" in everyday life, routinely and as a matter of course? Is he suggesting that ordinarily, say among family and friends, the individual views "life as theater"? If so, what shall we make of the fact that the mental patient experiences being "on" as an *interruption* of his "normal" perspective and as a source of anxiety and alienation? How shall we account for the patient's intense desire to get "off"?

We wish to suggest that no paradox is involved. In viewing "life as theater," the dramaturgic analyst does not present us with a model of the actor's consciousness; *he is not suggesting that this is the way his subjects understand the world.* Instead, the dramaturgic analyst invokes the theatrical model as a device, a tool, to permit *him* to focus attention on the consequences of the actor's activities for others' perceptions of the actor. The dramaturgic analyst finds this important because, according to *his* theory of social stability and change, others' "impressions" determine the ways they will act toward the actor. Thus, whether the actor self-consciously takes account of these "impressions" or not, whether or not

---

[13] Consider Goffman's statement to the effect that "when we observe a young American middle-class girl playing dumb for the benefit of her boy friend, we are ready to point to items of guile and contrivance in her behavior. But like herself and her boy friend, we accept as an unperformed fact that this performer *is* a young American middle-class girl. But surely here we neglect the greater part of the performance. . . . The unthinking ease with which performers consistently carry off such standard-maintaining routines does not deny that a performance has occurred, merely that the participants have been aware of it" (6, pp. 74–75).

he is even aware that he is creating an "impression," such "impressions" are demonstrably relevant to the fate of such interaction as the actor enters.

In one sense, then, the actor's "perspective," that is, the actor's view of what he is doing, is not relevant to the dramaturgic analyst. For whatever the actor believes he is doing, so long as he is engaged in interaction, the analyst finds and focusses on the "impression" the actor is making on others. The analyst's "frame of reference," his rules for converting the actor's motions into conduct (1), are given by the theatrical simile. This frame of reference, these rules, may be quite different than those used by the actor to understand his own behavior.[14] This feature of dramaturgic analysis seems to be frequently misunderstood, even by its appreciators.[15] At least in part, this seems to be due to a lack of explicitness, if not a lack of clarity,[16] on the part of those using the dramaturgic framework.

[14] In this respect, if in no other, the dramaturgic analyst's approach resembles that of the psychoanalytic psychiatrist. The psychoanalyst, too, is professionally engaged in attributing meanings to the behavior of individuals which are variant from the individuals' understandings of their own behavior.

[15] For example, Don Martindale (9, pp. 61–72) discusses Goffman's work as if it were a representation of the growing amorality of urban individuals. We are explicitly disagreeing with this interpretation and would hold that the dramaturgic approach is applicable to the analysis of moral conduct in any age. We agree with Martindale, however, that the growing amorality of urban individuals may help account for the emergence of the dramaturgic perspective.

[16] Surely it does little to clarify matters to suggest that "the *object* of a performer is to sustain a particular definition of the situation, this representing, as it were, his claim as to what reality is" (6, p. 85, italics added). "Performer" here refers to a person in everyday life carrying out his routine

In another sense, however, the actor's perspective is quite relevant to the dramaturgic analyst. As a social-psychologist, the dramaturgic analyst is little interested in documenting what "everybody knows." Instead he wants to get at *how* everybody knows what they know, at "hidden" effects or *latent* functions of interaction. The theatrical simile, like any of the similes invoked by the dramaturgic analyst, is revealing precisely insofar as it clarifies a latent function. Moreover, it seems to do so only when the actor is "unconscious" of the "impressive" effects of his activities, that is, only insofar as the actor "takes for granted" or "takes notice of without seeing" these effects. This may be appreciated by considering what a dramaturgic analysis of a theatrical performance might be.

A dramaturgic analysis of a theatrical performance would presumably *not* focus on how stage actors manage to bring a play "to life" for an audience. An analysis in these terms would be merely a technical analysis of the business at hand as the principles and the audience define this business. It would produce a manual of stage directions. In order to produce an account of interest to the dramaturgic analyst, what would have to be considered is how stage actors manage to keep the audience continually convinced that the play they are witnessing *is a play*. Such an analysis might point out, for example, that, by altering the segments of time within which events can "really" be accomplished, actors provide the audience with a sense of "play" as distinguished from "reality." It might document the gestures actors employ on stage which *interrupt* the audience

projects of action, *not* to someone who is "on."

member's sense of emerging character, which remind the audience that "character" and actor are not the same. It might note that returning for bows after the curtain has fallen not only services actors' egos, but also functions to remind the audience that there *is* someone "behind" the "appearance" they have been attending, for example, that the "appearance" of the dead man was "merely an appearance." Such an analysis might inquire as to which members of the audience, children under certain ages, for example, cannot retain the sense of the play *as* a play. And more. In general, a dramaturgic analysis of a theatrical performance would ask, what are the relations between the world in which the attitude of "play acting" prevails and that in which the attitude of "daily life" or "fundamental reality" obtains? What are the social devices whereby these worlds are kept distinct, and under what circumstances does this distinction collapse?

It should be noted that, insofar as the above is correct, the dramaturgic analyst seeks to describe the ways in which "impressions" are created, sustained, and ruptured under the condition that the actor is "unconscious" or only dimly "conscious" that this is a part of the business he is in. The other "models" used by the dramaturgic analyst reveal the same feature. Thus, the "con man" instructs us how, in everyday life, without being explicitly aware of it, those who do not conceive themselves as "con men" may sustain another's conception of themselves as "trustworthy" in the face of events which might lead him to conceive them quite differently. And persons who attach television aerials to their houses but do not own sets, those who put exotic travel labels on luggage that gets no further than the front door, in brief, those who *intentionally* misrepresent their qualities, thereby taking on a "character" for the audience to which they feel they have no "real" claim, are interesting to the dramaturgic analyst, not in themselves, but as persons who furnish "clear-cut evidence of the impressive function of presumably instrumental objects" and acts (6, p. 67).

Indeed, it does not seem too much to say that the power of dramaturgic analysis lies *in* the discrepancy between the perspective of the actor and that of the analyst. It is through this discrepancy that the analyst is able to elucidate matters that are beyond the immediate awareness of his subjects. It is when this discrepancy exists, when, for example, the actor provides "impressions" without being aware that he is doing so, that the theatrical simile is most revealing. What it reveals is this: the ways in which interactants *manage,* that is, *produce through their own activities,* that which they "take for granted" is "out there, really." Since the dramaturgic analyst aims to explore the conditions of constancy and change in others' impressions of actors as "being" what they claim, the theatrical simile seems exquisitely suited to his purpose. It focusses attention on that *aspect* of interaction of central interest to the analyst; affecting others' perceptions is the principal business of those in the theater. In the theater, creating appearances is regarded as a *task;* thus the analyst can more easily consider what individuals in everyday life *do* to create and sustain the realities they honor, even though they are not entirely aware of their doings. In the theater, the "expressive" and "impressive" functions of activity are *sep-*

*arated;* therefore the analyst can consider in isolation that function of interaction so central to his theory of social stability and change.

All this adds up to pointing out some of the ways in which the theatrical simile is a simile, not a homology. It is a simile, a frame of reference, invoked by the analyst to segregate and permit him to analyze *one* of the multiple functions of interaction: its "impressive" function. The purpose is facilitated *because* this function is segregated in the theater; in daily life, this function is a concretely inextricable part of a larger complex.

It is also worth noting that this frame of reference enables the analyst to himself abandon, if only for a while, the perspective of everyday life; it enables or forces him to *stop* taking for granted what his subjects *do* take for granted, thereby permitting him to talk *about* these matters. In this way, the perspective stands ready, as does the anthropologist's "tribe," to furnish a lens through which "what everybody knows" can be rendered problematic. We may then ask what we do that stabilizes Grand Central Station as a place for people with destinations, and not a place to live, subway cars as objects for travel, not for sleeping, a hotel lounge as a place to meet people in, a library for reading, a fire escape for survival, and more (7, p. 182).

But, as with any model, so the theatrical one has limits which, if not observed, pose dangers to analysis. The analyst and his readers run the risk of considering the dramaturgic framework to represent his subjects' model of the world. Because "impression management" is critical in the *analyst's* scheme of things, because in any situation it is this dimension that

*he* attends to, he may leave the impression that this is the way things "are" as his subjects see things—or at least that, if they could be brought to be honest for a bit, they would see and admit that this is the case. There is, of course, no justification for this. Indeed, within the dramaturgic framework one must address in all seriousness the subjects' view of self and world; this is, after all, the topic of analysis. On the other hand, there is no justification for overlooking the impressive function of daily activities in an analysis of human conduct. Adding the dramaturgic perspective to the social-psychological tool kit should go some way toward preventing this.

Second, if we are correct in asserting that the dramaturgic analyst does not present "life as theater" as his subjects' view of the world, then we must ask after the relation between his subjects' view and "life as theater." The dramaturgic analyst does not claim that the actor is aware of the impressive functions of his activities; indeed, he seems to claim that, to the extent that the actor is aware of these functions, he becomes alienated from interaction and, moreover, from himself (5). We concur with this view and have presented some observations by and about mental patients to help warrant it. But, although in the dramaturgic vision the actor does not attend to the impressive effects of his activities *as* impressive effects, he nonetheless exhibits a remarkable ability to produce the right effect at just the right time, or, short of this, to correct for the errors he and his teammates may make. How is this accomplished? More pointedly, what is the relation between the *actor's* model of the world and the *dramaturgic analyst's* model? Is the actor merely the outcome of a dynamicized set of "organizational principles" which shove and haul him about without his awareness? Anyone committed to an understanding of everyday life and of the "actor's world" must cope with such a question. The dramaturgic analyst is self-admittedly so committed.

Finally, the theatrical simile may encourage the analyst to forget another important aspect of any everyday actor's communications: the actor is communicating *about* himself; and this constrains the attitude he may take toward the qualities he projects.

The stage actor's obligations do not ordinarily include a belief that the character he projects be a "presentation of self." It is an "Anybody" that the stage actor presents, if a particular one: an other-than-himself. His task, as usually defined, is to employ whatever means will facilitate the "coming alive" of the character for the audience. This leaves the actor free, or relatively so, to select an attitude toward the character he plays. He may, for example, conceive that getting "inside" the character will aid the accomplishment of his task; he may conceive that this is not necessary, taking a "classical" stance rather than a "method" one. So long as he convinces the audience that the character he portrays is a plausible one, his obligations are fulfilled. It is presumably only "method" actors, however, who succeed in experiencing the characters they are projecting as their selves, however temporarily.

The everyday actor's obligations, at least so far as fundamental qualities are concerned, do not leave him free to select an attitude toward the character he communicates. He does not, finally, experience life as theater. He does not expect the curtain to ring down, returning what came before to the realm of make-believe. He is constrained to *be* what he claims, and mental patients suggest that these constraints operate "inside" the individual as well as "on" him. Indeed, his need to believe in himself seems even stronger than his need to be certain that others entertain a particular view of him. He is in the grip of an ethic, and he violates this ethic so long as he is "on."

The basic task joined by mental patients would seem to be the locating and fixing of the reality of themselves. In this, they differ from stage actors; they cannot remain "on" with impunity. And in this, mental patients represent us all.

## Bibliography

1. Burke, K., *A Grammar of Motives*. Englewood Cliffs, N.J.: Prentice-Hall, Inc., 1952.
2. Goffman, E., "Cooling the Mark Out: Some Aspects of Adaptation to Failure," *Psychiatry*, XXV (1952), 451–63.
3. ——, "Embarrassment and Social Organization," *The American Journal of Sociology*, LXII (1956), 264–71.
4. ——, *The Presentation of Self in Everyday Life*. Edinburgh: University of Edinburgh Social Science Research Centre, 1956.
5. ——, "Alienation from Interaction," *Human Relations*, X (1957), 47–60.
6. ——, *The Presentation of Self in Everyday Life*. Garden City, N.Y.: Doubleday & Company, Inc., 1959.
7. ——, *Asylums*. Garden City, N.Y.: Doubleday & Company, Inc., 1961.
8. Mailer, N., *Advertisements for Myself*. New York: The New American Library of World Literature, Inc., 1960.
9. Martindale, D., *American Society*.

Princeton, N.J.: D. Van Nostrand Co., Inc., 1960.

10. Sampson, H., S. L. Messinger, and R. D. Towne, "The Mental Hospital and Marital Family Ties," *Social Problems,* IX (1961), 141–55.

11. Wolfe, B., "Ecstatic in Blackface: The Negro as a Song-and-Dance Man," *Modern Review,* XI (1950), 196–208.

12. *Life,* XLV (December 22, 1958), 116.

13. *San Francisco Chronicle,* January 24, 1961, p. 32.

# PART II

# Social Differentiation

# Symbols of Class Status *†

*Erving Goffman*

With the publication of Vance Packard's best-selling book *The Status Seekers*,[1] the imagination and attention of the general public was captured by the everyday importance of a topic that has long been of central interest to many sociologists: the use of objects and practices by persons to act as interpersonal identifiers of their social rankings. These *status symbols* consist of a vast multitude of things that mark an individual's ranking in the social hierarchy from birth (by such things as the prestige level of the birthplace and doctor, and the kind of crib or baby carriage the child is placed in) to death (by such things as funeral size, type of gravestone, type of cemetery, etc.). The cars we drive, the foods we eat, the persons we marry, and even the places where we sleep, can all be indicators to others of our places in society. And as Thorstein Veblen so clearly portrayed, our leisure patterns, and especially our patterns of waste, tell others a great deal about our relative social statuses.[2]

Why are some objects and practices likely to be better indicators than others? Why do those of us who wish to make our status apparent through what Veblen called *conspicuous consumption* pick some things to consume rather than others? Why is a Cadillac automobile a better indicator than a 10 year supply of frozen pizzas, or some other commodity of comparable cash value? Professor Goffman takes up such questions as these in the following paper.

EDITOR

---

## I

The terms *status, position,* and *role* have been used interchangeably to refer to the set of rights and obligations which governs the behaviour of persons acting in a given social capacity.

In general, the rights and obligations of a status are fixed through time by means of external sanctions enforced by law, public opinion, and threat of socio-economic loss, and by internalized sanctions of the kind that are built into a conception of self and give rise to guilt, remorse, and shame. A status may be *ranked* on a scale of

* Reprinted from *The British Journal of Sociology*, II (1951), 294–304, by permission of the publisher. Footnotes renumbered.

† A modified version of this paper was presented at the annual meeting of the University of Chicago Society for Social Research in 1949. The writer is grateful to W. Lloyd Warner for direction and to Robert Armstrong, Tom Burns, and Angelica Choate for criticism.

[1] Vance Packard, *The Status Seekers* (New York: David McKay Co., Inc., 1959).

[2] Thorstein Veblen, *The Theory of the Leisure Class* (New York: Crowell-Collier & Macmillan, Inc., 1913).

*prestige,* according to the amount of social value that is placed upon it relative to other statuses in the same sector of social life. An individual may be *rated* on a scale of *esteem,* depending on how closely his performance approaches the ideal established for that particular status.[3]

Co-operative activity based on a differentiation and integration of statuses is a universal characteristic of social life. This kind of harmony requires that the occupant of each status act toward others in a manner which conveys the impression that his conception of himself and of them is the same as their conception of themselves and him. A working consensus of this sort therefore requires adequate communication about conceptions of status.

The rights and obligations of a status are frequently ill-adapted to the requirements of ordinary communication. Specialized means of displaying one's position frequently develop. Such sign-vehicles have been called *status symbols.*[4] They are the cues which select for a person the status that is to be imputed to him and the way in which others are to treat him.

Status symbols visibly divide the social world into categories of persons, thereby helping to maintain solidarity within a category and hostility between different categories.[5] Status symbols must be distinguished from

collective symbols which serve to deny the difference between categories in order that members of all categories may be drawn together in affirmation of a single moral community.[6]

Status symbols designate the position which an occupant has, not the way in which he fulfils it. They must therefore be distinguished from *esteem symbols* which designate the degree to which a person performs the duties of his position in accordance with ideal standards, regardless of the particular rank of his position. For example, the Victoria Cross is awarded in the British Army for heroic performance of a task, regardless of what particular task it is and regardless of the rank of the person who performs it. This is an esteem symbol. It rates above a similar one called the George Cross. On the other hand, there is an insignia which designates Lieutenant-Colonel. It is a status symbol. It tells us about the rank of the person who wears it but tells us nothing about the standard he has achieved in performing the duties of his rank. It *ranks* him above a man who wears the insignia of a Captain, although, in fact, the Captain may be *rated* higher than the Lieutenant-Colonel in terms of the esteem that is accorded to good soldiers.

Persons in the same social position tend to possess a similar pattern of behaviour. Any item of a person's behaviour is, therefore, a sign of his social position. A sign of position can be a status symbol only if it is used with some regularity as a means of "placing" socially the person who makes it. Any sign which provides re-

[3] The distinction between prestige and esteem is taken from Kingsley Davis, "A Conceptual Analysis of Stratification," *The American Sociological Review,* VII (June, 1942), 309–21.

[4] The most general approach to the study of status symbols known to the writer is to be found in H. Spencer, *The Principles of Sociology,* vol. II, part IV, "Ceremonial Institutions."

[5] See G. Simmel, "Fashion," *International Quarterly,* X, 130–55.

[6] See É. Durkheim, *The Elementary Forms of the Religious Life,* trans. S. W. Swain (New York, 1926), especially pp. 230-34.

liable evidence of its maker's position —whether or not laymen or sociologists use it for evidence about position—may be called a *test of status*. This paper is concerned with the pressures that play upon behaviour as a result of the fact that a symbol of status is not always a very good test of status.

By definition, then, a status symbol carries *categorical* significance, that is, it serves to identify the social status of the person who makes it. But it may also carry *expressive* significance; that is, it may express the point of view, the style of life, and the cultural values of the person who makes it, or may satisfy needs created by the imbalance of activity in his particular social position. For example, in Europe the practice of fighting a duel of honour was for three centuries a symbol of gentlemanly status. The categorical significance of the practice was so well known that the right of taking or giving the kind of offence which led to a duel was rarely extended to the lower classes. The duel also carried an important expressive significance, however; it vividly portrayed the conception that a true man was an object of danger, a being with limited patience who did not allow a love of life to check his devotion to his principles and to his self-respect. On the whole, we must assume that any item of behaviour is significant to some degree in both a categorical and an expressive capacity.

Status symbols are used because they are better suited to the requirements of communication than are the rights and duties which they signify. This very fact, however, makes it necessary for status symbols to be distinct and separate from that which they signify. It is always possible, there-fore, that symbols may come to be employed in a "fraudulent" way, i.e. to signify a status which the claimant does not in fact possess. We may say, then, that continuing use of status symbols in social situations requires mechanisms for restricting the opportunities that arise for misrepresentation. We may approach the study of status symbols by classifying the restrictive mechanisms embodied in them.

With this approach in mind, we may distinguish between two important kinds of status symbols: *occupation symbols* and *class symbols*. This paper is chiefly concerned with class symbols.

There appear to be two main types of occupation symbols. One type takes the form of credentials which testify with presumed authority to a person's training and work history. During the initiation of a work relationship, reliance must frequently be placed upon symbols of this kind. They are protected from forgery by legal sanctions and, more importantly, by the understanding that corroborative information will almost certainly become available. The other type of occupation symbol comes into play after the work relation has been established and serves to mark off levels of prestige and power within a formal organization.[7]

On the whole, occupation symbols are firmly tied to an approved referent by specific and acknowledged sanctions, much in the manner in which symbols of social caste are rigidly

[7] Examples would be private offices, segregated eating-rooms, etc. For a treatment of status symbols in formal organizations, see C. Barnard, "Functions and Pathology of Status Systems in Formal Organizations," in *Industry and Society*, ed. W. F. Whyte (New York, 1946), pp. 46–83.

bound. In the case of social class, however, symbols play a role that is less clearly controlled by authority and in some ways more significant.

No matter how we define social class we must refer to discrete or discontinuous levels of prestige and privilege, where admission to any one of these levels is, typically, determined by a complex of social qualifications, no one or two of which are necessarily essential. Symbols of class status do not typically refer to a specific source of status but rather to something based upon a configuration of sources. So it is that when we meet an individual who manipulates symbols in what appears to be a fraudulent way—displaying the signs yet possessing only a doubtful claim to what they signify—we often cannot justify our attitude by reference to his specific shortcomings. Furthermore, in any estimate we make of a person's class status, the multiple determinants of class position make it necessary for us to balance and weigh the person's favourable social qualifications against his less favourable ones. As we may expect, in situations where complex social judgments are required, the exact social position of a person is obscured and, in a sense, replaced by a margin of dissensus and doubt. Self-representations which fall within this margin may not meet with our approval; but we cannot prove they are misrepresentations.

No matter how we define social class we must refer to rights which are exercised and conceded but are not specifically laid down in law or contract and are not invariably recognized in practice. Legal sanctions cannot be applied against those who represent themselves as possessing a class status which an informed ma-

jority would not accord them. Offenders of this kind commit a presumption, not a crime. Furthermore, class gains typically refer to attitudes of superiority which are not officially or too openly discussed, and to preferential treatment as regards jobs, services, and economic exchanges which is not openly or officially approved. We may agree that an individual has misrepresented himself but, in our own class interests, we cannot make too clear to ourselves, to him, or to others just how he has done so. Also, we tend to justify our class gains in terms of "Cultural" values which everyone in a given society presumably respects—in our society, for example, education, skill, and talent. As a result, those who offer public proof that they possess the pet values of their society cannot be openly refused the status which their symbols permit them to demand.

On the whole, then, class symbols serve not so much to represent or misrepresent one's position, but rather to influence in a desired direction other persons' judgment of it. We shall continue to use the terms "misrepresentation" and "fraudulence"; but as regards matters of social class these terms must be understood in the weakened sense in which the above discussion leaves them.

## II

Every class symbol embodies one or more devices for restricting misrepresentative use of it. The following restrictive devices are among the most typical.

### (1) MORAL RESTRICTIONS

Just as a system of economic contract is made effective by people's willingness to acknowledge the legitimacy of the rights which underlie the system, so the use of certain symbols is made effective by inner moral constraints which inhibit people from misrepresenting themselves. This compunction is typically phrased in different but functionally equivalent ways. For example, in Western society, some of the persons who can for the first time afford to emulate the conspicuous consumption of the upper classes refrain from doing so on the grounds of religious scruple, cultural disdain, ethnic and racial loyalty, economic and civic propriety, or even undisguised "sense of one's place." [8] Of course these self-applied constraints, however phrased, are reinforced by the pressure of the opinion both of one's original group and of the class whose symbols one may misemploy. But the efficacy of these external sanctions is due in part to the readiness with which they are reinforced by internalized moral constraints.

## (2) Intrinsic Restrictions

One solution to the problem of misrepresentation is based on the kind of symbol which perceptibly involves an appreciable use of the very rights or characteristics which it symbolizes. We symbolize our wealth by displaying it, our power by using it, and our skill by exercising it. In the case of wealth, for example, racing stables, large homes, and jewellery obviously imply that the owner has at least as

[8] Moral restrictions apply to many types of status symbols other than class. For example, in Western society, women feel that it is seemly to refrain from using symbols of sexual attractiveness before reaching a given age and to abstain progressively from using them after attaining a given age.

much money as the symbols can bring on the open market.

The use of certain objects as intrinsic symbols of wealth presents a special problem, for we must consider why it is that a very high market value can be placed upon them. Economists sometimes say that we have here a case of "effective scarcity," that is, a small supply in conjunction with a large demand. Scarcity alone, however, does not qualify an object for use as a status symbol, since there is an unlimited number of different kinds of scarce objects. The paintings of an unskilled amateur may be extremely rare, yet at the same time almost worthless. Why, then, do we place great value on examples of one kind of scarce object and not upon examples of another kind of similar and equally scarce object?

Sometimes an attempt is made to account for great differences in the market value of objects that are of similar kind and are equally scarce by pointing to the "expressive" difference between them. (The same rationalization is sometimes employed to explain the difference in market value between "originals" and "reproductions." In many cases an identifiable difference of this kind not only exists but can also be used to rank the objects on a scale in accordance with some recognized æsthetic or sensuous standard of judgment. This difference in experiential value between relatively similar objects does not, however, seem to be important enough in itself to justify the widely different market value placed upon them. We must account for the high price placed upon certain scarce objects by referring to the social gains that their owners obtain by showing these possessions to other persons. The expressive superiority of an object merely accounts for the fact that it, rather than some other equally scarce object, was selected for use as a status symbol.

### (3) NATURAL RESTRICTIONS

The limited supply of some kinds of objects can be increased with relative ease but is not increased because persons do not have a motive for doing so or because there is a strong social sanction against doing so. On the other hand, the limited supply of certain kinds of objects cannot be increased by any means remotely available at the time, even though there may be a motive for doing so. These objects have been called "natural scarcities."

The natural scarcity of certain objects provides one kind of guarantee that the number of persons who acquire these objects will not be so large as to render the objects useless as symbols for the expression of invidious distinction. Natural scarcity, therefore, is one factor which may operate in certain symbols of status. Again we may note that not all scarce kinds of objects are valued highly. We must also note that not all highly valued scarce objects are status symbols, as may be seen, for example, in the case of certain radioactive minerals. Bases of scarcity in the case of certain status symbols nevertheless present a distinct analytical problem. If we think of it in this way we can appreciate the fact that while scarcity plays its most obvious role as an element in intrinsic symbols of wealth, there are symbols of status which are protected by the factor of natural scarcity and which cannot be directly bought and sold.

On the whole, the bases of natural scarcity may be sought in certain features of the physical production or physical structure of the symbol. More than one basis, of course, may be found combined in the same symbol.

The most obvious basis of scarcity, perhaps, can be found in objects which are made from material that is very infrequently found in the natural world and which cannot be manufactured synthetically from materials that are less scarce. This is the basis of scarcity, for example, in the case of very large flawless diamonds.

A basis of scarcity is found in what might be called "historical closure." A high value may be placed on products which derive in a verifiable way from agencies that are no longer productive, on the assumption that it is no longer physically possible to increase the supply. In New England, for example, family connection with the shipping trade is a safe thing to use as a symbol of status because this trade, in its relevant sense, no longer exists. Similarly, furniture made "solidly" from certain hardwoods, regardless of style or workmanship, is used as a symbol of status. The trees which supply the material take so long a time to grow that, in terms of the current market, existing forests can be considered as a closed and decreasing supply.

Another basis of natural scarcity is found in objects whose production requires an appreciable fraction of the total available means of production. This provides assurance on purely physical grounds that a large number of duplications will not appear. In non-industrial societies, for example, large buildings embody a significant portion of the total labour and building material available in a given region at a given time. This condition also applies in the case of some artists and craftsmen whose total life-output takes the form of a small number of distinctive objects which are characteristic of their producer.

We may consider, finally, the fact that the person who acquires the symbol may himself possess characteristics which connect him with the production of the symbol in a relatively exclusive way. This, for example, is the relation of its creator to a work of art that has become a symbol of status.

Similarly, children may share, in part, the status of their parents not only because the connection is demonstrable but also because the number of children a woman can bear is strictly limited. The family name may then be used as a symbol of status on the assumption that it can be acquired legally only by birth or by the marriage of a woman to a son of the house.

A similar basis of scarcity is found in the characteristics of social interaction. Generally speaking, personal association with individuals of high status is used as a symbol of status. The fact that there is a physical limit to the number of persons with whom any specific individual can be intimately related is one reason why this is possible. The limitation is based on the fact that personal relations imply mutual integration over a wide band of activities, and on the grounds of time and probability, an individual cannot be related in this way to a large number of persons.

Finally, a play produced by a given cast must "play to" an audience of limited size. This is related to the limitations of human vision and hearing. The cast may repeat their perfor-mance for a different audience, but the performance cannot be reproduced in the sense that is possible with a cinematic performance. It is only in the cinema that the same performance may be "given" at different places simultaneously. Play-going can thus be used as a symbol of status whereas a visit to the cinema, on the whole, cannot.

## (4) SOCIALIZATION RESTRICTIONS

An important symbol of membership in a given class is displayed during informal interaction. It consists of the kind of acts which impress others with the suitability and likeableness of one's general manner. In the minds of those present, such a person is thought to be "one of our kind." Impressions of this sort seem to be built upon a response to many particles of behaviour. These behaviours involve matters of etiquette, dress, deportment, gesture, intonation, dialect, vocabulary, small bodily movements and automatically expressed evaluations concerning both the substance and the details of life. In a manner of speaking, these behaviours constitute a social style.

Status symbols based on social style embody restrictive mechanisms which often operate in conjunction with each other. We tend to be impressed by the over-all character of a person's manner so that, in fact, we can rarely specify and itemize the particular acts which have impressed us. We find, therefore, that we are not able to analyse a desired style of behaviour into parts which are small and definite enough to make systematic learning possible.

We also find that symbolic value is given to the perceptable difference between an act performed unthinkingly under the invisible guide of familiarity and habit, and the same act, or an imitation of it, performed with conscious attention to detail and self-conscious attention to effect.

Furthermore the manner prescribed for the members of a class tends to be an expression in miniature of their style of life, of their self-conception, and of the psychological needs generated by their daily activity. In other words, social style carries deep expressive significance. The style and manners of a class are, therefore, psychologically ill-suited to those whose life experiences took place in another class.

Finally, we must note that members of a class frequently exercise exclusiveness in just those situations where the categorical significance of a particular act is taught. This accounts in part for the common social fact that one class may use as a symbol an act which another class does not know is being used in this way.[9] One-sided symbolism of this kind can occur even in cases where the persons who do the act are the ones who do not know of its significance.

### (5) CULTIVATION RESTRICTIONS

In many societies, avocational pursuits involving the cultivation of arts, "tastes," sports, and handicrafts have been used as symbols of class status. Prestige is accorded the experts, and expertness is based upon, and requires, concentrated attention over a long period of time. A command of foreign languages, for example, has provided an effective source of this sort of symbol.

[9] Perhaps the structural model for this kind of symbol is found in the "password" and fraternal sign.

It is a truism to say that anything which proves that a long span of past time has been spent in nonremunerative pursuits is likely to be used as a class symbol. Time-cost is not, however, the only mechanism of restriction which stands in the way of cultivation. Cultivation also requires discipline and perseverance, that is, it requires of a person that he exclude from the line of his attention all the distractions, deflections, and competing interests which come to plague an intention carried over an extended period of time. This restriction on the improper acquisition of symbols is especially effective where the period from preparation to exhibition is a long one.

An interesting example of cultivation is found in the quality of "restraint" upon which classes in many different societies have placed high value. Here social use is made of the discipline required to set aside and hold in check the insistent stimuli of daily life so that attention may be free to tarry upon distinctions and discriminations which would otherwise be overlooked. In a sense, restraint is a form of negative cultivation, for it involves a studied withdrawal of attention from many areas of experience. An example is seen in Japanese tea ceremonies during the Zen period of Buddhism. In Western society, the negative and positive aspects of cultivation are typically combined in what is called sophistication concerning food, drink, clothes, and furnishings.

### (6) ORGANIC RESTRICTIONS

Restrictions related to manner and cultivation provide evidence by means of relevant symbols as to how and where an individual has spent a great deal of his past time. Evidence concerning previous activity is crucial because class status is based not only on social qualifications but also on the length of time a person has possessed them. Owing to the nature of biological growth and development, acquired patterns of behaviour typically provide a much less reliable view of a person's past than is provided by acquired changes in his physical structure.[10] In Britain, for example, condition of hands and height in men, and secondary sexual characteristics in women, are symbols of status based ultimately on the long-range physical effects of diet, work, and environment.

## III

Persons in the same social position behave in many ways that are common to all the occupants of the position as well as particular to them. From the wide range of this activity certain items are selected and used for the special purpose of signifying status. These items are selected instead of other possible ones partly because they carry a strong expressive component and embody mechanisms for limiting misrepresentative use of them. The kind of class-consciousness which develops in a society can be understood in terms of the division between items of characteristic conduct that are employed as status symbols and those items which could be employed in this way but are not.

Six general devices for restricting misuse of class symbols have been

[10] The use of inherited characteristics as symbols of status is typically found, of course, in a society of castes not classes.

outlined. It must be said, however, that there is no single mode of restriction which can withstand too many contingencies; nor is there any restriction which is not regularly and systematically circumvented in some fashion. An example of this is the Public School System in Britain, which may be seen as a machine for systematically re-creating middle-class people in the image of the aristocracy—a task in which twenty-six Charm Schools in Chicago are similarly engaged, but with a somewhat different clientele and a somewhat different ideal image.

The presence of routine methods of circumvention may partly explain why stable classes tend to designate their position by means of symbols which rely on many different types of restrictive devices. It would appear that the efficacy of one type of restriction acts as a check upon the failure of another. In this way the group avoids the danger, as it were, of putting all their symbols in one basket. Conversely, social situations for which analysis of status symbols is important can be classified according to the type of mechanism upon which members of a class may be over-dependent or which they may neglect.

From the point of view taken in this paper, problems in the study of class symbols have two aspects, one for the class from which the symbol originates and the other for the class which appropriates it. As a conclusion to this paper, reference will be made to three of these two-sided problem areas.

## (1) CLASS MOVEMENT

Social classes as well as individual members are constantly rising and falling in terms of relative wealth, power, and prestige. This movement lays a heavy burden upon class symbols, increasing the tendency for signs that symbolize position to take on the role of conferring it.[11] This tendency, in connection with the restrictions that are placed upon the acquisition of status symbols, retards the rise to social eminence of those who have lately acquired importance in power and wealth and retards the fall of those who have lately lost it. In this way the continuity of a tradition can be assured even though there is a change in the kind of persons who maintain the tradition.

As already suggested, we find that sources of high status which were once unchallenged become exhausted or find themselves in competition with new and different sources of status. It is therefore common for a whole class of persons to find themselves with symbols and expectations which their economic and political position can no longer support. A symbol of status cannot retain for ever its acquired role of conferring status. A time is reached when social decline accelerates with a spiral effect: members of a declining class are forced to rely more and more upon symbols which do not involve a current outlay, while at the same time their association with these symbols lowers the value of these signs in the eyes of others.

The other aspect of this problem turns upon the fact that new sources of high status typically permit the acquisition of costly symbols before symbols based on cultivation and so-

cialization can be acquired. This tends to induce in the rising group expectations which for a time are not warranted and tends to undermine the regard in which costly symbols are held by members of other classes.[12]

## (2) CURATOR GROUPS

Wherever the symbolizing equipment of a class becomes elaborate a curator personnel may develop whose task it is to build and service this machinery of status. Personnel of this kind in our society include members of such occupational categories as domestic servants, fashion experts and models, interior decorators, architects, teachers in the field of higher learning, actors, and artists of all kinds. Those who fill these jobs are typically recruited from classes which have much less prestige than the class to which such services are sold. Thus there are people whose daily work requires them to become proficient in manipulating symbols which signify a position higher than the one they themselves possess. Here, then, we have an institutionalized source of misrepresentation, false expectation, and dissensus.

An interesting complication arises when the specialist provides symbol service for a large number of persons and when the symbol to which he owes his employment at the same time carries a strongly marked expressive

---

[11] The extreme case is found in so-called ritual transmission of charisma. See Max Weber, *Theory of Social and Economic Organization,* trans. T. Parsons (London, 1947), p. 366.

[12] This has been referred to as the problem of the *nouveau riche,* of which the community of Hollywood provides an example. See Leo Rosten, *Hollywood* (New York, 1941), especially pp. 163–80. See also Talcott Parsons, "The Motivation of Economic Activity," in *Essays in Sociological Theory* (New York, 1948), p. 215. An extreme case in the U.S.A. is the decrease in social value of the type of expensive car favoured by the rich criminal classes.

component. This is the case, for example, with the fashion model and interior decorator. Under these circumstances the curator comes to play much the same sacred role as those entrusted with the collective symbols of a society. It then becomes possible for the improper expectations of the curator to be realized and for the status and security of the patron class itself to be correspondingly diminished.

## (3) CIRCULATION OF SYMBOLS

The systematic circumvention of modes of restriction leads to downward and upward circulation of symbols.[13] In these cases, apparently, the objective structure of the sign-vehicle always becomes altered. A classification of these alterations or modes of vulgarization would be interesting to pursue but is beyond the scope of this paper.

From the point of view of this paper, circulation of symbols has two major consequences. First, those with whom a symbol originates must turn from that which is familiar to them and seek out, again and again, something which is not yet contaminated. This is especially true of groups which are smaller and more specialized than social classes—groups whose members feel inclined to separate themselves from their original social class, not by

moving up or down but by moving out. This may be seen, for example, in the attempt of jazz musicians to create a monthly quota of new fashion to replace items of their action and speech which laymen have appropriated.[14]

The second consequence is perhaps the more significant of the two. Status symbols provide the cue that is used in order to discover the status of others and, from this, the way in which others are to be treated. The thoughts and attention of persons engaged in social activity therefore tend to be occupied with these signs of position. It is also a fact that status symbols frequently express the whole mode of life of those from whom the symbolic act originates. In this way the individual finds that the structure of his experience in one sphere of life is repeated throughout his experiences in other spheres of life. Affirmation of this kind induces solidarity in the group and richness and depth in the psychic life of its members.

As a result of the circulation of symbols, however, a sign which is expressive for the class in which it originates comes to be employed by a different class—a class for which the symbol can signify status but ill express it. In this way conscious life may become thin and meager, focused as it is upon symbols which are not particularly congenial to it.

We may close with a plea for empirical studies which trace out the social career of particular status symbols—studies similar to the one that Dr. Mueller has given us concerning the transfer of a given kind of musical taste from one social grouping to

---

[13] It is not rare for practices which originate in one class to be adopted by the members of a higher one. Cases in point would be the argot of criminal, ethnic, and theatrical groups, and such fugitive social crazes as the Lambeth Walk. In most cases, these adopted practices serve only an expressive function and are not used as status symbols. Sometimes practices of low repute are adopted as status symbols in order to comment on those who cannot afford to be associated with them.

[14] From conversations with Howard Becker.

another.[15] Studies of this kind are useful in a period when widespread cul-

[15] J. H. Mueller, "Methods of Measurement of Aesthetic Folkways," *The American Journal of Sociology*, LI, 276–82.

tural communication has increased the circulation of symbols, the power of curator groups, and the ranges of behaviour that are accepted as vehicles for symbols of status.

# 3

# Speech and Social Status In America [*][†]

*Dean S. Ellis*

Some indicators of social status are more subtle and less easily intentionally achieved than others. One set of such indicators is to be found in the realm of language and communication. Probably the best known case of speech as an important indicator of social status is to be found in George Bernard Shaw's play *Pygmalion*, later made into the highly successful musical comedy and motion picture, *My Fair Lady*. A large portion of this dramatization represents the difficulties in teaching the lower-class, Cockney-speaking flower girl, Eliza Doolittle, how to speak in the upper-class British manner. Although somewhat caricatured in this comedy, the basic importance of speech patterns as indicators of social rank (as well as geographic ori-

gin) is common knowledge. Numerous sociologists have been interested in some of the class differences present in speech patterns, especially in instances of word choice and grammatical form.[1] It is only more recently, however, that various more subtle differences have been researched.

Human communication is usually broken down into three categories: language, paralanguage, and kinesics.[2] *Language* refers to the meanings ascribed to words according to the rules of grammar and syntax, and to the dictionary definitions of the words used. *Paralanguage*

[*] Reprinted from *Social Forces*, XLV (1967), 431-37, by permission of the publisher. Footnotes renumbered.

[†] This research was done while Professor Ellis was a research assistant in the Communications Research Center at Purdue University. It was conducted under the guidance of Dr. W. Charles Redding and with the financial support of a National Science Foundation grant to the Communications Research Center.

[1] In addition to the references given in Professor Ellis's article, cf. B. Bernstein, "Social Class, Speech Systems and Psychotherapy," *British Journal of Sociology*, XV (1964), 54–64; and his "Social Class, Linguistic Codes and Grammatical Elements," *Language and Speech*, V (1962), 221–40.

[2] Cf. George L. Trager, "Paralanguage: A First Approximation," in *Language in Culture and Society*, ed. Dell Hymes (New York: Harper & Row, Publishers, 1964), pp. 274–80; and Ray L. Birdwhistell, *Introduction to Kinesics. An Annotation System for Analysis of Body Motion and Gesture* (Washington, D. C.: Department of State, Foreign Service Institute, 1952).

refers to the meanings that are not cata-
logued in the dictionary, yet are attached
to words: that is, by stress, pitch, volume,
and other expressive meanings that we
indicate by the patterned sound of our
words. *Kinesics* refers to the meanings
found in gestures and body movements,
sometimes used independently but often
attached to oral communications. Although not present in a dictionary, it
would seem that there are cultural norms
surrounding the uses of paralanguage and
kinesics,[3] and although these can be
learned, their more subtle forms are not
easily brought to the attention of one who
wishes to learn them. It is a relatively
simple matter for any actor to learn his
lines. It is far more difficult for him to

capture the expressive qualities of the
vocal utterances and the subtle gestures
and body movements that must accom-
pany them if he is to fully capture the
multidimensionality of the character to
be presented.

The study below examines some of the
paralinguistic indicators of social class.
Contrary to much earlier thinking, which
belittled the importance of speech as an
indicator of social class, this study demonstrates not only the presence of such
indication, but also the subtlety of such
indicators, and the problems their presence would portend for those who wish
to assimilate members of the lower classes
into middle-class life.

EDITOR

---

Language has long been recognized
as a symbolic indicator of social class.
Barber[4] points out in his text, *Social
Stratification*, that in India the ability
to use written language, i.e. to read
and write, had long been a symbol
of Brahman caste membership. In
nineteenth-century Russia, the upper
classes spoke French, the language of
the court, in preference to their native
language which they shared with the
lower classes. In modern European
countries the speech patterns of the
different classes are often so gross as
to be considered different dialects.
The middle- and upper-class Germans
are expected to speak "Hoch Deutsch"
or high German. But it is acceptable
for the working and lower classes to

speak a regional variation of "Platt
Deutsch" or low German. George Bernard Shaw's play, *Pygmalion,* points
out how vital he thought language
was as an indicator of social status in
England.

The prominence of speech as an indicator of social status in foreign lands
seems to be fairly well accepted.
However, its prominence in America
seems to be more questionable, as is
indicated by the statement of Barber:

In American language and speech, as in
so many other kinds of American symbolic phenomena, the symbolization of
differences in social class position has
been subtle rather than gross. Regional
differences in accent and diction are probably greater than differences of social
class position. All social classes speak
roughly the same except that the better
educated upper and middle classes have
better diction and grammar. This is a
product of their superior education.[5]

The present paper will present research findings which are contrary to

---

[3] Cf., for example, E. D. Chapple, "The
Interaction Chronograph: Its Evolution and
Present Application," *Personnel*, XXV (1948–
49), 295–307; and Albert E. Scheflen, "The
Significance of Posture in Communicative
Systems," *Psychiatry*, XXVII (1964), 316–
31.

[4] Bernard Barber, *Social Stratification*
(New York: Harcourt, Brace and Company,
Inc., 1957), p. 151.

[5] *Ibid.*

Barber's statement. These will be followed by a discussion of additional research findings which show that Americans' speech does, rather nonsubtly, reveal social status and some possible implications of the way persons are affected by the social-status revealing aspect of their speech.

Barber states that regional differences in accent and diction are probably greater than differences of social class position. His statement seems to overlook the fact that listeners may be able to recognize the social-status cues in a person's speech in spite of the speaker's regional dialect.

Baltzell goes slightly beyond Barber's statement when he suggests in *The Philadelphia Gentleman* that there are some similarities in the speech patterns of upper-class persons which cut across regional dialects, but he limits such cross-regional speech patterns to the upper class.[6] Research findings suggest that there are actually similarities which cut across dialects for the middle and lower classes also. Putnam and O'Hern[7] recorded one-minute samples of speech from 12 Negroes of different educational and social backgrounds. The speech samples consisted of each speaker telling in his own words the fable, "The Lion and the Mouse." The speaker's social status was determined by the Warner index. After hearing these short recordings, 55 white university student

judges produced mean ratings of the speakers' social status which correlated .80 with the Warner index scores. This study shows that "whites" can identify the social status of Negroes. Putnam and O'Hern in discussing the findings pointed out that the various Negro speakers had a variety of regional dialects such as Southern, Eastern and "General American." Yet, these differences in the dialects of the speakers did not inhibit the judges' ability to identify the speakers' social status.

This same set of tape recordings used by Putnam and O'Hern was used by L. S. Harms in a study in the Midwest (Putnam and O'Hern's study was conducted in Washington, D.C.).[8] Harms found that the Midwestern listeners were as accurate as the Eastern listeners in identifying the social status of the Negro speakers.

A study by the present author also supports the contention that regional dialects of speakers do not inhibit the ability of listeners to identify the speakers' social status.[9] The speakers in this study were 12 college freshmen. Though the majority of the speakers spoke "General American," several speakers had an "Indiana twang," one speaker had a New York accent and one had a rural Southern accent. The social status of the speakers was determined by use of the Hollingshead *Two Factor Index of*

---

[6] "Accent clearly distinguishes the Southerner from his countrymen in the Middle West or New England. At the same time, there is a subtle upper-class accent in America which cuts across regional differences." E. D. Baltzell, *The Philadelphia Gentleman* (New York: The Free Press, 1958), p. 50.

[7] G. N. Putnam and E. M. O'Hern, "The Status Significance of an Isolated Urban Dialect," *Language,* XXXI (October–December, 1955), 1–32.

[8] L. S. Harms (Unpublished research reported on by Phillip K. Tompkins, "Speaking Ability and Social Class" a paper presented at the 1963 convention of the National Society for the Study of Communication, Denver, Colo.)

[9] D. S. Ellis, "The Identification of Social Status from Limited Vocal Cues" (paper, Purdue University, Communications Research Center, Department of Speech, 1963).

*Status Position.*[10] Each speaker made a 40-second recording of the fable, "The Tortoise and the Hare." These short recordings of the speakers' voices were played to groups of from 15 to 20 upper division students who served as judges. The judges produced mean ratings of the speakers' social status which correlated .80+ with the Hollingshead measure. The evidence from the three studies cited here all indicates that persons can identify social status regardless of the regional dialect of the speaker.

A second assumption made by Barber was that, "All social classes speak roughly the same, except that the better educated upper and middle classes have better diction and grammar." Putnam and O'Hern conducted a linguistic analysis of the 12 speakers used in their study. They brought out that the upper-class speakers had a marked sophistication in vocabulary and sentence structure and spoke with a clear, logical simplicity. The lower-class subjects used several sound substitutions such as the use of /ai/ and /æ/ as allophones of /ɑi/ and /au/, respectively and spoke with great weakening of the consonants, especially the stops. Their grammatical structure was extremely simple.[11] From the Putnam and O'Hern analysis, it appears that though grammar and diction are important status cues, the differences between the speech of upper- and lower-class persons in America is more complex than Barber's statement implies.

There is currently some work being done in England by Bernstein of the University of London, Department of Sociology, which suggests that persons of different classes and different backgrounds do not really share a common language, or as Bernstein states it, a common "code." This same concept is supported by general semanticists such as Wendell Johnson and S. I. Hayakawa.[12] The general semanticists point out that words do not have meanings; only people have meanings, and they assign those meanings to certain symbols, the most common of which we call words. The meaning a person assigns to a symbol depends upon the person's background. It seems obvious that the backgrounds of rich and poor are going to vary greatly. It should, therefore, be just as obvious that the meanings the rich and poor assign to symbols will vary greatly, and, thus, the symbols used by the two groups to express the same concepts should be expected to vary greatly.[13]

Osgood has conducted research, using his semantic differential scales which has shown that the meanings of words vary from group to group. The semantic differential studies, most highly related to this paper, are those that compare the meanings assigned to words by workers as compared to managers. These studies clearly are comparing the language codes of two different social classes. The findings consistently show that there are gross

[10] A. B. Hollingshead, *Two Factor Index of Status Position* (New Haven: Yale University Press, 1957), pp. 1–11. The two factors are the education and occupation of the head of the household.

[11] Putnam and O'Hern, *op. cit.*, pp. 27–30.

[12] An excellent review of general semantics can be found in Wendell Johnson's *People in Quandaries* (New York: Harper & Brothers, 1946).

[13] An example of the difference in the use of words to express an idea would be the two statements "I got a buck," and "I have a dollar"; or, "He's a cool swinger," and "He's a nice guy."

differences in the codes being used by the two groups.[14]

The evidence cited above indicates that there are major differences in the speech of different classes of Americans and the differences are neither subtle nor restricted to differences in diction and grammar as is suggested by Barber.

The discussion will now focus on studies which have directly investigated the effect of diction, grammar and other speech cues as indicators of social status.

In the Putnam and O'Hern study, it was reported that the major cues the listeners used in identifying the social status of the speakers were: "inclusion of aberrant vowel and diphthong allophones, consonant articulation, and the degree of sophistication of vocabulary and sentence structure. . . ."[15] They made no attempt to isolate the amount of independent effect any of these variables had in revealing the speakers' social status. They concluded, "Further research is needed to discover just what features are most diagnostic of social status."

L. S. Harms conducted a study using nine Midwestern, white speakers.[16] Instead of telling a fable, his speakers responded to printed cards which said such things as "How are you?" "Ask for the time." Harms pointed out that though his listeners could identify the social status of his speakers, the cues they based their

judgments on were not obvious.[17] He stated, "They could be based on word choice, pronunciation, grammatical structure, voice quality, articulation, and several other observable variables." The listeners could not indicate whether they based their judgments on one variable or several.

The study mentioned earlier by the present author found results similar to those of Putnam and O'Hern, and Harms. Two follow-up studies were conducted to partially isolate the effect speech cues—such as diction and grammar—had in revealing social status.[18]

In the follow-up study, instead of telling an impromptu version of the fable "The Tortoise and the Hare," as they had done in the first study, the speakers were instructed to role-play that they were honor students selected to conduct the university President and his guests on a tour of a new dormitory. The speakers were told to use their very best grammar and voice quality, and to try to "fake" their voices to make them sound upper class. The listeners were able to identify the social status of the speakers, in spite of the speakers' attempts at role-playing or "faking." However, the accuracy of the listeners' judgments dropped from a validity coefficient of .80+ in the first experiment to .65+ in this one.

It was assumed that since all of the speakers were college students, they could all use correct grammar and sophisticated sentence structures if they consciously attempted to. A later analysis of the speech samples proved

---

[14] C. E. Osgood, G. T. Suci, and P. H. Tannenbaum, *The Measurement of Meaning* (Urbana, Ill.: University of Illinois Press, 1957).

[15] Putnam and O'Hern, "Status Significance," p. 28.

[16] L. S. Harms, "Listener Judgments of Status Cues in Speech," *Quarterly Journal of Speech*, XLVII (1961), 164–68.

[17] Harms determined the social status of his subjects by using the Hollingshead *Two Factor Index of Status Position.*

[18] Ellis, "Identification of Social Status."

this assumption to be only partially correct. The subjects all used proper grammar, but their choice of vocabulary, sentence length, sentence structure, and their fluency varied greatly.

This experiment indicated that grammar may be a factor, but not the only factor giving cues to the speakers' social status. It also points out that speakers cannot easily hide or fake the social-status-revealing cues in their speech. A second follow-up experiment was designed which could more rigidly control the speech variables heard by the listeners.[19]

In this experiment the speakers each counted from one to 20 at a set rate of speed. This eliminated the speech variables of vocabulary choice, sentence length, sentence structure, grammatical usage, and fluency. Counting from one to 20 was chosen in preference to some other list of words because:

a. Counting from one to 20 requires a person to use almost every common sound in the English language;
b. The pronunciation of the numbers is well known to all classes and should not reflect one's educational background; and
c. The numbers are as well known and commonly used by the members of one social class as another.

The listeners were able to identify the social status of the speakers after hearing each speaker count for only 20 seconds. The ratings of the listeners correlated .65+ (significant at the .01 level) with the Hollingshead status position scores of the speakers.

These findings indicate that some of the cues listeners use in identifying speakers' social status are based on stimuli such as grammar or word

[19] Ellis, *op. cit.*

choice which were eliminated from this third experiment, since the accuracy of the listeners dropped from a validity coefficient of .80+ to .65+. But, a major part of the cues upon which listeners base their ratings of speakers social status comes from the way the subjects speak individual words. The cues may be in the pronunciation of the words or in some tonal qualities of the speakers' voices.

In relating these findings back to Barber's statement that "diction and grammar" are the two factors which differentiate the speech of upper- and lower-class individuals, it becomes apparent that his statement is not entirely false, but is rather a gross oversimplification. Even under the broadest definitions of the words "grammar" and "diction," it seems difficult to classify the list of speech variables discussed above, which could be used as cues for discriminating between upper- and lower-class speakers.

Barber's explanation of why the grammar and diction of the upper-class subjects is superior to that of the lower-class subjects also seems to lack empirical support. Barber states that it is due to the superior education of the upper-class speakers. Yet, in the three experiments by the present author, the speakers were all college freshmen. This indicates that they all had the same number of years of schooling and all had been in the upper one-third of their high school class scholastically. The S.A.T. scores of the speakers were not significantly related to their social status.

This indicates that formal educational differences, if a factor at all, are not the only factor which affect the social status revealing cues in speakers' voices. Nor is the intelligence of the speaker (as measured by S.A.T.

scores) the major factor which determines these status-revealing cues. It
seems logical to assume that the
speech qualities that which reveal
social status are not a product of anything so simple as "amount of education," but are rather a product of the
speakers' total environment. It seems
naive to assume that a lower-class
rural Negro who is fortunate enough
to receive a good education, but returns to work in his rural community,
would adopt the speech patterns of
the upper classes. It seems far more
logical and obvious that a person will
speak as the persons he intimately associates with and identifies with speak.

Now that the oversimplifications of
Barber's statement about language as
a symbolic indicator of social status
have been discussed, some additional
research findings not related to Barber's statement will be presented.[20]

Harms measured the social status of
his listeners as well as the social status
of his speakers. He found that there
was no significant difference between
the way high-status, middle-status,
and low-status listeners rated M.S.
speakers or L.S. speakers. But he did
find that the L.S. listeners rated M.S.
speakers significantly lower (sig. at
.05 level) than did M.S. or H.S. listeners. This difference was small and was
not explained by Harms.

Harms also had his listeners rate the
credibility of the speakers. Again, he
found that generally the M.S., H.S.

and L.S. listeners rated the credibility
of the speakers about the same. He
then correlated the ratings of the
speakers' social status with the ratings
of the speakers' credibility. He found
all correlations to be significant at the
.05 level, indicating that high-status
persons are perceived as being more
credible than low-status persons.

Highly related to those findings are
some of the findings in the series of
experiments by the present author. In
two of these experiments the listeners
rated how well they liked each
speaker. These ratings of "likableness"
of the speakers correlated with the
speaker's Hollingshead Status Position score .76 (sig. at the .01 level)
and the with the listeners' ratings of
the speakers' social status .60 (sig. at
.05 level). These findings tend to support Harms' findings,[21] i.e., they suggest that when listeners hear even
very short samples of a person's
speech, they are able to make a value
judgment about how well they would
like the person. These value judgments of the listeners are highly related to the social status of the
speakers.

The present author then constructed
a rating scale of "job-type best suited
for" to see if his listeners could make
a meaningful value judgment about
the type of work each speaker is best
suited for; and to see if these value
judgments are related to the social
status of the speakers. The job-type
scale used had seven different occupational categories described on it,
one to correspond to each of the seven

[20] These additional findings are drawn
from the works of the four authors already
cited, since these authors are the only ones
who have reported experiments dealing with
status cues in speech. One other study related to this area, but not reviewed here,
was recently completed at the University
of Chicago. The study used a sample size
of four. And those four were reported to be
extreme cases.

[21] These correlations are from the first experiment in the series on social status. In
this experiment, the listeners heard the
speakers tell a fable. In the experiment in
which the listeners heard the speakers count,
the correlations were smaller, but still significant at the .05 level.

levels or types of employment described by Hollingshead in the *Two Factor Index of Status Position*. The listeners heard the recording of the speakers' counting. The correlation between the Hollingshead Status Position score of the speakers and the listeners' ratings of the job-type the speakers were best suited for was .67 (sig. at the .01 level).[22] These findings suggest that listeners, when rating the type of job a person is best suited for, are actually identifying the general level of employment which corresponds to the social status of the person. A discussion of the possible implication of these and the other findings will be presented in the next section of this paper.

One fact seems obvious from the review thus far presented: much more research is needed in this area. The author has not been able to locate a single study conducted by a sociologist which investigates the symbolic-significance of speech as an indicator of social status. The studies conducted thus far have been done by persons in speech or linguistics: persons who lack an interest in social status as such. Donald G. MacRae, a sociologist, pointed out in an article in 1953 entitled "Social Stratification: A Trend Report," that sociologists have ignored the area of "vocabulary and speech structure." He said sociologists should devote more attention to this area. A review of the literature since 1953 suggests that the MacRae suggestions were not heeded.

To explain why speech should receive special attention as a symbolic indicator of social status, one need only ask himself, how many persons hear me speak every day? Speech is the primary medium which all persons use to affect the society in which they live, and the main medium through which they are affected by that society.

Research by Dusenbury and Knower[23] has shown that auditory cues provide more information about personality traits than do visual cues. And a study by the present author [24] has shown that when raters make judgments about speakers based on both auditory and visual cues jointly, the auditory cues strongly dominate over the visual cues. Barber has stated that the symbolic implications of American speech in relation to social class are subtle, but the research reported in this paper suggests that whether subtle or not they are easily recognized by all classes of Americans, and they label the speaker as belonging to a certain social class. The research further indicates that persons speaking one accent of American English can identify the social status of the speech of persons using different accents of American English. In short, the research implies that how ones speaks reveals his social class. This conclusion raises two other major questions: (1) is this label a handicap to the lower-status persons, and (2) if it is a handicap, how hard is it to change one's speech?

There is some research which indi-

---

[22] This correlation is exactly the same as and the listeners' (a different group of listeners) ratings of the speakers' social sta-speakers' Hollingshead Status Position scores the correlation reported earlier between the tuses.

[23] Delwyn Dusenbury and Frank H. Knower, "Experimental Studies of the Symbolism of Action and Voice," *Quarterly Journal of Speech*, XXIV (1938).

[24] Dean S. Ellis, "The Effects of Limiting the Amount of Exposure Between Interviewers and Interviewees" (paper, Communications Research Center, Purdue University, 1964).

cates that the label may be a handicap. The research of Harms and the present author, already reported in this paper, has indicated that listeners rated lower-status speakers as less credible than higher-status speakers. If these listeners make the same type of judgments in a nonexperimental situation—for example, in an interview—the lower-status person would have a disadvantage. There are over 170 million employment interviews conducted in the United States each year.[25] Much research has indicated that interviewers frequently based their decision about whether or not to hire a man on some personal whim, or a mannerism of the applicants which is totally unrelated to their qualifications for the position.[26]

In the series of experiments by the present author, the speakers were all college students. These students' social status was determined by the educational and occupational backgrounds of their fathers (the head of their household). So, in fact, the study shows that the children's voices reveal the status of their family backgrounds. The students in these experiments were all engineering students; in a few years they will all be interviewing for jobs which are classified by the Hollingshead index as upper-status jobs. The evidence thus far presented, though not conclusive, suggests that the student who comes from a lower-class family is likely to be discriminated against at hiring time. A controlled study is needed to investigate whether or not such discrimination

really takes place; but a study of engineers by Perrucci lends some support to this concept. He found that engineers from low-status backgrounds earn less than engineers from higher-status backgrounds.[27] However, there are many factors other than voice qualities of the speaker which could account for this difference in earning power, such as individual aspiration and family connections.

Though the evidence is not conclusive, it strongly suggests that the social acceptability of one's speech is a source of discrimination.

The discussion thus far has dealt with only one possible area in which a person may be discriminated against —the interview situation. The variety of other interpersonal situations which exist in our society could all be given as other possible examples: buying a house, joining a club, etc. Just how extensive such discrimination might be is a question which can be answered only by further sociological research.

We now turn to the second question. How hard is it to change the status-revealing qualities of one's voice? This question cannot be fully answered because research has not yet discovered exactly what the status-revealing qualities of speech are. Putnam and O'Hern's concluding statement to their article is not too encouraging.

The importance of speech as a mark of social status is a matter of great social significance. It is known that speech habits are not easily altered: the phonetic speech features, which proved to be most distinctive of social status, are probably

[25] Roger Bellows, The Psychology of Personnel in Business and Industry (Englewood Cliffs, N. J.: Prentice-Hall, Inc., 1961).
[26] A review of literature on this topic can be found in —— and M. F. Estep, Employment Psychology: The Interview (New York: Rinehart & Company, Inc., 1954), chapter 8.

[27] Robert Perrucci, "Social Class and Intra-Occupational Mobility: A Study of the Purdue Engineering Graduate from 1911 to 1956" (Thesis, Purdue University, 1959).

more resistant to change than non-phonetic speech habits. Persons who grow to adulthood as members of an underprivileged social group may carry a mark of their origin through life and suffer from the various forms of discrimination which society imposes on members of the lower socio-economic classes.[28]

This view seems a little pessimistic. The voices of students in the present author's experiments revealed the social status of these students' fathers. In the Harms, and the Putnam, and O'Hern studies the speech samples were of persons who were the heads of their own households. Their voices revealed their own social status; if any of the speakers in those two studies had fathers of a lower social status than their own, it indicates that with time and change of environment, the status-revealing qualities of one's voice may change to reveal the person's new status. Again no definite statement can be made due to a lack of research.

Harms suggests that voices can be changed, but Harms, who is a speech teacher, warns that, "when making a student aware of the different and unacceptable features of his speech, the teacher has a strong responsibility to assist the student systematically. Otherwise, the loss in confidence may far outweigh the possible gains of a partly learned new dialect." [29]

For the final thought on this subject the lesson from *Pygmalion* seems appropriate as a warning. Professor Higgins was able to change the flower girl's speech, but neglected or was incapable of changing her values. As a result, the girl was left with speech symbolic of the upper class, which, Shaw pointed out, would be as great a hindrance to her with her lower-class friends as lower-class speech would be in an upper-class gathering.

Speech is only one indicator of social class, and though it is an important one which should not be ignored, it should always be viewed in perspective. There is some evidence that the status-revealing cues in speech can be changed, but these changes, if not accompanied by complementary changes in the rest of the person's environment, may create as many problems as they alleviate.

[28] Putnam and O'Hern, "Status Significance," p. 23.

[29] Harms, "Speaking Ability," p. 168.

4

# The Secret Ranking *†

*Hans L. Zetterberg*

Although sociologists have explored the interrelations of a vast number of criteria by which human beings are hierarchically arranged in social life, a major dimension—at least insofar as immediate and everyday forms of interaction are concerned—is that of erotic stratification. We have all been aware of the important role of sexual attraction, especially since Freud; yet very little academic interest has been directed toward the role of physical attractiveness in social life,[1] or to the social importance of physical attractiveness when it cuts across other dimensions of social ranking.[2]

EDITOR

---

After all, what is marriage? . . . It completely regulates the life of passion . . . and closes the horizon. *Durkheim*

In a business enterprise the president wanted to fire his obvious crown prince. The board of directors objected, because they liked the up-and-coming man, had invested company funds in his training, and had gladly met the offers he had received from competitors by paying him a very high salary; in fact, they had done all this at the suggestion of the president who now wanted him fired. A look into the situation showed that the president's private secretary had fallen in love with the young man. As far as one could tell, it was a purely emotional surrender and involved no sex relations nor any proven attempts by the young man to get access to information that should remain confidential with the secretary and her boss. Nor was there any indication that the president and the secretary were or had been lovers. Yet the behavior of the parties resembled the triangle of a love story in which an older rival attempted to remove a younger one with

* Reprinted from *The Journal of Marriage and the Family*, XXVIII (1966), 134–42, by permission of the publisher. Footnotes renumbered.

† This study was presented as a plenary address at the annual meeting of the National Council on Family Relations in Toronto, October 22, 1965.

[1] Partial exceptions might be: J. R. Udry, "Structural Correlates of Feminine Beauty Preferences in Britain and the United States: A Comparison," *Sociology and Social Research*, XLIX (1965), 330–42; F. Densmore, "Conscious Efforts toward Physical Perfection among the Makah Indians," *American Anthropologist*, XXV, (1923), 564–67; and G. Roheim, "Professional Beauties of Normandy Island," *American Anthropologist*, XLII (1940), 657–61.

[2] An article that deals with this area somewhat indirectly is: William J. Goode, "The Theoretical Importance of Love," *The American Journal of Sociology*, XXIV (1959), 38–47.

aggressive unreason. After a consultation with a sociologist, the problem was readily solved at modest cost to the corporation by removing the secretary instead of the young man. She was helped to a better job with another company; a storm in an office teapot had been averted and a company had been saved from the high cost of replacing an executive.

This incident is trivial enough and on the surface hardly worth much attention from the consulting sociologist. However, conceptualizing a problem like this one to gain a basis for a recommendation is not simple. The ready-made sociological view of the above problem conceives of the young man as a charismatic leader who by the personal loyalties he can command, disturbs the formal authority of other offices and upsets the work flow in the organization.[3] Given this diagnosis, the alternative solutions to the problem, with the most preferable one last, would be to remove or isolate the young executive, keep him where he is but neutralize his charisma, or let him assume a formal authority within the organization that matches his charismatic authority so that his charisma works for organizational rather than personal aims.

In the above instance this sophisticated model appeared less relevant. Psychodynamic as well as common sense talk about love and jealousy seemed as close to the truth as theories of routinization of charisma; although, neither seemed entirely relevant. The sociological consultant had hit upon a helpful solution for his client, but he did not really know why it was helpful. The process of

[3] Amitai Etzioni, *A Comparative Study of Complex Organizations* (New York: The Free Press, 1961).

applying social theory to a practical problem had revealed a hole in his theoretical knowledge.

Wading through some similar problems, one eventually stumbles upon ideas for a new theory that allows a diagnosis more sensitive to the facts involved. In helping boards of directors to tackle problems such as major reorganizations or firing of the big executive, there is always a need to know the actual hierarchy and communication flow within the organizations. Because the organizational chart is too rough an approximation of these patterns, a consultant pursues other ways to establish who has power and prestige and who can talk effectively with whom. In the course of establishing the real hierarchy and the real communication pattern, he repeatedly encounters a latent but considerably significant rank order which, for want of a better term, might be called the *erotic ranking*. The young man in our illustration had bypassed his boss in the erotic ranking of the company. The reaction of the boss is understandable from the dynamics of interaction in hierarchies, and the solution recommended by the consultant is one of several compatible with well-known theories of relations between ranks. The missing link in our theoretical knowledge turns out to be the concept of erotic ranking.

We will now present a theory of erotic ranking. The evidence backing the theory is admittedly anecdotal. Nevertheless, a concept of erotic ranking can claim a status in science as a hypothetical entity that may be used to explain some findings, familiar events, and common sayings in stories about love. Today such a concept is only justified as a theoretical construct

—like the electron in early atomic theory—that forms necessary conceptual bridges between a variety of theory fragments. At some future day researchers may actually have found a way to measure it objectively and study it directly.

## Overcomeness and Secrecy

Erotic rankings enter into the "rating-dating complex" observed on some American campuses [4] as well as in other patterns of courtship. Its operation, however, is usually intermingled with and obscured by other more conventional rankings. The hero of the football field, the owner of the flashy sports car, the president of the fraternity, and the senior student, are ranking persons on campus not primarily because of their position in an erotic stratification, but because of their position in the hierarchies of athletics, publicity, consumption, power, and occasionally education. The rating-dating complex is highly visible; one advertises one's rank by being seen with a ranking figure in public. The point of the rating-dating game is to catch a high-ranking partner and be seen together. By contrast, the erotic ranking is incognito.

The secrecy of the erotic hierarchy, as we know it, may be reinforced by the puritan culture in which it is encountered. Yet the private nature of the erotic hierarchy is best seen as a part of its definition; the emotional overcomeness we here deal with thrives only in privacy. It stands to reason that the one who has surren-

dered emotionally is unwilling to have this fact advertised; but one may go further—although hesitantly—and say that to openly show this kind of overcomeness is to change its very nature. To preserve it, all parties must keep it from open inspection by others. The erotic hierarchy, as well as love, belongs in "the hidden society." The erotic rank is one of the secrets of love. "Love is sacred in that its secrets are essential and must remain secrets if the phenomenon is not to change character," says Aubert.[5] An erotic rank may also be one of the aspects of a profound sexual union and as such resist public analysis. What Doris Lessing in her *Golden Notebook* says about the difficulty in writing about sex for women applies particularly to the emotional overcomeness that defines erotic rank, "Sex is best when not thought about, not analysed. Women deliberately choose not to think about technical sex. They get irritable when men talk technically, it's out of self-preservation: they want to preserve the spontaneous emotion that is essential for their satisfaction."

The private aspect of the erotic ranking makes it an elusive topic of study. Novelists have, of course, dealt with it. In the classical erotic literature one may single out *Les liaisons dangereuses* (1782) as laying bare erotic stratification and describing the ascents and descents along its ladder. The steps up and down are not necessarily signalled in the form of sexual relations between the principals—such instances, although plentiful, are rather trivial from the point of view

---

[4] Wallace Walter, "The Rating and Dating Complex," *The American Sociological Review* (1937), pp. 727–34.

[5] Vilhelm Aubert, *The Hidden Society* (Totowa, N. J.: The Bedminster Press, Inc., 1965), p. 209.

of a person's placement in the erotic hierarchy—but as events when someone no longer is the master over his feelings. The critical events are the emotional surrenders, not the sexual conquests as such.

Throughout its long existence this book has been considered viciously immoral and pornographic. Although it lacks a close-up view of sexual acts, like pornography it violates a privacy taboo, the private quality of emotional surrender. The naked struggle for erotic hegemony—the pursuit of erotic success rather than erotic pleasure—among the characters in Laclos' book affects the readers so that they respond by putting the book into the pornographic category. It is precisely this strong reaction against making the erotic ranking public that suggests an element of privacy in its definition.

To sum up, a person's erotic ranking is the secretly kept probability that he can induce an emotional overcomeness among persons of the opposite sex. It is not altogether the same as love, for love is a many-splendoured thing; but it enters as an element in love.

A rank in the erotic hierarchy can presumably be assigned to an individual, but it is discernible only in his interaction with others. For a man and woman, we get two measures—one, her surrender to him and the other, his surrender to her. For larger groups the establishment of erotic ranks becomes more complicated, because we obtain more measures than there are persons. The problem of quantification of the ranks is not likely to get out of hand because of the requirement of privacy, which tends to keep the groups small.

Probably the mathematics used to compute sociometric ranks from friendship choices can be adapted to compute erotic ranks. For sexual minorities, such as homosexuals, the measures must relate to the object of their choice regardless of its gender.

In searching for the erotic hierarchy, one cannot expect to find it equally pronounced everywhere. In the lowest classes of society this hierarchy might be more salient than elsewhere simply because the poor, powerless, and uneducated have bottom positions in all other respects and, thus, may turn more to the rewards offered by erotic ranks. Erotic rankings are particularly significant among teen-agers, who have not yet grown into the ordinary community ranks that dominate adult life. One may surmise that teen-aging will forever remain puzzling unless we learn to understand interaction in erotic hierarchies. It also makes sense to assume that the erotic hierarchy is more salient in coeducational organizations, such as hospitals, laboratories, and offices, than in settings where one sex prevails. (The common conception of army life as preoccupied with erotic ranks may not be entirely correct.) The question in what settings this ranking becomes dominant remains puzzling. In some occupational communities, e.g. filmdom and advertising, the erotic hierarchy is part of the folklore, but in others it is not, as in publishing and banking. Variations seem great also between otherwise similar organizational structures. In one university department the erotic stratification may be so emphasized that the female graduate student who is offered an assistantship does not know whether

her academic or erotic competence has brought her the job. In the same university there may be other departments in which academic competence rules supreme. An easy—perhaps too easy—explanation for such differences is that the leaders of an occupational community or the heads of divisions and departments set personal examples which eventually spread among their subordinates.

Since erotic hierarchies are made up of secret ranks, everything we know about secrets, ranks, and stratifications should apply to them. Therefore, we turn our attention to the theories we have of these phenomena.

## Secret Societies

A secret group has several features. The political conspiracy, the guerrilla, the insiders trying to corner the stock market, the spy network, all engage in activities that, if revealed to the general public or its law enforcement agencies, would cause failure and disaster to the group. Common to all these, therefore, as shown by Georg Simmel,[6] are several societal devices to protect the secret.

When an erotic hierarchy is made public to the participants and their environment, there seems to spread among them an unusual amount of disgust and sense of degradation. This may again be mostly a result of our puritan culture, or, as previously suggested, this may be the nature of the beast. The erotic hierarchy never seems the same after it has been publicized; and making it visible generally leads to reorganiza-

[6] Georg Simmel, *Soziologie* (Leipzig: Dunker und Humbolt, 1908), Chapter 5.

tion of social relations. Hence, the erotic hierarchy is a secret to be preserved. Around it forms a group with the characteristic norm of secret societies—thou shall not squeal. Upon the observance of this norm depends the continued social relations of the group.

The preservation of the secret nature of erotic ranks is further guaranteed if the participants are also involved in other activities that require privacy. Lawrence Durrell concludes correctly in his Alexandria quartet that love reinforced by conspiracy is the most unbreakable kind.

The instability of love is otherwise proverbial. This may be due to the fact that the stability of a secret rank is no simple average of the stability of secrets and the stability of ranks. Secrets can be very stable; some family skeletons in the closet undoubtedly count their age in decades. Ranks can also be very stable; some count their age in centuries. But the chemistry of social life does not guarantee any more than the chemistry of matter that a compound formed by two stable elements will also be stable. Among the unstable sociological compounds, we count the secret ranks; for ranks do not naturally stay incognito but need public recognition, and secrets about glorious things urge to be told and thus lose their secrecy. Here then is a possible explanation for the fleeting quality of love—yesterday it was with us; today we are uncertain about it; and tomorrow it is gone.

The most heinous crime in a secret society is to inform outsiders. The informer threatens the very existence of his group. He gets the most despised status in the group. The outside world may give him some compensation for his loss of status in the in-group so long as he keeps informing. (Hence the pressure on the informer to fabricate evidence about the in-group.) In the end, however, the out-group distrusts him.

Those who gossip about erotic ranks and give them away are treated very much like informers, wreckers of something worthwhile. Even the one who takes a problem involving an erotic ranking to a marriage counselor or psychiatrist may be given the stigma of an informer, and, as such, he is never really welcome back into the group whose secret was revealed.

The norm against informing applies with equal force to an offended party who has lost his erotic rank. Smarting under jealousy and the pain of having been replaced, bypassed, or abandoned, those who complain publicly about their degradation will not readily be reinstated to their former rank. Thus, the old advice "to grin and bear it" applies to all such degraded persons who want to keep a realistic possibility of regaining a lost love.

The norm against informing applies also to the ones who have gained erotic rank. One must not brag about this rank if it is to be kept. If a person illicitly has made an advance, and guilt feelings have accompanied his climb in the erotic hierarchy, clinical practice gives him the advice to talk about it and get it off his chest. While a confession may help in coping with his guilt, the procedure may have the costly complication that he destroys his standing with the loved one and gives up his high erotic rank. Thus, the usual ideology of clinical counselling with its "let's-talk-about-it" and "tell-it-all" rules is not necessarily appropriate here.

## Visibility of Erotic Ranks

A general rule about the way in which we perceive hierarchies, first used by Max Weber,[7] may be formulated in this way: if a given dimension of ranking becomes less visible, associates tend to assume that a person's position on this less visible dimension is commensurate with his ranks on the visible dimensions. When, for example, the Calvinist theology made a person's religious standing invisible—no one but God knew who belonged among the elect or the damned—the ordinary Calvinist parishioners began to use their visible stratification criteria as a symptom of their religious standing. Economic success in particular was thought to be an indicator of religious standing. Ranks held on the visible dimensions thus suggested the rank on the invisible one.

This proposition is obviously relevant for erotic hierarchies since by definition they are private. We all have seen instances in which students fall for their teachers, airline stewardesses for their pilots, theater-going gentlemen for a ballerina or actress, men for the rich belle at the ball, nurses for their doctors, secretaries for their bosses, bobby socksers for a pop idol, laboratory assistants for a scientist, the females in the congregation for the minister, et cetera. In such instances they may be attracted to an assumed high erotic rank: ranks in the world of money, power, aca-

[7] Max Weber, *Gesammelte Aufsätze zur Religionssoziologie* (Tübingen: J. C. B. Mohr, 1922), I.

demic competence, sacredness, and artistic taste provide cues for assumed erotic ranks. Of course, the high community rank need not be real; it is enough if it appears high to start this process.

Many novels describe a seduction process that makes use of the likelihood of falling for visible ranks. The plot may show an ambitious but poor family banding together in an attempt to appear blue-blooded and honorable. They sacrifice to dress up one of the daughters to attract desired suitors. The prospect falls for the visible and is then stuck with the privately kept truth. Here is perhaps also the explanation why someone with a low erotic rank can be a little Casanova. For a man who has many conquests but who nevertheless lacks a commanding erotic rank can with the help of this process seduce his ladies by emphasizing his visible ranks, be they real or faked. Often enough such men give an appearance of riches not backed by a careful credit investigation, or academic honors not backed by a check in school or university records, or a noble background that is faked. The philanderer is called "false" and this may be true in more than one sense.

If a surrender to visible status is pursued into the private world of the object of infatuation, the actual erotic rank may end up very differently from the one inferred from visible status characteristics: the famous doctor may turn out to be a narrow-minded bore, the rich girl a drab lover, the celebrated actor or popular singer an insecure mother's boy, et cetera. That "disappointment in love" should be a prevailing theme is thus quite predictable.

The constellation of a high visible rank in the larger community but a modest erotic rank leads to a pattern of attracting partners all the time but soon finding that they are either dissatisfied and leave or that they hang on for reasons other than erotic ones. Persons with this constellation of ranks are thus changing partners quite often. One mistakenly speaks of their "high sex drive" or their "nymphomania" or "philandering." The truth is probably that they cut a painfully modest erotic rank. Perhaps the most stable relation or marriage they can have is with a "gigolo," that is, a person who uses and comforts the unhappy, lowly erotic state of another in return for money or the other advantages of his victim's high community rank.

The frequent failures of marriages formed after brief courtships may also be seen in this context. Both lay and professional marriage counselling holds that one should not make lasting commitments on the basis of a first love-impulse. We can perhaps refine this and say that love is fine as a basis for immediate commitment; but since it consists of rather private qualities, invisible to the outside, it takes time to cut through the visible misleading paraphernalia. "Love is blind," one says. Its blindness can be of two entirely different kinds: one can fail to see things that are there, and one can see things that are not there. The person who is falling in love is usually blind in the second sense: the presence of more visible desired things leads us to believe that the less visible desired quality is there. Great love can be blind in the other sense: our erotic rank exalts us so that no other consideration matters, concern over one's worldly station and the pursuit of ordinary goals become totally unimportant by comparison. As Antony says to Cleopatra, "We have kissed away kingdoms and provinces."

## The Psychodynamics of Erotic Ranks

Like other ranks, the erotic one is accorded a person by others. It cannot simply be taken, but must be granted. Those who say and act as if they were generals, kings, or physicians without being certified by others as occupants of such ranks are treated as fools or psychiatric cases. Erotic ranks are accorded by others; but the private, small groups in which this takes place make the process more personal—there the rank is personally given. Thus, love is said to be not a right but "a gift." Those who lay claim to erotic ranks that are not theirs, given them freely, are the fools of love.

We know from the theory of the looking-glass self[8] that a person's rank is reflected in his self-evaluation. Low-ranking strata of the population have a lower conception of their own worth than have the established high strata. Thus, we also expect a high self-esteem among persons who are superiors in the erotic hierarchy.

The dynamics of interaction in hierarchies are very much linked to the psychodynamics of the self-image. The topic is too complicated to cover here; but it should be pointed out that the direct relation between a person's downward move in the erotic hierarchy and threats to his self-esteem allows us to pursue a

number of psychodynamic mechanisms well-known in the clinical literature. The erotic downgrading leads to the whole web of aggression, projections, reaction-formations, regressions, distortions, rationalizations, etc., that fill the psychiatric and clinical dialogues.

A comfortable self-esteem is an asset in most social relations; it allows one to have greater tolerance for ambiguity, depart with greater ease from conventional ways, assume more readily the tasks of leadership, and be less anxious in new situations. To the extent that we need such persons to fill particular positions in society and organizations, we must pay attention also to their place in the erotic hierarchy. Common sense considerations about the importance of "virility" in a man and "poise" in a woman when they are judged for a job in this way can receive a theoretical rationale.

The pressure to equalize erotic rank with other ranks can also be observed. We have, in other words, a new application of the Rank Equalization Theorem.[9] A person who gets his self-esteem built up by community ranks signifying money, power, or knowledge will not tolerate a low erotic rank that hurts his self-conception. Throughout history the high and the mighty have usually extracted a tribute from the tender sex and considered it their fair due. Public opinion has usually accepted that the strong deserve the beautiful. Contrariwise, someone without high community rank who is firmly established in a high erotic rank can lay claim to

8 Charles H. Cooley, *Human Nature and Social Order* (New York: Charles Scribner's Sons, 1902), pp. 193–95.

9 Emile Benoit-Smullyan, "Status, Status Types, and Status Interrelations," *The American Sociological Review*, IX (1944), 151–61.

power, money, and other kinds of status. Public opinion as it is captured in fairy tales also rationalizes this tendency—he who wins the princess' heart gets half the kingdom, while the rivals who lost leave the court and the land to seek their fortune elsewhere. Whether some comings and goings of executives, politicians, white-collar workers, and professionals in the real world follow parallel principles is an open question.

However, among the norms that govern interactions in all hierarchies are always some that reduce the risk of capricious downgrading in rank. Arbitrary demotions lead to more than personal agonies for the degraded; they confuse the communication system and destroy morale among those who remain in their ranks. Hence, the pressure for tenure norms or other safeguards.

The Justice Proposition in theoretical sociology, formulated by George Homans,[10] says that resentments are generated among those who see others obtain high ranks without commensurate effort. Bitterness particularly besets those who in spite of committed strivings fail to advance and are left by the wayside. It is conceivable that this applies also along the erotic hierarchy. For the erotically high might be envied much like the very rich or the very powerful. Some lows may conceivably band together against someone high and plot his downfall. A high may behave like a typical snob and contemptuously ignore the lows; or, if someone is on the rise in an erotic hierarchy, an established high may put all kinds of blocks in his way. All this may be observed in adolescent society.

However, nowhere in history have we seen recorded an outright erotic class struggle. The reason for this is presumably the secret nature of the erotic ranking. What we do not know cannot be a basis for class consciousness. An individual or a small coalition of individuals can protest on the basis of indignation at their erotic ranks; but nothing can be observed on the level of the total society.

Hugh Duncan[11] has made a good case for the proposition that equals in rank have a broader spectrum of communication and also enjoy being together more than those who talk and meet as superiors and inferiors. While experimental support for this contention still is largely missing, we may take as a worthwhile assumption that equals in erotic rank get along best. They surrender to each other in equal shares and seem to have a wide range of conversation and fun. The matchmaker is probably most successful when pairing off equals. Yet minor assymetries in erotic ranks are as common as in other kinds of status; one person usually outranks another, and one usually surrenders more than the other. When the assymetries are large, the problems may be great; for there is immeasurable agony in loving without being loved in return. However, small rank differences also can have large emotional consequences. Baudelaire in his *Intimate Journals* pinpoints the torture these differences may bring.

For even when two lovers love passionately and are full of mutual desire, one of the two will always be cooler or less

---

[10] George C. Homans, *Social Behavior: Its Elementary Forms* (New York: Harcourt, Brace & World, Inc., 1961), Chapter 12.

[11] Hugh D. Duncan, *Communication and Social Order* (Totowa, N. J.: The Bedminster Press, Inc., 1962), Chapter 24.

self-abandoned than the other. He or she is the surgeon or executioner; the other, the patient or victim. Do you hear these sighs—preludes to a shameful tragedy—these groans. these screams, these rattling gasps? . . . A terrible pastime, in which one of the players must forfeit possession of himself.

The adviser in matters of the heart has to deal with interaction in hierarchies, although his work is not usually perceived in these terms. Marriage counselling may have much to learn from the general study of interaction in hierarchies, conducted on the level of organizations, markets, and communities. And the experience of marriage counsellors may benefit those who consult with large complex organizations. What is needed here is that we lift our thinking to a theoretical level with enough informative value to apply to all hierarchies.

## Achievement and Ascription in Erotic Stratification

The motivation to hold one's rank in the erotic hierarchy may be considered universal. However, the motivation to achieve higher ranks is something that only develops under special circumstances, if we are to assume that it follows the pattern of other varieties of achievement motivation. The circumstances that give rise to achievement motivation include a person's encounters with those who use more demanding scales of status symbols for the gauging of his standing than the ones to which he is accustomed. When he takes over these more demanding standards of self-evaluation he simply must do better. Since status symbols change

according to a dynamic of their own, the individual has little control over the process. For example, in an expanding economy an individual must achieve to keep up with the Joneses, to maintain his standing.

Applied to our problem, this means that the desire to climb the erotic ladder becomes more pronounced the more invidious comparisons of erotic ranks are made. By keeping the erotic hierarchy secret, society discourages a large scale emergence of erotic achievers.

The question of ascription, that is, the measures taken to keep persons in a given position, applies to all hierarchies, including the erotic one. In our culture the social norms allow to a person achievement along the erotic hierarchy during his courtship, but frown on efforts to make others surrender to him after he is married. Marriage thus follows the pattern of academic achievement—one is free to aim high, and once the chosen degree is achieved no one is allowed to remove it. What is gained through achievement becomes ascribed. A wedding in our culture is like a college commencement ceremony, transforming an achieved status into an ascribed one to last for better or worse until death does the parting. The present difficulties in upholding this pattern are apparent in the divorce statistics.

The secrecy of the erotic hierarchy keeps opportunities hidden from view, so that they do not generate temptations to pursue further heights of the hierarchy. That erotic achievement would stop, for all practical purposes, at the cutting of the wedding cake seems problematic; since the rest of society nowadays is arranged so that opportunities for erotic advancement are present in virtually every setting, particularly in the white-collar city. Love stories as well as pornography aid the process of breaking down secrecy, making it a less efficient check. The literature on love is not merely a more or less idle pursuit of more or less artistic value with more or less beneficial effects on the sexual imagination. It also helps to remove ascription from the erotic hierarchy. Since secrecy about the erotic ranking aids a conservative view of marriage, it is understandable that conservatives—although they do not usually know why—are against Kinsey-type research and favour censorship of books on love and sex.

## Anomie in Erotic Ranks

The most interesting insights into the conception of the erotic hierarchy come from its confrontation with the theory of anomie. Anomie as Durkheim used the term is what prevails outside our customary range of ranks. To suddenly lose all one's money would place a person outside his accustomed rewards. Likewise, to quickly come into a huge amount of money places him outside the security of the familiar range. Such sudden changes up or down leave a person without his bearings and are dangerous; in extreme cases they may result in suicide.

The secret nature of the erotic hierarchy implies that people in general have a very limited accustomed range of erotic scale. Breakouts into anomie territories are therefore possible for most. Feelings of, "Where have I been? I never knew anything like it," are thus predictable as new experiences are encountered. In love one discovers letters before *a* and others after *z*, and life translates into new languages. The sudden great falls into anomie, when the comfort of the familiar no longer embraces us, may of course be desperate. To be totally bereaved of erotic rank causes despair and in extreme cases, suicide. To suddenly gain rank beyond all imagination is also frightening and, in extreme cases, as we have heard, the great lovers seek death together.

Anomie, here as elsewhere, is countered by norms and social controls. Durkheim noted this in one of his striking insights into the sociology of marriage.

It [marriage] completely regulates the life of passion, and monogamic marriage more strictly than any other. For by forcing man to attach himself forever to the same woman it assigns a strictly definite object to the need for love, and closes the horizon.[12]

The horizon of the erotic hierarchy closes, restricting men to whatever have become their customary ranges. This Durkheim sees as a gain.

Thus we reach a conclusion quite different from the current idea of marriage and its role. It is supposed to have originated for the wife to protect her weakness against masculine caprice. Monogamy, especially, is often represented as a sacrifice made by man of his polygamous instincts, to raise and improve woman's condition in marriage. Actually, whatever historical causes may have made him accept this restriction, he benefits more by it. The liberty he thus renounces could only be a source of torment to him.[13]

[12] Emile Durkheim, *Suicide* (1897), in English trans. (New York: The Free Press, 1951), p. 270.

[13] *Ibid.*, pp. 273–74.

His argument that the restriction to a customary range is beneficial becomes more eloquent in an article written several years later.

> In assigning a certain object to desires, definite and unvariable, it prevents men from exasperating themselves in the pursuit of the ever new, the ever changing. . . . It prevents the heart from becoming agitated and from tormenting itself in a vain search for happiness . . . it renders more easily peace of heart, that inner equilibrium which is an essential condition for mental health and happiness.[14]

The phrase that "marriage kills love" can now be appreciated as an important half-truth: marriage restricts the pursuit of erotic rank to a customary range. Upon marriage, the spouses become members of castes, be they high or low, prohibited from leaving their accustomed territories.

Durkheim presumably wrote about the Frenchman who settles down after having established a fairly wide accustomed range. From his theory, one may also argue that the premature closure of the range to which one gets accustomed is equally inappropriate, since it leaves him vulnerable to any erotically ranking person who may cross his path. To be rigidly confined to one narrow ascribed range was called 'fatalism' by Durkheim and illustrated by the hopeless condition of a slave.

## The Social Norms of Sex

All this talk of an erotic hierarchy may have led some learned colleagues to visualize a sociometric ranking of who sleeps with whom within a community. Of course, every coeducational office, hospital, laboratory, or college has more or less appealing men and women; and the issue of who has access to whose bed is not an idle one. However, as we have seen, what is at stake in the erotic hierarchy, namely, emotional overcomeness, is different from sexual intercourse. This emotional surrender may, of course, lead to, be achieved with, or be confirmed in sexual intercourse. But the latter is not necessarily involved; and, as is well known, there are many sexual relations that do not involve any emotional surrender of either party. The connection we may have between the sexual sociometry and the erotic hierarchy must be specified by hypotheses and not taken as true by definition.

A person's place in an erotic hierarchy may be confirmed through a variety of activities; but some, such as flirtation and dancing, may place a person more readily than others. Sexual intercourse seems to produce an erotic rank for a person more easily than anything else. The fact that sexual intercourse can produce not only children, but erotic ranks is of the greatest importance to an understanding of the norms that govern it. One of the more interesting aspects of the theory of erotic hierarchies is the predictions it allows about the content of sexual norms.

Social norms range from conducive requests to coercive commands. The former are numerous and varied and seem to depend so much on accidents of tradition and situation as to escape systematic prediction. At any rate, we must here forego the attempt to explain the sexual norms that might be called the etiquette of seduction. We have to restrict our-

[14] Émile Durkheim, "Le divorce par consentement mutuel," *La Revue Bleue*, V (1906), p. 552.

selves to the ones having a more co-ercive quality, that is, to fundamental sexual morality.

It is clear that society wants to regulate something that produces its new members, particularly since human offspring need so much care and training before they can fend for themselves. Traditional sex norms served, among other things, to restrict unregulated conceptions and births. Some of these norms are being re-placed in our generation by norms requiring the use of contraceptives. Here, indeed, we notice a big change. However, the planned children that result from this pattern must still be cared for. The norms around "pro-creational" sex relations insure that parenthood is established, responsi-bility for the offspring assigned, and the offspring placed in the proper stratum of the society. These norms have not been changed much, except that they now tend to be phrased not in terms of "When and with whom may one have sexual intercourse?" but rather "When and with whom may one have sexual intercouse with-out using contraceptives?" The ques-tion that is currently much debated is entirely different. It is whether sexual activity not involving parent-hood—"recreational" sex—should be pursued freely, in the sense that one is free from social controls that go beyond the prescription to use con-traceptives.

The argument for erotic hier-archies which we have sketched gives us an answer. It is known that society regulates whatever places persons in any one of its dimensions of stratifi-cation. In all societies, norms govern the acquisition and assignment of economic, political, academic, and religious ranks. It seems entirely rea-sonable to assume that norms emerge to govern erotic ranks as well. If sexual relations produce ranks, that fact in itself will generate a set of social norms.

If our theory is correct, the norms of love must be those of a secret society and of hierarchy. From the theory of the secret societies, we trace the norms of privacy surrounding the sexual relation. From the theory of interaction in hierarchies, we trace the norms protecting the individual from capricious erotic degradation.

Such considerations lead us, first, to an explanation of the incest taboo. From the varying and sometimes fan-tastic explanations offered for this set of norms, we can now select the one that implicitly assumes an erotic hier-archy as the one deserving special at-tention. In other words, we follow Kingsley Davis.

Suppose that brothers and sisters were allowed to violate the incest taboos. Con-sider first the effect of the sexual rivalry which would develop between brothers and between sisters. If, for example, there were two brothers and only one sister in the family, sexual jealousy would prob-ably destroy the brotherly attitudes. . . . Moreover, since the number and sex dis-tribution of the siblings in different fami-lies is impossible to control, no standard institutional pattern could be worked out so that jealousy would be a support rather than a menace. . . . If sexual rela-tions between parent and child were per-mitted, sexual rivalry between mother and daughter and between father and son would almost surely arise, and this rivalry would be incompatible with the senti-ments necessary between the two.[15]

The family is only one of the pri-mary groups in which insurance

[15] Kingsley Davis, *Human Society* (New York: Crowell-Collier & Macmillan, Inc., 1949), pp. 402–3.

against erotic degradation emerges. Other groups in which we are also much involved, such as friendships, neighbourhoods, and work groups, develop similar prohibitions. A social norm that, in addition to the ordinary incest taboo, is irremovable from any society is, thus, a prohibition to steal a friend's, workmate's, or neighbour's spouse. In other words, the minimum sexual morality is an extension of the incest taboo to cover not only close relatives as before, but friends of the family, workmates, and neighbours. For sexual license in groups in which people are so intimately engaged makes for shifts in erotic hierarchies that cause too much agony to be tolerated.

The one who violates the incest taboo is certain to be abhorred in every society; the one who violates the extended taboo that puts a spouse beyond the sexual access of immediate friends, colleagues, and neighbours is also likely to be despised. This is true even where all other restrictions on sexual relations are dropped; friends, colleagues, or neighbours in prostitution consider it immoral to sleep with each others' pimps. Thus, there is always a minimum code of honour for sexual behaviour. Free love in the sense of sex unregulated by any social norms is a sociological anomaly. The sexual revolution of our times that abolishes conventional morality will predictably stop in front of an extended incest taboo covering all primary relations, not merely immediate blood relatives. Those in the current debate who formulate and teach the abolishment of conventional sexual morality in return for an extension of the incest taboo may well be judged as the wisest.

## Caveat

New theoretical ideas require special care. On the one hand, one must not believe in them and act as if they were true; for they have not yet met the test of research. On the other hand, one must show them much confidence and attention and help them grow strong before they are hit by tough formal logic and hard research data. Thus, there is an emotional ambivalence in the nursing of a new theoretical idea. It is not unlike the parental hypocrisy that calls the same child "a big boy" in the morning when he manages to get dressed by himself and "a little boy" in the evening when it is bedtime. This theory is presented in the happy morning hour when standards are generous. We have taken key ideas from sociological theory as developed by Durkheim, Simmel, Weber, and others and applied them to a new field. A theorist is supposed to link together ideas and propositions from various fields into a parsimonious bundle that then is handed over to the researchers, who guide further investigation, and to the practioners, who makes use of it in their recommendations to clients. What they say about it at the end of their working day must now be awaited.

PART III

Everyday Interactions

# 5

## Toward a Sociology of Telephones and Telephoners *†

*Donald W. Ball*

The telephone is a ubiquitous and central mode of communication in today's world. In addition to constituting a technological device for communicating immediately over great distances, however, the telephone presents numerous other special features of important consequence for its social uses, quite aside from its objective social importance as a status symbol. Since today almost everyone in the United States can have a phone, this importance does not center around mere ownership; it also comprises other characteristics such as phone color, shape, type of listing, number of phones in the house, etc. Thus the telephone has brought with it a variety of specialized forms of interaction.

Most of us have experienced occasions —especially those involving embarrassment—when telephoning a message appeared to be somehow "easier" or more appropriate than directly confronting the intended recipient. Whereas the telephone seems more impersonal in that the actors do not see each other's surroundings, facial expressions and other visual cues, it nevertheless has a uniquely direct aspect in that the parties can only hear each other, and do so alone in most cases, thereby bringing a degree of freedom and personal expression sometimes not present in face-to-face encounters; and this is especially true for those cases of periodic uses of the telephone for the communication of practical jokes, threats, and obscenities. The following paper attempts an examination and analysis of some of the routine grounds or underlying normative structures found in telephone conversations.

EDITOR

---

The sociologist has been slow to take as a serious subject of investigation what is perhaps the most distinctive feature of humans—talk.[1]

It has long been a truism among many social scientists that the major characteristic which uniquely distin-

* Prepared especially for this volume.

† I am grateful to Marcello Truzzi and Stanford Lyman for their criticical readings of an earlier draft and for their comments and suggestions, even those not incorporated in this version. Naturally, they are not responsible for any errors in substance or interpretation, for which I take all blame. Without the clerical assistance of Patricia Shinn, working under a very short deadline, this work might still be unfinished, while Bonnie Hoover has softened or corrected some of the harsher grammatical constructions and spelling miscues.

[1] Marvin Scott and Stanford Lyman, "On Accounts," mimeoed, April, 1967, p. 15.

guishes man from infrahuman species is his ability to converse: to produce, distribute, and consume symbols. Not social organization, but *culture* as it is manifested in a conversation-rooted economy of symbols is what binds and makes *human* society singular;[2] and for that matter, justifiable as a distinct area of scientific scrutiny separate from the biological sciences.

For sociologists, broadly, the essential object of their scholarly concern is with aggregates of organisms, the boundaries of which are defined by the member's communicative use of some common symbol system or language, and who become groups of *persons* by virtue of their trafficking in these shared symbols, primary among which are, of course, the words of idiomatic, everyday discourse.[3] It is through such symbols, embedded as

[2] G. H. Mead, *Mind, Self, and Society* (Chicago: The University of Chicago Press, 1934), is the classic statement of this position. This work also discusses the crucial distinction between signs and symbols. There are, of course, many infrahuman species that evidence social organization and a division of labor, e.g. ants, bees, the pecking order of chickens, etc.; but only humans manifest *symbolic* culture. Cf. John Paul Scott, *Animal Behavior* (Chicago: The University of Chicago Press, 1958).

[3] Floyd Matson and Ashley Montague write of the growing tendency of anthropologists to equate communication with culture, e.g., Edward Hall's *The Silent Language;* the works of Leslie White, e.g., *The Science of Culture;* and sociologists to make a similar conceptual equation regarding society and men in symbolic interaction. See Matson and Montague, *The Human Dialogue* (New York: The Free Press, 1967), pp. vii, 1–11. An excellent collection demonstrating the range of sociological and anthropological inquiry in this area is Dell Hymes, *Language in Culture and Society* (New York: Harper & Row, Publishers, 1964). For an overview and representative selections of the sociological, symbolic-interaction school, see Arnold Rose, ed., *Human Behavior and Social Processes* (Boston: Houghton Mifflin Company, 1962).

they are in communicative acts, that social structure itself is reified and given substance, and currency provided for social process. Put another way, *social reality occurs through conversational exchanges;* whether mundane and routine, dramatic and ritualized, or indirectly, as through written, printed, or electronic media, conversations are the stuff of which social order is constructed and maintained or altered and changed.[4]

As social phenomena, conversations are structured episodes of interaction: the mutually interdependent production, distribution, and consumption of shared symbols and their meanings, along with the resultant reciprocal influence of interactants or conversants upon one another; taking each other into account as the lines of communicative action shape, and are shaped, by the partners and the normative environment in which they and their conduct are located. It is in such transactions that organisms become persons, and persons become social actors; putting forth selves to be ratified and confirmed or disconfirmed and denied by their audience of others, while at the same time receiving or rejecting imputed identities assigned to them by these responding monitors.[5]

Ordinarily, when sociologists consider such interpersonal events, they have in mind direct social encounters in which the participants are physically copresent, i.e. face-to-face with

[4] See Peter Berger and Thomas Luckman, *The Social Construction of Reality,* (Garden City, N.Y.: Doubleday & Company, Inc., 1966), and Hugh Duncan, *Communication and Social Order* (Totowa, N.J.: The Bedminster Press, Inc., 1962).

[5] Gregory Stone, "Appearance and the Self," in Rose, *Human Behavior,* pp. 86–118, makes the distinction between *selves* that are presented by the actor, and *identities* that are imputed by his audience.

each other and able to visually and aurally, if not tactilely, audit the gestures, facial movements, postures, and so forth, of themselves and their audience.[6] Strictly speaking, of course, they can only *imagine* certain aspects of *their own appearance* because it is either inaccessible to their own visual range, i.e. facial expressions; or else appears to the audience from a different perspective than for the actor due to their differentiated spatial locations.[7] Still, what is important about such imaginings is not their accuracy or the lack thereof, but that valid or no, they are available to enter into the actor's own definitions of self and situation and the construction and evaluation of lines of face-to-face social action.[8]

However, the usual substantive preoccupations of conventional sociology with such copresent encounters should not blind us to the frequency, let alone importance, of another form of interaction: that which is not face-to-face, but only voice-to-voice, i.e. telephone conversations, where the participants are thrown back on their "linguistic wits" as it were. That such everyday communicative activities have their own generic rules, conven-

[6] Erving Goffman, *Behavior in Public Places* (New York: The Free Press, 1963), pp. 16ff. Some small group experiments are exempt from this description, e.g., when the subjects are visually shielded from one another and "talk" is via written messages, the timing and content of which are often one of the experimentally controlled variables.
[7] Maurice Merleau-Ponty, *The Structure of Behavior,* trans. Alden Fisher (Boston: Beacon Press, 1963); also, Mary Rose Barral, *Merleau-Ponty: The Role of the Body-Subject in Interpersonal Relations* (Pittsburgh: Duquesne University Press, 1965).
[8] The famous Thomas dictum that argues that if things are defined as real, their consequences are real; W. I. Thomas, *The Unadjusted Girl* (Boston: Little, Brown and Company, 1923).

tions, and attendant implications should perhaps go without comment, but suffice it to say, as a form of structured and normatively regulated conduct, telephoning is worth a full chapter in Emily Post.[9] And though telephonic phenomena are usually ignored by sociologists, there are almost four hundred million such conversations in the United States each day.[10]

In the following essay—and the discursive nature of this genre seems best suited to the tentative nature of the material herein—we wish to consider some *selected* aspects of telephones, telephoners, and telephonic conversations and their rules, as well as to suggesting more generally some of the social consequences of the telephone as a medium in and of itself. That the following discussion is selective needs emphasis—strictures of space preclude adequate consideration of many points and topics, some worthy of separate and complete coverage in their own right, which receive no more than textual asides or cursory footnote recognition in the material below which tends to focus upon typical, everyday aspects rather than the exceptional or bizarre.

Our sociological perspective is that of Georg Simmel, and his famous distinction between form and content; that is, we wish to focus upon the telephone and telephone conversations as *forms* which have their own social characteristics and functions irrespective of the substantive *content* of what may be said by any two persons so conversing, e.g. the meanings, purposes, etc. In other words, the fo-

[9] See Emily Post, *Etiquette: The Blue Book of Social Usage,* 9th ed. (New York: Funk & Wagnalls, 1955), Chapter 37, "Courtesy on the Telephone," pp. 441–48, also 27, 127, 275, 392, 404, 553, 554.
[10] U. S. Bureau of the Census, *Statistical Abstract of the United States: 1966,* 87th ed. (Washington, D. C.: 1966), p. 513.

cus will be upon the sociological structure of telephone talk, rather than the talk itself. Such a distinction is, of course, an analytic imposition rather than an empirical reality, a fiction for ordering the materials at hand. This is not to deny the relevance of what is said, but rather it is an attempt to specify some of the conditions and contingencies which regulate telephonic conversational exchanges, and thus structure the what of that which is said.[11]

Methodologically, as in Simmel's work, our materials are drawn from

1. The inductive data of observation as a participant in the heavily telephonic culture;
2. Sociologically informed deduction; and
3. The surprisingly sparse, sociologically relevant literature.

Although the materials are presented in essay form, they are, in many cases, hypotheses still awaiting the more precise formulation which is requisite to their testing. This is then, a working paper; as the title suggests this is an effort to build *toward* a sociology of telephones and telephoners.

Perhaps the first structural, macro-social fact which should be noted about telephones is their sheer distributional *pervasiveness*. The whole of the North American continent, for instance, is linked together through an ubiquitous direct-dialing system which involves over a hundred million instruments. With around 94,000,-000 in the United States (5,000,000 in New York City alone) and nearly

7,000,000 in Canada, North America has about 53 percent of the world's telephones; 43 per every hundred persons or 83 for every 100 households. As previously noted, in the United States alone between three and four hundred million calls are made each and every day; in fact, even as early as 1930 every telephone in the country averaged over three calls per day.[12]

Such widespread distribution is indicative of the telephone's explicit social definition: as a necessity. As long as forty years ago, in the 1920's, the Lynds found in their study of Middletown, a small midwestern city,[13] that even among the unstably and intermittently employed, only one out of every four families with a phone said they would have it disconnected in order to economize and save scarce funds; a response which proved to be predictively quite valid at the behavioral level when the depression struck a few years later.[14] Quoting an old-time Middletown resident of somewhat more comfortable means, they reported that as early as the Spanish-American War (1898), the telephone was considered something that one apologized for *not* having.[15]

It was at this time, around the turn of the century, that the socially *cen-*

[11] *The Sociology of Georg Simmel*, ed. and trans. Kurt Wolff (New York: The Free Press, 1950), pp. xxxiv–xxxvi, 21–23, and 40–43. I have attempted to deal more directly with one form of *talk* in a Simmelian manner elsewhere. See "Sarcasm as Sociation: The Rhetoric of Interaction," *Canadian Review of Sociology and Anthropology*, II (November, 1965), 190–98.

[12] *Statistical Abstract*, 1966, pp. 513–16, for all the figures in this paragraph except the last, which is from C. H. Cooley, Robert Cooley Angell, and Lowell Carr, *Introductory Sociology* (New York: Charles Scribner's Sons, 1932), p. 169.

[13] Robert S. Lynd and Helen Merrel Lynd, *Middletown* (New York: Harcourt, Brace and Company, Inc., 1929).

[14] Lynd and Lynd, *Middletown*, p. 62, and *Middletown in Transition* (New York: Harcourt, Brace and Company, Inc., 1937), pp. 201, 564. More recently, in 1966, even among those families whose aggregate income was *$1,000 or less*, over half had telephones in their residence. *Statistical Abstract*, 1966, p. 516.

[15] Lynd and Lynd, *Middletown*, p. 173.

*trifugal* effects of the telephone first started to be felt. For as the Lynds also noted, a steady historical decline in face-to-face neighboring in Middletown first began about then; direct confrontations being slowly replaced and superseded by the more attenuated voice-to-voice social contact of the telephone.[16]

However, any opposition toward the telephone was on more pragmatic non-social grounds; for instance, a fear in another midwestern town that the overhead lines would be all too good conductors of electricity in the event of lightning storms.[17] In spite of such sentiments, though, telephone lines became a major determinant of rural land use and settlement patterns, as families located themselves and their homes along these lines which would give them communicative access beyond their most immediate neighbors.[18]

Equally, if not more characteristic than the telephone's pervasive ubiquity is the *insistency*, under ordinary circumstances, of an activated, ringing instrument. To do otherwise than answer it is to risk missing a potentially important interaction as well being subjected to ringing which will otherwise be terminated only when the caller gives up and hangs up himself.

To repeat, in the usual case, to have a telephone is to be *accessible* to communications from others. Although it is only a physical object—a mechanical thing—a ringing telephone is something that calls out for a social response; the bell is a symbolic cue to the action of answering, and thus acknowledging and reacting to the caller on the other end of the line. Other than ordinary conditions may, of course, mute or void the usual telephone-induced felt sense of obligation and urgency regarding its answer. Engrossing involvements with others ranging from the dangerous consequences of leaving a half-bathed infant alone in a tub to the potential interruption of satisfactions derived from sexual intercourse provide one source of exception; being present when someone else's phone rings while they are out of the room is another, although observation suggests that for many persons the felt insistency is by no means lacking, but that to the extent they are hesitant, it is because of the involved explanation they predict their unauthorized action might entail. Still another concerns those situations where persons use prearranged codes, comprised of time of call and/or number of rings as a form of communication, e.g. as a way of transmitting messages at long-distance range, but without paying long-distance rates. Such expectations, and the above are merely suggestive and in no sense exhaustive, are explicitly beyond the scope of this discussion however.

Additionally, it is normatively defined that one is expected to, that one *should* answer a signaling phone's implicit invitation to interaction.[19] Most readers can verify this rule by trying not to answer their telephone the next

---

[16] *Ibid.*, p. 275. As such, this observation is a harbinger of contemporary Mass Society theory.

[17] James West (pseudonym), *Plainsville, U. S. A.* (New York: Columbia University Press, 1945), p. 17.

[18] *Ibid.*, p. 71.

[19] See *Amy Vanderbilt's New Complete Book of Etiquette* (Garden City, N.Y.: Doubleday & Company, Inc., 1963), p. 257. (As a cultural and sociohistorical datum completely irrelevant to this paper, it might be noted that one of the illustrators receiving credit on the title page for the neat, conventional line drawings that illustrate the text is Andrew—Andy of pop art and underground movie fame—Warhol.)

time it rings, and then monitoring their own experiencing of such conduct. Answering a phone involves, it should be made clear, not only the substance of speech; but is also a "performative utterance," [20] i.e. a verbal act, which by being spoken, also implies an additional activity by the speaker. As "I do" at weddings is a commitment as well as a promise, so too the "hello" of the telephone answerer is signal of willingness to converse as well as a sign of greeting.

Such characteristics have led Marshall McLuhan to observe that "the telephone is an *irresistible intruder* in time or place." [21] It is this potential for invasion and exploitation that has generated the set of various avoidance procedures which will be referred to in the discussions below; responses to the fact that not only is a caller a potential invader, but also a potential exploiter by virtue of the normative context of such conversations. This opportunity for victimage by the caller of the called is made possible by the important, though rarely made explicit, rule of telephone manners, one of the "background expectancies" as it were,[22] that *it is the initiator of a call who shall be its*

terminator, i.e. the person socially defined as being the one expected to do the hanging up.[23] Thus, to the extent that persons answering a phone are bound by the rules of the "telephone game," they are open to attempts to conversationally importune them which they cannot legitimately escape, but which etiquette dictates that they should endure.

Furthermore, one is expected to talk, to keep up one's *conversational obligations*; to participate by taking an active part in maintaining the flow of talk, even if only in the form of periodic ohs, grunts, sighs, etc., to denote one's continued orientation toward the action at hand. There is a simple experiment to test the presence of this rule for any reader who wishes to do so. All that must be done is to completely stop talking or responding during an ongoing telephone conversation and then sit back and record the response. And since one's definitions of self are fashioned out of what one does, one's conduct, such a breach is likely to have impact upon one's self as well as the person on the other end of the line. To engage in such conversational rule-breaking is to act in a way which potentially threatens definitions of self.[24] More generally, this fact of rule-breaking and threats to definitions of self is central to the operation of internalized noncoercive social control.

[20] J. L. Austin, *Philosophical Papers* (Oxford: Clarendon Press, 1961), pp. 220–39, especially 222; also *How to Do Things with Words* (New York: Oxford University Press, 1965).

[21] Marshall McLuhan, *Understanding Media: The Extensions of Man* (New York: McGraw-Hill Book Company, Inc., 1965) (paperback edition), p. 271; also see 268, 273.

[22] Berger and Luckman, *Social Construction of Reality;* Scott and Lyman, "On Accounts"; also, Harold Garfinkel, "Studies of the Routine Grounds of Everyday Activities," *Social Problems*, XI (Winter, 1964), 225–50, and *Studies in Ethnomethodology* (Englewood Cliffs, N.J.: Prentice-Hall, Inc., 1967). The primary works in this vein are those of the late Alfred Schutz.

[23] See Lois Irene Hutchinson, *Standard Handbook for Secretaries*, 7th ed. (New York: McGraw-Hill Book Company, Inc., 1964), p. 157. A nonrandom sample survey on this question by the writer found that, although many respondents didn't know, among those who did think they knew, all but a small minority designated the caller as the appropriate terminator.

[24] Erving Goffman, *The Presentation of Self in Everyday Life* (Garden City, N.Y.: Doubleday & Company, Inc., 1959).

If intensity is typically conveyed by a ringing telephone, interestingly, it is an *equalitarian intensity*: undifferentiated in terms of the caller's class, status, or any other social ranks vis-à-vis the person to whom he is calling. As Hall has observed, since it is impossible to tell from a ring who might be on the other end of the line or how important the call might be, people feel a compulsion to answer a jingling telephone, no matter who it may actually turn out to be.[25] Even though, because of time for instance, we may *expect* that it is a particular person who is calling, we cannot *know* in advance whether our expectations are correct or not. The momentous may be anticipated, but the trivial may await us.

Said another way, *unequals may call, but their calls are equal* (at least until answered). Furthermore, the signs and symbols of status are difficult to communicate over the phone (except by self-profession), save possibly for class-linked speech patterns —but even here, it must be remembered that the fidelity of telephonic voice reproduction is quite low, mitigating against such identifications by the listener. Thus, the telephone can become a strategic device in the hands of the lowly, allowing for stealthy, unseen telephonic approach toward those ordinarily unapproachable, subverting hierarchical elements in social order and organization.[26] Similar opportunities are also available for those persons whose visual appearance would disadvantage them in face-to-face encounters, as will be discussed below in more detail.

Therefore, lacking any opportunity for visual validation and to prevent such approaches by those deemed unworthy (for whatever reasons), and to maintain their unapproachability, the highly placed more and more employ *avoidance procedures;* juxtaposing intermediaries between themselves, their phones, and those who would so importune them. Such intermediaries may be persons, establishments, or machines; e.g. secretaries; answering services; or mechanical answering, message-taking and recording devices.

These last named machines are a belated technological response to a technology-created need; that is, the need to know: Who is the caller? What does he want? How important? How urgent? and so on. However, as Stanford Lyman (in a personal communication) has suggested, such mechanical contraptions are not without their drawbacks: not only for the caller, but also for the called who employ such machines.

For the caller, he is aurally confronted with the voice of an automaton; one who speaks and listens, i.e. receives messages, but one which does not, as would most human conversants, reply to the caller's utterances. The caller is also, in many such systems now on the market, limited in time as to the length of the message he can leave recorded. In sum, he is

---

[25] Edward Hall, *The Hidden Dimension* (Garden City, N.Y.: Doubleday & Company, Inc., 1966), pp. 131–32.

[26] Duncan defines social order itself as "the dramatization of relationships between superiors, inferiors and equals," *Communication and Social Order, passim*. On speech patterns and rank, see T. H. Pear, *Personality, Appearance, and Speech* (London: George Allen & Unwin Ltd., 1957), pp. 64–80; Dean Ellis, "Speech and Social Status in America," in this volume. On the erosion of hierarchies of taste and the "familiarization of everyone," see Louis Kronenberger, *Company Manners* (New York: Mentor Books, 1955). Something of this order seems to be involved in the first-naming of hosts by anonymous callers on the call-in radio shows.

"faced" with a dictatorial robot who tells him when and how long he may speak, but will not otherwise respond.

As regards the called, his situation too is made problematic by the use of such devices. Though he may have many and differentiated relationships with the population of callers to his number, his machine can present but one voice to them: the prerecorded statement of identification and unavailability, along with the summons to leave a message. To friends, enemies, colleagues, and strangers, the message is always the same: invariant, irrespective of the situational or personal characteristics of the caller and his abortive call. Thus, confronted with such a message, some frustrated callers have reported of their delight in cursing, leaving false messages, refusing to identify themselves and thereby mystifying the contrivance's user, and otherwise attempting to "get even." Perhaps one motivation for such conduct by the callers is the knowledge that there is no guarantee that even a legitimate, above-board message to the machine will result in the return of their call. The device's tape of the callers' messages can be played back in secret, and the call can be returned or not, at the user's convenience. In fact, one manufacturer devotes a full page in the owner's manual to this exploitative aspect of his product's usage.

As an alternative strategy, one may attempt to pick his callers in advance; this is the function of the unlisted number, issued only to the prejudged-as-acceptable potential caller. However, one takes this tack at his own risk. Not only is there the possibility of being inadvertently inaccessible to those whose calls would be desired, but there is frequently a degree of hostility toward those with unlisted numbers; for to do so is to deny or

attempt to control the right of others using the medium to have access to communicate with whomever they please.[27]

Conversely, as the obverse of avoidance procedures may be noted the legendary tales of actors and other celebrities having calls made to them in public places so that they might be paged and thereby call attention to themselves. Such cases illustrate the employment of the telephone to *avoid obscurity* rather than conversational involvement.

Finally, to escape callers, one may invoke the temporary, but only temporary, expediency of taking the phone off the hook. But this strategy is of only limited temporal utility, and will, in a relatively short time, provoke intervention by the telephone company either in the form of a warning buzz over the receiver or, in the long run, direct personal attention. In effect, the telephone company operates as a social control agency, making sure that accessibility is maintained. Currently then, technology lags behind itself, for these strategems are only piece-meal solutions to the real need generated by the telephone: a way to preview the identity of the caller so as to be able to screen out undesirable or inconvenient summons to conversation.

In connection with the above observations on exploitation, it should also be noted that such conversational activities are not necessarily directed from socially low to high only. To mention only a few examples: McLuhan quotes William S. Whyte, the author of the *Organization Man*, telling of an executive who confided to him that he liked to call his subordinates at their homes. "I like to call them up at night *when their guard's*

27 Hall, *Hidden Dimension*, p. 132.

*down*," he said.[28] In a similar vein, the Lynds in reporting on increased female aggressiveness and changing sex roles observed that the increased distribution and usage of the telephone had played an important part in this shift in between-sexes relationships, providing a semiprivate, partly depersonalized medium of approach to persons of the opposite sex.[29]

Since to have a telephone is to be open to conversational engagement, such possession automatically presupposes potential *scheduling* problems. The temporal order of social events is never completely in a person's control, always being at least partially contingent upon the actions of others. Thus, the person awaiting a call from someone else is, in effect, imprisoned until released by the incoming call. The problematics of scheduling is given picturesque but dramatic confirmation in Menotti's little two-voice opera, *The Telephone*.[30]

As Ben's repeated attempts to propose marriage to his sweetheart Lucy are constantly and repeatedly thwarted by her conversational involvement on the phone, both calling and being called, he becomes enraged at his mechanical tormenter which he blames for preventing his proposal. When Lucy momentarily leaves the room he cries in anguish that he would rather have to contend with a lover, or a husband, or in-laws than this "two-headed monster" which rings without invitation throughout the day, and which can't be challenged, poisoned, or drowned—which has "hundreds of

[28] McLuhan, *Understanding Media*, p. 270.
[29] Lynd and Lynd, *Middletown*, p. 140. To paraphrase a cliché, "They all *sound* alike when they ring."
[30] Gian-Carlo Menotti, *The Telephone* (opera buffa in one act) (New York: G. Schirmer, Inc., 1947), pp. 24–26. This source was suggested to me by Carol Jones.

lives and miles of umbilical cord." Finally, in frustration, Ben picks up a pair of scissors and menacingly approaches the phone; only to have it suddenly ring desperately and fearfully, summoning Lucy back into the room just in time to prevent its mutilation by the distraught Ben.

The point of this little cautionary tale is simple: In addition to the other problematic aspects referred to in the earlier discussion of accessibility, save with the help of intermediaries, we may expect, but we cannot know *when* someone will call. Lacking such information, temporal scheduling or planning is always subject to the vagaries and whims of those who may summon us to telephonic interaction, whether conveniently or not for our own potentially interruptible routines. And, of course, this problem is exacerbated by the "answer every call" and "caller is terminator" rules already mentioned.

Perhaps the most profound social structural consequence of the telephone has been what, for want of a better term, might be called the *decentralization of relationships*. This decentralization, the result of the social centrifugality referred to above, occurs both spatially and organizationally, and involves the spreading out of social networks, as well as the attenuation of direct social contacts.

Spatially, this decentralization can be seen macrosociologically in the territorial imperialism of those business concerns whose main headquarters function more and more as a central exchange for telephonically linked, farflung branches (where the action is), and less and less as a primary locus of decision-making activities. Furthermore, to the extent that the argument that there has been a historical decline in the importance of the extended family due to an industrialized society's need for a mobile, unencumbered labor force has been refuted or modified, such alteration has been forced by among other things, a belated recognition of the telephone's ability to vitiate separations of spatial distance.[31] In effect, families can afford greater spatial dispersion because of the possibility of maintaining relationships via the conversational linkages available through the telephone.

Somewhat more microsociologically, the decline of the brothel as a spatially delimited marketplace for prostitutes and their clients has been explained as a consequence of the telephone which makes such services, in the words of the commercial slogan, "as near as your phone."[32] Thus, regarding the rise in frequency of the role of call girl, Greenwald has observed that the telephone is first and foremost in the call girl's life; without it she could not practice her trade since call girls make almost all of their appointments with clients by phone. Additionally, many of the girls are afraid of being traced or arrested, and thus do not take calls personally, but handle their business via an answering service or exchange.[33]

Of course the telephonic facilita-

tion of the decentralization of such illicit activities more generally reduces their visibility, and perforce, the possibilities of disclosure and stigmatization for the client and arrest for the girl; and although the use of an answering service as an avoidance procedure furthers this end,[34] it would be a mistake to consider this the only or even primary function of such exchanges for the call girl. As one of Greenwald's informants put it, the primary item of business equipment is a telephone and an answering service, the latter to allow for a continuance of business even when the girl is with a client. Usually, as soon as the transaction with one client is completed, the girl will check with her answering service for the address of her next job, thus enabling her to handle a maximum number of transactions with a minimum loss of time.[35] Thus, the economics of client volume, no less than the avoidance of public scrutiny, makes the use of an answering service intermediary a necessity for the practitioners of this trade.

Turning to the decentralization of organizations: this may occur with or without a concomitant spatial spread. As it is related to the telephone, this tendency involves, among other things, the erosion of formal, bureaucratic structures of administration and control.

A primary defining characteristic of Max Weber's ideal-typical model of bureaucracy[36] was hierarchical au-

---

[31] For a summary of this debate and the relevant works of Litwak and Sussman, see Paul Reiss, "Extended Kinship Relationships in American Society," in *Marriage, Family, and Society,* Hyman Rodman, ed. (New York: Random House, Inc., 1965), pp. 204–10.

[32] McLuhan, *Understanding Media,* p. 267. A similar phenomenon may be observed regarding abortion clinics with geographically large referral systems. See D. W. Ball, "An Abortion Clinic Ethnography," *Social Problems,* XIV (Winter, 1967), 293–301. Also, mention might be made of want-ads offering illicit services with disguised descriptions, e.g., "masseur, young, muscular, day or night–phone #."

[33] Harold Greenwald, *The Call Girl* (New York: Ballantine Books, Inc., 1958), p. 16.

[34] This analysis will be developed in D. W. Ball, "Managing the Appearance of Respectability in Problematic Situations," in *Deviance and Respectability: The Social Construction of Moral Meanings,* Jack D. Douglas, ed. (New York: Basic Books, Inc., Publishers, forthcoming).

[35] Greenwald, *Call Girl,* p. 35.

[36] Max Weber, *The Theory of Social and Economic Organization,* trans. A. M. Henderson and Talcott Parsons (New York: Oxford University Press), pp. 329–41.

thority and communication: in the organizational pyramid each position, and therefore each positional occupant, was responsible *for* (and communicated down to) positions immediately *below*, and responsible *to* (and communicated up to) a position immediately *above*. The organizational diagram [37] was a normative flow chart of the expected authority and communication chain-of-command, indicating specifically prescribed relations among a limited number of positions, and proscribing all others.[38] According to the charts, direct relationships involved only positions immediately adjacent on the vertical plane; and relationships involving nonadjacent levels were prohibited. Only indirect contacts, mediated by the positions in-between, were legitimate in the Weberian model. Thus, privates talked to corporals, corporals to sergeants, sergeants to lieutenants, and so on up the line; privates did not converse with lieutenants, and *if* they did so, it was likely to be at the initiation of the man of the higher rank that the organization chart was short-circuited.

Now, although such a model provided stability and the assignment of responsibility and coordination of authority, it was in terms of communication that it proved frustratingly time-consuming; especially for those persons who, for whatever their reasons, wanted to communicate with vertically nonadjacent levels (usually, above theirs in the structure). However, as long as messages announced their source in advance, either through the visual appearance of a potential speaker, and thus his positional-organ-

izational identity, or in writing, e.g. "from the desk of . . .," potential violations of the hierarchical order could be spotted prior to their commission (and dealt with at the discretion of the potentially importuned). But as McLuhan has observed, the pyramidal shape of the structure of job-division and their descriptions and prescribed and proscribed powers and authority cannot long avoid the erosion brought about by the telephone's speed in bypassing hierarchical arrangements and involving people in depth.[39]

Not only can the telephone function in this way because of the speed which McLuhan rightly attributes to it, but also because, as we have earlier suggested, ringing telephones do not aurally differentiate their callers. Potential breaches of the hierarchy are ratified and become actualities as soon as a telephone is answered; the old warning devices of personal identification by sight and written-message-sender-addresses no longer suffice. Additionally, without necessarily subscribing to McLuhan's psychologistic inside-the-skin "involve people in depth" perspective, we can again note that there is an etiquette of telephoning which directly aids and abets such organizational subversion.

As will be recalled, it is a rule of telephone etiquette that they shall be answered, and further it is also normatively defined that the initiator of a call shall also be its terminator. Now, the very presence of these conventions means that, because they exist, they are at least potentially subject to manipulative exploitation, e.g. subordinates can use the telephone to hurdle over organization levels. Furthermore, it should be obvious that this exploitation potential is not limited to formal organization contexts

---

[37] For good discussion of these charts, see Theodore Caplow, *Principles of Organization* (New York: Harcourt, Brace & World, Inc., 1964), pp. 50–89, especially 50–60.

[38] On normative character of descriptions as becoming expectations, see the works of Goffman and Garfinkel cited herein.

[39] McLuhan, *Understanding Media*, p. 271.

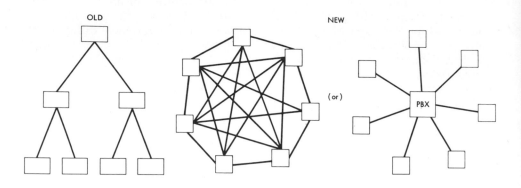

only, as anyone who has ever tried to extricate himself from telephone solicitations for magazine subscriptions while observing the conventional rules of polite discourse will bear testimony.

But to return to the organization and the effects of the telephone upon it, the point is this: no longer is the organization chart as a map of authority relationships isomorphic, i.e. in direct correspondence, with communication patterns; the pretelephonic, hierarchical pyramid tends toward becoming an equilateral polygon, with the vertical axis losing its convenient function of the *symbolization of hierarchy* and remaining as merely one of the coordinates of two-dimensional pictorial space. The ideal of vertical authority cannot survive as an actuality if it is no longer reinforced by communications patterns; its exercise cannot take place along only some of the possible lines of communications, but must pervade all the channels.

In other words, we can look at communications channels not only internally, but also as part of an environment to which the organization must structurally gear itself; the telephone provides a new web—one to which the organization and its normative chart of positional expectations must

adapt. It seems a not unwarranted conclusion (speculation if you must) that the shift from entrepreneurial, single-person, "man at the top" decision-making to the performing of such activity as a collective committee enterprise is more than a little related to the telephonic revolution of decentralization; whether functional or no, it represents a centrifugal movement not only of spatial patterns and social relationships, but also of authority, power, and influence.

If the reader finds much of the above discussion seemingly cynical and overly concerned with matters of manipulation and exploitation, he is in a sense justified. Obviously, the telephone has done much to extend, facilitate, and integrate social relationships and thus enrich human life. In many cases, the telephone has been a necessary prerequisite to the original establishment of any social contact between persons in the first place, e.g. the invalided, etc. Such are among the manifest, intended social functions of the telephone, the discussion of which is unfortunately essentially ignored herein due to considerations of space; this in no way to slight such concerns however. But certainly of equal interest and sociological relevance are the less immediately evident, latent,[40] often taken-for-granted characteristics of the instrument as a medium and their potential for social usage, exploitation and manipulation among them.

However, simply because some of these factors may have been generally less than instantaneously obvious, it does not follow that they have gone completely unnoticed in all sectors of society. We have previously seen how the structure of the telephonic communication medium provides for the opportunity of conversationally "working the system"; i.e. of callers importuning the called. A similar chance for social espionage occurs via the normative code surrounding telephonic conversation and its potential for deliberate breach by actors so inclined. But there is still another way in which the character of telephone interaction allows for its strategic utilization by those who would do so; this is because of its *strictly aural nature* as a medium of communication, and the *total absence of visual cues and signs* available to the participants, concerning one another; in essence, telephone conversations involve what might be termed "interaction in the dark."

Thus, telephonic communicants are (1) free to concentrate on their conversational presentations; and (2) able to ignore or misrepresent those aspects of appearance which might be not only relevant, but also damaging should they be seen and reacted to by the conversational other. They are, to use Goffman's felicitous phraseology, able to manage a potentially *dis-creditable* stigma from becoming an activated, *discrediting* one; [41] that is, the stigmas are concealed so that their interactional damage to the bearers is controlled. Such potential social disadvantages may be permanent or temporary, ascribed or achieved; they range from amputations, dwarfism, and other disfigurements to nose-picking, being unshaven or otherwise ill-groomed, from visible ethnic minority status to obscene tattoos, to note but a few of the possibilities.

An interesting institutional example of this latter feature is what is commonly called the "boiler room" mode of fraudulent stock and securities sales solicitation.[42] In such an operation, telephone solicitors representing themselves as agents of actually nonexistent, but supposedly reputable brokerage houses, call potential clients and attempt to persuade them to buy shares of ostensibly "hot" or high profit issues.

Rapid talkers, highly articulate in their field, these solicitors *sound* to their potential victims to be calling from the staid quiet of a conventional broker's office. Were these prospective purchasers actually able to *see* the pitchman and his immediate working environment, however, they would soon be dissuaded of their aural impression of legitimacy. For what they would see would be a group of several (sometimes up to forty) shirt-sleeved men in a single room or loft, clustered about a table or tables upon which there would be several phones, one for each solicitor, and an equal

---

[40] The classic statement on this distinction, and functional analysis in general is, Robert K. Merton, "Manifest and Latent Functions," in *Social Theory and Social Structure,* rev. and enlarged ed. (New York: The Free Press, 1957), pp. 19–84. Of course, not all latent phenomena are deviant or dysfunctional.

[41] Erving Goffman, *Stigma: Notes on the Management of Spoiled Identity* (Englewood Cliffs, N.J.: Prentice-Hall, Inc., 1963), pp. 41-42.

[42] For a more detailed description of this operation than the one given here, see Frank Gibney, *The Operators* (New York: Bantam Books, Inc., 1961), p. 12, and especially pp. 78–83.

number of boxes, these set upon their ends so that the opening of each box was on the side rather than the top (along the vertical plane instead of the horizontal), directly in front of the man using the phone.

When calling from this boiler room, as it is called, each pitchman leans forward, so as to place his head and the handset part of the telephone within the confines of the box. The purpose of this maneuver is to block out the external sounds of others in close proximity making similar calls otherwise surrounding the solicitor, and thus give the impression of a quiet, normal office. The sides of the box baffle sound so that they become functional surrogates for the walls of the private office he does not in fact have, nor which could he legitimately claim. He is thus free to focus upon his rhetorical presentation, knowing that the recipient of his call cannot know the true state of appearances or his business.

The boiler room operates upon the deliberate creation of mistaken identities assigned by the victim to the establishment; it relies upon the imaginings of its victims, i.e. that what sounds legitimate and respectable would also look so if it were to be seen. More mundanely, this same principle obtains in everyday affairs as when we step directly from a shower to answer a ringing telephone without benefit of nudity-canceling clothes or towels.

In effect, the telephone becomes a medium which involves and invokes a high degree of trust,[43] since the non-

vocal sources of impression validation present in face-to-face encounters are necessarily unavailable to the conversants. Knowledge of the other must be derived and inferred from sound, and sound alone; and similarly, it is the actor's only mode of conveying the definitions of himself he wants accepted, of manipulating the image he wishes consumed by his audience at the other end of the line.

Lest this Machiavellian view of the telephone and telephoning as an interaction form be thought to be limited to perfervid sociological imaginings only, it is useful at this point to examine the views on everyday conversational matters espoused by the telephone companies themselves, and also those who write instructional manuals on these mundane verbal transactions such as office handbooks and introductory speech textbooks. Both sources define the telephone it turns out, and its everyday use in highly exploitative and instrumental terms; if there be a difference, it is that the textbook authors are more subtle, the telephone companies more forthright.

Thus, the speech and secretarial texts *warn* of the implications of the communication restrictions for the speaker and listener, as for secretaries in the following:

Because the person you talk with on the telephone can't see you . . . he can only judge you by how you sound. His impression of you is gathered by your voice and your telephone habits.[44]

---

[43] On trust as a necessary requisite for interaction generally, see Harold Garfinkel, "A Conception of, and Experiments with, 'Trust' as a Condition of Stable Concerted Actions," in *Motivation and Social Interaction*, O. J. Harvey, ed. (New York: The Ronald Press Company, Inc., 1963), pp. 187–238. Thus, as Carol Jones has pointed out, when a switchboard operator asks us

to hold, we assume we shall receive equitable treatment at her hands and not be subjected to unduly lengthy waits. On exploitation in public, face-to-face situations, see Goffman, *Behavior in Public Places,* pp. 139–45.

[44] John Robert Gregg, *et al., Applied Secretarial Practise,* 5th ed. (New York: McGraw-Hill Book Company, Inc., 1962), p. 154.

Or from a textbook in speech:

Since in telephone conversation your voice must carry your meaning without the aid of facial expression, gesture, or body action, you need to be able to be particularly conscious of how your voice sounds to the person who is listening to you but cannot see you.[45]

Or again from a speech text:

The manner of speaking in a telephone conversation reveals the person. The tone of voice, the rate and care given to pronouncing words, and a pleasant or impatient attitude are perhaps emphasized more than when speaking face to face because the listener concentrates on the voice and manner of speech.[46]

By comparison, the brochures issued by the telephone companies positively *instruct*. It appears on analysis to be their view that a good "telephone voice" is consciously constructed, developed, and created; that it is a manufactured product of the person, produced for the furthering of instrumental ends. In a manner more than faintly reminiscent of Dale Carnegie,[47] telephoners are advised that

It's vital to *develop* a pleasing telephone personality.

but contradictorily,

Some people . . . change their personalities when they pick up a receiver. [So] when you telephone, *be natural*.

and

Be sincere. . . . It's . . . *better business*. Treat all calls *as though* they are important.

Furthermore (and this implies an interesting common-sense psychology of man),

Most people are like the rest of us—in love with their own names and titles. So where you can, use them frequently. [They] are sweet music to their ears. . . . You can't miss having your call remembered pleasantly.[48]

As regards techniques for the development of a successful telephone voice: its qualities include, according to another pamphlet (1) vitality, (2) expression, (3) naturalness, and (4) pleasantness.[49] Of these dimensions the reader is told,

Vitality is . . . *achieved by putting the proper emphasis into your speech*.[50]
Expression is . . . *acquired*. [51]
Naturalness . . . comes by *cultivating* [it].[52]

This last provides a particularly glaring contradiction, and finally,

Pleasantness . . . comes from *careful controlling* [of one's voice].[53]

Conveniently, the booklet from which the above quotations are taken provides sixteen pages of self-rating scales and exercises for the development of these qualities.[54]

---

[45] Roy Johnson, Marie Schalekamp, and Lloyd Garrison, *Communication: Handling Ideas Effectively* (New York: McGraw-Hill Book Company, Inc., 1956), p. 27.

[46] Margaret Painter, *Ease in Speech*, 3rd ed. (Boston: D. C. Heath & Company, 1954), p. 16.

[47] See *How to Win Friends and Influence People* (New York: Pocket Books, Inc., 1958); also the sociological analysis of this genre by Don Martindale, *American Society* (Princeton, N.J.: D. Van Nostrand Co., Inc., 1960), pp. 72–77.

[48] This and the two quotations preceding it are from "What Every Telephone User Should Know," General Telephone System (no publication information or pagination, emphasis added).

[49] "Your Voice is You," General Telephone Company (no publication information), p. 2.

[50] *Ibid.*, p. 3, emphasis added.
[51] *Ibid.*, p. 4, emphasis added.
[52] *Ibid.*, p. 5, emphasis added.
[53] *Ibid.*, p. 6, emphasis added.
[54] *Ibid.*, pp. 8–24.

While the textbooks caution, the company-produced brochures and pamphlets urge. But what they both have in common is an orientation to telephone conversation as a strategy for the instrumental presentation of self, and the control, through image-vending, of the other and his lines of action such that they are consonant with the actor's own goals and interests.[55]

Finally, in closing this highly selective discussion of telephones and telephoners, it seems most appropriate to give some consideration to the act of "hanging up" and its sociological implications. First of all, it should be remembered that telephone conversations are ordinarily two-person exchanges, i.e. *dyadic* interactions; and as Simmel has shown, such pair relationships have their own unique properties which differentiate them in theoretically meaningful ways from all other larger-sized groupings.[56]

And so it is with telephonic dyads; as Simmel long ago noted:

A dyad . . . depends on each of its two elements alone—in its death, though not in its life: for its life it needs *both* [parties], but for its death, only one. . . . It makes the dyad into a group, that [is] both endangered and irreplaceable.[57]

It follows then, of course, that a person's hanging up is a kind of interactional homicide, destroying by himself alone the electronically linked group. But what makes this of especial interest regarding telephonic dyads is its peculiarly irrevocable nature. While the person in a face-to-face pair who departs can be called out to, can be entreated and implored to return and thus restore the relationship; and even though he may choose to ignore such pleas, he is still (within the range of hearing) open to them.[58] However, this is not the case for those who terminate telephone conversations. In anger, for instance, not only is hanging up potentially a more abrupt closing of voice-to-voice interaction than even a heel-turning stalking-off in a situation involving copresence; but once the connection has been broken, the terminator is not even accessible to persuasion to reestablish the dyad, unless he chooses to be so. To even hear such overtures telephonically requires that a new connection be established, something which can be avoided by simply refusing to lift the receiver. It is thus that hanging up is the last best resort of those who are by telephone conversationally importuned; it offers a counterploy which is strategically unbeatable and simple to utilize, requiring a minimum of time or effort, and allows for a response on the potential telephone exploiter's own terms.[59] Of course, should the terminator have a change of heart he must know where the other can be reached, i.e. his telephone number, otherwise the breaching of the relationship may be permanent.

---

[55] This process of manipulating alter so that his conduct is consistent with ego's goals has been conceptualized as alter-casting; see Eugene Weinstein and Paul Deutschberger, "Tasks, Bargains, and Identities in Social Interaction," *Social Forces*, XLII (May, 1964), 451–56.

[56] "The Isolated Individual and the Dyad," in *Georg Simmel*, pp. 118–44. Although through extension phones and conference lines, larger groups than a dyad may converse, and are sociologically quite interesting, these are statistically rare cases. Similarly, although phones may be "bugged" by eavesdroppers, such persons are not interacting with their prey.

[57] *Ibid.*, p. 124, emphasis in original.

[58] Cf. Goffman, *Behavior in Public Places*, pp.131–39.

[59] On countercontrol in public, face-to-face settings, again see Goffman, *Behavior in Public Places*, pp. 145–48.

## A Caveat:

In this admittedly incomplete overview of some sociological aspects of telephones and telephoners, we have suggested several hypotheses, although they have been presented more as foregone conclusions. These have referred to such areas as pervasiveness, avoidance procedures, insistency, accessibility, scheduling, social centrifugality or the decentralization of relationships, hanging up, telephone etiquette, and several exploitive and manipulative potentials of the medium. It is now the task of sociology as a science to give more rigorous formulation and testing to them; though they are not necessarily contradictory at the substantive level, scientific proof is never the same thing as mere verbal exhortation.

Hopefully, however, we have demonstrated the utility of a sociological analysis of such telephonic phenomena, and the socially interdependent character of their initial contingencies and normatively defined features, along with the close intertwining of modern technology and this mode of conversation. If talk and the conditions surrounding it are a worthy object of sociological scrutiny, this is no less true when it is voice-to-voice rather than face-to-face.

# 6

# The Implications
# of Tipping in America *

*Leo P. Crespi*

In recent years much discontent about tipping has been reported by the American press. Unlike some countries which gravely frown on this practice (e.g., Australia, Soviet Russia, Communist China, Cuba), the United States now has more than one million persons who depend on tips as a major source of income. Despite strong negative attitudes toward tipping —such as those described in the paper below—the United States has only very lately seen any signs of organized opposition. A recent news story, carried nationally through the Associated Press, reported two antitipping organizations.[1] One organization, called NOTIP (Nationwide Operation To Instill Pride), sells small cards to be left by members instead of tips. These cards describe the nature of the organization, and tell the worker to give the card to his employer who is urged to rectify the wage discrepancy. According to the organization's founder, NOTIP is growing at the rate of about 100 members per month, with an average of 75 enthusiastic letters of sup-

* Reprinted from *Public Opinion Quarterly*, XI (1947), 424–35, by permission of the publisher. Footnotes renumbered.

[1] "No Tip Campaigner Says Project Gains," *Sarasota Journal* (Sarasota, Fla.), June 16, 1967, p. 25.

port received daily. A less revolutionary group called "Tippers Anonymous" has been organized in Boston. This group acknowledges the gratuity system but fights to keep tips at the current 15 per cent minimum.

Despite the ubiquity of tipping, we have very little research in the area. In his study of cabdrivers and their fares, Fred Davis pointed out that the tip's primary significance is not its symbolic value as an acknowledgement of appreciation for a service well performed; rather, Davis maintains, other regularities occur that can best be understood through an examination of the stereotypes of customers held by the cabdriver.[2] More quantitative relationships are described in a later study by Robert L. Karen.[3] Among the numerous findings in Karen's study are the following:

1. Most fares tip, and both those who do and those who don't maintain a consistent attitude toward tipping;
2. frequency of tipping is unrelated to the size of the fare;
3. tip percentage and fare size were inversely related, tip percentages varying from 19 to 44 per cent for most cases;
4. tipping frequency had no relation to the number of passengers or to special services performed by the cabdriver; and
5. women tipped less frequently than men.[4]

Though generalization from these particular tipping situations to others is surely limited, it seems likely that some regularities of a general sort do occur; and it is noteworthy that a stereotype of women as poor tippers (given some validation in the Karen study) is widely held in other tip-sensitive occupations.[5]

EDITOR

——————◆——————

That the custom of tipping has acquired no little significance in American life was indicated July 15, 1946 when *Life* magazine made it the editorial of the week—foregoing such currently inviting topics as the atom bomb, price controls, and the foreign ministers' conference in Paris. *Life* concluded from its inquiries that tipping was a national nuisance and as such should be eliminated.

In the light of the above it was a little surprising to read the Gallup results of April 12, 1947. Nationally, no clear majority was found opposed

to tipping—a full 49 per cent "believing in" the practice. And within urban areas (over 10,000 population), where tipping is largely to be found, a majority of 55 per cent believed in it. In the large city, where tipping reaches its maximum concentration, preponderance of approval apparently becomes even greater. A *Bulletin* poll in Philadelphia, employing Gallup's question, obtained a figure of 66 per cent.

What is the true story then? Is the custom of tipping in the minds of the American people a nuisance to be eliminated, as *Life* intimates, or on the contrary, is it a practice believed in by the majority of those most affected by it—the city-dwellers —as the Gallup and *Bulletin* polls suggest?

[2] Fred Davis, "The Cabdriver and His Fare: Facets of a Fleeting Relationship," *The American Journal of Sociology*, LXV (1959), 158–65. Among those stereotypes Davis includes "the sport," "the blowhard," "the businessman," "the lady shopper," and "the live ones."

[3] Robert L. Karen, "Some Factors Affecting Tipping Behavior," *Sociology and Social Research*, XLVII (1962), 68–74.

[4] *Ibid.*, p. 74.

[5] Cf. Frances Donovan, *The Woman Who Waits* (Boston: Badger, 1920).

TABLE 1.

A. DO YOU APPROVE OR DISAPPROVE OF THE PRACTICE OF TIPPING BY AND LARGE?

| Alternatives | Tipper Public N = 300 | Men N = 148 | Women N = 152 | Tippees N = 99 | Comparable Tippers from Public † N = 86 |
|---|---|---|---|---|---|
| Approve | 68.3% | 60.1% | 76.4%* | 95.0% | 69.8%* |
| Disapprove | 27.0 | 34.5 | 19.7* | 2.0 | 26.7* |
| No Opinion | 4.7 | 5.4 | 3.9 | 3.0 | 3.5 |

B. IF SERVICE WORKERS WERE GIVEN FAIR WAGES FOR THEIR WORK, DO YOU THINK THAT TIPPING SHOULD BE ELIMINATED?

| | | | | | |
|---|---|---|---|---|---|
| Yes | 69.7% | 69.5% | 69.8% | 56.6% | 66.3% |
| No | 26.3 | 27.7 | 25.0 | 40.4 | 31.4 |
| No Opinion | 4.0 | 2.8 | 5.3 | 3.0 | 2.3 |

† These tippers who are compared to tippees are members of the tipper public who are similar to the tippers in sex, age, and economic status.

* In this and the following table a starred figure indicates that the difference between adjacent columns passes the 95 per cent level of significance. If no stars appear, whatever differences are present are not reliably greater than chance.

The present writer and his associates [6] have completed a series of studies both among college students and the public of a large eastern city [7] which give the key to this puzzle of public attitude. In addition, these investigations answer some significant questions about the psychology and the social implications of the tipping institution.

And today tipping is an institution. It has come a long way from the occasional London coffeehouse practice of attaching coins to notes to the waiter, "To Insure Promptness," (T. I. P.). That tipping is now big business is clearly revealed in the present attitude of the Treasury Department. No longer does this agency overlook tips as casual unpredictable gifts. Now every effort is being made to tax tips as substantial and predictable sources of income.

It is remarkable that social psychol-

[6] Robert M. Brown, James B. Knight, and W. A. Tennermann of Princeton University.
[7] Trenton, New Jersey.

ogists who are generally so eager to examine every facet of social behavior have thus far overlooked the rich field of study that tipping offers. In the absence of scientific studies, journalistic accounts have held sway. These treatments are not without interest and insight. But based as they are upon unsystematic personal observation, their pronouncements upon the psychology of the public in tipping have been sketchy and conflicting. To supply the authoritative information which is needed, the crystal ball of personal observation must defer to public opinion measurement.

## What is the Real Public Attitude Towards Tipping?

We have already indicated that Gallup and *Life* give opposing views of the evaluation of tipping by American city-dwellers. Gallup's question went as follows: "Do you believe in the practice of tipping?" In our survey we asked a similar question, A in Table 1, and obtained 68.3 per cent approval—about the same as the 66 per cent figure that the Gallup question obtained on the *Bulletin* poll in Philadelphia. So far, then, the majority favor of tipping among urbanites indicated in the Gallup and *Bulletin* returns seems verified.

But further along in our ballot we had included an additional question bearing upon public attitude—B in Table 1. The returns to this query clearly exposed a mortal flaw in generalized "believe in" or "approve" questions about tipping, a flaw which renders Gallup's question valueless as a measure of attitudes toward tipping *per se*. Far from a majority of urbanites favoring tipping, fully 69.7 per cent would have tipping eliminated— with fair wages provided for service workers. The error in the simple "believe in" or "approval" question is the failure to factor out what might be termed *humanitarian tippers*—individuals who do not favor tipping in itself, but simply feel the necessity under present circumstances of augmenting in this fashion the inadequate salaries of service workers. What these people "believe in" or "approve" is simply fair wages, *not* the practice of tipping. When the question is worded so as to disentangle the two ideas the majority opposition to tipping is made evident.

With the humanitarian tippers parceled out, our results suggest very plainly that *Life* was in line with popular opinion in concluding that tipping should be eliminated.

If Table 1 is scrutinized it will be observed that the humanitarian "correction" not only affects the general conclusion about urban attitude toward tipping but also two more specific conclusions. It appears from the approval question that more women

than men approve of tipping. The unwary could go on to erect quite an edifice of theory upon this supposed result. But comparison of the answers to questions A and B discloses that in fact there is *no* sex difference in extent of favor of tipping. What there is is something quite different, simply a greater proportion of humanitarian tippers among women.

The second revision forced by the humanitarian correction stems from the tipper-tippee comparison. This point needs some introduction. One of the basic features of our study was an effort to obtain where possible the slant of the tipp*ee*—he who gets tipped—as well as of the tipp*er* on the facets of the tipping situation. Since obviously the two may differ in psychology, an adequate study must embrace both.[8]

On the basis of the approval question it appears in Table 1 that almost all tippees (95 per cent) approve of tipping, a far larger proportion than is to be found among tippers. If one's suspicions had not been aroused about the validity of the question, such a result could easily have been accepted as valid, indeed as obvious. For since tippees get more tips than they give, by and large it is no wonder that they are so widely approving of tipping and so greatly surpass the tippers in this respect.[9]

The true result as yielded by the more discriminating question gives a lesson on how the obvious may deceive. It is found that the apparently

[8] The difficult problem of constructing a representative tippee sample was bypassed in the interests of simplicity by using a sample solely of taxi drivers. While possibly not representative of all tippees, such a group is adequate for yielding valuable insights into tipper-tippee relationships.
[9] Only a negligible number of these tippers, it should be mentioned here, functioned to any extent in the role of a tippee.

TABLE 2. WHAT IN YOUR OPINION WOULD YOU CALL THE "MAIN" REASON
[FOR TIPPING] FOR MOST PEOPLE?

| Type of Reason | Tipper Public N = 300 | Tippees N = 99 | Comparable Tippers N = 86 |
|---|---|---|---|
| Incentive-reward | 38.0% | 47.5% | 38.4% |
| Fear of disapproval | 34.3 | 23.2 | 26.7 |
| Poor salaries | 13.0 | 15.2 | 22.1 |
| Others | 9.0 | 13.1 | 5.8 |
| No Opinion | 5.7 | 1.1 | 6.9 |

overwhelming approval of tipping by those who get tipped becomes, upon analysis, *a majority vote for its elimination* once service workers receive fair wages for their work. In addition it is revealed that tippees are not conclusively shown to differ from tippers in their extent of favor of tipping. The difference which appears in question B could readily have arisen by chance with samples of the sizes employed.

## Why Do People Tip?

Confident answers to the basic psychological question of why people tip have not been lacking in popular writings. Some representative pronouncements may be cited:

Tipping has been raised to its present absurd importance largely by the show-off mentality and the deadly fear of 99 out of 100 Americans of being thought pikers by their fellows. . . . It also gives the donor the opportunity to feel lordly and superior to the person tipped. . . .[10]

More often than not he [the tipper] gives either to gain special privileges or because he fears he will lose caste or be insulted if he does not.[11]

Most of us tip, not as an act of con-

descension, but as an easy expression of gratitude.[12]

People tip less from good will than from a sense of inferiority.[13]

The psychology of tipping may be stated more in detail in the following formula: to one-quarter part of generosity add two parts of pride and one part of fear.[14]

Probably the basic reasons for the lavish handing out of cash to people who give little or nothing in return is the human craving for recognition and the desire of the average man to be lifted, even momentarily, above his fellows.[15]

The ideas above exhibit more fertility than agreement. Diverse motives are posited in diverse proportions. This Babel of interpretations suggests that it is high time to forego intuition and unsystematic observation to employ quantitative public opinion measurement.

Since all these writers have had their say, it is only fair as a first tack to give the man in the street a try at estimating public psychology. Each subject was asked what in his opinion was the main reason for tipping

[10] A. F. Harlow, "Our Daily Bribe: the Degrading Practice of Tipping," *Forum*, XCIX (April, 1938), 231–35.

[11] C. B. Davis, "Tips," *Atlantic Monthly*, CLXXVIII (September, 1946), 126–27.

[12] Y. Y., "Tipping," *New Statesman and Nation*, XIX (March 30, 1940), 426–27.

[13] D. Macdonald, "Your Waiter Sizes You Up," *Reader's Digest*, XXXVIII (May, 1941), 27–29.

[14] W. R. Scott, *The Itching Palm: A Study of the Habit of Tipping in America* (Philadelphia: Penn Publishing Co., 1916).

[15] F. Sparks, "Headwaiter, Esq.," *Collier's Weekly*, CXVIII (November 23, 1946), pp. 26ff.

for most people. The results in Table 2 show that for both tippers and tippees two interpretations dominated—what might be termed the incentive-reward theory and the fear of disapproval theory. Proponents of the former imply by their answer that most people still tip for the same reasons which started the practice, namely considerations of incentive and reward. Proponents of the latter view hold, in effect, that whatever may have been the original instigating motivation, the force of custom i.e., the fear of social disapproval—is now the major motivant. It is finally to be noted under "poor salaries" in Table 2 that only a small group would go as far as to say that the humanitarian factor we have previously spoken of is the main reason why most people tip.

We may at this point leave the question of what people *believe* to be the reason most persons tip to inquire what is the reason in fact. An answer to this latter query will disclose which of the motivational notions held by the public is closest to the truth. It was thought advisable to avoid the direct question—Why do you tip?—as being too inviting to rationalization. Reward sounds so much more creditable than possibly more significant motives. Hence three questions with indirect bearing were utilized.[16]

The most convincing indirect indication of motive stemmed from the following question: "Do you generally tip (a waiter or waitress for example) even when you have received poor service?" In the writer's opinion an answer of *No* here supports the incentive-reward theory; an answer of

*Yes* challenges it. What was the finding? A definite majority of the public (55.7 per cent) answered *Yes*—that they do generally tip even with poor service. The comments made it abundantly clear that social pressure was the dominant motive at work. The only other that came in for any appreciable mention was the humanitarian reason of inadequate salaries.

It is worth making the aside here that the above finding calls into question one of the few defenses of tipping in the literature.[17] The heart of this defense is that, "Tipping works well when patrons have nerve enough to use it as discipline instead of an automatic gift—when they refuse tips to the inattentive, and when they send the waiter back for smaller change." This contention may be true; but our results show that people do not have the requisite nerve. Hence this defense of tipping, in depending upon a condition which is now shown to be lacking, boomerangs.

The second question giving an indirect basis for inferring why people tip was put only to those subjects who had expressed their disapproval of the practice. The question inquired, "Though you disapprove of the practice, do you tip anyhow?" Fully 83.3 per cent answered *Yes*, with most of their comments variations on the same theme—fear of social disapproval.

The third question of aid in dissecting out the actual motives for tipping went as follows, "Do you generally tip a shoe clerk or a salesgirl in a store?" The results to this query are not hard to predict, but are none the less relevant here. An overwhelming 97.0 per cent of the public answered *No* to the question, their most

[16] Unfortunately these were not included in the tippee ballot, but in all probability the conclusions that will be drawn apply substantially to tippees also.

[17] Anon., "Shall We Abolish Tipping? Pro and Con," *Reader's Digest*, XXXIII (October, 1938), 107–10.

frequent comment boiling down to the point that there is no social custom which makes it obligatory. So it becomes apparent that custom really calls the tune as to whether or not a service is tipped. Incentive-reward considerations, where they operate at all, function largely within the channels set by custom.

The results from these three indirect soundings for motive suggest rather strongly that custom, meaning primarily fear of social disapproval, is today the principal reason why people tip. If the arguments are accepted, a large proportion of the tipper public, and certainly the largest proportion of tippees, are quite wrong in their belief that the main reason for tipping is still the original motive of incentive and reward for good service.

The journalists that were cited are also not without error in their views. They went farthest off the track in their emphasis upon ego motives in tipping—"the showoff mentality," "desire of the average man to be lifted, even momentarily, above his fellows," "two parts pride," "the opportunity to feel lordly and superior to the person tipped." Analysis of the comments to various questions gave only very minor indications of the operation of such ego motives. The most conclusive evidence came from the answers to the following question: "Do you or do you not feel that tipping a person implies that you feel he is beneath you socially?" It was clear in the interviewing that people were answering this question in terms of whether or not they feel a superiority to the person they tipped. Only one person in ten (11.3 per cent) stated that he got such a feeling. Even supposing that some of the subjects were not entirely candid, the

position seems justified that ego motives play but a small role in tipping.

A parallel question put to the tippees strengthens the above conclusion. They were asked, "Do you or do you not feel that being tipped by a person implies that he feels he is above you socially?" Only one in ten (11.1 per cent) saw any such feeling in the tipping situation.

The overemphasis, in the light of our results, upon ego motives in tipping is not difficult to account for. It is simply the fallacy to which unsystematic observation is so prone—the exaggeration of the qualitatively striking to the neglect of the quantitative. Impressed by the attention-seizing actions of a few big and blatant tippers, some of the writers cited failed to consider how representative such instances may be of the bulk of tipping.

A final word on motivation. We have established that to the extent our public sample is representative, seven out of ten would have tipping eliminated. This fact implies that most people tip less from wanting to and more from having to. Which is precisely what we have now verified in the dominance of social pressure and humanitarian motives over incentive-reward and ego motives.

## Tipper Behavior

Digging out the motives for tipping proved to be a somewhat complex task. Tipping behavior, in contrast, is much more straightforward and hence need occupy us only briefly. In the present survey some information was gathered upon three of the most obviously significant questions of tipper behavior—How often do people tip, how widely, and how much?

TABLE 3. PUBLIC BEHAVIOR IN TIPPING SITUATIONS

|  | Restaurant | Nightclub | Taxi | Hatcheck Girl | Barber or Beautician | Shoeshine Boy |
|---|---|---|---|---|---|---|
| Number who have met situation | 271 | 137 | 189 | 130 | 204 | 100 |
| Those who don't tip | 3.8% | 11.0% | 12.7% | 13.1% | 13.2% | 20.0% |
| Those who tip | 96.2 | 89.0 | 87.3 | 86.9 | 86.8 | 81.0 |
| Most frequent tip | 10 % | 10 % | 25 % | 25 ¢ | * | 5 ¢ |
| Average tip | 12.5% | 13.8% | 18.4% | 18.4¢ | * | 9.1¢ |

* Most frequent tip to barbers by men is 10¢; average is 16.4¢. Most frequent tip to beauticians by women is 25¢; average is 20.7¢.

To the simple question, "How often do you tip?" two out of three in our sample of the public (67.3 per cent) checked "practically always," 9 per cent checked "often," 11.3 per cent "sometimes," 2.7 per cent "rarely," 7.7 per cent "practically never," and 1 per cent had no opinion. The trend is evident that the bulk of the public tip with great frequency with only one in ten tipping rarely or practically never.

The information upon how widely and how much people tip is presented in Table 3. Clearly in none of the possible tipping situations investigated does the proportion of people who generally tip drop below 80 per cent of those who have encountered the situation. The average amount of tip is in every case appreciable in terms of the service rendered, especially the 18.4 per cent average tip for taxi drivers.

This brief behavior survey suggests that most American urbanites tip frequently, widely, and substantially. In view of the fact that the big majority would like tipping eliminated, this finding adds up to a serious state of affairs—that a large and unremitting burden is being borne by the public without the free consent of most of those who must shoulder it.

## Is Tipping Democratic?

Having briefly considered the psychology of tipping, we may now devote our attention to a significant ethical question—is tipping democratic? It is instructive to cite a number of quotations bearing on this point which are illustrative of the consensus of published judgments.

When you, as an American citizen, present a tip to another American citizen, you are tacitly proclaiming, "I am a noble lord generously scattering largess to sub-human serfs." [18]

What, may I ask, is more un-American than tipping? It doesn't belong in American society; it doesn't belong in a Democracy. [19]

Americans would never stand for tipping and its servile implications if the system had not been gradually sneaked over them. [20]

Tipping is an offense against the spirit of equality. . . . Tips of small sums of money are relics of a world riven into classes. [21]

Tipping is a modern form of Flunkyism. Flunkyism may be defined as willing-

[18] Davis, "Tips."
[19] Harlow, "Our Daily Bribe."
[20] Anon., "Shall We Abolish Tipping? Pro and Con."
[21] Y. Y., "Tipping."

TABLE 4. DO YOU BELIEVE IT IS DEGRADING OR BENEATH ONE FOR PEOPLE
TO SEEK AND RECEIVE TIPS?

| Alternatives | Tipper Public N = 300 | Tippees N = 99 | Comparable Tippers N = 86 |
|---|---|---|---|
| Yes | 14.0% | 9.1% | 15.1% |
| No | 82.7 | 88.9 | 81.4 |
| No Opinion | 3.3 | 2.0 | 3.5 |

ness to be servile for a consideration. It is democracy's deadly foe.[22]

Nothing in America more certainly promotes class distinctions than tipping.[23]

Tipping tends to further stratify the social structure. It places a price tag on servility—or scurrility.[24]

The present writer and his associates are in substantial accord with these characterizations of the practice of tipping. We feel that tipping is an aristocratic hangover which is inconsistent with the democratic assumptions of the equality and dignity of men. But that tipping may be in fact undemocratic in its implications is no assurance that the public views the custom in such a light. It is on this point that some of the writers cited, particularly Davis, have gone astray. They have uncritically equated their studied judgment with public opinion, without in any adequate fashion surveying the latter.

To inquire directly whether or not tipping is democratic would have posed semantic difficulties with a cross section of the public. To avoid these, the heart of the undemocratic charge; namely, the invidious status implications, was embodied in a query. The question and the results appear in Table 4. The answer is apparent at a glance—more than four out of five of the tipper public see no status depreciation in the act of being tipped. And, it may be observed, tippees substantially concur with comparable tippers in this judgment. The conclusion seems inescapable that in the minds of American city-dwellers, so far as our sample is representative, tipping is not generally looked upon as an undemocratic practice.

The above result, it must be clearly understood, does not prove that tipping is democratic. It may only indicate that the rank and file tipper has not studied the custom sufficiently to appreciate its true implications and consequences. This latter interpretation is strongly supported by the fact that most commentators agree in their ethical denunciation of tipping and few writers have undertaken to defend the custom.

## The Elimination of Tipping

We already know that a majority of both tippers and tippees sampled by the present survey would have tipping eliminated once service workers receive fair wages for their work. The finding of the last section indicates that this majority opposition to the tipping principle cannot stem from any widespread feeling that tipping is undemocratic. From whence, then, does it derive?

Much of the objection to tipping can be easily deduced from the large element of social pressure that we have found to enter into its motivation. Nobody enjoys being pushed

[22] Scott, "Itching Palm."
[23] Samuel Gompers (quoted by Scott, Ibid.).
[24] Anon., Life, XXI (July 15, 1946), 30.

into actions through fear of social disapproval. Especially are people likely
to be irritated by what they feel to be
a compulsion to tip even when they
have received poor service. And, it
must be remembered, a majority of
our subjects did admit to tipping
under such circumstances.

But even when service is adequate
or excellent the continual necessity to
tip is probably a bother and an irri-
tation—in a word, a nuisance. To shed
some light on the extent of such a
reaction the following question was
asked: "Do you or do you not feel
that tipping is becoming more and
more of a nuisance?" In the process
of interviewing, it became clear that
this question was too vigorously
worded in that it missed people who
felt that tipping was a nuisance, but
did not feel justified from their experiences in saying that it was getting
to be more and more so. However, 45
per cent of those who would eliminate tipping took this stronger posi-

tion, so it is safe to conclude that a
substantial majority feel that tipping
is a nuisance.

The major problem in the elimination of tipping is of course, how?
With the appreciation of the fact that
a practical program must be something a majority of the public will go
along with, a series of suggestions
was presented to the public. The
questions and their results are listed
in Table 5.

It is plain from the returns to question A in Table 5 that however much
people wish to eliminate tipping they
do not accept as an adequate approach the good old "there ought to
be a law." It has become a commonplace in polling that people don't like
laws on anything. They dislike being
coerced by law even into doing things
they want to do. Laws against tipping
have been often tried in the recent
past and have in general been short-
lived and ineffective.

Question B in Table 5 poses an oft-

## TABLE 5.

### A. WOULD YOU FAVOR LAWS AGAINST TIPPING?

| Alternatives | Tipper Public N = 300 | Tippees N = 99 | Comparable Tippers N = 86 |
|---|---|---|---|
| Yes | 15.0% | 6.1% | 16.3% |
| No | 81.0 | 91.9 | 80.2 |
| No Opinion | 4.0 | 2.0 | 3.5 |

### B. DO YOU FAVOR OR OPPOSE THE PRACTICE OF THE MANAGEMENT HAVING A FIXED SERVICE CHARGE ADDED TO THE BILL FOR YOUR TIP?

| | | | |
|---|---|---|---|
| Favor | 18.0% | 23.2% | 17.9% |
| Oppose | 75.0 | 73.8 | 77.4 |
| No Opinion | 7.0 | 3.0 | 4.7 |

### C. MANY PEOPLE IN RESTAURANTS, HOTELS, BARBERSHOPS, ETC., DEPEND UPON TIPS FOR A PART OF THEIR PAY. DO YOU THINK IT WOULD BE BETTER TO HAVE THEM PAID LARGER WAGES OUT OF AN ADDITIONAL AMOUNT ADDED TO THE BILLS CUSTOMERS PAY?

| | | | |
|---|---|---|---|
| Yes | 57.3% | 53.5% | 60.5% |
| No | 33.7 | 37.4 | 31.4 |
| No Opinion | 9.0 | 9.1 | 8.1 |

suggested antidote to tipping, the imposition of a fixed service charge, e.g., ten per cent of the bill. Neither tippers or tippees, it may be seen, react favorably to such an idea. From the comments it appeared that the principal objection was the curtailment of personal choice. The plan was seen more as a fixed tip than as a fixed charge for service, and many subjects seemed to feel that there was enough compulsion in tipping already without adding another constraint. It is posssible that if the question had ended with the phrase, "instead of a tip," rather than its present, "for your tip," the results might have been different.

In evaluating the plan of a ten per cent service charge, a very real danger should be appreciated. In the words of one writer,[25] "It would be a disaster if tipping were forbidden by law and a charge of 10 per cent on the bill substituted for it and if, as a result of this, we were in danger of being bullied into gluttony by waiters eager to make us eat in order that they might live."

In question C[26] we finally have a proposal toward the elimination of tipping upon which a majority of the subjects, tippers and tippees alike, agree: have customers pay higher prices to eliminate the dependency of service workers upon tips for part of their pay. Our survey was taken during the current period of the highest prices in recent history. That under such circumstances the majority are willing to pay higher prices to minimize the necessity of tipping is in the writer's opinion a very significant indication of the strong opposition to the institution as it operates in American life.

It is clear then, that the desire of the majority of both tippers and tippees is to have employers eliminate the dependency of employees upon tips, even if such elimination necessitates rises in prices. The problem becomes one of persuading management to take this step. In the writer's opinion the necessary pressure can be obtained by the customer's refusal to tip in conjunction with an indication of his willingness to go so far as to pay higher prices to free service workers from bondage to tips.

So much for the impact that a plan must have upon employers. What requirements are necessary for a successful strategy in respect to the customer? He must above all be helped over the great psychological hurdle in the act of not tipping—the fear of social disapprobation. This necessity can be accomplished through three measures. First, publicize the fact that the majority of American tippers oppose the custom[27] and tip not so much because they want to, but ironically, because, fearing each other's disapproval, they feel compelled to. Publicize also the fact that tippees would rather have fair wages than tips. Secondly, devise a means of dignifying and putting upon a socially recognized footing the refusal to tip —this to make it clear that in not tipping one is not a piker but a conscientious objector. Lastly, give a basis for feeling that one is not fighting the system alone, but is a member of a group vigorously pursuing the common objective.

A concrete plan which embodies all the considerations we have held to be necessary for success is the initiation of an *antitipping league with*

---

[25] Y. Y., "Tipping."
[26] This question follows the wording of an early *Fortune* query.

[27] Of course prior to any serious campaign it would be wise to verify the results of this study upon a wider scale.

*a card which is left in lieu of a tip.*
The card might read as follows:

---

### FAIR WAGES—NOT TIPS!

PUBLIC OPINION POLLS SHOW THAT
THE MAJORITY OF THE AMERICAN
PEOPLE WANT TIPPING ELIMINATED
AND SERVICE WORKERS TO GET FAIR
WAGES FOR THEIR WORK. THE ONLY
WAY TO ACHIEVE THIS IS BY OUR
REFUSING TO TIP. IT'S UP TO YOU
TO GO TO YOUR EMPLOYER AND
SAY WE ARE WILLING TO PAY
HIGHER PRICES IF NECESSARY, BUT
NO MORE TIPS.
*National Anti-Tipping League*

---

On such a card the writer would personally like to see the additional point:

---

WE BELIEVE THAT TIPPING IS AN
UNDEMOCRATIC PRACTICE. WE DON'T
TIP OUR DOCTORS OR OUR DENTISTS,
BECAUSE WE CONSIDER THEM OUR
EQUALS. WE CONSIDER YOU THE
SAME.

---

This plan is not entirely novel, but it avoids certain psychological errors in past efforts. One Jean Charlot, for example, started in France a one man antitipping campaign based upon his tendering tippees a coin reading on one side, "Tipping is beggary," and on the other, "Get yourself paid by your employer." The time came, the *Christian Science Monitor*[28] reports, when M. Charlot couldn't get a shave within commuting distance of Paris or London.

Now Charlot has to wear a beard, and no wonder, with the psychological blunders in his strategy. To hand an expectant tippee a coin, which proves to be not a coin but an in-

[28] E. Billings, *Christian Science Monitor* (Boston), May 27, 1939.

sult, is hardly an auspicious method of eliminating tipping. Our card does not look like a tip that turns out to be otherwise; and our message is a conciliatory explanation, not an arrogant denunciation. Further, a one man campaign against any custom can hardly fail to look like the vagaries of a crackpot. For conviction, public opinion must be invoked and opposition raised upon a group basis.

The effectiveness of the plan that has been outlined must of course be tested through experiment. The writer is considering some studies to this end. Two questions from the tippee ballot, however, already yield some indication of what even a mere gesture toward explanation can do to tippee attitude. The first question asked, "What do you generally think, feel, or do when someone you have served does not tip you?" Fifty-three per cent responded "nothing" or words to that effect; 23.4 per cent said something equivalent to "think he's cheap"; 14.3 per cent "cussed mentally"; 7.1 per cent held that it was "O.K. if he hasn't got it"; and the remaining 3 per cent gave other responses. Tolerant reactions under these circumstances appear to add up to about 60 per cent.

The second question stated, "Suppose a person you had served gave you no tip with the explanation that he disapproved of tipping, what would your reaction be?" On this question the tolerant reactions rose to over 80 per cent. If such a decrease in antagonism can be occasioned with the bare statement that one disapproves of tipping, what can be expected with a message recognizing the necessity for fair wages and indicating a willingness to pay higher prices toward this end?

7

# Adult Talk
# About Newspaper Comics *

*Leo Bogart*

It has long been observed that the "funny papers" or "comic strips," often referred to as the "children's section" of the daily United States newspaper, are usually not funny or comic and are generally read by adults.[1] What accounts for this? If comic strips do not primarily amuse their audience, what do they do? The following paper directs us to some answers.
EDITOR

---

How and why do the newspaper comic strips figure in the talk of men in a low-income urban neighborhood? How do they bear upon the relations between one man and another? These are the questions this report seeks to answer.

As usually described, urban secular industrialized society has brought about increasingly impersonal human relations, specialized, and segmentalized. The significant others in an individual's life change as he picks up and drops the roles of neighbor, worker, churchgoer, club member.

It seems logical to assume that, to the extent that people have only limited and segmental knowledge of one another, it may be hard to find common interests to talk about, apart from the interests which brought them together in the first place. Thus there may be great need for "universal" topics of talk. Moreover, interpersonal relationships which lack intimacy call for superficial conversation on subjects remote from the real concerns of the speakers. Georg Simmel has described "talk for the sake of talking":

In purely sociable conversation, the topic is merely the indispensable medium through which the lively exchange of speech itself unfolds its attractions. . . . For conversation to remain satisfied with mere form it cannot allow any content to become significant in its own right. . . . [Talk] thus is the fulfillment of a relation that wants to be nothing but relation—in which, that is, what usually is the mere form of interaction becomes its self-sufficient content. Hence, even the telling of stories, jokes, and anecdotes, though often only a pastime if not a testimonial of intellectual poverty, can show all the subtle tact that reflects the elements of socia-

* Reprinted from *The American Journal of Sociology*, LXI (1955), 26–30, by permission of the University of Chicago Press. Copyright 1955 by the University of Chicago. Footnotes renumbered.

[1] For studies of other aspects of the culture of the comic strip, see: David Manning White, ed., *The Funnies: An American Idiom* (New York: The Free Press, 1963); and Arthur A. Berger, "Authority in the Comics," *Trans-Action*, IV (1966), 22–26.

bility. It keeps the conversation away from individual intimacy and from all purely personal elements that cannot be adapted to sociable requirements. . . .[2]

The mass media provide a natural source of such conversational material. They are by nature impersonal, there being no direct interaction between artist and audience. Their heroes, symbols, and themes are part of a common universe of discourse. They are familiar to all; their meanings are clear and stereotyped. They interest people without threatening them. Since they belong to the world of imagination, they are not obviously value-laden. Nonetheless, they are close enough to unconscious fantasies to permit identification and to create interest. Thus the newspaper comic strips, and the press generally, with television, radio, the popular magazines, and the motion pictures all provide grist for the mill of conversation in America today.

Intensive interviews were conducted in the summer of 1949 with 121 male readers of two New York newspapers, the *News* and the *Mirror*. All were residents of Lenox Hill, a low-income tenement neighborhood, ethnically mixed, on Manhattan's upper East Side.[3] Virtually all those in-

terviewed were wage earners in industry or service trades, divided about evenly among skilled, semi-skilled, and unskilled workers. Only two had more than a high school education. Twenty-six per cent were foreign-born, in approximately equal proportions in Great Britain and Ireland, Germany and Austria, Czechoslovakia, and Italy and eastern Europe. These were not the most avid comic-readers who might have been interviewed; earlier research shows reading to be highest in the middle-income range.

The conclusions drawn from so small and particular a sample are not intended as generalizations. They are reported here simply to indicate the place of the comics in the conversation of American workers.

The comics are as universally familiar as the daily newspaper. Unlike much else in the paper, they are fairly noncontroversial. They are read by four of every five urban adults in America.[4] Eighty-five per cent of those interviewed read them; 60 say that they have "talked about the things happening in the comic strips."

Significantly more of the high school educated respondents (71 per cent) report discussing the comics than those with less education (53 per cent).[5] Many studies of public opinion have shown that persons of superior education are most likely to discuss politics and current events. But the comics are popular symbols.

[2] *The Sociology of Georg Simmel*, trans. Kurt H. Wolff (New York: The Free Press, 1950), pp. 52–53. Another translation of Simmel's essay, "*Die Soziologie der Geselligkeit*," that by Everett C. Hughes, appears in "The Sociology of Sociability," *The American Journal of Sociology*, LV (November, 1949), 254–61. The paragraph referred to here is translated on p. 259.

[3] The method of the research is described at greater length in the writer's doctoral dissertation, "The Comic Strips and Their Adult Readers" (University of Chicago, 1950). The characteristics of the random sample selected for interviewing accord well with census data on the population characteristics of the census tracts in which the selected area falls. The neighborhood was

chosen for its social homogeneity to secure the highest possible concentration of tabloid readers. The tabloid *News* and *Mirror,* with New York's largest circulations, are specially analyzed in another portion of the same study.

[4] *America Reads the Comics* (New York: Puck, the Comic Weekly, n.d.).

[5] This difference could occur by chance with a probability between .01 and .001 by the chi-square test ($T = .38$).

One might well have expected to find the poorly educated *more* likely to talk about the comics because they presumably have fewer things to talk of. But the data show that to engage in discussion has less to do with a particular subject than with a generalized confidence or articulateness, which education helps to provide. The better-educated are better oriented to the mass media; they absorb more of their content, even the trivia.[6]

Discussion of the comics among middle-class persons may well be largely confined to the family circle. However, on Lenox Hill, conversation about the comics occurs typically among adult males—at work, in the tavern, at the street corner: "down by the garage"; "when we're on our way to work"; "in the shop"; "with my friends"; "barroom talk"; and "with a bunch of fellows on the corner."

Interest in the comics is no greater among fathers than among childless men. Only a few mention conversations with children or other members of the family:

[Restaurant headwaiter, age thirty-nine]: Yes, if there are some nice little jokes, I tell them to my daughter; she's about eight years old. She's started to follow them by herself now. When I get home, I read it to the daughter, and she gets interested now and always asks, "What's next?" or I have to go on and explain it to her.

The paucity of other shared experience in the family probably characterizes their social milieu.

The comics are usually discussed

[6] On this point see also O. N. Larsen and R. J. Hill, "Mass Media and Interpersonal Communication," *The American Sociological Review*, XIX (1954), 426–33; and Leo Bogart, "The Spread of News on a Local Event," *Public Opinion Quarterly*, XIV (1950), 769–72.

in terms of their literal content—the characters and the things they say or do. Though perhaps the least "realistic" of popular literature, their characters are invariably referred to as though they had an independent existence.

Any "serious" conversation about the comics would have to consider them as a form of art. Yet comments on the technique of the strips are rare. There is little place for discussion of style or artistic virtuosity which a middle-class audience might hold on the subject of movies, the theater, or literature:

[Policeman, age thirty-one]: I don't recall discussing any of the comic strips with the exception of "Prince Valiant" in the *Journal*. Most people remark on the way that strip is drawn—very authentic in detail; very nice drawing.

[Ice cream distributor, age twenty-seven]: A lot of people would come up to me and ask me whether I read this cartoon this morning. "Smokey Stover"—the cartoonist behind it is a genius for putting together phrases. Fellows used to comment about it.

The comics are not supposed to be taken seriously, and the respondent is a little defensive when questioned about them; phrases like "just trying to get a laugh" or "of course we all laugh at it" show how unimportant he considers them.

[Construction laborer, age thirty-one]: Yeah, with a bunch of fellows on the corner. I'd say, "Dick Tracy is in another scrape; I wonder how he'll get out of it." Of course we all laugh at it. And a guy will say, "Bet you half a dollar he gets out of it." Bunch of kids down at the café there.

The individual who takes the comics at face value, exhibiting a strong and genuine interest, is regarded as a deviant:

[Elevator operator, age thirty-seven]: Yes, Mother and myself and son get together talking about it. Just casually, of course; we don't go biting our fingernails about it. I've got one friend who actually bites his nails worrying how Dick Tracy is going to come out.

[Truck-driver, age twenty-six]: Last night a guy comes up and wonders how Li'l Abner was doing. The guys were talking all about it afterward, wondering whether the guy is nuts to wonder about how Li'l Abner is making out. He was really interested, and the boys had to tell him just what it was all about.

Actually, 36 per cent of those interviewed report that, on occasions when they have missed the paper, they have gone to some trouble to find out what had been happening in their favorite comic strips. But apparently such inquiries must be discreet and indirect. For it is an unusual person who admits reading the comics in order to use them as a conversation piece.

[Janitor, age fifty, mentions two comics which he reads regularly]: The other things I just read in case of conversation. When someone talks about them, you'll know about them. [Does that happen often?] Oh, yeah, quite regularly. Almost everybody reads the comics. Somebody says, "Did you read this, and did you read that?" and you can have a conversation for two hours after that on the funnies.

More often, the men take a more casual view of the habit. For example:

[Grocery clerk, age twenty-two]: Occasionally, we might discuss some funny article that might have happened. Very seldom, though. Just trying to get a laugh out of someone else that might have missed it. Just passing time talking, when there's nothing much to say.

Having something to talk about may make for companionship among people who are thrown together yet who share only a few common interests and associations. Moreover, among men working at jobs which are monotonous and repetitive, innocuous banter about the comics may fill empty moments.

[Mechanic, age forty]: Yes, we talk about how it would come out and how you think it's going to happen. If we have nothing else to do, we're standing around talking; we get into a conversation about it. Usually when we're on our way to work. It's in the Sunday paper now how they're going to break in the Sheriff [in "Mickey Finn"]. We just happened to discuss now how he's going to make out.

[Railroad baggageman, age thirty-five]: The fellows in work start talking about "Dick Tracy," and they imagine what's going to happen next. They like to kid around. In the meantime it makes work pleasanter and easier. We always did like that in work.

Such talk may be a reaching-out for fellowship, or the subject may be brought up to provoke response in another human being, to win his approval and friendship by making him laugh:

[Truck-driver, age twenty-two]: If a new character is introduced, if he's funny, if he's awkward, if he's portrayed good, you might mention it to somebody just for the effect of a laugh.

The comics are, in fact, an ideal subject for "kidding": their familiar protagonists are convenient targets of wit and irony in casual conversation. They offer ready-made satirical imagery, readily applicable to real people and problems.

[Machinist, age twenty-one]: We'd be talking about something, and then we would refer to it, like trying to make it the same way. Like seeing the way a fellow fell, a guy would say, "Just like in that comic strip."

[Laborer, age twenty-two]: I have often referred to ["The Flop Family"] when something happens in the strip that's like something that happens in the house, in the average family.

A broad distinction can be drawn between comic strips which are intended to be funny and which, like "Blondie," deal with the events of domestic life and those devoted to dramatic adventure. The latter may be either "realistic" and plausible, like "Terry and the Pirates," or clearly fantastic, like "Superman."

Comic strip characters, particularly in the domestic and fantastic strips, are often stereotyped caricatures of personality which arouse laughter insofar as their actions parallel actual events. In this respect, the humor is as described by Henri Bergson: the perception of incongruity between the living and the "mechanical."[7] To compare a policeman to Dick Tracy is to reduce him from a flesh-and-blood individual to a flat-paper image which is thrown into the trashbin each night.

[Bus-driver, age thirty-nine]: Well, down on the job if some of the other fellows talk about it, we talk about what happened. About a couple of weeks ago during lunchtime some guy was talking about what some guy on the street said. He got a ticket from a patrol car on One Hundred and Twenty-fifth Street, and he thought that was like what Dick Tracy would do. That thing was brought up.

[Ice-cream distributor, age twenty-seven]: There's a lot of things in comics that pertain to real life, and a guy says, "That's just like my wife or my mother-in-law."

[7] *Laughter* (New York: Crowell-Collier & Macmillan, Inc., 1924).

As suggested by the last quotation, a bantering analogy between a comic-strip character and a real individual may mask aggression. But, even where the reference is direct, the victim is not expected to take offense:

[Plumber, age thirty-seven]: Sometimes, to a friend. Like something happens, like a new character comes up in "Dick Tracy"; you see a guy who looks like that new character, and you give him a name. A guy that's short and round you call him "Pear Shape," first thing you know.

[Piano repairman, age twenty-two]: At times, barroom talk. When Dick Tracy had that character Mumbles, whenever someone had a mistake in speech, we'd call him "Mumbles"; or sometimes somebody might start talking like Li'l Abner.

In the last example the process is reversed; the young man who starts "talking like Li'l Abner" is momentarily assuming his identity in the same way as the small boy who flaps his arms and shouts, "I'm Superman!" Indeed, the comic strip hero may be talked about as a model to be emulated, for the comics are setting norms for behavior and aspirations in the same way that motion pictures, television, or magazines do.

[Chauffeur, age thirty]: Sometimes with my friends it would be like the phrase of the day: "Go out and do like 'Gasoline Alley'; get a loan like he did, or start a business like he did."

Here the irony, if any, lies in the bitter contrast between the respondent and his successful hero.

Fantasies involving the comic strip characters are often not openly admitted in conversation, yet, in talk itself, fantasy secures expression in disguised form. Identification with the characters is apparently not clear enough, and the emotions their adventures arouse not strong enough, to produce substantial reverie.[8] From the evidence it seems impossible to conclude that the comics are talked about *because* of the fantasies they arouse. We might, however, say that, *once* conversation turns to this subject, repressed or latent fantasies come into play.

Disguised identification is apparent in discussion about "What will happen next?—as the following instances suggest:

[Bus-driver, age forty-two]: Someone would bring it up, like "What happened to Skeeziks this morning?" "Did Nina Clock have her baby yet?" "Did Papa or Mama Clock take their vacation like they did a couple of weeks ago?"

[Truck-driver, age thirty-two]: Once in a while, when it's interesting, at work you ask the boys, "What are you following up? Is it interesting? How did he make out on it? What's going to be in the next day's issue? Is he going to get fired, the guy [a character in 'Gasoline Alley']?" Stuff like that.

But fantasy about how things will

[8] This point is documented in Bogart, "Comic Strips."

turn out is not necessarily a direct projection of one's own problems and motivations. Adventure and suspense, even in the cartoon narrative, may be in a vivid and attractive contrast to the uneventful lives of the readers. There, too, it may be socially more acceptable to talk about how Dick Tracy will get out of a trap than to confide one's personal concerns to street corner acquaintances. Be that as it may, the popular literature of our time may be said to provide an array of collective images which, like the heroes and legends of other places and times, can be introduced into conversation to provide analogies for the events of daily life, and to serve as vehicles for fantasy.

The subjects of conversation of urban workers are, of course, by no means typical, nor are its patterns or circumstances. The observations made here about the newspaper comics are not necessarily applicable to other popular media (for instance, motion pictures) which represent a more realistic and intense experience for the audience.

# 8

## Coolness in Everyday Life [*]

*Stanford M. Lyman* and *Marvin B. Scott*

From the now distant "Keep Cool with Coolidge!" to the more recent expressions such as "Cool it!" or "Don't blow your cool!" periodic statements have cropped

[*] Prepared especially for this volume.

up in American life to caution us, in one way or another, to avoid any display of emotionality. What do these expressions have in common? What does it mean to stay "cool"? Why should coolness be valued? And under what conditions? Has our image of coolness undergone change? These are some of the questions examined in the following essay by Professors Lyman and Scott.

EDITOR

---

Don't lose your cool!"

A common enough phrase and one easily recognized in contemporary urban America. But, sociologically speaking, what does this new moral imperative mean? What does one lose when he loses his cool? Our task is to answer these questions by analyzing the social arrangements whereby coolness gained and coolness lost are readily observable features in everyday life.[1]

Coolness is exhibited (and defined) as poise under pressure. By pressure we mean simply situations of considerable emotion or risk, or both. *Coolness, then, refers to the capacity to execute physical acts, including conversation, in a concerted, smooth, self-controlled fashion in risky situations, or to maintain affective detachment during the course of encounters involving considerable emotion.*[2]

We may distinguish three types of risk under which an individual might display coolness. First there is *physical* risk to the person in the form of danger to life and limb. The moral worth of many of the heroes of the Western world is displayed in their willingness and ability to undergo trials of pain and potential death with stylized equanimity and expert control of relevant motor skills. Modern fictional heroes, such as James Bond

and Matt Dillon, for example, face death constantly in the form of armed and desperate thugs and killers; yet they seem never to lose their nerve or skill. It is not merely their altruistic service in the cause of law and country that makes them attractive, but also, and perhaps more importantly, their smooth skill—verbal and physical—that never deserts them in times of risk.

Secondly, there is *financial* risk. Financial risk entails not only the possible loss of income and status, but also the loss of character associated with the venture. Captains of industry, professional gamblers and those who play the stock market are supposed to withstand the losses sometimes occasioned in the process with calmness, detachment, even cavalier abandon.

Finally, and most crucial for our concerns, there is *social* risk. Social risks may arise whenever there is an encounter. In every social encounter a person brings a "face" or "mask"—which constitutes the value he claims for himself.[3] Given that an individual stakes this value in every encounter, it follows that encounters are morally serious occasions fraught with great risks. Thus every encounter is a risk-taking situation where one puts on the line a public face. This is the most serious risk, for in risking it he risks his very selfhood. When the interactants are *aware* that each is putting on a public face, they will look for cues to glean some "real self" presumably lurking beneath the

---

[1] This paper explores a theoretical avenue opened up by Erving Goffman. Our orientation and some of the conceptual categories used here are derived from the various writings of this seminal thinker.

[2] This definition closely follows the one suggested by Goffman in "Where the Action Is" (University of California, Berkeley), p. 29.

[3] E. Goffman, "On Face Work," *Psychiatry*, XVIII (August, 1955), 213–31.

mask.[4] The capacity to maintain face in such situations constitutes a display of coolness.

As suggested, encounters are hazardous because of the ever present possibility that identity and status will be disconfirmed or damaged by behavior. Whenever an individual or a group has to stage an encounter before a particular audience in order to establish a distinctive identity and meaning, the management of the staging becomes crucial to the endeavor. The effort can fail not simply because of the inadequacies or the conflict of the presented material, but also, and perhaps more importantly, because of the failure to maintain expressive identity and control. Thus individuals and teams—for a successful performance—must not only manage what they have planned, but also carry off the presentation smoothly in the face of interruptions, intrusions, and prop failures.

Smoothness of performance can be seriously interrupted by "prop" fail-

[4] The hazards of social encounters are not universally recognized with the same degree of seriousness. Thus in Japanese culture the face engagements of individuals are always regarded as character tests. Individuals are expected to be aware at all times of the proprieties. Loss of face can occur at any time. On the other hand, in American culture it would appear that social risks are not recognized as an ingredient of every encounter, but only of those that have a retro- or pro-active effect on the participants. For an analysis of the Japanese as veritable models of poise under pressure, see Nyozekan Hasegawa, *The Japanese Character* (Tokyo: Kodansha International, 1966), especially pp. 29–34 and 90–94. See also George De Vos, "A Comparison of the Personality Differences in Two Generations of Japanese Americans By Means of the Rorschach Test," *Nagoya Journal of Medical Science*, August, 1954, pp. 164–65, 252–61; and William Caudill, "Japanese American Personality and Acculturation," *Genetic Psychology Monographs*, XLV (1952), 3–102.

ures. Some engagements involve the maintenance in good order of a particular setting. Included here at the minimum is the apparel of the actor. A professor lecturing before his class might be completely discomfited if he discovers his fly is unzipped, and he is indeed hard pressed to reestablish his seriousness of purpose if he is unable to repair the situation with discretion.

Smooth performance can also be challenged by interruption or intrusion. In certain societies—England, for example—public political speeches are traditionally interrupted by hecklers; and on some occasions, objects are flung at the speaker. English politicians try to develop a style that prepares them for responding to such interruptions by having in readiness a repertoire of clever remarks. Interruption can also be occasioned by a sudden and unexpected event that would normally upset the average man. During the second World War many actors and concert performers earned reputations for coolness under extreme situations when they continued to play out their performances after an air raid had begun.

Interruptions, intrusions, and prop failures are of two sorts with respect to coolness. The first type requires deft and casual repair of self or self-possessions in order for coolness to be displayed. The professor who, aware that the class perceives his unzippered fly, casually zips it up without interrupting the flow or tone of his lecture is likely to be recognized as cool. Similarly, the Walter Mitty-like flyer who sets the broken bone of his arm while maneuvering his plane to a safe landing under hazardous conditions will be known for his coolness.

The second type of intrusion, interruption or prop failure involves those situations that require immediate action because the entire situation has been altered by their presence. Fires in theaters, air raids, tornadoes, assassinations of presidents and other major calamities are illustrations. Those who maintain presence of mind in the face of the disastrous event, and especially those who by their own example prevent others from riotous or panicky behavior, place a stamp of moral worth upon themselves.

The exhibition of coolness under situations of potential panic can be a source of leadership. Formal leaders may be thrust from their posts because they panic, and unknown persons raised to political heights because of their publicly displayed ability to remain calm. Much popular folklore perceives calamitous situations as those providing just the right opportunity for a person otherwise unqualified to assume a dominant position. Indeed, if his acts are sufficiently skillful and smooth, the displayer of coolness may be rewarded with future rights of charismatic authority. A doctor who performs delicate surgery in the midst of an earthquake may by that act establish rights to administer the hospital in which he works. And a teacher who manfully but nonviolently prevents a gang of hoodlums from taking over a school may by his performance take over the school himself.

Embarrassment is one of the chief nemeses of coolness. Any encounter is likely to be suddenly punctured by a potentially embarrassing event—a gaffe, a boner, or uncontrollable motor response—that casts new and unfavorable light upon the actor's performance. In some instances, the audience will save the actor from needless embarrassment by studiously overlooking the event; however, this tactful inattention may itself cause embarrassment as each person in the engagement manfully seeks to overlook the obvious. In other instances, the actor himself will be on his mettle to attend or disattend to the disturbance in such a manner that it does not detract from his performance. A skillful self-rescue from a potentially embarrassing situation can win the actor more than he intended, since he may gain not only his directly intended objective but also a boost in his moral worth as well.

Thus coolness is both a quality to be lost and a prize to be gained in any engagement. That is, coolness may be lost or gained by qualities exhibited in the behavior. A failure to maintain expressive control, a giving way to emotionalism, flooding out, paleness, sweatiness, weeping, or violent expressions of anger or fear are definite signs of loss of cool.[5] On the other hand, displays of *savoir-faire*, aplomb, *sang-froid*, and especially displays of stylized affective neutrality in hazardous situations are likely to gain one the plaudits associated with coolness.

Coolness, therefore, involves more than routine performance in a role. However, an affectively manifest departure from a role can disconfirm the presence of an actor's coolness just as a remarkable exhibition of *sang-froid* can gain for one the reputation of having it—that is, to be cool is to exhibit a definite form of expressive control during the performance of a role. Thus, we can distinguish three kinds of role performance: *cool*

[5] The loss of cool is not everywhere a stigma. Among Shtetl Jews, for example, displays of overt emotionalism are culturally approved. See Mark Zborowski and Elizabeth Herzog, *Life is With People: The Culture of the Shtetl* (New York: Schocken Books, Inc., 1962), p. 335.

*role behavior, routinized role behavior, and role behavior that indicates loss of cool.*

Card playing is one type of social gathering in which all three kinds of role behavior might be exhibited. The "cool player" may push the deed to his family home into the pile of money in the center of the table with the stylized casualness of a Mississippi gambler, neither his smooth, softly smiling face nor his calm, unshaking hands indicating that he is holding only a pair of deuces. The "routine player" may make his bet with a grimace indicating seriousness of purpose and awareness of risk, but not entirely losing composure or calling undue attention to himself. The "uncool player" may become ashen, burst into tears, shriek obscenities, or suddenly accuse his opponents of cheating when his prized and final bet is raised beyond his ability to respond. The card game, like the battlefield, is a moral testing ground.

While the display of coolness is a potential in all encounters, there are certain typical situations that generate efforts for its display. These involve situations where the risks are patently obvious and where the display of coolness is itself a social expectation. Bullfighting, automobile racing, and war are examples. Literature dealing with these subjects typically portray characterological coolness and invest it with honor and virtue. Indeed, if one wishes to find examples and evidence of coolness one need but look in the literature about activities considered risky.

Two other types of situations calling for individuals to actively mobilize for a display of coolness are the "innovative" and the "anomic." Innovative situations include activities associated with the rites of passage—all those "first times" in the life cycle

in which one has to be poised in the face of the as yet unexperienced event. Examples include the wedding night for virgins, first days in school, and the first witnessing of death. Anomic situations are those in which at least one of the actors does not know the rules of conduct and must carry off an engagement in the face of those who do. Typically immigrants, newcomers, and parvenus find themselves in such situations—situations in which poise is at a premium.[6]

A display of coolness is often a prerequisite to entrance into or maintenance of membership in certain social circles. Since in nearly all societies coolness is taken to be part of the character syndrome of elites, we may expect to find a universal condition and a variety of forms of character testing of the elite. European nobility were expected to acquire adeptness at coquetry and repartee; the stylized insult and the witty return were highly prized and regularly tested.[7] Among would-be samurai in Japan, the martial skills were highly prized but even more highly prized was presence of mind. A samurai in training was constantly subjected to contrived sudden dangers, but if he exercised little cathectic control over his skill and strength he would be

[6] In some instances the fears and apprehension among newcomers are so great that not even ordinary calmness can prevail until special restorative measures are employed. For a most dramatic illustration of the point see *Equiano's Travels: The Interesting Narrative of the Life of Olaudah Equiano or Gustavus Vassa the African* (Originally published in 1789), ed. Paul Edwards (New York: Frederick A. Praeger, Inc., 1967), pp. 30–31.

[7] Repartee and word games apparently came into full bloom in courtly circles after women and intellectuals were admitted to participate. See Florian Znaniecki, *Social Relations and Social Roles* (San Francisco: Chandler Publishing Co., 1965), pp. 175–76.

severely reproved by his Zen master.[8] Another coolness test for membership —one involving sexual self-control— is a commonplace of college fraternity initiations. A "stag" film will be shown, and immediately upon its completion, the lights will be flashed on and the initiates ordered to stand up. Those who have "lost their cool" are then observable.

Tests of coolness among peers usually take the form of some contest relation. Teen-age Italian-American slum-dwellers engage in "a series of competitive encounters intended to assert the superiority and skillfulness of one individual over the other, which take the form of card games, short physical scuffles, and endless verbal duels."[9] And American ghetto-dwelling Negroes have developed a highly stylized dialogue of insult which reaches its quintessential manifestation in "sounding" or the game known as "the dozens."[10]

To successfully pass coolness tests one must mobilize and control a sizeable and complex retinue of material and moral forces. First one must master all those elements of self and situation whose unmastered presence constitutes the condition of embarrassment. These include spaces, props, equipment, clothing, and body.[11] Maladroit usages of these often constitutes a definite sign of loss of coolness, while deft and skillful management of any intrusive action by these can signify the presence of coolness.

Coolness tests also require one to control all those elements of self which, if evidenced, constitute the sign of emotional incapacity. In addition to the body—and here we refer to its carriage, litheness, deftness and grace—there is the special case of the face, perhaps the most vulnerable agent of, as well as the most valuable instrument for, poise under pressure.[12] The eyes, nostrils, and lips are all communicators of one's mental ease and personal control. Failures here—such as a look of fear in the eyes, a flare of the nostrils, or quivering lips—communicate characterological faults that deny coolness. Finally, the color of the face must be kept neutral if coolness is to be confirmed. Those who blush or pale quickly are

---

[8] Hasegawa, *Japanese Character*, p. 88.

[9] Herbert J. Gans, *The Urban Villagers* (New York: The Free Press, 1962), p. 81.

[10] See John Dollard, "The Dozens: Dialectic of Insult," *The American Imago*, I (November, 1939), 3–25; Rolph E. Berdie, "Playing the Dozens," *Journal of Abnormal and Social Psychology*, XLII (January, 1947), 120-21; Cornelius L. Golightly and Israel Scheffler, "Playing the Dozens: A Research Note," *Journal of Abnormal and Social Psychology*, LXIII (January, 1948), 104–5; Roger D. Abrahams, *Deep Down in the Jungle* (Hatboro, Pa.: Folklore Associates, 1964), pp. 41–65, 89–98, 259–62. Abrahams describes sounding as follows: Sounding occurs only in crowds of boys. One insults a member of another's family; others in the group make disapproving sounds to spur on the coming exchange. The one who has been insulted feels at this point that he must reply with a slur on the protagonist's family which is clever enough to defend his honor (and therefore that of his family). This, of course, leads the other (once again, due more to pressure from the crowd than actual insult) to make further jabs. This can proceed until everyone is bored with the whole affair, until one hits the other (fairly rare), or until some other subject comes up that interrupts the proceedings (the usual state of affairs), p. 50.

[11] Edward Gross and Gregory P. Stone, "Embarrassment and the Analysis of Role Requirements," *The American Journal of Sociology*, LXX (July, 1964), 6–10. See also, Erving Goffman, "Embarrassment and Social Organization," *The American Journal of Sociology*, LXII (November, 1956), 264–71.

[12] See Georg Simmel, "The Aesthetic Significance of the Face," in *Georg Simmel, 1858–1918*, Kurt Wolff, ed. (Columbus: Ohio State University Press, 1959), pp. 276–81. Also Goffman, "On Face Work."

hard put to overcome the outward physical sign that they are not poised.

Among the most significant instruments for coolness is the voice. Both form and content are relevant here, and each must be coordinated in the service of *savoir-faire* if that character trait is to be confirmed. In institutionalized verbal contests—such as the Negro game of the "dozens"—vocal controls are the principal element of style. For these games as for other verbal artistic endeavors "style is nothing if it is not an overtly conscious striving for design on the part of the artist." [13] To engage expertly in "the dozens," and other Negro word games, one has to employ "noncasual utterances"—*i.e.*, use of language for restricted purposes—in subculturally prescribed but seemingly effortless syntactic constructions and specified elements of diction. Of course voice control as an element of the establishment and maintenance of poise under pressure has its place in circles beyond that of the ghetto Negro. In parlor repartee, covert exchanges of hostility among colleagues, joking relations, and teasing, not only the content but also the tone and timbre count for much.

Courtship and dating are perhaps the most widespread institutions in which poise is expected and thus they require mobilization of those material, anatomical, physiological, and moral forces which together, under coordinated control, constitute the armamentarium by which the coolness game may be won.[14] Activities that require for their execution a mobilization of passions *e.g.*, sexual intercourse—are sometimes regarded as peculiarly valuable for testing poise through affective detachment. Italian-American men admire a person "who is able to attract a good-looking woman and to conquer her without becoming involved." [15] Chinese clan rules warn husbands about the dangers created by emotional expression in sexual relations with their wives.[16] And youthful male prostitutes count it as a proof of their strong character that they do not become emotionally excited during professional acts of sexual intercourse.[17]

Where coolness is considered a positive trait, attempts will be made to demonstrate it. However, there are those statuses and situations that typically are thought to be devoid of risk and whose incumbents must therefore search out or create situations in which coolness can be demonstrated if that trait is desired. For some, then, coolness must be staged. Since, as we have said, coolness is imputed to individuals only insofar as the person's actions are seen to occur in risk-taking situations, those who strive after a reputation for coolness will seek out risky situations wherein it can be manifested. Thus children often attempt to show emotional poise by "risky" riding on

---

[13] Charles T. Scott, *A Linguistic Study of Persian and Arabic Riddles: A Language-Centered Approach to Genre Definition* (Doctoral dissertation, University of Texas, 1963), p. 12.

[14] For a piquant instance in which these forces were unexpectedly tested by a Ki-

kuyu youth studying in America, see R. Mugo Gatheru, *Child of Two Worlds: A Kikuyu's Story* (Garden City, N.Y.: Doubleday Anchor Books, 1965), pp. 153–54.

[15] Gans, *Urban Villagers,* p. 190.

[16] Hui-chen Wang Liu, *The Traditional Chinese Clan Rules* (Locust Valley, N. Y.: J. J. Augustin, Inc.—Publisher, 1959), pp. 60–93.

[17] Albert J. Reiss, "The Social Integration of Queers and Peers," in *The Other Side,* ed., Howard S. Becker (New York: The Free Press, 1964), pp. 181–210.

merry-go-round horses.[18] Adolescents escalate both the nature of the risk and the poise required in games of "chicken." Not surprisingly we find that slum-dwelling adolescents—who highly prize the character attribute of coolness—distinguish time in terms of its potential for action (and, by inference, for displays of character). "Dead" time is time devoid of such potential.[19]

## CONCLUSIONS

Although the term "coolness" is of recent vintage, the phenomenon or trait to which it refers is universal, appearing under a variety of rubrics: nonchalance, sophistication, *savoir-faire*, "blasé character," and so on. For Simmel, coolness—or blasé character, as he called it—was a trait of urbanized man.[20] Although Simmel attributes this blasé character to the preponderance of a money economy, the rapidity of change, and the interdependence of roles in cities, it would seem that these are but major sources of risk that generate the conditions for displaying the character trait of coolness. These sources of risk may be matched by other types of risk, and thus other forms of coolness in character development appropriate to

them may be found in other than urban settings.[21]

Coolness is often associated with nobility, courage, and wealth; indeed, it is from among the ranks of the risk-taking rich that *savoir-faire* and finesse are usually noted and often expected, but it is not exclusively so. Bandits and burglars exhibit many of the traits associated with coolness and sometimes explicitly link these up to aspirations toward or identification with the nobility. Thus Robin Hood is portrayed as a wronged lord who, although forced to flee into the forest and adopt the outlaw life, remains noble, temperate, and capable of considerable finesse.[22]

Note, too, that coolness is not only associated with those of high rank but also among those who are so low in the social order that the most prized possession they have is personal character—a personal status that can be acknowledged or disconfirmed in everyday encounters and demonstrated particularly in the skill and finesse with which word games are played. Such

---

[18] For a discussion of the behavioristic elements in riding a merry-go-round and other games of equipoise see Erving Goffman, "Role Distance," in *Encounters* (Indianapolis: The Bobbs-Merrill Co., Inc., 1961), pp. 105–10.

[19] Gans, *op. cit.*, pp. 27–32; Jules Henry, "White People's Time, Colored People's Time," *Trans-Action*, March-April, 1965, pp. 31–34; John Horton, "Time and Cool People," *Trans-Action*, April, 1967, pp. 5–12.

[20] Georg Simmel, "The Metropolis and Mental Life," in *Sociology of Georg Simmel* (New York: The Free Press, 1950), pp. 413–14.

[21] One such setting is the chivalric ideal of the fifteenth century. See Diaz de Gamez, "The Chivalric Ideal," in *The Portable Medieval Reader*, James B. Ross and Mary M. McLaughlin, eds. (New York: The Viking Press, Inc., 1949), especially pp. 91–92.

[22] See Maurice Keen, *The Outlaws of Medieval Legend* (London: Routledge & Kegan Paul, Ltd., 1961). For further evidence of the generalized character of bandits and outlaws see Eric J. Hobsbawm, *Social Bandits and Primitive Rebels* (New York: The Free Press, 1959), pp. 1–29. For a characterological analysis of the modern-day fictional Robin Hood, namely, Raffles, see George Orwell, "Raffles and Miss Blandish," in *Dickens, Dali and Others* (New York: Reynal & Company, Inc., 1946), pp. 202–21. These legendary bandits—Robin Hood, Raffles, etc.—are characterized by taking extra risks in the name of sportsmanship, or for aesthetic reasons, and in so doing amply display strong character.

people, Negroes in America are an outstanding example, develop considerable vocal ability, a pervasive pride in their own individuality, and because of the permanent danger—of character as well as physical assassination—skill in social and personal defense. And it is among quite ordinary American Negroes and persons similarly situated that we find the creative imagination developed toward posturing and prevarication and characterological coolness.[23]

On the contemporary American scene, however, the trait of coolness is not limited to any one segment of the social order. Riesman and others have suggested that the era of moral absolutism, accompanied by the trait of inner-directedness, has declined; and among the concomitant changes is a shift in the concept of strong character.[24] In the era of inner-directedness moral character was summed up in the admonition to do one's duty. Today such a seemingly simplistic moral model has been exchanged for the chameleonlike, radar-attuned actor who keeps pace with the rapid changes in form, content and style. Although poise under pressure was an issue in the era of rugged individualism and unfettered capitalism, the nature of the risks involved was both different in content and differentially distributed. Modern society has changed the issue in risk and democratized it.[25] Keeping cool is now a problem for everyone.

[23] See Richard Wright, "The Psychological Reactions of Oppressed People," in *White Man, Listen!* (Garden City, N.Y.: Doubleday Anchor Books, 1957), pp. 17–18.
[24] David Riesman, Nathan Glazer, and Reuel Denney, *The Lonely Crowd* (Garden City, N.Y.: Doubleday Anchor Books, 1950, 1953).
[25] See Talcott Parsons and Winston White, "The Link Between Character and Society," in *Culture and Social Character,* S. M. Lipset

In the place of the earlier isolated individuality accompanied by morally clear doctrines of guilt and shame, there has arisen the coordinated group accompanied by loneliness and affected by a ubiquitous sense of anxiety. The fictional heroes of the eras reflect these changes. The Lone Ranger —perhaps the last fully developed prototype of morally correct inner direction—was a silent, skillful devotee of law and order. He traveled the uncharted trails of the frontier West accompanied only by an Indian, both in but not of their society. He spoke seldom and then in short, clipped, direct statements. He seemed to have no "social" needs: neither women, wealth, nor power attracted or wounded him. The problems he solved were simple in form; they were *only* dangerous to life and limb: a gang of evil-doers threatened the town. Only their removal from the scene would restore the unquestionably desirable *status quo ante.*

By contrast Maverick is a prototype hero of the modern age. He is a gambler and, like Riesman's other-directed man, a cosmopolitan. For Maverick, the problems are not simple. His interest is to get through life with the maximum of pleasure, the minimum of pain. He recognizes no moral absolutes except physical and characterological survival. For him the only weapon is his wits; the only skill, verbal repartee. Only if he loses his cool will he lose to his more powerful and often ill-defined and impersonal opponents. The moral lesson implied in Maverick is quite clear. The modern age is one of permanent complex problems. They neither lend themselves to direct solution nor do they

and L. Lowenthal, eds., (New York: The Free Press, 1961), pp. 89–135.

gradually disappear.[26] It is rather that the hazardous nature of life becomes ordinary, the impermanence of things and relationships becomes fixed, and to survive man must adopt the character associated with the routinization of anxiety. Its most salient feature is what we call coolness. Its manifestations are the recognition of danger in the *presentation* of self in everyday life, the risk in *attachment* to things or people, and the positive value of what Goffman calls "role distance." [27]

Despite the ubiquity of coolness in the modern world, its study may be enhanced if we look at the form and content of life for those who are relatively permanent outsiders in society.

[26] For an analysis of the modern world in these terms see Robert Nisbet, *Community and Power* (New York: Oxford Galaxy, 1962).

[27] Goffman, "Role Distance."

Career deviants must manifest a considerable display of *savoir-faire* if they are to survive and especially if—like abortionists [28]—they deal with a clientele who is only situationally deviant. Minorities whose status is both anomalous and precarious have evidenced a remarkable ability to build a subculture resting in large part on the artful development of coolness forms. Here, then, are the strategic research sites.

The study of coolness—its meaning, manifestations, and metamorphosis—is surely a topic deserving further investigation, for all men in society are subject to the problems of personal risk and the preservation of poise under pressure.

[28] See Donald Ball, "An Abortion Clinic Ethnography," *Social Problems,* XIV (Winter, 1967), 293–301.

# 9

# The Social Significance of Card Playing as a Leisure Time Activity *†

*Irving Crespi*

Given the recent interest in the routinized patterns of interaction used in the subtle contests of everyday encounters—

* Reprinted from *The American Sociological Review*, XXI (1956), 717–21, by permission of the author and the American Sociological Association. Footnotes renumbered.

† Revised version of paper read at the annual meeting of the American Sociological Society, September, 1956.

those that are now popularly called "the games people play" after the title of the recent psychiatric best-seller [1]—we turn our attention to the open competitions explicitly labeled games, in this instance, leisure time card playing. Much work has recently been conducted on the study of

[1] Eric Berne, *Games People Play* (New York: Grove Press, 1964).

games within a cross-cultural context.[2] These studies would suggest that games act as miniature models within a culture through which various socialization conflicts that are present among that society's members are assuaged. It would appear that, in general, games of strategy, chance, or physical skill (and their special combinations) perform quite different functions in a society, and are differentially present in societies depending on the kinds of socialization conflicts present within them.

Although such general studies of games do exist, we have had remarkably few examinations that attempted to discover the special functions, both social and psychological, performed for the players of particular games.[3] Card playing is certainly one of the most widely spread forms of entertainment to be found in the United States. What are the attractions of this game? What does its presence state about its players and the society that fosters it? Professor Crespi offers some suggestions.

EDITOR

---

Card playing is one of the most pervasive and persistent games played in the United States. A majority of Americans play cards, 56 per cent of a national sample reporting that they play cards either regularly or occasionally.[4] Another national survey revealed that cards are played in 87 per cent of American homes and that 83 per cent of American families play cards.[5] Over fifty million decks of playing cards can be expected to be sold annually, with a fad such as the canasta fad in 1950—raising the total to over eighty million decks.[6] Twenty per cent of the men and 18 per cent of the women of a national sample named card playing as one of their two or three favorite activities.[7] Most significantly, the number of card decks sold per hundred population has increased from twenty-two to over thirty during the past fifty years—that is, precisely during the period in which mass media and commercial activities underwent their greatest expansion.[8]

The confirmation of the popular image identifying card playing with gambling would be presumptive proof of a moral debilitation of the structure of American society. In order to

[2] E.g., John M. Roberts and Brian Sutton-Smith, "Child Training and Game Involvement," *Ethnology*, I (1962), 166–85; John M. Roberts, J. Arth, and B. R. Rush, "Games in Culture," *American Anthropologist*, LXI (1959), 597–605; and Brian Sutton-Smith and John M. Roberts, "Game Involvement in Adults," *Journal of Social Psychology*, LX (1963), 15–30.

[3] For one such study, see: John M. Roberts, Hans Hoffman and Brian Sutton-Smith, "Pattern and Competence: A Consideration of Tick Tack Toe," *El Palacio*, LXXII (1965), 17–30.

[4] American Institute of Public Opinion poll, December 13, 1947, in *Public Opinion Quarterly*, XII (Spring, 1948), 148.

[5] "Playing Cards—A National Survey," *Hobbies*, XLVII (December, 1942), p. 12.

[6] *Facts and Figures on Government Finance, 1950–51* (New York: The Tax Foundation, 1950), p. 131.

[7] The Fortune Poll, March 1949, in *Public Opinion Quarterly*, XIII (Summer, 1949), 354.

[8] Jesse Steiner, *Americans at Play* (New York: McGraw-Hill Book Company, Inc., 1933), p. 138; tax receipts reported in *Facts and Figures on Government Finance, 1950–51*; tax receipts reported in *The Budget of the U. S. Government for the Fiscal Year Ending June 30, 1953* (Washington, D. C.: Government Printing Office, 1952), p. 1161.

TABLE 1. CORRELATION BETWEEN INTENSITY OF INTEREST IN CARD PLAYING
AND FREQUENCY OF PLAYING

| Intensity of Interest | Frequency of Playing | | | | | Total | |
|---|---|---|---|---|---|---|---|
| | Three Times or More a Week | Once or Twice a Week | Two or Three Times a Month | Once a Month | Less Often | Number | Per Cent |
| Favorite | 10 | 15 | 1 | 1 | — | 27 | 10 |
| Like very much | 12 | 33 | 11 | 6 | 1 | 63 | 22 |
| Nice | 11 | 43 | 31 | 16 | 12 | 113 | 41 |
| Nothing else to do | 2 | 13 | 12 | 9 | 8 | 44 | 16 |
| Don't like | — | 5 | 6 | 8 | 9 | 28 | 10 |
| Total | 35 | 109 | 61 | 40 | 30 | 275 | 100* |

* N = 279, Includes 1 per cent "no answer."

test this belief, a study was designed to investigate exactly what role card playing performs in the leisure lives of Americans.[9] The study was conducted in a single community, Endicott, New York; therefore, it might be maintained that the findings are not immediately applicable to the entire nation. However, Endicott shares with the rest of the country the experience of rapid industrialization, urbanization, and metropolitanization, with all the attendant effects upon social stratification and social organization. Economically, it is part of the national market, while socially its characteristic modes of leisure are congruent with national patterns. More specifically, 57 per cent of the adult population of Endicott plays cards, almost identical with the national percentage; the same card games played nationally are played locally; and probably the same proportion as the national figure considers card playing

as one of its favorite activities.[10] Consequently, we are justified in making the heuristic assumption that whatever conclusions we reach concerning the functions of card playing in Endicott are applicable to the rest of the nation.

A survey, using a systematic 11 per cent sample of the adult population, revealed significant characteristics of card players and the conditions under which they played cards. The attitudes that card players have toward the game are one indicator of the place that card playing has in their lives. To get a rough index of such attitudes, the survey sample was asked whether card playing was their favorite pastime, whether it was one of the things they liked doing very much although not their favorite, whether they thought it was a nice way to spend time, whether they play when there is nothing else to do, or whether they play the game occasionally even though they do not really like the game. The intensity of interest in card playing, as measured by these items, was correlated with frequency of playing (See Table 1). The coefficient

[9] Irving Crespi, "A Functional Analysis of Card Playing as a Leisure Time Activity" (dissertation, The New School for Social Research, June, 1955). Hans Staudinger and Arvid Brodersen, of the Graduate Faculty of The New School, were of invaluable assistance in the formulation of the research design and the adaptation of analytical concepts.

[10] Ibid., pp. 20–28, 35, 51–53, 54, for a full description of these characteristics of Endicott.

of correlation, .47, is statistically significant ($P<.01$) but low enough to suggest that factors other than interest in the game are important determinants of how frequently card players actually play.

Undoubtedly, one of the factors accounting for the statistical significance of the correlation coefficient is the fact that the attitude items are partial indicators of frequency of playing. If a person says that an activity is a favorite of his, it is only natural that he will engage in it as often as possible. This is why almost all who say that card playing is their favorite activity play at least once a week. Similarly, the fact that most of those who say that they do not really like card playing also say that they play less than once a week is hardly surprising. But what is surprising is that the majority of card players who play at least once a week indicate that they have no more than a moderate interest in card playing. The high frequency with which these card players play cannot be satisfactorily explained unless we account for it by factors other than interest in the game itself.

The distinguishing characteristics of card players, the persons with whom cards are played, and the locus of card playing all indicate that these other factors have their root in primary group affiliations. Card players as contrasted with nonplayers tend significantly to be married (See Table 2). Furthermore, given the proportion of married people in the total sample who play cards, the proportion of spouses of card players who also play cards is greater than is to be expected through chance alone. The proportion of married men who play cards is .66; the proportion of married card-playing women whose husbands play cards is .85. The comparable propor-

tions of married women who play cards and of married card-playing men whose wives play cards are .47 and .65 respectively. The significance of the primary group relationship is further attested to by the fact that there is a significant relationship between being a card player and having relatives and having close friends who play cards (See Tables 3 and 4).

The fact that card playing is most often an activity carried on by primary groups is established when we consider with whom card players play and where. Only 7 per cent of the card players reported that they play with people they have met at card games. Friends are mentioned by 83

TABLE 2. COMPARISON OF CARD PLAYERS AND NON-CARD PLAYERS BY MARITAL STATUS

| Marital Status | Card Players | Non-Card Players | Total |
|---|---|---|---|
| Single | 24 | 29 | 53 |
| Married | 230 | 155 | 385 |
| Divorced and Widowed | 21 | 22 | 43 |
| Total | 275 | 206 | 481 |

$X^2 = 5.33$ Approaches significance at .05 level.

TABLE 3. ASSOCIATION BETWEEN BEING A CARD PLAYER AND HAVING CLOSE RELATIVES WHO PLAY CARDS

| Respondents | Relatives Play Cards | Relatives Don't Play Cards | Total |
|---|---|---|---|
| Card Players | 243 | 33 | 276 |
| Non-Card Players | 90 | 116 | 206 |
| Total | 333 | 149 | 482 |

$X^2 = 109.10$ Significant at .001 level.
$C = .60$.

TABLE 4. ASSOCIATION BETWEEN BEING A
CARD PLAYER AND HAVING BEST FRIENDS
WHO PLAY CARDS

| Respondents | Best Friends Play Cards | Best Friends Don't Play Cards | Total |
|---|---|---|---|
| Card Players | 257 | 18 | 275 |
| Non-Card Players | 108 | 99 | 207 |
| Total | 365 | 117 | 482 |

$X^2 = 109.72$ Significant at .001 level.
$C = .61$.

per cent, relatives by 67 per cent, and neighbors by 44 per cent. The locale of card playing is in the greatest number of cases where primary groups are to be found as a matter of course. Eighty-seven per cent of the card players said that they usually play in their own homes, and 73 per cent in the homes of their friends. Twenty-one per cent mentioned public card parties and only 2 per cent, tournaments. We can only conclude that card playing is most often engaged in by families and friends in each other's homes. That is to say, card playing is pre-eminently a primary group activity.

The fact that cards are most characteristically played by primary groups rather than by groups formed specifically for the purpose of playing is of major significance. If card playing is to be understood as a gambling activity, the moral integration of these groups, inferentially, is minimal. However, such does not seem to be the case. A series of fifty-one intensive interviews with card players was conducted to uncover underlying motives for card playing and the nature of involvement in card playing. In this way, the sociological functions of card playing could be ascertained.

The protocols of these interviews disclose that it is not gambling but the primary group which is the underlying factor explaining why and how most card players participate in the game.

A number of motives for playing can be delineated:

1. Motives directly related to the game itself and to the outcome of the game; the game or the rewards of winning are what attract the player.
2. Motives related to the fact that the group affiliation needs of the individual players can be satisfied while playing cards. What the player wants in these cases is the type of group life that card playing makes possible.
3. Motives related to the social status values that have become associated with card playing. What the player seeks here is the social acceptance, recognition, and even prestige that card playing bestows in certain situations.

The first motivational type of card player can be considered the gambler. He plays cards for the monetary reward that success brings: he has a lust to win a fortune through card playing. One man who plays regularly in a group in which losses up to two hundred dollars in one evening are possible commented:

The fellows I play with play for the sole purpose of winning. Social bridge has a different atmosphere compared with a poker game. Big stakes have the lure of money. I compare it to watching amateur and professional teams. One is the real thing.

In Endicott it appears that only a small minority of card players are gamblers. Only 23 per cent of the survey sample said that they play cards for money stakes, and not all of these are gamblers.

It might be objected that some respondents did not answer honestly because gambling is illegal. However it appears that most card players who play for money stakes do not do so in the hope of winning a large amount of money. Typically, they play for stakes so small that they cannot possibly entertain the thought of significantly adding to their income through winning at cards. Illustrative of such players are the following comments:

I get a lot of satisfaction at cards playing for pennies. I don't win or lose much, but I get a thrill.

We play for small stakes. The idea is not to win or lose a great deal. We can't afford it and it might create animosity . . . I am a mediocre player. Some of the others are excellent . . . We start playing immediately. The bastards are all after my money.

Playing for a monetary prize is an exciting and stimulating experience to players like these. Still gambling, because of their fear of losing, their mediocre playing, or their desire to avoid personal enmity, is "too rich for their blood." These players are "prize players" rather than gamblers. Even if we were to grant that more than one fourth of the card players in Endicott habitually play cards for money stakes, we would, according to these observations, be correct to say that only a small minority are gamblers.

A small category of card players are "skill players," who are attracted by the challenge of trying to win at cards through skilled performance. They seek to demonstrate their mastery of the necessary skills and, if possible, their skill superiority. Skill players, of necessity, play frequently and, by preference, with others who are also highly skilled. They confine their playing to games such as bridge, which are intrinsically difficult enough

to present a continuing challenge. Obviously, they can comprise only the small minority of card players who play very frequently and who consider cards a favorite.

The greatest proportion of card players are those included in the types "group player," "group-game player," "social player," and "accidental player." Group players like to play cards because it enables them to experience the conviviality that stems from playing a game with people with whom they want to spend their leisure time. In fact, few have any interest in attaining a level of skilled proficiency:

Cards are a universal game. It is something to pass the time. We play for the enjoyment of the game and the spirit of companionship. In a crowd it is the most congenial game.

I play poker not for the game but for the social relationships, getting together with friends, relaxation. Bridge is more difficult. You have to concentrate on the game. That takes the pleasure from playing.

The 41 per cent of the survey sample who said that card playing is a nice way to spend time, as well as the 16 per cent who said that they play cards when they have nothing else to do, are probably almost all of this type (see Table 1).

Group players feel that card playing is a congenial and entertaining way of being in groups for a number of reasons. One is the "atmosphere" of the game situation. Whether it is a group of relatives, a public card party, a male friendship group, or a gathering of married couples, players repeatedly mention that the card-playing situation has an air of friendliness and getting together in a group to enjoy themselves. Furthermore, the card game, by holding the group together in a common activity with a narrow focus of interest, acts as a substitute for conversation.[11] In this way group relationships among friends and relatives who have talked themselves out are eased. The basic contribution that the individual has to make once playing commences is to play more or less adequately; he is thus relieved of the personality demands of making conversation. By relaxing the tension resulting from boredom, card playing transforms the obligation of being a group member into an enjoyable opportunity to play a game. As an inexpensive and convenient alternative to "going out," card playing also holds some attractiveness. Finally, involvement in the process of competing to win, which sometimes reaches a high pitch, converts the players into impersonal technicians; in so doing, the card game facilitates the forgetting of personal worries and obligations. In this sense, it is a relaxing activity.

What card playing does, then is to permit families and friends to gather in the informal atmosphere of their homes in an inexpensive, relaxing, entertaining, and personally undemanding manner.

Intermediary between the group player, as we have described him, and those who are motivated by the game played for its own sake is the group-game player. Such players are equally motivated by the challenge of the game and the desire to win on one

hand, and the group values of playing on the other. One such player, for example, commented:

I'm glad I learned to play cards. If, a person can't play cards he is out of place in a crowd. I like cards as a game though I am not addicted to it. I like trying to win and the spirit of companionship.

Players of this type derive a dual gratification from playing cards. They are actively entertained in the group situation and so enjoy spending time with groups composed of relatives and friends. They also acquire a sense of satisfaction from having performed well in a technically demanding activity or having won money bet on an uncertain outcome. Most of the 22 per cent of the survey sample who said that they like card playing "very much" are probably of this type.

Social players are those who consider card playing a "social asset." They have discovered that by playing cards they can participate in the activities of groups that have social status value. They contend that the nonplayer is automatically cut off from much of the social life of the community. A few even recommend learning how to play cards in order to avoid social isolation.

There are three types of group situations in which card playing has a social status function. They are women's card clubs, public card parties, and the gatherings of married couples who have high-class status. In all these situations card playing is the mode of meeting, although involvement in playing is seldom developed to any appreciable degree, to the disgust of those few who are interested in playing the game. Card playing is a social asset in that the nonplayer is automatically restricted from entry to these groups. Hence, the opportunities to participate in the leisure-time

---

[11] The Lynds observed that in Middletown the vogue for bridge playing might be ascribable in part to a desire not to concentrate conversation on a single topic and to the monotony of small talk. See Robert S. Lynd and Helen M. Lynd, *Middletown in Transition* (New York: Harcourt, Brace & World, Inc., 1937), p. 270. This study has investigated why bridge, and other card games, can perform this substitutive function. See Crespi, "Functional Analysis," Chapter 4.

life of an appreciable portion of the higher social strata is reduced. The categories of group player and social player overlap to some degree. An analysis of the distinguishing characteristics of card players suggests that possibly one fifth of all card players can be included in this category.

Those card players for whom the group quality of card playing is the only reason for playing the game have been called "accidental players." The game itself is not only of no interest to them, it may even be obnoxious. Illustrative of this type of player is the following:

I definitely consider myself a non-card player. I avoid card games like the plague. Actually, I've played often with my aunt and uncle who love to play. I've been forced to play by the social situation. There's no way out.

Card players such as this woman never play if not forced to by their desire to belong, or felt obligation, to the group. They adjust to the specific group situation, sacrificing their personal pleasure. Some of these accidental players actually play often because members of their family or their friends play frequently. Judging from the responses to the survey schedule, 10 per cent of the card playing population—those who said they play even though they do not like the game are accidental players.

This analysis of motives for playing

cards demonstrates that it is the group intensification effect of card playing that underlies its being such a persistently widespread primary group activity. Gamblers and skill players, in an attempt to justify their intense interest in the activity, often maintain that only a minority of card players are not fully committed to playing cards for its own sake. Yet, in fact, it is they—the gamblers and skill players—who are the minority.

The great majority of card players, in opposition to popular misconceptions, play cards because they have discovered it to be an enjoyable and relaxing way of being together with friends and families and one which results in the strengthening of group ties. Another inducement to play cards is that the individual can hope to achieve acceptance into groups which will enhance his social position. We must conclude that card playing in Endicott, and probably in all of the United States, is essentially a group phenomenon and not a manifestation of social disorganization. The prevalence of card playing reflects not moral degeneracy but the struggle of primary groups to maintain their viability in the contemporary scene. Eager for friendliness and easy congeniality, many Americans appear to be incapable of generating such relationships without the artificial stimulation of impersonal, competitive group games.

# PART IV

# Occupations

# The Life Cycle of the Social Role of Housewife *†

*Helena Znaniecki Lopata*

Recent years have seen the emergence of a massive popular literature polemically concerned with the changing role of the housewife.[1] A great deal has been written arguing the merits and demerits of this particular social role; very little of this writing, however, has attempted objective empirical assessment.[2] Before any appraisal can be made of the conditions present in this role, we must have an analysis and description of the common properties present within this complex, its typical stages, and its relations to the other clusters normally surrounding it. This is the purpose of the following article.

EDITOR

---

This article[3] is devoted to the analysis of the life cycle of the social role of housewife, and of its placement in the role cluster of performers at different stages in their life cycles.[4]

* Reprinted from *Sociology and Social Research*, LI (1966), 5–22, by permission of the publisher. Footnotes renumbered.

† Appreciation is expressed to Erving Goffman and Joseph Gusfield for their advice concerning the role monograph that was the foundation of this and of other role papers.

[1] Most prominent here is the best-selling: Betty Friedan, *The Feminine Mystique* (New York: W. W. Norton & Company, Inc., 1963).

[2] For one such study dealing with the housewife, see: Robert S. Weiss and Nancy Morse Samelson, "Social Roles of American Women: Their Contribution to a Sense of Usefulness and Importance," Research Report, Survey Research Center, University of Michigan (Mimeo), 1957. There has been, on the other hand, much attention paid to the working mother. Cf. F. Ivan Nye and Lois W. Hoffman, *The Employed Mother in America* (Chicago: Rand McNally & Company, 1963).

[3] Revised version of paper read in the Sociology of Aging session of the Midwest Sociological Society meetings in April, 1965 in Minneapolis, Minn.

[4] The major contributor to the concept of life cycle of the family is Paul Glick, both in his *American Families* (New York: John Wiley & Sons, Inc., 1957) and in articles, including: "The Family," *American Sociological Review*, XII (April, 1947), 164–74, and "The Life Cycle of the Family," *Marriage and Family Living*, XVII (February, 1955), 3–9. Most of the textbooks on the family rely on this concept. This is a major focus of Evelyn Duvall's *Family Development*, 2nd ed. (Philadelphia: J. B. Lippincott Co., 1962) and Robert Winch uses it throughout his *The Modern Family* (New York: Holt, Rinehart & Winston, Inc., 1963). See also J. S. Slotkin, "Life Course in Middle Age," *Social Forces*, XXXIII (December, 1954), 171–76, for reference to the concept of "life course" developed in Germany by Charlotte Bühler.

It thus combines the concepts of social role and role cluster with three sets of life cycles: that of the role, that of the social person bearing the title of the role, and that of the participants in the social circle. The analysis is based upon the Znaniecki definition of social role as a set of patterned relations between a social person and participants of the social circle, involving sets of duties which are the functions of the role, and the sets of rights which enable their performance.[5] In all but new roles, a social role is entered into when more than one "other" (or Parson's "alter") accepts a person into culturally defined relations after tests have indicated that he is fit to carry out the duties and to receive the rights. The title of the role is assigned to this person who is the center of the relations, toward whom rights are directed, and from whom duties are expected. The role is based upon cultural expectations, but it is the actual set of relations. Members of the society and sociologists select only certain generalized and patterned actions in describing a role and in indicating it by the use of the title.

Although the title of a social role is assigned to the one person who is the center of the relations, the role does not exist if only that person carries out a system of actions.[6] It requires at least two more persons who interact with him because of the role. Thus roles require relational duties and, usually, task duties, but never the latter alone. The rights include the permission to carry out the duties, certain actions by circle members, and the facilities they provide in order to enable the functioning of the role.

Social roles can be located in a variety of systems. They are always assigned positions in status or prestige systems and, in the case of associational groups, in organizational charts.[7] They can also be seen as having location in clusters of all the social roles carried out by their participants. Each human being performs, usually, if not always, several social roles at any stage of his life, each role within a different social circle, but often among the same aggregates of human beings. The role clusters tend to be focused by the individual around a central role, with relative degrees of importance assigned by him to other roles which are placed in different locations from this center. Each role, of course, can take the center stage briefly every time attention is focused on it. However, it is the thesis of this paper that the individual tends to focus on one or at the most two, roles in any cluster he maintains. The life cycle of a human

[5] The definition and the theoretical framework for the concept of social role are contained in the work of Florian Znaniecki. They first appeared in English in *The Method of Sociology* (New York: Farrar & Rinehart, 1934) and were developed fully in his posthumous *Social Relations and Social Roles: An Unfinished Systematic Sociology* (San Francisco: Chandler Publishing Co., 1965). The last prior published reference to it is contained in "Basic Problems of Contemporary Sociology," *The American Sociological Review*, XIX No. 5 (October, 1954), 519–42.

[6] The assumptions that a role can be limited to expectations of actions, or to the behavior of one person, or to the consequences of status placement is an important factor in the inability of sociologists to utilize it meaningfully in their analyses of social interaction. This deficiency results in an uneven and restricted use of a concept which could be vital to the field and which renders comparisons of roles impossible or at best limited.

[7] See Helena Znaniecki Lopata, "A Restatement of the Relation Between Role and

being can be seen as involving shifts in the components of his role cluster when new roles are added and old ones dropped, and shifts in the location of each role in the cluster. Modifications in the characteristics of each role occur as the individual enters different stages of its life cycle or changes his definition of the role, or as a consequence of shifts in the cluster. Changes in the role definition can, of course, be brought about by events external to the person, such as modifications in the components or characteristics of the social circle or in their definitions of the role or of their part in it.

The title "housewife" is assigned, in Western European and American societies, to women who are, or have been, married and who "run" their own households, clearly differentiating between them and daughters who care for the homes of their fathers, "housemothers" in sororities, or "housekeepers" running the households of their employers.[8] The matter of proprietal rights over the household is an issue in our society, as evidenced by the aged mother who feels that she has lost some vital rights as a housewife when she moves into the household of her daughter. A person may be designated as a housewife even when she no longer performs the role of wife, although it is assumed that only women who have been married are rightful holders of the title.

The social role of housewife is an indeterminate one, to use Mack's classification of occupations, binding together a variety of "others" through diversified sets of relations.[9] The role cannot be performed by a woman herself, although she may carry out many of the actions through which the maintenance of the home is accomplished without the immediate presence of others. It requires that several persons relate to the title holder through the duties and the rights. The housewife in modern American society maintains her home for and/or with the cooperation of: members of her family of procreation and other residents; guests, such as kin, neighbors, friends, husband's work associates, persons involved in the lives of offsprings, members of voluntary associations, etc; persons or groups who enter the home to provide services, such as servants, repair experts, or delivery men; and persons or groups whose services or goods she seeks outside of the home in order to maintain it.

The social role of housewife has an interesting cycle compared to other roles, involving relatively little anticipatory socialization, very brief time devoted to the "becoming" stage and a rather compressed and early peak. It can be performed during the major part of the life cycle of a woman, yet its entrance, modifications, and cessation are usually not a consequence of its own characteristics or rhythm but of those of other roles.

---

Status," *Sociology and Social Research,* XLIX (October, 1964), 58–68, for the theoretical foundation and definition of *status role.*

[8] American women often react negatively to the term "housewife." Women's magazines have used the word "homemaker" to accentuate creativity and action; but pilot interviews indicated that the women themselves find the term artificial and seldom use it to define their role. The objection to the term "housewife" is not due to the presence of a more satisfactory title, one suspects, but to the low level of prestige assigned to the role.

[9] Raymond W. Mack, "Occupational Determinateness: A Problem and Hypotheses in Role Theory," *Social Forces,* XXXV (October, 1956), 20–24.

## "Becoming a Housewife" [10]

The first stage of any role which is to become important for the person is really composed of two phases, frequently lumped together under the term "novice." It involves not only the process of learning to perform the duties and to receive the rights in a satisfactory and unselfconscious or sophisticated manner, but also the process of gradual placement of the self within the role. The latter phase requires the ability to see the self as a "natural" center of a role circle and the role as a part of one's own role cluster.

The dual aspect of the first stage are in great evidence in the social role of the housewife. In modern American society a young woman typically enters the role upon marriage, due to the neolocal residence of each family of procreation. The housewife is not "adequately" trained for the role according to Chicago urban and suburban women whose depth interviews, collected over the past few years from the base of this paper,[11] and to numerous other com-

mentators.[12] Although each young girl usually lives in a home run by her mother up till the time of marriage, the American system of education and occupation removes her from its walls for most of her conscious hours starting at the age of five, and even impinges upon her time within it. Training in "home economics" and the voluntary learning of homemaking skills are not highly evaluated by the society and especially by teen-aged school-work-boy-leisure oriented girls. Attention tends to be directed "outside" of the home, and the focal point of interest in the role cluster of each teen-ager tends to be not a role, but the individual.

The process of becoming a housewife includes the phase of the learning the various skills used in maintaining the home and relating to those who are involved in its maintenance. The process of shifting identifications and space placements is also important to the young woman. The stress upon the location of the self "inside" the home as opposed to "outside" life roles, or persons, so important to housewives in the next stage of the cycle, begins with a gradual shift of the image of the self from a rather functionally diffused "outside" existence to a role-focused and geographically placed identity within a home.

The newly married bride, still en-

---

[10] The term "becoming" is not meant to indicate a teleological reaching for completed bloom of being, the closed frame of existentialist writers. Howard Becker's "Becoming a Marihuana User," *The American Journal of Sociology*, LIX (November, 1953), 235–42, expresses more of the intended stress upon a process involving self-indication and placement.

[11] The study involves 1000 interviews with Chicago area housewives. The first 300 were obtained with the help of funds from *The Chicago Tribune,* and formed an area probability sample drawn from newly developed sections of 12 socio-economically divergent suburbs. It included only full-time housewives who owned their homes and had pre-high-school children. The additional 700 interviews came from as broad a range of racial, ethnic, socio-economic, residential and role focusing women as was available in the Chicago area and to Roosevelt University students.

[12] The most famous proponent of "home economics" training for women was Lynn White, Jr. His *Educating Our Daughters* (New York: Harper & Brothers, 1950) created a storm of controversy over the relative values of different systems of education for future homemakers. Almost every study of role expectations and preparation on the part of American girls concludes that training in housekeeping knowledge and skills is not a present focus of choice or even interest, although the popularity of "adult education" courses in related fields indicates increasing interest in later years.

gaged in occupational or school roles typical of the American pattern, sees herself as located outside of the home. Living in her own place is important, but it is seen mostly as part of being a wife, and then in terms of primary relations with the husband, rather than as a potential center of multiple relations. She talks of her life in terms of personality changes and feelings to a degree not used again till very old age.

The role of housewife begins to enter her life pattern with a growing awareness of the complexity of duties involved in the role of wife, duties beyond those of primary attitudes, and, with shifting significance, the role of customer. The meaning of money does change, reflecting and perhaps even leading the changes in the role cluster. The role of worker becomes used more instrumentally than before, as a source of obtaining means for housekeeping activities. The role of consumer begins to involve purchasing for a unit, budgeting, and accounting to the self for expenditures. The role of customer no longer serves only the ends of personal pleasure and adornment. Although "fixing up the apartment" is accomplished with external eyes, the process of bringing the self and purchases "inside" the house begins to acquire a symbolic tone.

The shifting of roles into new clusters often results in the placement of the role of wife in the center, and in the pushing of the roles of daughter, worker, and colleague into the background. The role of housewife or "homemaker" and of consumer are gradually pulled into the foreground.

## The Expanding Circle

The increase of importance assigned to the role of housewife in the role cluster comes with pregnancy. Outside employment "fades out" as an important role for most women, and the role of mother antecedes actual birth. The length of time involved in pregnancy performs the important function of "anticipatory socialization."

As Le Masters points out, and interviewees emphatically echo, the birth of the first child is a dramatic event, changing the whole life pattern of the woman.[13] One of the consequences is the shift of focus in the cluster of roles as new ones are added and old ones are dropped. Because of the utter dependence of newborn infants upon practically twenty-four-hour care by an adult, the number of activities such care necessitates, and the society's preference for its being undertaken by the biological mother, the young housewife suddenly finds herself confined to her house, carrying on a variety of housekeeping tasks; often inexpertly and alone.

Not only does the infant require many housewifely actions, and its birth expand the social circle to include new people, but new sets of duties arise in new role relations with people already present in other circles. The husband now becomes also the father of the child and must relate to the mother on that level. The shift of attention often pushes the role of wife to the background, temporarily if not permanently.[14] One of the characteristics of the role of housewife is the

[13] E. E. LeMasters, "Parenthood as Crisis," *Marriage and Family Living*, XIX (November, 1957), 352–55.

[14] Two thirds of the Chicago area women interviewed in this study, as reported in Helena Znaniecki Lopata, "Secondary Features of a Primary Relation," *Human Organization*, (Summer, 1965), pp. 116–23, did not assign the role of wife first place when asked to list the roles of women in order of importance.

fact that competence acquired in the previous stage of the role may not actually help the new mother. A housekeeping schedule, for example, may be dysfunctional to, or made ineffective by, the demands of a newborn baby in a society which stresses its needs above those of adults.

## The Peak Stage

The stage of the role of housewife in which the woman has several small children, that is, the peak stage, varies considerably in actual practice, depending on a combination of the following factors:

1. The number and ages of the children.
2. Their special needs.
3. The kinds of duties undertaken by the housewife in relation to these children, because of societal, circle, or self-imposed demands.
4. The kinds of duties undertaken by the housewife in relation to other members of the household.
5. The size of the home which must be maintained.
6. The number of items which must be maintained and the activities required to keep them in a desired condition.
7. The number of persons helping in the performance of the duties and the type of assistance each provides. Such assisting circle segments may include employees, relatives, friends and neighbors, and members of the household involved in a regular or emergency division of labor.
8. The number and variety of "labor-saving" devices or "conveniences" designed to decrease the effort or the time required to perform any of the tasks.
9. The location of the household and of each task in relation to the assisting segment of the circle and to the useful objects, plus the versatility of these services as a source of shifting duties and activities.

The role of housewife, being an indeterminate one, can be performed in a variety of styles, with great complexity or with simplified standards of care of the house and persons within it.

## The "Full House" Plateau

The next major stage in the role of housewife starts, according to interviewers, when the youngest child enters school and ends when the children start leaving home to live somewhere else. The women with small, pre-school children had anticipated this stage with hopes for "relaxation" and "time for myself." Their statement reflected their reaction to the stage in which they were engaged, one of shift from "outside" to "inside," accompanied by the addition of new roles and hectic hours.

The stage when there are no babies in the home is not reached for most women as soon as the Glick tables of average life cycles led us to expect.[15] At least, the range of time between the birth of the first child and the year when the youngest child starts school, for the 1,000 Chicago interviewees, indicates wide variations in the ages of women when this stage occurs.

Furthermore, the "full house" stage does not turn out to be as restful as the mothers of pre-schoolers had anticipated. It seems to be true that, as children grow older, the housewife tends to be relieved of certain household activities. A child's gradual increase in self-control, and in the ability to care for himself and his belongings, plus the decrease in the amount of time he actually spends in the home, may decrease the number or complexity of actions performed by

[15] Glick, "The Life Cycle of the American Family," p. 4.

the adult in the house. However, the presence of school-aged children often results in the expansion of the housewife's circle with additions of duties toward each member. Playmates, teachers, tutors, or organization leaders may ask for special attention or impose special demands upon the child, requiring more work of its mother. Other roles may impinge on the time she has to devote to housekeeping tasks. For example, many of the interviewed mothers stated that the supervision of their teen-aged daughters, who are entering a new stage of life, took more time than the supervision of small children. Allowing for the warping of memory and for the probability that these women are not really talking of the amount of time involved in direct supervision but of the amount of worry and conflict, we still must caution ourselves from accepting an oversimplified image of the "full house" stage of the role of housewife—one of decreased activity and increased leisure.

The housewife's activities in this stage, when new members are not likely to be added to the household through birth, and when residing members are all still there and functioning in a relatively self-sufficient manner, are highly dependent on the size of the social circle, the cultural and personal demands as to what she must do for each person, the kind and amount of assistance provided her, and the time other roles leave her for this function.

For example, the career cycle of the husband is likely to have resulted in a consistent improvement of the family's economic position, due to increased expertness in occupational role performance or upward mobility in role sequences. Such affluence was frequently mentioned by interviewees, but its consequences upon the role of housewife varied; it became a source of more work if more objects were added for the sake of beauty, comfort, or class status, or a source of less work if the money was converted into services or work-simplifying objects.

Standard variations in the role of housewife in the "full house" stage depend also on solutions to a "inside-outside" continuum of role clusters. The fact that the husband and the children are now all "outside" of the home a great deal of time, and have many outside identifications and orientations may leave the housewife as the only person with a basically "inside" location. She can continue focusing on any of the three roles of wife, mother, or housewife. An interesting focus is developed by women who generalize their relations with the husband and with each child into "family" relations, involving mostly the performance of duties for it. Such women tend to separate themselves, as performers of certain home-maintaining actions, from those who are the recipients, defining all as "the family" and seldom during the interview, if ever, isolating individual relations. Such women speak of "cooking for the family," "sewing for the family," or "waiting for the family to come home."

Other women with growing children place themselves on the "outside" of the home for the majority of the day, taking full-time employment or devoting themselves with complete dedication to volunteer work. As a number of sociologists have pointed out, especially in the analysis of The Working Mother,[16] the kinds of out-

[16] The lack of importance given to their occupational roles, and especially to the task components of such roles, on the part of American women is a conclusion researched by many sociologists, as reported in F. Ivan Nye and Lois W. Hoffman, eds., *The Em-*

side roles undertaken, and the ways in which these are clustered depend on several factors. We can analyze the influence of these by seeing how they contribute to the balance between the pull of the activities and gains from each direction. Some women never become "inside-located," so that the return to work or other community life after the birth of children is rapid and complete. Women who have placed themselves in the home and for whom the housewife role became important may be attracted to the outside or forced out of the inside by a feeling of obligation to help in the financial support of the family, or through crises such as widowhood. This study of housewives suggests that the factor of personal influence is very important in furnishing a bridge and an impetus for the breaking down of psychological barriers between the home and the rest of the world. The example and urging of friends and relatives who return to work help offset inertia of a woman who fears that she could no longer function in the occupational world. As in other instances of personal influence, decisions to undertake new roles requiring new skills and behavioral traits tend to take the form of fashion.[17]

Those who do not go out completely, but do so part-time include women who have never cut off ties with the outside, or who develop new lines of connection. They most frequently combine both orientations through the addition of some outside roles, such as that of PTA member, or part-time worker, without letting such identifications grow into total commitments. They continue their focality of a home-based role, such as a wife, mother, housewife or "carer" of the family. The women utilizing the last two categories of role foci tend, however, to least often combine inside with outside orientations; and they continue being home oriented.

One of the factors which must be considered in the analysis of role clustering on the part of women who no longer have small, dependent children and who have a choice in activities they may undertake is the low, if not negative, evaluation of the role of housewife in American society. Such an evaluation has been built up into whole systems of ideology by such writers as Betty Friedan.[18] The role tends to be seen as an instrumental, or servile one, whose function is to help other people perform more vital and interesting roles—away from the home.

ployed *Mother in America* (Chicago: Rand McNally & Co., 1963). The same point is made by Cumming and Henry, especially in their chapter on "Retirement and Widowhood." Elaine Cumming and William E. Henry, *Growing Old* (New York: Basic Books, Inc., Publishers, 1961).

[17] The Elihu Katz and Paul E. Lazarsfeld statement of the significance of informal communication appeared in *Personal Influence* (New York: The Free Press, 1955) and it has been the foundation of a great deal of research, especially in consumer behavior. I had the pleasure of participating in a search for an effective technique for getting to the content of "the recommendation process" through interviews, under the

direction of Nelson Foote of General Electric in the summer of 1955. This experience, combined with the study of Polish-American associations, "The Function of Voluntary Associations in an Ethnic Community: Polonia" in Ernest Burgess and Donald Bogue, *Contributions to Urban Sociology* (Chicago: University of Chicago Press, 1964), and the study of housewives have convinced me of the importance of friends and other personal links between the woman and any form of "outside" activity.

[18] Betty Friedan, *The Feminine Mystique* (New York: W. W. Norton and Company, Inc., 1963). See also, Simone de Beauvoir, *The Second Sex* (New York: Alfred A. Knopf, Inc., 1963).

Some prestige can come to a housewife if she runs the home of persons judged important by the society. The increase in the number of persons benefiting from the activities of a housewife is also a source of prestige, as it is assumed to increase the significance of what she does. So are, to some extent, the degree of dependency of these people, and the excellence of performance of the role.

All of these bases for prestige in the role of housewife make difficult the next stage for women who have invested their lives in that role, as many have, and who do not have alternative sources for the focusing of identity. The number of alternatives, however, decreases with increased separation from the "outside." The role of mother cannot become a satisfactory focus at this stage of the child's life, because, in American society especially, one of its basic functions is to decrease its own importance.

## The Shrinking Circle

The next stage in the social role of housewife starts when the first child is married or when he has left home. The previous years actually prepared the way for this stage, since modern American children tend to spend less and less time in the home as they progress through their teens. This stage can last for many years; and it often contains a pause after the last child has left and before the death of the husband.

The shrinking of the circle seriously affects the role. It removes many of the sources of prestige without any choice or control on the part of the woman whose identity is bound with it. No matter how well she performs it, how many and how important are the persons for whom it is performed, or how significant is the role in the lives of recipients, modern society automatically decreases the ability of the role of housewife to serve as a center of relations. The housewife ceases to perform the role at a peak, and even at a high plateau level, long before capacity to carry out its duties decreases, providing a reason or excuse for its cessation. Changes in the role come basically and primarily from changes in characteristics of the circle prior to any changes in her which could provide justification for decreasing functionality.[19]

The shrinking of the role importance of housewife and mother cannot always lead to a shift of self and of role-focus to a concentration on the role of wife, if such an emphasis was absent, since the husband tends still to be highly involved in his role of worker. Thus a gap develops between importance assigned to the husband's functions and those of his wife. She now has the time she desired before, but not necessarily the means of converting it into meaningful roles. An increase in self-directed or in house-directed activities is not a source of roles unless it is accomplished by entrance into new circles. In the case in which the woman does not have satisfactory role substitutions, or in which she does not have an acceptable reason for not being the center of several circles, the life cycles of the role and of the person are not synchronized. This withering of roles and circles leaves her feeling useless and functionless. It is within this stage of the role's cycle that a

[19] One must bear in mind that the fact the circle shrinks through a decrease in the number of persons within it may not automatically decrease the significance of the role to the person, even when the society evaluates roles by using the numbers game.

sharp difference in expressed life satisfactions occurs among different women because of availability of alternative activities and of expectations. Barring ill health, the women who can be located in the higher socio-economic strata express greater enjoyment of their lives than their less well-positioned counterparts. They make frequent references to the tasks of entertaining and visiting, and to community activities. They look forward to their husband's vacations and future retirement. As one interviewee explained: "I have the ability, both physical and financial, to do and go pretty much as I please." On the other hand, women of the lower socio-economic strata tend to list more dissatisfaction with life, and to either see the future in negative hues, or to refuse to predict changes in it.[20]

A source of satisfaction for some women whose circles inside the home had shrunk was that of grandmother. The interview did not specifically refer to this role, so we cannot know why so few women who had children 25 years of age or over, and who can be presumed to be grandmothers, actually spoke of the role. Older women tended to make more references to it, regardless of the age or number of children. Future studies will attempt to learn more of the significance of this role. An interesting hypothesis is that younger women

[20] The importance of a feeling of competence in life satisfaction has been of interest to several University of Chicago social scientists, including Nelson Foote, Robert Havighurst, and Bernice Neugarten. Lee Rainwater, Richard Coleman, and Gerald Handel contrast The Workingman's Wife (Dobbs Ferry, N.Y.: Oceana Publications, Inc., 1959) whom they find filled with feelings of inadequacy, powerlessness, and incompetence with the middle-class woman who expects to be able to deal with the world and to solve problems.

do not identify with the role of grandmother, either because of its aging stereotype, or because they are so busy with other roles as not to assign much significance to it. The distance between the family units is, of course, one factor. It is possible that the present trends in marriage and childbearing are producing grandmothers who are too young to take up the role voluntarily until the grandchildren are too old to need them.

The role of worker does not draw positive comments from women in this stage of life, except on the part of the few who identify with their occupation, all of whom are in professional roles. Most women see their jobs as a source of money and personal contact, but, as they get older, they refer to the role more frequently as something they can leave, or from which they may retire. The comments bear some analysis, since they are very different from the desires of younger women with small children; who see happiness in future roles away from home; and since they indicate a probable source of difference in attitudes of men and women facing retirement.

Women with shrinking housewife roles who are working outside the home frequently explain that they want to "return home" where they "belong," and where they "always want to be." They feel that they have been deprived of a certain set of rights because they "had to go to work." Previous complaints about home restrictions (if actually made by the same woman) are forgotten; and working away from home is seen as an imposition, not a choice. It is quite possible that the man, lacking this feeling of rightfully belonging in the home, has a much more difficult time adjusting to the substitution of this location of the "self" for one in the "world of work." Retirement automatically tends to place the focus of life inside the home. The woman who has always had the role of housewife, with its location "inside," as one of the roles in her cluster and sometimes as the focal role, finds herself inside the home more comfortably than the man for whom this focus is foreign.

The first phase of the "shrinking circle" stage in the social role of housewife ends with adjustment to the absence of the last child to leave home. During the pause preceding the next stage when she is left alone in the home, before aging becomes a real problem, and if she is not bothered by special difficulties as ill health, the housewife tends to experience gradual changes due to the process of growing older. The factors bringing about these changes and the manner in which aging is evaluated by those who experience it, is of particular interest to modern society because of the increasing percentages of populations who do, or will, face the variety of problems connected with it. Sociological literature dealing with the process is recent, but expanding.[21] This study of the life

[21] The aging literature which is most pertinent to this study includes: James Birren, ed., *Handbook of Aging and the Individual* (Chicago: University of Chicago Press, 1959); Clark Tibbits, ed., *Handbook of Social Gerontology* (Chicago: University of Chicago Press, 1960), especially Chapter 9 by Richard Williams; Clark Tibbits, Wilma Donahue, eds., *Process of Aging* Vol. I (New York: Atherton Press, 1963); E. W. Burgess, ed., *Aging in Western Society* (Chicago: University of Chicago Press, 1962); Peter Townsend, *The Family Life of Old People* (London: Routledge & Kegan Paul, Ltd., 1957); Elaine Cumming and William E. Henry, *Growing Old*, and Arnold Rose in *Old People and their Social World*, Arnold Peterson and Warren Peterson, eds. (Philadelphia: F. A. Davis Co., 1965).

cycle of the role of housewife indicates that there are several phenomena connected with not only the process but also with the societal and self-definitions of its characteristics, stages, and consequences. Such definitions influence social roles in several different ways.

The roles a person performs are affected, of course, by physiological processes experienced in aging, since certain duties are no longer possible or have become modified. The interviewees who were in their latter 60's for example, frequently commented on the fact that they were getting "slower," or that it was taking them longer to do the things they had to do, although the evaluation of this fact ranged from negative, through neutral to even positive.

The societal definition of "symptoms" of aging and classification of a person who has reached a certain chronological age as "old" may have any of the additional consequences upon social roles.

One, it may result in modifications in permitted duties or in rights offered within roles the person is already performing. Fewer demands for help or entertaining may be made on the part of offsprings of a housewife. She may even be forbidden to perform certain actions. Women mentioned that they now were "eating out" a lot, or that husbands wouldn't let them shop alone.

Two, the person may be removed from certain social roles because of the assumption on the part of others, or of the self, that qualifications necessary for satisfactory behavior in those roles are lost. The interviewees frequently referred to retirement, or withdrawal, from active participation in voluntary associations and "community life," due to aging.

Three, the person may be assigned

special social roles due to the societal assumption that the process of aging automatically develops qualities judged necessary for the roles. As many observers have pointed out, the American society has no social role for the aged person, not even a *status role.*[22] It does not have a function to be performed by an aged person. It does not even have a noun which could be the title of such a role, toward which preparatory stages would train the candidate.

Finally, it may make necessary a shift in the concentrations or clusters of social roles, with or without serious modifications of their components.

The aging housewife experiences all forms of changes but the process is gradual and the phenomena connected with it so complex that, until the final stages, its relation to the life cycle is not automatic and the manner in which it affects a particular woman depends upon many factors. A surprising finding was the level of satisfaction expressed by many women in their 50's and 60's who have remained healthy, have husbands still living and no serious problems. Aging frequently provides a rational and virtuous excuse for not expanding roles. Statements by women in this phase of the stage often lack the implication of emptiness and on nonfunctionality of statements made by women in the early phase of circle decrease. Fewer decision-making problems, a lack of pressure from demanding and often conflicting roles, satisfaction with past performance of the role of housewife and with the products of the role of mother, and prior adjustment to the lack of centrality in the lives of children, have

[22] Helena Znaniecki Lopata, "Role and Status."

all contributed to a relatively high degree of satisfaction contained in the interviews with women in this segment of the cycle. For those who are not widows, the focality of the role of wife is increased with the retirement, or "fadeout" from occupational roles on the part of the spouse. The roles of grandmother and of association member continue to provide sources of satisfaction but demand decreasing contribution. Actions are slowed down gradually so that regular self- and house-maintenance activities take more time and attention, and are less frequently seen as things which must be finished in order to clear the ground for something "important."

Widowhood causes a major transformation in the social role of housewife, especially if it occurs after everyone else but the couple have left the household. Being a widow with small children is very different from becoming one in later life, when the removal of the role of wife is likely to be permanent and when it adds to the effects of the prior withering of the social circle of housewife.

## The Minimal Plateau

The final stage in the role of housewife can be delineated as one in which she is the only person for whom the house is regularly maintained, though others still contribute to the performance of the role and enter it as guests or in order to provide services. It lasts until the death of the housewife, or until the time she breaks up *her* household and moves into a residence being "run" by someone else, be it an offspring or a paid administrator. For its duration the woman tends to devote decreasing energies to external affairs and she tends to see and relate to a decreasing number of persons, depending upon size and closeness (both social and geographic) of kin and friends.[23] The society expects of her lessening contributions while it increases her rights. No one seriously expects the "old widow" or "old woman" to be giving a role outside of her home the focal place in her cluster. The process involves some "disengagement" from organized "outside activities" but it basically changes role clusters.[24] The society, and, reflectively, she herself, justifies her existence in terms of itself, and her functionality in terms of self-maintenance. The older she gets, the more pride she can gain from such tasks, and from continued contacts with others. Strain occurs if her expectation of what roles she should

[23] The importance of kin for the older person is indicated in the national and cross-cultural research of Ethel Shanas, in the Cumming and Henry and in the Townsend studies. Marvin Sussman and Eugene Litwak have also contributed to our understanding of the interaction with, and assistance dependencies of, members of a kin.

[24] The theory of disengagement, as developed by the several authors of Growing Old, suffers from a confused use of the concept of social role. Based on the ideal-typical Parsonian separation of roles on the basis of a single dimension, for example, "instrumental-emotional"—a separation that speaks only of the manner of behavior or attitude forming part of the duties or means—they neglect to distinguish between several forms of role-related phenomena. They thus speak of disengagement as involving the following processes as if they were all the same: a decrease in the number of duties that are performed, a change in the manner in which all duties are performed, a change in the manner in which rights are granted and received, shifts in the relation between one role and another performed simultaneously or in sequence by one person, the shifting focus of life from one role to another, the dropping of roles entirely, and the removal of persons with whom the individual is involved in a multiplicity of roles as if his absence eliminated only one role.

perform or what level of performance can be expected of her, does not match that of her social circle which either "restricts" her, or does not grant her "sufficient consideration" rights. The society has not, as the students of aging have pointed out, developed a satisfactory set of sub-roles or standardized variations of regular roles for its older persons. The lack of *status roles* or of other functional assignments for the aging may thus be only part of the problem facing the society and the person. It is possible that more attention ought to be paid by problem solvers to the development of, and training into, satisfactory modifications of ongoing in addition to the creation of new roles for our aged population.

One of the basic problems leading to difficulties in role assignment or modifications is the fact that this stage of life is surrounded, as Goffman has pointed out, by "stigma" of such proportions that younger circle members are often incapable of understanding the needs of a mother, hostess, customer, etc., who obviously looks old.[26] The emphasis upon idiosyncratic characteristics of appearance, and the suspicion of on-coming senility interfere with role relations.

The end result of this process of adjustment of performance is that no social role is expected to form the focus of the role cluster of the very aged. The person is considered as not "having to" or not "needing to" be vitally concerned with any role. The role of wife and mother have already been left behind entirely or significantly. The role of worker and association member are no longer a source of action or identity. The role of

[25] Erving Goffman, Stigma: Notes on the Management of Spoiled Identity (Englewood Cliffs, N.J.: Prentice-Hall, Inc., 1963).

daughter as well as many others are impossible to maintain. Because of concerns with the self, because of the slowness with which tasks are performed, and because of the relative isolation of an old woman from the flow of active adult life, she is often described in terms quite similar to those assigned to teenage girls.[26] The content and the location of the roles each undertakes in her cluster are almost exclusively different. Both women, however, are expected to be concerned mostly with themselves and society assigns neither a focal role nor a focal place in its scheme. The society excuses each if she neglects some aspect of a role and even expects negligence—if such behavior provides the active, often harried adult with a motivation to "keep his shoulder to the wheel." Role-oriented, wheel pushing activity belongs to those who prove virtue by non-negligence and who judge themselves as well as being judged by others on the basis of their performance within specific social roles, of the unique roles they select, or of the unique clusters they make of them.

A right which is often taken away from the aging housewife is that of running her own home or of deciding the duties she should undertake to run it. When this happens she loses one of the important rights by which housewives contrast this role

[26] Although Cumming and Henry draw a comparison between the old person and the child, my interviewees lead me to the comparison of the old woman to the teen-age girl because my population contained only housewives. Those women who were judged able to perform this role, to run a home, at least in a minimally effective manner, by those who would have had the right to remove them from the role, or to encourage or permit them to remove themselves had not disintegrated in their abilities sufficiently to warrant analogies of childlike behavior or attitudes.

to that of working outside, the right to "be my own boss," to "plan my own work."

## Summary

The social role of housewife is, in summary, peaked early in the life cycle of a woman, preceding sufficient anticipatory socialization, training, and identification. She must "be" a housewife before she has shifted her role clusters and herself inside the home through a process of "becoming." Placement of the self in the home as the center of its relations, because of house maintenance functions, is frequently a slow and painful process for the young American woman. Her successful adjustment to such placement may not, however, draw societal approval after the period of time judged normal, especially if it involves additions of "extra children." Some women never move inside. They do not build role clusters around the role of housewife or even assign it an important location. A number of women combine "inside" and "outside," especially after the peak stage, due usually to the influence of friends, neighbors or relatives, and to the outside location of husband and children. Most of the Chicago interviewees, even those who had full-time employment outside of the home, expressed an "inside" identity. Such a placement did not necessarily solve all strains as it involves several roles and is often combined with some external activities. Thus, in all but the last two stages the housewives felt rushed and busy, expecting the next stage to give them "time for themselves." Many expressed the desire to "go out," especially during the peak period, but not in terms of a complete shift in the role cluster.

# 11

## The Executioner:
## His Role and Status
## in Scandinavian Society *

*Finn Hornum*

Although much attention has been given by opponents of capital punishment to the plight of the condemned prisoner,[1] as well as to the moral condition of states imposing the ultimate sanction of death upon those who would violate their major norms,[2] it is remarkable that very little attention has been given to the social role of the executioner.[3] Today, with the abolition of capital punishment having made great headway, especially in the United States,[4] his

is a disappearing occupation. Many questions easily present themselves: What sort of men took these positions, and how did they get them? How were such men perceived by other members of their communities? Was theirs a profitable business?

Considering the unusual quality of the executioner's task, that is, the enforcement of the normative values of the community through means usually perceived as necessary but nonetheless distinctly unpleasant by the general populace, one might expect the incumbent of the role of executioner to be entrapped within an interesting social conflict. For although he is the upholder and enforcer of societal values—and should therefore be seen as a cultural hero—his occupational task is so odious that he is usually seen as the opposite social type, as a villain.[5] It is interesting to note that the status of this public servant appears universally low, not only for the Scandinavian executioners discussed below, but also, seemingly, for English hangmen, French and German guillotiners, Spanish garroters, and

* Reprinted from the *Graduate Sociology Journal of the University of Pennsylvania,* IV (1965), 41–53, by permission of the author and publisher. Footnotes renumbered.

[1] E.g., Edward G. McGehee and William H. Hildebrand, eds., *The Death Penalty: A Literary and Historical Approach* (Boston, D. C. Heath & Company, 1966), pp. 1–49. For a most unusual paper along such lines, see: Antonin J. Obridlik, " 'Gallows Humor' —A Sociological Phenomenon," *The American Journal of Sociology,* XLVII (1942), 709–16.

[2] Cf. McGehee and Hildebrand, *op. cit.,* pp. 52–152.

[3] The major exception to this statement is the excellent paper by Gerald D. Robin, "The Executioner: His Place in English Society," *British Journal of Sociology,* XV (1964), 234–53.

[4] Cf. Hugo Adam Bedau, ed., *The Death Penalty in America* (Garden City, N.Y.: Doubleday Anchor Books, 1964), pp. 13–32.

[5] Cf. Orrin E. Klapp, *Heroes, Villains, and Fools* (Englewood Cliffs, N.J.: Prentice-Hall, Inc., 1962), pp. 27–67. It is interesting to note that the executioner does not fit neatly into either the Hero or Villain social type as outlined by Klapp.

United States electrocuters.[6] Similar status incongruities are probably present in many other occupations wherein the role incumbent performs an important or valuable social role that involves tasks generally labeled "unclean," e.g., the garbage collector, whose role carries with it low status despite its important social functions in the community. Unlike the duties of garbage man, however, the role of the executioner has sometimes involved very special skills not usually found within the general population. Therefore, the executioner's low status poses some especially interesting problems for theories of social stratification arguing that social rewards should be highest for those roles that are important for the maintenance of the social system and also difficult to fill.[7]

EDITOR

---

## Introduction

In 1692, Robert Molesworth, Envoy Extraordinary from William III to the Danish Court, wrote the following account of the conditions in Denmark:[8]

In criminal Matters a great Severity of Justice is practiced. You never hear of any person guilty of the Crime of Treason against the King; the Government has riveted itself so fast upon the Bottom it now stands, that no body offers to wag as much as the Tongue against it. There are no Clippers or Coiners, no Robbers upon the High-way, nor House-breakers; which Conveniency of arbitrary Government, among the Multitude of Mischiefs attending it, I have likewise observed in France. . . . The most usual Capital Crimes are Manslaughter and Stealing. Execution is done upon Offenders by beheading them with a Sword at one Stroke very dexterously. The Headsman, tho' infamous by his Place, so that no body will come into his company, yet is commonly rich, having other advantageous Employments that no body else dares undertake, viz. the emptying all the Necessary Houses, the removing all dead Dogs and Horses out of Houses and Stables, or from before Doors; for no Danish Servant will upon any Terms, set a hand to either of these Works; and the Executioner has his own Rates for these base Offices, which he performs by his under Servant called the Racker [sic].

This brief reference to the role and status of the executioner in Scandinavia is one of the few in English and reflects the scarcity of information relative to this topic of investigation. It is perhaps not strange that scholars have shown little or no interest in the executioner—possibly they share the reluctance of the public toward unveiling a chapter in history which seems best forgotten. The executioner, nevertheless, played a considerable role in the life of the Scandinavian community and it is this role and the accompanying status position we shall examine in the following pages.[9]

---

[6] Cf. Robin "The Executioner," pp. 234–38.

[7] Kingsley Davis and Wilbert E. Moore, "Some Principles of Stratification," *The American Sociological Review*, X (1945), 242–49.

[8] Robert Molesworth, *An Account of Denmark (1692)* (London: Tho. Longman, 1738), pp. 153–54.

[9] For the purposes of this paper, Scandinavia includes Denmark, Norway, and Sweden, three countries characterized by considerable homogeneity of population and culture. At times Iceland and Finland are also included. The differences in culture between Iceland and Finland and the other three countries make comparisons difficult. The author is also unable to read original sources in Icelandic or Finnish.

## The Evolution of
## Capital Punishment

But before examining the role and status of the executioner, it seems useful to provide a brief review of the history of capital punishment in Scandinavia. The prevalence of executioners is of course closely related to the extent of capital punishment and the brief historical sketch should enable us to see the executioner in an appropriate perspective.

Generally, punishment in Scandinavia passed through three consecutive stages. During the first phase the use of the death penalty was a rarity. The second phase was characterized by such an increase in the use of capital (and corporal) punishments that it became the predominant method of penalizing offenders. In the third stage, finally, decrease in the use of the death penalty and eventual abolition was typical.

No definite date can be established for the first use of capital punishment in Scandinavia but it seems to have been a rare event until about 1400.[10] During the 11th and 12th centuries, unwritten (or customary) law established trial by combat, the ordeal and the oath. Criminal defendants proved their innocence by duel with the victim, his relatives, or his champion. Guilt was proven and punishment carried out if the defendant lost. Guilt or innocence could also be determined through the ordeal by fire; or, in some cases, the wrong-doer might clear himself by oath provided certain impartial peers swore that they believed him innocent.[11]

Although these particular procedures were abolished during the thirteenth and fourteenth centuries, the principle of private redress continued. The Jutland Code in Denmark, which remained in effect until 1683, the Gulatings-Law and the Frostatings-Law in Norway, and similar laws in Sweden sought to bring the victim and wrong-doer into agreement. Only in cases where the state was directly interested (such as treason, murder and repeated theft) did it intervene. In some cases vengeance by the victim or his kin was allowed; in others the defendant could buy off the victim, and only in exceptional cases would the offender be punished by a fine going to the king, by loss of his life, or by outlawry. The death penalty was rarely used,[12]

During the fifteenth century this view of punishment began to change. With the development of towns during the late Middle Ages and the accompanying rise in criminality, the good burghers became increasingly concerned with retaliation. At first executions were carried out by the enraged population. From Ribe comes the following story reminiscent of western "lynch-law":[13]

The thief was placed standing on a wagon and this was driven to the tree where the hanging was to take place. The farmers put the rope around the sinner's neck and everyone now had to touch the rope which was then fastened to one of the branches of the tree. The mob withdrew a bit and opened a bombardment of the horses with lumps of earth and stones until these rushed

---

[10] See several places in *Saxo Grammaticus,* trans. Oliver Elton and F. Y. Powell; and N. M. Peterson *Danmarks Historie i Hedenold* (København: J. S. Schubothes, 1855), III, 194–95.

[11] L. B. Orfield, *The Growth of Scandinavian Law* (Philadelphia: University of Pennsylvania Press, 1953), p. 44.

[12] *Ibid.,* pp. 44–45.

[13] Hugo Mathiessen: *Boddel og Galgefugl* (København: Gyldendal-Nordisk Forlag, 1910), p. 3.

frightened away, dragging the cart. The sinner lost his balance and strangled in the rope.

But later the centralization of authority with the growth of the monarchy's power demanded a more dignified manner of execution. A professional executioner was needed to symbolize the power and wrath of the state. The public was now seen as the offended party and retribution and deterrance became the primary aims of punishment. Torture, corporal and capital punishments fitted these requirements to perfection. In the beginning of the sixteenth century, Christian II of Denmark (1513-1523) issued laws that penalized all cases of deliberate homicide with death,[14] and when ecclesiastical jurisdiction was taken over by the state after the Reformation, such crimes as rape, adultery, witchcraft, vagrancy, incest, and concealment of childbirth were included.[15] Christian V's Danish Law of 1683 and Christian V's Norwegian Law of 1688 maintained and expanded the use of the death penalty and a parallel development took place in Sweden. In the seventeenth century the dominant principles of punishment were said to be:

1. *lex talionis* is the highest justice according to the Law of God;
2. the legislator should endeavor to frighten prospective criminals by the most severe penalties; and
3. the legislator shall seek to appease the Deity by the most severe penalties.[61]

It was not until late in the eighteenth century that the philosophy of

punishment began to change. As late as 1734 the Swedish Code, "Sveriges Rikes Lag", carried the death penalty for 68 offenses. The reform ideas of Beccaria, Bentham, and Howard began to make themselves felt in Scandinavia in 1789 when two principles of punishment were enunciated for Denmark and Norway: "punishment as mild as compatible with public safety and the object of punishment should be the redemption of the offender."[17] The last vestiges of torture were abolished. Imprisonment became the predominant form of punishment and capital punishment was the exception.

The nineteenth century saw a further reduction in the use of the death penalty. The Norwegian Penal Code of 1842 made capital punishment possible for treason, intentional homicide and other grave forms of murder but also provided an alternative: penal servitude for life.[18] Torture had already been abolished in the Constitution of 1815.[19] The Danish Penal Code of 1866 has parallel provisions. Criminal statistics show the change. In Denmark, 389 persons were sentenced to death, but only 38 were actually executed from 1841 to 1866, from 1866 to 1892 the figures were 51 and 4.[20] In Norway, 89 received the death sentence from 1846 to 1885, but from 1859 to 1885 only 10 were executed.[21] In Sweden, the figures from 1800 to 1864 show more than 600 ex-

---

[14] Orfield, *Scandinavian Law*, p. 45.
[15] *Ibid.*, p. 46.
[16] Salmonsen, *Salmonsens Konversations Leksikon* (København: Galge, 1917) Vol. III.

[17] Orfield, *op. cit.*, p. 46.
[18] Aschehoug, *Aschehougs Konversasjons Leksikon* (Oslo: Dødsstraff, 1956), Vol V.
[19] Orfield, *op. cit.*, p. 197.
[20] Stener Grundtvig, *Dødsdommene in Danmark, 1866–92* (København: J. Frimodt, 1893), p. vii.
[21] Norges Officielle Statistik, Tredie Raekke no. 70: *Oversigt over de vigtigste Resultater af Norges Kriminal statistik for Aarene 1846–1885*, Aschehoug, Kristiania, 1888, p. 10.

ecuted while there were only 15 such deaths from 1866 to 1910.[22]

Norway abolished capital punishment in 1905 (last execution: 1876)[23], Sweden in 1921 (last execution: 1910)[24] and Denmark in 1930 (last execution: 1892)[25]. The re-introduction of the death penalty for war-criminals and collaborators in Denmark and Norway after World War II has no particular significance for our purposes since the executions took place by shooting performed by a troop of policemen.

## The Executioner

Various terms have been employed to designate the executioner in Scandinavia. The two most frequently applied are "Bødel" (Swedish: "Bödel") and "Skarpretter" (Swedish: "Skarprättare"). "Bødel" comes from the German term "Bodel," "Skarpretter" from the German form "Scharfrichter" and some authors have assumed that there was a distinction made between the two terms. The "Skarpretter," supposedly, was the skilled executioner who performed beheadings with the sword while the "Bødel" handled the more dishonoring executions such as hanging, breaking on the wheel, living burial, etc. In Scandinavia, however, the terms seem to have been used indiscriminately at least at a later time. A more general term was "Mestermanden" (Swedish: "Mästermannen") and he was some-

times referred to by titles indicating his other occupations.[26]

### THE EXECUTIONER'S BACKGROUND

During the early Middle Ages, when capital punishment was an exception, the executioner seems to have been recruited from among the kin of the victim or, without any special qualifications, from the general population.

In the later Middle Ages, however, the executioner was hired from among the gallows-birds themselves. It was quite common to ask the convicted offender, as he was standing on the scaffold ready to receive his punishment, to serve as hangman. Mathiessen cites the following example:[27]

In the year 1470, a poor thief stood at the foot of the gallows in the Swedish town Arboga and was waiting to be hanged. The public attending the spectacle had pity on the sinner and when he, to save his neck, offered to become executioner in the town, it was agreed. He was pardoned and the red-hot iron was used to brand his body with both thief and executioner mark.

This practice was also used with recidivists:[28]

In 1608, an *old* thief from Grönsö, Mickel Matsson was placed before Stockholm's town-hall court. He was asked if he would like to keep his life and become executioner in Uppsala or be hanged on the gallows. He answered that he would take the job as executioner and was led to the scaffold where both his ears were cut off, and was sent on to Uppsala.

[22] G. A. Dalman and G. O. Gunne, *Skarprättaren* (Stockholm: Special-Förlaget, 19466), pp. 42–43. The first figures mentioned are questionable.
[23] Aschehoug, *Konversasjons Leksikon*, Vol. V.
[24] *Evensk Uppslagsbok*, Norden AB (Malmö, Dödsstraff, 1948), Vol. VII.
[25] Orfield, *Scandinavian Law*, p. 47; and Salmonsen, *op. cit.*, Vol. VI.

[26] *Svensk Uppslagsbok*, "Skarprättare," Vol. XXVI; Lars Levander, *Brottsling och Bødel* (Stockholm: Ahlen & Söners, 1933), p. 216. *Kulturhistorisk Leksikon for Nordisk Middelalder*, "Bodel" (København: Rosenkilde og Bagger, 1957), Vol. II.
[27] Mathiessen, *Bøddel og Galgefugl*, p. 63.
[28] Levander, *op. cit.*, pp. 222–23.

It was not until the seventeenth century that this doubtful method of recruitment began to die out. In Sweden, the use of criminals for hangmen was not made illegal until 1699.[29] For several centuries, then, the executioners' backgrounds were identical with those of the criminal they were called upon to punish.

The migration of German executioners to Scandinavia began a new phase in the executioner's history. With the growth of Absolutism in Europe many towns lost their right to appoint their own executioners; the appointment became a royal prerogative and executioner-dynasties grew up. This trend had begun in Germany already at the time of the Reformation and as the dynasties there grew ". . . and the number of younger sons passed the number of vacant positions, an inner pressure forced the members to seek new pastures."[30] Names such as Freimuth, Sell, Reburghk, Höcker, Conrad, Liebeknecht, Bröchner, Mühlhausen, Pflugh, etc. appear in Danish accounts. A new ethnic group replaced the native executioners. These men had been trained by their fathers and possessed considerable skill and experience:[31]

When the old Høcker in Aarhus died after having served the county for 34 years, his son, Hans Henrich Høcker, inherited the territory—and with justice, since he could not only refer to his father's deeds, but also to his own as he was tried in his art and had "shown his skill on many sinners and wrongdoers abroad, in Brandenburg, Poland, Sachsen, and in Silesia and now, last, on June 6 in Viborg, on a woman who was shipped and burned on the back." 21

other delinquents in this country had experienced his skill and no complaint had been launched against him. Such qualifications deserved consideration and he was given monopoly in 1705 within the Høcker territory.

A dynasty was even present in Sweden as late as the 19th century. Carl Gustaf Hafström, who was executioner in Stockholm from 1820 to 1832, was replaced by his son Carl-Ludwig Hafström who served in the same post from 1832 to 1859.[32] During the 19th century, however, the executioner "aristocracy" died out in most places. With the decrease in the number of capital punishments only very few, and at last one, professional executioner was needed in each country.

The Swedish executioners during the 19th century and the beginning of the 20th century have been analyzed fairly intensively and we thus have some evidence about their backgrounds. Sweden's last executioner, Anders Gustaf Dalman (1885 to 1920) came from a family of craftsmen and farmers. His grandfather was a shoemaker and his father a farmer, both solid middle class.[33] The former occupations of the last five executioners in Sweden also show predominant middle class status position. In chronological order they were: ornaments-sculptor, joiner's apprentice, prison guard, poor-farm principal and top-sergeant in the Swedish army.[34] When the position became vacant in 1883, 28 persons applied for the job. The majority of the applicants were soldiers and the remainder came from such occupations as butcher, baker, policeman, copper-smith, etc.[35] By

[29] Svensk Uppslagsbok, Vol. XXVI.
[30] Mathiessen, Bøddel og Galgefugl, p. 126.
[31] Ibid., p. 128.

[32] Dalman, Skarprättaren, p. 44.
[33] Ibid., p. 57.
[34] Ibid., pp. 44, 49, 55, 58.
[35] Ibid., p. 55.

this time, apparently, the executioner-profession had become a respectable middle class position and there was competition for the "good" job.

## THE EXECUTIONER'S TASK

The executioner had several different jobs in the Scandinavian community. Primarily, of course, he was the "arm of the law" and carried out corporal and capital punishments. Secondly, however, there were certain tasks which the community's respectable citizens would not undertake and which therefore were required of the hangman. Thirdly, there were some jobs which the executioner held because he desired to expand his activities and his income.

The occupational roles of the executioner, then, began in Scandinavia in the 14th to 15th centuries. Throughout the latter Middles Ages and into the 17th century, the executioner was a municipal official appointed by and responsible to the town's mayor and council. Christian II ordered that every town should keep an executioner.[36] After the introduction of the Absolute Monarchy he became, in most areas, appointed by the county in the name of the king and his territory increased proportionately.[37] During the 19th century, finally, the executioner became a civil servant whose territory sometimes included the entire country. Anders Gustaf Dalman, for example, served in the beginning of his term only in Stockholm and Västmanland County, but was later given the appointment for Gotland, Kalmar, Gävleborg, Jämtland, Västernorrland and Blekings counties. In addition, he often served in other parts of Sweden.[38]

36 Mathiessen, *Bøddel og Galgefugl,* p. 28.
37 *Ibid.,* pp. 122–23.
38 Dalman, *Skarprättaren,* pp. 61–62.

Throughout the centuries, then, he was a true public servant.

It seems reasonable to expect that such an official position would have attained certain status symbols, such as a uniform. Until the 17th century, however, there is no indication that the executioner wore a special dress. Pardoned criminals were used and they already carried distinguishing marks! Whenever a dress appears to have been reserved for the executioner, it was not used to increase his dignity but rather to mark him with shame and dishonor. With Absolutism, however, an appropriate uniform did come to be used to add dignity to the profession.[39]

The methods of execution used in Scandinavia do not differ from those of other countries in Europe. At the height of the use of capital punishment, the following methods were employed: hanging, beheading, burning, breaking on the wheel, live burial, and drowning. Beheading became the dominant method after hanging was abolished (in Norway 1815, in Sweden 1858). The axe or the sword was used but a guillotine was built in Sweden in the beginning of this century—though only used once, in 1910.[40] Executions took place, until very recently, on the gallows hill outside of town. Public executions were never abolished in Denmark, but in Sweden the last public execution took place in 1862.[41]

A single illustration should suffice to show the method of execution and the barbaric spectacle which took

39 Levander, *Brottsling och Bødel,* p. 227; Dalman, *op. cit.,* p. 14; Mathiessen, *op. cit.,* p. 133.
40 Levander, *op. cit.,* pp. 235–66; Dalman, *op. cit.,* p. 32; Mathiessen, *op. cit.,* pp. 45–46, 50–57; Salmonsen, "*Galge,*" Vol. IX; *Svensk Uppslagsbok,* "Hangning," Vol. XIII; Aschehoug, "Galge," Vol. VII.
41 Dalman, *Skarprättaren,* p. 50.

place in front of large audiences. The following is taken from a contemporary account of the executions of Count Struensee and Count Brandt. Struensee was the benevolent despot who ruled Denmark (and the Danish queen) during the insanity of Christian VIII:[42]

Struensee and Brandt were executed on the 28th of April, 1772. The scaffold was constructed near the East Gate of the town; and they were conducted to the spot in two separate carriages, through an immense concourse of people. They arrived at the place of execution about 11 o'clock. . . . Godschkay, the executioner, was bred a surgeon, and articled to his trade; wore a sword, and was not held infamous; the axes he used were very sharp and heavy; he had two by his side covered in bags. Struensee was really convulsed and therefore could not hold himself still; his face and right arm were of necessity placed in the cavities purposely cut into the block to receive them; the executioner's assistant held the hand by the fingers, and the head by the hair; it was no wonder if the headsman was a little nervous; but the hand was struck off at a blow; the axe was fixed tight in the block; he seized his other and the neck of Struensee being very short, part of his chin was cut off; it is probable he was insensible before the fatal blow was given.

Were the executioners qualified for their job? Beheading, especially with the sword which was used on the kneeling defendant without any block to support the head, was an extremely difficult task. The execution was often bungled, a dangerous matter for the executioner as indicated in the following story:[43]

A woman by the name of Johanne had been sentenced to die because she had been the mistress of her brother-in-law, and she was to be executed with the sword on the plain outside the town. Master Anders Aalborg should perform the beheading. When the poor Johanne should die—he bungled the first blow and merely cut a small ring into the neck so that the woman fell over and gave a pitiful scream; and thereafter he gave her 5 or 6 blows and still could not decapitate her. Then fear took hold of the executioner and he threw the sword of justice away, shouted in mortal fear "Mercy! Mercy!" and fled away. But the furious mob of people . . . set off after him and he was beaten brutally and killed.

Master Aalborg appears to have had a bad arm; but other reports give evidence that such occurrences were far from rare. The German executioners, however, seem to have had sufficient skill.

The executioner was also in charge of corporal punishments, flogging, branding, mutilations, banishment and torture, being the most common sorts.

The Scandinavian townspeople, however, demanded more from the executioner than law enforcement. During the Middle Ages and far into the 17th century, he was charged with the duty of taking care of prisoners. While many towns gradually began to use a town jail, usually located in the cellar of the town hall, certain offenders were put in the executioner's charge and imprisoned in his house. Along with those who were to be put to death, troublemakers, drunks, and violators of the strict sabbath-regulations were sentenced to "Bøddeliet," the executioner's home.[44]

[42] John Brown, *Historic Court Memoirs 2, Courts of Sweden and Denmark* (Paris, Boston: The Grolier Society, 1818), I, 175–77.

[43] Mathiessen, *Bøddel og Galgefugl*, p. 73.

[44] *Ibid.*, pp. 34–36; and Troels-Lund, *Dagligt Liv in Norden* (Gyldendal: København-Kristiania, 1914), II, 130.

Another duty which from the beginning was given to the hangman was the sanitation and night-renovation of the town. This duty involved a number of different activities. All dead animals, horses, cats and dogs, had to be removed from the streets or from people's houses. In this line, the executioner was known as the "Rakker." [45] Another task was the removal of trash and the contents of the privies. This task took place at night, thus the nickname "Natmanden." [46] Related to these activities was the need for elimination of town pests. Troel-Lund reports that swine and wild dogs were the plagues of the towns in the 16th century and "in its need the government transferred the hunt to a new official, the executioner, with the promise that he may keep everything he can catch".[47]

Then there were the kinds of jobs that the executioner took upon himself for financial and/or prestige reasons. These generally grew out of his role as supervisor of the gallows. He was responsible for the upkeep of his tools and was also in charge of disposing of the bodies of convicted criminals and suicides. This enabled him to take advantage of the superstition attached to the gallows, the bodies of criminals and his tools. The finger of the dead, their, or the hand, armbone or teeth of same were re-

puted to have magical curative value as was the gallows-rope, the soil around the gallows, and the little plant, the "galgeurt," usually found on the gallows-hill. One may be sure that the executioner realized this opportunity to increase his income. He became the "shaman" of the town and in the course of time he was even able to set up a virtual pharmacy in his house.[48]

The German executioners who settled in Scandinavia even managed to establish themselves in the medical profession. Dissections were outlawed by the regular physicians; but the executioner had plenty of opportunity to establish himself as an expert anatomist. It is interesting to note that Frederik II, in 1579, gave "Anders Freymuth, executioner in Copenhagen, permission to help anyone who visits him with broken bones in putting them together and to heal old damages." [49] Soon many surgical tasks were in the executioner's hands. The barbers and later the established surgeons objected strenuously but to no avail until the 19th century.[50]

The range of jobs held by the executioner disappeared in more recent times. The dignity with which the German executioners held their jobs increased their social standing and the dishonorable tasks of "Rakker" and "Natmand" were delegated to assistants until separate agencies were set up to handle these matters. In the 19th century the civil service position did not permit such varied activities.

[45] Ibid., pp. 11, 12, 37–38. "Rakker" is used in Scandinavia today to refer to rascals and rabblerousers.
[46] Ibid., pp. 40–41; Levander, Brottsling och Bødel, pp. 233–34; B. J. Hovde, The Scandinavian Countries, 1720–1865 (Ithaca, N.Y.: Cornell University Press, 1948), II, 234. "Natmand" is translated as night-man, but the term seems to have been dropped from usage.
[47] Troels-Lund, Dagligt Liv i Norden, II, 104–6; see also Mathiessen, Bøddel og Galgefugl, pp. 39–40.

[48] Mathiessen, op. cit., pp. 93–102, 105–8.
[49] Ibid., p. 113.
[50] Ibid., pp. 110–21; Levander, Brottsling och Bødel, pp. 234–35; E. Holm, Danmarks-Norges Indre Historie—Enevaelden 1660–1720 (København: G. E. C. Gad, 1907), p. 342.

## THE EXECUTIONER'S INCOME

It is apparent that the executioner had numerous opportunities to establish a sizeable income. The sources agree that this was one of the few attractive circumstances of the profession.

At the time that the executioner was a municipal official his income varied greatly from town to town. In general, however, he was well salaried in comparison with other municipal occupations. "In Elsinore," for example, "the executioner drew 48 Mark for the year 1580 while the two teachers at the Latin School merely received 40 each." [51] In addition, he was almost everywhere free of taxes and the municipality gave him free living-quarters and upkeep. [52]

Extra income at this time came first of all from the executions he carried out. Each particular method of execution or corporal punishment had a fixed rate. Disposal of bodies was similarly rewarded, and increments from the occupations as "Rakker," "Natmand," Swine and Dog Catcher, and Jailer were also quite substantial. Income in goods rather than money came from various sources. The executioner was entitled to keep the clothing of the executed offender. He possessed traditional rights to visit the citizens on such special occasions as Christmas, St. Martin's Day, and at Weddings and demand a contribution from each. He also collected "taxes" from incoming ships and traveling merchants. [53]

With the coming of Absolutism and the executioner's promotion to royal civil servant, the income became somewhat more standardized. In the provinces and in the towns a special tax, "Mestermandspenge," was collected and each municipality gave yearly donations to the executioner. A fixed rate for executions was set for the entire country. For Denmark it was set as follows in 1698: [54]

For a head with a sword to cut .. 10 Dlr.
For a head with an axe to cut ... 8 Dlr.
For a hand or a finger to cut off .. 4 Dlr.
A Head and one Hand to set on the Stock, for each 2, is ...... 4 Dlr.
For One to hang .............. 10 Dlr.
For One of the Gallows to take down .................... 4 Rdl.
For a whole body to set on the Wheel, to bury and set on the Stick .................... 7 Rdl.
For One to break Arms and Legs in Pieces and put on the Stock 14 Rdl.
For a Body to bury in the earth 3 Rdl.
For a dead Body to lead out of Town .................... 2 Rdl.
For One to cut up and put on the Stock .................... 12 Rdl.
For "each pinch" with glowing tongs .................... 2 Rdl.
For a Branding ............... 4 Rdl.
For Flogging ............... 5 Rdl.
For Whipping out of Town ..... 7 Rdl.
For Banishment of Town and County .................... 4 Rdl.
For Burning a Body ........... 10 Rdl.
For Burning "Pasquiller" or similar 3 Rdl.
For putting Name on the Gallows 2 Rdl.

That this formed a substantial part of the executioner's income is apparent from the number of complaints which came forth as the number of executions decreased. [55] The executioner-profession did not lack applicants and incumbents were constantly trying to increase their territory. [56]

[51] Mathiessen, *Bøddel og Galgefugl*, p. 32.
[52] *Ibid.*, p. 34; Levander, *op. cit.*, p. 228; *Kulturhistorisk Leksikon*.
[53] *Ibid.*, pp. 30–42, 50.

[54] *Ibid.*, pp. 123–24 and Levander, *Brottsling och Bødel*, p. 229.
[55] E. Holm, *Danmarks-Norges Indre Historie–Kristian VII* (København: G. E. C. Gad, 1907), VI, 483.
[56] Mathiessen, *Bøddel og Galgefugl*, pp. 129–32; Holm, *Enevaelden*, p. 137.

During the 19th century, the executioner's income possibilities were much more limited. The municipal duties disappeared but his fixed salary grew with time and increase in territory.[57] The salary of the Swedish executioner, Hjort, was 1,376 Rdr. plus 10 Rdr. for each execution and this was a solid income for the time.[58] Dalman earned about 1700 Kr. per year.[59]

From the financial point of view, then, the executioner ranked in a high class throughout his history. To the extent that wealth was a significant status criterion, we might expect the executioner to have high status.

## The Executioner's Power

The executioner's occupational role must have brought a certain amount of power with it. Fear was always connected with his position. He was the enforcer of the law and had monopoly on the executions within his territory, a monopoly which was carefully guarded.[60] The superstition which surrounded his person, moreover, also earned him some respect.[61] But as long as the executioner was an integral part of the community, his power was limited. His power was at its height during the time of the German dynasties. These executioners spoke a foreign language, wore a fancy uniform, were wealthy and appointed by the king. They only appeared before the population in the most frightening manner and kept their distance from the lay-people in the community.[62]

## The Executioner's Social Behavior

A person's reputation is related to his behavior within a normative context. In the 16th or 17th century community, everyone's private life was public. The executioner's social behavior was closely scrutinized by the population. The evidence is not in his favor. In 1651, the magistrate in Køge found it necessary to order the executioner and his subjects to refrain from stealing wood from people's fences.[63] In Falun, Sweden, Master Gudmund was ordered not to cause harm to any of the townspeople and later he was threatened with prison if he did not behave politely.[64] In general, executioners were reputed to be drunks, troublemakers and even criminals,[65] and his house was the gathering place for prostitutes, thieves and troublemakers.[66]

This poor reputation changed with the times. As the executioner became more and more absorbed into the middle class, he no longer found it necessary to find associates among the criminal elements. The county executioners may have been greedy but they were also financially successful. Their social behavior improved. In more recent times, the Swedish executioners appear to have had a fine reputation partly due to their quiet, unassuming, and law-abiding lives.[67]

---

[57] Cf. Dalman, *Skarprättaren*, p. 50.

[58] *Ibid.*, p. 50.

[59] *Ibid.*, p. 63.

[60] Mathiessen, *op. cit.*, p. 30.

[61] Troels-Lund, *Dagligt Liv in Norden*, VI, 38.

[62] Mathiessen, *Bøddel og Galgefugl*, p. 133.

[63] *Ibid.*, p. 29.

[64] Karl-Gustaf Hildebrand, *Falu Stads Historia 1641–1687* (Falun, 1946), pp. 542–43.

[65] Mathiessen, *op. cit.*, pp. 61–76; Georg Hansen, *Saedelighedsforhold* (København: Det Danski Forlag, 1957), p. 101.

[66] Mathiessen, *op. cit.*, p. 68; Levander, *Brottsling och Bødel*, p. 220; Troels-Lund, *Dagligt Liv in Norden*, XII, 165.

[67] Dalman, *Skarprättaren*, pp. 11–12, 22.

## THE EXECUTIONER'S STATUS

In the previous pages we have investigated who the executioner was, what he did, what he earned and how he behaved himself. The conclusions we can draw from these data, and supporting evidence, will constitute the remainder of this inquiry.

We have seen there was a whole range of attitudes toward the roles of the executioner: pity, disgust, fear and respect are each characteristic at different times. How did these feelings manifest themselves in the social life of the community?

During the Middle Ages, the executioner was viewed as a sinner of unmeasurable magnitude. As self-redress disappeared, the sins which had been committed by everyone through the spilling of blood were transferred from the individual citizen to the executioner. His deeds were viewed with pity and the Catholic Church recommended pilgrimage to Rome or Jerusalem as a method by which he could wipe out his guilt.[68]

The Reformation and the increasing secularization of society led to a change in this view. The criminal became "unclean" and "dishonorable" and this was contagious. It touched everyone who came into contact with the wrong-doer, including the executioner. Disgust became the prevailing attitude toward this servant of justice, a feeling which manifested itself in all areas of life. The executioner might have to wear a "shame" suit or be branded to show everyone that he was "different." In effect, the executioner became a social outcast.[69] His House was located outside of town and the surrounding land was avoided by passers-by. In the towns where the house was located inside the gates, the street became infamous and to warn the uninitiated it was named "Bøddelstraede" or even "Helvede."[70] When the hangman wanted to eat or drink in the local tavern or in the town-hall cellar, he had a separate plate and mug, so that no one would become contaminated.[71] In church, his place was isolated from the rest of the community's pews and when he died it was extremely difficult for the magistrate to get someone to carry the coffin.[72] The contamination spread to his family. The executioner's wife found it next to impossible to get a midwife and his children were baptized without godparents to carry them to the font. The executioner's children were also excluded from craft and merchant guilds and in this manner the infamy continued. Only the executioner-profession or something lower, "Rakker" or "Natmand," was open to them.[73] The executioner and his family had become "untouchables."

What were the reasons for this attitude? This has already been indicated in the previous discussion. The executioner was often an "unclean" criminal himself and even if he was not, he certainly kept delinquents and deviates for company. His secondary jobs supported the view. He was doing the jobs, after all, which the good burghers could not get themselves to do. The power that he enjoyed as a municipal official and the wealth he possessed were not in themselves enough to outweigh the

[68] Mathiessen, *Bøddel og Galgefugl,* pp. 6–10.
[69] *Ibid.*, pp. 15–16. See also, Levander, *Brottsling och Bødel,* p. 22.

[70] Mathiessen, *op. cit.,* p. 36.
[71] *Ibid.*, p. 16; see also, Levander, *op. cit.,* p. 218.
[72] Mathiessen, *op. cit.,* p. 19; and Levander, *op. cit.,* p. 219.
[73] Mathiessen, *op. cit.,* pp. 16–17.

odium of his occupation and his behavior.

But the status situation changed. Though there are still reports of prejudices in the local community during the 17th and 18th centuries,[74] they were on the way out. The central government could not allow one of their civil servants such an inferior status and made efforts to stamp out the label of "infamy." [75] They wanted to divorce themselves from the native hangmen and sought admittance to the middle class. This was not easy, but they were largely successful. The fact that the executioners now also divested themselves of menial jobs, and their speculation in such things as medicine increased their reputation as respectable citizens. Wealth, finally, had become a much more important criterion of status with the rise of the middle class. The executioner had the income to "buy friends and influence people." This improvement in status is particularly apparent in the letters written to executioners during this period. They show considerable respect for the profession.[75]

The 19th and 20th centuries see the executioner as a member of the middle class. It is no longer the solid mercantile middle class, however. Whatever the executioner had gained through his wealth during Absolutism, he lost as his wealth decreased. He is still respected but only as a civil servant, a "bureaucrat," and this evaluation lowers his position. Another reason for this decrease in prestige may be the lack of fear which formerly attached to his position. He is becoming anonymous. People no longer enjoy watching executions and in two of these countries they can not. But emotion is still attached to the profession. Dalman mentions a childhood experience of name-calling[78] and tells about the reactions of curiosity and horror he encountered when traveling with his father to an execution.[79] But the nameplate on Dalman's door said clearly: A. G. DALMAN—Skarprättare; indeed a far cry from the earlier outcast position.

[74] *Ibid.*, pp. 18–22.
[75] Holm, *Enevaelden*, pp. 316–17.

[76] Mathiessen, *Bøddel og Galgefugl*, p. 21.
[77] *Ibid.*, p. 134.
[78] Dalman, *Skarprätturen*, pp. 12–14.
[79] *Ibid.*, pp. 21–22.

# 12

## Trust and the Cab Driver * †

*James M. Henslin*

One form of social interaction has largely gone unexamined, that is, the everyday, hurried, unrenewed, and random series of relationships, devoid of usual social constraints, in which most of us daily engage, whether it be with waiters, elevator operators, bellhops, telephone operators, or airline hostesses. A fleeting relationship that has undergone sociological study, however, is that of the cab driver and his fare; [1] even this, however, has been largely the result of some sociologists' practical experience as cab drivers (often working their way through graduate school) rather than with a much needed concern with the more mundane social situation.

The following study is typical in that information was obtained through the technique of *participant observation,* a method whereby the researcher partici-

pates as a member of the group he is observing for study. In this instance, the author drove a cab for the Metro Cab Company (a pseudonymous name) in St. Louis, Missouri, using a hidden tape recorder to gather much of his data. Neither the other drivers, the customers, nor the management knew that he was anything other than a college student working at a part-time job.

Should a criminal wish to rob him or otherwise do him injury, or should a customer wish to misuse him, the cab driver is in an unusually vulnerable position. Therefore, the relationship of trust (an important social variable in all our lives) is an especially salient part of the cab driver's life. It is this relationship that will be examined here.

EDITOR

———◆———

Although trust is a generalized phenomenon in society, *i.e.*, it is found throughout society, and this analyst

assumes that trust is one of the fundamental elements of social interaction, an element without which most interaction as we know it could not exist and without which the world

* Prepared especially for this volume by the author from his: "The Cabdriver: An Interactional Analysis of an Occupational Culture," Unpublished Doctoral dissertation, Washington University, St. Louis, 1967.

† I am indebted to George Psathas for his comments on an earlier version of this paper.

[1] E.g., cf. Fred Davis, "The Cabdriver and His Fare: Facets of a Fleeting Relationship," *The American Journal of Sociology*, XLV (1959), 158–65; and Robert L. Karen, "Some Factors Affecting Tipping Behavior," *Sociology and Social Research*, XLVII (1962), 68–74; George Psathas and James M. Henslin, "Dispatched Orders and the Cab Driver: A Study of Locating Activities," *Social Problems*, XIV (1967), 424–43; and James M. Henslin, "Craps and Magic," *The American Journal of Sociology*, in press.

would be an entirely different place,[2] it has been subjected to very little scientific investigation or analysis,[3]

[2] This is essentially the point made by Isaacs, Alexander, and Haggard (1963), whose definition, with Garfinkel's comes closest to my own, when they state ". . . trust is one of the important determinants of the subjective world" (p. 468) and ". . . trust forms such an important part of the basis of the current social structure that without trust and trustworthiness we could not have our form of society," (p. 462), and that trust "determines the over-all basis for both degree and quality of perceptions of, and orientations to, the world" (p. 461).

[3] The major exceptions are in the field of psychology; and this only recently, primarily in the last decade and a half. The few attempts at studying this phenomenon (either direct studies of or passing references to) include those by Brehn and Lipscher (1959), Deutsch (1954, 1958, 1960, 1962), Evans (1964), Farr (1967), Garfinkel (1963), Harford (1965), Hughes and Hughes (1952), Isaacs, Alexander, and Haggard (1963), Kamm (1960), Kelley and Ring (1961), Lawton (1964), Loomis (1958, 1959), Mullinger (1956), Murdock (1966), O'Donovan (1965), Read (1962), Rekosh and Feigenbaum (1966), Sandler (1966), Secord and Backman (1964), Solomon (1957, 1960), and Wrightsman (1966).

In these studies there is no agreement as to what trust actually is, or of what it consists. Consequently, trust has been conceptualized and defined in the literature in a number of differing ways. These include viewing trust as the willingness to wait for a preferred reward under various circumstances (Lawton 1964); as cooperation (Wrightsman 1966); as the expectation of the occurrence of an event where this expectation leads to behavior which the individual perceives to have positive motivational consequences if the expectation is confirmed, and negative motivational consequences if it is not (Deutsch 1954, 1960, 1962; Solomon 1957; Loomis 1958); as an affective attitude primarily directed outward, involving a sense of comfort, confidence, and reliance that certain acts and behavior will or will not occur (Isaacs, Alexander, and Haggard 1963), as free and confidential communication (Hughes and Hughes 1952), as a feeling—not further defined (Secord and Backman 1964); and as taking for

but has been part of the "taken-for-granted" aspects of "life-in-society." In this paper we shall attempt to explicate what trust means for the cab driver, and, more specifically, what determines whether a cab driver will accept an individual as a passenger.

Erving Goffman in *The Presentation of Self in Everyday Life* [4] has made observation about and developed useful concepts concerning the "front" of performers (the expressive equipment that serves to define the situation for the observer) that can be utilized as a conceptual framework in analyzing how a cab driver determines whether an individual can be trusted to become a passenger or not. Goffman says that there are three standard parts to front: a general aspect, (a) the *setting* (background items which supply scenery and props for the performance, *e.g.*, furniture, décor, and physical layout), and two personal aspects, (b) the *appearance* of the performer (the stimuli that tell the observer the social statuses of the performer, *e.g.*, clothing); and (c) the *manner* of the performer (the stimuli that tell the observer the role that the performer will play on this occasion or how he will play the role, *e.g.*, being meek or haughty). Goffman adds that the audience ordinarily expects a 'fit" or coherence between these standard parts of the front.

Actors are continually offering definitions of themselves to audiences.

granted the constitutive expectancies or the basic rules of the game (Garfinkel 1963).

One can readily see the lack of agreement that currently exists among social scientists on defining the concept of trust. Accordingly, a definition of trust will be developed in this paper, a definition that will of necessity not include all previous uses of the term, but a definition that, we hope, is useful in analyzing certain behaviors of the cab driver.

[4] Goffman (1959), pp. 22–30.

The audience, by "checking the fit" of the parts of the actor, determines whether it will accept or reject the offered definition. *Where an actor has offered a definition of himself and the audience is willing to interact with the actor on the basis of that definition, we are saying trust exists.* Where the audience, on the other hand, does not accept the definition of the actor and is not willing to interact with the actor on the basis of his proffered definition, the situation is characterized by distrust.

Thus trust is conceptualized for our purposes as consisting of:

a. The proffering of a definition of self by an actor;
b. Such that when the audience perceives fit between the parts of the front of the actor;
c. And accepts this definition as valid;
d. The audience is willing, without coercion, to engage in interaction with the actor;
e. The interaction being based on the accepted definition of the actor, and;
f. The continuance of this interaction being dependent on the continued acceptance of this definition, or the substitution of a different definition that is also satisfactory to the audience.

## Trust and Accepting
### Someone as a Passenger

The major definition that actors offer of themselves that cab drivers are concerned with is that of "passenger." An individual, in trying to hire a cab, is in effect saying to the cab driver, "I am (or more accurately, want to be) a passenger," *i.e.*, I will fulfill the role-obligation of a passenger. In the driver's view, the role obligations of "passenger" include having a destination, willingness to go to a destination for an agreed-upon rate, ability and willingness to pay the fare, and not robbing or harming the cab driver. If a cab driver accepts someone as a passenger, *i.e.*, is interacting with him on the basis of this definition, it means, according to our conceptualization of trust, that trust is present. How does the cab driver know whether he can accept someone's definition of himself as a passenger and interact with him on the basis of that definition, *i.e.*, how does he know whether he can trust him? This is the major concern of this paper and in the rest of the paper we shall explicate as specifically as we possibly can exactly what enters into such a decision for the cab driver.

In most situations, cab drivers will accept a potential passenger as a passenger, *i.e.*, will accept an actor's definition of himself as belonging to the category "passenger," and they almost without exception will do so when they are dispatched to an order. However, under some circumstances, especially "flag loads," the cab driver will sometimes not allow the potential passenger to become his passenger, and will refuse to allow him to ride in his cab. How does the cab driver differentiate between those he allows to become his passengers and those he does not? Difficulties that arise in answering this problem are: a given man will be refused as a passenger by one cab driver but be accepted by another, and the same man will be refused by a cab driver under one set of circumstances but be accepted by this same cab driver under another set of circumstances. In other words, the difficulty seems to be that there is nothing constant, in either the passenger or the circumstances that would offer a solution. If this is so, how can we solve the problem?

The solution lies not in looking for constants in the passenger or in the situation that are invariant in leading to trust or distrust, but rather, in taking the view of the audience, the one who is doing the trusting or distrusting, which in this case means to take the driver's perspective, in looking for the way the driver defines the features of the situation or passenger. If we follow this approach, it seems that there are four criteria that serve as the basis for accepting passengers and five for rejecting them. (To better understand what is involved in the criteria for accepting passengers, compare them with the analysis of the criteria for rejecting someone as a passenger.) The potential passenger must meet each of the four criteria successively if he is to be accepted as a passenger, i.e., only if he satisfactorily meets (a) does his meeting (b), (c), or (d) count; he must meet both (a) and (b) for (c) or (d) to count, he must meet (a), (b), and (c) for (d) to count. Cab drivers *will accept* as passengers those who in the driver's view:

a. Desire a destination or service that the driver is both willing and able to provide;
b. Appear as if they are able to provide an exchange for the driver's services that the driver defines as being equal to or more than the service was worth under the circumstances, this exchange not necessarily being monetary;
c. Appear as if they will in fact provide such an exchange; and,
d. Offer to provide an exchange that represents little or no risk to the driver (costs not too high).[5]

[5] The above analysis is essentially in exchange theory terms. For a simplified, schematic presentation of exchange theory, see Secord and Backman (1964), pp. 253 ff. For a more complete analysis see Blau (1964).

Thus, if the driver thinks that the potential passenger meets these criteria, the result will be trust on the part of the driver, i.e., he will view the individual as wanting to "really" be a passenger, and will be willing to interact with him on that basis. This means that, because he has accepted as valid the individual's definition of himself as belonging to the category "passenger," that he will accept him as a passenger and will trust that he will meet a passenger's obligations (i.e., will play the role of a passenger in an acceptable fashion), especially paying his fare, and not robbing or harming the driver. Failure to meet criteria (b) and (c) will lead the driver to distrust the individual and to refuse to allow him to become a passenger. (Failure to meet criterion (a) will lead the driver to refuse the individual but probably not to distrust him.)

If this analysis is valid, we should expect that drivers will not accept as passengers those who, in the driver's view:

a. Want a service or destination that the driver is unwilling or unable to deliver, e.g., a prostitute, or a destination that is too far, or in the wrong part of town for the time of day;
b. Appear to be unable to give what the driver would call a "fair exchange" for the service or trip, this being insufficient money, insufficient sexual attractability, or insufficiency in some other area that the driver would otherwise except as "exchange," e.g., friendship or favors; or
c. Have the "exchange" but are unwilling to part with it, e.g., "Bucket loads";[6] or

[6] A "bucket load" is the cab drivers' term for a passenger who refuses to pay his fare, generally by leaving the cab "to get some money" and never returning or getting out of the cab while it is stopped at a light and "melting into" the crowd.

d. Meet the criteria of (a), (b), and (c), but whose exchange represents too much risk for the driver *e.g.*, "getting caught" concerning a sexual exchange; or

e. Appear not to be wanting to "really" be passengers, *i.e.*, they do not want to be taken to a destination for an exchange but want to get in the cab for a purpose that is unacceptable to the driver. In this latter case would be included those whom the driver thinks might be planning on robbing him or would be more likely to do so, and also those who want to use the cab or the cab driver for personal purposes that are unacceptable to the driver, *e.g.*, the homosexual who wants the driver as his sexual partner.

On what basis does the cab driver decide that a potential passenger satisfactorily meets the positive criteria? Why does he trust that someone's definition of himself as a "real" passenger is legitimate or valid, *i.e.*, if the cab driver is actually utilizing these criteria in determining whether an individual who says he wants to "be a passenger" is acceptable as a passenger, as we are here positing, what underlies this decision on the part of the driver? It is here, in analyzing how the cab driver "validates" a potential passenger's claim to membership in the category "passenger" that Goffman's conceptual tools prove useful.

Because the cab driver's work takes him throughout the city and forces him to interact with people of all social statuses, he is constantly exposed to many different fronts. Because of this exposure, he becomes extremely sensitive to the meaning of front and to any misfit between the parts. This sensitivity is also developed because part of his livelihood depends on it, *e.g.*, being able to "size up" a potential customer and

his ability to pay for the destination he has ordered,[7] and even his life can depend on sensitivity to fit and misfit, *e.g.*, being able to pick up interactional cues by a potential or actual passenger in order to avoid being robbed or murdered, *i.e.*, becoming aware of a misfit between appearance and manner.

The following ordinary example can illustrate how a lack of coherence between the three parts of the front of the potential passenger results in distrust by the cab driver.

I had let off a passenger in the middle of the block in a business district and was writing down information on this fare when a poorly dressed crippled man on crutches walked up to the cab and said:

P: You busy?
D: No.
P: Can you give me a ride?
D: Yeah, where you going?
P: Kingsland and Lotus in Wellston.

[7] The cab driver, like other members of society, isn't always correct in his "sizing up" of potential passengers. He, too, is subject to being taken in by con men, by those who convince their audience that they have the "fit" of a trusted category (cf. Goffman, 1959, footnote p. 18). This can be very costly for the driver, as witness the following:

"A Chicago taxicab driver showed up at police headquarters yesterday with a meter reading $368.05 and a passenger with an empty wallet.

"The driver, Andrew Jones, said he picked up his fare at a Chicago hotel about 6 a.m. Sunday and arrived with him in Washington at 8 a.m. yesterday after spending 26 hours and $14 for gasoline en route.

"He said the passenger, a Washington man whom police declined to identify, told him he had friends in Washington who would cash his check. On arrival, he said, the passenger admitted that this was not so.

"Officers at the Hack Inspectors Bureau were trying to determine whether a crime had been committed, and if so, who had jurisdiction." (*St. Louis Post-Dispatch,* March 22, 1966)

D: Kingsland and Lotus?
P: Yeah.
D: You know what it usually runs?
P: A dollar and a quarter.
D: Yeah, that's about right.

This is a fairly typical conversation except for the question by the driver, "You know what it usually runs?" This is a question that ordinarily would not be asked, but is here being asked because the driver did not trust the man who approached the cab, who was attempting to define himself as a passenger to the driver. The driver distrusts accepting this definition because the expected fit between the parts of the front is lacking. The *setting* in which the cab driver will ordinarily accept someone's definition that he is or wants to become a passenger is when the cab driver is parked at a cab stand waiting for passengers, is dispatched to an order, or is cruising about the streets looking for passengers. In this case, however, the cab driver was sitting in a cab parked in the middle of the block taking care of some personal business, and since this setting was one in which he wouldn't ordinarily expect to be approached by a passenger, he was hesitant to accept the proffered definition. In addition, the *appearance* of the performer did not fit that expected by the driver of a passenger, *i.e.*, the driver ordinarily expects that a passenger will "look like" he can afford to pay for the trip or at least that he has the money to do so, but this passenger looked as if he couldn't afford to ride in a cab. Finally, the expected coherence between *manner* and the proffered definition of the performer as a passenger was lacking, *i.e*, his first question, "You busy?" was acceptable, but his second, "Can you give me a ride?" was not. It was a question, that in conjunction with the setting

and appearance, made the driver think that the performer was perhaps asking for a free ride. In addition, the man did not "look like" he was wanting a cab. He was just walking down the street, and when he saw the cab, he stopped. If he had been standing on the corner attempting to "flag" a cab, the setting would have fit the definition of himself as a passenger and would have "overridden" his appearance, *i.e.*, would have "communicated more" to the driver than his appearance such that the driver would have been willing to accept this man's definition; and his question would then also have fit the rest of his front.

Accordingly, since there was this lack of coherence between setting, appearance, and manner with the definition of himself which he wished the driver to accept, the driver did not trust that this man was a passenger, *i.e.*, could afford to pay for a trip, and he asked, "You know what it usually runs?" in order to find out whether this man intended to and was willing to state that he could afford to pay for the trip. Only when he had received an answer that was satisfactory to the driver, the man giving an amount that both seemed reasonable and that also communicated his intention to pay for the service, did the driver accept this actor's definition of himself and "let him become a passenger" by allowing him to enter the cab and then "treating him as a passenger" by "throwing the meter" and starting to drive toward his destination. Only then was there a trust-relationship developed such that the driver could accept this man as a passenger and take him to his destination.

Thus, when someone defines himself as a passenger, and there is fit between the parts of his front, the cab driver accepts this as evidence that the individual satisfactorily meets the four criteria, and he trusts him enough to let him become a passenger. When, however, in the driver's view, this fit is lacking, he takes this as evidence that the person has not met the criteria, and he refuses to allow him to become a passenger.

Thus, a lack of fit between the parts of the front and the proffered definition of the performer can lead to distrust. In the above case, there was no reason to distrust the man because of the parts of this front *per se.* It was only when these parts of the front did not fit the acceptable definition of the performer that distrust resulted. Thus if this man had continued walking down the street, the driver would have had no reason to distrust him. But when he tried to define himself as a passenger, the lack of fit was such that distrust resulted.

Ordinarily the cab driver accepts as passengers those to whom he has been dispatched. This is because in the vast majority of dispatched orders there is a fit between the parts of the front of the potential passenger, *i.e.,* he is where the dispatcher said he would be, and to the driver he appears to meet the four criteria listed above. This is especially the case when the driver is to pick up a passenger from a middle or upper-class residential area during daylight hours and becomes progressively less so as the time becomes later or the neighborhood becomes more lower-class or more Negro, especially when these last three variables are combined.

From his past experiences the driver assumes that he is safer as the neighborhood becomes better. He seems to assume greater "trackability," and a corresponding greater responsibility or trustworthiness, on the part of the caller for a cab in such neighborhoods. This is especially the case when the passenger emerges from the residence to which the driver has been dispatched. The driver assumes that there is a connection between such a caller and his point of departure, *i.e.,* responsible people whom one can trust to be "good passengers," live in homes like these, and if this caller lives there, he is that kind of person; and if he doesn't live there, he must be "known" by those who do live there since he presumably made the call from the location from which he is now emerging. It is, therefore, unlikely that this individual would be anything other than a "good passenger" because he can be "traced back" to his point of origin and his association with the residence or with the people who live in that residence, *i.e.,* great "trackability" exists here. Those who possess the greatest amount of trackability, and in whom the drivers place the greatest trust, are "regular riders," those who routinely use cabs in their activities and who consequently become "known" to the drivers. (In many of these cases the interaction between cab drivers and regular riders moves into the personal sphere.[8])

[8] The above is true for Metro Cab which does not allow "personals," *i.e.,* a passenger who is allowed to phone the company and ask for "his" driver and the company will dispatch that particular driver to "his" passenger, regardless of spatial rules. Where this is allowed, it is obvious that this is one step closer to "maximum trust." Personals would be more common in smaller towns; but they also exist in St. Louis with some of the smaller cab companies.

A specific type of regular rider is the "charge customer," the passenger who has a charge account with Metro, and, instead of paying cash, he fills out and signs a charge slip. Like many other charge accounts in our society, he is billed monthly by the company.

However, this is not the case when the driver is dispatched to a potential passenger in a neighborhood where, in the driver's view, less responsible types of people live, people who are not as financially established, who do not own their own homes, people whose trackability is less. Thus, in the driver's view, the origin of his passenger is highly important in determining trust. As the neighborhood becomes poorer or "blacker," i.e., the proportion of Negroes increases, the driver views this as an indication of correspondingly less responsibility and trackability on the part of potential passengers. Accordingly, he trusts persons from these origins less, and the likelihood increases that he will reject them as passengers.

The same is true with time of day. The driver feels that daylight provides greater trackability. He is able to "get a better look at" the passenger which would serve for easier identification if it were necessary. In the daylight he is also able to observe much more about his passenger than at night which means that he can become more aware of any discrepancies or lack of fit between the parts of the front of the passenger, especially his appearance and manner. Where these parts of the front become hard to observe in darkness, they are the easier observed during daylight. Thus, in a given lower-class neighborhood, even a lower class Negro neighborhood, the cab driver can "look over good" any potential passenger, whether the passenger has phoned for a cab or is trying to flag down the driver. This means that he is able to observe quickly and well any discrepancies between the parts of his front and, especially in the case of a flag load, determine quickly whether to stop or

not. When it is night the driver is not as easily able to observe such discrepancies, and he becomes progressively with the lateness of the hour less likely to stop for passengers in such areas.

This works out in practice the following way. There are certain neighborhoods in which a driver will always enter, at any time of the night or day, for a dispatched order to a residence. These are the upper and middle class neighborhoods of the city. He is, however, less likely to accept a passenger who is calling from a phone booth in this area because the trackability becomes much less, because the connection between the caller and the residents of that neighborhood becomes more tenuous, i.e., it could be anyone calling from a public phone booth, including, and probably more likely, someone who doesn't "belong there."

There are other neighborhoods which drivers will both enter during the day for a dispatched order and will stop for a flag load, but to which they will go at night only for dispatched orders. It is assumed by the drivers that one can trust people in this neighborhood who call at night from their apartment for a cab, but that one cannot trust anyone flagging a cab here at night. In this type of neighborhood, novice drivers are frequently exhorted by veteran drivers to be very careful that they observe that their passenger is actually coming from the house to which they were dispatched and not from an area by the house, e.g., from between houses or by or on the porch, and if the house has a light on inside, so much the better. (If it doesn't have a light on inside it becomes difficult to tell whether the person is coming from inside the house or not. If a light is on inside, the driver can see the individual emerge from the house when he opens the door.)

Finally, there are other neighborhoods which drivers will enter for a dispatched order during the day, and perhaps reluctantly stop for flag loads during the day, but which they will not enter at night to pick up any passengers, dispatched or otherwise. This is primarily the hard core ghetto of St. Louis. (What demand there is for cabs from this area is serviced primarily by the Negro cab firms of St. Louis. Perhaps this is partially because the inhabitants have learned that Metro and other primarily "white" companies will ordinarily not enter the area at night.)

Along with the variables of time and type of neighborhood in determining the acceptance of one's definition of himself as a passenger is also the variable of sex. A driver, under almost all circumstances, will exhibit greater trust for a female passenger than for a male passenger.[9] The following comment by a driver illustrates this trust of the female:

I was driving down Union and Delmar about two o'clock this morning, and this woman hollered "Taxi." I wouldn't have stopped at that time in the morning, but I saw it was a woman, so I stopped for her. At least I thought it was a woman. And she gets into the cab, and she turns out to be a guy all dressed up like a woman.

Aside from the humor present in this case of deviance, the driver furnishes us with a good illustration of the differential trust cab drivers have of the female. Union and Delmar is on the fringe of the ghetto,

[9] This was evidenced by the incredulity and shock Metro drivers expressed when during the Christmas season of 1964 it was learned that a female passenger had robbed a cab driver.

and drivers would ordinarily stop for flag loads during the day, but would not at this time of night. This driver, however, typically stops for a woman in this area at a time when, according to his own statement, he would not think of stopping for a male who was trying to flag him down.

A variable that is similar to sex that also goes into the determinants of trust is that of age. If a passenger is quite aged, the driver will have greater trust for him. I was unaware of the influence of this variable until the following took place:

About midnight I was dispatched to an apartment building where I picked up two men who appeared to be in their seventies or eighties. As we drove along I started to count the money that was in my pocket. Ordinarily every time I accumulated five dollars over enough to make change for a ten I would put the excess away to make certain that it would be safe in case of robbery. I thought to myself, "I should put this away," but then I thought, "No, these guys aren't going to rob me." It was at this point that I realized that I felt safe from robbery because of their ages.

One does not ordinarily think of a robber as being an old man. These men were not too "spry." They walked with the aid of canes and didn't look as if they were physically able to rob me.[10]

[10] I assume that the health of an individual would be another such variable, that is, if an individual were sick or weak the driver would have fewer reservations about accepting him as a passenger. One's perception of health could of course be erroneous. The individual could be faking his illness or even be forced into robbery, due to needs caused by his illness. He could, of course, also be faking his sex (see quote above), his residence, his social class, and his agedness. But we are here speaking of the driver's perceptions as they relate to trust and the acceptance of a passenger, not the accuracy of his perceptions.

The same applies at the other end of the age continuum: children would be more trusted by drivers than adults. They, too, at least the very young children, are physically incapable of carrying out a robbery or of harming the driver, and, as they became older, until they reach a certain age or size, they could do so only with difficulty.

A variable that operates in a similar fashion is the degree of sobriety of the passenger. This variable does not operate by itself, however. It operates much as a "potentiator." [11] The passenger's degree of sobriety takes on meaning for the driver only in conjunction with other variables. Thus sobriety allows the other variables to retain their meaning, but different levels of intoxication intensify the meaning of the other variables. The level of intoxication that is described as "He is high" makes those who in the driver's view meet the criteria of a passenger even more trusted. They are more likely to increase their tips and/or to be amenable to the driver's suggestions. At the same time, this level of intoxication makes those who do not meet the criteria of a passenger even less trusted. The driver views them, when they have been drinking, as being more likely than ever before to "try something funny." When intoxication is greater than "high," and one could be called "drunk," the driver has less trust of both those who meet the criteria of a good passenger and those who fail to meet the criteria. This is because of a basic unpredictability of a drunk, or as the drivers say, "Ya

don't know what a drunk is gonna do." However, when intoxication is beyond a certain point and the passenger has little control over his actions (is close to being "dead drunk" or "passed out"), trust again increases. These persons become defined by the driver as those who are unable to carry out evil intentions even if they wanted to. The person inebriated to this degree, of course, easily becomes prey for the cab driver.

The secondary location, the destination to which the passenger is going, is another variable determining trust for the cab driver. In the driver's view, the passenger's destination is frequently considered to be part of the passenger himself.[12] Thus, if the driver picks up a passenger in an area that is acceptable and the passenger is going to an area that he distrusts, his distrust of the area can be transferred to the passenger whom he otherwise trusted. That is, if this same passenger were going to a location that the driver trusted, the driver would not give a second thought about this passenger, but if everything else is the same except that the passenger wants to go to an area that the driver doesn't trust, the driver will now begin to wonder about the trustworthiness of his passenger, and will begin to question the correctness of his original deci-

[11] A potentiate or potentiator is a term used by chemists to refer to a substance that makes the action of the other chemicals more powerful or effective or active. It is different from a catalyst because it is consumed in the reaction. I am indebted to Elliot G. Mishler for this analogy.

[12] Since cab drivers have low trust of Negroes, i.e., are reluctant to enter interaction with them on a cab driver-passenger relationship, Negroes, even in good neighborhoods, have a difficult time getting a cab. Godfrey Cambridge writes about this problem in "My Taxi Problem and Ours," *Monocle*, VI No. 1 (Summer, 1964), 48–52, where he corroborates the point above by saying that a reason for this difficulty in New York is that the cab drivers think that the passenger might be wanting to go to Harlem. I am indebted to Marcello Truzzi for bringing this article to my attention.

sion to trust this individual as a passenger. He will wonder why this passenger is going into that area, an area which the driver himself doesn't like to enter.[13] Usually the reason will become apparent, sometimes the driver eliciting the information, either directly or indirectly, and sometimes the passenger, aware of the driver's concerns, volunteering the information. Usual reasons for this discrepancy involve such things as one's place of residence versus one's place of work, e.g., a Negro domestic returning by cab to the ghetto, or continuing relationships with friends and relatives who have been unable to move out of the ghetto, or "slumming," persons who are out for "kicks" that they can't receive in their usual "haunts."

Other ways that the passenger's given destination can communicate distrust to the driver include the driver's perception of the destination as a non-location, i.e., one in which there is no "match" between the location given and a corresponding location in physical reality, e.g., a street address is given, and the driver is aware that that street doesn't run as far as the number indicates. In this case, too, he will seek an explanation for the discrepancy, and many times a plausible explanation exists, e.g., the person has read the number incorrectly. If a plausible explanation is not readily available, or if the individual is one for whom low trust exists, this "fiction" will lead to distrust.

[13] In addition to the ghetto and other lower-class "tough neighborhoods," other areas of the city that will elicit distrust, unless there is an adequate "account" given, are areas of the city that are relatively deserted, especially at night, such as a small back street or dead-end street with few or no lights, or a warehouse or riverfront section of town.

If no specific destination is given, this, too, can lead to distrust. A passenger telling a driver to "just drive around" is suspect unless there is a satisfactory explanation for this unusual type of destination, e.g., a tourist who wants to see various parts of the city, a woman who wants to be driven around the park because it is a beautiful day. Where the explanation is not available, the driver is likely to suspect that the passenger might be setting him up for a robbery.

The secondary location can communicate distrust or questions on the part of the cab driver that must in some way be answered, as above, or it can also communicate trust. A passenger who gives as his destination a "good" part of town, or an area that the driver already trusts, is less likely to be under the driver's suspicion than in the above case. In some instances, the secondary location can even mitigate distrust which has developed for other reasons. For example,

It was about one A.M. I had taken a practical nurse home after her work shift and ended up in part of the ghetto. Since I was next to a stand, I decided to park there. As I was pulling into the space, I saw a man standing at the bus stop which was next to the stand, with his arm held out horizontally and wagging his finger a bit. He was a large Negro male wearing a dark blue overcoat. He opened the back door of the cab, and my first thought was, "Well, here goes! I'm going to be robbed. I'd better turn on the tape recorder and get this on tape!" After he got in the cab, he said, "I want to go to Richmond Heights. You know where Richmond Heights is?"

Although there was originally a high level of distrust of this passenger, when he gave his destination I was much assured. My perception at that time of the Negro community of Richmond Heights was that of a small community of Negroes in the midst of middle class whites, a Negro community that was "solid," composed of Negro professional and working people. His destination was "paired" with him, and I figured that if he was going to where this class of Negro lives, I did not have to worry about being robbed.

There are many variables that affect trust that are not as easily analyzable as the above variables. Many of these are subtle interactional cues that communicate much to the driver but which are difficult to explicate. Such a variable is the "sitting behavior" of the passenger, i.e., how the passenger sits. It is possible for the passenger to sit in such a way that he communicates "evil intention" to the driver, i.e., this part of his manner doesn't fit the rest of his front or his definition of himself as a trustworthy passenger. In the above case, for example,

After I was reassured about this passenger because of his destination, I noticed in the mirror that he was sitting in a slumped-over position in the extreme right-hand side of the back seat. It seemed that he could be sitting this way in order to hide his face from me. I decided to turn around and get a good look at him. I turned around and made some innocuous comment about directions, and as I did so I noticed that he was sleeping. When he heard my question his eyes popped open, and he began to respond. It was then obvious that he was just starting to go to sleep. I was again reassured.

Another type of sitting behavior that lessens a driver's trust of his passenger concerns single passengers. A single passenger will almost invariably sit on the right-hand side of the back seat (the side diagonal from the driver), or, at times, in the front seat opposite the driver. The driver views either of these positions as being appropriate for his passenger. Occasionally, however, a passenger will sit directly behind the driver in the back seat. This ordinarily makes the driver somewhat uncomfortable and somewhat wary of the passenger. He begins to wonder why the passenger is sitting there. Interaction between the driver and passenger is more difficult in this position, and it is more difficult for the cab driver to "keep tabs" on what his passenger is doing. One reason for this sitting behavior that strikes the cab driver is that the passenger might be sitting in such a position in order to cut his visibility (unable to be easily seen through the rear view mirror or when the driver turns around while he is driving) and thus his trackability through indentification. The passenger's sitting behavior is important for the driver because it makes certain activities possible. Thus, in this case, the driver feels uncomfortable because this is one way he could be set up for a robbery. Consequently, he attempts to determine if this is the reason or not, and in so doing he searches for other logical reasons that might explain his passenger's sitting behavior. A reason that is acceptable is that the passenger is trying to view something on the street (e.g., particular buildings, scenery) that can be best viewed from that side of the cab. Another reason that helps explain the behavior, but is less acceptable, is that the passenger climbed into the cab from that side instead of the usual side, frequently the case with flag loads or when the driver has pulled up on the wrong side of the street for a dispatched order. This reason is less acceptable, however, because most passengers when they enter the cab from the "wrong" side slide across the seat to the usual position. The driver must still account for the passenger's failure to move to this position. One such satisfactory account is that the passenger is going on an extremely short trip. Another is that the passenger wishes to minimize the communication opportunities for personal reasons, e.g., he just doesn't feel like talking to anyone.

Very similar to "sitting behavior" would be all the subtle interactional cues which members of society learn and come to associate with "intention" of an actor, cues that give direction for appropriate response, whether these cues communicate happiness, anger, trust, unfamiliarity, distrust, or whatever. Cab drivers, as individuals who have been socialized into both "general" society (i.e., they have learned the applicable general cultural traits such as gestures), and into a particular subculture (i.e., they have learned all the nuances of a particular occupational group's speech, gestures, etc.), possess, along with other members of society, standardized ways of interpreting the interaction in which they are involved or which they witness. This would range from the "look" of somebody, e.g., "sneaky, slitty eyes," to body posture and beyond. Cab drivers, then in stereotypical ways, interpret and react to others on the basis of symbols into which they have been socialized. These include those that apply to trust. It is obvious that there are any number of such cues, gestures, or symbols that lead to trust or distrust. Most of these are beyond the scope of this analysis except to state the obvious, that when those appear to which the driver has the "feeling of distrust attached," he will distrust the bearer of the communi-

cation, the passenger in this case.

An example of something to which the meaning of distrust has become attached is the sound of one's voice. This was the manifest variable leading to distrust in the following case:

Dispatcher: Twenty third and Choteau (( )). . .
Driver: (( ))
Dispatcher: It's fine if you can't. Don't take any chances . . .
Driver: (( ))
Dispatcher: I don't like the order myself. *I don't like the sound of the man's voice* . . .

This order was given at 1:10 a.m., and the dispatcher himself was answering incoming calls. According to his statement, there was something about the caller's voice that made the dispatcher reluctant to dispatch a cab. But what was it about the caller's voice that led to this reaction? It is this type of variable, although it is both interesting and important in determining trust, to which our data unfortunately does not lend itself for analysis.

As the dispatcher has a vital role in the communication process of dispatching drivers to passengers, so the dispatcher can play a crucial role in determining whether a driver will trust a potential passenger to become an actual passenger or not. For example, there are times when the dispatcher alerts the driver to his own distrust of the passenger, as in the above case. The above recorded conversation concluded with:

Dispatcher: No. It is not a Missouri Boiler order! It is not a Missouri Boiler order! It's a terminal railroad man on Twenty third and Choteau, on twenty third street north of Choteau . . .
Driver: (( ))
Dispatcher: Let me know if you get the man or if you do not get him . . .

The driver, who wants and needs the order at this slack period of his shift, tries to tie the order in with the "known and trusted." That is, workers getting off the swing shift at Missouri Boiler sometimes take cabs, and they can be trusted. Perhaps this is such an order. But the dispatcher, showing his impatience with the driver's lack of knowledge that the address he gave is not that of Missouri Boiler, tells him that it is not that kind of order and that the man should be carefully approached if the driver is going to take the order. The dispatcher then does an unusual thing, he makes the dispatched order optional at the discretion of the driver. Ordinarily a dispatched order becomes a "sacred thing" to the driver. It is the opposite of optional. It is a responsibility for which the driver assumes completion and for which he can be fired if he fails to complete. Yet here the dispatcher openly announces that this order is optional. The caller, because of some unrevealed aspect of his voice, is not trusted. In the view of the cab driver and of the dispatcher, the cab driver does not need to accept the responsibility for completing an order when the passenger cannot be trusted.[14]

The dispatcher when he is able, offers assurance to drivers when they do not have enough cues to know whether they can trust a passenger or not. The following illustrates how trust can develop such that the dispatcher is able to assure the driver that he can trust the potential passenger:

Dispatcher: You have to go in the rear to the court to get in there, Driver. We had that last night, so it's alright . . .

_____
[14] It is again, of course, irrelevant whether the passenger can, in fact, be trusted. It is the driver's perception of trust that matters.

The dispatcher is assuring the driver that the order is acceptable, that the people will be waiting, *i.e.*, that it won't be a no-go, and that the people waiting are acceptable as passengers, *i.e.*, although the driver must drive where he is reluctant to go, in the back where it is perhaps dark, that it is all right to do so, that this is not a set-up for a robbery. How can the dispatcher give such assurance? As he states, they had an order out of there the night before, and it turned out to be an acceptable passenger. In this case, the setting, "in the rear of the court at night," did not fit the driver's estimation of acceptability for trusting someone to become a passenger, "in the rear of the court at night," but because the dispatcher has had a previous rewarding experience with this lack of fit he knows that it is all right and is able to so assure the driver.

The passenger whom I had who best incorporates most of the above variables of distrust within a single case and who illustrates a couple of variables which have not been explicated was the following:

About 2:00 A.M. I was dispatched to just within the ghetto, to a hotel which also serves as a house of prostitution. My passenger turned out to be an elderly male Negro, quite drunk, who chose to sit in the front seat. He ordered me to take him to East St. Louis and said, "We're going to a rough neighborhood. Lock your doors. Roll up your windows."

The passenger then began talking to himself. As he did so I thought he was talking to me, and I said, "What did you say?" He looked up and said, "None of your business!" He then continued talking to himself. As we passed the Atlas Hotel in 4200 block of Delmar, he made the comment that he should have stopped there and seen someone, but that since we had already passed it I should go on.

I said, "No, that's all right. I'll take you there," and I drove around the block to the hotel. He got out and was about to leave when I said, "I'll wait for you, but you'll have to pay what's on the meter." He became rather angry, gave me some money, and then urinated against the side of the cab. I drove on without him.

This man was distrusted because he was a stranger, a male, a Negro, at night, had been drinking, was coming from the edge of the ghetto, going to a ghetto area, which area was "unknown" to the driver, and acted irrationally by speaking aloud to himself.

The driver has less trust for someone who acts irrationally just as most members of society would have less trust for someone who exhibited this type of behavior, i.e., because the individual is irrational, predictability of his behavior decreases. And to trust someone means that one can predict his behavior on the basis of acceptance of his identity. This is what cannot be done with someone who is irrational, i.e., who does not act as we have learned that "ordinary" persons will act.

The driver has less trust for an area that he does not "know," i.e., an area in which he lacks previous experience with its "layout" and thus in which he cannot easily maneuver his cab and plan and carry out routes, because "control" in such situations passes from the driver to the passenger who possesses such knowledge. To enter an interaction with someone with greater control over the situation requires trust that the other individual will not use this control to his advantage and your disadvantage, in this case such things as robbery or not paying the fare.

The variables leading to greater or lesser trust on the part of the cab driver, and his corresponding willingness to allow someone to become his passenger are summarized in Table 1.

## Trust by the Passenger of the Cab Driver

Trust, in most interaction situations, is reciprocal, i.e., the actors, to varying degrees, trust their role partners to fulfill their role obligations. We have examined certain variables that lead the cab driver to trust an individual enough to allow him to become his passenger. Although we do not have as much data on the variables determining passengers' trust of cab drivers, we shall attempt to specify the amount of trust passengers exhibit when they enter into the passenger-relationship, when they play the role of a passenger. Not all passengers, of course, exhibit the same degree of trust of cab drivers, but even the actor who enters only with reluctance into such a relationship, who is suspicious of cab drivers, is exhibiting much trust. This type of passenger might distrust the cab driver in many areas, e.g., he might not trust the driver to take the most economical route, might suspect him of gouging him economically if he gets the chance, but at the same time he is trusting certain definitions of the situation to be what the cab driver "says" they are. For example, even a reluctant passenger trusts that the man who is wearing a certain cap and who is driving an automobile with certain insignia and lights actually is a cab driver, one who will take him to a desired destination for a fee. In addition to accepting this definition ("He is a cab driver."), he also exhibits trust that could have far-reaching ramifications for his own life, e.g., he trusts the driving ability of the cab driver, and in becoming a

# TABLE 1. THE VARIABLES WHICH, IN THE CAB DRIVER'S VIEW, LEAD TO GREATER OR LESSER TRUST OF ONE WHO WANTS TO BE (OR HAS BECOME) A PASSENGER

## Characteristics of Location

| Trust | Type of Order | Time | Match with Physical Reality | Social Class | Racial Make-up | Driver's Knowledge of | Illumination and Habitation |
|---|---|---|---|---|---|---|---|
| HI | Dispatched order (caller) / Regular rider or charge customer | Day | Matches (a location) | (a) Upper class (b) Middle class | White | Known to driver | Light, inhabited area |
| LO | Flag load | Night | Doesn't match (a non-location) | Lower class (poverty area) | Negro (ghetto area) | Strange to driver | Dark, deserted area |

## Characteristics of Passenger / Behavior of Passenger

| Trust | Social Class | Sex | Race | Age | Sobriety | Emergent Behavior | Where | How | Rationality of Behavior |
|---|---|---|---|---|---|---|---|---|---|
| HI | (a) Upper class (b) Middle class | Female | White | (a) Very old (b) Very young | (a) Sober (b) "High" (c) Very drunk | Seen to emerge from primary location | (a) In rear, diagonal from driver (b) In front | "Open sitting" | Acts rationally |
| LO | Lower class (poverty) | Male | Negro | Ages between above | (a) Sober (b) "High" (c) Drunk | Not seen to emerge from primary location | In rear, behind driver | Sitting that seems to conceal passenger | Acts irrationally |

## Previous Experience with a Given Variable / Summary of the Variables of this Table

| Trust | Dispatcher | Previous Experience | Summary |
|---|---|---|---|
| HI | (a) Dispatches order without comment (b) Offers assurance | Positive experience: "Known that can be trusted" | Matches any stereotype the driver has of a trusted category |
| LO | Dispatches order with a warning | (a) Negative experience: "Known that cannot be trusted" (b) No experience: "Not known whether can be trusted" | Matches any stereotype the driver has of a distrusted category |

passenger he is actually entrusting his physical safety to this stranger. Trust to this high degree exists on the part of a suspicious or reluctant passenger, one who perhaps would state that you can't trust cab drivers very far, that they'll "take you" if they get the chance.

Most passengers do not exhibit much suspicion of cab drivers and, correspondingly, trust the cab driver with much more than the type of passenger above. For example, women passengers, by becoming passengers, are trusting that the cab driver will not molest them sexually.[15] Actually, female passengers frequently exhibit much more trust than this. They not only trust that the cab driver will not do something negative to them, but that he will do something positive for them. It is common for women, returning home by cab late at night from work, from visiting, or from a bar, to ask the cab driver to wait until they get inside their house or until they get a light turned on. In other words, they have defined the situation such that someone, usually a male, may be wanting to rob or molest them, but that this someone is not going to be the cab driver. Not only will it not be the cab driver who will do such a thing in their estimation, but they even define the cab driver as one who will protect them from such events.

There are many variables that could be utilized in explaining such trust on the part of exploitable passengers; especially important would be the past experiences of each passenger with cab drivers and the passenger's resultant present expecta-

tions of the behavior of cab drivers in such situations. However, another of the most important would be trackability, that is, this cab driver, although he is a stranger to the passenger, is someone who has an identity with others in the community, is someone who ordinarily cannot simply appear from nowhere and then disappear into nothingness, but is a man who is traceable to an organization that is easily found, the cab company. Records of calls are kept, and when a driver is dispatched to an order, it is recorded who was sent to the caller at what time. If something negative happens, the complainant can get in contact with the offender. Another would be the "timing" of events, the close proximity of the temporally separate events of calling for a cab and the arrival of a cab. This proximity "validates" for the passenger both the trust he places in the cab driver and the trackability that he assumes is present.

There is, on the other hand, much less trackability of a driver who picks up a flag load. The company has no record of this transaction to which it can refer in the event of a complaint. But the driver himself is aware of certain trackability in such cases, his lack of anonymity due to the high visibility of the number of his cab which is written both on the inside and outside of his cab. I cannot say from the data I have that trust on the part of passengers is less in the case of a flag load than in the case of a dispatched order. But I can say, from evidence I have, that the driver is more likely to engage in questionable activities in such cases because he is cognizant of his lessened tractability, e.g., "rolling" a drunk or overcharging in some way.

The data also indicates that passengers' trust of cab drivers does not

[15] Actually this same trust is technically exhibited by male passengers also. But since the likelihood of such an event is much more remote, there is less trust involved in the same act.

extend equally to all cab drivers. Many female passengers, for instance, conceptualize "male Negroes" as a social-category-that-cannot-be trusted, even when the male Negro is a cab driver. Thus even though they will trust a cab driver in many ways and with much, this trust extends only or primarily to white cab drivers.

I was parked in the cab line at the Ambassador Hotel one night and was sitting with the next Metro driver who was "ace man." A middle-aged white woman walked slowly past the cab, peering into the cab. She passed the cab, but I thought perhaps she wanted a cab, and I said, "Ya want a cab?" and she said, "Yes. But I want a white driver. Is he white?" I said, "He looks pretty white to me, Lady." She then climbed into the cab saying that she didn't trust Negro cab drivers.

In this case the woman had cab drivers broken down into at least two categories, "white" and "colored," the one to be trusted and to be interacted with on the basis of a passenger-cab driver relationship, and the other to be distrusted and not be interacted with on this basis.

Partially because of the fears expressed above by the white female passenger, Negroes have only recently been permitted to drive at night for Metro. According to one informant Negroes began driving at night in July 1965. At some time prior to this they had been permitted to drive at night, but because of a white woman's complaint that a Negro driver had "bothered a woman" this right was taken away from all Negro drivers.

Passengers' conceptions of Negro drivers as a category-not-to-be-trusted extend also to the perceptions of some Negroes. Thus on one occasion a young Negro male who looked like a college student was trying to flag down a cab in the 5200 block of Delmar. Both a "colored cab" and I stopped for him. He quickly entered my cab, looked relieved when he got in, and said, "I'm scared of those nigger cabs." He did not elaborate on the basis of his fears. The point here is that just as passengers do not form a unidimensional category in cab drivers' perception neither does the cab driver in the passengers' perceptions of the social actors of his world.

Most of the ways in which passengers demonstrate trust of cab drivers, as explicated above, are manifest. There are, however, several latent demonstrations of trust, for example, ways by which passengers communicate information to the driver about themselves and their activities that could be used to their detriment. Passengers, by ordering the cab to come to a particular address, communicate to the driver information about their probable past activities and by taking the cab to another address communicate information about their future or intended activities. Most of the information communicated in this way is innocuous and is of little value to someone who wanted to misuse it. However, frequently such obvious situations as the "openness" to blackmail of a married, respectable male who was picked up at a house of prostitution to more subtle communications such as the cab driver becoming aware, by precautions the passenger takes in locking her house or apartment, that no one else is present and there exists a perfect set-up for burglary.[16]

[16] The cab driver is in an ideal situation to "case" burglary prospects, and I am surprised that I have never come across such a use of information. For example, a middle-aged female passenger whom I was taking to Union Station revealed to me that she was going to Kansas City, that she had pur-

Cab users, like most members of society, have "routines," fairly standardized "timing" of their activities. It is also this "routine" of individual passengers to which the cab driver often gains access and which he could utilize to the disadvantage of the passenger. It is probably true that most "regular riders" are unaware of the extent to which they are communicating such information by the very fact that they are using a cab in a particular way. But their very "unawareness" can be taken as evidence of trust of the cab driver because if they did not trust the cab driver they could use various subterfuges to avoid giving such information, *e.g.*, being picked up at a location other than their home and dropped off at a location other than their destination. This does happen on occasion when passengers do not trust the cab driver and want to minimize their own trackability. The very fact that it is rare is evidence of the fact that the passenger is unaware of the extent of information he is communicating about himself, the use to which it could be put, and to his acceptance or trust of the cab driver. The following instance demonstrates the cab driver's access to such potentially useful information. A woman who owned a Dairy Queen was a "regular rider" of Metro Cabs. She would take a Metro Cab home every morning between 1:30 and 2:00 after she had closed her business. The "regularity" of the call became apparent to me when the same address was given at approximately the same time night

after night. After I had her as a passenger just once I was acquainted with her work schedule, her home address, the time she usually arrived home, the door by which she entered her house, and was fairly certain that she lived alone. It would have been very simple for any driver with this knowledge to either go to this house and burglarize it when she was not there, perhaps even checking at the Dairy Queen to make certain that she was at work, or to be waiting for her inside the house when she returned from work. Missing from this block of information was the certainty that she lived alone. This was only an impression, but it could have been easily verified by waiting in the area of the Dairy Queen at the right time of the morning to make certain that one received that order, and then in conversation picking up the missing information. This information could then, at one's leisure or convenience, be used for one's own purpose.

## Summary and Conclusion

The purpose of this paper has been to examine a very common, ordinary, everyday variable, a fundamental element of social interaction, that of trust. The specific framework that has been utilized in this examination and analysis has been that of the world of the cab driver, the specific setting being that of cab driver-passenger interaction. A conceptualization and definition of trust was formulated. This conceptualization was then examined by asking and answering the basic question, "What leads to trust or distrust for the cab driver such that he will accept or reject an individual as a passenger?" Various variables going into the make-up of trust for the cab driver were then

chased her ticket twelve days ago. She came from an upper middle-class residence (single dwelling), and there was an indication (by the care with which she locked her house and by her taking her dog with her) that the home would be unoccupied for a period of several days. What a "natural" for a burglary!

specified as they had been observed when the author drove a cab. The major variables include the type of order, the time, the characteristics of the location type, the characteristics of the passenger, the behavior of the passenger, and the behavior of the dispatcher. These variables were seen to be correlated with positive or negative experiences which lead to the formation of stereotypes held by the cab driver which, in turn, when examined for "fit" with a proffered definition, lead to trust or distrust. Finally, trust or distrust of the cab driver by the passenger was briefly examined. This was a more cursory examination because the basic point of view in the paper is that of the cab driver, not that of the passenger.

Although this investigation of trust has been within the framework of a specialized setting, that of cab driver-passenger interaction, the reader should have little difficulty relating to this analysis since the reader's world is also composed of situations in which persons are continually offering a definition of themselves to the reader, and the reader must, and does, continually evaluate that definition and react according to his evaluation. To specify components that go into such an evaluatory process has been the goal of this paper. Hopefully, then, the reader should have a clearer perception of his own social world and a more complete understanding of his reactions to others in that world.

## Bibliography

Blau, M., *Exchange and Power in Social Life*. New York: John Wiley & Sons, Inc., 1964.

Brehm, Jack W., and David Lipsher, "Communicator - Communicatee Discrepancy and Perceived Communicator Trustworthiness," *Journal of Personality*, XXVII, No. 3 (1959), 352–61

Deutsch, Morton, "Trust and Cooperation —Some Theoretical Notes." New York: Research Center for Human Relations, New York University, 1954.

——, "Trust and Suspicion," *Journal of Conflict Resolution*, II (1958), 265–79.

——, "Trust, Trustworthiness, and the F Scale," *Journal of Abnormal and Social Psychology*, LXI (1960), 138–40.

——, "Cooperation and Trust: Some Theoretical Notes," in *Nebraska Symposium on Motivation*, ed. M. R. Jones. Lincoln, Neb.: University of Nebraska Press, 1962.

Evans, Gary, "Effect of Unilateral Promise and Values of Rewards upon Cooperation and Trust," *Journal of Abnormal and Social Psychology*, LXIX, No. 5 (1964), 587–90.

Farr, James N., "The Effects of a Disliked Third Person upon the Development of Mutual Trust." Paper read at the American Psychological Association, New York, September, 1957.

Garfinkel, Harold, "A Conception of and Experiments with, 'Trust' as a Condition of Stable Concerted Actions," in *Motivation and Social Interaction: Cognitive Determinants*, ed. O. J. Harvey. New York: The Ronald Press Company, 1963, pp. 187–238.

Goffman, Erving, *The Presentation of Self in Everyday Life*. Garden City, N.Y.: Doubleday Anchor Books, 1959.

Gouldner, Alvin H., and Helen P. Gouldner, *Modern Sociology: An Introduction to the Study of Human Interaction*. New York: Harcourt, Brace & World, Inc., 1963.

Harford, Thomas C., Jr., *Game Strategies and Interpersonal Trust in Schizophrenics and Normals*. Doctoral dissertation, Boston University Graduate School, 1965.

Hughes, E. C., and Helen M. Hughes, *Where People Meet*. New York: The Free Press, 1952.

Isaacs, Kenneth S., James M. Alexander, and Ernest A. Haggard, "Faith, Trust, and Gullibility," *The International Journal of Psycho-Analysis,* XLIV, No. 4 (1963), 461–69.

Kamm, B. A., "Confidentiality in Psychoanalysis," *Samiska,* XIV, Nos. 1–4 (1960), 24–27.

Kelley, Harold H., and Kenneth Ring, "Some Effects of 'Suspicious' versus 'Trusting' Training Schedules," *Journal of Abnormal and Social Psychology,* LXIII (1961), 294–301.

Lawton, Marcia Jean, *Trust as Manifested by Delay of Gratification in a Choice Situation.* Doctoral dissertation, Northwestern University, 1963.

Loomis, James L., *Communication and the Development of Trust.* Doctoral dissertation, New York University, 1958.

——, "Communication, the Development of Trust and Cooperative Behavior," *Human Relations,* XII (1959), 305–15.

Mellinger, G. D., "Interpersonal Trust as a Factor in Communication," *Journal of Abnormal and Social Psychology,* LIII (1959), 304–9.

Murdock, Peter H., *The Development of Contractual Norms in the Interdependent Dyad with Power Differentiation.* Doctoral dissertation, University of North Carolina, 1965.

O'Donovan, Dennis, "Detachment and Trust in Psychotherapy," *Psychotherapy: Theory, Research and Practice,* II, No. 4 (1965), 174–76.

Read, William H., "Upward Communications in Industrial Hierarchies," *Human Relations,* XV (1962), 3–15.

Rekosh, Jerold H., and Kenneth D. Feigenbaum. "The Necessity of Mutual Trust for Cooperative Behavior in a Two-Person Game," *Journal of Social Psychology,* LXIX, No. 1 (1966), 149–54.

Sandler, David, *Investigation of a Scale of Therapeutic Effectiveness: Trust and Suspicion in an Experimentally Induced Situation.* Doctoral dissertation, Duke University, 1965.

Secord, Paul F. and Carl W. Backman, *Social Psychology.* New York: McGraw-Hill Book Company, 1964.

Solomon, Leonard, *The Influence of Some Types of Power Relationships on the Development of Trust.* Doctoral dissertation, New York University, 1957.

——, "The Influence of Some Types of Power Relationships and Game Strategies on the Development of Interpersonal Trust," *Journal of Abnormal and Social Psychology,* LXI (1960), 223–39.

Wrightsman, Lawrence S., "Personality and Attitudinal Correlates of Trusting and Trustworthy Behaviors in a Two-Person Game," *Journal of Personality and Social Psychology,* IV, No. 3 (1966), 328–32.

# PART V

Youth

# Beatlemania—The Adulation and Exuberance of Some Adolescents *

*A. J. W. Taylor*

The entertainment world has periodically seen the rise of unusual figures that set off national crazes that constitute important case studies for students of collective behavior. Whether we examine the cases of Frank Sinatra in the 1940's, Elvis Presley in the 1950's, or the Beatles in the 1960's, the patterns of youthful adoration and excitement have been markedly similar in their expressions. Although some sociologists have credited the rise to national prominence of these persons to their functions as symbolic figures that focused the attention of youth in their rebellions against the adult world's authority and values, other people most notably elements in the popular press—have stated that these incidents reflect serious personality difficulties among the youthful followers.

What do the Beatles do for their fans? What makes a Beatles' enthusiast? How are enthusiasts different from those less enthusiastic? Professor Taylor suggests that the existence of some personality correlates among Beatles' fans would indicate that these entertainers perform psychological functions for their fans other than merely presenting them with a special music.

EDITOR

---

This research was an attempt to unravel some of the complex factors that underlie the Beatle stimulus and the response of "Beatlemania." The data was collected shortly after the visit of the Beatles to New Zealand in 1964, and its analysis was supported by a grant from the Research Committee of Victoria University of Wellington.

Three hundred and forty-six sub-

* This article is a revised and somewhat updated version of the author's earlier article "Beatlemania—A Study in Adolescent Enthusiasm," *The British Journal of Social and Clinical Psychology*, V (1966), 81–88, reprinted here with the permission of the publisher.

jects between the ages of 15 and 20 were given a series of psychological tests in a search for relationships between their personality factors and social background, and their enthusiasm for the Beatles as measured by a test of "Beatlemania." The 50 who were most enthusiastic formed the "high" group, 122 moderately interested formed the "middle" group, and the 50 least interested formed the "low" group or resisters. The groups were then divided further into males and females and their test data were examined. Statistically significant differences were found between the three groups of females on the factors of

"Beatlemania," age, and various factors of personality. Only the factor of "Beatlemania" and one factor of personality were statistically different among the male groups. There was no evidence from the Hysteria Scale of the Minnesota Multiphasic Personality Inventory to support the popular opinion that the enthusiasts were hysterics, and, although there was some evidence of neuroticism on the Maudsley Scale in some of the groups, there was no supporting clinical evidence of neurotic behavior. There were also no significant social differences between the groups. It was concluded that "Beatlemania" is the passing reaction of predominantly young adolescent females to group pressures of such a kind that meet their special emotional needs.

## Introduction

The Beatles are a group of four entertaining musicians who have met with considerable success with audiences in different parts of the world. They had played together in England and Europe for some years before they produced a particular type of universal audience reaction that came to be known as "Beatlemania." The reactions were exhibited primarily by adolescent girls, and they consisted of screaming, hysterical, and involuntary behavior. Similar reactions had been produced by singers and "rock-and-roll" groups in the postwar years but none had been so successful at producing them as had the Beatles. History is, however, replete with examples of involuntary behavior being induced by groups of musicians, dancers, and singers from Dionysius (Winnington-Ingram, 1948) to the various religious and pathological dances of the Middle Ages (Hecker,

1844; Backman, 1952). However, there had been no clinical and sociological studies of such group behavior as "Beatlemania," and an attempt to remedy the matter was made in June 1964 when the Beatles passed through Wellington on a worldwide concert tour.

## Research Method

### 1. THE STIMULUS

The Beatle stimulus seemed to consist of a complex variety of personal, musical, social, and commercial factors. Arrangements were therefore made to obtain direct interviews with the Beatles and to attend their Wellington press conferences, concerts, and public appearances. Letters of authority were also obtained from the Vice-Chancellor of the University, the Commissioner of Police, and the Superintendent of the Traffic Department in order to facilitate movement in restricted areas. The cooperation of the editors of the local papers was also sought in an attempt to prevent any zealous reporter making enquiries that might have disturbed the respondents.

### 2. THE RESPONSE

Alternative methods were prepared for obtaining subjects in case members of the audience were reluctant to take part in this research. Psychological research that is based on "captive" samples of eager Stage I university students, hospital patients, or prisoners avoids the practical problems that are associated with research with less readily available subjects and leads to biased sampling.

## Methods for Obtaining Subjects

1. Ten senior students of psychology were stationed at vantage points in places such as the airport, outside the Beatles' hotel, where crowds could be expected to gather. Other observers attended the concerts in the Town Hall. Each observer was instructed to seek and hand letters of invitation to subjects whose "near-hysterical" behavior could be gauged by involuntary body movements and persistent screaming or roaring and to others who remained apparently calm despite the furore around them. The "enthusiasts" and the "resisters" were given invitations to join separate discussions on the Beatles at convenient times on the nearby university campus during the weekend. The invitation to the enthusiasts was less formally expressed than that to the resisters in an attempt to obtain the collaboration of the respective groups.

2. The following additional method of obtaining subjects was prepared in case of a poor initial response to Method 1 above:

1. An estimate was made of the ages of subjects who could be described as "enthusiasts" or "resisters" from their performances at various vantage points during the Beatles' tour.
2. Plans were then made to approach large groups of people of the same age as the subjects who performed in (1) above in the hope that the groups would contain both "enthusiasts" and "resisters."

Four checks on the legitimacy of the obtained sample were then to be applied. The first check was to depend upon the agitated or tranquil reaction of subjects as they listened to Beatle music from a tape recorder while they entered the test room. The second was to be assessed from the verbal interchange between various groups of those who were enthusiastic, resistant, or moderately interested in the Beatles as the psychological testing proceeded. The third check was to be derived from the scores of the subjects obtained on a new scale of Beatlemania that the author developed. The final check was to be deduced from the eagerness or disdain with which the subjects accepted a photostat copy of the Beatles' autographs as their reward for completing the testing programme. The Test Battery consisted of the following objective psychological tests and questionnaires:

1. I, P.A.T.  16 P.F.  Test
2. "Hysteria" scale of the Minnesota Multiphasic Personality Inventory
3. Eysenck Scale of Neuroticism
4. Social Background Schedule
5. Scale of Beatlemania
(Items 4 and 5 above may be had on request to the author.)

## The Outcome

### 1. The Personal Stimulus

At press conferences and interviews the four Beatles were a friendly, quick-witted group of young men with overgrown hair and marked "Liverpudlian" accents. They wore "sharp" clothes in good taste, and they appeared to be relatively unaffected by their financial success. They seemed to be quite unruffled by the reaction of the crowds and audiences to them and their music and, in fact, they were somewhat disappointed if people did not respond to them excessively. The Beatles knew that other singers and groups had produced excessive reactions among their audiences, but they considered themselves to be the first group to have maintained such a widespread effect. The Beatles felt intuitively that young people needed opportunities and situations in which they could be aroused, and admitted that they only became successful as a group when they began to strike a particular throbbing beat which brought their audiences to screaming and roaring point and they "began to move." They estimated that their audiences consisted of 80% teenage girls and 20% young men in most parts of the world except for the Continent of Europe where the audiences were older and more evenly balanced between the sexes. They suggested that the composition of the audiences on the Continent was a function of greater parental control and the consequent delayed adolescence of the children there than elsewhere.

## 2. The Musical Stimulus

The two-and-a-quarter-hour non-stop programmes had been skillfully arranged so that the audience participation increased as the concerts proceeded. The electric guitars and the drums of two early minor bands throbbed at a changing tempo and volume, and their leaders exhorted the audience to stamp their feet, clap their hands, and to shout. This now classical technique for manipulating groups of people had the effect of lowering levels of individual resistance and of establishing group conformity. A climax was reached when the Beatles appeared for the final half-hour of each performance, and the whole audience became noisy and restless. The din increased to such a pitch that the Beatles could not be heard but were merely seen opening their mouths as they rocked backward and forward. Members of the audience then broke through a massive cordon of policemen around the front of the stage, and there was pandemonium. Order was quickly restored when the Beatles were escorted off the stage by their security guards and the house lights were turned on to expose a noisy, dishevelled audience.

The beat seemed so significant in arousing the stimulus in audiences that its disorganizing effect as reported by Sargent (1957, pp. 92-93), and experimentally demonstrated by Kneutgen on animals (1964) and Salk on humans (1962) requires more experimental investigation than was possible in this study. However, in a preliminary enquiry, McLeod of Victoria University of Wellington found a beat frequency variation of 67 to 200 per minute in the Beatle rhythms with a mean beat frequency of 135.4 and an S.D. of 26.67.

No decibel recordings were taken in New Zealand, but the readings in Australia were reported as fluctuating between 98 and 114 decibels (*Daily Telegraph*, Sydney, 20.6.64), and it is well known that this level is close to that of a jet aircraft taking off.

A passing comment might also be made that the changing proportion of percussion and beat to melody and rhythm in the Beatle music might render Herskovits's distinction between the music of Euro-American and non-literate societies invalid (1948, pp. 435–439, and Reed, 1966).

According to Davis (1965), the Beatles based their music extensively on modal progressions and archaic scales, and arranged their words in phrases of classical rhythms and meter. The Beatles who actually composed the music and lyrics used a less sophisticated analysis when they said that they merely wrote simple tunes for people who constantly fall in and out of love.

### 3. Social Factors

Many subjects commented on the apparent success of the Beatles in breaking social class barriers, and it was interesting that such an observation should have been made in New Zealand where the social class barriers are not so rigidly defined as they are in other countries. The Beatles were admired by adolescents for the ease with which they were able to communicate with different people. The publicity about the response of young people towards the Beatles helped to create international bonds between adolescents, but it also helped to create barriers between different generations in different countries. Adolescents knew that the Beatles would give them an opportunity for conformity in exhibitionism, and adults in authority expressed their resentment and apprehension in advance. In fact, the extensive plans and reinforcements that the police and civic authorities made to control the crowds and the traffic were similar to those that were made for a Royal Tour of New Zealand. The publication of traffic routes, the buttressing of fences at the airport, and a full muster of uniformed personnel, all contributed to the air of expectancy and anxiety.

### 4. Commercial Factors

The daily newspapers began to carry reports of Beatle concerts for nearly two years before they arrived in New Zealand. The Beatles were referred to frequently on the radio, and sundry domestic products were advertised as if under Beatle patronage. Long-playing records were released,

John Lennon's book, *In His Own Write* appeared, and an announcement was made about the first Beatle film. The Beatle image of ubiquity and success in the artistic, literary, and commercial world was well to the fore when the Beatles alighted in Wellington from their aircraft.

### The Response

*Method I*

The ten observers distributed a total of 85 invitations to 38 "enthusiasts" and 47 "resisters" in the audiences and crowds. Only 10 people responded to the invitations by attending appropriate sessions at the university and, because the number of respondents was so small, the additional method for obtaining subjects was adopted.

*Method II*

Enquiries were made at different schools in the Wellington area to discover the approximate ages of those pupils who were most enthusiastic or indifferent about the Beatles. A sample of 336 subjects was then selected of pupils and student teachers which included both the "enthusiasts" and the "resisters," and permission was obtained to administer the same Test Battery that had been prepared for use in Method I. The fact that the subjects were "captive" proved not to be too great a criticism of the present research because the respondents happened to be chiefly younger adolescents for whom school attendance was compulsory. However, the research would have been more complete had it been possible to sample the reactions of older people to the Beatles, and precautions will be taken in future to obtain the addresses and to follow up the tardy respondents.

## ANALYSIS OF DATA

### 1. Psychological tests

All of the four check scales were positive at each of the 10 testing and interview sessions. The following is an indication of the range of responses on the test of Beatlemania:

#### ENTHUSIASTIC BEATLE FANS

*Question 4.* If you could have got up on the stage, what would you have done?

*Answer.* "Touched their hair or clothes"—"Screamed"—"Because it is not often you can scream and get away with it." "I would have tried to touch or hold them until the police dragged me away."

*Question 5.* How did you *feel* about the Beatles?

*Answer.* "I can't describe the feeling very well, except to say that the beat and their personalities moved me so that I had to scream my appreciation. I was very excited." "Teenagers wanted something like this to happen, and here it is." "They made me feel as if I wanted to laugh and cry at the same time." "After singing and clapping with them I felt I knew them."

*Question 6.* How different are they from any other group that you have known?

*Answer.* "They are original and not carbon copies of other groups." "They have a real pounding beat." "Their form of music has its own piquant quality that is almost brilliant in its simplicity. The lyrics of the songs have their own style." "Their singing has a wild, uninhibited sound that no other music has got." "They made me feel wonderful."

*Question 9.* Did you mind standing up to dance or scream in the Town Hall?

*Answer.* "I screamed only between songs and did not approve of people standing up and twisting." "I enjoyed screaming with the rest—I would have minded by myself." "You can forget your troubles and let off steam." "I was stirred up." "I didn't mind screaming—it seemed automatic—I wasn't conscious."

#### BEATLE RESISTERS

*Question 4.* If you could have got up on the stage, what would you have done?

*Answer.* "Cut their hair." "Called for a decent singer." "Couldn't be bothered getting on to the stage."

*Question 5.* How did you *feel* about the Beatles?

*Answer.* "Good luck to them." "Anyone who screamed wanted their heads looked at." "Their singing—if it can be called that—was lousy." "Only interested to see them because such a fuss was made of them."

*Question 6.* How different are they from any other group that you have known?

*Answer.* "They rely on sheer volume of sound—not a fancy effect." "They are followed by girls screaming." "They are a lot worse than any group I have known." "They are so different that it makes them ridiculous."

*Question 9.* Did you mind standing up to dance or scream in the Town Hall?

*Answer.* "I'm not easily carried away by mob hysteria." "Couldn't hear them because of the screaming."

In an attempt to preserve the audience ratio which the Beatles themselves had assessed, the 40 females with the highest scores on the Beatlemania scale and the ten males with the highest scores were regarded as the group of "enthusiasts," and the 50 females with the lowest scores and the ten males with the lowest scores

TABLE 1. FEMALES: RESULTS OF TESTING

| | | | | t scores | | |
|---|---|---|---|---|---|---|
| Variable | High or enthusiastic | Middle | Low or resisters | High to low d.f. 78 | High to middle d.f. 97 | Middle to low d.f. 97 |
| N. | 40 | 59 | 40 | | | |
| Beatlemania | 17.65 | 9.75 | 2.1 | 16.14*** | 8.45*** | 5.10*** |
| Age | 16.3 | 16.12 | 18.3 | 3.006** | .3185 | 3.5*** |
| 16 P.F.:A | 10.375 | 10.15 | 9.125 | 2.267* | .354 | 2.002 |
| B | 7.625 | 8.37 | 7.15 | 1.084 | 1.024 | .928 |
| C | 15.625 | 15.97 | 16.6 | 1.459 | .358 | .938 |
| E | 14.125 | 13.10 | 12.225 | 2.508* | 1.224 | 1.045 |
| F | 18.25 | 16.14 | 13.45 | 6.059*** | 2.489* | 3.492*** |
| G | 11.675 | 11.66 | 11.475 | .285 | .024 | .30 |
| H | 12.325 | 12.20 | 10.25 | 1.844 | .122 | 1.92 |
| I | 12.4 | 13.00 | 12.05 | .977 | .938 | 1.784 |
| L | 9.075 | 8.36 | 8.0 | 1.395 | 1.036 | .48 |
| M | 10.825 | 11.63 | 10.875 | .105 | 1.14 | .953 |
| N | 9.275 | 9.66 | 9.025 | .484 | .711 | .619 |
| O | 12.575 | 11.53 | 10.55 | 2.875** | 1.437 | 1.51 |
| $Q_1$ | 10.275 | 10.29 | 9.5 | 1.337 | .02 | 1.31 |
| $Q_2$ | 9.275 | 9.73 | 10.375 | 1.735 | .642 | 1.123 |
| $Q_3$ | 9.0 | 9.17 | 10.10 | 1.817 | .255 | 1.800 |
| $Q_4$ | 14.5 | 13.32 | 11.025 | 3.739*** | 1.158 | 2.700** |
| Maudsley N | 12.275 | 11.42 | 8.45 | 3.391*** | .751 | 2.616** |
| M.M.P.I. Hy | 21.05 | 20.22 | 19.875 | 1.232 | .877 | .371 |

*** p < .001.    ** p < .01.    * p < .05.

TABLE 2. MALES: RESULTS OF TESTING

| | | | | t scores | | |
|---|---|---|---|---|---|---|
| Variable | High or enthusiastic | Middle | Low or resisters | High to low d.f. 18 | High to middle d.f. 71 | Middle to low d.f. 71 |
| N. | 10 | 63 | 10 | | | |
| Beatlemania | 16.4 | 9.97 | .09 | 9.831*** | 8.371*** | 13.52*** |
| Age | 16.0 | 16.5 | 16.4 | 1.077 | 1.674 | .220 |
| 16 P.F.:A | 7.8 | 8.24 | 8.1 | .212 | .398 | .136 |
| B | 7.5 | 7.72 | 6.7 | .959 | .386 | 1.482 |
| C | 17.9 | 17.31 | 17.1 | .410 | .428 | .137 |
| E | 17.6 | 14.63 | 14.5 | 1.557 | 1.842 | .095 |
| F | 16.8 | 15.59 | 14.2 | 1.207 | .900 | .931 |
| G | 9.8 | 10.75 | 10.2 | .262 | .645 | .854 |
| H | 12.5 | 11.32 | 10.5 | .839 | .821 | .408 |
| I | 10.6 | 9.67 | 8.5 | 1.192 | 1.06 | .724 |
| L | 8.8 | 9.78 | 9.1 | .225 | .893 | .716 |
| M | 11.1 | 10.94 | 10.1 | .569 | .149 | .556 |
| N | 11.1 | 11.04 | 11.7 | .729 | .076 | 1.158 |
| O | 9.6 | 11.53 | 10.7 | .569 | 1.545 | .531 |
| $Q_1$ | 13.3 | 11.77 | 11.1 | 1.882 | 1.839 | .911 |
| $Q_2$ | 9.5 | 10.50 | 12.6 | 1.730 | .988 | 1.341 |
| $Q_0$ | 9.1 | 8.96 | 9.9 | .529 | .129 | .812 |
| $Q_4$ | 12.4 | 13.44 | 11.9 | .249 | .635 | .966 |
| Maudsley N | 6.9 | 10.51 | 5.9 | .449 | 1.698 | 3.487*** |
| M.M.P.I. Hy | 18.7 | 18.28 | 18.6 | .041 | .263 | .220 |

*** p < .001.

were set aside to form the "resisters."

The group of 122 that fell midway on the Beatlemania scale was accepted as a middle or third group for comparative purposes.

The initial data on the groups was as follows:

| | Beatle- mania | Score | Fe- males | Males |
|---|---|---|---|---|
| Enthusiasts | Mn. | 17.4 | 40 | 10 |
| | S.D. | 2.54 | | |
| Middles | Mn. | 9.9 | 59 | 63 |
| | S.D. | .91 | | |
| Resisters | Mn. | 1.86 | 40 | 10 |
| | S.D. | .36 | | |

Comparisons were then made between the scores of the three groups on the remainder of the tests in the manner of A-B, A-C, B-C (Tables 1, 2, and 3), and the following number of statistically significant differences were found between the groups:

| | High to low | High to middle | Middle to low |
|---|---|---|---|
| Females | 8 | 2 | 5 |
| Males | 1 | 1 | 2 |

In more detail:

I. The females of the high or enthusiastic group were significantly higher than those of the low group or resisters on:

1. Beatlemania.
2. 16 P.F. Test, Factor A, cyclothymia.
3. 16 P.F. Test, Factor E, assertiveness.
4. 16 P.F. Test, Factor F, surgency.
5. 16 P.F. Test, Factor O, worrying, anxious.
6. 16 P.F. Test, Factor $Q_4$, tense, excitable.
7. Maudsley Neuroticism, inclined to emotional instability.
8. The enthusiasts were also younger than the resisters.

II. The females of the high or enthusiastic group were significantly higher than those of the middle group on:

1. Beatlemania.
2. 16 P.F. Test, Factor F, surgency.

III. The females of the middle group were significantly higher than those of the low group or resisters on:

1. Beatlemania.
2. 16 P.F. Test, Factor F, surgency.
3. 16 P.F. Test, Factor $Q_4$, tense, excitable.
4. Maudsley Neuroticism, inclined to emotional instability.
5. The middles were also younger than the resisters.

IV. The males of the high or enthusiastic group were significantly higher than those of the low group or resisters on:

1. Beatlemania.

V. The males of the high or enthusiastic group were significantly higher than those of the middle group on:

1. Beatlemania.

VI. The males of the middle group were significantly higher than those of the low group or resisters on:

1. Beatlemania.
2. Maudsley Neuroticism, inclined to emotional instability.

## Social background schedules

The majority of the subjects in all groups were living at home, and only five indicated that they had been in trouble with the police (Table 3).

TABLE 3. SOCIAL HISTORY DATA

| | | In trouble with the police | Living away from home |
|---|---|---|---|
| Females: | High | 1 | 7 |
| N = 139 | Middle | 1 | 13 |
| | Low | — | 18 |
| Males: | High | 1 | 1 |
| N = 83 | Middle | 2 | 7 |
| | Low | — | — |

## Conclusions

People may be stirred to heights of enthusiasm and excess if they are intellectually or emotionally involved in groups. Their involvement may be encouraged on an intellectual plane if they can be persuaded to adopt a unifying theme or cause, and it may be induced on an emotional plane if they are given opportunities for satisfying basic needs. Individual reserve and resistance can be reduced by leaders who encourage audiences to participate actively in group proceedings until such time as the subjective experience of group conformity becomes sufficient to ensure group cohesion. However, the rate of personal involvement in a group may be a function of individual differences of group members as well as a function of group pressures and manipulative techniques to which they may be subjected. From the objective psychological test data presented in this research, it seems clear that those females who conformed to the considerable direct and indirect group pressures of the Beatles were neither hysterics in the strict clinical sense (Mayer-Gross *et al.*, 1960, pp. 131-146) nor in the psychometric sense. Rather, the personality pattern of the keen Beatle girls was such that they were younger, more gregarious, assertive, active, worrying, excitable, and inclined towards emotional instability than both the "moderates" and the "resisters." There were no similar differences between the male groups, except that the middle group of males was more inclined towards emotional instability than either of the others. There was no evidence to suggest that the keen Beatle fans of either sex were antisocial and living away from parental control.

Perhaps the girls were attracted by the masculine image of the Beatles, and a corresponding group of female musicians would have changed the responses of the boys. However, the fact that the older adolescent girls were relatively unresponsive to the Beatle stimulus encourages one to think that the enthusiasts themselves may grow through their stage of immaturity and flagrant conformity to group pressures. The findings reported in this research were in line with the clinical findings of Ausubel (1954, p. 50, ⅞) that girls consistently show more emotional instability than boys and, reassuringly, that the instability is mostly a transitory reaction of each generation to various developmental strains. Furthermore, each generation seems to need its own musical stimulus for group identity and emotional release. The musical styles have already shifted from "the beat" to sounds of Tijuana Brass, sitar type and psychedelic mood music, and the future must be of perpetual change if it is to satisfy adolescents.

## References

Ausubel, D., *Theory and Problems of Adolescent Development.* New York: Grune & Stratton, Inc., 1954.

Backman, E. L., *Religious Dances in the Christian Church and Popular Medicine.* London: George Allen & Unwin, 1952.

Davis, E., "Psychological Characteristics of Beatlemania: The Beatle Phenomenon." Unpublished paper, University of New South Wales, Australia, 1965.

Hecker, J. F. C., *The Epidemics of the Middle Ages,* trans. B. G. Babbington. London: George Woodfall and Son, 1844.

Herskovits, M. J., *Man and His Works: The Science of Cultural Anthropology.* New York: Alfred A. Knopf, Inc., 1948.

Kneutgen, V. J., "Beobachtungen über die Anpassung von Verhaltensweisen an gleichförmige akustische Reize," *Zeitschrift fur Tierpsychologie*, XXI, No. 6 (1964), 763–79.

Mayer-Gross, W., E. Slater and M. Roth, *Clinical Psychiatry* (2nd ed.). London: Cassell & Company, Ltd., 1960.

Reed, G. F., "The Psychology of Jazz,"

*Bull. Brit. Psych. Soc.*, XIX, No. 63 (1966), 58-59.

Salk, L., "Mothers' Heartbeat as an Imprinting Stimulus," *Trans. N.Y. Acad. Sciences*, XI, No. 24 (1962), 753–63.

Sargant, W., *Battle for the Mind*. London: Pan Books Ltd., 1957.

Winnington-Ingram, R. P., *Euripides and Dionysius*. Cambridge: Cambridge University Press, 1948.

# 14

## Teen-agers, Satire, and *Mad* [*]

*Charles Winick*

Much has been said about national character through analysis of a country's humor. Yet despite the everyday importance of humor, especially as a mechanism of social control, relatively little attention has been given it by sociologists.[1]

Even a cursory examination of foreign humor periodicals (e.g., the Soviet Union's *Krokodil*, or England's *Punch*) shows a vast number of differences with regard to what is perceived as funny or laughable in these countries. Although little has been done in the way of comparative study, the following article attempts an analysis of the appeals and satirical targets of the leading humor periodical in the United States, *Mad* magazine.[2] A great many humor magazines have been unsuccessfully launched into the American mass market in the last twenty years, including such titles as *Trump*, an attempt at major invasion of the humor field by the fantastically successful *Playboy* magazine; *Bounty*, an attempt at reproducing the more intellectual style of *Punch* for an American audience; plus a host of imitators of *Mad*, some of which have even been repro-

[*] Reprinted from *Merrill-Palmer Quarterly of Behavior and Development*, VIII (1962), 183–203, by permission of the author and publisher. Footnotes renumbered.

[1] Some of the more notable studies include: Milton J. Barron, "A Content Analysis of Intergroup Humor," *American Sociological Review*, XV (1950), 88–94; J. H. Burma, "Humor as a Technique in Race Conflicts," *American Sociological Review*, XI (1946), 710–15; Jacqueline D. Goodchilds, "Effects of Being Witty on Position in the Social Structure of a Small Group," *Sociometry*, XXII (1959), 261–72; Orrin Klapp, "The Fool as a Social Type," *The American Journal of Sociology*, LV (1949), 157–62; R. Middleton and J. Moland, "Humor in Negro and White Subcultures: A Study of Jokes Among University Students," *American Sociological Review*, XXIV (1959), 61–69; Richard M. Stephenson, "Conflict and Control Functions of Humor," *The American Journal of Sociology*, LVI (1951), 569–74; and Charles Winick, "Space Jokes as Indications of Attitudes Toward Space," *Journal of Social Issues*, XXVII (1961), 43–49.

[2] Cf. B. R. Manago, "*Mad:* Out of the Comic Rack and into Satire," *Add One*, I (1962), 41–46.

duced in three-dimensional art work (to to viewed through special glasses accompanying the magazine). The often more elaborate trappings of competitors, notwithstanding, however, few of these products have been able to stay on the scene very long—the one great exception is *1000 Jokes Magazine,* which has been in existence much longer than *Mad,* but whose sales are a great deal smaller; but several of the imitators of *Mad* are still reasonably successful. What accounts for *Mad's* success? Who reads it? And what does it do for its readers? Professor Winick suggests some interesting answers. EDITOR

———◆———

This is a report on some aspects of American teen-agers' perception of their world via a content analysis and some interviews with regular readers of the satirical magazine *Mad.*

Goethe once observed that nothing shows a person's character more than the things at which he laughs. This thought has recently been translated into psychiatry by measures of personality, based on a patient's ability to respond to humor (Redlich, Levine & Sohler, 1951) and on his favorite joke (Zwerling, 1955). How people respond to satire should be a revealing clue to their character, because satire is the form of humor most concerned with comment on the norms of a society. Jonathan Swift's epitaph on his Dublin grave, "Where savage indignation can no longer tear his heart," suggests the nature of the satirist's work expressing savage indignation, usually stemming from a firm sense of morality. There have been times in a literature—as in the age of Pope—when satire was the dominant literary form. Some satirists, like Lord Byron, have become international celebrities as a result of their wit.

Although satire has often flourished in America since James Russell Lowell first acclimated it, the writers and artists of today do not seem to respond with satire; in contrast to the tradition of Americans like Mark Twain, Thorstein Veblen, Kin Hubbard, E. W. Howe, Robert Frost, and Sinclair Lewis.

Television performers have generally addressed their satire to peripheral themes, rather than to the central social concerns of our times. It is possible that sponsors have feared that claims made for their products would suffer if linked with the derision of satire. Another contributor to the decline in satire seems to be a decrease in the incidence of "wisecracks," an almost indigenous form of satire. Satirical movies are seldom made, or are usually unsuccessful commercially even when successful artistically.[3] The character actors who provided humor and satire in movies have almost completely disappeared.

Although satirical magazines for adults flourish in other countries, the United States has no such magazines.[4] Today the only satire magazine published in this country which has any considerable circulation is *Mad,* a magazine in comics format, which is geared toward adolescents.

Why adult satire has not been suc-

[3] For example, *Beat the Devil* (1954), or Preston Sturges's films.

[4] Writers like Anatole France, G. K. Chesterton, Oscar Wilde, G. B. Shaw, and A. P. Herbert have contributed to European satire magazines. They include France's *Bizarre* and *Le Canard Enchaîné,* England's *Punch,* Germany's *Simplicissimus,* Italy's *Candido, Travaso* and *Marc Aurelio,* and the Soviet Union's *Krokodil.*

cessful in the last several decades can only be a subject for speculation. The areas of national life in which ridicule is acceptable have diminished steadily. The preoccupation with un-Americanism, and, thus, with Americanism, can only be seen in perspective if we consider how we might feel if we heard of "Englishism" and "unEnglishism" and "Frenchism" and "unFrenchism." James Thurber, who began as a satirist and spent his last years as a moralist, commented that it is almost as if patriotism were a monopoly by Americans (Thurber, 1958). Such a climate is not one that fosters satire. Another possible reason is that satire is like a soufflé. It must be done well; and there is no audience for an average performance.

Other reasons for the decline in American satire may reflect larger cultural trends. The American audience for even better-than-average satire may be smaller than the European audience, because Americans read less than Europeans. Even in the theater, American audiences do not go to satire, unless it is set to music, in contrast to European audiences, who enjoy the work of satirical dramatists. It is, therefore, less surprising that the only viable format for American satire is *Mad,* which is in comic-book format.

Satirical magazines other than *Mad* have only limited circulation.[5] There are many college satire magazines;

---

[5] Among the satirical magazines published recently, *Cracked* and *Sick* are imitators of *Mad; Caterpillar* published only a "preview" issue; *Ad Lib, Trump,* and *Bounty* collapsed after one, two, and three issues, respectively; considerable time has elapsed since *Ape* and *Babel* published their first issue; the future of *Monocle* is uncertain; and *For Laughing Out Loud, 1,000 Jokes,* and *Help,* which are published regularly, can be classified as satire only with difficulty. *The Realist* is more a free-thought publication than a satirical magazine.

but few enjoy much extramural circulation. Many imitate *Mad,* while disdaining it. The *New Yorker* used to be a satirical magazine; but only a diminishing proportion of its content is satirical or even humorous. Perhaps the only format in which American satire has continued to appear over the decades is the editorial page political cartoons (e.g., Herblock). Some satirical cartoonists (e.g., Jules Feiffer, Saul Steinberg) have achieved commercial success.

The absence of a national, adult satirical magazine, at a relatively prosperous time like the present, is puzzling, because such magazines seem to flourish with prosperity. *Puck,* which established the traditional text and cartoon format of so many other satire magazines, was most successful during the Gilded Age. The satirical magazine *Life,* at its peak in the 1920s, had a circulation of 250,000 (Peterson, 1956). *Life* was a major vehicle for satirists, and ran articles on subjects like Anthony Comstock, trusts, and Christian Science. *Judge* also reached its top circulation of 250,000 in the 1920s. In the same decade, *Vanity Fair's* famous satirical "We Nominate For Oblivion" department was widely influential. One *Vanity Fair* cartoon, at the time of Japan's attack on Manchuria, showed the Japanese emperor pulling a rickshaw containing the Nobel Peace Prize. It was headed "Unlikely Happenings." The cartoon elicited a formal protest from the Japanese government. The *American Mercury,* which was a magazine of irreverence as well as of satire, reached a peak circulation of 77,000 copies in 1927, under H. L. Mencken's editorship. It is possible that satire could flourish in the 1920s because of the widespread awareness of institutions like "speakeasies" and "gangsterism" which so conspicuously flaunted current morality.

In that same period, *Ballyhoo* gleamed more brightly than any previous American satirical magazine. By the time of its sixth issue in 1931, *Ballyhoo* had reached a circulation of two million. It was read by adults and developed an array of rings, ties, and other objects sold by the magazine. The magazine inspired a successful Broadway show "Ballyhoo Revue." A number of advertisers paid to be satirized in the magazine. Thus, one manufacturer paid to have his radio identified as the one which gave you "all the crap in the world at your finger tips." *Ballyhoo* made a household word of "Elmer Zilch," a silly-looking man whose picture it displayed prominently. All the editors on the masthead were called Zilch. The creator of *Ballyhoo* could not account for its success (Anthony, 1946). Its success is probably attributable to a combination of a shock reaction to the depression, the public's reaction against advertising as the most visible symbol of our economy, and to the psychological spark of its "slapstick" approach.

## *Mad*

*Mad* has some characteristics of *Ballyhoo*. Advertising and other media are among its major targets. It has a masthead on which "Fumigator," "Bouncer," and "Law Suits" are among the staff titles listed. It sells special identifying materials. It has a character somewhat like Elmer Zilch in "Alfred E. Neuman," who is a foolish-looking boy often shown in the magazine. He usually appears with the caption, "What—Me Worry?" He is always grinning, has tousled hair and a missing tooth. The face

was originally used in an advertising slide at the turn of the century and adopted by *Mad* several years ago. His name was given him by a member of the magazine staff. Neuman has become a symbol of the magazine, just as Zilch became associated with *Ballyhoo*. The name "Melvin" appears occasionally, as does an avocado plant called "Arthur," and a child in a cart. The nonsense word "potrzebie" appears from time to time in the magazine. On one recent cover, Alfred E. Neuman's girl friend, "Moxie," who looks much like him, is dressed as a drum majorette. She is beating a drum on which there is a picture of Neuman with a black eye. The drum belongs to Potrzebie High School, the Latin motto of which is "Quid, me vexari?" (i.e., "What—me worry?").

*Mad* started in 1952 as a comic book which lampooned other comics (e.g., *Superman*) and sold at the regular comic price of ten cents. It changed its format and raised its price to twenty-five cents in 1955. Its format of the extended comic magazine story differs from the text emphasis of earlier satire magazines, although its vocabulary level is fairly high. An average story has perhaps ten panels covering three pages, and an average issue has 17 stories. Some authors are well-known comedians like Steve Allen and Orson Bean. Its circulation has increased steadily and in 1960 reached 1,400,000, of which 97 percent are sold on newsstands. The magazine receives over 1,500 fan letters a week. Surveys have indicated that the bulk of the readership is probably concentrated among high school students, although there is some readership in colleges and among adults (Gehman, 1960). Fifteen *Mad* anthologies have been published success-

[6] December, 1959.

fully. There are few areas of the country in which it does not enjoy some popularity, although it is most popular in urban areas. *Mad's* stemming from comic books was probably responsible for its initially having more boy than girl readers, but both sexes are now equally represented among its readers. *Mad's* ability to institutionalize satire and to develop an audience seemed to provide a clear-cut opportunity to study some parameters of satire's appeal to teen-agers.

## CONTENT ANALYSIS

A content analysis of the magazine was conducted in order to determine the relative incidence of various kinds of subject matter. All eight issues published during 1959 were examined and each story was placed into one of eleven subject categories, which had been established on the basis of preliminary analysis of previous issues. Table 1 gives the incidence of each theme.

TABLE 1. CONTENT ANALYSIS OF ISSUES PUBLISHED IN 1959

| Theme | *Proportion of total percentage* |
|---|---|
| U.S. leisure time activity, other than media | 21 |
| Advertising | 19 |
| Magazines, newspapers, and radio | 18 |
| Television | 10 |
| Biographies of noted persons | 10 |
| Movies | 6 |
| Transportation | 5 |
| Politics and international relations | 4 |
| Business customs | 3 |
| Special groups in the population | 2 |
| Education | 2 |
| Total | 100 |

Each of the categories shown in Table 1 represents a satirical treatment of a subject; laughing at it by using its established vocabulary or trappings. Although satire includes both the understatement of *irony* and the exaggeration of *parody,* there is less irony than parody in *Mad.* However, much of *Mad* is in the form of parody, since it treats the same subject as the original but burlesques its style. Thus, the category "Advertising" would include what appear to be real advertisements. Readers who know the original can easily recognize that the manner of presentation of the advertisement is satirical.

For example, one story classified as advertising was called "The Hip Persuaders," and presented "hip" versions of ten, very familiar, advertising campaigns, each one treated in one panel.[7] One such advertisement showed a man wearing earphones with antennae coming out of his spectacles and about to put a wicked-looking pizza pie into his shining teeth. The headline read, "He lays on only *GLEEM,* the choppergrease for cats who can't sand after every scoff." The reader can respond to this on three levels. He can recognize the well-known advertisement which recommends a toothpaste for people who can't brush after every meal. He can also identify "hip" people who are in touch with the secret language of a deviant subculture. He can also comprehend the translation of the advertising slogan into "hip" language.

Another popular format for a *Mad* story is like Fielding's approach in *Jonathan Wild,* in which the actions of a highway man are described in mock admiration, in the language usually bestowed on statesmen; and the satire consists in the linking of disparates.

[7] April, 1959, pp. 20–22.

An example of such high satire is "The National Safety Council's Holiday Weekend Telethon," in which a telethon is the theme.[8] An announcer urges people to go out and get themselves killed in a highway accident, so that the Safety Council's quota for the holiday weekend will be met. Drivers are told that the program will pay their toll if they crash into another car while on a toll bridge. Children are told that they can contribute to the total even if they have no automobile by going out and playing on a highway after dark, when it will be easier for them to be hit. Similar appeals are used throughout the rest of the story (i.e., "The family that drives together—dies together." As in *Jonathan Wild*, the mood is sustained; viewers of the telethon are urged not to tie up the lines by telephoning nonfatal accidents, because only fatal accidents can be used. As the story progresses, the number of deaths listed on the scoreboard mounts.

Over half of *Mad's* contents are concerned with leisure and adult mass media. The central role of media in socializing adolescents makes this major theme of *Mad* of special interest. The leisure and media activities and problems of adolescents, however, receive little coverage. Other adolescent problems are either not treated or treated without much gusto. Thus, the teen-age reader can enjoy his spectatorial role as he reads about how sick and silly is the rest of society. One possible reason for the relative absence of satirical material of direct interest to adolescents is that adolescents may have difficulties in perceiving comic elements in situations in which they are involved.

[8] January, 1959, pp. 11–13.

The teen-ager can laugh at those younger than himself, as well as those who are older. One article on magazines for younger children, for example, featured a magazine called "Pedal Trend, The Tricycle Owner's Magazine," with articles on customizing tricycles, the *Grand Prix de Disneyland*, and similar subjects.[9] Much of the satirical material on younger people is not separate but is worked into the details of the panels of stories on other subjects. Thus, one panel in a 14-panel story on "halls of fame" dealt with a copywriter who wrote advertisements for babies, with slogans like "ask the kid who wets one."[10] The artist who regularly draws a child in a cart in his stories never offers an explanation of why the child is there.

## PERSONAL INTERVIEWS WITH READERS

Although readers of *Mad* range from eight year-olds to college students and adults, the most typical *Mad* reader is a high school student. Personal interviews were conducted in 1959 with 411 regular readers of *Mad* with a mean age of 16.2, in order to determine the readers' attitudes toward the magazine, pattern of reading, and participation in other typical activities of teen-agers.[11] The

[9] January, 1959, p. 15.
[10] June, 1959, p. 34.
[11] The sample was selected by administering a screening questionnaire on reading habits to the total population of a high school which services a large and fairly heterogeneous population in the metropolitan New York area. A personal interview was conducted with each student who met the criterion of a regular reader (i.e., having read at least five of the last eight issues). The age range was 15.2 to 17.7. There were 218 boys and 193 girls. Weighing equally the three criteria of residence, parents' in-

respondents were asked questions on stories they would have published in *Mad* "if editor," what they liked most about it, how they read an issue, with whom they discussed it, how often they read magazines for teen-agers and comic books, and how they liked rock-and-roll music. The sequence of questions was rotated in order to minimize the effect of the sequence of questions. Background data on other and previous media use were also obtained.

*Stories in* Mad *if editor.* The average respondent gave eight stories which he would run "if editor," with a range from four to 22. The responses were coded into the categories developed in the content analysis. Most respondents cited stories which had already appeared in *Mad*. Table 2 gives their specific choices.

There was a high degree of agreement between what actually appeared in *Mad* and what the readers would put in the magazine.[12] The only major category which *Mad* readers said they would like to see in the magazine and which had not been previously coded was Alfred E. Neuman. In the content analysis, there was no category for Neuman because he has not been the subject of stories, although often figuring in them.

TABLE 2. WHAT READERS WOULD PUT IN ISSUE OF *Mad* IF THEY WERE EDITOR

| Theme | Proportion of Total Percentage |
|---|---|
| Advertising | 17 |
| Business customs | 14 |
| Leisure time activity, other than media | 14 |
| Movies | 12 |
| Alfred E. Neuman | 11 |
| Education | 7 |
| Biographies of noted persons | 6 |
| Television | 5 |
| Transportation | 4 |
| International relations | 4 |
| Special groups | 3 |
| Magazines, newspapers, and radio | 2 |
| Miscellaneous | 1 |
| Total | 100 |

Readers would, however, like more of some subjects and less of others. They want more satire on business customs, education and movies and less attention to other mass media. Respondents expressed no interest in seeing problems of adolescence like parents, vocational choice or sex, treated by the magazine. Its readers seem to prefer that matters close to them not be satirized, with the exception of movies and education, which are both relatively external institutions. The magazine occasionally carries articles on parents, in which parents and the family are presented as being relatively unattractive.[13]

Cross-tabulations by sex, status, and school performance yielded no significant differences, except that more boys than girls selected the business customers area ($p < .01$). Boys might be expected to be more aware of business. Their interest in business customs may reflect ado-

---

come, and father's vocation, 102 were classified as lower class, 243 were described as middle class, and 66 upper class. In terms of their school performance, they were divided into those doing relatively well (82), average (241), and relatively poor (88).

[12] The Spearman rank correlation coefficient between the content analysis by theme and what the readers would put in the magazine was .69. Student's $t$ was .98. As another check on the relationship between the content and the readers' preferences, the coefficient of concordance between the two ranked groups was computed to be .568. Snedecor's $F$ (1.26) confirmed that there was no significant degree of variation in rank between the two groups of themes.

[13] For example, a story on "How to Deal With Parents from Ages 21 to 60" in the December 1960 issue, pp. 39–47.

lescents' special fascination with adult business behavior; much of which *Mad* has helped them to perceive as foolish and immoral. The readers may regard such stories as clues and "how to" guides to the world of business which they may soon be entering. Some readers may want stories on business because of the inadequacies of high school instruction on business and their feeling that this is an important and mysterious area of American life that they do not understand. Others may want more on business, because the work done by their fathers is increasingly removed from the children's "ken" and less product-oriented, so that the children have a relatively dim impression of just what their fathers do in the business world.

The interest in movies reflects teen-agers' extreme "movie-going" activity; only the 15–19 age group has increased its movie-going in the last ten years (Opinion Research Corp., 1957). The teen-age 11 percent of the population accounts for approximately half of all movie tickets. Movies are important for teen-agers as the traditional "safe" date. It is also possible that the procedures whereby the movie stars of today are made into stars, have been so widely publicized that teen-agers are cynical about the techniques of making stars, and would like to see them satirized. There is often so little to say about the artistic qualities of some movie stars that their publicity stresses how they were "discovered," and teen-agers may wish to see more satire on this aspect of the movies.

The interest in education perhaps reflects readers' feelings that the subject should get more treatment in *Mad*, so that they might have a better vocabulary for laughing at it. Another possibility is that some teen-agers feel that their schools and teachers

are quite inadequate, and that the sensationalist criticism of education in popular media is wide of the mark. *Mad's* integrity might seem to these teen-agers to make it an ideal vehicle for candid and informed criticism of the schools.

Since the respondents are regular readers, their general acquiescence in *Mad* content is not surprising. It is curious that readers did not mention major social issues of our time, like "desegregation" and "atomic war," as subjects for satire. There seems to be a tacit understanding that there are some subjects which are best left alone, even satirically. The readers may sense that the traditional *Mad* procedure of satirizing both sides of a controversy would lead to obvious difficulties in the case of desegregation. Some may be apathetic about the issue while others may be so ego-involved in it that they would not want it satirized. Teen-agers may be so fatalistic about nuclear war that they could not face even a satirical treatment of the subject.

*What liked about* Mad? The reasons given by the respondents for liking *Mad* were coded into several categories. The average respondent gave approximately four reasons. The proportion citing each reason is shown in Table 3.

The respondents described the appeal of the magazine mainly in generalities and the third person. Relatively few responses refer to the reader's response in the first person ("relaxing, makes me laugh, fun, cheers me up"): In view of the complex and perhaps threatening nature of satire and of humor, it is hardly surprising that the readers did not verbalize many details of the magazine's appeal. Over half of the reasons cited clearly refer to the magazine's satirical and witty content.

TABLE 3. WHAT READERS LIKE ABOUT
*Mad*

| Reason | Proportion of Readers Who Cited Reason<br>*Percentage* |
|---|---|
| Makes fun of and satirizes things | 44 |
| It's funny, comedy | 37 |
| Stories on famous people | 25 |
| Like everything in it | 24 |
| Makes me laugh | 22 |
| Makes fun of itself | 22 |
| The ads | 21 |
| Tells how things work | 19 |
| Not afraid to attack things | 19 |
| It's crazy | 19 |
| The jokes | 19 |
| Alfred E. Neuman | 18 |
| Has current events | 18 |
| Well done, well written | 17 |
| Not like other magazines | 17 |
| The stories | 16 |
| It's fun | 12 |
| It's relaxing | 8 |
| It's silly | 7 |
| Cheers me up | 2 |
| Miscellaneous | 2 |
| Total | 388 |

One reason for liking *Mad* ("famous people, how things work") is its role as socializing agent. Some teen-agers may be learning skills for functioning in our society by acquiring the procedures for survival in America today which are spelled out in witty detail by *Mad*. They may, thus, covertly be learning rules for antisocial behavior, while overtly laughing at those engaged in such behavior. *Mad* has carried seventeen different articles with titles beginning "how to" and many other articles with similar themes. At their best, they range from the bitter satire of Schopenhauer's enumeration of the many ways to win a controversy without being right (1942) to the inspired buffoonery of Rabelais' Panurge's de-

bate with "a great English scholar" (1952).

Reading *Mad* may thus be a kind of problem-solving activity. The teenager may feel that he is learning to emulate "gamesmanship" while laughing at it. He can be an inside "dopester" while chivying inside dopesters. It would be analogous to, for example, a reader of Ovid's *Art of Love* or Castiglione's *Book of the Courtier* studying them for the apparent purpose of ridiculing love-making and the courtier's life, respectively, but actually sopping up much "how to" information on these subjects. Thus, a recent *Mad* article on the "Practical Scout Handbook" is a parody of the *Boy Scouts' Handbook* in terms of various social situations.[14] A discussion of scout teamwork urges the reader to keep on the alert for accidents, so that he can call an ambulance and then a lawyer. The reader is advised to act surprised if the lawyer offers him part of his fee, but to turn him in to the police for "ambulance chasing" if he doesn't. The reader can thus smile at the advice; which is typical of the literalist content of much of *Mad*. He can also experience dislike of people who behave in this way, while at the same time absorbing the advice. The same appeal can be seen, for example, in recent books which deplore prurience and consist largely of examples of prurience to which the reader can feel superior while enjoying them.

Few respondents said that they discuss the details of their enjoyment of the magazine with their peers. They said that they did often discuss it in general terms (i.e., "did you see the last issue, did you see the story on —?"). There appears to be no specific social context of teen-agers within

[14] October, 1961, pp. 43–47.

which the magazine is unusually likely to be discussed.

A number of respondents (22 percent) praised the consistency of the magazine, which manifests itself in *Mad's* making fun of or attacking itself in "house" advertisements. Such advertisements seem to say, "We can't criticize others without criticizing ourselves." A typical advertisement urges readers to buy a picture of Alfred E. Neuman, so that street cleaners may be kept busy gathering up the pictures when they are thrown out. An anthology from the magazine is called "The Worst from *Mad*" and refers to "sickening past issues" from which it is culled. The editors run their own pictures and laugh at them. These are examples of what many readers perceive as the infectious high spirits and enthusiasm with which the magazine is edited. Such enthusiasm seems to have a special appeal for young people, who are likely to respect competence in any form and apparently interpret the self-mocking advertisements as expressions of consistency and competence. The respondents commenting on how well written *Mad* was (17 percent) also are praising the competence of the editors. The implication may be that the authors of *Mad* are professional enough to have absorbed all the skills of the people they are satirizing, but have chosen to use their expertise in making fun of society and even of themselves. Inasmuch as there is considerable agreement that a distinctive feature of juvenile delinquency is its celebration of prowess (Matza, 1961), it is possible that the teen-age reader perceives *Mad* as a kind of delinquent activity which has somehow become successful; and, thus, one way of demonstrating prowess by antisocial activity.

Relatively few readers (3 percent) volunteered any features of the magazine which they did not like. These features were relatively independent of their enthusiasm for the magazine. Thus a reader liking a great many features might still mention some which he did not like. Alfred E. Neuman heads the list of least-liked features; one half of those who expressed some dissatisfaction did so because Neuman "runs too often," "looks too dopey," and similar reasons.

Cross-tabulations—by sex, socioeconomic status, and degree of success at school—of the various reasons for liking the magazine did not yield any significant differences, with two exceptions: Alfred E. Neuman and current events.

Of the 74 respondents who cited Alfred E. Neuman as a reason for liking the magazine, 56 percent were in the group which was not doing well at school ($p < .01$). It can be speculated that the less successful students are more likely to identify with Neuman because he conveys a feeling of failure, defeat, defensiveness, and uninvolvement. His non-worry slogan has a "let the world collapse, I don't care" quality, and his appearance suggests stupidity. One fan admiringly said that "If Alfred E. Neuman jumped off the Empire State building, he would be laughing." A few readers thought that Neuman was a functionary of the magazine, although he does not appear on the masthead. It is possible that his silliness and appearance of being someone who doesn't know any better, helps to make the magazine more acceptable, by making its attack less committed.

An adolescent who is doing well at school might enjoy the magazine because of its "joshing" of the very symbols of status and achievement to which he is attracted. The less effective adolescent may like *Mad* because of Neuman, who represents fecklessness and nonachievement. The magazine may thus appeal to teen-agers at opposite ends of the scale of achievement for quite different reasons, while giving each one a chance to feel superior.

Most of the respondents (71 percent) who commented on the magazine's basing its stories on current events, were in the group which was doing relatively well at school ($p <$ .01). The more alert readers, thus, seem to derive pleasure from their ability to recognize the relationship between an actual happening and its being satirized by *Mad*. A few called such consonance between *Mad* stories and current events to their parents' attention, perhaps as one way of making their parents feel that the magazine has some educational value. It might be speculated that the identification of such current events material may help to assuage guilt feelings which the magazine's satirical content may evoke.

Even though doing well at school does have some status among teenagers, it is more important for them to achieve good grades by appearing to do little work *without* making any special efforts to get good grades (Coleman, 1959). Adolescents' group norms operate to keep effort down. Therefore, if a *Mad* reader can scoff at his elders and society, by seeming to learn something about current events, he is deriving multiple dimensions of satisfaction.[15]

*How read an issue.* Another question put to respondents was intended to determine their traffic through the magazine. Over half (62 percent) of the regular readers go through *Mad* soon after getting it. Twenty-eight percent read the magazine in two or three sittings. Ten percent read it intermittently. Readers often reread their favorite articles.

The large proportion of respondents who read *Mad* through is another confirmation of the loyalty of its readers, which is not unexpected in view of adolescents' fierce loyalties to group, team, and school.

It can be speculated that one way in which the group can give vent to nonconformism is by regular readership of a magazine which largely mocks the adult world. This is a world which the magazine's readers have not yet engaged directly, but which they are approaching during a period when they are trying to learn who they are and what their feelings are. By enjoying satire on this adult world, they can approach it while mocking it. They can also mock the world of younger children.

This ability of adolescents to take a socially acceptable medium, the format of which involves conformity to group norms—like a comic magazine or rock-and-roll—while using the medium to express hostility and aggressiveness, is in line with what is known about adolescents' needs. They want both, to belong and not belong, to have and have not, to enjoy but also to attack.

The very name of *Mad* implies not only aggression ("mad at") but also

---

[15] In spite of the great success of *Mad*, it would not be safe to assume that all teenagers are interested in laughing at the ways of adult society. The largest selling teen magazine is *Boy's Life*, sponsored by the Boy Scouts, with a circulation of 1,790,000. Magazines like *Boy's Life* and *Scholastic*

were not included, because they have institutional affiliations and are not bought on the open market. The magazines tabulated were *Dig, Teen, Flip, Hep Cats, Modern Teen, Seventeen, 16, Datebook, Teen Parade, Teens Today,* and *Teen World.*

the foolishness ("mad as a hatter") of much civilization. This kind of ambivalence—enjoying media which imply conformity while at the same time using them to rebel against it—is a special kind of escape, which is strongly developed in adolescents.

Adolescence has long been known to be a period of contradictions, and of the growing awareness of contradictions. Materialism and idealism, egoism and altruism, and sociability and loneliness are among the contradictory feelings, which are likely to be emerging simultaneously. A major problem of adolescents is how to express their hostility while seeming not to do so. One noted expression of this conflict was "Hound Dog," probably the most successful single phonograph record ever made. This rock-and-roll record sold 5,500,000 copies, almost all to teen-agers. Its lyrics represent pure hostility, although the format in which it is expressed is the socially acceptable one of the rock-and-roll record. Elvis Presley, the nonpareil exemplar of the rock-and-roller's hostility toward the adult world, is the first performer in history to make a long-playing record that sold over one million copies. Another example of adolescents' ability to use media in this way is the extent to which they will *seem* to read all of a school circulated magazine (i.e., *Reader's Digest*) which has both serious and humorous material, but will pay attention to the jokes and cartoons, and largely ignore serious material.

This ability to *express* aggressiveness seems to have found some relatively recent outlets, but the *presence* of the aggressiveness has often been noted by other investigators. The most intensive study ever made of adolescent fantasy—using cartoon-like picture stimuli—found that its major theme was aggression, which was described as "practically universal" (Symonds, 1949). Even "mild" boys and girls told extremely aggressive stories, with considerable destructive violence. There were over three times as many themes of "aggression" expressed by the adolescents studied, as "eroticism," the next most popular theme. Anxiety, Oedipal conflict, moral issues, success striving and turning stories into jokes, were other common themes; all of these elements can be found in *Mad*.

A study conducted before the "heyday" of comic books suggested that high school students are less likely to respond to pictorial humor than to verbal and intellectual humor (Harms, 1943). *Mad* would seem to represent a combination of these elements. The use of the comic format may help to remove some sting from the aggressive content for some readers because of the association of comics with "kid stuff." Another reason for the special appeal of the comic format is suggested by previous studies of adolescent humor, which report that visual presentation of humorous material facilitates the ability of adolescents to respond to it (Omwake, 1937). Many adolescents have had much experience with the comic format in their preadolescent years. The great majority (89 percent) of the respondents had read comic books before *Mad*. A convincing case could probably be made for the comic book's having supplanted the fairy tale as a major carrier of our culture's ethos to young people! *Mad*, along with some other comic books, is not permitted in schools by many teachers and even by some parents in their homes, thus adding the lure of the forbidden to the magazine.

During the interviewing, a number of respondents referred to *Mad* as "our magazine." They meant that *Mad* expressed their point of view so effectively that they had almost a proprietory feeling about it. *Mad* reinforces membership in the teen-agers' peer group—it's the "thing to do." As one respondent said, "All the kids read *Mad*. The cats and the frats both make it." This suggests that the less, as well as the more, staid teeners enjoy it. There is so much interest in *Mad* that one fan has published a complete cross-index to the magazine (von Bernewitz, 1961). It is likely that this in-group feeling is strengthened by the several personalities in the magazine who are never explained: Neuman, Arthur, the plant, the child, and potrzebie. A number of the respondents mentioned that they had "discovered" these features by themselves. Their having done so seemed to contribute to their feeling of being a member of an in-group.

Practically no respondent referred to the magazine's commercial success, which did not seem to have made much of an impression on readers. Many explicitly commented on the extent of peer-group readership as a positive feature. "Most of the other kids read *Mad*" and "we swap old copies back and forth," were typical comments. The wide readership of the magazine by other teen-agers helps to legitimize its appeal; especially in the face of the considerable opposition to it by parents and other institutionalized figures of authority. Readership of *Mad*, thus, reinforces membership in a kind of ritual nonconformity.

This use of media to obtain membership in an in-group of outsiders is one way in which the adolescent can make tolerable his need both to assent and dissent. It is perhaps this sensitivity and response to the near-intolerable which has helped to make what is now called "sick" humor, an established part of adolescent humor. Stories like, "I stepped on my mother because I wanted a stepmother," have been told by teen-agers for decades. A similar kind of gallows humor appeared in World War II among French adults faced with the extreme situation of the Resistance. It is probably no accident that this kind of "sick joke" has appeared among American adults, coterminously with the near-intolerable situation of the threat of atomic annihilation.

A special appeal of a magazine of satire like *Mad* is that *the satirist can say things which even a reformer or critic cannot easily say. It may be easier to laugh at something than to discuss it objectively.* The adolescent both wants to make contact with the symbols of success in the outside world, as some do by autograph collecting and fan clubs, and, at the same time, wants to believe ill of them. *Mad* provides its readers with an opportunity to "go away a little closer" from some important American institutions.

This hostility seems to have a special need to find expression in high school and college students. They enjoy the absurd and satirical, as well as the opportunity to release pent-up emotional energy, and feelings of superiority (Kambouropoulou, 1930). Satire may have a special appeal to relatively young people, because it can be viewed psychoanalytically, as a reflection of the inner dependence of childhood, which is projected onto noted individuals and institutions, in order to attack them (Bergler, 1956). Satire is often described metaphorically as "biting," because it is a method of communication for persons who respond orally. It can be regarded as a weapon of the weak; and adolescents may regard themselves as being relatively weak. *Mad* offers an opportunity for a kind of counterphobic, defensive reaction to social institutions. The adolescent readers of the magazine face the prospect of going out into the adult world, not with anxiety but with an opportunity for gratification through laughter, as they achieve symbolic mastery over the adult world by continually assuring themselves that its institutions and personalities cannot be taken seriously (Wolfenstein, 1957). The gratification comes from reenacting mastery over anxiety (Kris, 1938), for which the *Mad* story provides the occasion. It is traditional to say that adolescents "quest for new people to love and new forms of functioning." By its exposés of the latter, *Mad* gives its adolescent readers new targets for their ambivalence.

## ENTHUSIASM SCORE

Even within a group of such regular readers of the magazine, it was considered useful to obtain a measure of comparative degree of enthusiasm. Each interview was read through independently by two analysts, who considered how the magazine was read, what the respondent said about it, the respondent's feeling tone about the magazine, and the extent of his ego involvement in it.[16] The interviewee was rated on a scale with one representing the lowest and ten the highest score. The range of scores was from four to ten, with an average of 8.0.

Boys had an average enthusiasm score of 8.7, girls of 7.8 ($p < .05$). The upper-class readers had a score of 8.6, middle-class readers also

averaged 8.6, and lower-class readers 7.1 ($p < .01$). The group which was doing relatively well at school averaged 8.2, the average students 8.4, and the poorest students averaged 7.5 on enthusiasm. The difference between the poorest students and each of the other two groups was significant ($p < .05$).

The readers whose families are faring better economically and who are better students, thus seem to like *Mad* better. Why? We might speculate that these students are likely to be expecting, consciously or otherwise, to be assuming more active and significant roles in their society and community once they leave school and college. Similarly, boys are likely to be more aware of their potential involvement with and functioning in the community than girls, because the boys face decisions on jobs and military service. The very closeness of these groups to the opportunity of functioning in our society may make them more than usually alert to the dissonances and moral ambiguities of society. It is this kind of alertness which makes satire possible.

It is no coincidence that our wealthiest universities have also spawned some of the best college satire and humor magazines (e.g., Columbia *Jester*, Vassar *Igitur*, MIT *Voo Doo*, Stanford *Chaparral*, Harvard *Lampoon*). The student body at the Yale Law School in New Haven, which is perhaps as sensitized to power as any American student body, created *Monocle*, which is the only American political satire magazine. Thus, universities with students likely to achieve power also have publications which sneer most enthusiastically at manifestations of power. These publications represent one method of absorbing role strain on the part of groups other than the lower-class

[16] Acknowledgment is made of the cooperation of Regina Pezzella and Elliott Winick.

marginal groups, which have traditionally showed strain in adolescence. How cautious even such elite groups may be, can be seen in a recent issue of *Monocle*, in which *over half* the contributors use pseudonyms.[17] The editors dedicate the issue to the contributors' skill in selecting pen names! It is a vivid commentary on satire in our time, and a magazine of satire in which most of its authors do not wish to be identified. The caution of these contributors to Yale's *Monocle* makes especially relevant George S. Kaufman's observation, that "satire is what closes in New Haven."

Another possibility for the greater interest in *Mad* of the higher socio-economic groups and better students is that satire is the end result of indignation, and indignation is based on the awareness of standards. The higher status and education group may be more aware of the standards which contemporary society is implicitly said to be violating by *Mad*, because of its greater exposure to literature, other art forms, and other facets of society.

The existence and success of *Mad* does not necessarily mean that from an adolescent's point of view there is more to satirize today than there has been in the past. What it does mean is that this particular kind of satire has found a market at this time, because it serves some significant function for the teen-agers who are its primary market. There have been some changes in the life situation of teen-agers that probably contribute to their greater receptivity to satire. The number of teen-agers increased from 15 to 20 million during the 1950s. They currently spend ten billion dollars a year and are the targets of many marketers, so that they are

more aware of marketing. They save their money less than previous generations did, start dating earlier, and marry earlier. Teen-age girls spend $300 million on cosmetics each year. The first magazine specifically for teen-agers, rather than for boys *or* girls, appeared in 1955.

The 1950s appeared to provide a climate that was especially hospitable for the approach of a satirical magazine. Cynicism among the middle classes was certainly a significant characteristic of the post-World War II national mood; to which, on another level, the late Senator McCarthy responded. *Confidential* strengthened this mood by becoming the most successful magazine in American history, with its exposés of "irregularities" among the famous. This combination of factors may have helped to contribute to the mood of criticism of society, which is necessary for satire. A clue to how teen-agers feel about the morality of their elders can be obtained from the comments of teen magazines on the charge that their leading television master of ceremonies, Dick Clark, had accepted "payola." None of the magazines that commented on the charge had anything adverse to say about Clark, because they saw nothing wrong in payola.

The teen-agers of the 1950s are the "war babies" of the World War II period. Not only were their fathers often away, but their mothers were likely to be working. Even after the war, many teen-agers of the 1950s may have grown up in suburban communities, where fathers were at home less often than the fathers of previous generations. The effect of moving from one place to another, which 20 percent of the population engages in each year, may be related to the feelings of deracination that many

[17] Summer-Fall, 1960.

teen-agers experience; and that may have contributed to teen-agers' feeling more critical of their elders, and closer to each other.

Inevitably, the success of *Mad* and the new sick comedians during the same decade suggests some comparison between the two.[18] *Mad* and the new comedians are both nihilistic, and level their burlesque at so many targets that they hardly seem to have any time or energy left to deal with alternatives to the lunacy they attack. They must both therefore continue to charge harder at their targets. They both engage in irony and reinforce their audience's feeling of being "in." Both see corruption everywhere. Both enjoy attacking mass media. The sick comedians, however, regularly attack intolerance, domesticity, religion, and self-improvement, which are seldom butts of *Mad*. Although politics represents a target for the sick comedians, it constitutes a small proportion of *Mad's* content. *Mad* actually does not comment on substantive political matters, but deals with personalities in politics. Thus, it might joke about Senator McCarthy's heavy beard, President Eisenhower's golf, or President Kennedy's haircut, but not about their policies.

It is curious that, with the possible exception of the sick comedians, satire has not found a market among adults since *Ballyhoo*. In a democracy in which the dissident voice may be a sign of healthy differences in points of view, and awareness and examination of alternatives, *Mad* has not only entertained dissident theories but made them feel at home and helped to get them into millions of homes. Its very success, however, may have a boomerang effect. As *Mad* achieves greater success and recognition as a vehicle for teen-agers, adults may reinforce their image of satire as a juvenile medium. Satire as an adult format may thus become less possible in this country for this generation. Another possibility, of course, is that the millions of teen-agers who have read *Mad* may develop into adults who will constitute a ready audience for sick comedians and other satire. It is also possible that the reason teen-agers enjoy *Mad* is that school has sensitized them to standards, but today's nonschool, adult world is so normless that adults cannot respond to an art form that implicitly is based on departures from the norm. Yet another possibility is that the magazine's continuing attacks on so many targets will give its satire almost a good-natured quality, and thus ultimately blunt its impact. For at least the next few years, however, it appears likely that *Mad* will maintain its unique status of being respected, if not quite respectable.

## Bibliography

Anthony, N., *How to Grow Old Disgracefully*. New York: Eagle Books, 1946, p. 126.

Bergler, E., *Laughter and the Sense of Humor*. New York: Intercontinental Medical Book Corp., 1956, pp. 161–65.

Coleman, J. S., "Academic Achievement and the Structure of Competition," *Harvard Educational Review*, XXIX (1959), 330–51.

Gehman, R., "It's Just Plain Mad," *Coronet*, XLVIII, No. 1 (1960), 96–103.

Harms, E., "The Development of Humor," *Journal of Abnormal Sociology and Psychology*, XXXVIII (1943), 351–69.

[18] It is an interesting commentary on our culture's attitudes toward satire that these comedians have been completely unsuccessful in their attempts to be called "truth" comedians.

Kambouropoulou, P., "Individual Difference in the Sense of Humor," *The American Journal of Psychoanalysis,* XXXVII (1930), 268–78.

Kris, E., "Ego Development and the Comic," *International Journal of Psychoanalysis,* XIX (1938), 77–90.

Matza, D., "Subterranean Traditions of Youth," *Annals of the American Academy of Political and Social Sciences,* CCCXXXVIII (1961), 102-18.

Omwake, L., "A Study of the Sense of Humor," *Journal of Applied Psychology,* XXI (1937), 688–704.

*The Public Appraises Movies.* Princeton, N.J.: Opinion Research Corporation, 1957, p. 12.

Peterson, T., *Magazines in the Twentieth Century.* Urbana: University of Illinois Press, 1956, pp. 147–52.

*The Portable Rabelais.* New York: The Viking Press, Inc., 1952, pp. 306–10.

Redlich, F., J. Levine, and T. P. Sohler, "A Mirth Response Test," *American Journal of Orthopsychiatry,* XXI (1951), 717–34.

Schopenhauer, A., "The Art of Controversy," in *Complete Essays of Schopenhauer.* New York: John Wiley & Sons, Inc., 1942, pp. 1–98.

Symonds, P. M., *Adolescent Fantasy.* New York: Columbia University Press, 1949.

Thurber, J., "A Subversive Conspiracy," *The Realist,* I, No. 1 (1958), 25–26.

von Bernewitz, F., *The Complete* Mad *Checklist.* Silver Spring, Md.: Published by the author, 1961.

Wolfenstein, M., "A Phase in the Development of Children's Sense of Humor," in *The Psychoanalytic Study of the Child.* New York: International Universities Press, Inc., VI, 336–50.

Zwerling, I., "The Favorite Joke in Diagnostic and Therapeutic Interviewing," *Psychoanalytic Quarterly,* XXIV (1955), 104–14.

# 15

## Draftee Behavior
## in the Cold War Army *†

*Eugene S. Uyeki*

A major factor confronting today's male youth is the probability of his being inducted into the military service of his country. Considering the massive impact of this socialization process on the minds of the nation's most physically fit young men, it is remarkable that so little atten-

* Reprinted from *Social Problems,* VIII (1960), 151–58, by permission of the author and The Society for the Study of Social Problems. Footnotes renumbered.

† This is a revised version of a paper read at the annual meeting of the American Sociological Association held in Seattle, Washington, August 1958. It is based on my own recorded observations during 21 months duty in the U. S. Army from February 1954 to November 1955, most of the time as a Pvt. and Pfc. The recorded material is in the form of weekly letters which were filed for me in the Department of Social Studies, Case Institute of Technology.

tion has been paid to the effects of this process on American life. Although the draft has clearly had an impact on the life career patterns of those eligible for military service—as well as on women whose lives are affected—we know little about the social processes involved.

Since the second World War, when numerous major studies were conducted on such questions,[1] there have been many studies of the military as a social system and as a part of the state,[2] and research has been conducted on its leadership,[3] but little attention has been given to the average nonprofessional soldier.[4]

EDITOR

---

This article attempts to conceptualize a sociological perspective useful for viewing draftee behavior in the cold-war army. In the following sections, two assumptions are made. The first assumption is that a particular configuration of elements making up a social structure elicits a pattern of individual responses which may be typed as being modal for that social structure (5). The second assumption is that the structural requisites of the cold-war army are different from other armies, specifically from the peacetime volunteer army or the total-war mass army.

The army is a special-purpose organization, bureaucratically structured, whose major purpose is that of fighting and winning wars. This deadly mission differentiates the army from other non-militaristic organizations (9). As a bureaucracy, it is based on rigid definitions of duties and responsibilities, allocated by an authoritarian system of ranking (2). Theoretically, it makes no difference what particular individual is filling any position, so long as he fulfills the prescribed responsibilities of that position. These two characteristics of the army maximize organizationally structured behavior, and, in the ideal case, eventuate in the total submersion of the individual in military ways and his loss of identity as a civilian. This ideal type of individual commitment occurs only under a specific set of conditions in the United States: when the society is engaged in total war.[5] In this case, there is a transformation of the relation between the army and other institutional structures

---

[1] Most noteworthy is the now classic study by Samuel A. Stouffer, *et al.*, *The American Soldier* (Princeton, N.J.: Princeton University Press, 1949), Vols. I and II.

[2] E.g., see Morris Janowitz, *Sociology and the Military Establishment* (New York: The Russell Sage Foundation, 1959).

[3] E.g., ———, *The Professional Soldier* (New York: The Free Press, 1964).

[4] For a related work, see, Frank E. Jones, "The Infantry Recruit: a Sociological Analysis of Socialization in the Canadian Army" (Doctoral dissertation, Harvard University, 1954).

[5] The attitude of the draftee in the Korean War where it was accepted policy to rotate him after nine months' combat duty, is instructive. Huntington comments as follows: "In World War II, soldiers were in for the duration: they could only achieve their personal goal of getting home when the government achieved its political goal of military victory. In Korea, however, rotation divorced the personal goals of the troops from the political goals of the government. The aim of the soldier was simply to endure his nine months at the front and then get out. The war was a necessary evil, and he acquiesced and accepted it as such. His attitude was brilliantly summed up in that classic expression of Stoic resignation which emerged out of the front lines: 'That's the way the ball bounces.' For the first time in American history the common soldier fought a major war solely and simply because he was ordered to fight it and not because he shared any identification with the political goals for which the war was being fought" (3. pp. 388–89).

of the society. In a sense, the whole society is mobilized and the military becomes the key institution. At other times, the function of the army is potential. These considerations suggest that differences in societal conditions result in

a. differences in social structure of the army and
b. differences in individual commitment of the ordinary soldier to the army organization.

It may be useful to conceive of three ideal types of army-social situations:

a. the peace-time army,
b. the total-war army, and
c. the cold-war army.

The peace-time army is in being when there is no major threat of overt or covert conflict. It is staffed by professionals (volunteers) in both the officer and enlisted ranks; and it is small in total size compared with the other two armies.[6] Promotions are slow, and rank distinctions become very important. It occupies its historically low status in relation to other organizations and institutions in the larger society (1; 8). Its solidarity lies between the other two armies since it is composed of professionals.

The total-war army is a mass army which is organized when the whole society is engaged in overt total conflict. The great influx of amateurs into both the officer and enlisted ranks outnumbering the professional soldiers occurs under the motivation of intense patriotic sentiments.[7] These

are supported by a great mobilization of the total resources, both human and physical, in the society. Promotions are rapid. Solidarity is high among the personnel in the army. It is under these conditions that the army's manifest and latent functions coincide.

The cold-war army is marginal between the other two types. The relations between nations are tense and the possibility of overt conflict is real. There is much discussion in the mass media about the adequacy of military readiness. The function of the cold-war army is deterrence. The quantity of societal support is dependent upon whether the cold war threatens to erupt into armed conflict or whether the continuity of peace seems assured. It is populated by a large number of amateurs among the enlisted men and a fair number among the officers.[8] It is numerically quite large in numbers though it does not approach the size of the total-war army.[9] Voluntary enlistment is not enough to keep it at required strength and the draft is utilized. The amateurs move in and out of the army as their terms of service expire. The orientation of the amateur soldier to the army is less emotional, more matter of fact.

## Social-Psychological World of the Cold-War Draftee

What has happened during the cold-war period has been the institu-

[6] In 1916, the authorized strength of the U. S. Army was 175,000 (1, p. 171); in 1925, the total strength was 136,356, and in 1940, it was 267,767 (6, p. 734).

[7] Including the Air Force, in 1945, the U. S. Army totaled 8,267,958 (10, p. 245).

[8] My limited observation of officers leads me to believe that the "amateur officers" (usually ROTC and non-regular army medical officers) have somewhat the same range of attitudes as the draftees.

[9] The U. S. Army reached its top strength after World War II during the Korean conflict in 1952 when it totaled 1,569,419. It held about this strength until 1955 when it fell to 1,109,296. In 1957, its strength fell below a million to 997,994 (10, p. 245).

tionalizing of the marginal and ambiguous status of the cold-war army. Certain regularities of adjustment in the social system of the army organization have been made to this ambiguity in cultural values of the larger society. And these regularities in the social system requisites of the army have had their effect in eliciting from the draftee a modal type of adjustment which may be characterized as segmental, individualistic, and detached.[10] This modal draftee commitment to the army organization during the cold-war period results from the following factors:

a. the routinization of the army career,
b. the two-year limitation of service,
c. the individualization of the army career, and
d. the inadequate motivation of the reward system.

This differential pattern of draftee behavior in the cold-war army is recognized and accepted by the regular army man.

[10] Even during the total-war period, there may be a number of amateur soldiers who would resist their socialization into the army organization. But the net effect of the societal pressures during the total-war period would result in a greater frequency of the total commitment responses than during the cold-war period. In terms of the framework being utilized here, a total commitment response by the draftee would be a "deviant" (not used invidiously) adjustment in the cold-war army. I also recognize the analytic differences between "private" and "public" attitudinal acceptance or rejection and overt behavior, all of which may vary independently. My data do not allow me to type situations which allow for extensive analysis of various combinations of these dimensions of behavior. However, since many social-psychological studies have pointed to the "strain for consistency" of attitudes and behavior, I feel justified in dealing with a combination of these dimensions in the observed behavior of the draftee.

## THE PRIMARY VALUE OF THE CIVILIAN WORLD: THE ARMY AS A JOB

The real world of the citizen-soldier is the civilian world. Upon being inducted into the army, the draftee becomes subject to the army social organization to which he is tied by legal and military sanctions of a punitive nature. During the first few weeks of basic training, disruptions in his previous self-concept occur for the draftee as he is subject to all the indignities and harassments that attend this period of de-individualization. He is actually kept away from contact with the civilian world by restricting him to the military post and his only contacts with the outside world are through letters, long-distance telephone, and newspapers. The initial period is one of becoming accustomed to military ways, of doing everything collectively, living in close quarters, being dressed alike, addressing officers as "sir," and so on.

Whenever individuals are taken away from the social situations that give rise to and sustain their definitions of their appropriate roles there is a systematic elaboration of these definitions in a particular direction. Since the civilian world is more attractive than the military world, favorable memories of the former are elaborated and unchecked by any consistent involvement in it. The favorable projections about the civilian world provide meaning and support for resisting the complete identification by the draftee as a soldier, while easing his acceptance of military training. The resistance to the military identification would be difficult to maintain without some contacts with the civilian world which permit the retention of identity with the latter. These contacts are possible even during the basic training period, for shortly after about a month of service, the draftee may receive passes and leave the army post. Although for most of the eight weeks of basic training the citizen-soldier has to be on call for military duty twenty-four hours a day, it is possible for him on weekends to re-enter the civilian world. Having no civilian clothes and forced to dress in ill-fitting khaki with his hair not yet grown out from the close cropping given to each inductee, he is quite self-conscious about his appearance. These physical differences are enough to symbolize the fact that he is no longer the complete civilian. But these visits to the civilian world during basic training permit the draftee to reinforce his affinity for civilian values because of their obvious attractiveness in comparison with the enforced norms of military life.

As soon as the basic training period is over, the status of the inductee changes. This varies between eight weeks for a few and sixteen weeks for most. The draftee then becomes a member of a permanent organization, and he is given a permanent pass to be used on off-duty hours and is allowed to keep civilian clothes for wear at such times. For most draftees the army becomes an eight-hour job with the rest of the hours in the day free for his own purposes. From time to time, field problems may demand greater than the normal eight-hour involvement. Details like guard duty and KP impinge periodically upon the draftee. But these become mere deviations from the routine.

The duties of soldiering, in effect, become comparable in many respects with a regular job in the civilian world. It approaches a five-and-one-half day work week for most and a five-day work week for a few. The

weekends are usually free. This is the actual social-psychological reality for the citizen soldier. He comes to look upon any demands which are greater than the normally expected as intrusions upon his own time, with a great amount of attendant griping. After hours the individual can wear civilian clothes and leave the military post, "passing" for a civilian. The possibility of having one's own car facilitates the ease with which one can leave the military post, enhancing the ability to indulge individual needs.

These factors are maximized for the married draftee. It is possible for him to live off the post and commute daily to his duty station. Once he is away from the post, his time is his own, and it is easy to forget the stringency of military discipline. Even if he lives on post, his housing is usually away from the troop area. The proximity of his family dilutes the pressures for acceptance of the military identification. Whatever status degradations he may face while on duty is compensated for by having his affectionate needs taken care of by his family. To be sure, hostility which is suppressed by the draftee rather than expressed to officers or NCO's because of possible consequences is often released to his wife, much to her surprise and chagrin.

These conditions make it easy for the draftee to validate daily the primacy of the civilian world. He is able to segmentalize his military role and relegate this to a secondary value in favor of a primary civilian identification, since in fact, the military is only a part of his actual social-psychological reality.

## Two-Year Limit on Service: Time Perspective of the Draftee

The limitation of service for the draftee to two years (21 months for those who have either a job or school waiting) is another factor which lessens the necessity for a deep identification with the role of soldier. Once the individual is drafted, he looks ahead to the time when he can leave military service. The army experience is perceived as a series of short-run tests, each of which must be endured until the days become weeks; the weeks, months; until the required number of months have been accumulated. This time perspective is quite different from that of the draftee serving in a time of total war—for the latter, the time perspective is indefinite and vague, for the duration.

The common denominator for all draftees becomes one of finishing the necessary tasks required by the army in two years. The major hurdle is basic training which is physically and psychologically difficult. One is able to endure this since the rest of the army experience becomes one of waiting out the required time in duty comparable to a civilian job.

In the course of a day, one is usually asked, "How much time you got left, Joe?" The response to this question varies with the various stages of the draftee's army career. At the beginning, it turns out to be in terms of months; after a year, in terms of weeks; and during the last few weeks, in terms of days. The really ingenious draftee has his remaining time broken down into hours. Other ways of counting the remaining time utilize the regularly scheduled events: so many inspections, so many full-fields, so many KP's, and so many field problems. The draftee often overtly flaunts his remaining time to superior officers and regular army men. Those who work at jobs in offices with official calendars have the days numbered backward in terms of decreasing days until time for release. A great amount of ritual and ceremony is attached to turning over the calendar to the next page or to crossing off another day. On a Friday afternoon a draftee may cross off the Saturday and Sunday dates, thereby drawing some psychological satisfaction at crossing off non-duty days and "speeding" the time of release from service. For a non-duty day counts the same as a duty day toward the date of separation from service.

The importance of these activities to the draftee is in categorizing the two years into a limited and definable (and therefore psychologically manageable) series of events with a predetermined conclusion—the return to civilian life. Once the individual is drafted, the passage of time will permit him to return to the civilian world.

## INDIVIDUALIZATION OF THE ARMY CAREER

As many social scientists have pointed out, intimate and rewarding relations with members of a small group facilitate the acceptance of values and roles common to that group. The role of the primary group in giving support to the individual has been detailed in a number of studies of military organizations in the second World War (4; 7). This type of primary group support is *weakened* in the cold-war army.

Except for basic training, the draftee is not participating in common tasks with a group of individuals having the same fate as he does over any length of time. Soon after basic training, the company is split up and groups of individuals are sent to separate stations. Even when a group from the basic training unit is sent to the same permanent station, before their army career is over, it is highly probable that there will occur further transfers among them, thus atomizing the group which may have common memories and a certain amount of solidarity. The draftee sees other individuals being transferred from unit to unit. There grows up an expectation that shifting of duty stations is a routine occurrence in the army. The draftee prepares himself for this by not committing himself more than necessary to any group to which he happens to be transferred. Any great psychological involvement in a single primary group, when a shift is possible at any moment, is apt to be frustrating.

A second factor that reinforces individualizing behavior is that the individual draftee's time for separation from service *is known* and is usually *different* from most others in the units to which he is shifted after basic training. This weakens the close ties between individuals. Why should the draftee band together in close solidarity with other draftees to ease the psychological frustrations that assault them, when his time for departure from service nears? It is better to suffer the indignities individually and wait patiently until the separation date when he can take his leave of military life. Some type of solidarity and group identification is generated among the draftees by their facing of common problems. But the point is that the frequent transfers and individual departure dates from army service increase the pressures for an individualistic approach by the draftee to his military career.

## THE INADEQUATE MOTIVATION OF THE REWARD SYSTEM

Regardless of the draftee's psychological alienation from his identification as a soldier, he cannot escape completely the values of the military organization. One way whereby an individual comes to accept the values of a group to which he is ascribed, but originally rejects, is when the rewards which accrue to him from the new group become attractive. Identification with the military role would be facilitated if the draftee were able to receive training which might be translated into richer esteem-gaining skills in the civilian world, or if there were sufficient monetary returns that resulted from acceptance of military ways.

There are very few positions in the army that draftees can fill which can serve as preparation for civilian jobs. Most of these positions are taken over by people trained in the civilian world who are then assigned to these specialist positions. Because of the limitation of service to two years for the draftee, it does not pay the army to train the draftee for about nine months, only to have him leave service in the space of another year. Consequently, it is the regular army man or the three-year enlistee who is sent to the special schools which require long periods of training.

The attraction of monetary rewards in the army is tied up with the ranking system. Theoretically, it is possible for the inductee to become a sergeant at the end of a year, receiving about $150 a month. But reaching this rank by the draftee is contingent upon the following conditions:

a. that the individual be in a unit continuously,

b. that the individual is filling a position in the Table of Organization (i.e., is not "surplus"),

c. that the individual is recommended for promotion at the necessary time, and

d. that at the time of recommendation, there is an allocation for promotion to the next grade.

It is rare when all of these four conditions occur at the same time for any draftee. There is at least one transfer for each inductee (this is from his basic training unit to a permanent unit) and usually more than one in his military career. Often an individual is "surplus"—that is, he is not filling a position that is provided for in the T.O. and therefore is ineligible for promotion. (Some Commanding Officers made efforts to shift men in and out of positions provided for in the T.O. in order to promote their men.) It is a rare draftee who is recommended for promotion each time he is eligible. With the army in process of stabilizing after the ending of the Korean conflict, there was a restriction in the number of openings for promotion. Individuals were often recommended for promotion before having sufficient time in grade by recourse to "waivers." But these were not acted upon because of lack of allocations for promotion to the next higher grades. Realistically, the typical draftee can look forward to promotion to Pfc. or to Cpl. (Sp-3) some time before his release from service, receiving about $100 a month in the former position and $120 a month in the latter position. The reward system of the army does not have a great attraction to motivate individuals to accept military ways.

It should be noted parenthetically at this point, however, that the individual draftee cannot completely escape involvement with the ranking system of the army. For at least eight hours of the day, the individual is attached to the army and the evaluations of this membership group has its claims, however tenuous they may be in the individual case. And a higher grade has its compensations within the army structure in terms of an increase in pay, higher prestige,

and exemption from the more onerous duties of military life. That these rewards were of some importance may be evidenced by the frequency and intensity of gripes by the draftee when promotion time came and his name was not on the list.

## RA-US DISTINCTION: RECOGNITION OF DIFFERENTIAL BEHAVIOR

The distinctiveness of the behavior patterns and identification with the military role by the draftee in comparison with that of the regular army man is accepted by both groups. The terms which are frequently used by enlisted men are "RA" and "US." As the draftee uses it—US refers to an "involuntary" who did not choose the military life, who gives little of his "real" self to the army, being "psychologically AWOL," and who does his duties in an impersonal way. For the draftee, the depiction of a soldier as being RA (whether or not the person actually carries the serial number of RA——) implies a soldier who has chosen the military life, who enjoys taking orders, who lacks independence and initiative, and who adheres to the spit and polish of army rituals.

To the regular army man, the term US refers to a young man, full of mischief, who refuses to do anything ordered unless he feels like doing it, and who gives only lip service to identifying with the military. The regular army man conceives of himself as an individual who feels that the military is a masculine way of life and the army as an organization devoted to an important patriotic mission, and who has made his choice in a positive way for this style of life.

Needless to say, the actual behaviors of individual draftees and regular army men do not fit completely into these characterizations. But the widespread use of these stereotypes are indicative of differences in perspectives that account for differences in behavior patterns and identifications. The regular army man actually does not expect as much from the draftee as he does from others like himself. He often explains away a "mistake" made by a draftee by saying, "He's a US!" This suggests that *there is a certain looseness in the cold-war army social structure* which permits the draftee to engage in behaviors that are not strictly according to military ways.[11] This is a mutual accommodation that has emerged because of the recalcitrance of the draftee in resisting acceptance of the military identification and the willingness of the regular army man in not insisting upon it. This emergent norm shared by both the regular army man and the draftee recognizes the necessity for greater conformity of overt behavior to army expectations, but less demand for rigid attitudinal conformity.

## Conclusion

The bureaucratic nature and the special mission of the army are useful perspectives for explaining many aspects of army life. The importance of the primary group in formal organizations is also a fruitful way of looking at army life. This article has at-

[11] An additional development which operates in the same direction has been conceptualized by Janowitz as the "civilianizing" of the miliary. This is based in part upon the greater role of technology in the modern military with consequent organizational stress upon manipulation rather than domination as the basis of authority and discipline (4, pp. 36–42).

tempted to demonstrate that a focus upon changes in the larger societal situation from which the army derives its degree of functionality is a useful perspective for explaining individual behavior in the organization, specifically in terms of the cold-war army and draftee behavior in it.

## References

1. Ekrich, A. A., Jr., *The Civilian and the Military*. New York: Oxford University Press, Inc., 1956.
2. Feld, M. D., "Information and Authority: The Structure of Military Organization," *The American Sociological Review*, XXIV (February, 1959), 15–22.
3. Huntington, S. P., *The Soldier and the State*. Cambridge: Harvard University Press, 1957.
4. Janowitz, M., *Sociology and the Military Establishment*. New York: The Russell Sage Foundation, 1959.
5. Merton, R. K., *Social Theory and Social Structure*. New York: The Free Press, 1949.
6. New York World Telegram, *The World Almanac and Book of Facts* (1958).
7. Shils, E. A., "Primary Groups in the American Army," in *Continuities in Social Research*, R. K. Merton and P. F. Lazarsfeld, eds. New York: The Free Press, 1950, pp. 16–39.
8. Smith, L., *American Democracy and Military Power*. Chicago: University of Chicago Press, 1951.
9. Speier, H., "The Sociology of Military Organizations," in *Continuities in Social Research*, pp. 106–32.
10. U. S. Bureau of the Census, *Statistical Abstract of the United States, 1958*, Washington, D. C.: U. S. Government Printing Office, 1958.
11. Waller, W., *The Veteran Comes Back*. New York: Dryden Press, 1944.

# PART VI

# Minority Groups

# Lilliputians in Gulliver's Land: The Social Role of the Dwarf *

*Marcello Truzzi*

The majority of works in the massively burgeoning literature on minority groups have concentrated on the study of ethnic and racial groups. There have, of course, been studies conducted of other specialized groups including everything from homosexuals [1] to the physically handicapped,[2] but few of these studies attempt any analytic integration with the literature developed around ethnic and racial groups.[3]

One neglected subject of sociological concern is the dwarf.[4] The effects of the

stature of these persons have had numerous social and personal consequences for them, although there has been gross distortion of the problems encountered through folklore, and misrepresentation by those who have publicized dwarfs as entertainment attractions. Examination of the special problems of these small persons soon reveals that they share many of the social difficulties and problems of self-presentation found among other stigmatized minority groups.

EDITOR

---

Although the folklore and mythology of the dwarf [5] have been of great interest to those in the literary and

organization, Little People of America, and primarily surveys the functions this organization serves for its membership.

[5] The term dwarf is used here in the non-medical sense referring to any adult person whose height is so low as to socially entail perceptible drawbacks in the form of reduced strength and striking appearance. There appears to be some cross-cultural difference in the demarcation of such heights.

As regards the definition a number of figures . . . have been stated as limits of dwarfism. . . . The most rational procedure, however, would be to reckon from the mean figure of a large normal material, using the standard deviation as a measure since the conception of dwarfism must be a function of the normal height. It goes without saying that a dwarf is of another height among Lapps than among Swedes or Anglo-Saxons. (Paul Horstmann, "Dwarfism: A Clinical Investigation," *Acta Endocrinologica*, Supplement 5 [Copenhagen: Einar Munksgaard, 1949].)

* Prepared especially for this volume.

[1] E.g., Maurice Leznoff and William A. Westley, "The Homosexual Community," *Social Problems*, III (1956), 257–63.

[2] E.g., Fred Davis, "Deviance Disavowal: The Management of Strained Interaction by the Visibly Handicapped," *Social Problems*, IX (1961), 120–32.

[3] In addition to the works by Goffman cited in the paper below, a notable exception is: John Cumming and Elaine Cumming, "On the Social Psychology of Stigma," paper read at the Annual Meeting of the American Sociological Association (Washington, D.C.: 1962).

[4] A notable exception is an unpublished paper by Martin S. Weinberg, "Midgets and Dwarfs, The Organization of a Minority and the Alleviation of Their Social Problems," 1966 (Mimeo). This paper reports questionnaire responses by members of the dwarf

artistic realms,[6] social science has shown only a minimum of interest in this very specialized social role. There have been historical surveys of a general variety,[7] some biographical studies of individual dwarfs of eminence,[8] and there is a reasonable literature dealing with medical cases;[9] but a

[6] E.g., concerning literary criticism and history, cf. Joseph Ritson, "On Pigmies," in his *Fairy Tales, Legends and Romances Illustrating Shakespeare and Other Early Writers* (London: Frank and William Kerslake, 1875); or Vernon J. Harward, *The Dwarfs of Arthurian Romance and Celtic Tradition* (London: E. J. Brill, 1958). With respect to the visual arts, cf. Erika Tietze-Conrat, *Dwarfs and Jesters in Art,* trans. Elizabeth Osborn (London: Phaidon Press Ltd., 1957).

There has also been some utilization of dwarfs in fiction, often for symbolic purposes: e.g., Walter De La Mare, *Memoirs of a Midget* (New York: Alfred A. Knopf, Inc., 1922); Aldous Huxley, *Chrome Yellow* (New York: George H. Doran, 1922); or Carson McCullers, *The Ballad of the Sad Cafe* (Boston: Houghton Mifflin Company, 1951).

It is noteworthy that the social roles in which the dwarf has been cast have been expanded in recent years—a trend well reflected in the literary treatments—from what Orrin Klapp has called the role of the *deformed fool* to what today can also often include heroic and villainous roles. Cf. Orrin Klapp, *Heroes, Villains and Fools* (Englewood Cliffs, N.J.: Prentice-Hall, Inc., 1962), p. 80.

[7] Edward J. Wood, *Giants and Dwarfs* (London: Richard Bentley, 1868); C. J. S. Thompson, *The Mystery and Lore of Monsters* (London: Williams and Norgate, 1930); and Eduard Garnior, *Les Nains et les Géants* (Paris: Hachette et cie, 1884).

[8] E.g., Alice Curtis Desmond, *Barnum Presents General Tom Thumb* (New York: Crowell-Collier & Macmillan, Inc., 1954). The closest approximation to an autobiography of a dwarf that this reviewer has been able to unearth is that of Henry Viscardi, Jr., *A Man's Stature* (New York: The John Day Company, Inc., 1952), but Viscardi's affliction was limited to his legs and therefore makes him rather untypical.

[9] E.g., Horstmann, *op. cit.;* Ernst Trier Mørch, *Chondrodystrophic Dwarfs in Den-*

review of the literature dealing with these persons has revealed only one investigation into this corner of humanity by a psychologist,[10] and the closest approximation to a sociological or social psychological investigation is a somewhat sensationalistic but nonetheless valuable journalistic report.[11]

Despite the paucity of work on the social psychological dimensions of dwarfism, there has been some attention given by social psychologists to the more general interpersonal relationship characterized as *stigma*,[12] and many of the special aspects of these persons' social interactions can be subsumed under the broader rubric of deviance and minority group studies.[13] It is only within such a broader analytic framework, in fact,

*mark* (Copenhagen: Einar Munksgaard, 1941); Hans Grebe, *Chondrodysplasie* (Rome: Edizione dell' Instituto Gregorio Mendel, 1955); and P. G. Seckel, *Bird-Headed Dwarfs* (Springfield, Ill.: Charles C. Thomas, Publisher, 1960). The Horstmann study is especially valuable since it includes a variety of dwarf types as well as a large number of cases (74).

[10] Walter L. Wilkins, "Pituitary Dwarfism and Intelligence," *Journal of General Psychology*, XVIII (1938), 305–17.

[11] Walter Bodin and Burnet Hershey, *It's a Small World* (New York: Coward-McCann, Inc., 1934).

[12] Erving Goffman, *Stigma: Notes on the Management of Spoiled Identity* (Englewood Cliffs, N.J.: Prentice-Hall, Inc., 1963); and John Cumming and Elaine Cumming, "On the Social Psychology of Stigma," paper read at the Annual Meeting of the American Sociological Society (Washington, D.C.: 1962), Mimeo. Whereas Goffman centers attention upon stigma as a discrediting attribute (cf. pp. 1–3), the Cummings treat stigma as the actual loss of social competence (cf. pp. 1–3). Goffman's definition stems from his more general approach, and we shall follow his usage.

[13] Cf. Howard S. Becker, *Outsiders* (New York: The Free Press, 1963); and E. M. Lemert, *Social Pathology,* (New York: McGraw-Hill Book Company, Inc., 1951).

that any scientifically fruitful results —aside from the value of systematic description—can be obtained. For although the social lives of these small people are fascinating in their departures from conventional life histories, their great value lies in the unique conditions of variable characteristics which they offer to any future theoretical scheme enjoined to explain human behavior. For example, cursory examination of the cross-cultural literature on instances of very small persons (both real and mythological) in a society dominated by persons of normal size would seem to indicate important restrictions of social roles as well as common forms of social types.[14] It is these kinds of generalizations which might be disclosed through intensive study of these groups, and even a lack of such generalizations would be an important factor in the shaping of any future theory of social relations such as that envisioned by Goffman around concepts such as stigma.[15] Let us begin, therefore, with a review of the findings about small stature as a factor in social relations.

Although studies have been conducted on relating height to psychological characteristics such as I.Q., with some slight correlations being found,[16] the range of heights in these studies did not include those of dwarf dimensions, and it is doubtful that the slight generalizations made there can be extended to include these very small persons. In fact, such positive correlations as have been found between physical size and social activity and aggressiveness, and with non-criminality, and the negative relation to popularity,[17] might very well be strongly reversed in regard to persons of dwarf dimensions. And the inconsistent and weak correlations found between height and personality inventory scores might be greatly strengthened in the special cases of dwarfs, due to the narrower role restrictions with which they must cope.[18]

Before a more detailed examination of the social conditions of the dwarf can be attempted, it will be necessary to clarify some of the distinctions in *types of dwarfs*. The general term *dwarf* is used in this paper to refer to persons under four feet six inches in height. This definition is not a medical one[19] but refers to the social labeling which occurs among dwarfs themselves and among persons having professional dealings with them in their role as dwarf.[20] The term dwarf is used, therefore, to include *all* persons under this height whether normally proportioned or not. The term is also used here in its usual social

---

[14] E.g., the characteristics of the mythical Mehehune of Polynesia bear remarkable resemblances to the leprechauns of Ireland, as well as to other fictional small people of Oceania. Cf. Katherine Luomala, "The Mehehune of Polynesia and Other Mythical Little People of Oceania," *B. P. Bishop Museum Bulletin 203* (Honolulu: Bernice P. Bishop Museum, 1951), pp. 68–69.

[15] Cf. Goffman, *op. cit.*, pp. 126–47.

[16] Cf. J. A. Harris, *et al.*, *The Measurement of Man* (Minneapolis: University of Minnesota Press, 1930), pp. 140–49; or Roger G. Barker, B. A. Wright, and M. R. Genick, *Adjustment to Physical Handicap and Illness: A Survey of the Social Psychology of Physique and Disability* (New York: Social Science Research Council, 1946), Bulletin 55, pp. 13–15, 19–21.

[17] Studies cited in *ibid.*, p. 14.

[18] This would seem to be indicated in the study by W. L. Wilkins, "Pituary Dwarfism and Intelligence," pp. 314–15.

[19] A variety of medical classifications exist, some of which can be found in Horstmann, "Dwarfism," pp. 10–12.

[20] This demarcation at four feet six inches would appear to be very widespread; it is consistent in the writing on the subject by nonphysicians as well as in the interview data I have obtained.

meaning to exclude hereditary or racial forms of dwarfism such as the African pigmy. It seems likely that some structural similarities can be found between dwarf-normal and pigmy-normal interaction patterns; but the special problems in the socialization of the dwarf by normal-sized parents are important variable characteristics which sharply differentiate the life cycle of the dwarf from the pigmy. Thus, the dwarf's own initial primary group (his family) is already part of the normal-sized world into which he must emerge as an adult.

Although there are many medical typologies of dwarfs, our concern will not be with many of these subtle distinctions. Instead, our concern here will be only with the usually perceived categories of dwarfism—that is, the socially distinguished categories. Although the biological differences present might have importance for fully understanding the behavioral components of the dwarf's world, the definition of the situation perceived by normals interacting with dwarfs is almost completely unaffected by such subtleties of medical taxonomy; and it would appear that they make little difference to the dwarfs themselves. Thus, in terms of most role relations, it makes little difference for example, if a dwarf is a result of rickets or chondrodystrophy.

The two categories of dwarfism that will concern us here are: (1) the proportioned dwarf, or *midget,* usually the result of a dysfunction of the pituitary gland; and (2) the disproportioned dwarf, or what is sometimes termed the *true dwarf,* usually the result of achondroplasia, a dysfunction of the thyroid gland. Within each of these major categories, the social problems of each being quite different, there are many sub-cate-

gories including those of mental level, sexual potency, etc.; but our concern will be centered around those whose deviation from normalcy is *primarily* that of height. Therefore, we shall begin our examination of this group with a discussion of the proportioned dwarf, or midget.

## The Midget

Data on midgets which is presented here is based largely upon the literature described above and upon a series of interviews conducted with a well-known impressario and agent for midgets [21] and several of the midgets in his employ. Other material is based upon contact with midgets had by this investigator in the circus milieu over a period of many years.

It has been estimated that midgets, who are a great deal more rare than disproportioned dwarfs, constitute about one-millionth of the earth's population.[22] Thus, there are approximately 3,000 midgets in the world. Though this estimate is based on the status of medicine in 1934, science has made only small inroads into the treatment of this growth infirmity,[23]

[21] The entrepreneur, Mr. Nate Eagle, has had business and personal dealings with literally hundreds of midgets and has had charge of many troops of midgets, one group including 187 midgets. His role is essentially very similar to that of the late Leo Singer, the international impressario for midgets from about 1910–1935. Both men have acted in many important buffer roles and functions for the midget community. Re Singer's role in midget history, see: Bodin and Hershey, *Small World,* pp. 281–97. For information on Mr. Eagle, see: Robert Lewis Taylor, "Profile: Talker," *The New Yorker,* XXXIV (April 19 and 26, 1958), 47f. and 39f.

[22] Bodin and Hershey, *op. cit.,* p. 41.

[23] E.g., cf. Horstmann, "Dwarfism," pp. 55–67. A difficult problem in this area—and one not mentioned in the physicians' works

and the reported decreases of midgets in show business [24] are probably due to the development of new social roles now open to midgets rather than any startling decrease in their frequency.

Contrary to some folklore, midgets would appear to be evenly distributed in their births throughout the globe. Their survival into adulthood, however, has depended upon their potential "fit" into the cultural roles available to them in their societies. These roles have historically been known to include those of the shaman, king, artisan, soldier, entertainer, scholar, painter, and revolutionary; there have even been midget deities.[25] Most of these historically noteworthy midgets, however, have been rather exceptional persons in somewhat specialized circumstances (e.g., the sons or protégés of nobility) which have made it possible for them to escape what were probably the unhappy and certainly the unrecorded lives of most of their fellows. As late as 1934, most professions were closed to midgets,[26] thus forcing many of them to seek employment in exhibitionism through the theater, carnivals, and circuses. Even in 1934, however, there were numerous midgets reportedly employed as watch and clock makers and gold and jewelry workers, largely due to the excellent adaptation of their hands to such intricate tasks; and several other midgets were re-

ported to have had employment in more common occupations including shopkeeping, restaurant ownership, clerking, selling, real estate, brokerage, and even architecture.[27] But these midgets were definitely viewed as exceptional by other midgets, the majority of whom had gone into exhibitionism.[28] And even those outside the theatrical world still often capitalized on their attraction as midgets in their various other businesses. Today, the situation has greatly changed. Few midgets are now on exhibition,[29] but this has been the function of factors other than the acceptance of midgets as fully equal human beings, one of these additional considerations being a decline in public interest in seeing such human anomalies.[30]

## THE LIFE HISTORY OF THE MIDGET

Before any discussion can be undertaken of the typical midget, it must be first pointed out that there are actually four varieties of midget, and these are differentiated by those

---

we have cited—is the lack of controls in the treatment studies, since dwarfs have often been known to suddenly grow several inches without any treatment at all.

[24] Cf. "Goodbye, Tom Thumb," *Time*, LXXIX (May 18, 1962), 53; or John Lentz, "Passing of the Side Show," *Today's Health*, XLIX (March, 1964), 48–51.

[25] An excellent brief review of midgets in history can be found in Bodin and Hershey, *op. cit.*, pp. 189–207.

[26] *Ibid.*, p. 90.

[27] *Ibid.*

[28] This would seem to be borne out by inference from the fact that over half the midgets in Mr. Eagle's troop of 187 midgets were United States born (and this excludes other midget troops in the country which were smaller and therefore less able to afford the importation of foreign midgets), and our estimation that there should only have been about 150 or less midgets born in the United States who were present in this country in the late 1940's. This is also corroborated by Bodin and Hershey's placing the 1934 population of foreign- and native-born midgets in the United States at no more than 300. Cf. Bodin and Hershey, *Small World*, p. 263.

[29] See footnote 24.

[30] This is part of the larger industrial change which has brought with it the decline of the "rube mentality." For a lengthier discussion of the topic, cf. Marcello Truzzi, "The Decline of the American Circus: The Shrinkage of an Institution."

socially involved with any large number of midgets.[31] First, there is the *true midget,* a normal born child whose body growth stops at any time from infancy to the immediate pre-adolescent years. These midgets constitute the vast majority of the earth's midget population, and are adults in most particulars except for their size.

A second variety of midget is the *primordial midget* whose dwarfism exists from birth. These midgets develop perfectly normally except for height, like the true midget; but since their growth does not abruptly stop in childhood as does that of the true midget, they (1) are not initially brought up as normal children, (2) are naturally the smallest of the midget population (e.g., Miss Adele Ber of Yonkers, New York, was only one foot six inches tall, probably the world's smallest person), and (3) have closed bone ends and therefore never continue to grow as do most other types of midgets who sometimes even grow at amazing rates in their thirties.

A third variety of midget is the *infantile midget* who is intellectually normal but has not developed into sexual maturity either in physical appearance (facial hair for the male, breast and hip development for the female) or in erotic desire.

A fourth type is the *hyper-metabolic midget* whose bodily rate is about one and one-half times that of the average person's. This kind of midget is very vigorous and usually lives only about thirty years, unlike most other midgets, who sometimes

even live into their eighties and nineties. In fact, many midgets believe that midget longevity is greater than that for normal-sized persons, largely because most midgets take excellent care of their health (this being enhanced by the fact that many leisure patterns like the neighborhood bar are closed to them).

A possible fifth kind of midget is the *feeble-minded midget,* one who fails to develop in mental level as well as in stature. This type, who is not common, shall not concern us here since his major disability is his mental rather than his physical deficiency.

### The Initial Realization

The age of onset, as we have noted, can vary a great deal, but it would appear that the most frequent ages are from three to five. The usual pattern of parental response is to assume that the child is late in his growth, that he is merely physically backward. An exception to this pattern occurs when the child has a midget brother or sister already, a not uncommon occurrence, or in the rare case of a midget's own offspring being a midget. In these latter cases, the parent may be expectant of such a possibility and notice it sooner. Parental reactions to the recognition of their child's malady varies a great deal. It often takes an extreme form of either violence or shielding overprotection. The intelligent parent usually consults medical help, whereas the less educated have all too often viewed the affliction as an instrument of God's wrath against themselves and have tried to hide the fact of their abnormal child, frequently pretending that he is younger, removing him from the school, and going to a strange community.

The greatest shock, however, is that experienced by the child upon his

[31] This classification incorporates the three types of midget mentioned by Bodin and Hershey, *op. cit.,* p. 46, as well as those derived from interviews with midgets themselves. It should be mentioned that Bodin and Hershey unfortunately seem to have in some cases made false generalizations to all midgets from some of these specific types.

learning of his affliction. Many midgets never fully recover from this experience.[32] Since the child is quite young (usually about nine or ten) when he experiences this fateful revelation, its full implications are usually not immediate; and there is often a hopeful disbelief and an expectancy that growth may still come. It is not uncommon for those who seek medical advice and, normally, fail to receive any benefit, to turn to quacks.[33]

Before we can understand the nature of the life careers adopted by the midget, some description must be made of the special problems of his condition, aside from the psychic difficulties.

## THE MATERIAL PROBLEMS OF THE MIDGET

The most important material problem of the midget is the oversized nature of most of the socially produced items that he needs in his daily life. Whether it be the massive bathtub (in which some midgets have been said to drown), the impossibility of obtaining the appropriate ready-made clothes (children's clothes are very limited as a substitute because of differences in the adult's physical shape and his style of fashion—even shoes must be especially made at a cost of about fifty dollars per pair), the necessity of making mechanical adjustments on an auto-

mobile before it can be driven (raising the seat level and the operation pedals), or merely the everyday little nuisances such as the too highly placed elevator buttons or telephone in the pay station, the midget finds himself constantly confronted with the symbols of his smallness. And the life of a midget is an expensive as well as a frustrating one. The simple fact is that most midgets simply cannot afford to take many everyday jobs (even where they are open to them), jobs which can provide them with some preservation of their self-picture as a normal human being but not enough pay to meet their many special expenses. Aside from the need for custom-made clothes (which most midgets have learned to partly circumvent by becoming experts with a needle and thread), another basic problem is food. Midgets eat as much as or more than normal-sized persons, but usually must do so in smaller quantities at one time; thus, many eat four or five times a day instead of the usual two or three times. This creates some waste even at home, and is much worse for the midget who eats in commercial establishments. Pride almost always precludes the ordering of a child's-size portion; and this means even greater waste and expense. This is one of the main reasons for the great attraction for midgets of the world of exhibitionism; for despite its cost to the psyche, it often has meant remarkable financial rewards, as well as other compensations to be discussed below.

## THE PERSONALITY OF THE MIDGET

As might be expected, the typical midget has developed under a socialization process which is highly hazardous to his ego development. In

[32] As Goffman well put it: "The painfulness . . . of sudden stigmatization can come not from an individual's confusion about his identity, but from his knowing too well what he has become," Goffman, *Stigma*, pp. 132–33.

[33] No statistics are available on midgets' consultations with quacks; but Mørch found that 43 per cent of all cases of chondrodystrophic dwarfism in Denmark had consulted quacks. Cf. E. T. Mørch, *Dwarfs in Denmark*, p. 111. The number of consultations by midgets is probably less since their disorder is somewhat easier to live with.

his investigations, Wilkins applied the Thurstone *Personality Schedule (Clark revision)* to thirty midgets. He found that:

All but two of these scores indicate . . . some degree—marked or mild—of maladjustment . . . [And] the extreme deviation upon the personality scale showed, beyond peradventure, lack of personality growth which makes social adjustment difficult for most midgets and impossible for many.[34]

As might be expected, such a physical maladjustment often produces strong overcompensatory characteristics. Bodin and Hershey baldly stated in their 1934 work (which included many nonexhibitioning midgets) that:

Midgets, to survive decently in an oversized world, must be egotists.
When they have finally equipped themselves to survive in what will always be an alien world, they frequently emerge as insufferable egotists.[35]

This overcompensation, however, is centered about their concern with the normal-sized world's recognition of their status as *adult, fellow human beings.* That is, there seems to be not so much a blown-up self-picture (such as that which characterizes some conceited persons), but rather, an overuse made of what Goffman has termed *disidentifiers,* that is:

a sign that tends—in fact or hope—to break up an otherwise coherent picture but in this case a positive direction desired by the actor, not so much establishing a new claim as throwing severe doubt on the validity of the virtual one.[36]

This disidentification centers about their demonstrating that they are

34 Wilkins, "Pituitary Dwarfism," pp. 314–15.
35 Bodin and Hershey, *Small World,* p. 162.
36 Goffman, *Stigma,* p. 44.

1. *adults* and not children, and
2. *fellow human beings,* and not some sort of freak.

Their insistence that they be treated as adults often involves the invoking of numerous disidentifiers such as hats, canes, cigars, and facial hair by the men; high fashions and elaborate makeup and hairdo by the women; and more formal attire for both sexes than normal-sized persons might generally wear. This defensiveness about being confused with children sometimes has its disadvantages. We have already mentioned the usual refusal to order a child's portion, despite the desire for a limited quantity of food. But this is only one of the many cases where pride precludes the buying of children's things, e.g., such limited clothing as might in fact prove adaptable is often scorned. This hatred for treatment as though they were children is evident in many actions which are usually taken by normals to indicate extreme arrogance. This can prove rather embarrassing to one who first meets midgets, since many of our actions toward small persons are habitually those we would extend toward children, e.g., the offering of one's hand when crossing the street, or other forms of help offered quite unmaliciously by normal-sized adults. Too, this drive for the recognition of full adulthood sometimes results in the midget male's showing a certain degree of bravado, or boasting about sexual activities, especially with normal-sized women.

The importance of disidentification by the midget from the world of what are often termed freaks or monsters is a second major motivation in the midget's dealings with normal-sized persons. Like most minority groups, midgets have accepted the dominant group as their reference point in the creation of their values. Thus, the midget does not refer to himself as a dwarf at any time. This term is strictly restricted by him to those disproportioned small persons who, to him as well as to most normals, appear somewhat aesthetically grotesque. Thus, midgets see themselves as merely *small persons*. This is well evidenced in their conversations, and in the name given their organization of the Small Men's Association at the Los Angeles County Fair in 1927. Calling a midget a dwarf is considered an insult by most midgets. It seems to be largely because of this fact that midgets seldom have much to do with dwarfs or the professions of dwarfs. Thus, midgets are very seldom found in circuses as clowns, as professional wrestlers, or in other jobs which often falsely advertise themselves as "midget" exhibitions but in fact include only the disproportioned dwarf. On the other hand, many dwarfs prefer to be referred to as midgets even though they are not technically such.

It is in conjunction with this motive to stress his fellow-humanity that the midget in show business has found some conflict. For the midget in show business has classically been asked to present somewhat of a caricature to his audience, a "minstrelization" [37] or clown role of the happy and talented little man mixed with that of the precocious child. Midgets have always resented this role, and have tried to stress their talents as singers, dancers, and musicians. But the audience has always responded to these performers—many of whom are truly exceptional in their professional abilities—as midgets first and performers only second. It is this conflict which has probably done most to drive the midget from show business. And as more midgets have found greater personal freedom and satisfaction in new social roles, there has developed a negative reaction by many midgets against show business in general and against midgets who have turned to it, much in the manner of many Negro Americans' rejection of those Negroes who gave white Americans a stereotyped image of their race and culture.[38]

## SEXUAL AND MARITAL PATTERNS

No elaborate survey having been conducted on the sexual activities of midgets, our information about such behaviors must remain somewhat clouded. Two main sources of obfuscation other than the paucity of materials exist:

1. the tendency of some midgets to elaborate upon their sexual exploits because of their symbolic value as proof of their adulthood, and
2. lack of knowledge of whether many midgets from whom information has been obtained are, in fact, true, primordial, or infantile midgets.

As we have noted, the infantile midget has no sexual development;

[37] Cf. *ibid.*, pp. 109–10. The term "minstrelization" comes from A. Broyard, "Portrait of the Inauthentic Negro," *Commentary*, X (1950), 59–60.

[38] It is interesting that this attitude towards "minstrelization" is still quite new among midgets, and a reaction against this "deminstrelization" or role inversion has not yet been exhibited, except, possibly among the ranks of current show business midgets. Show business midgets, however, have an odd form of midget pride since it is also valuable for a midget—given that he must be small all his life—to be as small as possible. Thus, many midgets who relied upon exhibitionism as their livelihood lived in fear that they might (as did some midgets) grow into that intermediary height where they were minimally valuable as midgets but not normal sized either. Thus, one could achieve a strange sort of vested interest in being one of the smallest midgets.

but this impotency is something which is usually hidden and is sometimes covered by elaborate fictions. Bodin and Hershey found in their extensive interviews that the true midget male's sexual potency develops only in his late teens or early twenties. This late onset only adds to his maturational problems; and his early learning of the covering process:

The midget has arrived at the age of puberty, but does not stand on the threshold of maturity, as do his friends. Their smutty stories, their girl-ogling, their growing preoccupation with things of the flesh are foreign to him. He patterns after them in outward behavior, but has no valid reason for doing so. These pubescent boys, so soon to be initiated into the ritual of sex, act and talk instinctively; the midget, with his sexual awakening still a half dozen or more years in the future, apes them to save face.[39]

This kind of artificial role playing is thus begun early, and makes it difficult to objectively ascertain much from the midget male's later tales of conquest.

Bodin and Hershey also reported that impotency comes early to the midget male, usually present by the age of fifty.[40] This fact also makes

[39] Bodin and Hershey, *Small World*, p. 87. Because of the *visibility* of his stigma, the midget cannot pass as a normal sized person, as can persons with some other kinds of stigma. His stature is very evident to anyone; and this perceptibility of his stigma is present even on the telephone since the voice of most midgets is quite shrill and distinctive compared to the normal adult. The midget is therefore forced to concentrate on minimizing the *obtrusiveness* of his stigma (cf. Goffman, *Stigma*, pp. 48–51, for an excellent discussion of the nuances of visibility). He therefore learns many *covering techniques* which he can use to reduce tension and normalize interaction (cf. *ibid.*, pp. 102–4, for a fuller discussion of the covering process).

[40] Bodin and Hershey, *Small World*, p. 101.

objective information difficult to obtain in lieu of the exceptional value placed on masculinity as a symbol of adulthood for the midget.

Midget women also develop late, seldom reaching menstruation before nineteen or twenty. But this probably creates few comparable problems for the female. Her great conflict has classically been the fear of pregnancy, for the child would have to be removed by Caesarian section. Although many of the midgets that Bodin and Hershey surveyed led complete sexual lives, they also found that many females had chosen celibacy at the time of their 1934 interviews because of the dangers involved in a pregnancy. With modern advances in medicine and contraception, however, it is unlikely that this latter pattern is common today. And even in these 1934 cases, there is some lack of clarity as to the possibility that these celibate women might have been infantile midgets.

In their 1934 interviews, which surveyed 233 midgets in the United States, Bodin and Hershey found that only slightly over 22 per cent of the midget population married at all, that 56 per cent of these married other midgets, the remaining 44 per cent marrying normal-sized persons.[41] Fifty-nine per cent of all the marriages were childless with fruitfulness greatest in marriages between midgets and normals (70 per cent), with a great decrease in fruitfulness in marriages between midgets (just under 11 per cent). Marriages of midget women to normal males were slightly less fertile than those of midget males and normal women; but this difference was not significant, and can probably be explained by the preg-

[41] These and other percentages given in their survey can be found in *ibid.*, pp. 148–50.

nancy fear of the female midget. Despite these very crude statistics presented by Bodin and Hershey to show relatively small fertility between midgets, history has reported tremendous variations in these patterns. Thus, to cite an extreme and probably exaggerated case, in the eighteenth century Judith Skinner (two feet two inches tall) reputedly gave her husband Robert (two feet one inch tall) fourteen normal-sized healthy childen over a twenty-three year period, all of whom survived to adulthood.

Although the reason for marriage by midgets varies with their idiosyncratic personalities, the range of which should not be underestimated, some common patterns can be found here, as in most matings. Probably the most interesting pattern, however, is that of the normal-midget intermarriage. Here it would probably be wise to sharply differentiate whether the midget member was male or female. In the case of the male midget, as we have already noted, there is some desire on his part to prove to normal-sized males that he can engage in relations with normal-sized females on a basis equal to their own. It also must be remembered that the majority of a midget's daily contacts are with normal-sized persons, and not other midgets. Midgets cannot usually live in an insulated world of their own, nor do they usually so desire. In fact, many of the ideas held of the midget living in an apartment or house with his furniture and other personal objects scaled down to his size are purely mythological, often part of the spiel fed to the gullible public by the men who have exhibited midgets in such bogus surroundings. The midget, like most of us, has internalized the basic values and aesthetic judgments of his general culture; and this includes the

usual notions of feminine beauty. Thus, a midget is no less impressed by the strains of a popular song with its ideal of the girl as "five foot two, eyes of blue . . ." just because he is a mere two feet eight.

It is probably true that strong maternal feelings are a component to be found in the normal-sized woman who marries a midget male. Interviews with midget males, many of whom have sexual careers rivaling that of Don Juan, indicate that a strong force in their favor is the curiosity of many normal-sized women. However, it seems unlikely that such curiosity is an important factor in bringing about intermarriage.

The midget female probably presents a different pattern of intermarriage. A diminutive size for a wife and mother is somewhat more expected than it is for a husband and father, and although a woman of midget proportions is exceeding the expectation, she is nonetheless in line with the expected direction. The midget male, on the other hand, has actually reversed the expected pattern in the family, and must cope with the many conflicts his size presents in symbolically limiting and even denying his masculinity. The midget female has no such problems. There is no direct conflict between her size and her role as wife and mother.

Although divorce is not unknown in midget marriages, whether they be between midgets or between midgets and normals, no figures are available. Like the reasons for the original marriage, there are a multitude of causes. But it is likely that, in the case of intermarriages, there is not always a clear understanding by the midget of the difficulties inherent in his assimilation.

Frequently midgets so marry, in part, at

least in the belief that union with one of the "big people" will convince the world of their normality and thus gain its tolerance. Quite the reverse is true. Such matings invariably magnify the midget's incongruity and further arouse the onlookers' curiosity as to the sexual experience involved in such alliances.[42]

Finally, a word might be mentioned regarding sexual deviation among midgets. Information on this point is, as one might expect, almost nonexistent. There are numerous cases which have been reported of midget females who have been employed in prostitution, posing in some cases as children for the Humbert Humberts' jaded appetites. As for other deviations, they are probably rare, in light of the exaggerated response of the midget to otherwise attain all the symbols of normality. This would be especially true of male homosexuality, which would be blatantly in conflict with the ultramasculine projection of most midget males; and this is confirmed by the lack of any such cases reported by Bodin and Hershey's 233 informants.[43] Cross-cultural materials may provide some exceptions, of course; but in Western society, as the old joke goes, the midget has quite enough trouble by just being a midget.

## The Disproportioned Dwarf

The disproportioned dwarf presents us with quite different problems than the midget; for other than medical (usually physiological) investigations, we have very little knowledge about these people's lives. The disproportioned dwarf can take many forms and his malformation can be the re-

sult of many conditions, including chondrodystrophy, cretinism, rickets, Silfverkiöld-Murguios disease, gargoylism, phocomelia, Kashin-Beck's disease, multiple cartilaginous exostoses and chondromata, as well as other rarer causes.[44] By far the most common of these forms of dwarfism, however, is chondrodystrophic dwarfism; and it is only with this form of disproportionate dwarfism that we shall be dealing in this paper.

The chondrodystrophic man is what many persons think of as the *true dwarf*, the dwarf often pictured in Norse mythology. He has a normal-sized torso and head but small arms and legs. This disproportion gives many persons the false impression that his head is actually larger than it should be. This disorder appears to be hereditary, and is actually present from birth. There are also some minor characteristics often present such as bowleggedness and a typical head shape.[45]

Although an organization for dwarfs called Little People of America Incorporated was founded in 1957,[46]

---

[42] *Ibid.*, p. 151.
[43] *Ibid.*, p. 107.
[44] Cf. Mørch, "Dwarfism in Denmark," pp. 57–77.
[45] A full description can be found in *ibid.*, pp. 28–38.
[46] This group held its seventh national convention in Philadelphia in 1965. An investigation of this group is currently being made, but this author must thus far rely on limited information from its newsletters, personal correspondence with its president, and a highly popularized article: Alvin Adams, "The Little People—A Tiny Minority with Big Problems," *Ebony*, XX (October, 1965), 104–13. It is noted in this article that less than 1 per cent of this organization's members (some 700 according to information from personal correspondence with its president) earn their living in show business (p. 110). This presents some question about the representativeness of this membership. Although these little people strongly reject show business as "minstrelization," informant dwarfs in show business

and although this organization probably has mostly chondrodystrophic persons as members [47] (thus making a control data source for research on dwarfs now possible), little objective data are currently available on the social problems of the dwarf in the United States.

The findings of Mørch's excellent 1941 survey of all the 86 living chondrodystrophic persons in Denmark, however, are probably generalized in most ways to the chondrodystrophic population elsewhere, since it is quite well established that their frequency is unaffected by parents' race, geography, or class structure.[48] According to Mørch's findings, chondrodystrophics number one person per 44,000.[49] Thus, there are about 65,000 present in the world today, and about 4,450 in the United States.

Although chondrodystrophic persons are encumbered by their low stature, this problem is at least equaled by their disproportioned appearance, especially in the case of the female, since beauty is normally an important variable in the life of a woman. This lack of physical beauty is an important factor for the social adjustment of the chondrodystrophic person; and it is probably this factor

which is reflected in the marital figures given by Mørch. Only about one third of the Danish chondrodystrophic men were married, and only one chondrodystrophic woman, she to a chondrodystrophic man.[50] In the Danish cases this has led to illegitimate pregnancies among these women, a situation similar to that reported as being present in the United States.[51]

In regard to the occupational roles, Mørch found that of the thirty-nine men, there were twenty-one artisans, three tradesmen, four office clerks, one musician, one circus clown, one souffleur, and eight unskilled laborers. Among the thirty-eight women, there were nine seamstresses, one married woman, one owner of an embroidery shop, one teacher of housekeeping, one music student, one farm owner, one music hall performer, two housemaids, and seventeen untrained women.[52] Although the occupational pattern is probably quite similar in the United States, insofar as women are less trained than the men, the situation is otherwise probably quite specific to Denmark and other socialist countries which provide special aid and training for these people. Thus, the picture may well be less bright in the United States, where training is not provided by the government.

Finally, it should be noted that Mørch found his chondrodystrophic persons of normal mental development; and, although they experience great psychological stresses, he found that "The great majority of them have a pleasant, well-balanced disposition of a quite normal emotional nature." [53] However, he also states:

---

were asked about this new organization and gave it a somewhat negative description as a club for maladjusted dwarfs. Thus, the show business role, which usually places a dwarf in the company of other dwarfs—unlike many other jobs, which isolate the dwarf—often functions to give him a therapeutic milieu within the limits allowed by the show business role.

[47] Unfortunately, there is no breakdown of its over 700 members by dwarf type. It might be noted that this organization sets its membership height maximum at four feet ten inches, unlike the four feet six inches we have set in this discussion.

[48] Mørch "Dwarfism in Denmark," pp. 103–11, 122.

[49] Ibid., p. 101.

[50] Ibid., p. 46.
[51] Cf. A. Adams, "The Little People," p. 113.
[52] Mørch, op. cit., p. 56.
[53] Ibid., p. 55.

As is to be expected in patients with such a marked degree of malformation, one will sometimes meet with suspicion, hypersensitiveness to offense—real or imaginary—and aversion to society.[54]

## Conclusion

In our examination of the dwarf, we have found that these persons must encounter a variety of problems. The midget represents the true variable condition of stature diminished to the point of having serious interpersonal consequences. The chondrodystrophic dwarf, on the other hand, presents us with a case of this condition plus the presence of a malformation whose grotesque qualities also have their influence.

Although the data are very limited, the compounding of deviant characteristics in the chondrodystrophic person (both his stature and aesthetic appearance) creates much greater problems for him than for the midget. Though both show normal intelligence and ability, both have found social roles and occupations closed to them, and both find their physical stature creating conflict in some of the social roles they can successfully maintain; but the midget seems to have generally found his conflict somewhat smaller. Of the female members of these minority groups, the midget woman, too, has found a great deal less conflict, for she may still retain beauty despite her lack of normal height; thus, marriage is usually available to her, even if she might not choose to take it.

The dwarf presents a unique case for social science investigation. As we have seen, the dwarf undergoes a socialization process which, because of the many roles closed to him, probably represents a greater uniformity

than that undergone by most normal-sized persons. What are the implications of this social tightening? From what little we know, this uniformity should have its counterpart in the personality structures of dwarfs. One would also predict, in lieu of their limited access to the achievement of life goals,[55] that dwarfs should be highly anomic. Investigation of this and many similar personality questions awaits our collection of more information.

The dwarf clearly fits the criteria set for definition of a minority group,[56] yet the importance of this group, as well as other nonethnic categories of persons that would fit the definition, has been seriously neglected. It might also be mentioned, in this regard, that, although dwarfs are not a race of people, this has sometimes been thought of them by the general population; thus, some cases of dwarf-normal interactions might fit under the sociological category (if such it can be called) of race relations. However, the point being made here is that these persons, and the reactions of normals to them, constitute important sources for the testing of some of our propositions about minority groups developed elsewhere. Thus, some of our notions about prejudice, as for example in Frank R. Westie's normative theory,[57] would include the

[54] *Ibid.*

[55] Cf. Dorothy L. Meier and Wendell Bell, "Anomie and Differential Access to the Achievement of Life Goals," *The American Sociological Review*, XXIV (April, 1959), 189–202.

[56] Cf. Louis Wirth, "The Problem of Minority Groups," in *The Science of Man in the World of Crisis*, ed. R. Linton (New York: Columbia University Press, 1945), pp. 347–72.

[57] Frank R. Westie, "Race and Ethnic Relations," in *Handbook of Modern Sociology*, ed. Robert E. L. Faris (Chicago: Rand McNally & Company, 1964), pp. 581–603.

commonly held attitude toward the dwarf as one who is an inferior person fitted only for limited roles, but would find this case a difficult theoretical fit. For it is quite possible that the prejudice against the small person has a quite different etiology than that which we find against Negroes or ethnic groups. Thus, Westie's theory states that:

Individuals are prejudiced because they are raised in societies which have prejudice as a facet of the normative system of their culture. Prejudice is built into the culture in the form of normative precepts—that is, notions of "ought to be"—which define the ways in which members of the group ought to behave in relation to the members of selected outgroups.[58]

It seems likely, however, that the false generalizations held about the dwarf are not directly learned—how many people have ever actually been told the proper behavior toward a dwarf?—but may be the result of something more basic in man's predisposition, e.g., a sense of dominance over the small (superiority), and a repugnance toward the malformed (negative affect). In any case, we have no right to assume a simple fit for our theories of prejudice developed in other areas when we attempt to apply them to the case of dwarfism. Though this writer believes that it is probably true that we deal here with the same kind of prejudice found elsewhere, this has simply not been established. Empirical questions are thus posed which need to be answered; for it is not impossible that, for example, persons scoring high on the F scale (authoritarianism) might in fact be less prejudiced toward dwarfs.

The remarkable thing is not that we know so little about dwarfs themselves—although this is certainly regrettable—but that we know so little about attitudes toward them. Clearly, prejudice exists, role expectations are limited, and strong affective reactions can be elicited; but the domain is unmapped. Almost every culture has special roles for the very small person; but the similarities in these social typings have never been investigated.

Social science must broaden its focus to include investigations of groups such as the dwarf. For if it fails to examine the whole of man in all his forms, including his less common ones, its theoretical development will be parochial; and it will fail to analytically encompass but a corner of social life.

[58] *Ibid.*, pp. 583–84.

# 17

## Sexual Modesty, Social Meanings, and the Nudist Camp *†

### Martin S. Weinberg

Among the numerous types of *sign equipment* discussed by Erving Goffman in our earlier selection on "Symbols of Class Status," was clothes. The changing symbolic values in clothes are clearly reflected by the presence of fluctuations in what is considered fashionable dress.[1] The social functions of clothing have long been of interest to sociologists;[2] but we can often discover the importance of social objects most clearly by studying those cases where they are absent. This is well demonstrated by the following study.[3]

EDITOR

---

Deviant sub-systems have norms that permit, organize, and control the behavior which defines them as deviant. The nudist camp is an example of such a deviant sub-system, nudists being defined as deviant by their disregard for clothing when in the presence of others, particularly members of the opposite sex. This paper will describe the normative system of the nudist camp, its consequences for sustaining the definition of the situation common to this group, and the way it maintains those interaction patterns this sub-system shares with the outside society.

* Reprinted from *Social Problems*, XII (1965), 311–18, by permission of The Society for the Study of Social Problems and with several minor changes added by the author. Footnotes renumbered.

† Revision of a paper presented at the annual meeting of the Midwest Sociological Society, Kansas City, 1964. This represents one aspect of a theoretical treatment and study on Sex, Modesty, and Deviants. I am grateful to John I. Kitsuse for his encouragement, suggestions, and criticisms. I would also like to thank Raymond Mack, Scott Greer, Arnold Feldman, Walter Wallace, and Richard Schwartz for their valuable comments.

[1] Such fashion fluctuations have been intensively but not extensively studied. Cf. A. L. Kroeber and J. Richardson, *Three Centuries of Women's Dress Fashions; a Quantitative Analysis* (Anthropological Records, Vol. V, No. 2, University of California at Berkeley, 1940).

[2] For some of the classic early statements, see: W. I. Thomas, "The Psychology of Modesty and Clothing," *The American Journal of Sociology*, V (1900), 246–62; J. C. Flugel, *The Psychology of Clothes* (London: The Hogarth Press, 1930); E. B. Hurloch, *The Psychology of Dress* (New York: The Ronald Press Company, 1929); and F. A. Parsons, *Psychology of Dress* (New York: Doubleday & Company, Inc., 1921).

[3] For more recent works of relevance, see: Martin S. Weinberg, "Becoming a Nudist," *Psychiatry*, XXIX (1966), 15–24; and Fred Ilfeld, Jr. and Roger Lauer, *Social Nudism in America* (New Haven, Conn.: College and University Press, 1964).

The general sociological framework to be used emphasizes the study of "social meanings" as a salient subject for understanding the realm of social organization. Such an approach was set forth by Weber: [4] in order to understand social organization it is not sufficient to look at stable and recurrent patterns of social behavior alone; one also must look at the subjective meanings attached to behavior, i.e., those meanings by which social behavior is oriented in its course. The assumption underlying this focus is that stable social meanings are products of a social standardization process, being controlled by the "molds" which social organization imposes on patterns of association.[5]

The institutionalized patterns of sexual modesty will be viewed as an aspect of social organization, with attention given to the social meanings linked to normative breaches, i.e., immodesty. A study of the deviant case of social nudists will then be presented, illustrating how members of this social system are re-socialized in the meaning attributed to one form of immodesty. It is hoped that this study will contribute to a better understanding of the nature and essence of sexual modesty, as well as to the general processes of social organization.

## Modesty and Meanings

Modesty is a form of reserve. Sexual modesty is sexual reserve (or a communication of non-availability for sexual interaction). This quality of meaning results from the social actor's following the dictates of sexual propriety—the common-sense constructs of proper or "decent" behavior. From the point of view of this paper, sexual modesty is thus defined as an institutionalized pattern of social interaction.[6] It imposes a pattern of ten-

---

[4] Max Weber, *The Theory of Social and Economic Organization* (New York: The Free Press, 1947), pp. 88ff. Also see: Alfred Schutz, *Collected Papers I: The Problem of Social Reality* (The Hague: Martinus Nijhoff, 1962), p. 59. Schutz insists that in considering these social meanings the sociologist develop "constructs of the second degree" out of the meaning constructs which typically guide the social actor. That is, the sociologist should abstract his more generalized model of social order out of the "order" which channels individual actors in their social behavior.

[5] Cf. Harold Garfinkel, "The Routine Grounds of Everyday Activities," *Social Problems*, III (Winter, 1964), 237.

[6] An "institutionalized pattern of social interaction" will be defined as an organized way of doing something: a formal, legitimized, recognized, established, and stabilized way in which an aspect of behavior is expected to be performed. (Cf. Robert Bierstedt, *The Social Order* [New York: McGraw-Hill Book Company, Inc.], pp. 299ff.)

Modesty may additionally be viewed as a pattern of deference, i.e., conducting oneself with good demeanor is in general a way of showing deference to those present (cf. Erving Goffman, "The Nature of Deference and Demeanor," *American Anthropologist*, LVIII [June, 1956], p. 492). This could be labeled "deference through non-initiation" of sexual overtures. This interpretation of modesty leads us to inequalities in the social structure, since patterns of deference point to the relative positions of the actor and alter in the social hierarchy. Therefore, as women gain more equality in the social structure we would expect the "double standard" of modesty to decline— i.e., women gain more rights to "initiate" or suspend patterns of deference.

A more extreme degree of deference may, however, lead to immodesty rather than modesty. This is "deference through subservience." Thus women who dress or act immodestly solely for the benefit of the male may also demonstrate deference. Deference through both non-initiation and subservience should decrease with equalization of the social structure.

sion management by which social control is maintained over the sexual interests latent in any heterosexual encounter.

In the sexual realm, acts of immodesty take the following basic forms, all of them communicating a boldness or lack of inhibition: (1) verbal communications; and (2) non-verbal communications,[7] which typically are differentiated into (a) a display of body or bodily functions, and (b) other forms of erotic overture (e.g., the way one actor looks at another).

Common-sense definitions assume an interrelationship between verbal and non-verbal expressions of immodesty. Rightly or wrongly, most men regard a woman who will curse in their presence—that is, use the proscribed four letter words—as a woman who will suit action to her language.[8] At one time this imputation went so far that if a woman talked about the "legs" of a table or the "breast" of a chicken, she was immediately typed as being *immodest and unrefined*.[9] The preceding examples illustrate, respectively, two meanings commonly attributed to immodest acts:

1. the act may be perceived as communicating sexual availability; and
2. the act may be perceived as a projection of bad breeding.

These types are not mutually exclusive, but they do seem most typically differentiated by the *blatancy* of display.

[7] See Erving Goffman, *The Presentation of Self in Everyday Life* (Garden City, N.Y.: Doubleday Anchor Books, 1959).
[8] Shailer Upton Lawton and Jules Archer, *Sexual Conduct of the Teen-Ager* (New York: Spectrolux Corporation, 1951), p. 111.
[9] Alexander M. Gow, *Good Morals and Gentle Manners for Schools and Families* (New York: American Book Co., 1873).

Immodest acts may also be analytically differentiated along the dimension of "commission—omission."[10] That is, acts may be classified as immodest because of one's *active* performance of an act, or because of one's *passiveness* or failure to manage effectively an impression of restraint in regard to another's immodest act. Thus, the girl who stares at a nude man is defined as immodest, as well as the girl who displays herself nude; the girl who listens to "dirty" jokes (and, if unable to escape the social gathering, fails to display inattention), as well as the girl who tells them; the girl who allows herself to be grabbed, as well as the girl who does the grabbing. Although it may appear contradictory to define *passiveness* as nullifying *reserve*, this may be clarified by viewing such an omission as invalidating an impression of *sexual* reserve (i.e., non-availability for sexual interaction).

TYPOLOGY OF IMMODEST BEHAVIOR

| Act of: | Display of body | Verbal expression | Erotic overtures |
|---|---|---|---|
| Commission | Shows 1-1 | Says 1-2 | Does 1-3 |
| Omission | Looks at 2-1 | Listens to 2-2 | Lets do 2-3 |

HYPOTHESIS AND METHOD

The manifest function of sexual modesty (i.e., those consequences evaluated by common-sense rationality) is maintenance of social control over latent sexual interests. Common-sense conceptions of modesty also put most emphasis on the covering of the body when in the presence of the op-

[10] Weber, *Social and Economic Organization*, p. 88; Schutz, *Collected Papers I*, pp. 6ff.

posite sex for the performance of this function.[11] Considerations of a breakdown in clothing modesty bring forth images of rampant sexual interest, promiscuity, embarrassment, jealousy, and shame.

Social nudists (i.e., those who practice nudism in a nudist camp) are thus defined as "deviants" by their disregard for body covering, falling in cell 1-1 of our typology of immodesty. The remainder of the paper will discuss an empirical study of this group of systematic deviants.[12] The following general hypothesis provided the foundation for this research:

If nudists effectively change the societal definition of the situation regarding nudity, and are also able to maintain the forms of modesty pertaining to the other cells of our typology, then social control over latent sexual interests will still be maintained.

If we take as given that the nudist camp only changes the definition of one of our cells of immodesty, then when other forms of modesty are not maintained the *indubitableness* or taken-for-grantedness of the changed definition of the situation (regarding nudity) will be called into question.[13]

For an examination of this hypothesis, three nudist camps located near the Chicago metropolitan area were

contacted, and readily agreed to be the objects of research. Field work was undertaken in these camps over the course of one summer. During the period of participant observation, nudist members were asked to fill out cards which requested their name and address, so that they could be contacted at a later date for purposes of an interview. These formalized interviews were a supplement to the more exploratory field work, serving as a systematic technique by which to gather the specific data desired. Although nudists tend to be wary of revealing personal data such as last name or address, rapport was high and, when given a promise of confidentiality, very few refused to fill out these sample cards.

After the observational data were organized, an interview schedule was constructed. Selection of respondents was limited to those living within a hundred mile radius of Chicago; a total of one hundred and one interviews were completed.[14]

## The Nudist Camp

The ideology of the nudist camp provides a new definition of the situation regarding nudity, which in effect maintains that:

1. nudism and sexuality are unrelated
2. there is nothing shameful about exposing the human body
3. the abandonment of clothes can lead to a feeling of freedom and natural pleasure
4. nude activities, especially full bodily exposure to the sun, leads to a feeling of physical, mental, and spiritual well-being.

[11] See Lawrence Langner, *The Importance of Wearing Clothes* (New York: Hastings House Publishers, Inc., 1959); René Guyon, *The Ethics of Sexual Acts* (New York: Blue Ribbon Books, 1941); Havelock Ellis, *Studies in the Psychology of Sex*, Vol. 1 (Philadelphia: F. A. Davis Co., 1930).

[12] For a discussion of the concept "systematic deviant," see Edwin Lemert, *Social Pathology* (New York: McGraw-Hill Book Company, Inc., 1951).

[13] See Schutz, *Collected Papers, I*, pp. 94–95, for a summary discussion of the process by which presuppositions get called into question.

[14] Many of the nudists interviewed had attended or held membership in a number of different camps. Thus, experiences from at least twenty camps provided concurrent data for our conclusions.

These definitions are sustained by nudists to a remarkable degree, illustrating the extent to which adult socialization can function in changing long-maintained meanings; in this case regarding the exposure of one's nude body in heterosexual situations. The tremendous emphasis on covering the sexual areas, and the relation between nudism and sexuality which exists in the outside society, however, suggest that the nudist definition of the situation might, at times, be quite easily called into question. The results of the field work and formal interviews indicate how the social organization of the nudist camp has developed a system of norms that contributes to sustaining the official definition of the situation. Since the major concern of this paper is modesty, we will restrict our discussion to the first two declarations of nudist ideology (i.e., that nudism and sexuality are unrelated, and that there is nothing shameful about exposing the human body). These are also the elements which lead to the classification of nudists as deviant. The normative proscriptions which contribute to the maintenance of this definition of the situation will be described.

*Organizational Precautions.* Organizational precautions are initially taken in the requirements for admission to a nudist camp. Most camps do not allow unmarried individuals, especially single men, or allow only a small quota of singles. Those camps that do allow male-singles may charge up to thirty-five per cent higher rates for the single's membership than is charged for the membership of an entire family. This is intended to discourage single memberships but, since the cost is still relatively low in comparison to other resorts, this measure is not very effective. It seems to do little more than create resentment among the singles. By giving formal organizational backing to the definition that singles are not especially desirable, it also might be related to the social segregation of single and married members that is evident in nudist camps.

An overabundance of single men is recognized by the organization as threatening the definition of nudism that is maintained. The presence of singles at the camp is suspected to be for purposes other than the "nudist way of life" (e.g., to gape at the women). Such a view may call into question the denied relation between nudity and sexuality.

Certification by the camp owner is also required before anyone is admitted on the camp grounds. This is sometimes supplemented by three letters of recommendation in regard to the character of the applicant. This is a precaution against admitting those "social types" which might conceivably discredit the ideology of the movement.

A limit is sometimes set on the number of trial visits which can be made to the camp; that is, visits made without membership in some camp or inter-camp organization. In addition, a limit is usually set on the length of time one is allowed to maintain himself clothed. These rules function to weed out those guests whose sincere acceptance of the "nudist" definition of the situation is questionable.

*Norms Regarding Interpersonal Behavior.* Norms regarding patterns of interpersonal behavior are also functional for the maintenance of the organization's system of meanings. The existence of these norms, however, should be recognized as formally acknowledging that the nudist definition of the situation could become problematic unless precautions were taken.

*No staring.* This rule functions to prevent any overt signs of "overinvolvement." In the words of a nonnudist who is involved in the publication of a nudist magazine, "They all look up to the heavens and never look below." This pattern of civil inattention[15] is most exaggerated among the females, who manage the impression that there is absolutely no concern or awareness that the male body is in an unclothed state. Women often recount how they expect everyone will look at them when they are nude, only to find that no one communicates any impression of concern when they finally do get up their nerve and undress. One woman told the writer: "I got so mad because my husband wanted me to undress in front of other men that I just pulled my clothes right off thinking everyone would look at me." She was amazed (and somewhat disappointed) when no one did. Thus, even though nudists are immodest in their behavior by "showing" their bodies, which falls in cell 1-1 of our typology of immodesty, they are not immodest in the sense of cell 2-1 of our table. "Looking at" immodesty is controlled; external constraints prohibit staring.

(Have you ever observed or heard about anyone staring at someone's body while at camp?) [16] I've heard stories—particularly about men that stare. Since I heard these stories, I tried not to, and even done away with my sunglasses after someone said, half joking, that I hide behind sunglasses to stare. Towards the end of the summer I stopped wearing sunglasses. And you know what, it was a child who told me this.

[15] See Erving Goffman, *Behavior in Public Places* (New York: The Free Press, 1963), p. 84.
[16] Interview questions and probes have been placed in parentheses.

*No sex talk.* Sex talk, or telling "dirty" jokes, is not common in the nudist camp. The owner of one of the most widely known camps in the Midwest told the writer: "It is usually expected that members of a nudist camp will not talk about sex, politics, or religion." Or in the words of one single-male: "It is taboo to make sexual remarks here." Verbal immodesty was not experienced by the writer during his period of field work. Interview respondents who mentioned that they had discussed or talked about sex qualified this by stating that such talk was restricted to close friends, was of a "scientific" nature or, if a joke, was of a "cute" sort. Verbal immodesty, represented in the second column of our typology of immodesty, is not common to the nudist camp.

When respondents were asked what they would think of someone who breached this norm, they indicated that such behavior would cast doubt on the actor's acceptance of the nudist definition of the situation:

One would expect to hear less of that at camp than at other places. (Why's that?) Because you expect that the members are screened in their *attitude for nudism*—and this isn't one who prefers sexual jokes.
They probably don't belong there. They're there to see what they can find to observe. (What do you mean?) Well, their mind isn't on being a nudist, but to see so-and-so nude.

*Body contact is taboo.* Although the degree to which this rule is enforced varies among camps, there is at least some degree of informal enforcement. Nudists mention that one is particularly careful not to brush against anyone or have any body contact, because of the way it might be interpreted. The following quotation illustrates the interpersonal precautions taken:

I stay clear of the opposite sex. They're so sensitive, they imagine things.

One respondent felt that this taboo was simply a common-sense form of modesty:

Suppose one had a desire to knock one off or feel his wife—modesty or a sense of protocol prohibits you from doing this.

When asked to conceptualize a breakdown in this form of modesty, a common response was:

They are in the wrong place. (How's that?) That's not part of nudism. (Could you tell me some more about that?) I think they are there for some sort of sex thrill. They are certainly not there to enjoy the sun.

If any photographs are taken for publication in a nudist magazine, the subjects are allowed to have only limited body contact. As one female nudist said: "We don't want anyone to think we're immoral." Outsiders' interpretations of body contact among nudists would cast doubt on the nudist definition of the situation or the characteristics set forth as the "nudist way of life."

A correlate of the body contact taboo is the prohibition of dancing in the nude. This is verbalized by nudist actors as a separate rule, and it is often the object of jest by members. This indication of "organizational strain" can be interpreted as an instance in which the existence of the rule itself brings into question the nudist definition of the situation, i.e., that there is no relationship between nudism and sexuality. The following remark acknowledges this: "This reflects a contradiction in our beliefs. But it's self protection. One incident

and we'd be closed." Others define dancing in the nude as an erotic overture which would incite sexual arousal. Such rationalizations are common to the group.

Returning to our typology of immodesty, it can be seen that incitements heightening latent sexual interest that would fall in column three of the typology (i.e., "doing" behavior), are to some extent controlled by prohibiting body contact.

*Alcoholic beverages are not allowed* in American camps. This rule also functions in controlling any breakdown in inhibitions which could lead to "aggressive-erotic" overtures (column three of immodesty). Even those respondents who told the writer that they had "snuck a beer" before going to bed went on to say, however, that they fully favored the rule. The following quotation is representative of nudists' thoughts:

Anyone who drinks in camp is jeopardizing their membership and they shouldn't. Anyone who drinks in camp could get reckless. (How's that?) Well, when guys and girls drink they're a lot bolder—they might get fresh with someone else's girl. That's why it isn't permitted, I guess.

*Rules regarding photography.* Taking photographs in a nudist camp is a sensitive matter. Unless the individual is an official photographer (i.e., one photographing for the nudist magazines), the photographer's definition of the situation is sometimes suspect, especially when one hears such remarks as the following: "Do you think you could open your legs a little more?"

There may be a general restriction on the use of cameras and, when cameras are allowed, it is expected that no pictures will be taken without the subject's permission. Members especially tend to blame the misuse of cameras on single men. As one nudist said: "You always see the singles poppin' around out of nowhere snappin' pictures." In general, however, control is maintained, and any infractions which might exist are not blatant or obvious. Any overindulgence in taking photographs would communicate an over-involvement in the nude state of the alters and bring doubt on the denied connection between nudism and sexuality. This, like staring, would fall in cell 2-1 of our typology of immodesty; like staring, it is controlled by the norms of the nudist camp.

The official photographers who are taking pictures for nudist magazines recognize the impression communicated by forms of immodesty other than nudity, i.e., for the communication of sexuality. In regard to the erotic overtures of column three of our typology, the following statement of an official photographer is relevant: "I never let a girl look straight at the camera. It looks too suggestive. I always have her look off to the side."

*Accentuation of the body is suspect* as being incongruent with the ideology of nudism. The internalization of the previously discussed principles of nudist ideology would be called into question by such accentuation. Thus, one woman who had shaved her pubic area was labeled as disgusting by those members who talked to the writer about it. Women who blatantly sit in an "unladylike" manner are similarly typed. In the words of one female nudist:

It's no more nice to do than when you are dressed. I would assume they have a purpose. (What's that?) Maybe to draw someone's attention sexually. I'd think it's bad behavior and it's one thing that

shouldn't be done, especially in a nudist camp. (Why's that?) Because it could lead to trouble or some misfortune. (Could you tell me some more about that?) It could bring up some trouble or disturbance among those who noticed it. It would not be appreciated by "true nudists."

*Unnatural attempts at covering any area of the body* are similarly ridiculed, since they call into question the actor's acceptance of the definition that there is no shame in exposing any area of the human body. If such behavior occurs early in one's nudist career, however, it is responded to mostly with smiles. The actor is viewed as not yet able to get over the initial difficulty of disposing of "outsiders'" definitions.

*Communal toilets* are also related to the ideological view that there is nothing shameful about the human body or its bodily functions. Although all camps do not have communal toilets, the large camp at which the writer spent the majority of his time did have such a facility, which was labeled "Little Girls Room and Little Boys Too." The stalls were provided with three-quarter length doors. The existence of this combined facility helped, however, to sustain the nudist definition of the situation by the element of consistency: if you are not ashamed of any part of your body, or of any of its natural body functions, why do you need separate toilets? Thus, even the physical ecology of the nudist camp is designed in a way that will be consistent with the organization's definition of modesty.

## Consequences of a Breakdown in Clothing Modesty

In the introductory section of this paper it was stated that common-sense actors anticipate breakdowns in clothing modesty to result in rampant sexual interest, promiscuity, embarrassment, jealousy, and shame. The field work and interview data from this study, however, indicate that such occurrences are not common to the nudist camp. The social organization of the nudist camp provides a system of meanings and norms that negate these consequences.

## Conclusions

Our results make possible some general conclusions regarding modesty: (1) Covering the body through the use of clothes is not a necessary condition for a pattern of modesty to exist, nor is it required for tension management and social control of latent sexual interests. Sexual interests are very adequately controlled in nudist camps; in fact, those who have visited nudist camps agree that sexual interests are controlled to a much greater extent than they are on the outside. Clothes are also not a sufficient condition for a pattern of modesty; the manipulation of clothes and fashion in stimulating sexual interest is widely recognized. (2) Except for clothing immodesty, which represents one cell of our typology of immodesty, all other forms of modesty are maintained in a nudist camp (e.g., not looking, not saying, not communicating erotic overtures). This suggests that the latter proscriptions are entirely adequate in achieving the functions of modesty when definitions regarding the exposure of the body are changed. (3) When deviance from the institutionalized patterns of modesty is limited to one cell of our typology, (i.e., clothing is dispensed with), and the definition of the situation is changed, the typically expected consequence of such a breakdown in this normative pattern does not occur. Rampant sexual interest, promiscuity, embarrassment, jealousy, and shame were not found to be typical of the nudist camp.

# PART VII

# Religion

# 18

# The Flying Saucerians:
# An Open Door Cult *†

*H. Taylor Buckner*

With heightened interest in outer space and the advanced technology that will soon allow man to explore it, many have noted great potential sources of explanation for unusual aerial sightings. Such sightings have been going on for centuries, evoking a vast number of explanations, from Divine intervention in the form of miracles to the midnight flight of participants in a witches' Sabbath. Although many groups and organizations have undertaken to investigate these phenomena, some of these investigators (including academicians and government agencies) have shown less skepticism than others, especially about reports alleging actual contact with visitors from other worlds. Some of these persons have formed groups that have taken the form of new religious cults. Professor Buckner examines one such organization below. **Editor**

---

## I

Insofar as its social impact is concerned the flying saucer might as well have been a flying Rorschach blot. Any interpretation of its "true" meaning can be advanced, indeed probably has been advanced, and since there are no externally verifiable facts, no interpretation can be refuted. This fact has had an important effect on the organizations founded by flying saucer believers, or flying saucerians, and on the flying saucerians themselves. Before speaking of this, however, let us briefly review the history of the flying saucer. There are two main phases, popular excitement and occult colonization.

The phase of popular excitement has three main periods. There is a period of sensitization which lasted from 1947 to 1951. There is a period of hysteria in 1952, and a period of secondary hysteria following Sputnik in the last months of 1957. This is a phase of truly *popular* excitement. Many of the people, indeed probably most, who saw flying saucers were in all other ways quite normal. As a result many people to this day are unwilling to completely reject the idea that there is "something up there."

The course of the phase of popular excitement was as follows: When Kenneth Arnold saw something from

223

his airplane near Mount Rainier in June 1947, he gave them the happy name of flying saucers.[1] This concrete name defined a previously undefined class of phenomena and people began fitting their experiences to it. Just as in the Seattle Windshield Pitting Epidemic where people looked *at* their windshields for the first time instead of *through* them, events which would otherwise excite no notice became cause for speculation.[2] Through the rest of 1947, 1948, 1949, 1950 and 1951 reports of flying saucers continued to come in at a rate of 100 to 200 a year. During this period of sensitization the public at large came to be aware of the word flying saucer, and to be unsure of its reality or meaning. On May 20, 1950, toward the end of the period of sensitization 94 per cent of the respondents of the regular American Institute of Public Opinion poll claimed to have heard of flying saucers. The largest portion of these people said they didn't know what they were, and those who thought they knew guessed wildly.[3]

In April to July of 1952 *Life* magazine and the United States Air Force managed to trigger the flying saucer hysteria which we all remember. On

April 7 *Life* printed an article which argued that the flying saucers came from another planet. Then the Air Force began to report seeing flying saucers. Through a series of incredible public relations blunders which ranged from giving official sanction to wild reports to advancing patently absurd "explanations" the Air Force managed to fan the hysteria. By the end of 1952 1501 sightings had been reported for the year.[4]

The hysteria fell away rapidly, though not to the low level of the sensitizing period, and was briefly revived when people began looking at the sky after Sputnik went up in October, 1957. This ended the phase of popular excitement. There are still people who report seeing flying saucers but their numbers are quite small.

The second phase, which overlaps the first, is the phase of occult colonization. It consists, in brief, of people who report not that they have seen something in the sky but that they have had personal contact with beings from another planet who were piloting the flying saucers. This is clearly quite a different phenomenon.

The definition of the situation in occult terms began in 1950 with the publication of two books, one of which was the first saucerian book complete with little green men.[5] These two books, particularly Frank Scully's *Behind the Flying Saucers*, are looked upon by saucerians as the beginning of the tradition.

The publication explosion hit the

[1] Described in Donald Keyhoe, *The Flying Saucers are Real* (New York: Fawcett Publications, Inc. 1950), pp. 23–24.

[2] Nahum Z. Medalia and Otto N. Larsen, "Diffusion and Belief in Collective Delusion: The Seattle Windshield Pitting Epidemic," *The American Sociological Review*, XXIII, No. 2 (April, 1958), 180. See also, D. M. Johnson, "The Phantom Anesthetist of Mattoon," in *Readings in Social Psychology*, ed. Guy E. Swanson, T. M. Newcomb, and Eugene H. Hartley (New York: Henry Holt and Company, 1952), pp. 208–19; and Hadley Cantril, "The Invasion from Mars," *ibid.*, pp. 198–207. Norman Jacobs, "The Phantom Slasher of Taipei: Mass Hysteria in a Non-Western Society," *Social Problems*, XII, No. 3 (Winter, 1965), pp. 318–28.

[3] "The Quarter's Polls," *Public Opinion Quarterly*, XXIV (Fall, 1950), 597–98.

[4] The source of saucer sighting data is Lt. Col. Lawrence J. Tacker, *Flying Saucers and the U. S. Air Force* (Princeton, N.J.: D. Van Nostrand Co., Inc., 1960).

[5] Gerald Heard, *Is Another World Watching?* (New York: Harper & Brothers, 1950); Frank Scully, *Behind the Flying Saucers* (New York: Henry Holt and Company, 1950).

flying saucer field in 1953 and 1954. Ten important books claiming contact with the flying saucers were published in these two years.[6] These books found a ready audience of interested people who were still wondering what flying saucers were after the hysteria of 1952 had passed. Many people read these books, few believed them. Being as charitable as possible most of these books would not convince a rather dull ten year old. But many people were convinced. Who were they? I think that the answer must be that they were people who were already believers in the occult and psychic.

Those people who believed the flying saucer books began, starting in 1955 and 1956, to band together in flying saucer clubs and to hold flying saucer conventions. A large chain of saucer clubs, Understanding Incorporated, was started in 1956. As a natural consequence of the existence of this public a number of magazines devoted to flying saucers began to be published. This was a period of great growth for flying

saucer organizations. Organizations of people interested in the scientific study of "saucers" also grew up at about this time. These organizations are not included in this study.

The existence of flying saucer clubs meant that there was a ready market for lectures given by those who had been contacted by flying saucers. It became common for flying saucer contactees to go from club to club telling of their "experiences" with the "space brothers" starting as early as 1956. This pattern persists, though in greatly modified form, to this day.

## II

A social world is a culture area, a universe of regularized mutual response, whose boundaries are set by the limit of effective communications. Each social world has a universe of discourse in which pertinent experiences are categorized in particular ways. Social worlds have norms of conduct, sets of values, prestige ladders, and perspectives or world views.[7] The social world of the occult "seeker" is a very unusual one.[8] The seeker moves in a world populated by astral spirits, cosmic truths, astrologers, mystery schools, lost continents, magic healing, human "auras," "second comings," telepathy, and vibrations. A typical occult seeker will probably have been a Rosicrucian, a member of Mankind United, a Theosophist and also a member of four or

---

[6] Desmond Leslie and George Adamski, *Flying Saucers Have Landed* (New York: British Book Center, 1953); Daniel W. Fry, *The White Sands Incident* (Los Angeles: New Age Publishing Company, 1954); ——, *Alan's Message to Men of Earth* (Los Angeles: New Age Publishing Company, 1954); Truman Bethurum, *Aboard a Flying Saucer* (Los Angeles: DeVorss & Co., 1954); George Adamski, *Inside the Space Ships* (New York: Abelard-Schuman, Limited, 1955); George Hunt Williamson and Alfred C. Bailey, *The Saucers Speak* (Los Angeles: New Age Publishing Company, 1954); Orfeo M. Angelucci, *The Secret of the Saucers* (Amherst, Wis.: Amherst Press, 1955); George W. Van Tassel, *I Rode a Flying Saucer* (Los Angeles: New Age Publishing Company, 1952); Harold T. Wilkins, *Flying Saucers on the Attack* (New York: Citadel Press, 1954); Cedric Allingham, *Flying Saucers from Mars* (London: Frederick Muller, Ltd., 1954).

[7] Tamotsu Shibutani, "Reference Groups and Social Control," in *Human Behavior and Social Processes*, ed. Arnold Rose (Boston: Houghton Mifflin Company, 1962), pp. 136–37.

[8] This idea of occult seekers is quite similar to that used by John Lofland, "The World Savers" (Doctoral dissertation, Department of Sociology, University of California at Berkeley, 1964).

five smaller specific cults. The pattern of membership is one of continuous movement from one idea to another. Seekers stay with a cult until they are satisfied that they can learn no more from it, or that it has nothing to offer, and then they move on. Seekers know one another having seen each other at various meetings over the years, so that there is an occult social world which contains all of the various philosophies and all the people who restlessly move from one to another of them. Any new philosophy can gain a large first-time audience simply by letting it be known among the seekers that it exists. There are very few occult philosophies, however, which are so well organized as to keep the interest of the seeker over many years. If the seeker doesn't feel that she is learning anything, or that something is being hidden from her, she will move on. The limits of the occult world are the limits of the communication structures provided by the occult organizations and the informal face-to-face contacts of occultists.

## III

The flying saucer movement started as just another distinct occult philosophy but it gradually changed and is now an open door cult. How did this come about?

The most important single fact about the flying saucer clubs I have had contact with is that they were organized by people who were functioning within the occult social world. One particular club which I have followed for several years, personally, and whose records I have been able to examine is perhaps typical in this regard. Its organizer was a late-middle aged lady whose formal education had ended with the fourth

grade. She uses the title "Reverend" which she was given by a man who claims the title himself, and who has been taken to task by the State of California for dispensing titles for a fee. She had been a member of Mankind United before the war and had been president of the Theosophist Club. She was familiar with all of the other major occult philosophies. When she decided that this new field of flying saucers was of more than passing interest, after reading some of the volumes of the publication explosion, she decided to start a club. Apparently this was entirely on her own as no other organizations of any size existed then. She rented a small hall for the first meeting, and immediately ran into difficulty. The owner objected to having "Flying Saucer" on his bulletin board. The name was changed to "Space-Craft Club" to satisfy this difficulty. Having a hall she then mailed out postcards "to her friends." Her friends, of course, were people she knew from her contacts in the world of occult seekers. To this first meeting of a new club in February 1956 from a single mailing of post cards came thirty-five people. The first three meetings consisted of quite straightforward flying saucer information. The fourth meeting was on "Space People in the Bible."

What is the flying saucer story? The flying saucer clubs were organized around a fairly simple idea. In brief it is that intelligent beings from other planets, disturbed by mankind's development of atomic energy, have appeared above earth in flying saucers with the intent of saving man from himself. In its original formulation, which was the formulation current when most clubs were formed, the flying saucer is a material object which operates on magnetic energy and is free of the laws of acceleration and inertia. They also "vibrate" in some way so that they can disappear. The pilots bring a new message to the men of earth which is roughly "do unto others as you would have them do unto you." Even space people seem to have a norm of reciprocity.

Even given all of its ramifications and variations this is not a very complex revelation, and the occult seekers who joined the club were probably soon able to look elsewhere for new revelations. The response of the club was to tie flying saucers up with occultism of various types. Thus flying saucers were supposed to be the way of travel between Atlantis and Venus and between Mu and Venus. Also flying saucers are supposed to travel between various astral levels and thus the ascended spirits of one's departed relatives can talk to you over a radio-like communications system from a flying saucer. When beliefs like this become diffused throughout a social world it becomes very difficult to determine what is distinctively a property of flying saucers. The flying saucer thus becomes a Rorschach blot. Any one with any occult line to sell can hook it up to flying saucers in some way to have it accepted in the flying saucer club. For several years this took place, with speakers moving around the Understanding Incorporated lecture circuit with progressively further-out connections with flying saucers. Then, around 1960, a strange thing began to happen. The audience in the flying saucer clubs began to lose interest in flying saucers. A common remark was "we all know about that!" Which implies that they were no longer interested in hearing about it. In the terms used by club members "we have advanced" from those ele-

mentary insights to more complex insights. These more complex insights were the various occult philosophies which everyone was already familiar with. The occult lines were presented from the flying saucer platform in a nonexclusive fashion with no particular emphasis on one line or another. For many seekers the seeking was over. They could stay in one place and have the various lines of the occult world paraded before them without having to move from one group to another.

Through this process of the gradual elimination of interest in flying saucers the flying saucer clubs have become a permanently constituted audience. In many ways it is a selective audience, but it is an audience which is willing to listen to just about anything occult.

The personal characteristics of the audience are of particular significance because they relate to the survival of the flying saucer organization. My data have been gathered by observation over a period of three years of attendance at conventions and one year of continuous attendance at meetings with sporadic attendance of meetings during the other two years. The observations I have made could be presented in statistical form but I feel that this would only obscure the fact that most of them are based on judgments and on talking with limited numbers of people in something less than a cross-sectional survey design.[9]

[9] No survey was taken for two reasons. First, one must be functionally literate to answer a questionnaire (resources did not allow for interviews) and many saucerians are not. Second, one must be willing to "play the survey game" of internally categorizing slices of the self to fit them into survey categories, and these people are not practiced in thinking of themselves as objects.

First of all the members are old. The average age is probably around 65 and there are very few people under fifty. Most of the members, perhaps 90 per cent of the regulars, are women. The ordinary meeting, then, will have an audience which is at least 80 per cent composed of women over fifty years old. Secondly, and this is less firm, most of the members seem to be widowed or single. There are very few couples who attend, and there are a few who attend who are married to non-believers who do not attend. Third, the socio-economic status of the members seems to hover around the upper-working class and lower-middle class line with, perhaps, a greater dispersion downward than upward. Fourth, the formal education level of most members is quite low. This has a consequence in that although they spend all their time learning, and they consider themselves "students," they do not learn things in an ordered and disciplined way, but build up chunks of disconnected knowledge which they cannot bring to bear on a problem and which they cannot systematize. Fifth, the physical health of the audience appears to be bad, even worse than would be accounted for by the high average age. Many members are deaf, many have very poor vision, many walk with the aid of sticks and many more display obvious physical handicaps of other types. Sixth, by any conventional definition the mental health level of the audience is quite low. Hallucinations are quite common, though people may be drawn to the environment by the fact that "seeing things" is accepted as a mark of special sensitivity and explicitly called this.[10]

[10] Field Notes, 27 March 1965. Clark La Verne Wilkerson, the speaker, solicited "visions" from the audience and praised those

If one were to attend a meeting and watch the action without knowing in advance whether the audience was in a mental hospital or not, it would be very difficult to tell, because many symptoms of serious illness are displayed. Seventh, the audience, as a group, has a norm of "anything goes" in several areas. No behavior and no ideas, except those in bad taste, are considered illegitimate. All human defects are treated with kindness even to the extent of disrupting a meeting, so that a late-arriving person with hearing difficulties can be given a front row seat.

## IV

The flying saucer clubs as organizations have difficulties. Having few members who are explicitly interested in flying saucers is one thing, but having an audience that on one level is willing to learn about anything occult but that would gradually drift away if only one line were emphasized, and on another level having an audience that will drift away if they don't feel that they are being benefited, is quite another. It poses problems for the person who must choose the speakers: they must always have something "new" to say and it must be helpful. The club has no line of its own to sell which is so important that it would exclude any other even contradictory line. Enclosed in a recent newsletter was the following statement which illustrates the latitude given to other lines:

who came forth. Even if the visions produced in such a setting are a collective delusion, one who has visions anyway will feel at home. Exactly the same phenomenon was found by Lloyd H. Rogler and August B. Hollingshead, "The Puerto Rican Spiritualist as a Psychiatrist," *The American Journal of Sociology*, LXVII, No. 1 (July, 1961), 17–21.

The "Bay City" Space-Craft Club, as such, may not always share the views of extra and varied statements placed in the envelope for distribution, but the Club is always ready to serve its patrons, in any plan that will build a "Better World" for the present and future generations.

In the past this open door policy has been wide enough to include socialism, birchism, peace, retirement plans, anti-communism, new-age economics, and the saucerians' own Universal Party all at more or less the same time. In addition to political lines where contradictory characteristics may be clear, occult lines have included: Lemurianism, astrology, Rosicrucianism, Yoga, Baha'i, Christian Yoga, Unity, Divine Principles, UFOlogy, health food, ascended masters, the Master Aetherius, technical metaphysics, Negro history, color healing, free energy, Akashic records, celestial music and hypnotism.[11] The strain toward variety is clear. But unrestrained variety is chaotic and would lead to a small average attendance as any single line may attract a fairly specific audience. A decision must be made whether or not to present a line and the decision is made in large part on the basis of whether it will attract an audience. Some things, such as political lines, can be presented in a convention where people will sit still for them, but could not be presented in a meeting, where no one would come. The founding of the Universal Party, the saucerians' very own political party, drew exactly 11 people, six of whom had set it up, four members of the "audience," and me.[12] Attend-

ance like that doesn't pay the rent.

Since in theory the flying saucer club is a really open platform for the presentation of anything that will build a "better world" the people who choose the speakers do not explicitly choose those who draw a big audience. They do, in fact, choose speakers that draw a large audience, but I think the process is largely unconscious. Speakers are not characterized as being popular or unpopular but as being good or bad. This has nothing to do with their speaking ability but with the interest the audience has in their topic.

The characteristics of the audience affect what they want to hear. Time after time the "good" speakers are the healers. Anything which has to do with physical disease will draw a good sized audience, and if the speaker presents a line of magic healing with mental power the audience will be large and interested. The healers on the Understanding lecture trail are all con-men of some talent, and they use the flying saucer club platform to make their public pitch for private, expensive treatments or therapy. Thus, given limited amounts of money, healing speakers are a self limiting group. Flying saucer clubs will never become exclusively devoted to healing speakers but they will continue to drift toward an exclusive interest in the magic healing of the problems, social, economic, political, physical and mental, of the aged. And this drift will continue without anyone making a conscious organizational decision to do so.[13]

The process of organizational survival could almost be described as a stochastic process, whereby speakers

[11] For specific documentation see H. Taylor Buckner, *Deviant-Group Organizations* (Master's thesis, University of California at Berkeley, 1964, mimeographed), pp. 72–88.

[12] Field notes, 18 May 1963.

[13] No one ever makes conscious organizational decisions in flying saucer clubs. Things just come up and happen.

are chosen more or less at random, and the effect of the speaker observed, and taken into account in the selection of other speakers. This process is limited by the available speakers, by the open door policy, and by the overall goals of the organization, but it works. The flying saucer clubs have maintained themselves in the face of the loss of interest in flying saucers by choosing a goal so general, building a better world, that it can legitimate anything. Then drifting with the interests of the audience the organizations manage to survive. They are not prospering however; it takes more than drift to build.

# 19

# Magic, Sorcery, and Football Among Urban Zulu: A Case of Reinterpretation Under Acculturation *†

*N. A. Scotch*

Religious institutions, like all others, are subject to the pressures of social change. Sometimes this involves unusual synthesis or accommodation, especially in the case of those preliterate societies now undergoing rapid change because of assistances and cultural intrusions from technologically more advanced countries. There are often reinterpretations of older elements that will allow the acculturation of new ones. Many such instances can be seen in the pattern of immigrant adjustment into American society.[1] The following article represents a somewhat unusual case, involving as it does the elements of magic, medicine, and sport.

EDITOR

---

In discussing beliefs in witchcraft in Africa, Gluckman[2] points out that patterns and identification with the native beliefs in witchcraft not only

* Reprinted from *The Journal of Conflict Resolution*, V (1961), 70–74, by permission of the publisher. Footnotes renumbered.

† I wish to thank M. J. Herskovits, A. Vilakazi, R. LeVine, and W. Elmendorf for having read and made valuable suggestions regarding this paper. The responsibility for this final version is, of course, completely my own. I also wish to thank the National Institute of Health, the Program of African Studies at Northwestern University, Washington State University, and the Russell Sage Foundation for the financial support that made possible the field work and analysis of data on which this paper is based. This is a revised version of a paper read at the 1959 meetings of the American Anthropological Association.

[1] For one such interesting case, see: E. D. Beynon, "The Voodoo Cult among Negro Migrants in Detroit," *The American Journal of Sociology*, XLIII (1938), 894–907.

[2] M. Gluckman, *Custom and Conflict in Africa* (London: Oxford University Press, 1955).

persist in the face of continuing acculturation but often expand and
change to meet the exigencies of new
life situations. In fact, the impact of
science, and particularly the impact
of modern medicine, on previously
nonliterate Africans actually inhibits
their traditional beliefs and practices
much less than might be expected;
and although it would be incorrect
to assert that Africans have rejected
modern medicine—rejected, say modern germ theories of disease—the fact
remains that they sustain the basic
structure of their traditional beliefs
in spite of elemental contradictions
between those beliefs and scientific
explanations.

But how can opposing explanations
of cause and effect be held simultaneously? According to Gluckman,
concepts of science and witchcraft
fulfill different functions: science explains *how* a given process occurs, as
in the course of a disease, for example; whereas witchcraft explains *why*
the process occurs at all, or why one
man and not another contracts the
disease. From the African point of
view, modern medicine is extremely
limited in explaining total situations.
It may contribute dependable proba-
bilities, as when it predicts that ten
per cent of a tribal population will
die of tuberculosis, or when it prog-
nosticates a specific disease in the
individual; but it fails to explain,
from the African perspective, why
one particular child among ten shar-
ing the same conditions contracts
tuberculosis whereas the remaining
nine do not, and it is this last explanation that witchcraft continues
to provide with assurance for modern
Africans. As Gluckman [3] observes:
"The difficulty of destroying beliefs
in witchcraft is that they form a

system which can absorb and explain
many failures and apparently contradictory evidence."

This functional aspect of witchcraft
may explain, to a very great extent,
its persistence in the belief system of
Africans, its expansion and peculiar
adaptability to industrialized Euro-
American modes of life. As Gluckman
points out:

African life nowadays is changing rapidly, and witchcraft accusations now involve circumstances arising from Africa's
absorption in Western economy and
polity. Conflicts between old and new
social principles produce new animosities,
which are not controlled by custom, and
these open the way to new forms of ac-
cusation. Charges, previously excluded,
as by a Zulu against his father, are now
made. The system of witchcraft beliefs,
originally tied to certain social relations,
can be adapted to new situations of conflict—to competition for jobs in town, to
the rising standard of living, made possible by new goods, which breaches the
previous egalitarianism, and so forth.[1]

One example of such innovation in
the application of magic and sorcery
—terms which I prefer to witchcraft
—to cultural change and urban living
came to my attention during my
recent research among the Zulu in
South Africa. It illustrates not only
how the changing pattern of magic
is related to the changing way of
life, but it does the reverse as well,
and shows how innovations can only
be built on previous cultural patterns.
In Durban the Africans show a great
enthusiasm for soccer, or, to use the
local term, football. Much of the
limited leisure of the native male
population is devoted to watching,
discussing, and participating in this
game, and organized football leagues
resembling, in their hierarchies of

[3] *Ibid.*, p. 101.                                    [4] *Loc. cit.*

skill, our own major and minor leagues in baseball, engage in complex rivalries no less extreme, bitter, and unremitting than in Chicago or Cleveland. This exemplifies the "new situations of conflict" to which Gluckman refers. Interpersonal and intergroup hostility and aggression are much greater in an urban setting than in the more traditional rural Zulu community. Unnaturally crowded conditions and competition for scarce employment opportunities lead to more frequent accusations of sorcery in the city. Football, it may be hypothesized, serves a dual function in this context: first, it is one of the few opportunities open to the Zulu for release from the anxiety and tensions of anomic urban life; and more specifically, it allows the expression of the increased aggression and hostility that arise in the city between Africans, within the framework of a modern, acceptable form.

It is common knowledge, and not surprising, that in an effort to produce winning teams each of these football teams employs an *inyanga*, or Zulu doctor, who serves the dual purpose of strengthening his own team by magic and ritual, and of forestalling the sorcery directed at his team by rival *inyangas*. Although no *inyanga* with whom I talked would admit that he employed sorcery against opposing teams, each was convinced that this was the practice of rival *inyangas*. Actually magic in Durban football is so widespread that although in searching for players there exists at least a minimal recognition of individual talent, few players known to be the object of *umtagathi*, or sorcerers, would be considered by a team regardless of their ability; moreover, success or failure of a team is invariably attributed to the skills of the *inyangas*, as

well as to the natural talent of the players. However, when a team consistently loses it is the *inyanga* who is replaced, not the players. When, on the other hand, an individual player is suspected of being the object of sorcery he may be dropped from the team for fear that the spell might generalize to include the teammates of the unfortunate victim.

That football holds a place of extreme importance to the African community is demonstrated in several ways. Players of considerable talent are much sought after; and part of the work of the trainer is to scout other teams and to attempt to entice skilled players of opposing teams into joining his own. In fact, although ostensibly this is an amateur sport, players of promise are frequently paid a salary from the treasury of the team as a means of keeping them. If a skilled player has had difficulty in finding employment, it is incumbent on all members of the team to find suitable and well-paying employment for the star. So involved are the efforts of teammates to keep them happy that star players are known to pass from club to club for the "best deal."

Because of this, and for other reasons as well, strict discipline is maintained on the team. The trainer—or what we would call coach—is in a position of supreme authority. All the normal rules of status and interpersonal relationships which have long traditions and history may be discarded in the interests of winning games. Thus, it is even possible for a trainer to strike a man older than himself—perhaps considerably older— if the trainer feels he is not doing his share. This, of course, is a gross transgression against important Zulu norms regarding seniority and status. The supernatural is enlisted in every possible way to aid in the production of a successful football team. Thus, ritual and ceremony are used on a number of occasions connected with football, and serve the functions of sanctioning and supporting the efforts of a team. Before the season even opens, the team slaughters a goat "to open the doors to luck" and the season's end is marked by another slaughter.

Much of the ritual is propitiative as in the example of the slaughter cited above, but most ceremonies combine propitiation with positive attempts to combat sorcery. The following is an account, related by an educated Zulu health educator, of the ritual conducted by *inyangas* on the night preceding a match:

All the football teams have their own *inyanga* who doctors them all for each match. The night before a match they must "camp" together around a fire. They all sleep there together, they must stay naked and they are given *umuthi* and other medicines by the *inyanga*. Incisions are made on their knees, elbows, and joints. In the morning they are made to vomit. They must all go together on the same bus to the match, and they must enter the playing grounds together. Almost every team I know has an *inyanga* and does this—it is necessary to win. Even though players are Christians and have lived in towns for a long time, they do it, and believe in it.

Another informant gave as the reasons for this practice of camping-out the following account:

The purpose is to avoid liquor, sexual intercourse, mixing with enemy players who might bewitch them, and mixing with other persons who might affect them with ill-luck.

The camping group is composed of the starting team and reserves, plus administrative members of the club,

loyal and enthusiastic supporters, and the *inyanga*. The morning after the camping the whole group moves to the playing grounds together. A certain procedure is followed: the group keeps a very tight formation with every man touching the man in front of, behind and beside him; the pace is very slow and stylized and the group may be likened to a millipede —one organism with a million legs. Even when the group has to take a bus from one part of town to another where the football field is, they still make every effort to maintain their formation. The players themselves are placed right in the center of the group in order that they might be protected. Moving out onto the actual playing field with their stylized trotting step, the group acts very hostile to outsiders for fear that intruders will attempt to bewitch the players or in some way to weaken the "umuthi" or the medicine of the *inyanga*.

Now, when we compare the description of the ritual magic involved in "camping-out" with accounts by Bryant [5] and Krige [6] of doctoring of Zulu warriors in the time of Shaka during the early 1800's, we perceive many elements of unmistakable similarity: the circle around the fire; the medicines to endow strength and courage; the medicines on the weapons (currently, on football jerseys and shoes) to increase their potency (currently, to make them slippery); and the purificatory emetic which, in Shaka's time, was taken on the morning of the battle, and nowadays on the morning before the football match.

[5] A. T. Bryant, *The Zulu People* (Pietermaritzburg, S. Africa: Shuter and Shooter, 1949), p. 501.
[6] E. J. Krige, *The Social System of the Zulus* (London: Longmans, Green & Co., Ltd., 1936), p. 272.

Further, the formation followed in reaching the playing field derives, without doubt, from historical military formations. The avoidance of sex on the eve of battles can also be traced back to earlier customs connected with warfare. These are but a few examples of the basic similarities of the ritual and ceremony used currently by football teams and formerly by army regiments.

There is an interesting parallel to be found to the above example of cultural syncretism. Sundkler,[7] in describing Zulu leadership patterns in separatist churches, has shown that the traditional roles of chief and medical specialist are carried over into the modern Christian church in much the same way as these roles are found in modern football teams.

Returning to the point made earlier —why does a belief in magic in football exist at all? As Gluckman says, because such a belief explains the inexplicable. Why does one football team win consistently and another lose? Certainly the winning team will have players who are more talented —but why, in the first place, do these teams manage to gather more talented players; and, in the second place, why are these players more talented, where does their skill come from? Why is it that the talented players avoid sorcery? These are the questions with which magic deals.

That beliefs in magic help to explain the inexplicable is illustrated by the following account:

We health educators started a team and did very well. We made a point of not using an *inyanga*. We advertised the fact that we did not use one. We even invited a few outsiders on to our team so that they would see that we used no

[7] B. Sundkler, *Bantu Prophets in South Africa* (London: Lutterworth Press, 1948).

witchcraft, and we hoped that they would tell others about this. Well, we won a lot of games—and do you know what the people said? They said that because we work with European doctors we were given injections to make us strong so that we could win. We could not convince them otherwise.

By this account a number of things are made clear. Modern medicine is viewed as essentially similar to the magic of the Zulu doctor, except in this case it is the magic of the European. Formerly, Zulu avoided European doctors (except in the case of trauma) in the belief that they could only help or cure Europeans. Today, they accept the fact that an African can be helped in many cases by modern Western medicine. Nonetheless, it is still believed that there are some diseases—which they refer to as Bantu diseases—which cannot be helped by the European. Such diseases as *umfufuyana, chayiza* and *spoiliyana*, which are essentially psychosomatic, hysterical-type personality disorders, are rarely taken to the European doctor.

On the other hand, the injections used by European doctors are viewed as being entirely magical, and Zulu who come to the European doctor for help of any kind always insist on a *jovo*—an injection—as part of any treatment. No distinction is drawn between the *jovo* of the white jacketed European doctor or the roots or herbs of the *inyanga* clad in skins. Thus, when we view the football team we clearly see how the winning of matches is almost always explained by references to magic. In usual cases it is magic of the *inyanga*, while in unusual cases, like that of the health educator team, the magic of the European doctors.

Retention by urban Zulu of magical beliefs and practices also throws some light on the persistence of conflict patterns in a changing culture. The use of sorcery practices and warfare rituals within the framework of the game of soccer introduced by Europeans illustrates the adaptation of old methods of expressing hostility to the new and highly frustrating urban situation.

# 20

## What Kind of People Does a Religious Cult Attract? *

*William R. Catton, Jr.*

H. L. Mencken once said that the surest way to get rich quick in America, next to robbing a bank, was to start a new religion. The public imagination is periodically captured by journalistic reports of persons declaring themselves to be divinities, new messiahs, or lesser prophets.[1] A few of these people have been judged psychotic and have been placed in mental institutions. A recent study, by a social psychologist, concerned the reactions of three men, each of whom claimed to be Jesus Christ, when they were forced into interaction with each other.[2] Many such persons, however, are functioning members of society, some with large followings, despite the unusual claims of their leaders—some of which appear wholly outlandish to the outsider.[3] Professor Catton examines some of the attractions held by such groups for their followers.[4]

EDITOR

◆

On the basis of existing theory of institutional behavior, is it possible to predict what classes of people may be attracted to a new religious cult?

Consider the following propositions about religion:

(1) Religion is a spontaneously appearing, perennial, and universal attribute of man. . . . The element of chance, here

* Reprinted from *The American Sociological Review*, XXII (1957), 561–66, by permission of the author and the American Sociological Association. Footnotes renumbered.

[1] For a highly readable account of some of these, see: Richard Mathison, *God is a Millionaire* (New York: Charter Books, 1960).

[2] Milton Rokeach, *The Three Christs of Ypsilanti: A Narrative Study of Three Lost Men* (New York: Alfred A. Knopf, Inc., 1964). Unfortunately, in this case the three lost men stayed lost.

[3] For good examples, see: Mathison, *op. cit.*; and Sara Harris, *Father Divine: Holy Husband* (Garden City, N.Y.: Doubleday & Company, Inc., 1953).

[4] For other relevant works of general interest, see: Vittorio Lanernari, *The Religions of the Oppressed: A Study of Modern Messianic Cults* (New York: Alfred A. Knopf, Inc., 1963); and Eric Hoffer, *The True Believer* (New York: The New American Library of World Literature, Inc., 1958).

and hereafter, everlastingly must be contended with. (2) From earliest known times, religion has assumed institutionalized forms. Apparently it . . . cannot exist without social expression and social organization. (3) Organized religions tend to become over-organized, from the very fact of their organization as "going concerns". . . . They become ends in themselves rather than means. (4) . . . it is easier to administer the affairs of an organization than it is to keep creeds flexible, codes of conduct clear and uncompromised, and the life of the spirit immanent. Historically this has meant either the eventual disappearance of the particular religious organization, or more commonly, reform or schism, especially in the form of new sects or cults.[5]

From these propositions we may deduce that any sufficiently large and varied population is likely to contain a number of individuals whose religious interests are intense but are not adequately served by existing religious institutions. These would include persons we should predict might be attracted to a new religious cult. But can such persons be identified in terms of objective characteristics observable prior to their actual affiliation with the cultist movement? The study reported here suggests an affirmative answer.

## A Research Opportunity

An opportunity to study public reaction to a man whose small band of followers regarded him as Christ (and who himself acknowledged that status) arose when such a group visited Seattle, Washington, in the winter of 1952. Their presence was first announced by a two-column 8-inch advertisement in both Seattle

[5] J. O. Hertzler, "Religious Institutions," *Annals of the American Academy of Political and Social Science,* CCLVI (March, 1948), 1, 3, 12.

newspapers. The ad contained a photograph of a bearded man in a long robe, resembling the traditional portraits of Christ. Beside the picture were the words: "We Believe THIS IS CHRIST The Begotten Son of God. What MORE can we say!!! Listen to the words of Christ." The time, place, and auspices for a public appearance were specified in smaller print at the bottom.

The writer and a friend [6] attended the meeting. The audience numbered about 300. We watched and listened, but asked no questions of anyone. At subsequent meetings our investigation included direct personal conversation with the "Christ," Krishna Venta. We were able to establish sufficient rapport to facilitate fairly systematic study of this embryonic cult with tape recorder and questionnaires.[7]

## The Meetings

The first meeting, on January 20, was quietly conducted by several "disciples" dressed in plain robes,

[6] The author wishes to acknowledge the cooperation of Lynn B. Lucky in the execution of this study, from the original decision to attend the first of this unusual series of meetings, to the analysis of the questionnaire data. Acknowledgement is also due the Washington Public Opinion Laboratory, by which both the author and Lucky were then employed, for the use of its facilities. The criticism of Melvin L. DeFleur, Indiana University, was of great help in preparing this report.

[7] This rapport was close enough, in fact, to be slightly embarrassing, and may have influenced some of the responses to our questionnaires. Some audience members regarded us as followers of Krishna. Weeks after the last meeting, when this group had left Seattle, the irate husband of one woman (whose attendance at several meetings had convinced her Krishna was really Christ) threatened us by telephone: "I'll have the law on you."

moving about on bare feet, wearing beards and long hair, and embracing each member of the audience upon entrance. One of them, called "Peter," gave a quiet, lengthy introduction of the "Master" who made a dramatic entrance. In an hour-long lecture he reprimanded the crowd for having paid him so little heed 1,900 years before, and stated his present mission as the "gathering of the elect," disclaiming any present intent to "save souls." During an ensuing question session, several members of the audience sought to ridicule the speaker, but the majority of the audience seemed content to enjoy the show.

At the second meeting the following evening Krishna's entry was unexpectedly interrupted by the minister of the liberal church in which the meeting was being held. He disclaimed all personal connection with the affair by announcing his discovery since the previous meeting that Krishna had a criminal record. Krishna was, however, permitted to speak. His lecture was defiant, referring repeatedly to persecutions inflicted on him by so-called Christians. The audience, containing many people who had attended the first meeting, reacted very differently on this occasion. In addition to those who had come just to see a show and the few who sought to ridicule the "Master," as at the first meeting, there now appeared to be a highly motivated and articulate minority who saw him as a serious threat to their own orthodox Christian beliefs. They fought him aggressively, armed with Bible verses. Their questions were of the type: "If you're really the Christ, show us the scars of your crucifixion!" In short, they seemed exclusively concerned with *reassuring*

themselves that Krishna was an imposter.[8]

A different meeting place was obtained for the third and subsequent meetings. The third meeting (on January 27, Sunday) dealt with prophecy.

At the fourth meeting (Wednesday evening, January 30) Krishna lectured on "Hypnotism and Mental Telepathy" in rather abstract terms.

In his fifth lecture (Sunday, February 3) Krishna informed the audience that Christ and Jesus were two different people; that Christ assisted God in the creation of the universe, has been with men since their beginning; and that Christ, not Jesus, was crucified. Krishna reasserted that he himself was Christ: "I am Christ, the son of the living God. The eternal Christ. The one that was crucified 1,900 years ago, died and was buried and on the third day rose again."

In addition, the speaker devoted himself to a lament for the current state of freedom-of-the-press in the United States. Both Seattle newspapers had refused to carry further advertising about his group, due, Krishna asserted, to pressure from interests that were afraid of his power.

At the sixth and last meeting on Sunday, February 10, Krishna discussed his criminal record,[9] describ-

[8] Elizabeth K. Nottingham, *Religion and Society* (Garden City, N.Y.: Doubleday & Company, Inc., 1954), p. 5, points out that the unholy is often closely associated with the holy in religious thought. The devout persons who thought Krishna was a wicked imposter seemed especially anxious to obtain proof that he was not the genuine Christ.

[9] Krishna was fond of the Book of Revelation, which attributes to Christ the following words: ". . . I will come like a thief, and you will not know at what hour I will come upon you." Rev. 3:3.

ing himself as a martyr for humanity at the hands of a cruel and selfish society. His remarks were tape-recorded, and included the following words spoken in a quiet tone, weary from long suffering:

It is true, children, I have served time for committing that bad check. I served . . . nine months, in a road gang, three years on probation. It is true, children, that I . . . was convicted for a so-called burglary. . . . The truth cannot be in someone like that because that person is bad, and society says he is bad, and condemns him for everything he has done. And yet it has not stopped me from my mission, and my work. As much as society has said that I was guilty of those crimes, I say I was not guilty.—Why?—It's good for all of you. You know why I'm telling you this today? I want you to condemn me too and show your true "Christian" spirit. I want to see how much Christian you are and how much Hypocrite you are.

Several members of the audience wept throughout Krishna's talk. At the close of this last meeting, a member of the audience once again challenged Krishna: "Are you the embodiment of Christ?" Krishna answered:

If I were to say "no" to you, you would be pleased, because you are not willing to accept. If I were to say "yes" that I am, you would be very highly displeased and say, "No, it isn't possible!" So I have to make my choice between you and God. I fear not what man might say about me. In all of his rejections I do not fear; but I do fear God. Therefore, I cannot lie to you to please you. I must tell the truth in the sight of God. I *am* the Son of God.

A woman in the audience cried out ecstatically, "I knew it!" Shortly afterward Krishna and his disciples de-

parted in their Buick station wagon for their home base, a utopian colony in southern California.

## The Audiences

From our informal observations at the first two meetings, it seemed that while many people attended as mere spectators, others were genuinely concerned whether or not this man was really Christ.[10] The degree to which persons accepted Krishna's claim seemed to depend more on their own predilections than on what he said. Our first questionnaire, therefore, was designed to measure *degree of acceptance* of his claim, and to obtain some indication of *predispositions*.

The audiences appeared to range from middle to lower socio-economic status, with men and women about equally represented. Very few non-white persons were present at any of the meetings. Questionnaire responses showed that collectively the audiences included one or more adherents of each of the following faiths: Baptist, Catholic, Christian, Christian Scientist, Church of the People, Congregational, Episcopal, Greek Orthodox, Jehovah's Witnesses, Latter Day Saints, Lutheran, Mental Science, Methodist, Open Bible Standard, Pentecostal Assembly of God, Presbyterian, Quaker, Rosicrucian, Seventh Day Adventist, Spiritualist, The Church, United Brethren, and Unity. In size the audiences ranged as shown in Table 1.

[10] This was true also of the "secondary audience"—persons who heard of the affair second-hand through us. Many of them were chiefly concerned to know whether *we* thought Krishna really was Christ.

TABLE 1. SIZE OF AUDIENCE AND NUMBER
OF QUESTIONNAIRES RETURNED
BY DATE OF MEETING

|  | Size of Audience | Question-naires Returned |
|---|---|---|
| Sunday, Jan. 20 | About 300 | . . . |
| Monday, Jan. 21 | No count taken | . . . |
| Sunday, Jan. 27 | 420 | 125 |
| Wednesday, Jan. 30 | 132 | 70 |
| Sunday, Feb. 3 | 120 | 58 |
| Sunday, Feb. 10 | 84 | 37 |

Each questionnaire included the open-ended query: "What was your main interest in coming to this meeting?" With very few exceptions [11] it was possible to divide the respondents into two rather clear-cut categories: those who said "To learn," "To seek the truth," or "To gain an understanding of God," etc. were classified as *seekers;* those who said "To see a show," or "I was curious," etc. were designated *observers.*

What kind of people were these seekers and observers? Other questions showed that seekers were less likely to be church members, attended church less often than did observers, more frequently read the Bible, were more inclined to believe in the possibility of a second coming, devoted somewhat more of their idle thoughts to questions of where and how they would spend eternity, were lonelier, were slightly more apprehensive about war and depression. In short, seekers tended to be those who had strong religious interests that were

[11] The exceptions probably included a small group of relatives and friends of two of Krishna's robed followers who happened to be from Seattle. Responses: "I came on account of a friend," or "To see Brother Gene," etc. These appear under "N.R." in the tables.

not being satisfied through normal institutional channels. These were the people, as identified by questionnaire items, whom we would predict as most likely to become followers of Krishna, according to the theoretical position stated at the beginning of this paper.

## The Questionnaire Findings

Did any of these people in fact become "followers" of Krishna? A total of 129 names and addresses were obtained from the questionnaires; and each individual's questionnaires were assembled into a single unit. The number of meetings attended by seekers and observers is shown in Table 2.

If the nine "no responses" are eliminated and the table is condensed into a four-fold contingency table (seekers vs. observers, and one meeting vs. more-than-one-meeting attended), this condensed table yields a Chi-square of 12.05, which for one degree of freedom is significant beyond the .001 level. This indicates that seekers were more prone to return to subsequent meetings after

TABLE 2. PREDISPOSITION OF RESPONDENTS BY FREQUENCY OF ATTENDANCE [*]

| No. of Meetings Attended | Seekers | Observers | N.R. | Totals |
|---|---|---|---|---|
| 1 | 61 | 37 | 9 | 107 |
| 2 | 10 | — | — | 10 |
| 3 | 11 | — | — | 11 |
| 4 | 1 | — | — | 1 |
| Totals | 83 | 37 | 9 | 129 |

[*] Includes only those who gave their names.

first exposure to "the Master" than were observers. Returnees can be re-

TABLE 3. PREDISPOSITION OF RESPONDENTS BY DATE OF FIRST ATTENDANCE *

| First Attendance | Seekers | | Observers | | N.R. | | Totals | |
|---|---|---|---|---|---|---|---|---|
| | No. | % | No. | % | No. | % | No. | % |
| Sunday, Jan, 27 | (56) | 71 | (17) | 22 | (5) | 6 | (78) | 100 |
| Wednesday, Jan. 30 | (14) | 61 | (9) | 39 | . . . | . . | (23) | 100 |
| Sunday, Feb. 3 | (10) | 53 | (7) | 37 | (2) | 11 | (19) | 100 |
| Sunday, Feb. 10 | (3) | 33 | (4) | 44 | (2) | 22 | (9) | 100 |
| Totals | (83) | | (37) | | (9) | | (129) | |

* Restricted to those who gave their names.

garded, in a limited sense, as "followers."

Despite the greater proneness of seekers to return to Krishna's lectures, the proportion of *new observers* in successive audiences appears to have increased, as shown by Table 3.

Based on the same "voluntary sample" as Table 2, Table 3 indicates that successive audiences included proportionately fewer *new* seekers, and proportionately more *new* observers. Since the later meetings were held without benefit of newspaper advertising, it may be hypothesized that word-of-mouth recruiting of new audience-members was more effective in bringing in additional observers than seekers. This hypothesis is supported by responses in the mailed follow-up questionnaire to the item: "I *first* found out about Krishna by (a) hearing about him from another person, (b) reading his ad in the papers" (see Table 4).

By eliminating the N.R. row and column, Table 5 can be reduced to a four-fold contingency table that yields a Chi-square of 4.71, which is significant for one degree of freedom at the .05 level. Thus Table 4 indicates a significant tendency for seekers to learn of Krishna predominantly via newspaper advertising and for observers to learn principally via word-of-mouth.

For both categories, however, the median number of persons *told* was two; and if we compare telling versus not telling by seekers and observers we obtain Table 5.

The first four cells of this table, taken as a four-fold contingency table, yield a Chi-square of .032, which is far from significant. Therefore, we cannot argue that seekers were any more, or less, talkative than observers.

It was hypothesized that once present in the audience, *seekers would be more inclined to accept Krishna's claim to be Christ than would observers*. The degree of acceptance of this claim was measured by an item

TABLE 4. SOURCES OF INFORMATION FOR SEEKERS AND OBSERVERS

| | Word-of-Mouth | Advertisement | N.R. | Totals |
|---|---|---|---|---|
| Seekers | 13 | 32 | 7 | 52 |
| Observers | 10 | 7 | 1 | 19 |
| N.R. | 1 | 3 | — | 4 |
| Totals | 24 | 42 | 9 | 75 |

TABLE 5. COMPARISON OF SEEKERS WITH OBSERVERS AS ORAL COMMUNICATORS

| | Told Nobody | Told Somebody | N.R. | Totals |
|---|---|---|---|---|
| Seekers | 17 | 28 | 7 | 52 |
| Observers | 6 | 11 | 2 | 19 |
| N.R. | 2 | 2 | — | 4 |
| Totals | 25 | 41 | 9 | 75 |

involving a thermometer-like diagram. The top of its column was labeled "Absolutely certain," and the bottom, where it joined the thermometer bulb, was labeled "Absolutely impossible." Above the thermometer diagram were the words, "Degrees of likelihood." Respondents were asked to blacken the tube up to a height that would indicate "how likely you think it is that Krishna is Christ." While this constituted a very unsophisticated attitude-scale, it had the merit of being clearly meaningful to the respondents.

This item appeared twice on each questionnaire, and respondents were instructed to indicate their degree of belief both *before* and *after* the meeting. The markings were converted later to a numerical index ranging from 0, "absolutely impossible," to 1.0 "Absolutely certain."

The signed questionnaires enabled us to observe individual opinions before and after *one or more* exposures to Krishna. For the 51 seekers and 29 observers who put their names on their questionnaires *and* gave at least two responses on the likelihood (thermometer) question, definite shifts of opinion occurred, as shown in Table 6.

TABLE 6. OPINION SHIFTS AMONG
IDENTIFIED RESPONDENTS

*Likelihood Krishna is Christ*

|  | Mean First Response | Mean Last Response |
|---|---|---|
| Seekers (N = 51) | .44 | .51 |
| Observers (N = 29) | .10 | .04 |

The initial level of belief differed significantly between seekers and observers (C.R. = 12.09) in the direction one would expect. More than this, the initially favorable seekers became more favorable (C.R. = 2.25) through exposure to Krishna's lectures, while the initially skeptical observers became still more skeptical (C.R. = 2.85) in response to "the same" stimuli.

In response to the questionnaire item, "What do you think was the main thing you got out of coming [to this meeting]?" one respondent—a non-church member—wrote, "Satisfaction of Krishna being the Christ." Another said, "A lovely friendly feeling and a light heart." Still another—a church member—wrote, "Satisfaction that he is a fraud. . . ." Several respondents indignantly called him "anti-Christ."

## Summary and Conclusion

When a man who claimed to be Christ gave a series of public lectures in Seattle, his audiences consisted largely of two kinds of persons: *seekers,* persons who wanted to consider him seriously as a religious leader and many of whom were not affiliated with a church, and *observers* who came because of curiosity. Seekers were more inclined than observers to return to subsequent meetings. Initial announcement of the meetings was by newspaper advertisement; but audience members could later be recruited only by word-of-mouth. The latter means of communication was more effective in bringing in observers to the lectures, while seekers were mainly brought in by the printed advertising, so successive audiences contained increasing proportions of observers. The acceptance of his claim to be Christ was initially higher among seekers than among observers, and increased among seekers upon exposure to the lectures, whereas the lectures decreased acceptance among observers.

It can be argued theoretically that any religious organization that is "successful" institutionally must "fail" religiously for at least some of its constituents. These people will be more prone than others to accept the claims (at least temporarily, until institutionalization sets in) of a cultist leader. The present research has indicated that it is possible, even with relatively unsophisticated techniques, to identify these persons in the larger population, and to predict their responses to religious stimuli. Often, of course, there are a number of different cults "on the market" at the same time. It is plausible that important differences exist between the sort of person who was attracted to Krishna Venta and

those who find themselves aroused by a different sort of appeal.[12] The evidence reported in this paper would not enable us to predict which of several competing cults might be selected by a cult-prone (institutionally alienated but religiously intense) person. Much further research would be required before such specific prediction could be attempted.

[12] The possibility that some persons may have a generalized cult-proneness seems implied by the previous involvement with dianetics of several of the members of the cult studied by Leon Festinger, Henry W. Riecken, and Stanley Schachter in *When Prophecy Fails* (Minneapolis: University of Minnesota Press, 1956). There are seekers, apparently, who move from cult to cult in a never-ending quest.

# 21

# What Is the Meaning of Santa Claus? *

*Warren O. Hagstrom*

Unlike Father's Day and Mother's Day, Christmas was not developed in the minds of Madison Avenue advertising men. And yet, despite its religious importance, it must be acknowledged—if sadly—that the economic importance of this holiday is not to be denied, especially today when banks encourage us to start banking money for next year's Christmas on December 26, and stores recommend that we begin our shopping immediately after Halloween.

* Reprinted from *The American Sociologist*, I (1966), 248–52, by permission of the author and publisher.

The major symbol, magical though secular, representing the commercial side of this otherwise spiritual occasion is, of course, Saint Nicholas, alias Kris Kringle, alias Santa Claus. What is the significance of the magical figure who bridges the sacred and secular realms at this festive time? Professor Hagstrom, in what is in large part a parody of sociological writings, takes on the question of the remarkable and near-universal importance of this symbolic figure. The meaning and implications of his analysis, however, are quite straightforward.
**EDITOR**

What is the meaning of Santa Claus? A simple and naïve answer to this question would be something like the following: "Santa Claus is a fat man with a white beard in a red suit who brings gifts at Christmas and rides in a sleigh drawn by reindeer and—who either exists or doesn't exist." This is the kind of answer a child might give. More sophisticated children (among whom I include many of my readers) might answer the question of the meaning of Santa Claus either in terms of *Clauseology* or *Positivism*.

## Clauseology and Positivism

The Clauseologist position is that Santa Claus exists but that his essential nature ("meaning") cannot be empirically ascertained. The empirical phenomena associated with Santa are likely to be illusory and deceptive. It is instead necessary to rely on nonempirical methods of investigation, of which there are two types: inner experience and revealed sources. I cannot report here my inner experiences of Santa Claus, since it has been so long since I've had any *genuine* experiences of this type. In any case, sorting the genuine from the spurious Claus-experiences is one of the major problems of the Clauseologist. Another major problem is collecting authentic revealed sources and reconciling apparent inconsistencies among them. Thus, works like Clement C. Moore's "A Night Before Christmas" can certainly be accepted as part of the revealed canon; and I believe that Jean de Brunhof's *Babar and Father Christmas* can likewise be accepted as authentic. The latter source, however, suggests that Santa is known as Father Christmas (Père Noël), that he lives in Prjmneswe, Bohemia, and that

he uses a flying machine instead of a reindeer-drawn sleigh. Such minor inconsistencies with American stories do not discourage the Clauseologist, who is able to detect temporal change, symbolism, and consistency among apparent inconsistencies. The Clauseologist, however, will reject from his revealed canon works like "Yes, Virginia, there is a Santa Claus," by Francis Church. Such works of higher criticism, by giving metaphorical interpretations to Santa, concede the essential elements of belief.

The Positivist (19th century version) accepts the Clauseologist's definition of Santa Claus but rejects the use of nonempirical methods. Belief in Santa Claus is defined as erroneous; and the problem of the Positivist is to discover how such erroneous beliefs arise. The Positivist, arguing that all beliefs arise by inference from experiences, finds the meaning of Santa in false inferences from actual experiences. An Animist, following E. B. Tylor and Herbert Spencer, might say that the child, confronted with the experience of receiving gifts from anonymous donors, and given many images and even dreams of Santa, makes the logical, if false, inference that Santa brings these gifts.[1] Such inferential processes undoubtedly exist. One boy, at age 4, lived in a family in which gifts were opened Christmas Eve after lying under the Christmas tree for some days. He inferred that Santa brings the gifts to the department stores and can be seen in such places; parents then pick up gifts there in the stores. He was unable to convince friends of this interpretation, and was somewhat disturbed by his failure to do so; but he

[1] Note the sympathetic reference to Tylor's theories in Renzo Sereno, "Some Observations on the Santa Claus Custom," *Psychiatry*, XIV (1951), 387–96, at 396.

would not accept cultural relativism as an explanation of the differences.

The Naturism of Max Müller is a variety of Positivism which finds the origin of figures like Santa in natural phenomena. Children, like primitive men, tend to personalize the abstract forces of nature.[2] Santa, or Father Frost as he is known in the Soviet Union, is then likely to be a representative of the benevolent aspects of midwinter—the Winter Solstice heralding the return of the sun. While small children may find it difficult to conceptualize the winter solstice, they find it easy to conceptualize Santa Claus. (Ask any child questions about the two phenomena.)

The social scientist can accept neither Clauseology nor Positivism. Since he relies on empirical evidence, he cannot accept the results of Clauseological investigations—nor can he reject them, for that matter. The scientific reasons for rejecting the Positivist interpretation are more complex and can only be hinted at here.[3] Three reasons may be mentioned. First, the Positivist theories do not account for the "sacred" aspects of Santa Claus; as we shall see below, Santa may be profaned, and Positivist theories cannot account for this. Second, if Santa is an expression of natural forces, "it is hard to see how it has maintained itself, for it expresses them in an erroneous manner"[4]—as any eight-year-old knows.

[2] The best evidence on this is from Jean Piaget. See his *The Language and Thought of the Child* (London: Routledge & Kegan Paul, Ltd., 1926).
[3] See Émile Durkheim, *The Elementary Forms of the Religious Life*, trans. J. W. Swain (London: George Allen & Unwin, 1915), Chapters II and III; and Talcott Parsons, *The Structure of Social Action* (New York: The Free Press, 1937), the argument summarized on pp. 728 ff.
[4] Durkheim, *op. cit.*, p. vi.

Third, it seems unlikely that beliefs in Santa and similar figures, of immense importance in history and in family relations, can be merely illusory; the persistence of the beliefs implies a social meaning and a social function.

## Historical Approaches

The naïve historian finds the meaning of anything in its origins: The meaning of the oak is to be found in the acorn. The more sophisticated historian looks for the unique characteristics of anything in its origins and history; while the meaning of oaks in general cannot be interpreted in terms of acorns in general, the characteristics of *this* oak is to be found in its acorn, and subsequent experiences. Since the historian does not present empirical generalizations (or does so only implicitly and in a simpleminded fashion), the historical meaning of Santa is an incomplete meaning from the point of view of the scientist. Nevertheless, the work of the historian can suggest and delimit problems for the scientist and provide evidence for general hypotheses.

Historians find, in brief, that Santa Claus is a thoroughly American figure who appears for the first time in the early 19th century. The alleged descent from Saint Nicholas, Bishop of Myra and patron saint of children (as well as maidens, lovers, merchants, sailors, robbers, and scholars) is mythical.[5] Saint Nicholas does

[5] A few items about Saint Nicholas may be of interest, however. He is alleged to have played an important role in establishing Trinitarian doctrine at the Council of Nicaea, where he died of a stroke after vanquishing his opponents in the midst of debate (A.D. 345?). See John Shlien, "Santa Claus: The Myth in America," *Human De-*

play a role similar to Santa Claus in the Netherlands, but he neither looks like Santa nor acts like him—he is a much more punitive figure and appears on December 6th—and there is no direct historical connection between him and Santa. The early Dutch settlers of America were Calvinists and hagiophobic in the extreme.[6] The attribution of Santa to the Dutch was made by Clement Moore, who wrote " 'Twas the Night Before Christmas" in 1822, and by other early 19th century American writers who created a mythical and sentimental picture of Dutch life in America a century earlier.[7] Washington Irving is perhaps the best known member of this group. Our current picture of Santa was not provided until 1863, when the political cartoonist Thomas Nast published his first drawing of Santa.

---

*velopment Bulletin*, No. 6, Spring, 1953, Committee on Human Development (Chicago: University of Chicago), 27–32. Christmas itself became established as an important holiday only at this time; previously Epiphany, the commemoration of Jesus's baptism or enlightenment, had been the more important holiday. Christmas, by emphasizing the divinity of Jesus from conception and birth and by de-emphasizing any later enlightenment, is a kind of Trinitarian and anti-Unitarian holiday. Ludwig Jekels has suggested that Christmas and Trinitarianism may represent a resolution of the Oedipus problem: The Trinitarians elevated the Son to a level with the Father. Why did they do this in the fourth century A.D.? Because, says Jekels, on the one hand they were still a rebellious minority, resentful of the Emperor father figure, and, on the other, they felt powerful enough to partly displace authority figures. "On the Psychology of the Festival of Christmas," *International Journal of Psychoanalysis*, XVII (1936), 57–72.

[6] Eric R. Wolf, "Santa Claus: Notes on a Collective Representation," in *Process and Pattern in Culture*, ed. Robert A. Manners (Chicago: Aldine Publishing Company, 1964), pp. 147–55, at pp. 147 ff.

[7] *Ibid.*

This American Santa Claus is quite different not only from Saint Nicholas but from the mythical Christmas or midwinter figure found in other cultures. He is not involved in ceremonies of role reversal, like the Saturnalia celebrated by the ancient Romans in late December—Santa is no relative of the Lord of Misrule, or the Boy Bishop of the Western Middle Ages.[8] Santa has no connection with the Latin Three Kings; and he "would not be seen dead in the company of light-bringing and gift-bearing female spirits, such as the Swedish Santa Lucia, the Russian Babushka, or Befana, the Italian witch."[9] Thus, when Santa Claus appears in person in department stores in Paris, Rome, and Lima, he is almost certainly diffusing from the United States.[10] This diffusion suggests some interesting questions that can only be noted in this paper. Although some Italians oppose Santa as an alien, Santa rites sometimes coexist with Befana rites, which occur in January. Santa may also coexist with the Three Kings in Mexico or Peru. Is there a differentiation of functions in such cases, with Santa bringing gifts in the nuclear family and Befana or the Three Kings bringing them in the extended family? If so, when Befana or the Three Kings decline in relative importance, as they appear to, is this symptomatic of a change in the importance of the extended family? Santa evidently does not displace the Jultomten of Sweden; does this imply

[8] The Protestant Reformation put a stop to these practices. It has, however, been suggested that providing gifts for children originated as a form of bribery in such role-reversal ceremonies, something like our own tricks-or-treats on Halloween. See Wolf, "Santa Claus," p. 148.

[9] *Ibid.*

[10] Sereno, "Santa Claus Custom," pp. 387 ff.

the functional equivalence of Santa and the Jultomten? When Peruvians adopt Santa Claus, does this represent a desire to appear like United States citizens; or does Santa fill a need in the evolving Peruvian family system that cannot be filled by traditional figures such as the Three Kings?

Santa Claus is originally American; and in the United States his acceptance by minority groups probably facilitates and indicates the assimilation of minority groups into the larger American community.[11] But why does he exist only in America and other areas that have become Americanized? What is his *meaning* for Americans?

## Approaches in the Behavioral Sciences

Although behavioral scientists have unjustly neglected the study of Santa Claus, theories developed for other reasons can be applied to him very neatly.

### PSYCHOANALYSIS

Psychoanalysts have written surprisingly little about Santa Claus; and as a result I have been compelled to concoct my own half-baked theory

instead of using someone else's. Richard Sterba,[12] however, has suggested the obvious place to start from by noting that Santa Claus, "no doubt, is a father representative." However, he goes on to suggest that Santa Claus and the rest of Christmas is an "acting out of childbirth in the family." There is a period of "expecting" involving much secrecy, a Christmas rush involving great "labor," the exhibition and admiration of presents, and the obvious sexual symbolism of having Santa come down the chimney and through the fireplace. This last suggests that Santa is not entirely masculine, as does his fat belly and bag of gifts (is he pregnant?).[13] Sterba's theory implies the hypothesis that Santa Claus should be especially significant when the facts of childbirth are kept secret from children and should be less significant when children are well informed. This can be tested and is probably true. (There is no Santa Claus in the Trobriand Islands.) However, like many psychoanalytic explanations, Sterba's unduly neglects interpersonal relations and is incapable of explaining many variations within and among cultures. To generate better explanations, it is necessary to use neo-Freudian or post-Freudian theories.

Young children have ill-formed personifications of their parents. On the one hand, they may not clearly distinguish fathers and mothers, and, on the other, they may distinguish be-

[11] Eric Wolf says there is no Negro Santa Claus (*op. cit.*, p. 153), something which might appear to inhibit the assimilation of Negroes. However, Wolf is mistaken. Department stores in the Negro areas of Chicago have used Negro Santas, although one store owner pointed out "Now that we've used both white and black it doesn't seem to matter which he is—the children think it's Okay." And there are some Negro Santas on Christmas cards. See Shlien, "Myth in America," p. 30.

[12] Richard Sterba, "On Christmas," *Psychoanalytic Quarterly*, XIII (1944), 79–83.
[13] This argument would probably be attractive to Bruno Bettelheim, who has argued elsewhere that many male initiation rites in primitive societies involve a symbolic acquisition of female sexual characteristics and stem from masculine envy of female sexuality. See his *Symbolic Wounds* (New York: The Free Press, 1954).

tween a "good Mother" and a "bad Mother."[14] It is not easy to construct a consistent image of a parent. Children's myths often clearly differentiate images of consistently good parents from images of consistently bad parents. The prevalence of witches, goblins, and giants allows children to express hostility and anxiety toward parent figures which they are not allowed to express toward their actual parents.[15] But why Santa Claus? Isn't it permissible to express affection toward the real father? No, for two reasons. First, the real father doesn't deserve the affection. Santa represents a wish-fulfilling fantasy. Second, the real father tends to reject excessive affection because it is associated with excessive dependency. Fathers are relatively incompetent nurturant figures and confine affection from children within limits, so that children will be unable to make dependent demands on them. Thus, Santa is a consistently benevolent father image toward whom affectionate and dependent feelings may be expressed.[16]

[14] See Tamotsu Shibutani, *Society and Personality* (Englewood Cliffs, N.J.: Prentice-Hall, Inc., 1961); and Harry S. Sullivan, *The Interpersonal Theory of Psychiatry* (New York: W. W. Norton & Company, Inc., 1953).

[15] On the prevalence of witches and bogey-men, see Beatrice Whiting, ed., *Six Cultures: Studies of Child Rearing* (New York: John Wiley & Sons, Inc., 1963).

[16] One of my critics has argued that I have here followed a persistent tendency of psychoanalytic thinkers in emphasizing the nuclear family to the neglect of the extended family in discussing child socialization. This critic points out that many of Santa's characteristics are more befitting a grandfather figure or an uncle figure than a father figure; grandfathers and uncles often play the role of Santa in family ceremonies. I believe American grandfathers and uncles are seldom salient figures in child socialization, although I might be wrong; we lack good data on this point.

This approach suggests that Santa beliefs are especially likely to be salient when the child finds it difficult to construct a consistent image of his father. This is especially likely to be so in American society, where fathers and mothers both express affection toward children and where they both order children about, but where the father tends to be more punitive and less affectionate than the mother.[17] Fathers in other societies tend to be more consistently authoritative and more distant emotionally,[18] so that there is less cause for children to respond intensely to images like Santa Clause. The relative "dedifferentiation"[19] of parental roles in American families not only makes Santa an appropriate figure, it has also led to the increasingly frequent appearance of *Mrs.* Santa Claus.[20]

Although the figure of Santa Claus may have an important psychological meaning for children, this is only a small part of his meaning in society. "Children don't make culture," and if Santa beliefs persist it is because they have meaning for adults as well as children—or, rather, because they have meaning for adults in their relations to children.

[17] See Charles E. Bowerman and Glen H. Elder, Jr., "Variations in Adolescent Perception of Family Power Structure," *The American Sociological Review*, XXIX (1964), 551–67.

[18] See B. Whiting, *Six Cultures;* and E. C. Devereux, Jr., U. Bronfenbrenner, and G. J. Suci, "Patterns of Parent Behavior in the United States of America and the Federal Republic of Germany," *International Social Science Journal*, XIV (1962), 488–506.

[19] Philip E. Slater, "Parental Role Differentiation," *The American Journal of Sociology*, LXVII (1961), 296–308.

[20] One wonders what the Bishop of Myra would have had to say about her.

## Marxism

On the one hand, belief in Santa is an ideology of parents to facilitate the control of children, and, on the other, it is an expression of the distress of children. On the former, Friedrich Engels might have written, religion

. . . became more and more the exclusive possession of the ruling classes, and these apply it as a mere means of government, to keep the lower classes within bounds. Moreover, each of the different classes uses its own appropriate religion: the landed nobility—Catholic Jesuitism or Protestant orthodoxy; the liberal and radical bourgeoisie—rationalism; parents —Santa Claus; and it makes little difference whether these ladies and gentlemen themselves believe in their respective religions or not.[21]

On the latter, Karl Marx might have written,

The belief in Santa Claus is at the same time the *expression* of real distress and the *protest* against real distress. Belief in Santa is the sigh of the oppressed children, the heart of a heartless world, just as it is the spirit of an unspiritual situation. It is the *opium* of childhood. The abolition of Santa Claus as the *illusory* happiness of children is required for their *real* happiness. The demand to give up the illusions about their condition is the *demand to give up a condition which needs illusions.*[22]

Parents use the belief in Santa Claus to control children, to induce children to defer demands for gratification to Christmas and to make it

appear that Santa, not the parents, causes the deprivation of children.

Although Marx and Engels didn't make the above statements, they might have. Numerous later writers on Santa Claus have expressed themselves in such a vein. For example, Eric Wolf writes,

A long time ago Marx criticized the 'commodity fetishism' of Smith and his followers, their tendency to conceptualize the dance of commodities as a reality independent of the social relations that make up the market. In Santa Claus, this commodity fetishism has found an appropriate collective representation. . . . [As] God has been replaced by society, so the word of God has been replaced by the morality of the market place that governs the production and distribution of goods. Of this morality Santa Claus is both emblem and agent.[23]

Renzo Sereno has presented a similar argument, adding that the adult emphasis on the exchange of commodities at Christmas stems from their feelings of loneliness and worthlessness. Sereno not only argues that children are the "innocent victims" of Santa Claus beliefs, but that they are unwilling victims. He argues that children are distressed by Santa and anxious in his presence, and that adults can recall only unhappiness in their own childhood experiences with Santa.[24]

These arguments have serious weaknesses, which will be discussed below. However, there is some indirect corroborating evidence. While

---

[21] Engels, "Ludwig Feuerbach and the End of Classical German Philosophy," in Marx and Engels: *Basic Writings on Politics and Philosophy,* L. S. Feuer (Garden City, N.Y.: Doubleday Anchor Books, 1959), p. 240.

[22] Marx, "Toward the Critique of Hegel's Philosophy of Right," in *ibid.,* p. 263.

[23] Wolf, "Santa Claus," pp. 153 and 154.

[24] Sereno, "Santa Claus Custom," pp. 389–92. Sereno conducted interviews about Santa beliefs in central Illinois; the credibility of his work must be qualified by his admission that, "My investigation required no intensive interviews, because in most cases the candor of the adults matched the candor of children." *Ibid.,* p. 391.

there have been no systematic studies of Santa Claus as a child control device, belief in God has been studied in this way. Clyde Z. Nunn reports a study [25] in which a good sample of adults in eastern Tennessee were asked, "Do you tell your child that God will punish him if he is bad?" In 27 per cent of 367 families both parents said they did, and either father or mother did in an additional 40 per cent. The data show a slight tendency for parents affiliated with sectarian religions to use this "coalition with God" as a child control device more frequently than parents associated with denominational religions, except in the lower income groups.

Nunn's data suggest that parents are most likely to attempt to form a coalition with God when their power is hampered in other respects. Thus, a coalition with God is most likely to be attempted when family income is low and when the mother is employed outside the home; if only one parent attempts to form a coalition with God, the mother is most likely to do so when the child is more affectionate to the father than to her, and the father is most likely to do so when the child is more affectionate to the mother.

Children tend to believe parents who tell them they will be punished by God for misbehavior. Thus, a considerably larger proportion of children who were told this by their parents than of those who were not, responded affirmatively to the question, "Do you believe God punishes you when you get angry?" Believing this, they also tend to blame themselves more when they do get angry. There is also a slight tendency for

children whose parents form a coalition with God to believe that "A child should obey his parents without question" more than other children.

This study deserves to be replicated for such figures as Santa Claus and bogey-men; and it deserves to be elaborated to other areas of personality. Casual observation suggests considerable variation in the degree to which Santa is used as a child control device, in the degree to which parents tell children that rewards from Santa are contingent upon good behavior. (This variation is limited in two ways. First, the idea that Santa's behavior is contingent on good behavior is prevalent in the larger culture and manifested in such songs as "Santa Claus is coming to town." Children may acquire the belief from other sources than their parents. Second, *in fact* Santa's rewards are generally not contingent upon good behavior; parents who assert otherwise are bluffing.) We need information on the social determinants of these aspects of the behavior of Santa Claus.

Nunn suggests that the parental coalition with God produces *compliance* to rules on the child's part (and self-blame for noncompliance) but that it does not produce inner *commitment* to rules. It is also possible that parental coalitions with God or Santa generate anxiety and a sense of inner worthlessness in children; the child cannot rely on the unconditional support of his parents or other figures, and he is rewarded not for what he is but for what he does. This is an as yet untested hypothesis. Even if true, it is likely to be true only of a minority of American Santa Clauses. Santa Claus is generally a benevolent figure, and not only children but their parents regard him as such. Parents do not use Santa in a cynical fashion but tend to accept him themselves.

[25] Clyde Z. Nunn, "Child-Control through a 'Coalition with God,' " *Child Development*, XXXV (1964), 417–32.

This fact is a critical weakness of Marxist approaches. Engels to the contrary notwithstanding, it does make a difference if parents believe in Santa Claus.

## DURKHEIM

Santa Claus satisfies Emile Durkheim's definition of a religious object: the distinction between the sacred and the profane is made with regard to him, belief in him is closely related to a set of rites, and these rites are acted out in an organized social group, the family.

The sacred character of Santa Claus may explain Sereno's observations of apparently negative reactions by children to him. The sacred is often approached with awe and anxiety, not with informality and glee. This does not imply that the sacred is negatively valued. In the absence of systematic data, some observations of John Shlien [26] can be used to support the idea that Santa is a sacred figure.

1. During the second World War, the coal miners went on strike shortly before Christmas. A news commentator dramatized his announcement of the event by saying, "John L. Lewis just shot Santa Claus." Within an hour NBC network offices received 30,000 phone calls from frantic children and their parents. A little boy in Texas drank a bottle of castor oil in despair. NBC put Morgan Beatty on the air with an interview of Santa, who said reassuringly, "John L. Lewis just missed me." This reassured everyone except John L. Lewis, who called this the foulest blow of all. Evidently some children do have strong positive sentiments toward Santa.

2. In 1948, *Time* magazine published a picture of several hooded and robed members of the Ku Klux Klan

surrounding an elderly negro couple to whom they had just presented a radio as a Christmas present. The Grand Dragon of the Klan, in Santa Claus costume, stood front and center holding the hands of the old Negroes. *Time* called it "The most incongruous picture of the week"; and when Shlien showed the photographs to his professional acquaintances, one turned away in disgust and said it made him want to spit, and another said, "It's a perversion. . . . There is such a thing as the Devil." "That which is sacred is shown to be so if it is capable of being profaned by misuse or by contact with its opposite." [27]

3. Shlien performed a kind of experiment in which a plate of chocolate squares, fruit, animals, and Santa Clauses (all of chocolate) were placed before three different groups.[28] Among eleven 4 and 5 year old nursery school children, only one ate a Santa Claus, and she had an older brother. In a group of nine seven- and 8 year olds, all ate the Santa Claus. And, at a bridge party of twelve young parents, only one person ate a Santa Claus, and his wife criticized him for it. There is evidently a curvilinear relation between age and acceptance of Santa Claus. (It is likely that Sereno interviewed mostly 7 to 9 year old children.)

Santa Claus is a sacred figure. Like the totemic figures of the Australian aborigines which were analyzed by Durkheim, eating him or his representations is taboo. Like the Australian totems, he does not represent natural objects but a social group. Groups need such representation, since they are real but often invisible; the group exists even when its members are

[26] Shlien, "Myth in America," pp. 29–31.

[27] *Ibid.,* p. 29.
[28] David Schmitt has suggested to me that this technique could be generalized into a larger class of "projective eating" tests.

dispersed. Unlike Australian totems, Santa Claus does not represent the total society or the clan; however, he represents the group most important to small children, the nuclear family. Santa Claus beliefs and rituals represent the family and serve to enhance its solidarity.

To derive testable hypotheses from these statements, it is necessary to go beyond the theories of Durkheim. This can be done best by following the lead of Durkheim's associate Marcel Mauss [29] and considering the most important ritual associated with Santa Claus, gift-giving. The exchange of gifts (and, in an attenuated form, cards) is one way in which the solidarity of American extended families is maintained. It is not the economic value of these gifts that is important, but their symbolic value; the gifts symbolize positive familial sentiments, sentiments that are often latent (not affecting overt behavior) but which are nevertheless important.[30] Gifts are freely given, and by definition they are not given in expectation of a return gift. But, implicitly, reciprocity is expected, either in the form of a gift or in the form of feelings of gratitude and deference.[31] If reciprocity is not extended, feelings are hurt or hostility is aroused; in any event, the social relation is broken. Gift-giving is obviously capable of abuse, and gifts may be given in the

[29] Mauss, *The Gift: Forms and Functions of Exchange in Archaic Societies*, trans. Ian Cunnison (New York: The Free Press, 1954).

[30] Sociologists will notice a revision of Durkheim here. The exchange of commodities, which Durkheim felt to be especially important for organic solidarity, turns out to be important for maintaining mechanical solidarity when it takes the form of gift-exchange.

[31] Cf. Alvin W. Gouldner, "The Norm of Reciprocity," *The American Sociological Review*, XXV (1960), 161–78.

conscious expectation of a return and in the absence of favorable sentiments. Most people can make the distinction, however, between a gift and a bribe. Some of the condemnation of the "commercialism" of Christmas rests on just this feeling that alleged exchanges of "gifts" are often forms of barter or bribery. Recognition of this in no way weakens the importance of gift-giving for the maintenance of solidarity in families and similar groups.

Gifts exchanged between adults are generally acknowledged publicly. It is almost necessary that they be so acknowledged if they are to perform the functions described above. The problem of Santa Claus is that he is associated with anonymous gift-giving. Santa does not stay around to be thanked for his gifts, and parents are enabled to give gifts, not in their own names, but in his. Why? The Marxist answer would be that the parent prevents his children from bugging him for gifts all year long by the assertion that he is incapable of giving any and that the children must rely on another figure, Santa Claus (who is, fortunately, in league with the parent). (Santa Claus may also be a scapegoat if a child's wishes are denied.) There may be something to this, but why should the parent make any gift at all in this case? It seems more likely that the parent expresses a real affection toward his children in the form of the anonymous gift. An acknowledged gift always carries the possible suspicion of an expectation of reward—especially when the gift is made to a child, who may be unable to distinguish between the explicit denial of an expectation of reciprocity and the implicit acceptance of a norm of reciprocity. The anonymous gift is much less likely to arouse such suspicions, on the part of the donor as well as others. Thus, whenever we place a high value on the possession of certain positive sentiments we are likely to value the anonymous gift. Some of the attraction of many Christmas stories resides in this—stories like "The Juggler of Tours," or the dispatch by the reformed Scrooge of an unacknowledged turkey to the Cratchit family.

Christmas rites permit the expression of positive sentiments in extended and nuclear families. Santa Claus, by accepting responsibility for our gifts, allows us to express morally uncontaminated sentiments toward children. He is an especially important figure in American families because of the great emotional importance of the small family group for Americans. Santa Claus is likely to become important in other Western societies to the extent that their family systems become more like the American—to the extent that the power of extended families loses importance, and to the extent that the nuclear family becomes the center of the emotional life of all its members.

## NEEDED RESEARCH

The behavioral science approaches to Santa Claus that have been presented here need not be inconsistent with one other. It is conceivable that Santa Claus can be simultaneously a benevolent father figure, a child-control technique, and a symbolic representation of affection in small family groups. Santa's very complexity may account in part for his importance as a cultural figure. However, the apparent compatibility of these theories is also a sign of their weakness. They are not stated in a form that will permit their refutation. Additional work of a theoretical nature would be valuable, either to provide a genuine

synthetic theory or to generate hypotheses, the test of which would make it possible to reject one theory while retaining others.

Some needed empirical research has been suggested on the preceding pages. We need to know the conditions leading parents to form a coalition with a Santa Claus threatening to withhold rewards from children who misbehave; and we need to know the consequences of this Santa belief. We need studies like those reported by Shlien to show the extent to which Santa Claus is regarded in a sacred light. And we need to know which types of families in other societies are most likely to adopt the American Santa Claus system of beliefs and rites.

It is unlikely that studies of the distribution of Santa Claus beliefs in American society would be interesting in terms of the theories stated above. It seems likely that the most important determinant of these beliefs among young children is the religion of their parents. Parents of strict orthodox beliefs—obviously orthodox Judaism but also orthodox Christianity—and parents who are militant atheists are probably most likely to reject Santa Claus. The middle ranges of religiosity are probably most likely to be associated with belief in Santa.

The age at which children cease to believe in Santa, and the process by which disbelief develops, does deserve study. The presence or absence of older siblings is probably an important determinant of age of disbelief. Whatever the age, disbelief may have consequences for child behavior. Does the child feel taken in by his parents, and does he tend as a result of disbelief to question the legitimacy of his parents' authority? Or does he feel guilty for not believing as he is expected to? (A nine-year-old subject pretended to believe in Santa Claus, perhaps so that he would not disillusion his parents.) Or is disbelief a functional "belief" in its own right, enabling the child to identify himself as a more mature and sophisticated figure, one who can accept the symbolic meaning of gifts in the manner of an adult? Contrary to the beliefs of Clauseologists and Positivists, the meaning of Santa Claus does not depend solely on his existence or non-existence. The question, "Does Santa Claus exist?" may be misleading. As George Herbert Mead said, "Reality is itself a social process."

# PART VIII

# Deviance and Crime

# 22

# Apprenticeships in Prostitution *†

*James H. Bryan*

Although prostitution is often referred to as "the oldest profession in the world," little study has been made of how its practitioners enter the occupation. A vast literature on prostitution exists; [1] much of it, however, has been concerned only with the personality structure of the prostitute [2] or with the practice as a social problem. [3] Some of the latter literature still promulgates the picture of induction into this occupation usually found in folklore, especially in the largely mythological tradition surrounding what used to be called "white slavery." The following paper presents one of the few empirical investigations into this question.

EDITOR

Although theoretical conceptions of deviant behavior range from role strain to psychoanalytic theory, orientations to the study of the prostitute have shown considerable homogeneity. Twentieth century theorizing concerning this occupational group has employed, almost exclusively, a Freudian psychiatric model. The prostitute has thus been variously described as masochistic, of infantile mentality, unable to form mature interpersonal relationships, regressed, emotionally dangerous to males and as normal as the average women. [4]

* Reprinted from *Social Problems*, XII (1965), 287–97, by permission of the author and The Society for the Study of Social Problems. Footnotes renumbered.

† These data were collected when the author was at the Neuropsychiatric Institute, UCLA Center for the Health Sciences. I wish to acknowledge the considerable aid of Mrs. Elizabeth Gordon, Miss Carol Kupers, and Mr. Saul Sherter in the preparation and the analysis of these data. I am greatly indebted to Dr. Evelyn Hooker for both her intellectual and moral support, and to Vivian London for her excellent editorial advice. I particularly wish to express my great gratitude to my wife, Virginia, for her tolerance, encouragement, and understanding.

[1] For two of the best sociological pieces dealing with the general issues involved, see: Kingsley Davis, "The Sociology of Prostitution," *The American Sociological Review*, II (1937), 744–55; and Travis Hirschi, "The Professional Prostitute," *Berkeley Journal of Sociology*, VII (1962), 33–49.

[2] E.g., see: Norman R. Jackman, Richard O'Toole, and Gilbert Geis, "The Self-Image of the Prostitute," *Sociological Quarterly*, IV (1963), 150–61; and Harold Greenwald, *The Call Girl* (New York: Ballantine Books, Inc., 1958).

[3] E.g., see: Judge John M. Murtagh and Sara Harris, *Cast the First Stone* (New York: McGraw-Hill Book Company, Inc., 1957); ————, *Who Live in Shadow* (New York: McGraw-Hill Book Company, Inc., 1959); and Sara Harris, *They Sell Sex: The Call Girl and Big Business* (Greenwich, Conn.: Fawcett Publications, Inc., 1960).

[4] H. Benjamin, "Prostitution Reassessed," *International Journal of Sexology*, XXVI (1951), 154–60; ———— and A. Ellis, "An Objective Examination of Prostitution," *International Journal of Sexology*, XXIX

The call girl, the specific focus of this paper, has been accused of being anxious, possessing a confused self-image, excessively dependent, demonstrating gender-role confusion, aggressive, lacking internal controls and masochistic.[5]

The exclusive use of psychoanalytic models in attempting to predict behavior, and the consequent neglect of situational and cognitive processes, has been steadily lessening in the field of psychology. Their inadequacy as models for understanding deviancy has been specifically explicated by Becker, and implied by London.[6] The new look in the conceptualization and study of deviant behavior has focused on the interpersonal processes that help define the deviant role, the surroundings in which the role is learned, and limits upon the enactment of the role. As Hooker has indicated regard-

ing the study of homosexuals, one must not only consider the personality structure of the participants, but also the structure of their community, and the pathways and routes into the learning and enactment of the behavior.[7] Such "training periods" have been alluded to by Maurer in his study of the con man, and by Sutherland in his report on professional thieves. More recently, Lindesmith and Becker have conceptualized the development of drug use as a series of learning sequences necessary for the development of steady use.[8]

This paper provides some detailed, albeit preliminary, information concerning induction and training in a particular type of deviant career: prostitution, at the call girl level. It describes the order of events, and their surrounding structure, that future call girls experience in entering their occupation.

The respondents in this study were 33 prostitutes, all currently or previously working in the Los Angeles area. They ranged in age from 18 to 32, most being in their mid-twenties. None of the interviewees were obtained through official law enforcement agencies, but seven were found within the context of a neuropsychiatric hospital. The remaining respondents were gathered primarily through individual referrals from previous participants in the study. There were no

---

(1955), 100–5; E. Glover, "The Abnormality of Prostitution," in *Women*, ed. A. M. Krich (New York: Dell Publishing Co., Inc., 1953); M. H. Hollander, "Prostitution, The Body, and Human Relatedness," *International Journal of Psychoanalysis*, XLII (1961), 404–13; M. Karpf, "Effects of Prostitution on Marital Sex Adjustment," *International Journal of Sexology*, XXIX (1953), 149–54; J. F. Oliven, *Sexual Hygiene and Pathology* (Philadelphia: J. B. Lippincott Co., 1955); W. J. Robinson, *The Oldest Profession in The World* (New York: Eugenics Publishing Co., 1929).

[5] H. Greenwald, *The Call Girl* (New York: Ballantine Books, Inc., 1960).

[6] H. S. Becker, *Outsiders: Studies in the Sociology of Deviance* (New York: The Free Press, 1963). Also see H. S. Becker, ed., *The Other Side* (New York: The Free Press, 1964); P. London, *The Modes and Morals of Psychotherapy* (New York: Holt, Rinehart & Winston, Inc., 1964). For recent trends in personality theory, see N. Sanford, "Personality: Its Place in Psychology," and D. R. Miller, "The Study of Social Relationships: Situation, Identity, and Social Interaction," in *Psychology: A Study of a Science*, ed. S. Koch, Vol. 5 (New York: McGraw-Hill Book Company, Inc., 1963).

[7] Evelyn Hooker, "The Homosexual Community," *Proceedings of the XIV International Congress of Applied Psychology*, 1961, 40–59. See also, A. Reiss, "The Social Integration of Queers and Peers," *Social Problems*, IX (1961), 102–20.

[8] D. W. Maurer, *The Big Con* (New York: Signet Books, 1940); H. S. Becker, *Outsiders*; E. H. Sutherland, *The Professional Thief* (Chicago: University of Chicago Press, 1937); A. R. Lindesmith, *Opiate Addiction* (Evanston, Ill.: Principia Press, 1955).

obvious differences between the "psychiatric sample" and the other interviewees on the data to be reported.

All subjects in the sample were call girls. That is, they typically obtained their clients by individual referrals, primarily by telephone, and enacted the sexual contract in their own or their clients' place of residence or employment. They did not initiate contact with their customers in bars, streets, or houses of prostitution, although they might meet their customers at any number of locations by prearrangement. The minimum fee charged per sexual encounter was $20.00. As an adjunct to the call girl interviews, three pimps and two "call boys" were interviewed as well.[9]

Approximately two thirds of the sample were what are sometimes known as "outlaw broads"; that is, they were not under the supervision of a pimp when interviewed. There is evidence that the majority of pimps who were aware of the study prohibited the girls under their direction from participating in it. It should be noted that many members of the sample belonged to one or another clique; their individually expressed opinions may not be independent.

The interviews strongly suggest that there are marked idiosyncrasies from one geographical area to another in such practices as fee-splitting, involvement with peripheral occupations (e.g., cabbies), and so forth. For example, there appears to be little direct involvement of peripheral oc-

cupations with call girl activities in the Los Angeles area, while it has been estimated, that up to 10 per cent of the population of Las Vegas is directly involved in activities of prostitutes.[10] What may be typical for a call girl in the Los Angeles area is not necessarily typical for a girl in New York, Chicago, Las Vegas, or Miami.

Since the professional literature (e.g., Greenwald; Pomeroy) concerning this occupation and its participants is so limited in quantity, and is not concerned with training *per se*, the present data may have some utility for the social sciences.[11]

All but two interviews were tape recorded. All respondents had prior knowledge that the interview would be tape recorded. The interviewing was, for the most part, done at the girls' place of work and/or residence. Occasional interviews were conducted in the investigator's office, and one in a public park. Interviews were semistructured and employed open-ended questions. One part of the interview concerned the apprenticeship period, or "turning out" process.

## The Entrance

I had been thinking about it [becoming a call girl] before a lot. . . . Thinking about wanting to do it, but I had no connections. Had I not had a connection, I probably wouldn't have started working. . . . I thought about starting out. . . . Once I tried it [without a contact]. . . . I met this guy at a bar and I tried to make him pay me, but the thing is, you can't do it that way because they are roman-

[9] This definition departs somewhat from that offered by Clinard. He defines the call girl as one dependent upon an organization for recruiting patrons and one who typically works in lower-class hotels. The present sample is best described by Clinard's category of high-class independent professional prostitute. M. D. Clinard, *Sociology of Deviant Behavior* (New York: Holt, Rinehart & Winston Inc., 1957).

[10] E. Reid, and O. Demaris, *The Green Felt Jungle* (New York: Pocket Books, Inc., 1963).

[11] Greenwald, *Call Girl;* W. Pomeroy, *Some Aspects of Prostitution* (unpublished paper).

tically interested in you, and they don't think that it is on that kind of basis. You can't all of a sudden come up and want money for it, you have to be known beforehand. . . . I think that is what holds a lot of girls back who might work. I think I might have started a year sooner had I had a connection. You seem to make one contact or another . . . if it's another girl or a pimp or just someone who will set you up and get you a client. . . . You can't just, say, get an apartment and get a phone in and everything and say, "Well, I'm gonna start business," because you gotta get clients from somewhere. There has to be a contact.

Immediately prior to entrance into the occupation, all but one girl had personal contact with someone professionally involved in call girl activities (pimps or other call girls). The one exception had contact with a customer of call girls. While various occupational groups (e.g., photographers) seem to be peripherally involved, often unwittingly, with the call girl, there was no report of individuals involved in such occupations being contacts for new recruits. The novice's initial contact is someone at the level at which she will eventually enter the occupation: not a street-walker, but a call girl; not a pimp who manages girls out of a house of prostitution, but a pimp who manages call girls.

Approximately half of the girls reported that their initial contact for entrance into the profession was another "working girl." The nature of these relations is quite variable. In some cases, the girls were friends of long standing. Other initial contacts involved sexual relations between a Lesbian and the novice. Most, however, had known each other less than a year, and did not appear to have a very close relationship, either in the sense of time spent together or of

biographical information exchanged. The relationship may begin with the aspiring call girl soliciting the contact. That is, if a professional is known to others as a call girl, she will be sought out and approached by females who are strangers: [12]

I haven't ever gone out and looked for one. All of these have fell right into my hands. . . . They turned themselfs out. . . . They come to me for help.

Whatever their relationship, whenever the professional agrees to aid the beginner, she also, it appears, implicitly assumes responsibility for training her. This is evidenced by the fact that only one such female contact referred the aspirant to another girl for any type of help. Data are not available as to the reason for this unusual referral.

If the original contact was not another call girl but a pimp, a much different relationship is developed, and the career follows a somewhat different course. The relationship between pimp and girl is typically one of lovers, not friends:

. . . because I love him very much. Obviously, I'm doing this mostly for him. . . . I'd do anything for him. I'm not just saying I will, I am. . . . [After discussing his affair with another woman] I just decided that I knew what he was when I decided to do this for him and I decided I had two choices—either accept it or not, and I accepted it, and I have no excuse.

Occasionally, however, a strictly business relationship will be formed:

Right now I am buying properties, and as soon as I can afford it, I am buying stocks. . . . It is strictly a business deal. This man and I are friends, our relation-

[12] A point also made in the autobiographical account of a retired call girl. Virginia McManus, *Not For Love* (New York: Dell Publishing Co., Inc., 1960), p. 160.

ship ends there. He handles all the money, he is making all the investments and I trust him. We have a legal document drawn up which states that half the investments are mine, half of them his, so I am protected.

Whether the relationship is love or business, the pimp solicits the new girl.[13] It is usually agreed that the male will have an important managerial role in the course of the girl's career, and that both will enjoy the gains from the girl's activities for an indefinite period:

Actually a pimp has to have complete control or else it's like trouble with him. Because if a pimp doesn't, if she is not madly in love with him or something in some way, a pimp won't keep a girl.

Once the girl agrees to function as a call girl, the male, like his female counterpart, undertakes the training of the girl, or refers the girl to another call girl for training. Either course seems equally probable. Referrals, when employed, are typically to friends and, in some cases, wives or ex-wives.

Although the data are limited, it appears that the pimp retains his dominance over the trainee even when the latter is being trained by a call girl. The girl trainer remains deferential to the pimp's wishes regarding the novice.

## Apprenticeship

Once a contact is acquired and the decision to become a call girl made,

the recruit moves to the next stage in the career sequence: the apprenticeship period. The structure of the apprenticeship will be described, followed by a description of the content most frequently communicated during this period.

The apprenticeship is typically served under the direction of another call girl, but may occasionally be supervised by a pimp. Twenty-four girls in the sample initially worked under the supervision of other girls. The classroom is, like the future place of work, an apartment. The apprentice typically serves in the trainer's apartment, either temporarily residing with the trainer or commuting there almost daily. The novice rarely serves her apprenticeship in such places as a house of prostitution, motel, or on the street. It is also infrequent that the girl is transported out of her own city to serve an apprenticeship. Although the data are not extensive, the number of girls being trained simultaneously by a particular trainer has rarely been reported to be greater than three. Girls sometimes report spending up to eight months in training, but the average stay seems to be two or three months. The trainer controls all referrals and appointments, novices seemingly not having much control over the type of sexual contract made or the circumstances surrounding the enactment of the contract.

The structure of training under the direction of a pimp seems similar, though information is more limited. The girls are trained in an apartment in the city they intend to work and for a short period of time. There is some evidence that the pimp and the novice often do not share the same apartment, as might the novice and the girl trainer. There appears to be two reasons for the separation of

[13] Two of the pimps denied that this was very often so and maintained that the girls will solicit them. The degree to which they are solicited seems to depend upon the nature and extent of their reputations. It is difficult to judge the accuracy of these reports as there appears to be a strong taboo against admitting to such solicitation.

pimp and girl. First, it is not uncommonly thought that cues which suggest the presence of other men displease the girl's customers:

Well, I would never let them know that I had a lover, which is something that you never ever let a john know, because this makes them very reticent to give you money, because they think you are going to go and spend it with your lover, which is what usually happens.

(Interestingly, the work of Winick suggests that such prejudices may not actually be held by many customers.) [14] Secondly, the legal repercussions are much greater, of course, for the pimp who lives with his girl than for two girls rooming together. As one pimp of 19 years experience puts it:

It is because of the law. There is a law that is called the illegal cohabitation that they rarely use unless the man becomes big in stature. If he is a big man in the hustling world, the law then employs any means at their command. . . .

Because of the convenience in separation of housing, it is quite likely that the pimp is less directly involved with the day-to-day training of the girls than the call girl trainer.

The content of the training period seems to consist of two broad, interrelated dimensions, one philosophical, the other interpersonal. The former refers to the imparting of a value structure, the latter to "do's" and "don'ts" of relating to customers and, secondarily, to other "working girls" and pimps. The latter teaching is perhaps best described by the concept of a short range perspective. That is, most of the "do's" and "don'ts" pertain to ideas and actions that the call girl uses in problematic situations.[15] Not all girls absorb these teachings, and those who do incorporate them in varying degrees.

Insofar as a value structure is transmitted it is that of maximizing gains while minimizing effort, even if this requires transgressions of either a legal or moral nature. Frequently it is postulated that people, particularly men, are corrupt or easily corruptible, that all social relationships are but a reflection of a "con," and that prostitution is simply a more honest or at least no more dishonest act than the everyday behavior of "squares." Furthermore, not only are "johns" basically exploitative, but they are easily exploited; hence they are, in some respects, stupid. As explained by a pimp:

. . . [in the hustling world] the trick or the john is known as a fool . . . this is not the truth. . . . He [the younger pimp] would teach his woman that a trick was a fool.

Since the male is corrupt, or honest only because he lacks the opportunity to be corrupt, then it is only appropriate that he be exploited as he exploits.

Girls first start making their "scores"—say one guy keeps them for a while or maybe she gets, you know, three or four grand out of him, say a car or a coat. These are your scores. . . .

The general assumption that man is corrupt is empirically confirmed when the married male betrays his wife, when the moralist, secular or religious, betrays his publicly stated values, or when the "john" "stiffs" (cheats) the girl. An example of the

[14] C. Winick, "Prostitutes' Clients' Perception of the Prostitute and Themselves," *International Journal of Social Psychiatry,* VIII (1961–62), 289-97.

[15] H. S. Becker, Blanche Geer, E. C. Hughes, and A. L. Strauss, *Boys In White* (Chicago: University of Chicago Press, 1961).

latter is described by a girl as she reflects upon her disillusionment during her training period.

It is pretty rough when you are starting out. You get stiffed a lot of times. . . . Oh sure. They'll take advantage of you anytime they can. And I'm a trusting soul, I really am. I'll believe anybody till they prove different. I've made a lot of mistakes that way. You get to the point, well, Christ, what the heck can I believe in people, they tell me one thing and here's what they do to me.

Values such as fairness with other working girls, or fidelity to a pimp, may occasionally be taught. To quote a pimp:

So when you ask me if I teach a kind of basic philosophy, I would say that you could say that. Because you try to teach them in an amoral way that there is a right and wrong way as pertains to this game . . . and then you teach them that when working with other girls to try to treat the other girl fairly because a woman's worst enemy in the street [used in both a literal and figurative sense] is the other woman and only by treating the other women decently can she expect to get along. . . . Therefore the basic philosophy I guess would consist of a form of honesty, a form of sincerity and complete fidelity to her man [pimp].

It should be noted, however, that behavior based on enlightened self-interest with concomitant exploitation is not limited to customer relationships. Interviewees frequently mentioned a pervasive feeling of distrust between trainer and trainee, and such incidents as thefts or betrayal of confidences are occasionally reported and chronically guarded against.

Even though there may be considerable pressure upon the girl to accept this value structure, many of them (perhaps the majority of the sample) reject it.

People have told me that I wasn't turned out, but turned loose instead. . . . Someone who is turned out is turned out to believe in a certain code of behavior, and this involves having a pimp, for one thing. It also involves never experiencing anything but hatred or revulsion for "tricks" for another thing. It involves always getting the money in front [before the sexual act] and a million little things that are very strictly adhered to by those in the "in group," which I am not. . . . Never being nice or pleasant to a trick unless you are doing it for the money, getting more money. [How did you learn that?] It was explained to me over a period of about six months. I learned that you were doing it to make money for yourself so that you could have nice things and security. . . . [Who would teach you this?] [The trainer] would teach me this.[16]

It seems reasonable to assume that the value structure serves, in general, to create in-group solidarity and to alienate the girl from "square" society, and that this structure serves the political advantage of the trainer and the economic gains of the trainee more than it allays the personal anxieties of either. In fact, failure to adopt these values at the outset does not appear to be correlated with much personal distress.[17] As one girl describes her education experiences:

[16] The statements made by prostitutes to previous investigators and mental helpers may have been parroting this particular value structure and perhaps have misled previous investigators into making the assumption that "all whores hate men." While space prohibits a complete presentation of the data, neither our questionnaire nor interview data suggest that this is a predominant attitude among call girls.

[17] There is, from the present study, little support for the hypothesis of Reckless concerning the association of experience trauma and guilt with abruptness of entry into the occupation. W. C. Reckless, The Crime Problem (New York: Appleton-Century-Crofts, 1950).

Some moral code. We're taught, as a culture . . . it's there and after awhile you live, breathe, and eat it. Now, what makes you go completely against everything that's inside you, everything that you have been taught and the whole society, to do things like this?

Good empirical evidence, however, concerning the functions and effectiveness of this value structure with regard to subjective comfort is lacking.

A series of deductions derived from the premises indicated above serve to provide, in part, the "rules" of interpersonal contact with the customer. Each customer is to be seen as a "mark," and "pitches" are to be made.

[Did you have a standard pitch?] It's sort of amusing. I used to listen to my girl friend [trainer]. She was the greatest at this telephone type of situation. She would call up and cry and say that people had come to her door. . . . She'd cry and she'd complain and she'd say "I have a bad check at the liquor store, and they sent the police over," and really . . . a girl has a story she tells the man. . . . Anything, you know, so he'll help her out. Either it's the rent or she needs a car, or doctor's bills, or any number of things.

Any unnecessary interaction with the customer is typically frowned upon, and the trainee will receive exhortations to be quick about her business. One girl in her fourth week of work explains:

[What are some of the other don't's that you have learned about?] Don't take so much time. . . . The idea is to get rid of them as quickly as possible.

Other content taught concerns specific information about specific customers.

. . . she would go around the bar and say, now look at that man over there, he's this

way and that way, and this is what he would like and these are what his problems are. . . .

. . . she would teach me what the men wanted and how much to get, what to say when I got there . . . just a line to hand them.

Training may also include proprieties concerning consuming alcohol and drugs, when and how to obtain the fee, how to converse with the customers and, occasionally, physical and sexual hygiene. As a girl trainer explains:

First of all, impress cleanliness. Because, on the whole, the majority of girls, I would say, I don't believe there are any cleaner women walking the streets, because they've got to be aware of any type of body odor. . . . You teach them to French [fellatio] and how to talk to men.
[Do they (pimps) teach you during the turning out period how to make a telephone call?] Oh, usually, yes. They don't teach you, they just tell you how to do it and you do it with your good common sense, but if you have trouble, they tell you more about it.

Interestingly, the specific act of telephoning a client is often distressing to the novice and is of importance in her training. Unfortunately for the girl, it is an act she must perform with regularity, as she does considerable soliciting.[18] One suspects that such behavior is embarrassing for her because it is an unaccustomed role for her to play— she has so recently come from a culture where young women do *not* telephone men for dates. Inappropriate sex-role behavior seems to produce greater personal distress than does appropriate sex-role behavior even when it is morally reprehensible.

[18] The topic of solicitation will be dealt with in a forthcoming paper.

Well, it is rather difficult to get on the telephone, when you've never worked before, and talk to a man about a subject like that, and it is very new to you.

What is omitted from the training should be noted as well. There seems to be little instruction concerning sexual techniques as such, even though the previous sexual experience of the trainee may have been quite limited. What instruction there is typically revolves around the practice of fellatio. There seems to be some encouragement not to experience sexual orgasms with the client, though this may be quite variable with the trainer.

. . . and sometimes, I don't know if it's a set rule or maybe it's an unspoken rule, you don't enjoy your dates.
Yes, he did [teach attitudes]. He taught me to be cold. . . .

It should be stressed that, if the girls originally accepted such instructions and values, many of them, at least at the time of interviewing, verbalized a rejection of these values and reported behavior that departed considerably from the interpersonal rules stipulated as "correct" by their trainers. Some experience orgasms with the customer, some show considerable affection toward "johns," others remain drunk or "high" throughout the contact.[19] While there seems to be general agreement as to what the rules of interpersonal conduct are, there appears to be considerable variation in the adoption of such rules.

A variety of methods is employed to communicate the content described above. The trainer may arrange to eavesdrop on the interactions of girl and client and then discuss the interaction with her. One trainer, for example, listened through a closed door to the interaction of a new girl with a customer, then immediately after he left, discussed, in a rather heated way, methods by which his exit may have been facilitated. A pimp relates:

The best way to do this [teaching conversation] is, in the beginning, when the phone rings, for instance . . . is to listen to what she says and then check and see how big a trick he is and then correct her from there.

. . . with everyone of them [trainees] I would make it a point to see two guys to see how they [the girls] operate.

In one case a girl reported that her pimp left a written list of rules pertaining to relating to "johns." Direct teaching, however, seems to be uncommon. The bulk of whatever learning takes place seems to take place through observation.

It's hard to tell you, because we learn through observations.
But I watched her and listened to what her bit was on the telephone.

To summarize, the structure of the apprenticeship period seems quite standard. The novice receives her training either from a pimp or from another more experienced call girl, more often the latter. She serves her initial two to eight months of work under the trainer's supervision and often serves this period in the trainer's apartment. The trainer assumes responsibility for arranging contacts and negotiating the type and place of the sexual encounter.

The content of the training pertains both to a general philosophical stance and to some specifics (usually not sexual) of interpersonal behavior

[19] In the unpublished paper referred to above, Pomeroy has indicated that, of 31 call girls interviewed, only 23 per cent reported never experiencing orgasms with customers.

with customers and colleagues. The philosophy is one of exploiting the exploiters (customers) by whatever means necessary and defining the colleagues of the call girl as being intelligent, self-interested and, in certain important respects, basically honest individuals. The interpersonal techniques addressed during the learning period consist primarily of "pitches," telephone conversations, personal and occasionally sexual hygiene, prohibitions against alcohol and dope while with a "john," how and when to obtain the fee, and specifics concerning the sexual habits of particular customers. Specific sexual techniques are very rarely taught. The current sample included a considerable number of girls who, although capable of articulating this value structure, were not particularly inclined to adopt it.

## Contacts and Contracts

While the imparting of ideologies and proprieties to the prospective call girl is emphasized during the apprenticeship period, it appears that the primary function of the apprenticeship, at least for the trainee, is building a clientele. Since this latter function limits the degree of occupational socialization, the process of developing the clientele and the arrangements made between trainer and trainee will be discussed.

Lists ("books") with the names and telephone numbers of customers are available for purchase from other call girls or pimps, but such books are often considered unreliable. While it is also true that an occasional pimp will refer customers to girls, this does not appear to be a frequent practice. The most frequent method of obtaining such names seems to be through contacts developed during

the apprenticeship. The trainer refers customers to the apprentice and oversees the latter in terms of her responsibility and adequacy in dealing with the customer. For referring the customer, the trainer receives forty to fifty per cent of the total price agreed upon in the contract negotiated by the trainer and customer.[20] The trainer and trainees further agree, most often explicitly, on the apprentice's "right" to obtain and to use, on further occasions, information necessary for arranging another sexual contract with the "john" without the obligation of further "kick-back" to the trainer. That is, if she can obtain the name and telephone number of the customer, she can negotiate another contract without fee-splitting. During this period, then, the girl is not only introduced to other working colleagues (pimps and girls alike) but also develops a clientele.

There are two obvious advantages for a call girl in assuming the trainer role. First, since there seems to be an abundant demand for new girls, and since certain service requirements demand more than one girl, even the well established call girl chronically confronts the necessity for making referrals. It is then reasonable to assume that the extra profit derived from the fee-splitting activities, together with the added conveniences of having a girl "on call," allows the

[20] The fee-splitting arrangement is quite common at all levels of career activity. For example, cooperative activity between two girls is often required for a particular type of sexual contract. In these cases, the girl who has contracted with the customer will contact a colleague, usually a friend, and will obtain 40 to 50 per cent of the latter's earnings. There is suggestive evidence that fee-splitting activities vary according to geographical areas, and that Los Angeles is unique for both its fee-splitting patterns and the rigidity of its fee-splitting structure.

trainer to profit considerably from this arrangement. Secondly, contacts with customers are reputedly extremely difficult to maintain if services are not rendered on demand. Thus, the adoption of the trainer role enables the girl to maintain contacts with "fickle" customers under circumstances where she may wish a respite from the sexual encounter without terminating the contacts necessary for re-entry into the call girl role. It is also possible that the financial gains may conceivably be much greater for most trainers than for most call girls, but this is a moot point.

A final aspect of the apprenticeship period that should be noted is the novice's income. It is possible for the novice, under the supervision of a competent and efficient trainer, to earn a great deal of money, or at least to get a favorable glimpse of the great financial possibilities of the occupation and, in effect, be heavily rewarded for her decision to enter it. Even though the novice may be inexperienced in both the sexual and interpersonal techniques of prostitution, her novelty on the market gives her an immediate advantage over her more experienced competitors. It seems quite likely that the new girl, irrespective of her particular physical or mental qualities, has considerable drawing power because she provides new sexual experience to the customer. Early success and financial reward may well provide considerable incentive to continue in the occupation.

A final word is needed regarding the position of the pimp vis-à-vis the call girl during the apprenticeship period. While some pimps assume the responsibility for training the girl personally, as indicated above, as many send the novice to another girl. The most apparent reason for such referral is that it facilitates the development of the "book." Purposes of training appear to be secondary for two reasons:

1. The pimp often lacks direct contact with the customers, so he personally cannot aid directly in the development of the girl's clientele;
2. When the pimp withdraws his girl from the training context, it is rarely because she has obtained adequate knowledge of the profession.

This is not to say that all pimps are totally unconcerned with the type of knowledge being imparted to the girl. Rather the primary concern of the pimp is the girl's developing a clientele, not learning the techniques of sex or conversation.

The apprenticeship period usually ends abruptly, not smoothly. Its termination may be but a reflection of interpersonal difficulties between trainer and trainee, novice and pimp, or between two novices. Occasionally termination of training is brought about through the novice's discovery and subsequent theft of the trainer's "book." Quite frequently, the termination is due to the novice's developing a sufficient trade or other business opportunities. The point is, however, that no respondent has reported that the final disruption of the apprenticeship was the result of completion of adequate training. While disruptions of this relationship may be due to personal or impersonal events, termination is not directly due to the development of sufficient skills.

## Discussion and Summary

On the basis of interviews with 33 call girls in the Los Angeles area, information was obtained about entrance into the call girl occupation and the initial training period or apprenticeship therein.

The novice call girl is acclimated to her new job primarily by being thoroughly immersed in the call girl subculture, where she learns the trade through imitation as much as through explicit tutoring. The outstanding concern at this stage is the development of a sizeable and lucrative clientele. The specific skills and values which are acquired during this period are rather simple and quickly learned.

In spite of the girls' protests and their extensive folklore, the art of prostitution, at least at this level, seems to be technically a low-level skill. That is, it seems to be an occupation which requires little formal knowledge or practice for its successful pursuit and appears best categorized as an unskilled job. Evidence for this point comes from two separate sources. First, there seems to be little technical training during this period, and the training seems of little importance to the career progress. Length or type of training does not appear correlated with success (i.e., money earned, lack of subjective distress, minimum fee per "trick," etc.). Secondly, the termination of the apprenticeship period is often brought about for reasons unrelated to training. It seems that the need for an apprenticeship period is created more by the secrecy surrounding the rendering or the utilization of the call girl service than by the complexity of the role. In fact, it is reasonable to assume that the complexity of the job confronting a streetwalker may be considerably greater than that confronting a call girl. The tasks of avoiding the police, sampling among strangers for potential customers, and arrangements for the completion of the sexual contract not only require different skills on the part of the streetwalker, but are performances requiring a higher degree of professional "know-how" than is generally required of the call girl.[21]

As a pimp who manages both call girls and "high class" streetwalkers explains:

The girl that goes out into the street is the sharper of the two, because she is capable of handling herself in the street, getting around the law, picking out the trick that is not absolutely psycho . . . and capable of getting along in the street. . . . The streetwalker, as you term her, is really a prima donna of the prostitutes . . . her field is unlimited, she goes to all of the top places so she meets the top people. . . .

The fact that the enactment of the call girl role requires little training, and the introduction of the girl to clients and colleagues alike is rather rapid, gives little time or incentive for adequate occupational socialization. It is perhaps for this reason rather than, for example, reasons related to personality factors, that occupational instability is great and cultural homogeneity small.

In closing, while it appears that there is a rather well-defined apprenticeship period in the career of the call girl, it seems that it is the secrecy rather than the complexity of the occupation that generates such a period. While there is good evidence that initial contacts, primarily with other "working girls," are necessary for entrance into this career, there seems no reason, at this point, to assume that the primary intent of the participants in training is anything but the development of an adequate clientele.

[21] Needless to say, however, all of the sample of call girls who were asked for status hierarchies of prostitution felt that the streetwalker had both less status and a less complex job. It *may* well be that the verbal exchange required of the call girl requires greater knowledge than that required of a streetwalker; but the nonverbal skills required of the streetwalker may be considerably greater than those of the call girl.

23

# From Mafia to Cosa Nostra *

*Robert T. Anderson*

Some sociologists have questioned what one has called the "myth of the Mafia." [1] More recent information, however, especially that disclosed in the Joseph Valachi hearings about Mafia activities in New York State, would appear to disallow further questioning of the importance of this criminal force on the American scene. But, as the following article argues, the traditional type of formal organization once present in the Mafia has been replaced by a new bureaucratized structure, both in Sicily and, especially, in the United States. **EDITOR**

---

Sicily has known centuries of inept and corrupt governments that have always seemed unconcerned about the enormous gap between the very rich minority and the incredibly poor majority. Whether from disinterest or from simple incapacity, governments have failed to maintain public order. Under these circumstances, local strong men beyond reach of the government, or in collusion with it, have repeatedly grouped together to seek out their own interests. They have formed, in effect, little extra-legal principalities. A code of conduct, the code of *omertà*, justified and supported these unofficial regimes by linking compliance with a fabric of tradition that may be characterized as chivalrous. By this code, an "honorable" Sicilian maintained unbreakable silence concerning all illegal activities. To correct abuse, he might resort to feud and vendetta. But never would he avail himself of a governmental agency. Sanctioned both by hoary tradition and the threat of brutal reprisal, this code in support of strong men was obeyed by the whole populace. The private domains thus established are old. After the 1860's they became known as "Mafias."[2]

[2] Giuseppe Pitrè, *La famiglia, la casa, la vita del popolo siciliano* (Palermo: Stabilimento Tipografico virzi, 1913), I, 289–91; George Wermert, *Die Insel Sicilien in volkswirtschaftlicher, kultureller und sozialer Beziehung* (Berlin: Dietrich Reimer [Ernest Vohsen], 1905), pp. 397–402, 437; Gaetano Mosca, "Mafia," *Encyclopaedia of the Social Sciences* (London: Macmillan & Co., Ltd., 1933), X, 36; Margaret Carlyle, *The Awakening of Southern Italy* (London: Oxford University Press, 1962), pp. 111–12; Jerre Mangione, *Reunion in Sicily* (Boston:

* Reprinted from *The American Journal of Sociology*, LXXI (1965), 302–10, by permission of The University of Chicago Press. Copyright 1965 by the University of Chicago. Footnotes renumbered.
[1] Daniel Bell, "Crime as an American Way of Life," in his *The End of Ideology* (New York: P. F. Collier, Inc., 1961), pp. 138–41.

As an institution, the Mafia was originally at home in peasant communities as well as in pre-industrial towns and cities. (Sicilian peasants are notable for urban rather than village residence.) The Mafia built upon traditional forms of social interaction common to all Sicilians. Its functions were appropriate to face-to-face communities. Mafias persist and adapt in contemporary Sicily, which, to some extent, is industrializing and urbanizing. Mafias also took root in the United States, where industrialization and urbanization have created a new kind of society, and here, too, they have persisted and adapted. But can a pre-industrial peasant institution survive unchanged in an urban, industrial milieu? May we not anticipate major modifications of structure and function under such circumstances? The available evidence on secret organizations, though regrettably incomplete, inconsistent and inaccurate,[3] suggests an affirmative

answer. The Mafia has bureaucratized.

Formal organizations of a traditional type, whether castes in India, harvesting co-operatives in Korea, monasteries in Europe or other comparable groups, normally change as they increase the scale of their operations and as their milieu urbanizes.[4] They often simply disappear, and their surviving activities are taken over by other institutions. In the Japanese village of Suye Mura, for example, Ushijima finds that work formerly done by co-operative exchange is now done by wage labor.[5] Alternatively, however, these traditional associations may survive by being reconstituted as rational-legal associations or by being displaced or overlain by such associations, as castes in India, traditionally led by headmen and councils (panchayats), are now being reconstituted by the formation of caste associations.[6] The substitution of rational-legal for traditional organization is of world-wide occurrence today.[7]

Because models of rational-legal organization are almost universally known, and because modern states provide the possibility of regulating organizations by law, bureaucratization rarely occurs now by simple evo-

---

Houghton Mifflin Company, 1950), p. 74; Francis M. Guercio, *Sicily, the Garden of the Mediterranean: The Country and Its People* (London: Faber & Faber, Ltd., 1954), p. 69; *Time* (August 15, 1960), p. 25; E. J. Hobsbawm, *Primitive Rebels. Studies in Archaic Forms of Social Movement in the 19th and 20th Centuries* (Manchester: Manchester University Press, 1959), p. 40; Antonino Cutrera, *La Mafia ed i mafiosi: origini e manifestazion, studio de sociologia criminale* (Palermo: Alberto Reber, 1900), p. 177; Norman Lewis, "The Honored Society," *New Yorker* (February 8, 15, 22, 1964).

[3] As Hobsbawm has pointed out, information about the Mafia, and especially quantitative and detailed information, does not meet standards normally set for institutional analysis. It is, after all, a secretive criminal organization. But while one cannot speak as authoritatively as one would like, this type of organization does need to be considered by social theorists, both as an important kind of institution and as a powerful force in Sicily and elsewhere. Hobsbawm, *Primitive Rebels*, p. 40.

[4] Peter M. Blau, *Bureaucracy in Modern Society* (New York: Random House, Inc., 1956), p. 36; Robert T. Anderson, "Studies in Peasant Life," *Biennial Review of Anthropology* (1965), ed. Bernard J. Spiegel (Stanford, Calif.: Stanford University Press, 1965).

[5] M. Ushijima, "Katari in Suye Mura—Its Social Function and Process of Change," *Japanese Journal of Ethnology*, XXVI (1962), 14–22.

[6] Robert T. Anderson, "Preliminary Report on the Associational Redefinition of Castes in Hyderabad-Secunderabad," *Kroeber Anthropological Society Papers*, No. 29 (Fall, 1963), 25–42.

[7] Anderson, *op. cit.*

lution. The Mafia is one of the few exceptions. Because it is secret and illegal, it cannot reorganize by reconstituting itself as a rational-legal organization. Yet it has changed as it has grown in size and shifted to an urban environment. Analysis of this change assumes unusual importance, because the Mafia is a significant force in modern life and because, as a rare contemporary example of the reorganization of a traditional type of association without recourse to legal sanctions, it provides a basis for comparison with potential other examples. Much of the present controversy about the Mafia, particularly about whether such an organization exists in the United States, is the result of confusing a modern, bureaucratic organization with the traditional institution from which it evolved.

## The Traditional Mafia

A Mafia is not necessarily predatory. It provides law and order where the official government fails or is malfeasant. It collects assessments within its territory much as a legal government supports itself. While citizens everywhere often complain about taxation, these Mafia exactions have been defended as reasonable payment for peace. The underlying principle of Mafia rule is that it protects the community from all other strong men in return for regularized tribute.[8]

To illustrate, the Grisafi band of the Agrigento countryside, led by a young, very large man called "Little Mark" (Marcuzzo Grisafi) formed a stable, though illicit, government that oversaw every event in his area for a dozen years (1904-16). An excellent marksman, he was able by his strength and with the aid of four to eight gunmen to guarantee freedom from roving bandit and village sneak alike.

On a larger scale, between approximately 1895 and 1924, a group of eleven villages in the Madonie Mountains were also ruled by a Mafia. The head and his assistants had a private police force of as many as 130 armed men. A heavy tax resembling official annual taxes was imposed upon all landowners. As with the Grisafi band, this Mafia was not a roving body of terrorists. Their leaders, at least, were well-established citizens, landowners, and farmers. While they might mount up as a body to enforce their tax collections, they stayed for the most part in their homes or on their farms. They assumed supervision of all aspects of local life, including agricultural and economic activities, family relations, and public administration. As elsewhere, the will of the Mafia was the law. The head, in fact, was known locally as the "prefect" ("U Prefetto").[9]

Although not necessarily predatory, Mafias seem always to be so, despotisms possessed of absolute local power. Many in the band or collaborating with it may find it a welcome and necessary institution in an otherwise lawless land. But multitudes suffer gross injustice at its hands. No one dares offend the Mafia chief's sense of what is right. The lines between tax and extortion, between peace enforcement and murder, blur under absolutism. Many would claim that the Agrigento and Madonie mafiosi were

[8] Cutrera, Mafia, Mafiosi, p. 116; Gavin Maxwell, Bandit (New York: Harper & Row, Publishers, 1956), pp. 31–33; Mangione, Reunion in Sicily, p. 73.

[9] Cesare Mori, The Last Struggle with the Mafia, trans. Orlo Williams (London: Putnam & Company, 1933), pp. 113, 130–33, 165–67, 179.

mostly involved in blackmail, robbery, and murder. An overall inventory of Mafia activities leaves no doubt that it is a criminal institution, serving the interests of its membership at the expense of the larger population.[10]

In organizational terms, the Mafia is a social group that combines the advantages of family solidarity with the membership flexibility of a voluntary association.

The most enduring and significant social bond in Sicily is that of the family.[11] Its cohesiveness is reinforced by a strong tendency to village endogamy. Only along the coast, where communication was easier, was it common to marry outside of the locality. The tendency to family endogamy further included some cross-cousin marriage.[12] Family bonds are not necessarily closely affectionate ones, but the tie has been the strongest social relationship known. It is the basic organizational group both economically and socially, functioning as

a unit of production as well as of consumption.[13]

Family ties often bind members of the Mafia together. The Mafia of the Madonie included two sets of brothers, as did the core membership of the Grisafi group. Not only are members of the Mafia frequently concealed and aided by their families, but their relatives commonly speculate on their activities and profit from them so that a clear line cannot be drawn between the criminal band on the one hand and the circle of kinsmen on the other.[14]

Family ties have a certain utility for organizing social action. Brothers are accustomed to work together. They possess a complex network of mutual rights and obligations to cement their partnership. The father-son and uncle-nephew relationships, equally enduring and diffuse, possess in addition a well-established leader-follower relationship. Cousins and nephews may be part of the intimate family; and it has been suggested that the children of brothers are especially close as indicated by their designations as *fratelli-cugini* (brother-cousins) or *fratelli-carnale* (brothers of the flesh).[15]

The family has one major drawback as a functioning group: its membership is relatively inflexible. Typically, family members vary in interests, capabilities, and temperaments. While this may be of little consequence for running a farm, it can constitute a serious handicap for the

[10] *Ibid.*, pp. 130–33; Cutrera, *Mafia, Mafiosi*, p. 116; August Schneegans, *La Sicilia nella natura, nella storia e nella vita* (Florence: G. Barbera Editore, 1890), p. 291.

[11] Pitrè, [P]*opolo siciliano*, p. 30; William Foote Whyte, "Sicilian Peasant Society," *American Anthropologist*, XLVI (1944), 66; Giovanni Lorenzoni, *Inchiesta parlamentare sulle condizion dei contadini nelle provincie meridionale e nella Sicilia*," VI: *Sicilia* (Rome: Tipografia nazionale di Giovanni Berlero, 1910), 462.

[12] At the turn of the century, an explicit preference existed for cross-cousin marriage. Such marriages, forbidden both by secular and canon law, were actually rare. But more remote consanguineous relatives did marry, and more commonly (one marriage in a hundred) than in most other parts of Italy. Figures for marriages between affinal kin are not available (Lorenzoni, *op. cit.*, pp. 464, 467; Whyte, *op. cit.*, p. 66; Vincenzo Petrullo, "A Note on Sicilian Cross-Cousin Marriage," *Primitive Man*, X, No. 1 [1937], 8–9).

[13] Pitrè, *op. cit.*, pp. 38–39; Salvatore Salomone-Marino, *Costumi ed usanze dei contadini di Sicilia* (Palermo: Remo Sandron, 1897), pp. 5–10; Lorenzoni, *op. cit.*, pp. 462, 469–73.

[14] Mori, *Last Struggle*, pp. 130, 166, 172, 218; Wermert, *Insel Sicilien*, p. 398; Gaston Vuillier, *Le Sicile, Impressions du présent et du passé* (Paris: Hachette, 1896), p. 165; Maxwell, *Bandit*, p. 160.

[15] Petrullo, "Cross-Cousin Marriage," p. 8.

successful operation of a gang. Some offspring may be completely devoid of criminal capacity, while good potential *mafiosi* may belong to other families. To a certain degree this drawback is countered by the extension of ties through marriage. But often a desirable working alliance cannot be arranged through a suitable wedding.

Throughout Europe a technique is available for the artificial extension of kinship ties. The technique is that of fictive or ritual kinship. Godparenthood, child adoption, and blood brotherhood make it possible to extend kin ties with ease. These fictive bonds are especially notable for the establishment of kinlike dyadic relationships. Larger social groups have not commonly been formed in this way in Europe except as brotherhoods, the latter with variable, sometimes minimal, success. The Mafia constitutes an unusual social unit of this general type in that the fictive bond is that of godparenthood, elsewhere used for allying individuals, but only rarely for forming groups.[16]

The godparenthood tie has had a variable history in Europe. In the Scandinavian countries it is a momentary thing, with few implications for future interaction. But in the Mediterranean area, and especially in Sicily, it is usually taken very seriously. An indissoluble lifetime bond it is often claimed to be equal or even superior to the bond of true kinship.[17] While the godparenthood (*comparatico*) union may cross class lines to link the high and the low in a powerful but formal relationship, it is more often a tie of friends, affective in an overt way that contrasts with the lesser open affection of the domestic family.[18] Above all, the relationship is characterized by mutual trust.

Sicilians in general, then, live with greatest security and ease in the atmosphere of the family with its fictive extensions. The Mafia is a common-interest group whose members are recruited for their special interests in and talents for the maintenance of a predatory satrapy. As noted above, this tie of shared interest often originates within a kinship parameter. When it does not, a kinlike tie is applied by the practice of becoming co-godparents. Although the Mafia *setta* (cell) may or may not be characterized by other structural features, it always builds upon real and fictive kinship.[19]

The Mafia of nineteenth-century Sicily practiced a formal rite of ini-

[16] Friedrich notes for the Tarascans that "every man strongly needs a certain number of intimates, many of whom are usually his ceremonial coparents, or compadres—the fathers of his godchildren and the godfathers of his children." (Paul Friedrich, "Assumptions Underlying Tarascan Political Homicide," *Psychiatry: Journal for the Study of Interpersonal Processes*, XXV, No. 4 [November, 1962], 316). The Mexican-Americans of Salsipuedes, California, normally feel insecure until they have established godparenthood ties with neighbors (Margaret Clark, personal communication). These Mexican and Mexican-American groups appear to be ego-oriented, however, and not well-defined corporate bodies. Eugene Hammel is presently studying godparenthood groups in Yugoslavia (personal communication).

[17] Various ways of contracting godparenthood ties are known to the Sicilians. See Whyte, "Peasant Society," pp. 66–67; Henry Festing Jones, *Castellinaria and other Sicilian Diversions* (Plymouth, England: William Brendon, 1911), pp. 131–34; Giuseppe Pitrè, *Usi e costumi credenze e pregiudizi del popolo siciliano* (hereinafter cited as "*Usi e costumi*"), "Biblioteca delle tradizione popolare siciliane," XV (Florence: G. Barbera Editore, n.d.), 255.

[18] This utility of fictive kinship for psychological release is a striking feature that merits further attention but cannot be dealt with here. See Cutrera, *Mafia, Mafiosi,* pp. 58–59; Pitrè, *Usi e costumi.*

[19] Cutrera, *op. cit.,* p. 59.

tiation into the fictive-kin relationship.[20] Joseph Valachi underwent the same rite in 1930 in New York.[21] In addition to the "baptism of blood," the chief at the first opportunity normally arranges to become the baptismal godfather of the tyro's newborn child. Lacking that opportunity, he establishes a comparable tie in one of the numerous other *comparatico* relationships. The members among themselves are equally active, so that the passing years see a member more and more bound to the group by such ties.

Ritual ties seem to function in part as a temporizing device. Although efficacious in themselves, they are usually the basis for the later arrangement of marriages between sons and daughters, and thus ultimately for the establishment of affinal and consanguineous bonds. The resultant group is therefore very fluid. It utilizes to the utmost its potentialities for bringing in originally unrelated individuals. Yet it possesses the organizational advantage of a lasting body of kin.[22]

Mafia family culture supports membership flexibility additionally by providing for the withdrawal of born members. The criminal family passes on Mafia tradition just as the farming family passes on farming traditions. Boys are taught requisite skills and attitudes. Girls are brought up to be inconspicuous, loyal, and above all silent. The problems of in-family recruitment are not greatly different from those of non-criminal groups. Just as a son without agricultural propensities or the chance to inherit land leaves the countryside to take up a trade or profession, the Mafia son lacking criminal interests or talents takes up a different profession. Indeed, sometimes Mafia family pride comes to focus upon a son who has left the fold to distinguish himself as a physician or professor. But while such an individual might not himself take up an illegal occupation, he is trained never to repudiate it for his kindred. In the Amoroso family, who controlled Porta Montalto near Palermo for many years in the nineteenth century, Gaspare Amoroso, a young cousin of the chief, degraded himself by joining the police force *(carabiniere)*. When the youth was discharged and returned to his family home, the Amoroso leaders removed this dishonor by having him killed in cold blood.[23]

The headship of a Mafia is well defined. Referred to as *capo* ("head") or *capomafia* ("Mafia head"), and addressed honorifically as *don,* the chief is clearly identified as the man in charge. Succession to this post, however, is not a matter of clear-cut procedure. In some cases family considerations may result in the replacement of a *capo* by his son or nephew. Commonly, an heir apparent, who

[20] Alexander Rumpelt, *Sicilien und die Sicilianer,* 2d ed. (Berlin: Allgemeiner Verein für Deutsche Literatur, 1902), pp. 141–42.

[21] *Organized Crime and Illicit Traffic in Narcotics: Report of the Committee on Government Operations, United States Senate, Made by Its Permanent Subcommittee on Investigations, together with Additional Combined Views and Individual Views* (hereinafter cited as "Organized Crime and Illicit Traffic in Narcotics"), Senate Report No. 72, 89th Cong. 1st Sess. (Washington, D.C.: Government Printing Office, 1965), p. 12.

[22] Frederic Sondern, Jr., *Brotherhood of Evil: The Mafia* (New York: Farrar, Straus & Giroux, Inc., 1959), pp. 5, 242–43; *Organized Crime and Illicit Traffic in Narcotics,* pp. 39–43.

[23] Cutrera, *Mafia, Mafiosi,* pp. 152–60; Sondern, *op. cit.,* pp. 5–6, 24; Maxwell, *Bandit,* p. 34.

may or may not be related consanguineously, is chosen on an essentially pragmatic basis and succeeds by co-optation. Generally, promotion is by intrigue and strength. It must be won by the most powerful and ruthless candidate with or without the blessing of family designation or co-optation. Only the *capo*, in any case, is formally recognized. The appointment of secondary leaders and ranking within the membership are informal.[24]

In sum, the traditional Mafia may be described as family-like. It would not be considered a bureaucratic organization. Of the four basic characteristics of a bureaucracy (according to Blau), the Mafia lacked three —a hierarchy of authority, specialization, and a system of rules.[25] Impartiality, the fourth characteristic, requires a special note. Impartiality requires that promotion, reward, and job assignment ideally be uninfluenced by the pervasive ties of a primary group and determined solely by individual performance-achievement. The Mafia is a kind of kin group. The individual, once a member, belongs for life with a family member's ineluctable rights to group prerogatives. Yet, the Mafia seems always to have been ruthlessly impersonal when it mattered. A criminal association survives by making its best marksmen assassins, its best organizers leaders, and by punishing those who are disloyal or not observant of *omertà*. Impartiality in the Mafia is not fully developed, but bureaucracy in this sense has no doubt always been present. The Amoroso murder of the *capo-*

*mafia's* cousin, for example, illustrates extreme impartiality for a family group.

## Bureaucratization of the Mafia

Though still seriously underdeveloped, Sicily seems poised for industrialization with its concomitant changes. To the extent that change has already occurred, the Mafia has adapted and expanded its techniques of exploitation. Claire Sterling writes of the intensification of urban activities: "Today there is not only a Mafia of the *feudo* (agriculture) but also Mafias of truck gardens, wholesale fruit and vegetable markets, water supply, meat, fishing fleets, flowers, funerals, beer, *carrozze* (hacks), garages, and construction. Indeed, there is hardly a businessman in western Sicily who doesn't pay for the Mafia's 'protection' in the form of '*u pizzu*.' "[26]

Mafia formal organization seems at a turning point. The Mafia so far has remained essentially a hodgepodge of independent local units confined to the western part of the island, although cells have been established outside of Sicily. Co-operation among localities in Sicily has an old history. The more successful *capi* have at times established hegemony over wider areas. But it appears that large-scale groupings could not endure in an underdeveloped milieu with notoriously poor communication systems.[27] Modernization, however, is breaking down this local isolation. The scale of operations is expanding. The face-to-face, family-like group in

[24] Guercio, *op. cit.*, p. 69; Sondern, *op. cit.*, p. 6; Burton B. Turkus and Sid Feder, *Murder, Inc.: The Story of "The Syndicate"* (New York: Farrar, Straus & Giroux, Inc., 1951), pp. 78–87.

[25] See Blau, *Bureaucracy*, p. 19.

[26] Claire Sterling, "Shots in Sicily, Echoes in Rome," *The Reporter* (August 4, 1960), pp. 35–36. See Danilo Dolci, *Outlaws*, trans. R. Munroe (New York: Orion Press, 1961), p. 319.

[27] Hobsbawm, *Primitive Rebels*, p. 33.

which relationships on the whole are diffuse, affective, and particularistic is changing into a bureaucratic organization.

The best-documented example of early bureaucratization concerns the Mafia of Monreale. Known generally as the *Stoppaglieri,* or facetiously as a mutual-aid society *(società di mutuo soccorso),* and world famous later for the criminal success of some members who migrated to America, the group first formed in the 1870's, when one of Monreale's political factions, in danger of losing local power, formed a Mafia that succeeded in wresting control from the older Mafia of the area. The basic group consisted of 150 members in the city itself. As they prospered they expanded into the surrounding area. Affiliated chapters were established in Parco San Giuseppe Iato, Santa Cristina, Montelepre, Borgetto, Piana dei Greci, and Misilmeri. A hierarchy of authority was created by the formal recognition of three ranked leadership roles rather than only one. The head of the whole organization was designated *capo,* but each area, including the various quarters of Monreale, was placed under the direct jurisdiction of a subhead or *sottocapo.* Each subhead in turn had an assistant, the *consiglio direttivo.* The rules of the association were made somewhat more explicit than those of other Mafias in providing for the convocation of membership councils to judge members charged with breaking the regulations of the group. And these regulations, completely traditional in character, were very precise, binding members:

1. To help one another and avenge every injury of a fellow member;
2. To work with all means for the defense and freeing of any fellow member who had fallen into the hands of the judiciary;
3. To divide the proceeds of thievery, robbery, and extortion with certain considerations for the needy as determined by the *capo;*
4. To keep the oath and maintain secrecy on pain of death within twenty-four hours.

Group intimacy among the *Stoppaglieri* appears to have been less than that of a smaller Mafia. The whole membership could not be easily convoked as they grew in size and territory. Patterns of universalism intruded upon those of particularism so that, according to some reports, a secret recognition sign was devised. On the whole, however, third-party introductions were more common than secret recognition signs.[28]

This, then, is what we know of one Mafia that bureaucratized to some extent at a relatively early date. Other and recent Mafias in Sicily display similar bureaucratization when they expand their operations.[29] Whatever the terminology—it tends to vary—these larger organizations are all char-

[28] Cutrera, *Mafia, Mafiosi,* pp. 118–22, 132–41; Ed Reid, *Mafia* (New York: The New American Library of World Literature, Inc., 1952), p. 100; Albert Falcionelli, *Les Sociétés secrètes italiennes* ("Bibliothèque historique" [Paris: Payot, 1936]), p. 208; "Mafia," *Encyclopaedia Britannica* (1951), XIV, 622; Hobsbawm, *Primitive Rebels,* pp. 41–42; Peter Maas, "Mafia: The Inside Story," *Saturday Evening Post* (August 10, 1963), p. 21.

[29] Cutrera, *op. cit.,* pp. 165–75; F. Lestingi, *La Fratellanza nella provincia di Girgenti* (Archivo di Psichiatria, Scienze penale ed antropologia criminale), Vol. V, No. iv; Salvo di Pietraganzili, *Rivoluzione siciliane dei 1848 à 1860* (Palermo: Bondi, 1898), II, 59. See Pasquale Villari, *Le lettere meridionale ed altri scritti sulla questione sociale in Italia,* 2d ed. (Turin: Fratelli Bocca, 1885), p. 28; Pitrè, [P]*opolo siciliano,* p. 292; Jones, *Castillinaria,* p. 163; Vuillier, *La Sicile,* p. 84.

acterized by an embryonic hierarchy of authority. They also continue a degree of impartiality and operate in terms of the traditional, explicitly elaborated, though unwritten rules. Specialization and departmentalization do not appear much developed. The problem of succession to authority continues to be troublesome. Journalists tend to designate one or another chief as the head for all of Sicily. A high command on this level does not seem to have developed beyond irregular councils of autonomous *capi*.

One may observe further bureaucratization of the Mafia in the United States. Mafias were first established in America in the latter part of the nineteenth century. During the prohibition era they proliferated and prospered. Throughout this period these groups continued to function essentially like the small traditional Mafia of western Sicily.

Recent decades in the United States have witnessed acceleration of all aspects of modernization. Here, if anywhere, the forces of urbanization impinge upon group life. But while American criminals have always been quick to capitalize upon technological advances, no significant organizational innovation occurred until the repeal of prohibition in 1932, an event that abruptly ended much of the lucrative business of the underworld. Small face-to-face associations gave way over subsequent decades to the formation of regional, national, and international combines, a change in which American *mafiosi* participated.[30]

As always, information is incomplete and conflicting. Bureaucratization, however, seems to have increased significantly beyond that even of bureaucratized Sicilian groups. Specialization, generally undeveloped in Sicily, became prominent. Personnel now regularly specialize as professional gunmen, runners, executives, or adepts in other particular operations. Departmentalization was introduced and now includes an organizational breakdown into subgroups such as narcotics operations; gambling; the rackets; prostitution; and an enforcement department, the infamous Murder, Inc., with its more recent descendants.[31]

The hierarchy of authority has developed beyond that of bureaucratized Sicilian Mafias. Bill Davidson describes a highly elaborated hierarchy of the Chicago Cosa Nostra, which he compares to the authority structure of a large business corporation. He points to the equivalent of a three man board of directors, a president of the corporation, and four vice-presidents in charge of operations. He also notes a breakdown into three geographical areas, each headed by a district manager. District managers have executive assistants, who in turn have aides. Finally, at the lowest level are the so-called sol-

[30] Walter C. Reckless, *Criminal Behavior* (New York: McGraw-Hill Book Company, Inc., 1940), p. 135; Donald R. Taft, *Criminology*, 3d ed. (New York: Macmillan Company, 1956), p. 233; Robert G. Caldwell, *Criminology* (New York: The Ronald Press Company, 1956), pp. 77–82, 86; *Life* (Feb. 23, 1959), p. 19; Estes Kefauver, *Crime in America* (New York: Doubleday & Company, Inc., 1951), p. 14; Daniel P. Moynihan, "The Private Government of Crime," *The Reporter* (July 6, 1961), p. 15.

[31] Sidney Lens, "Labor Rackets, Inc.," *The Nation* (March 2, 1957), pp. 179–83; Martin Mooney, *Crime Incorporated* (New York: McGraw-Hill Book Company, Inc., 1935), pp. 5–6; Harry Elmer Barnes and Negley K. Teeters, *New Horizons in Criminology* (Englewood Cliffs, N.J.: Prentice-Hall, Inc., 1959), pp. 24–28.

diers.[32] National councils of the more important *capi* apparently meet from time to time to set up territories, co-ordinate tangential activities, and adjudicate disputes. They serve to minimize internecine strife rather than to administer co-operative undertakings. The problem of succession has still not been solved. The Valachi hearings revealed an equally complex hierarchy for the state of New York.[33]

A written system of rules has not developed, although custom has changed. Modern *mafiosi* avoid the use of force as much as possible, and thus differ strikingly from old Sicilian practice. The old *"mustachios"* are being replaced by dapper gentlemen clothed in conservative business suits. But as a criminal organization, the Mafia cannot risk systematizing its rules in written statutes.

A major element of bureaucratization is the further development of impartiality. Mafiosi now freely collaborate on all levels with non-Sicilians and non-Italians. The Chicago association includes non-Italians from its "board of directors" down. In these relationships, consanguineous and affinal ties are normally absent and co-godparenthood absent or insignificant. Familistic organization, the structural characteristic that made for the combination of organizational flexibility with group stability in the traditional associations of Sicily—and that goes far to explain the success of Mafias there—apparently proved inadaptive in urban America. When it became desirable and necessary to collaborate with individuals of different criminal traditions, it sufficed to rely for group cohesion on the possi-

bility of force and a business-like awareness of the profits to be derived from co-operation.[34] Family and ritual ties still function among Sicilian-American criminals to foster co-operation and mutual support within cliques, but pragmatic considerations rather than familistic Mafia loyalties now largely determine organizational arrangements.[35]

## Conclusion

The Mafia as a traditional type of formal organization has disappeared in America. Modern criminals refer to its successor as *Cosa Nostra*, "Our Thing." The Cosa Nostra is a lineal descendant of the Mafia; but it is a different kind of organization. Its goals are much broader as it exploits modern cities and an industrialized nation. The real and fictive kinship ties of the old Mafia still operate among fellow Sicilians and Italians, but these ties now coexist with bureaucratic ones. The Cosa Nostra operates above all in new and different terms. This new type of organization includes elaboration of the hierarchy of authority; the specialization and departmentalization of activities; new and more pragmatic, but

[34] Lens, "Labor Rackets, Inc.," pp. 179–83; Mooney, *Crime Incorporated;* Barnes and Teeters, *Criminology;* Paul W. Tappan, *Crime, Justice and Correction* (New York: McGraw-Hill Book Company, 1960), p. 232; Kefauver, *Crime in America,* pp. 24–25 *et passim;* Turkus and Feder, *Murder, Inc.,* pp. xiii–xiv, 6, 44, 85–87, 426, 431; Sondern, *Brotherhood of Evil,* pp. 104–6; L. McLain, "Mafia: A Secret Empire of Evil," *Coronet,* November, 1958, pp. 60, 62. See Reckless, *Criminal Behavior;* Sondern, *op. cit.,* p. 181; Joseph N. Bell, "Exploding the Mafia Myth," *Pageant;* May, 1960, p. 52.

[35] *Organized Crime and Illicit Traffic in Narcotics,* pp. 37–38, 43.

[32] Bill Davidson, "How the Mob Controls Chicago," *Saturday Evening Post* (November 9, 1963), pp. 22–25.
[33] *Organized Crime and Illicit Traffic in Narcotics,* pp. 19–32.

still unwritten rules; and a more developed impartiality. In America, the traditional Mafia has evolved into a relatively complex organization which perpetrates selected features of the older peasant organization but subordinates them to the requirements of a bureaucracy.

# 24

# Rape and Social Structure *†

*Kaare Svalastoga*

One of the most severely punished and most publicized of crimes—if one can judge from reports appearing on the front pages of our newspapers—is rape. In general, these violations are depicted as the results of highly idiosyncratic conditions of spontaneous passion that emerge from the psychological problems of individual rapists. The crime is usually pictured as an irrational act committed by a mad man, one that is viewed as generally unrelated to other aspects of society. In the following study, however, Professor Svalastoga demonstrates that these incidents appear to have systematic connection with variations in social structure. Thus, as in the case of Émile Durkheim's classic study of suicide (another social action generally described as solely the irrational act of a deranged mentality, unconnected with other features of the social order),[1] it would appear that rape is a *social fact* (to use Durkheim's phrase) that can, in large part, be explained in terms of other *social facts*, i.e, sex ratio in the community, and the relative social statuses of the rapist and his victim.

EDITOR

## The Problem

Rape, as shown by J. S. Brown, is a behavior pattern that is nearly universally met by very strong social sanctions.[2] Only incest, among sex offenses occurring in modern societies, encounters equally severe and universal social opposition.

Rape is commonly defined as enforced coitus.[3] But this very definition

* Reprinted from *The Pacific Sociological Review*, V (1962), 48–53, by permission of the publisher. Footnotes renumbered.

† Revised version of paper presented at the American Sociological Association meetings, St. Louis, 1961. The author is strongly indebted to Professor Clarence Schrag of the University of Washington, who read the first version of the paper and gave numerous valuable suggestions concerning form and content. For defects still present, the author is of course solely responsible.

[1] Émile Durkheim, *Suicide: A Study in Sociology* (1897), English trans. (New York: The Free Press, 1951).

[2] J. S. Brown, "A Comparative Study of Deviations from Sexual Mores," *The American Sociological Review*, XVII (April, 1952), 135–46.

[3] We shall in this paper limit the concept to a consideration of the typical sex constellation—rapist: male, rapee: female.

suggests that there is more to the offense than the use of force alone. This must be so, since no society has equipped itself with the means for measuring the amount of force applied in an act of coitus.

Hence, rape, like any other kind of crime, carries a heavy social component. The act itself is not a sufficient criterion. The act must be interpreted as rape by the female actee, and her interpretation must be similarly evaluated by a number of officials and agencies before the official designation of "rape" can be legitimately applied. Furthermore, rape is somewhat unique in that its negative evaluation in public opinion is very frequently extended to the victim as well as the offender.[4] This aspect of the crime is clearly instrumental in reducing the number of such offenses that are brought to the attention of the police.

This paper is not primarily concerned with force or the degree of its use in rape offenses. Rather, it investigates the role of *anonymity* and of *status differentials* between offenders and their victims as important components of the social situation that ordinarily accompanies this type of offense. In addition, variations in the *sex ratio* will be utilized in order to account for the unequal regional distribution of crimes of rape.

In formulating hypotheses concerning the variables mentioned, we have used an axiomatic-deductive procedure, assuming that this method will facilitate our search for invariances in the behavior under investigation.[5]

## Review of Pertinent Research

The author has been able to locate only one previous sociological treatment of rape, although several discussions of sex crimes in general are on record. For example, Hoegel found that Austrian sex offenders in 1900–1901 were chiefly from the class of manual workers and had a maximum incidence in the age group 16-20 years. Again, Wulffen found the highest incidence of rape and similar offenses in the warmer seasons of the year, the maximum occurring in July and the minimum in January, according to German data for the years 1883–1892. He also cites French data for the years 1827–1869, which reveal a maximum of sex crimes in June and a minimum in November. A study from Vienna, also reported by Wulffen, shows a maximum number of sex crimes and violent offenses on Sundays and a minimum number on Thursdays. Somewhat similar results have been reported in a number of other studies.[6]

Herz, an Austrian criminologist, stressed the sex ratio as a factor in the explanation of sex crimes, maintaining that these offenses increase according to the amount of deviation in either direction from an equilibrium ratio of 100. Herz's own data, however, show that the sex ratio is

---

[4] As an illustration we may cite the experience of a seventeen-year-old shop assistant from a small town who was raped in a nearby big town. She said that she had to leave the small town for some time because of public gossip—in the street, people would make hints about her "big town experiences."

[5] H. Zetterberg, *On Theory and Verification in Sociology* (Stockholm: Almquist and Wiksell, 1954).

[6] E. Wulffen, "Sexual Kriminalstatistik," in *Der Sexual Verbrecher* (Berlin: 1910), Chapter 4. Also, cf. S. Kaplan, "The Geography of Crime," in *Sociology of Crime*, J. S. Roucek, ed. (New York: Philosophical Library, 1961), pp. 160–92.

a rather poor predictor of sex crimes. Much better is the percentage of bachelors among males 24 years of age and older. This suggests that overall imbalance is not as crucial as sex ratio imbalance among unmarried adults in the peak marital propensity period. Hoegel's data for Austria in 1902–1903 point in the same direction.[7]

The most comparable previous study is that of LeMaire, whose study of Danish offenders includes 104 rapists for the period 1929–1939. LeMaire demonstrates striking variations among ecological factors that are related to sex offenses. Thus, rape, incest among siblings, coitus with minors, and indecent behavior toward females all show a maximum concentration in rural areas, whereas other sex offenses are either concentrated in urban areas or are relatively evenly distributed in both rural and urban areas.[8] Rape, according to LeMaire's findings, occurs most frequently on Saturdays and Sundays, between the hours of midnight and six o'clock in the morning, among persons 15 to 19 years of age, the unmarried, and persons in low status rural occupations. Rapists were rarely psychotic or mentally deficient, and alcohol was considered a dominant factor in only 22 per cent of the cases. Unfortunately, LeMaire was unable to make any observations concerning the victims of rape.[9]

## Major Findings of the Present Study

Before proceeding to the derivations and tests of hypotheses, a concise description of the data collected in our study will be given in terms of time, place, people involved, violence used, and some characteristics of the victim and the offender.

### TIME, PLACE, AND PEOPLE

Our data are from the complete and original records of 141 cases of rape and attempted rape coming before the court in Denmark in the years 1946 through 1958.[10] These cases constitute a nearly complete enumeration of the rape offenses brought before the criminal courts during the years 1956–1958 and a 50 per cent nonrandom sample for the preceding years. Comparison indicates that the sample may underrepresent the milder offenses and cases of attempted rape; but it also shows that none of our major conclusions would be modified by a fuller coverage of cases.

Our data show that rape is predominantly, although not exclusively, a nocturnal crime. The hours from 12 to 2 o'clock in the morning have the greatest rape risk and exactly ⅗ of all rapes occurred between 10 in the evening and 4 in the morning. Satur-

[7] Wulffen, op. cit., pp. 293–96.

[8] The American crime rates for 1958 reveal that forcible rape is relatively more frequent in the rural than in the urban environment for all cities below 250,000. Above this size, the urban crime rate is higher and, considering cities alone, tends to increase with the size of the city. See, Kaplan, op. cit.

[9] L. LeMaire, Legal Kastration (Copenhagen, 1946). Mean age of rapists was given as 23 years in a Los Angeles report and as

26 years in a New York report (N = 30). See, M. Guttmacher, Sex Offenses (New York, 1951), p. 67.

[10] The author is indebted to the Danish Ministry of Law for granting permission to use the original criminal records of each of the 141 cases. He also wishes to thank the Danish police represented by Kriminalkommisaer Bang, and the Danish Bureau of the Census, represented by Sekretaer Rita Knudsen for their helpfulness. Preben Wolf gave valuable criminological advice with usual helpfulness.

day through Monday as well as Wednesday have higher than average incidence. Sunday is the day of maximum incidence and rapes occur then with about twice the frequency observed for Tuesday, the day of minimum incidence (25 : 13). Furthermore, there is a confirmation of the so-called "thermic law of crime" in as much as the four lowest figures occur for December through March. Rape is in most cases an open-air event.

We may list the place and frequency of occurrence as follows:

| Place of Offense | Per Cent of Cases |
|---|---|
| Out-doors. Isolated place | 48 |
| In densely populated area | 24 |
| In-doors. Isolated house | 11 |
| In densely populated area | 13 |
| In automobile | 4 |
| Not ascertained | 1 |
| Total | 101 |
| (N = 141) | |

Most rapes are pair events, i.e., the rapist approaches his victim alone. However, both the constellation two males—one female, and the constellation three males—one female occurs. There were no cases where more than one victim was involved. We have:

| Group Constellation | Per Cent of Cases |
|---|---|
| One male, one female | 84 |
| Two males, one female | 10 |
| Three males, one female | 6 |
| | 100 |
| | (N = 141) |

## Amount of Violence

Even a casual reading of the police reports on rape reveals that rapists vary quite widely in the amount and seriousness of violence used.

It should be mentioned that in our sample there were no cases in which violence resulted in the death of the victim. The following ranking was developed and then tested by two outside criteria:

| Degree of Violence | Per Cent of Cases |
|---|---|
| 1. Interference with general body movement, disequilibration | 35 |
| 2. Interference with vocalization | 24 |
| 3. Interference with respiration | 20 |
| 4. Producing traumas by beating or kicking [11] | 21 |
| | 100 |
| | (N = 141) |

The first three levels seem to function as a logical rank order considering the situation. The fourth category was empirically seen to be accompanied in most cases by either the second or the third, while it logically implies the first.

We may use as one criterion for this ranking the rapidity with which the police were alarmed (within 12 hours or later):

| Degree of Violence | Per Cent of Cases Police Notified within 12 hours | N |
|---|---|---|
| 1 lowest | 55 | 49 |
| 2 | 71 | 34 |
| 3 | 93 | 28 |
| 4 highest | 87 | 30 |

[11] With one single exception no tools were used. The exception is represented by a 19-year-old worker, a former butcher's assistant, who in the early night entered through the window where he in the daytime had observed a young woman. He was equipped with a heavy iron hammer and directed two violent blows at the head of a young woman asleep in the room without any prior attempt at securing sexual privileges in other ways. He seems, however, to have been shocked by his own deed, because no traces of coitus could be determined. Although the female was severely hurt and remembered nothing of the event, she recovered later.

Another possible criterion is leniency of social sanction. This comparison will be limited to cases of completed rape:

| Degree of Violence | Per Cent of Cases Offender Receiving 3 Years Prison or Less | N |
|---|---|---|
| 1 | 54 | 26 |
| 2 | 61 | 18 |
| 3 | 17 | 12 |
| 4 | 21 | 14 |

One interfering factor here is previous criminal record. In general similar crimes will be punished more severely on repetition than as first offense. On the whole, these comparisons suggest that there may be less difference between levels 3 and 4 on our scale than between the other levels.

One difficulty in a coitus situation is that what the stronger partner may perceive as bashful mockery the weaker partner may interpret as a maximum of resistance. Thus the medical analyst writes about one of our cases (21 years old, 6 feet tall, weight 190 pounds, skilled worker): "In his work as . . . , he is used to handling (objects) weighing 140-150 pounds with ease and swiftness. It is therefore highly probable that a girl's resistance would not penetrate to his consciousness with the same strength as might have been the case, had he been weaker." He was actually acquitted in court. A contributing factor might be that the girl in question was described as "loose" by local authorities. (Violence level 1.)

## The Victim [12]

The most likely victims of rapists seem to be those females who for some reason have to walk alone or go by bicycle alone to their home at a time of the day when most people are asleep.

The next most likely victims are those who on such occasions are accompanied by casual male acquaintances but still using the above modes of transportation. It is probably significant that no single case of rape in our data refers to females who used motorized vehicles.

Since the females with higher than average risk are mostly younger and unmarried persons returning home from visits, dances, restaurants, etc., it is a reasonable finding that about one half of all victims belonged to the age category 15 through 19 years, and 77 per cent were between 10 and 24 years of age, although the range spans from 8 to 77 years.[13] At least 85 per cent of the victims were single. Furthermore, at least in 37 per cent of the cases the rape experience is reported to be the victim's first sex experience.

## The Rapist

The rapist is most likely to be a youth or young adult. Seventy-one per cent of our rapists were 15-29 years old, while another sixteen per cent were between 30 and 34.[14] As one might expect, the majority (70 per cent) are single or (5 per cent) previously married,[15] but still there is a surprisingly high remainder of married rapists (24 per cent). He is likely to possess some previous sex experience. He is neither taller nor shorter than the average male.

[12] A female is counted as one victim each time a new rapist approaches her. Hence there are somewhat below 141 different females in our data.

[13] Data from New York, 1937–1941, corroborate the tendency for rape victims to be young. See, H. Hentig, The Criminal and His Victim (New Haven: Yale University Press, 1948), p. 402.

[14] Top risk: 20–24 years.

[15] Here including separated persons.

Intelligence tests on 87 persons of the group gave a median score of 88. When the unfavorable testing conditions are taken into account, as well as the fact that many of the supposedly more "normal-looking" were not tested, it is doubtful whether the group as a whole is less intelligent than the average male.[16]

Most rapists were examined by one or more psychiatrists. Serious mental deviation (insanity or imbecility) could only be documented in 11 cases. The modal psychiatric diagnosis was that of minor deviation from normality either in the form of mental retardation or in the form of some psychopathy. However, one third of the group was classified as normal and another 10 per cent were not examined.

The rapist is more often a man with a criminal background than a novice in deviant behavior. Only 33 per cent had no previous criminal record, while 22 per cent had received two or more prison sentences prior to the rape. His family background will be discussed below.

## Derivation of Hypotheses

Our major postulates are as follows:
1. A sex ratio for unmarried persons aged 15-49 years at or near 100 defines a condition of social equilibrium. Small departures from this equilibrium are relatively unimportant. However, larger departures, particularly those in the positive direction (male surplus), lead to social tensions which tend to find outlet in increasing efforts at securing efficient sexual approaches. Von Hen-

tig is the major source for this postulate.[17]

2. The means by which males secure coitus outside of marriage depends on social status. With increasing male status the action potential of the male increases. In particular he can choose between many more social techniques in his sexual approach.[18]

3. Parallel with this correlation goes a differential attitude towards violence by social status. In the middle and upper classes violence is more readily delegated to police monopoly, and the use of violence is socially unacceptable under normal conditions. In the lower classes, by contrast, the use of violence, since it frequently appears to be the only method promising success, is not so readily dismissed.

A similar contention has recently been set forth by J. E. H. Williams, who writes: " . . . there is probably a sub-culture of violence among a certain portion of the lower socioeconomic group, in which quick resort to physical aggression is a socially approved and expected concomitant of certain stimuli and in which violence has become a familiar but often deadly partner in life's struggles." [19]

4. Violence is more readily condoned in a solidary and highly interactive group than in a plural of little or no interactivity.

The definition of "rape" used, is the following: *Rape* (completed + attempted) *is a successful or unsuc-*

[16] For a different conclusion see Hentig, *op. cit.*, p. 104.

[17] H. Hentig, "The Sex Ratio," *Social Forces*, XXX (May, 1951), 443–49.
[18] Compare J. Thurber, *Men, Women, and Dogs* (New York, 1946).
[19] J. E. H. Williams in a review of M. Wolfgang, *Patterns in Criminal Homicide* (Philadelphia, 1958), in the *British Journal of Sociology*, XI (1960), 95.

TABLE 1. SEX RATIO AND RAPE BY PLACE OF OCCURRENCE

| Place | Sex ratio among un-married persons 15–49, 1957 | Number of rapists | Rapist ratio per million of all males 15–49, 1950 |
|---|---|---|---|
| Capital | 93 | 10 | 43 |
| Provincial cities | 91 | 35 | 130 |
| Elsewhere in Denmark | 163 | 96 | 175 |

*cessful attempt at securing coitus by the method of more or less violence, which in a society creates sufficient disturbance to be reported to the police and brought before a law court.*

From the above postulates, we derive the following hypotheses to be tested by our data:

1. Rape will be more frequent in communities with a large sex ratio than in communities with a sex ratio of about 100, assuming that there are no important differences in class structure.

2. The rapist will most likely be a member of the lower social classes.[20]

3. The female victim will be most likely to belong to the upper or middle classes, because in these classes the negative evaluation of violence will be most likely to insure that the case be brought before the police.

4. Between a rapist and his victim anonymity or a condition of low interactivity prevailed prior to the event.

5. As a consequence of derivations 2 and 3, a rapist-rapee status matrix as compared with data for marital unions will reveal an abnormally high incidence in the cells designating

[20] In contrast to derivation 1 and postulate 1, which evolved in the course of the study, the rest of the postulates and derivations were developed prior to the study. It will be seen below that derivation 3 fails to receive support from our data.

lower male status as compared with female's status.

## Tests of the Hypotheses

### THE SEX RATIO

The regions with highest positive departures from equilibrium sex ratio (rural communities) have the highest relative rape incidence. Hence derivation 1 is confirmed.[21]

The great difference in the frequency of rapes in regions having roughly the same sex ratio, such as in the capital and in the provincial cities, indicates that the sex ratio is not a sufficient explanation. It seems likely that the higher availability of sex satisfaction on commercial terms (prostitution, call girls etc.) in the capital may help to explain the dif-

[21] In fact, direct reference to the extreme sex ratio is found in the court record of one of the cases here studied. This is also the single example of a case where rape is associated with homicide, the persons killed by the rapist being not the rape victim but her employers—a farmer and his wife who tried to help the rape victim. The day before the tragic event, the 18-year-old future life prisoner was working in the hay fields with the later victim and a married female helper. These two women both asked the young boy, "what he sought here in Western Jutland, because here there were no girls." The young man responded that there had to be some. Whereupon the younger of the females said, "There is at most three."

ference observed between the capital and the other Danish cities.

## Social Status of Rapist

Using the stratification system described by Svalastoga,[22] and in particular placing vagabonds and persons imprisoned twice or more in the lowest stratum, we arrive at the following status distribution of rapists:

| Social Status of Offender | Per Cent of Cases |
|---|---|
| (1 highest, 9 lowest) | |
| 4 (upper middle) | .7 |
| 6 (small enterprisers, white collar employees) | 3.5 |
| 7 (skilled worker and apprentices) | 6.4 |
| 8 (unskilled or rural workers) | 58.9 |
| 9 (criminal repeaters and/or vagabonds) | 30.5 |
| | 100.0 |
| | (N = 141) |

Reference to the status distribution of the Danish adult population in derivation 2 is amply confirmed (see footnote 21). It is true that part of the difference might be explained by the relative youthfulness of the rapists; but this is of no great importance in this connection because we deal with a group which to an exceptional degree is characterized by mobility handicaps.

The rapist is an underprivileged person in several respects. At least 80 per cent have only 7 years of schooling not even including training for any craft, and only 3 per cent possess an intermediate high school diploma (9 or 10 years).

A repeated theme in the reconstruction of the offender's childhood is his desire to engage in some kind of craft training (4 years apprenticeship

[22] K. Svalastoga, *Prestige, Class, Mobility* (Copenhagen: Gyldendal, 1959).

with modest pay) and the frustration of this desire due to the poor family economy. Seventeen per cent of the group were born out of wedlock. Also characteristic is a large sibling group. Where the number was given its median value was 6; and no less than 20 per cent of 102 rapists with known sibling size stemmed from sibling groups numbering from 10 to 17 children.

The social and economic status of the parents or foster parents was on the average very low. Only 11 per cent had a middle-class origin, while 85 per cent were working class people, mostly unskilled. Information is missing for the remaining 4 per cent.

Poverty, disorderly home, and criminal or other deviant behavior among family members are frequent, although not invariable, childhood experiences of the rapist.

It is hard to escape the conclusion that the violence of this group is a tool used by a category of people who have less chance than most people to learn more refined ways of social persuasion or to acquire the means whereby favors are bought and not taken by force.

The highest ranking rapist in our sample strikingly illustrates how a high status person intent on sexual adventures has other methods at his disposal, which are barred to the low status male.

The records reveal that this high ranking person several times utilized sexually females who were economically dependent on him, and how he (even if parents of the victim protest) was able to appease them with payoffs which did not mean much to him. Furthermore, it appears that several of his victims avoided reports to the police or to other people because they pitied his wife or felt that a police report might completely ruin

TABLE 2. DEGREE OF ACQUAINTANCE AT TIME OF OFFENSE AND TIME OF NOTIFYING POLICE

| | Police Notified Within 12 Hours | | Police Notified Later | | Total N % (Base: 141) | |
|---|---|---|---|---|---|---|
| | N | % | N | % | | |
| No mutual acquaintance | 66 | 86.8 | 10 | 13.2 | 76 | 54 |
| Mutual acquaintance but brief, superficial or indirect | 24 | 82.8 | 5 | 17.2 | 29 | 21 |
| Long acquaintance | 9 | 45.0 | 11 | 55.0 | 20 | 14 |
| Relatives | 2 | 18.2 | 9 | 81.8 | 11 | 8 |
| N.A. | 2 | 40.0 | 3 | 60.0 | 5 | 4 |
| Totals | 103 | 73.0 | 38 | 27.0 | 141 | 101 |

him and his family. In fact, when finally arrested on the basis of rumors becoming more and more loud in his town, he was immediately fired from his high ranking position.

## SOCIAL STATUS OF VICTIM

Derivation 3 fails to obtain support from the data as the following tabulation shows.

In contrast to the contention of derivation 3, most rape victims have a lower (working) class background. It is true that the method of classification is somewhat slanted against derivation 3 insofar as a classification of young females on the basis of their own occupation (where their social origin is unknown) leads to a higher

| Social Status of Victims [23] | | Number of Cases | Percentage of Cases |
|---|---|---|---|
| Upper or middle classes | 3 | 1 | .7 |
| | 4 | 4 | 2.8 |
| | 5 | 5 | 3.5 |
| | 6 | 20 | 14.2 |
| Lower classes | 7 | 30 | 21.2 |
| | 8 | 77[24] | 54.6 |
| | 9 | 4 | 2.8 |
| | | 141 | 99.9 |

[23] Based on the occupation of female's father or husband, or, in case of no data, on the occupation of the female herself.

[24] Includes three cases with incomplete information.

proportion of low status females than a classification by parental occupation solely would have given. However, the data show that even if we limit comparison to cases where the latter classification is possible, we arrive at the same result: Derivation 3 is false.

## PRIOR RELATIONSHIP

Derivation 4 does stand up (Table 2) but not as well as expected. In about one fifth of the sample, the rapist and his victim were in the long acquaintance + relatives category. Although this could not be definitely ascertained, it seemed that the rate of previous interaction, even in the long acquaintance category, had been modest in most cases.

An indirect indication tending to support derivation 4 appears when we consider the correlation between acquaintance level and speed of alarming the police (Table 2). It appears that in most cases where the partners do not know each other, the offense is reported to the police within 12 hours, whereas this is rarely done where the partners are relatives.

In addition incestuous rapes are frequently reported to the police only several years after the event, and even then the report often occurs after some other event has caused a reduction in family solidarity.

One of our rape cases offers a remarkable illustration of the principles involved in hypothesis 4. The case concerns a female factory worker. She was surprised in her unlocked bedroom one night by an intruding male whom she did not recognize with certainty due to darkness. He proceeded to have coitus with her (violence degree 2). The following day (or possibly later) the female looked up the person with whom she last had willingly had coitus. She asked him whether he had been at her house the night of the enforced coitus, because she did not see the person. And she added that in case he was the person, "she would not report the case to the police." In fact, this is a case where no report was given to the police within the first 12 hours of the incident. The rapist proved, however, to be another person. He, too, was a long time acquaintance of the victim, but clearly not on the same level of intimacy as the person previously mentioned.

### Rapist-Rapee Status Relationship

Reference to Table 3 shows that derivation 5 is confirmed. The status-relationship between rapist and victim reveals an abnormally high frequency of cases where the female enjoys higher social status than the male.

From Table 3, the following compilation comparing male and female status may be reported:

| Female Status Is: | Observed | Expected [25] |
|---|---|---|
| | % | % |
| Higher | 51 | 19 |
| Same | 38 | 67 |
| Lower | 11 | 14 |
| | 100 | 100 |
| | N = 141 | |

[25] From Svalastoga, *Prestige*, table 5.14, p. 388.

This finding is of course in part due to the fact that rapists are recruited so overwhelmingly from the lower social strata making a majority of all females their social superiors. However, even for constant social origin it can be shown that rapists are abnormally likely to seek their female partners far removed in social space.

To show this we shall limit our attention to the 90 per cent of the rapists who belong to the two lowest social strata. The other strata are so under represented that they do not have much evidential value treated in isolation.

TABLE 3. COMPARISON OF THE SOCIAL STATUS OF RAPIST AND VICTIM

| Social Status of Female Victim | Male Rapist Social Status | | | | | | |
|---|---|---|---|---|---|---|---|
| | 9 | 8 | 7 | 6 | 5 | 4 or 3 | Total |
| 3 or 4 (highest) | 2 | 2 | 1 | | | | 5 |
| 5 | 3 | 2 | | | | | 5 |
| 6 | 8 | 11 | | 1 | | | 20 |
| 7 | 8 | 17 | 3 | 2 | | | 30 |
| 8 | 21 | 48 | 5 | 2 | | 1 | 77 |
| 9 (lowest) | 1 | 3 | | | | | 4 |
| Totals | 43 | 83 | 9 | 5 | 0 | 1 | 141 |

TABLE 4. SOCIAL STATUS OF VICTIM FOR
RAPISTS IN STRATUM 8 OR 9

| Social Status | Observed % | Expected [26] % |
|---|---|---|
| 1 - 5 | 7.1 | 1.1 |
| 6 | 15.1 | 21.3 |
| 7 | 19.8 | 36.9 |
| 8, 9 | 57.9 | 40.7 |
| Totals | 99.9 | 100.0 |
| | (N = 126) | (N = 263) |

The author is not inclined to attribute any importance to the apparently lower upward move to strata 7 and 6 among lower class rapists. It should be remembered that rapists are mostly to be found within the lower part of the two strata. They should therefore be expected to have fewer chances of contacts with fc males of higher status than most males in the strata mentioned.

It will be seen that among our five derivations four were confirmed while one, derivation 3, had to be rejected. This again means that there is something wrong with postulate 3 as stated

[26] Unpublished data from table relating social status of husbands at time of interview to social status of wife's father. Same nation-wide sample as used in Svalastoga, op. cit.

above, which provided the basis for derivation 3.

It seems likely that the postulate exaggerates the working class non-working class distinction. The chief distinction should perhaps be drawn further down the status scale. Another possibility is that since young females of working class background frequently have middle class employers the latter will in fact increase the probability of a rape against a working class female being reported to the police. Absence of relevant research makes it impossible at the present time to test the implications of these explanations. There is also the further possibility that derivation 3 should be reformulated to read as above, but with the addition "sex ratio in approximate equilibrium."

This explanation may be tested directly on our data by analyzing the urban material separately. Although the proportion of females of upper and middle class status thereby increases from 21.2 to 26.7 per cent (N=45), still the majority of victims, even in an environment where the sex ratio is in approximate equilibrium, belong to the working classes.

Hence only further research can provide a more adequate axiomatization than was achieved in this study.

# PART IX

# Social Change

# 25

# The Sociology of the Bicycle *

*Sidney H. Aronson*

Numerous sociologists have been interested in the impact of inventions on social change.[1] But just as inventions bring with them innovations that quickly permeate the general culture, so, too, are they often replaced. Such was the case with the once ubiquitous bicycle: Although still popular outside the United States, its presence is hardly felt in this country today. But, just as the automobile has displaced the bicycle in importance as a major means of everyday transportation (and most of us are aware of the tremendous impact of the automobile on American life—including its far-reaching and often noted effects on our courting practices), so too did the bicycle create numerous changes in other areas of social life, changes that, the following article argues, left an important legacy for the automobile soon to replace it.

EDITOR

---

The bicycle came to America three times. The first two models, of 1819 and 1869, were duds, but the third, brought here in 1879, was the real thing, and brought an explosion which can only be—and, indeed, was—called a "bicycle boom."[2]

Perhaps the primary reason for this phenomenon was a mechanical one: the 1879 "bike" was the best made. The 1819 model, known first as the "dandy-horse" and later as the velocipede, was brought to this country from England. It consisted of two wheels of equal size connected by a long wooden bar; the operator straddled this bar and propelled the machine by walking or running along the ground. Once the rider built up some speed, he would lift up his legs and glide until the force petered out. Going downhill, the cyclist did not have to do anything but coast and hope that he would not run into anything—for the machine had no brakes.[3] There was a brief flutter of excitement over this vehicle, centering in Boston and Philadelphia where riding schools opened; but soon the novelty wore off and the machine disappeared from sight.[4]

With the 1869 model, the rider's foot power was used somewhat more subtly; cranks were placed on the

* Reprinted from *Social Forces*, XXX (1952), 305–12, by permission of the publisher. Footnotes renumbered.

[1] The most famous of these is probably W. F. Ogburn, J. L. Adams, and S. G. Gilfillan, *The Social Effects of Aviation* (Boston: Houghton Mifflin Company, 1946).

[2] "Effect of the Bicycle Boom on Trade," *Scientific American*, LXXIV (June 27, 1896), 407.

[3] Luther H. Porter, *Cycling for Health and for Pleasure* (Boston, 1890), p. 23.

[4] Axel Josephsson, "Bicycles and Tricycles," *Twelfth Census of the United States, 1900, Manufactures*, William R. Merriam, director (Washington, D. C.: 1902), part IV, 331.

front wheel. This machine had wooden wheels with iron tires; it was heavy and cumbersome, and did not ride smoothly, especially over the roads of the seventies. For these reasons the machine was called, not too affectionately, the "bone crusher."[5] By 1871 it, too, passed from the American scene.[6]

But in 1879 came the first successful wheel, again from England, and soon afterward, Colonel Albert A. Pope, the father of the American bicycle, began to manufacture it in Boston.[7] This machine, known as the ordinary or high bicycle, made good speed, and its solid rubber tires gave a smoother ride. But it was awkward to mount because the seat was perched on top of the front wheel, which was four to five feet in diameter. Balance, too, was very difficult and a quick stop or the slightest roughness on the road would throw the driver in a fall which, in the popular jargon, became known as a "header."[8] The vehicle was propelled by pedals on the front wheel, another factor which made smooth braking a rarity. This bicycle became only moderately popular and mostly among young and athletic males.[9] It lingers on today as a favorite prop of clowns and vaudevillians.

Finally, in 1885 the safety bicycle, which made cycling possible for young and old of both sexes, was developed in England. Several factors made this machine simpler and safer to ride. The two wheels were each about two feet in diameter and hence the vehicle was easier to mount; a saddle rested on an iron frame between the wheels. The machine was driven by a sprocket and chain attached to the rear wheel and moved by pedals below the saddle.[10] In 1890 the invention of the pneumatic tire assured its success by greatly increasing its speed, comfort, and ease of propulsion.[11] It was in fact substantially the same bicycle that we use today.[12]

This is not to say that the adoption of the bicycle came spontaneously and without the opposition that so often accompanies social innovation. As has been shown above, the first group of cyclists in the eighties was an eager and athletic one, which gave little regard to the rights of others as they "scorched" over the highways training for record-breaking attempts.[13] Later cyclists, though tamer, inherited the antagonism of horsemen and teamsters. The latter, accustomed to having the roads to themselves, resented the intrusion, especially because the newcomers frightened horses and caused runaways.[14] The hostility between the two groups took various forms. Often the horsemen and teamsters deliberately turned on the cyclists and ran them down.[15] Fist-fighting between wheelmen and

[5] Ibid., p. 331.
[6] Ibid.
[7] A. G. Batchelder, "The Story of the Bicycle," Harper's Weekly, XL (April 11, 1896), 359.
[8] Albert A. Pope, "The Bicycle Industry," in One Hundred Years of American Commerce, ed. Chauncey M. Depew (New York: 1895), II, 551.
[9] Ibid.

[10] Archibald Sharp, Bicycles and Tricycles (London, New York, and Bombay, 1896), pp. 153–59.
[11] Ibid., pp. 159–60.
[12] The suspension wheel, the ball bearing, weldless steel tubing, and the coaster brake were all introduced in this period. Josephsson, "Bicycles and Tricycles," p. 332.
[13] W. E. W. Mollins, "My Friends Who Cycle," Blackwood's Edinburgh Magazine, CLIX (June, 1896), 884.
[14] Charles E. Pratt, The American Bicycler (Boston: 1879), p. 193.
[15] The New York Daily Tribune, July 1, 1895.

draymen was frequent and fierce.[16]

Sometimes pedestrians, who were irked by the cyclists, teamed up with the horsemen and passed laws prohibiting the riding of bicycles in public parks and drives. But in 1879 wheelmen won an important victory when a Massachusetts court ruled that "bicycles cannot be deemed as nuisances but are entitled to the reasonable use of the highways." [17] A few years later the Treasury Department classified bicycles as carriages rather than as steel products, which meant a 10 per cent reduction in the tariff.[18]

To further this legal struggle as well as for other reasons, the League of American Wheelmen was formed on May 31, 1880.[19] American cyclists were fortunate in having the aggressive and influential League to protect their interests. Throughout its history, the L.A.W. kept its pledge "to promote the general interests of bicycling; to ascertain, defend, and protect the rights of wheelmen." [20] It was through the League's efforts in several test cases that the laws which were applied to carriages came to be applied to bicycles as well.[21]

Another group was not so much opposed to cycling as it was to using the "bike" on Sundays. Perhaps it would not have been so terrible to break the Sabbath if the offense had consisted in carrying the riders to church instead of to the country. On the contrary, according to a New Haven clergyman, the road of the cyclists led "to a place where there is no mud on the streets because of its high temperature." [22] Such admonitions were of no avail, and one writer cleverly noted that "one curious effect which should afford some consolation to Sabbatarians is that theatres in certain cities which were formerly open on Sundays have been closed permanently." [23]

Not all men of religion opposed the bicycle, however. Henry Ward Beecher, as early as 1869, when asked about the coming man and how he would come, answered, "I think he is coming on a velocipede. I shall not be at all surprised," he continued, "to see in a short time a thousand velocipedists wheeling their machines to Plymouth Church." [24] Clergymen themselves started to take up the exercise—Beecher was among the first [25] —and the editor of the *Spectator* wrote that it was proper for a bishop to cycle provided, of course, he didn't "coast downhill on his bicycle with his legs up." [26] And by 1896 the *Boston Daily Advertiser* could write, "It seems to be settled that the majority of the clergymen are in favor of Sunday cycling." [27]

The bicycle was the subject not only of religious but also of medical dispute. In this debate both sides made extravagant claims. The anti-bicyclists said that the cycle path led straight to the hospital or the grave. They discovered all sorts of new ailments which the cyclist was heir to, including kyphosis bicyclistarum, or

[16] Charles E. Pratt, *What and Why* (Boston, 1884), p. 15.

[17] *Ibid.*, p. 45.

[18] *Ibid.*, p. 15.

[19] *Ibid.*, p. 56.

[20] *Ibid.*

[21] *Ibid.*, pp. 45–48; Porter, *Cycling*, p. 154.

[22] Joseph B. Bishop, "Social and Economic Influence of the Bicycle," *Forum*, XXI (August, 1896), 683.

[23] *Ibid.*

[24] Quoted by J. F. B., *The Velocipede* (London, 1869), p. 99.

[25] *Columbia Bicycle Catalogue* (Boston, 1888), Appendix.

[26] "Dignity and Indignity," *The Spectator*, LXXVII (August 29, 1896), 267.

[27] *The Boston Daily Advertiser*, May 13, 1896.

bicycle stoop, which was acquired by pedaling in a bent-over position.[28] Cyclist's sore throat was found to occur after a long ride on a dusty road.[29] Perhaps worst of all was bicycle face, a result of the wheelmen's continuous worrying about keeping his equilibrium while he rode.[30] The *Christian Intelligence* added that another cause of bicycle face was the habitual violation of the law of the Sabbath by cyclists.[31] Many more "normal" diseases were also laid to the exercise.[32]

The proponents of the bicycle, on the other hand, likened its effects to that of a wonder drug. Among the more important illnesses that it could cure were rheumatism, indigestion, alcoholism, anemia, gout, liver trouble, and "nerves."[33] At the same time, though not altogether denying the existence of such ills as bicycle face or bicycle stoop, the advocates of the wheel minimized their danger or told how to avoid them. At a meeting of the Academy of Medicine in 1895, doctors advised the average American cyclist that he would not be troubled by bicyclist's stoop if he sat erect.[34] Indeed, Dr. Graeme M. Hammond, in a paper before the same academy, reported that detailed physical examinations of cyclists revealed

them to be unusually healthy.[35] An article in the *New York Daily Tribune* maintained that bicycle face was not an illness to be avoided but to be sought after and that

. . . anybody who rides every day on a wheel and does not acquire the bicycle face lacks character, and is a menace to himself and everybody else when on the road or on the track. The bicycle face denotes strength of mind in the persons who possess it. It means alertness, quick perception and prompt action in emergencies. The idiotic grin of some of the cigarette smoking fellows who make fun of bicycling can never be mistaken for the bicycle face.[36]

There were saner elements among medical authorities; and most of these agreed that cycling for the normal person was a healthful form of exercise. It was especially good because, unlike many forms of athletics, the performer (the cyclist) did not have to be phenomenally muscular or robust.[37] Of course, these doctors warned, if carried to excess, cycling, like any physical activity, could be harmful.[38] Most people came to accept this view. An editorial in *The Literary Digest* expressed the common feeling when it said, "The notion has been exploded, happily, that wheeling is a panacea for all ailing folks and for all ailments."[39]

Having thus reviewed the mechanical, legal, religious, and medical skirmishes that preceded the full acceptance of the bicycle, what were

[28] "Kyphosis Bicyclistarum," *Scientific American*, LXIX (July 1, 1893), 10.
[29] "Cyclist's Sore Throat," *The Literary Digest*, XVII (August 13, 1898), 197.
[30] "The Bicycle Face," *The Literary Digest*, XI (September 7, 1895), 548–49.
[31] *Ibid.*
[32] A. L. Benedict, "Dangers and Benefits of the Bicycle," *Century Illustrated Monthly Magazine*, XXXII (July, 1897), 471–73; B. W. Richardson, "How Cycling Injures Health," *The Review of Reviews*, I (April 1890), 287–88.
[33] Porter, *Cycling*, pp. 11–19.
[34] John G. Speed, "The Bicycling Era," *Scientific American*, LXXIV (August 24, 1895), 124.

[35] Porter, *op. cit.*, pp. 179–88.
[36] *The New York Daily Tribune*, July 14, 1895.
[37] "In Praise of the Wheel," *The Literary Digest*, XIII (July 18, 1896), 378.
[38] Henry Smith Williams, "The Bicycle in Relation to Health," *Harper's Weekly*, XL (April 11, 1896), 370; Porter, *Cycling*, pp. 187–90.
[39] "In Praise of the Wheel," p. 378.

the consequences of this acceptance in certain areas of social life? Perhaps the bicycle's greatest impact was upon the American woman. As soon as the safety and the drop frame made it easier for the fair sex to mount and ride, women seized upon the vehicle as a new means of defying tradition. This was the period, it must be remembered, of the suffragettes, when the genteel female was on her way out and women were demanding every form of equality with men. Thus, for example, probably because of the reluctance of elderly ladies to learn to ride, it became socially proper for a boy and girl to go cycling without a third party.[40] (Or was it because the bicycle built-for-two had no room for a chaperone?)

For the sake of both comfort and safety, women's clothing was drastically changed. As one female cyclist put it, "On the [bicycle] excursion a special adaptation of dress is absolutely necessary, for skirts, while they have not hindered women from climbing to the topmost branches of higher education, may prove fatal in downhill coasting."[41] Some of the bolder among the sex easily adapted their dress to cycling by shortening their skirts, shockingly exposing their ankles to view.[42] The courage of some yet more daring women gave America the famous bloomer girl.[43] "Skirts," as one advocate of dress reform was quoted in the Tribune, "long or short . . . are bound to go. It is merely a

question of time when an unadulterated man's suit . . . will be the universal garb for women, and all this talk and agitation of the question will be forgotten."[44] And bloomers did resemble men's knickerbockers, though they were wider and more flowing. Despite the censure and ridicule directed at them, the women stuck doggedly to the new fashion. "The time for a woman to faint if a man caught sight of her ankle," said the new woman, "has passed."[45]

Public opinion was not entirely unfavorable to this new turn in women's fashion. An editorial in The Philadelphia Item was perhaps typical of some of the more tolerant comments. "Let the women alone," it began; "they can work out their own salvation, if they desire to wear bloomers why let them bloom."[46]

The effect of the bicycle on women's clothing was truly revolutionary —within a period of two or three years the bicycle gave the American woman the liberty of dress which reformers had been seeking for generations.[47]

Because women rode bicycles, new problems of etiquette presented themselves. One difficulty which appeared for the first time—and which still plagues us today—was whether it was a man's duty to fix a flat tire for a woman. An editorial in Harper's Weekly tried to resolve this problem:

It is recognized as befitting a gentleman to offer his services in repairing a punctured tire, adjusting a nut, or arrang-

[40] Bishop, "Social and Economic Influence of the Bicycle," p. 683.

[41] W. H. Fenton, "A Medical View of Cycling for Ladies," The Nineteenth Century, XXXIX (May, 1896), 800.

[42] Henry J. Garrigues, "Woman and the Bicycle," Forum, XX (January, 1896), 583.

[43] Although the bloomer had been introduced many years earlier, it was not until women adopted the garment for cycling that it became socially acceptable. Ibid.

[44] The New York Daily Tribune, July 7, 1895.

[45] "Crusade against the Wheel for Women," The Literary Digest, XIII (July 18, 1896), 361.

[46] "The Revolutionary Bicycle," The Literary Digest, XII (July 20, 1895), 335.

[47] Scribner's Magazine, XIX (June 1896), 783; Garrigues, "Woman and the Bicycle," p. 578.

ing something that has gone astray with a woman's wheel, and it is not considered improper for a woman to accept his politely proffered services for the mending of a wheel, which he can do better than herself.[48]

But this friendliness and familiarity of the road should not be carried too far; the same editorial frowned on the practice of a male cyclist tipping his hat to a woman rider he did not know.[49] The rule of the right of way at an intersection was a problem, in those days as in ours. But this magazine's solution was simple and gallant. "A woman," wrote Harper's, "should always have the right of way."[50]

Yet, as late as 1896, there continued to be opposition to these newly won freedoms for women. The dissent was led by the Woman's Rescue League of Washington, D. C. This organization claimed that cycling prevented married women from having children, that the new dress was shocking and indecent, and that the new familiarity and companionship with men led to immorality. "Bicycling by young women," a spokesman for the League wrote, "has helped more than any other medium to swell the ranks of reckless girls, who finally drift into the army of outcast women of the United States."[51] But this was definitely a minority opinion; many more of the fair sex considered cycling a step toward even greater freedom. "Many a woman," wrote Mrs. Elizabeth Cady Stanton, "is riding to the suffrage on a bicycle."[52]

As would be expected, the bicycle was an innovation of considerable importance for the American economy. In 1880 the manufacture of bicycles and tricycles [53] was not even listed as a separate industry in the census reports on manufacturing.[54] We may adduce here another reason for the failure of the old ordinary. Every cyclist required a different size of driving wheel, so that this vehicle was not easily adaptable to mass-production techniques.[55] The invention of the safety, however, with its pedals in a position that could be reached by any cyclist, allowed the use of factory methods in bicycle production. In 1889 the volume of orders received by wheel manufacturers and jobbers in Boston, which was then the center of the industry, was unprecedented.[56] And in 1890 the census reports listed the manufacture, as well as the repair of bicycles and tricycles, as separate industries.[57]

A few statistics will show the phenomenal expansion of the cycling industry after the introduction of the safety bicycle. In 1890 there were 27 establishments making bicycles and tricycles.[58] By 1900 this number had

[48] "The Etiquette of the Road," Harper's Weekly, XL (October 3, 1896), 974.
[49] Ibid.
[50] Ibid.
[51] "Crusade against the Wheel for Women," p. 361.
[52] "The Revolutionary Bicycle," p. 334.

[53] President Cleveland himself appeared on the streets of Buffalo riding a tricycle—for in these days tricycles were not just toys for children but were expensive gigantic vehicles with the sole advantage of being easier to ride and to dismount than two-wheelers. Columbia Bicycle Catalogue, Appendix.
[54] Josephsson, "Bicycles and Tricycles," p. 325.
[55] Lacy Hillier, "The Cycle Market," The Contemporary Review, LXXII (August, 1897), 184.
[56] The Boston Daily Advertiser, June 4, 1889.
[57] Report of Manufacturing Industries in the United States at Eleventh Census, 1890 (Washington, D. C.: 1902), part I, 82.
[58] Ibid.

risen to 312.[59] The total capital investment in 1890 was $2,058,072;[60] in 1900 it was $29,783,659.[61] In 1890 establishments manufacturing bicycles employed 1,797 people and paid them a total of $1,105,728.[62] In 1900 they hired 17,525 and the wage bill had risen to $9,358,904.[63] Reliable estimates put the total number of bicycles in use during the nineties at ten million in a population approaching seventy-six million.[64] Cycle repairing underwent a similar growth.[65] Furthermore, many companies began to turn out bicycle accessories and found a lucrative market for them. Bicycle lamps, bells, saddles, tools, tires, trouser-clips, rear-view mirrors are typical of the extras of the nineties.[66] All sorts of bicycle clothing were manufactured: bloomers, bicycle stockings, bicycle caps, bicycle shoes, bicycle pants—with reinforced seats; even bicycle corsets were sold.[67] Employment opportunities were offered in riding schools to which thousands flocked.[68] Jordan Marsh and Company of Boston converted one of its floors into a riding academy and offered free lessons to anyone who purchased a wheel there.[69]

At the same time the price of the safety dropped to about $60 compared to the $150 for the ordinary; and by 1900 new bicycles could be purchased for as little as $18.[70] In addition, the fashion of trading the machine in every year or two had already been established, so that a secondhand "bike" was within the reach of all.[71]

Some industries actually suffered adverse effects from the bicycle boom.[72] Fortunately, many retailers were able to bolster their sagging sales by taking in a stock of roadsters (another name for bicycles). Soon jewelry, shoe, gun, hardware, and department stores were all selling wheels.[73]

The bicycle had its effect on the United States Army, too. Some military men predicted bicyclized warfare. "It is in rapidly moving considerable bodies of infantry," wrote one officer, "that the bicycle will find its highest function in time of war."[74] Military maneuvers were held in which the bicycle was used. The Colt automatic rifle was mounted on the handlebars of a wheel. The Medical Corps received training in evacuating

[59] Report of Manufacturing Industries in the United States at Twelfth Census, 1900 (Washington, D. C.: 1902), part I, 82.
[60] Report of Manufacturing at Eleventh Census, part I, 126–27.
[61] Report of Manufacturing at Twelfth Census, part I, 82.
[62] Josephsson, op. cit., p. 325.
[63] Ibid.
[64] Lloyd Morris, Not So Long Ago (New York, 1949), p. 243.
[65] Report of Manufacturing at Eleventh Census, part I, 126–27; Report of Manufacturing at Twelfth Census, part I, 78–79.
[66] Porter, Cycling, pp. 118–76; The Boston Daily Advertiser, May 2, 1896.
[67] The Boston Daily Advertiser, May 16, 1889; June 11, 1896; April 4, 1889.
[68] The New York Daily Tribune, July 14, 1895.

[69] The Boston Daily Advertiser, June 15, 1896.
[70] Columbia Bicycle Catalogue pp. 6–44; The Boston Daily Advertiser, March 31, 1896; April 4, 1899.
[71] "Cheaper Wheels," The Literary Digest, XIII (June 13, 1896), 197; The New York Daily Tribune, April 26, 1896.
[72] Bishop, "Social and Economic Influence of the Bicycle," p. 685; "Effect of the Bicycle Boom on Trade," p. 407.
[73] Scribner's Magazine, XIX (June, 1896), 783; "Bicycles and the Book Trade," The Literary Digest, XIII (July 11, 1896), 347.
[74] Major Howard A. Giddings, "The Bicycle in the Army," Harper's Weekly, XL (April 11, 1896), 364.

men on the bicycle.[75] And in 1896, 200 wheels were shipped to Cuba and were probably used in the fighting there.[76]

It was to be expected that bicycling would make its mark in the world of sports. Because of limited space, only the slightest summary will be made here of the bicycle's impact on the American sporting scene. Race tracks cropped up throughout the country, and thousands of tournaments enabled amateurs and professionals to vie for honor and reward. Many colleges had bicycle teams which engaged in school meets.[77] The six-day bicycle race attracted thousands to Madison Square Garden each year.[78] Arthur A. Zimmerman was the Di Maggio of bicycle racing, and the idol of a considerable segment of American youth. His speed on the wheel earned him $40,000 annually.[79] To help keep the sport honest, the League of American Wheelmen took charge of professional racing in 1895.[80]

But easily the greatest significance of the bicycle was the interference it ran for the automobile. The bicycle did the dirty work for its mechanized successor in a variety of ways. We may first mention the adoption in cycle manufacturing of assembly-line techniques. Standardization had been perfected to such a degree that the manufacturing company no longer constructed the entire bicycle under its own roof, but had merely to assemble the parts which smaller com-

panies had contracted to make.[81] The importance of this method for automobile manufacture is obvious. As a matter of fact, the census of 1900 noted that 56 automobiles had in that year been made in bicycle factories.[82] The census report even classified the auto under the general heading of bicycle.[83]

The abundance of repair shops— there were 6,328 of them in 1900— was another of the bicycle's gifts to the automobile.[84] Not only did these become the logical repair places for the auto, but they were the training schools for a group of mechanics who could easily turn from the bicycle when the new vehicle became popular. Charles and Frank Duryea owned such a bicycle repair shop in Springfield, Massachusetts; and it was here that they built the first American automobile.[85]

By carrying on effective agitation for road repairs and construction, the cyclists rendered still another inestimable service to future autoists. Without good roads, the automobile could never have succeeded: the earliest autos had had to be put on tracks because they could not be made to run effectively on the English highways of their day; hence they became locomotives, with all the limitations that tracks entailed.[86] Privately built and operated turnpikes, which had once given the United States good roads, had become unprofitable because of the railroads.[87] Furthermore,

[75] Ibid.

[76] The New York Daily Tribune, May 1, 1896.

[77] The Boston Daily Advertiser, May 25, 1896.

[78] The New York Daily Tribune, December 10, 1897.

[79] The Bicycling World (April 20, 1894), p. 665.

[80] The New York Daily Tribune, July 13, 1895.

[81] Josephsson, "Bicycles and Tricycles," p. 328.

[82] Ibid.

[83] Ibid.

[84] Report of Manufacturing at Twelfth Census, part I, 78.

[85] Morris, Not So Long Ago, p. 229.

[86] A. L. Kroeber, Anthropology (New York: Harcourt, Brace and Company, Inc., 1948), pp. 358–59.

[87] Nathaniel S. Shaler, American Highways (New York, 1896), pp. 93–95.

road construction and maintenance were the responsibilities of the cities and towns and not of the federal or state governments.[88] As a result, the roads were rough and rutted, muddy in the spring, sandy and dusty all summer.[89]

To the League of American Wheelmen goes most of the credit for road reform in the eighties and nineties. Under its direction, pamphlets and books—including the *Good Roads* magazine—urging reform were written and distributed.[90] In Washington the League lobbied unsuccessfully for a federal highway, but did succeed in 1893 in getting the national government to create the Office of Public Roads Inquiries.[91] Other returns for this effort began to roll in. By 1896, 16 states appropriated money to improve their roads.[92] Several states— Massachusetts and New Jersey were the first—also established state control of roads through a central highway commission. In Massachusetts, all the members of the State Highway Commission belonged to the L.A.W.[93] In Iowa and Kentucky, the custom was begun of putting convicts to building and repairing roads.[94]

In still other ways the League of American Wheelmen sought to improve roads. The League backed legislation for lighted streets and for erecting guideposts at intersections with the names of streets.[95] This remarkable organization even built signs on the road marking the danger spots; these signs would be sent free to any place in the country by the Committee on Danger Signs.[96] In like manner, the League constructed signposts with important travel information, such as direction and distances of neighboring cities.[97] League members were asked to record their mileage on cycling trips, so that this information would be available.[98] These services were important not only to cyclists but also to riders of the new horseless carriages.

The pressure of millions of wheels on the road during the nineties compelled the passage of a new series of laws regulating their use. Many states required cyclists to purchase licenses for their wheels; in some cases the money derived from this source was used to keep roads in repair.[99] New Jersey was the first state to require bicycles to be lighted at night and also be equipped with a bell to give a warning signal.[100] Riding on sidewalks was prohibited in virtually all states.[101] Successful lobbying on the part of the League of American Wheelmen brought about statutes requiring that names and addresses be exchanged in case of accidents.[102] Wheelmen in Massachusetts, Michigan, and New Hampshire were obliged to keep to the right side of the road except when passing.[103] Though not yet a matter of law, many cyclists voluntarily began the practice of passing on the left and giving hand signals when turning.[104]

[88] *Ibid.*, pp. 89–90.

[89] Morris, *op. cit.*, p. 241.

[90] Isaac B. Potter, "The Bicycle's Relation to Good Roads," *Harper's Weekly*, XL (April 11, 1896), 362.

[91] Morris, *op. cit.*, p. 242.

[92] Potter, "The Bicycle's Relation to Good Roads," p. 362.

[93] *Ibid.*

[94] *Ibid.*

[95] Isaac B. Potter, *Cycle Paths* (Boston, 1898), pp. 6–23.

[96] *Ibid.*, p. 80ff.

[97] *Ibid.*

[98] Potter, "The Bicycle's Relation to Good Roads," p. 362.

[99] Potter, *Cycle Paths*, p. 72.

[100] *Ibid.*, p. 77.

[101] *Ibid.*

[102] *Ibid.*, p. 80ff.

[103] Potter, *Cycling*, p. 158.

[104] "The Etiquette of the Road," *Harper's Weekly*, XL (October 3, 1896), 973.

Speed limits were set at ten miles per hour on the highways and eight miles in the public parks; but these laws were apparently frequently violated and the phrase "fined for scorching" became a familiar one.[105]

Along with these laws and practices and their infractions, the system of enforcement was part of the legacy which the bicycle bequeathed to the automobile when the latter began its reign in the twentieth century. For the speed demon, so familiar to the modern American scene, dates back to the coming of the bicycle and jeopardized the lives of pedestrians and other wheelmen. So many accidents occurred that a new obituary column entitled "Death by the Wheel," appeared in newspapers.[106] Cyclists boasted about the close shaves they experienced on the road.[107] Since the scorchers could outdistance police on horseback, police methods had to be modernized.

Many cities coped with this problem by equipping squadrons of bicycle cops.[108] Daring races between bicycle policemen and scorchers became common; the public enjoyed these free contests and, more often than not, cheered the speedster—especially a female one—and hissed the officer.[109] Not only was the wheel effective in combating scorchers, but policemen also found it an efficient instrument when covering their beats— a foreshadowing of the patrol car.[110]

It was the bicycle which gave rise in the nineties to that new type of mobility that became so characteristic of the twentieth century. In the earlier part of the century, horses and carriages were only for the more well-to-do. The average city worker and his family, except for an occasional railroad trip, rarely left their place of residence. But the wheel made it possible for Americans to visit the countryside and neighboring towns.[111] Despite the inadequacy of the roads, the cyclist thought little of covering twenty-five to fifty miles in the course of a Sunday.[112] Often the whole family participated in these outings; the children all had bicycles of their own, and the parents might have had a convertible—a tandem bicycle that could also be used as a single safety.[113] The wayside inn, so much a part of the American scene today, was rescued from oblivion by the bicycle. The hostelry, because of the railroads, had been on the point of extinction, until hordes of hungry and thirsty wheelmen in the nineties thronged the country roads.[114]

In the summertime many people went on bicycle journeys in much the same way as we today go on automobile trips.[115] Of course, they didn't cover as much mileage as we do; but these hardy Americans did cover several hundred miles.[116] The League of American Wheelmen provided its two hundred thousand members with maps that marked out the best roads

[105] *The Boston Daily Advertiser*, May 16, 1896.

[106] "Cyclomania," *The Living Age*, CCXV (November 13, 1897), 470.

[107] *Ibid.*, p. 471.

[108] *The Boston Daily Advertiser*, May 14, 1896.

[109] *The New York Daily Tribune*, May 2, 1896.

[110] *The Boston Daily Advertiser*, May 14, 1896.

[111] "The Charm of the Bicycle," *Scientific American*, LXXX (May 13, 1899), 292; Garrigues, "Woman and the Bicycle," p. 578.

[112] Garrigues, *op. cit.*, p. 578.

[113] Porter, *Cycling*, pp. 163–64.

[114] Garrigues, "Woman and the Bicycle," p. 578; Potter, "The Bicycle's Relation to Good Roads," p. 362.

[115] J. Cleveland Cady, "The Vacation Awheel," *The Outlook*, LVI (June 5, 1897), 304–5.

[116] *Ibid.*

and listed hotels at which members received discounts, and even took the trouble of advising members not to disclose their League affiliation until their stay was over lest they be put in poorer accommodations because of the rebate.[117] "Unlike the steam car," wrote one cycling vacationist, "the bicycle takes one to the out-of-the-way places and scenes; unlike the horse, it is not a source of care and anxiety, or liable to serious ills on the way.[118]

But not only were many Americans enabled to visit the country, but many also found it possible to live on the outskirts of the city and cycle into and home from work.[119] Many could

afford to make this change because suburban rents were still as low as tenement rents.[120]

Thus it can be concluded that the bicycle provided a preview on a miniature scale of much of the social phenomena that the automobile enlarged upon. Of course the automobile, for the most part, displaced the bicycle as a means of transportation, but made full use of the institutions that accompanied the two-wheeled vehicle. At any rate, an early cyclist hardly realized how right he was when he said with the bicycle in mind, "Walking is now on its last legs." [121]

[117] Porter, op. cit., p. 179.
[118] Cady, op. cit., pp. 304–5.
[119] Bishop, "Social and Economic Influence of the Bicycle," p. 689; Benedict,

"Dangers and Benefits of the Bicycle," p. 472.
[120] Benedict, op. cit., p. 472.
[121] J. F. B., The Velocipede, ii.

# 26

# Of Time, the City, and the "One-Year Guarantee": The Relations Between Watch Owners and Repairers *†

*Fred L. Strodtbeck* and *Marvin B. Sussman*

Students of social change, especially those who have concentrated on modern-

* Reprinted from *The American Journal of Sociology*, LXI (1956), 602–9, by permission of The University of Chicago Press. Copyright 1956 by the University of Chicago. Footnotes renumbered.
† Incidental direct expenses incurred in this study have been met from a Ford Foundation grant-in-aid.

ization with its key process of industrialization, have primarily concerned themselves with transitions in the major social institutions of society, e.g., the family, the economy, and the polity. But along with the changes found in the macroscopic arena, one can also observe the impact of modernization on numerous more mundane and microscopic areas of social life, especially on occupations. For just as the advent of the automobile diminished the importance of the bicycle or the horse, so, too, did it diminish the importance of the blacksmith.

In addition to the occupations and professions that have been eradicated because of new technological devices, there have been those whose professions are retained by the changing society but whose functions have been severely limited. And with this decrease in functions, there has come a decline in status. Such an occupation is that of the watch repairer.[1] What does the practitioner do when he sees his professional status being threatened? How does he respond to his approaching obsolescence? How does such change affect the practitioner's relations with his clients? These are the questions taken up by Professors Strodtbeck and Sussman in the following study.

EDITOR

The amount a watch owner pays for the repair of a watch is not closely related to the repairer's costs. In classical economic theory, discriminative pricing is believed to be a short-run instance of imperfect competition; and it is therefore predicted that a service priced to reflect more closely the cost to the repairer will eventually be brought about. In this paper the writers present the basis for the prediction that a generalized and, in an economic sense, discriminatory price will continue to be charged for watch-repair services.

In each of the three sections that follow, a primary consideration is given the technology of the watch. The groundwork of the argument rests upon the obsolence of certain previously prestigeful skills and the limited risk to a repairer who guarantees a repair. The repairer's work situation is developed in terms of the historical position of the craft, the requirements of daily operations, and the repairer's ultimate occupational aspirations. Finally, the typical watch owner's perspective to watch mechanisms is presented, to complete the matrix of factors used in the interpretation of current price practices.

## The Watch Mechanism and Repair Technology

The evolution from the clock operated by weights to the modern watch involved essentially three inventions: the mainspring, the spiral balance spring, and jewel bearings. The mainspring is believed to have been invented by Henlein, between 1500 and 1510. The principle of motive power involved in this invention, i.e., the use of a coiled steel spring for the source of power, has not been altered since 1700, although improvements in the size, tension, and quality of mainsprings have been made.

The accuracy of the modern watch is dependent on the invention of the spiral balance spring by Huygens and Hooke in the seventeenth century, and on the promotion of its widespread use by the watchmaker Julien

[1] Numerous other occupations have been caught in a similar dilemma. Cf., e.g., Thelma H. McCormack, "The Druggist's Dilemma: Problems of a Marginal Occupation," *The American Journal of Sociology*, LXI (1956), 308–15; and Paul Dommermuth, "Retail Pharmacists: Professional Contingencies in a Business Setting" (Paper read at the Annual Meeting of American Sociological Association, Miami, Fla., 1966).

LeRoy a century later. This spring, popularly known as the "hairspring," is a delicate, coiled steel spring, "set" on the balance wheel to control the circular motion of the balance. Without the constant harmonic motion of the balance wheel (to and fro, back and forth), accurate timekeeping would be impossible.

Other improvements in the watch mechanism that came after the mainspring and hairspring include the perfection of wheels, gears, pinion teeth, and pivots. The most notable of these was the use of jewels (pierced rubies or synthetic corundum) as pivot holes by Nicholas Fatio, the Swiss geometer, in 1704. Jewel bearings reduced friction between moving parts so that watch pieces could be made smaller, their size being determined by the strength of the steel pivots set in jeweled pivot holes.

By the beginning of the eighteenth century, Henlein, Huygens, and others had discovered the basic principles of watch construction. Watches made for Queen Elizabeth I had been in operation for more than two hundred years. The watchmaker, associated with royalty and with the prestige of the sciences of geometry and mechanics, was a skilled craftsman working at the most advanced technology of his time. Although from that time forward development of the theoretical science of watchmaking virtually stopped, the rapid and continuous advance of general machine technology made it possible by 1860 to drill plate holes and manufacture jewels with precision sufficient to allow the setting of jewels by pressure alone.[2]

[2] A recent and readable history of the watch is given in James R. McCarthy, *A Matter of Time* (New York: Harper & Row, Publishers, 1950).

Up to the turn of the twentieth century, the watchmaker, with some salvage parts and bits of metal, could duplicate the wheels, pinions, or any other part needed for repair. The skill required for this task was almost equal to that of earlier times, when the watchmaker started the manufacture of a handmade watch by scratching out pivot locations on a blank metal base plate. Experience and ability to operate complex hand tools were essential. But, by 1900, machine tools adequate for producing the 125 standardized interchangeable parts that go into the average watch were perfected by Swiss technologists.

In America, after World War I, supply-parts catalogs and channels for the distribution of interchangeable watch parts manufactured in Switzerland were rapidly developed. Today a judiciously organized portable cabinet can contain most of the tools and watch parts required to repair a large variety of standard watch models. The other parts a repairman needs in his work can be obtained through material-supply houses. If he needs a hairspring vibrated (a skilled operation of coiling the spring and curving of the brequet loop according to the weight of the balance) or a radium-figured dial repainted, or if he has a watch that he has failed to repair after several tries, a "sticker," he can obtain the services of more experienced workmen. If a smashed or rusted watch movement, the present of a loved one, must for sentimental reasons be replaced, the repairer can obtain another movement.

There have been no contrasting developments in recent years to complicate watch repair and offset the very great reduction in mechanical skill that this availability of spare parts has involved. This holds despite the increased distribution of very small ladies' watches. The smaller watches demand only slightly more careful handling to insure that parts will not be damaged in the process of repair. The one major innovation in repair technology during the last twenty years is the electronic timer. By placing a watch in this machine and adjusting it to various positions the repairer can, in about one minute, extrapolate the accuracy of time performance of the mechanism over a 24-hour period. Differential performance in three positions provides a diagnostic test for a number of causes of watch stoppage, e.g., binding gears, oily or bent hairspring, balance out of true and poise, etc. Yet, while the electronic timer is a recent and helpful innovation, the very great simplification of watch repairing may be attributed almost entirely to the availability of spare parts. The extent of this simplification is illustrated by the ordnance training program utilized during the second World War: in 15 weeks inexperienced men with mechanical aptitude could be taught to use spare parts in the maintenance and repair of army timepieces.[3]

The use of whatever machine skills the repairer may possess to make wheels, pinions, or other watch parts is now "obsolete." Parts are available at very low cost: winding stems for standard model watches, for example, cost as little as 75 cents a dozen. The price is far less than the value of the time required to make a stem from steel stock. If parts are not available, a substitute movement of equal quality can usually be obtained for less than $10.00. If none of these courses

is practical, a new watch can be had at low cost, e.g., a new seventeen-jewel, waterproof watch with shock-resistant movement, compactly designed, timed to a probable tolerance of 10–15 seconds a day, is available for less than $20.00. Thus, during the last thirty years the watch repairer has ceased to be a craftsman and is virtually an assembler and adjuster—a person with primary knowledge of spare-parts supply channels, plus experience and a degree of kinesthetic co-ordination.[4]

## The Repairer's Work Situation

In the trade literature two recurrent themes are used to justify watch repairing as an occupation: freedom of action as a self-employable, and security. Typical expressions from two interviews in a pilot set of fifteen are given here:

There is nothing like being your own boss. When I come down to the shop in the morning, if I feel like working hard or if I have to, I can run them off the griddle like hotcakes. If I don't feel like working, I can take in a ball game and even close down the shop. As long as you get the work done when you promise it, you can do it on your own time. Nobody knows what you put into it.

As long as you have the skill, you can always do enough repairs to pay the rent, light, and get enough to live on. The rest is gravy. If you sell a watch now and then, you make a 100 per cent profit—

[3] *War Department Technical Manual, TM 9-1575: Ordnance Maintenance, Wrist Watches, Pocket Watches, Stop Watches, and Clocks* (Washington, D.C.: War Department, April, 1945).

[4] Lay conceptions of watch repairing emphasize the visual activity, but actually "touch" becomes extremely important in many operations. Pearl H. H. King has previously described the disposition to overestimate the visual component of a precision job in hosiery manufacture (see "Task Perception and Inter-personal Relations in Industrial Training," *Human Relations,* I [1947], 121–30, 373–412).

it's a gift. Why should I work for someone else?

Virtually all repairers have sales sidelines. Secondhand watches, standard watches, bracelets, and cigarette lighters are the first items stocked. If the repairer is successful, he will increase his sales, rent larger space, and may eventually hope to own a jewelry store.

The repairer at the bench is virtually certain of being able to "make his time" at straightforward repair work. During the spring and summer of 1953 at current rates in New England, a good worker turned out forty repairs and twenty to thirty adjustments per week, which grossed between $150 and $200. If the repairer hires another worker, he may make an additional $75–$100 per week. This income compares favorably with skilled machinist jobs in industry. There are seasonal slumps when work is not available, which reduce this income, but this threat is more than counterbalanced by the possibility of a retail sale.

The nature of the "best practice" to be taught watchmaker trainees is continually under debate in the technical journals of the British and American horological societies. One of the most interesting controversies has dealt with the use of watch-cleaning machines. The conventional way of cleaning disassembled watch parts was to string them on a fine wire, then dip them successively into a cleaning solution and two rinses, then dry them with a hand blower. The cleaning machine utilizes a small wire basket into which the disassembled parts can be dumped, then successively whirled in the three solutions, and dried. The machine is semiautomatic, so the repairer can be working at another job while the cleaning takes place; the parts get a uniform finish, and the repairman is spared the inconvenience of getting his fingers in the various solutions. Watch manufacturers and horological societies generally oppose the use of these machines.

Carpenters' opposition to power saws and painters' opposition to wider brushes are understandable as resistance to the contractor's effort to reduce labor costs; but it is not clear why the horological societies would resist an innovation that would save time for the self-employed watch repairer. The watch repairer, not a contractor, would profit from the economy of time. As we explored this problem with representatives from both sides of the argument, we discovered an interesting variance in the use of the term "cleaned." To clean a watch implies complete disassembly, including the removal of all capped jewels and covered parts. However, it is apparently not unknown for watch repairers to compromise by only partially disassembling the watch. Experts all agree in informal conversation that *if the watch is completely disassembled,* there is no objection to the cleaning machine if the repairer continues to hand-clean with peg wood the pivot holes, jewels, and other crevice parts. Thus it appears that the rejection of the cleaning machine because of its possible misuse is a primitive control mechanism that would not be invoked if there was in fact, an effectively operating system of internal regulation.[5]

[5] The watch manufacturers have attempted to raise levels of competence and integrity by lending their support to the United Horological Association of America, Inc., which works for licensing laws and related occupational controls. The growth in the number of watchmakers from a prewar total of about 25,000 to 40,000 in 1949 has hampered efforts to maintain high repair standards. This increase is an oversupply,

## Watch Owner's Reactions to Watches and Repairers

In 1941, *Reader's Digest* sent a male and female investigator to 462 watch repairmen in 48 states. To each repairman they presented a well-known American watch in first-class running condition except for an obvious defect. Just before entering the shop they would loosen the crown wheel screw, disengaging the gears so that the watch would no longer wind. In the watches used, the screw is conspicuous and accessible. If the repairer failed to replace the crown screw immediately, he was defined as cheating the customer. Of the 462 watchmakers, 236 made the repair immediately. However, 226, or 49 per cent, "lied, overcharged, gave phony diagnoses, or suggested extensive and unnecessary repairs." On the basis of this evidence Roger William Riis, the *Reader's Digest* editor, chose to title his report, "The Watch Repair Man Will Gyp You If You Don't Look Out." A criterion of value that results in classifying half the shops contacted as "gyp shops" must be more stringent than the criterion of value that patrons use. This article undoubtedly did not improve the public's attitude toward watch-repair shops. Indeed, the instituting of the study and the tenor of the report may be taken as evidence of generally unfavorable public relations.

A man known to the writers to have a broad command of general technology commented: "Watch repairers are all crooks. They substitute poor parts or works for good. I knew a little old man in Boston. He could

---

since replacement needs are estimated to be only 1000 per year (*Occupational Outlook Handbook*, U.S. Department of Labor and the Veterans' Administration Bull. No. 998 [Washington, D.C., 1951]).

be trusted, but he is dead. Now I don't know where to go." It is hard to believe that if he had known the low value of watch parts he would have feared the substitution of parts. The mechanism in a $75 and $200 watch by the same manufacturer is approximately the same, the differences being confined to the case and the trimmings.

The association of the number of jewels with the price of a watch has given rise to the belief that the jewels themselves have intrinsic value. To determine the extent of this belief, the writers administered a questionnaire to 140 adult students in an evening college and found that only 22 per cent knew that watch jewels were synthetic stones or hard glass of little intrinsic value. The remainder believed watch jewels were semiprecious or precious stones. Replacement jewels are obtained by the repairer at costs varying from 5 to 25 cents each. Since watch jewels are easily damaged in removal, and the replacement of a jewel takes about a half-hour, it would appear that concern about watch jewels while a watch is in the repairer's custody is unfounded.

The opportunity for exercise of a salesman's guile arises in the conversation in which the watch is accepted for repair. During this conversation, the repairer searches for cues to the motivation of the watch owner. If there is a complaint about previous unsuccessful repair attempts, after checking the marks inside the case to insure that he has not worked on the watch before, the repairer suggests that the previous repairers were "butchers." If the watch owner brings in the watch as a challenge to the repairer's skill, the watch can be taken in with the suggestion that the repair may be expensive; and if a great compulsion by the watch owner to have the "correct" time is revealed, then the idea of buying a new watch will be introduced.

Of the 80 persons in our sample of 140 who had had experience with watch repairers, approximately two thirds received and believed what appears to be poor counsel. For example, one respondent who had been troubled by a series of broken mainsprings, on advice of his repairer, retired his expensive American watch to a bank vault because it was so "sensitive" that changes in temperature broke it. Even though poor technique in installation is a more probable explanation, this respondent described his repairer as "an excellent craftsman." A girl informant had been convinced by her repairer that it was the magnetism of her body that caused her watch to stop. Another informant, who still believed his repairer was "very honest," reported that for a time he had to have his watch "cleaned" every month. When the repairer finally told the owner that "his skin was rough on a watch," the owner complained only that he should have been told sooner that he couldn't wear wrist watches. In the watch industry it is well known that body magnetism and skin condition can have no effects on watch operation.[6]

To obtain a more representative set of the discussion between the watch owner and the repairer when watches are brought in for repairs, the writers arranged to have a concealed microphone placed in a moderate-sized repair shop for a two-week period. While interviewing repairers concerning the time required for common repair operations, additional field ob-

[6] Watches can be made inoperative by magnetism; but such changes cannot be effected by magnetic potentials of the human body. These misconceptions are frequently discussed in the horological literature.

servations were made in six other shops. A model discussion is well exemplified by the following:

A customer approached the repairer and told him that her watch would not wind and that she thought the mainspring was broken. The repairer, while seated at his bench, removed the movement from its case and examined it carefully, peering through his eye loop. After a minute or so he turned to the customer and said: "The mainspring is not broken. It is the click spring that is gone."

"Oh! I thought it was the mainspring because I couldn't wind it," replied the customer.

"No," said the repairer, "it is the little click spring which holds the click in place—this is broken." He continued: "When did you have this watch cleaned? It is dirty and dry, and probably the click spring broke because the old oil dried up."

"Well, I don't remember when I had it cleaned but it was running fine before it broke."

The repairer, "I won't want to take it in for just a click spring and then guarantee it. If I replace the click, it may break again in a week, or some other part may go at any time. The oil is dried out and the watch should be taken apart, thoroughly cleaned and oiled, and then timed. If we overhaul it, we will replace worn parts and then guarantee it for one year. This is a fine watch and it will give you many more years of good service."

"How much will that cost?"

"The complete job, the watch will be overhauled, is $8.50."

"Well, all right, you will guarantee it then?"

"Yes, for one year, if you have any trouble with it, we will take care of it."

"When can I have it?"

"A week from today."

"Oh! Can't I have it for Saturday?"

"Well, I will try. If you are downtown, why don't you drop by?"

Here the owner volunteered a diagnosis involving the mainspring: mainspring breakage is often suggested by people with little mechanical sophistication. Then the repairer corrected the owner's diagnosis before accepting the work, and he assumed certain obligations by promising to overhaul the watch for $8.50. From the owner's standpoint, confirmation was received that repair was possible and that her financial obligation would not exceed $8.50. The "guarantee for one year" was mentioned just before she relinquished her watch.

The click spring in question is a standard part usually purchased in gross lots. Replacement of a click spring takes less than 10 minutes; careful disassembly, cleaning, and reassembling of the watch take less than 90 minutes. Why did the watch repairer in this instance insist on the excessive delay? Do such delays impress the watch owner that the repairer is a busy man, or does the watch owner believe that the repairer is going to check the performance of the watch at different times? One might guess that the delay has the partial justification of enabling the repairer to work when he chooses and at his own rate of speed. Delay may also enable him to obtain the spare parts he requires; but our experience strongly suggests that the delay is often utilized as a technique to conceal the simplicity of many repair operations. Such delays are the regular procedure even when spare parts are available and there is no backlog of work on hand.

The owner often questions whether his watch is worth repairing. The common practice is to tell him what it would cost to buy an equivalent new watch. When the watch owner has been negligent, e.g., permitting his watch to become rusty, he is chided by the repairer, "Why didn't you bring this in right away? This is certainly a mess now." If the owner responds as if he does feel guilty for dropping or neglecting the watch, the watch repairer does not work hard to establish the legitimacy of the charge he proposes. He proceeds to sell his service as if he enjoyed the full confidence of the owner; and the owner may reciprocate by expressing his relief to learn that the negligence can be rectified.

When the watch owner questions the repairer's diagnosis, the repairer has his defense. He may introduce technical descriptions with which the layman cannot argue. A spokesman for the industry has recently illustrated this use of technical jargon in remarking:

George Bennett's contention in taking in a watch was . . . no use in telling a customer his watch needs cleaning, give him a good story, mostly something like "Your watch can be repaired all right, fusee chain is causing friction on the barrel, making the third wheel bind on the center wheel" or "the hairspring is rubbing on the third wheel, causing friction on the roller jewel." Don't think he ever took in a watch for a mainspring without saying that the center wheel of the third pinion was broken. . . . Surprisingly enough, he never seemed to lose a customer.[7]

[7] Kenneth C. Saalmans, "General Repairs and the Public" (Address given to the international meeting of the Horological Institute of the American and Canadian Jewelers' Institute, October 2, 1950, Dearborn Inn, Mich., printed in *Horological Institute of America Journal*, December, 1950). The humor of Bennett's story depends on knowledge of timepiece nomenclature: fusee chains were once used in watches, but in

Actually, the use of technical terms with the client is not increasing. In the more modern shops the trend is to suggest simply that the watch be cleaned and adjusted (e.g., over-hauled) and to guarantee the repair for one year. A price of from $6.00 to $10.00 is quoted for the job, depending on the location of the shop and the status of the clientele. With a ceiling on the possible cost and mention of a guarantee, the owner turns the watch over to be repaired without further conditions.

## Discussion

Most simply stated, watches are mechanisms for slowly releasing tension on springs. They tend to work for long periods without repair of any kind. This essentially technological characteristic enters into the social matrix of owner-repairer relations insofar as it prevents the owner, in most cases, from developing the personalized relation with the repairer that he would with service agents who are visited more often.

The technology of the watch—once the claim of the watchmaker to the highest status in the craftsman hierarchy—is now the point of entry for threats to the watch repairer's status. Interchangeable parts have so reduced the value of metalworking skills that it is fair to say that the bench lathe is more frequently used as a showpiece than as a tool. The continued mechanization of watch manufacture by the Swiss has held the price of serviceable timepieces very low. A further ceiling upon the value of the watch repairer's service is the

elasticity of the supply, for if the rewards for watch repairing were to rise sharply, technical school graduates, who could enter repairing after a year's training, would be quickly attracted to the field.

Since the sale of watches and jewelry is at present widely dispersed, and since at each point of retail distribution the services of a repairer are required, there is little prospect that there will be in the near future an integration of watch repairing into a centralized bureaucratic enterprise. This interdependence of the repairer and the jewelry store has social consequences. A repairer can observe that the jeweler doesn't sell all items for the same markup; and, by analogy, he can ask: Why should I charge in direct relation to bench time?

The outright shift from being a watch repairer to operating a jewelry store is not usually possible because the repairer lacks the $20,000 capital normally required for the original investment in equipment and stock in a modern jewelry store.[8] Jewelry has a high markup and a slow turnover. As much as fifteen years may be required to develop a firmly established business. The repairer starts with watch bands and lighters; and, if this is successful, more jewelry may be added. This mode of expanding into a jewelry business is now threatened by the very successful expansion of department stores into the jewelry field. Although it is difficult for the repairer to achieve the goal of operating a jewelry store, the importance of the possibility of making profit "like

---

modern times their only equivalent is the chain used to wind weight-operated cuckoo clocks.

[8] Sam Mintz, *Establishing and Operating a Jewelry Store*, U.S. Department of Commerce (Washington, D.C.: Government Printing Office, 1946); and *The Jewelry Trade*, U.S. Department of Commerce, Bulletins 3–7, "Trade Series," U.S. Census of Business (Washington, D.C.: Government Printing Office, 1948).

a jeweler" cannot be overemphasized. The sideline sales, the chance of personally profiting from a transaction that involves no bench time—this is what the watch repairer really alludes to when he says, "You're your own boss."

Whenever an owner appears before a repairman's counter, a conflict of interest is potentially present. The position of confidence attributed to the repairman in such negotiations is strengthened each time he successfully repairs a watch for a particular customer; but it is almost equally true that each time a watch stops, the owner's confidence in the repairer is threatened. The repairer may have worked on component A, and the watch may stop because of a failure of component B; the owner does not recognize these distinctions. The training of the owner into more informed expectations is unlikely, because in many cases he is little interested in detail. His position is pragmatic: he wants his watch in running order. The repairer, on the other hand, avoids discussions which involve possible exposure of the simple exchange of parts that is the base of most repairs.

The horological societies, which have the charter function of improving the watch repairer's "hazy, undefined and rather unfavorable" relationship to the public, do little to discipline repairers.[9] They attempt to create favorable public opinion by stressing the continuation in modern watch repairing of the old craftsman traditions. If the repairer has lost the pride in workmanship of the craftsman, he nonetheless clings to the philosophy of individualism that Veblen

and others have associated with handicraft social organization.[10] He does not recognize that his personal profit is related to the public relations objectives that may be sought as supra-individual organizational goals. Collateral organizations have not grown to regulate standards and reduce invidious comparisons. Licensing in seventeen states is the closest approach to internal control that has evolved.[11] In the main, the repairer faces the "self-other" dilemmas of his operations outside the framework of a protective or regulative institutional context.

It is almost axiomatic, in the face of the possible exploitation of the watch owner by the repairer, that a means for controlling and regularizing their relations would arise. The point of interest is the form this means will take. The solution now being adopted throughout America emerges quite clearly. Without discussion of the details of the repair, the repairer offers to clean and adjust the watch for a fixed sum. The owner is reassured by a social contract, the continued operation of his watch for one year is guaranteed. The guarantee, quickly given and confirmed by a stub, is an impersonal matter at the time of its issue; but it is at the same time a bona fide promise of performance directed at the very core of the owner's concerns.

At first glance, a repair guarantee appears to have some relation to law and legal authority; but the question

[9] United We Stand (New York: United Horological Association of America, Inc., April, 1952) (brochure).

[10] See Thorstein Veblen, The Instinct of Workmanship (New York: Crowell-Collier & Macmillan, Inc., 1914), particularly Chapter VI, "The Era of Handicraft."

[11] In this connection Wisconsin has pioneered with a model law (see State of Wisconsin Board of Examiners in Watchmaking, Regulations Relating to the Practice of Watchmaking [1946]) (pamphlet).

of whether or not a particular guarantee is enforceable in the courts is strictly academic. The demonstrable loss that a watch owner might suffer from a failure of the repairer to work further on a watch would not exceed $10.00. In practice, the only loss which threatens the repairer, if he fails to recognize the guarantee, is the loss of a customer and some increment of business good will. On the other hand, if the repairer chooses to recognize the guarantee, as most of them do, the owner is relieved, and the repairer creates a favorable impression as a responsible workman. Even in the absence of the present-day combination of watch repairing and various sales lines, the repairer has little to lose by taking the time to do an "N.C.," a no-charge job. Now, with the increasing emphasis upon sales on the side, the honoring of a guarantee becomes an asset insofar as it predisposes the watch owner, both by his presence in the store and by his closer and now "tested" relationship with the repairer, to make other purchases.

In summary, Riis's finding that 50 per cent of the repairers wanted to accept the test watch on some grounds unrelated to the immediate difficulty emerges in a new light. What Riis in his popular treatment considered unmitigated chicanery may be alternately viewed as an attempt to use a "clean-and-adjust" job, guarantee included, as a basis for regularizing the business relationship between the watch owner and the repairer.

The emergent business pattern is an amalgam of matters of *time* and the *city*. The old craftsman tradition, the new spare-parts technology, the owner's naïveté, the limited risk of the guarantee, and the similarity in causes of different watch failures are all intertwined in the technology of timekeeping. The threat of exploitative relations, and the anonymity arising from mobility and infrequent experience with specialized crafts are a part of the social complex of the city. The "one-year guarantee," serving as it does to meet different, but complementary, needs of the owner and repairer, causes standard costs to be charged for very different services. Noting the increasing use of the "clean-and-adjust, one-year guarantee" practice, and noting also the cost to a customer of collecting sufficient watch information to permit him to defend his claim to a particularized price, one doubts that this trend will be arrested. Despite the contrary predictions of competitive economic theory, it is believed that the present case constitutes a valid instance in which a matrix of social and technological factors now support, and will in the foreseeable future continue to support, a discriminatory pricing system.

27

# The Decline of the American Circus:
# The Shrinkage of an Institution *

*Marcello Truzzi*

Despite a growing literature on the subject of leisure,[1] comparatively little academic attention has been given to the social structure of the entertainment world.[2] A vast popular literature stresses the glamor and excitement of show business and its leading figures; yet sociologists have generally neglected examination of its specific subcultures, and the social changes undergone by these institutions. This is especially true of the lower ranking and more insulated sectors of this largely marginal and often normatively deviant set of subcultures. Although some sophisticated ethnographic attention has been given to the interna-

tional world of the gypsies,[3] little similarly detailed attention has been given to their analytic counterparts in the world of legitimate entertainment: carnivals and circuses.[4]

What has happened to the circus in America? What accounts for the demise of the massive spectacles that traversed the United States prior to this mid-century? Was the circus the victim of the same forces that "killed" vaudeville?[5] Or have both these one-time giant industries been transplanted to the world of television?

EDITOR

---

* Prepared especially for this volume, an earlier version of this paper was read at the Annual Meeting of the Eastern Sociological Society in New York City, April 15, 1967.

[1] E.g., Eric Larrabee and Rolf Meyersohn, eds., *Mass Leisure* (New York: The Free Press, 1958).

[2] Notable exceptions include: Sidney Wilhelm and Gideon Sjoberg, "The Social Characteristics of the Entertainer," *Social Forces*, XXXVII (1958), 71–76; David Dressler, "Burlesque as a Cultural Phenomenon," (Doctoral dissertation, New York University, 1937); and Jack R. Conrad, "The Bullfight: The Cultural History of an Institution," (Doctoral dissertation, Duke University, 1954).

[3] E.g., Jean-Paul Clébert, *The Gypsies*, trans. Charles Duff (New York: E. P. Dut-

ton & Co., Inc., 1963); and Jan Yoors, *The Gypsies* (New York: Simon and Schuster, Inc., 1967).

[4] These two worlds should be carefully distinguished. The circus is essentially an extension of theater, whereas the carnival is primarily an extension of the medieval fair; the functions and organizations of circus and carnival are quite different. See Witold Krassowski, "Social Structure and Professionalization in the Occupation of the Carnival Worker" (Master's thesis, Purdue University, 1954); and Marcello Truzzi, "The Circus as a Source of Folklore: An Introduction," *Southern Folklore Quarterly*, XXX (1966), 289–300.

[5] See Douglas Gilbert, *American Vaudeville: Its Life and Times* (New York: Dover Publications, Inc., 1963); and Abel Green

The social institution of the American Circus,[6] despite its great interest for students of Americana, has somehow been neglected by sociologists. This is the case despite its many unique variable characteristics which one would have thought might prove especially attractive, if only to the early Park and Burgess Chicago School which took special interest in the deviant subculture. As those within the subculture have long recognized, the true nature of this organizational structure has been heavily obscured by hosts of romanticized fictions and histories, especially by those circus fans who have sought to perpetuate knowledge of it.

The first problem in an analytic approach to this institution is its definition. Following the historians, as well as the folk classifications used by the members of circuses themselves, *a circus is a traveling and organized display of animals and skilled performances within one or more circular stages known as "rings" before an audience encircling these activities.* Thus, the American circus has included the great early Wild West Shows and excludes the carnival which, though it shares some early origins with the circus, is socially a

very distinct organization.[7] It might be added that, from the viewpoint of its employees, the circus very much resembles those varieties of Erving Goffman's *total institutions* which are established "better to pursue some worklike task and justifying themselves only on these instrumental grounds."[8]

Before an examination of the social conditions which brought about the disappearance of the circus from the American scene, be undertaken, it will be necessary to first present some information as to the scope and history of this institution. There have been over 1100 circuses and menageries in America since 1771.[9] By America we mean to include the United States, Canada, and Mexico. It would not be feasible here to distinguish these three countries' circuses because of frequent border crossings and difficulties in the data. A plotting of the frequencies of known American circuses from 1771 to 1956 reveals that the peak was in 1903, with some 98 circuses and menageries; by 1956 there were only 13 (see Figure 1). Except for some postwar rises, the pattern since 1903 has been one of clear decline. One might contend that although quantity of circuses had declined possibly the quality had risen. To some limited extent this was true. Many circus partnerships and amalgamations were involved which resulted in *The Greatest Show on Earth* (Ringling Bros., Barnum and Bailey Combined Shows); but it must be realized that this giant enterprise grew upon

and Joe Laurie, Jr., *Show Biz from Vaude to Video* (New York: Henry Holt and Company, 1951), pp. 268–84.

[6] The American circus is an "institution" in the sense used by L. T. Hobhouse, *Social Development* (London: George Allen & Unwin, 1924), p. 49; or by J. O. Hertzler, *Social Institutions* (New York: McGraw-Hill Book Company, Inc., 1929), p. 7; and not as used by T. Parsons, *The Social System* (New York: The Free Press, 1951), p. 39; or R. M. Williams, Jr., *American Society* (New York: Alfred A. Knopf, Inc., 1963), pp. 30–33. The circus might better be termed an "association," as used by R. M. MacIver and C. H. Page, *Society* (New York: Rinehart & Company, Inc., 1949), p. 15.

[7] Cf. William F. Mangels, *The Outdoor Amusement Industry* (New York: Vantage Press, 1952).

[8] Erving Goffman, *Asylums* (Garden City, N.Y.: Doubleday Anchor Books, 1961), p. 5.

[9] Cf. George L. Chindahl, *A History of the Circus in America* (Caldwell, Ohio: The Caxton Printers, Ltd., 1959), pp. 240–72.

the bankruptcies of its competitors; and even this tyrannosaurus has undergone depression since 1930, including its abandonment of the Big Top, Side Show, most of its menagerie, and all but its skeleton by 1957.

In the discussion which follows, much of our concern will be centered around the Ringling Circus. Although some circuses in America are older

have also, at various times, headed different circuses, e.g., Arthur Concello managed the Clyde Beatty and Cole Bros. Circus, the Russel Bros. Circus and the Ringling Show all within a five year period. Finally, it must also be understood that from the viewpoint of circus personnel, the Ringling Show was "the big one," the pace setter and example for the other

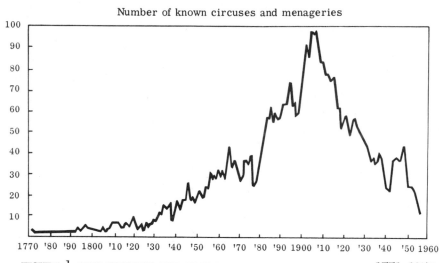

FIGURE 1. THE GROWTH AND DECLINE OF AMERICAN CIRCUSES, 1771–1956

Source: G. L. Chindahl, *A History of the Circus in America* (Caldwell, Ohio: The Caxton Printers, Ltd., 1959), pp. 240–72.

(e.g., Hunt Bros. Circus, which plays only the Northeastern United States), there is little social structural difference among circuses, partially because there is much mobility of persons among them. There is also a great historical overlap in management. Thus, there is not only a circus syndicate,[10] but the same persons

shows; and its condition had great effects in determining the perceived social situation of everyone in the circus world.

Our examination of the American Circus will lean heavily for its data upon:

1. interviews and participant observations;

[10] The current business syndicate which owns several circuses and controls the routing practices of others is very limited in its power compared to 1929 when John Ringling bought the American Circus Corporation and thus had title to almost all the circus property in the United States. Cf.

Marian Murray, *Circus! From Rome to Ringling* (New York: Appleton-Century-Crofts, Inc., 1956), p. 279. Circus syndicates have existed since the "Flatfoots" in 1830–1880. Cf. Earl Chapin May, *The Circus From Rome to Ringling* (New York: Dover Publications, Inc., 1963), pp. 40–48.

2. several journals and magazines devoted to circus history; [11]
3. route books published by various circuses;
4. historical surveys; [12] and
5. museum materials. [13]

## A Brief History of the Circus

The cultural diffusion which has produced what is the American Circus has been extremely complex. Origins of various circus acts have commonly been traced to the ancient Orient, early Greece and Rome, medieval fairs, and the Italian Commedia dell Arte. [14] The extensive geographical mobility of circus performers has given these essentially folk arts a widespread territorial diffusion despite the almost exclusive reliance upon oral transmission. Examination of the individual types of acts reveals their extensive connections with long chains of world-wide tradition as well as a complexity in technique that would seem to preclude independent invention. For example, juggling is far too complex—in its advanced form—to be easily developed without instructions in the techniques used to maximize the efficient manipulation of the objects, and some elements in this art are easily traceable to diverse cultures. Thus, the great Italian juggler Rastelli was much influenced by the ball manipulations of the Japanese juggler Takashima in England around 1910.

The true circus is usually designated by historians as originating in England in 1770 under the direction of Philip Astley, commonly spoken of as the Father of the Circus. It is from this beginning that one can directly trace all contemporary circuses, except possibly the Chinese Peking Circus (though some connections do exist). Astley developed the pattern of the one-ring circus, usually in a permanent building, that still dominates the European scene. There emerged a fandom that appreciated the sometimes subtle distinctions important for appraisal, e.g., a recognition of the rarity of the triple somersault, the juggling of nine balls, and the fact that a forward somersault on a tightwire is more difficult than a backward somersault.

The American Circus began following the European model under John Bill Ricketts in 1793. Following Astley, Ricketts, who was an excellent horseman who often rode with his friend George Washington, centered his circus around its equestrian elements. In this early period, it should be noted, it was not uncommon for

[11] *The White Tops* is a bimonthly magazine put out by The Circus Fans Association of America, founded in 1926. *The Bandwagon* is a monthly journal published by the Circus Historical Society, founded in 1939. An excellent listing of other articles and magazines dealing with the American Circus can be found in Chindahl, *History of the Circus*, pp. 277–79.

[12] Chindahl, *op. cit.*, is the major work dealing with the American Circus history. Two other works of especial importance are Murray, *op. cit.*, and the earlier May, *op. cit.*, originally published in 1932. Regarding the circus internationally, cf. Raymond Toole-Stott, *Circus and Allied Arts: A World Bibliography*, 3 volumes (Darby, England: Harpur, 1958–1962).

[13] Several noteworthy circus collections exist. Primary is the Ringling Museum of the American Circus in Sarasota, Florida. In addition, there are the Harry Hertzberg Collection in the San Antonio, Texas, Public Library; the New York Historical Society Collections; the Wisconsin State Historical Society Collection; the Circus World Museum; the Sauk County Historical Society at Baraboo, Wisconsin; the Miami County Historical Society at Peru, Indiana; and the Circus Hall of Fame at Sarasota, Florida.

[14] Cf. Murray, *Circus!*, pp. 29–77.

foreign circuses to visit America and American shows to go to Europe. During this time, the American Circus was, like its European counterpart, still viewed as an artistic and prestigeful one-ring display. In addition to Ricketts' semi-royal patronage from President George Washington,[15] one can also cite the command performances in Drury Lane for Queen Victoria in 1839 by Isaac A. Van Amburgh's Circus when it visited England.[16] Thus, during this early period, circus people enjoyed relatively high social status, unlike the later "gypsy" ascription of the 1900's.

The first landmark in the emergence of the uniquely American Circus was in 1830 when Aron Turner took his show out under a round tent 90 feet in diameter—the first such tent ever used.[17] The second major innovation—and the one which was to radically transform the American Circus—was the interjection of three rings under the Big Top in the Barnum and Bailey Circus of 1881.[18] The third element which distinguished the American Circus from the European was the rise of the railroad as its carrier. Although there were early experiments carried on with the railroad as early as 1853, the first Railroad Circus to make a transatlantic tour was Dan Castello's Circus and Menagerie in 1868.[19]

The period from 1871, when P. T. Barnum (then sixty-one and famous for his museums and hoaxes) was persuaded by W. C. Coup to go into the circus business, until about 1915 is usually referred to as the Golden Age of the Circus in America.[20] It was during this period that the rise of the great and massive circuses was seen as they dotted the nation (see Figure 1). And it was during this period that there rose and fell the magnificent circus parade with its miles of animals, bands, tableaux, forty-horse teams, gilded wagons (costing up to $40,000 each), and its closing trademark, the calliope.[21]

But with this Golden Age came the death of the European style of circus performance with its intimacy and audience of discriminating viewers.

. . . old timers are in agreement with many professionals that a great glory passed with the one-ring show; that split-second performances in which a dozen riders, acrobats or aerialists must time their routine so they can finish together on a whistle, have killed most of their artistry.[22]

But more important is the fact that it is impossible to see and appreciate the individual act with the intensity needed for discriminating its artistic worth. This problem was already noticeable in the first performance of the three-ring show of 1881. As the New York *Herald* noted:

The only drawback to the performance was that the spectator was compelled to receive more than his money's worth; in other words, that while his head was turned in one direction he felt he was losing something good in another.[23]

A shift had been made from the intimate art form of the European tradition to the massive and glittering spectacle and panorama of the *Greatest Show on Earth*.

Beginning with the passing of the circus parade following World War I, the frequency of these immense

[15] Cf. May, *Rome to Ringling*, pp. 15–22.
[16] Cf. Murray, *Circus!* p. 135.
[17] *Ibid.*, p. 131.
[18] *Ibid.*, p. 242.
[19] Cf. Chindahl, *History of the Circus*, pp. 88–89.
[20] Cf. May, *Rome to Ringling*, pp. 224–35; and Chindahl, *op. cit.*, pp. 118–57.

[21] As long as three miles, a pageant might move through the streets for five hours. Cf. Murray, *Circus!*, pp. 251–57.
[22] May, *op. cit.*, p. 226.
[23] Quoted in Murray, *op. cit.*, pp. 242–43.

enterprises has shown a sharp decline. By 1956 there were only two railroad shows as compared with at least thirty-eight in 1910, and only thirteen circuses as compared with at least ninety-eight in 1903 (see Figure 1). Today, the *Greatest Show on Earth*, the Ringling Bros., Barnum and Bailey Circus, is without its tents, the parade is gone, (though it was briefly and minutely revived by several minor circuses in the 1950's), and the menagerie is small. Though not yet dead, the American Circus is but a pale shadow of its former glory. Circus fans and performers might argue that the circus is not dying;[24] but in terms of the usual criteria by which circuses have been judged in the past (size of tent and menagerie, number of elephants and trains, etc.), and the decrease in the number of American circuses currently touring, there seems little doubt of decline.[25] One can argue that the American Circus has undergone metamorphoses and has been absorbed by other entertainment forms, but the American Circus of the Golden Age has not survived.

## The Shrinking of an Institution

Many statements have been made as to the causes of decline of the American Circus. Three events have frequently been suggested as causes:

1. the Hartford Fire of 1944,
2. the so-called "Hollywoodization" of the circus, and

3. the emergence of television as a competitive media.

A common belief among outsiders is an attribution of the decline in the American Circus to the great fire which set Ringling Bros. ablaze in 1944 at Hartford, Connecticut. This event resulted in the killing of 185 persons and the injury of some 450, thereby bringing lawsuits totaling some four million dollars. This argument has little explanatory value since: (1) circuses have all had a long history of fires, (2) the show went out the next season under a fire-proof canvas, and (3) the full four million dollars was paid off by 1951, entirely out of profits.

Many circus performers and fans attribute the decline to the "Hollywoodization" of the circus.[26] By "Hollywoodization" it is meant that the circus management has forgotten the circus' original sources of glamour and has substituted a facade of glittering music, ballet, and pseudo-sophisticated art through such devices as the incorporation of a George Balanchine ballet, music by Igor Stravinsky, and the singing of theme songs. However, as early as 1889 Barnum and Bailey gave a performance in the Olympia in London, followed by *Nero, or the Destruction of Rome,* a ballet directed by the famous master Imre Kiralfy, with over 1600 persons participating.[27] These critics also overlook the many songs, especially those sung by the then vocal clowns, heard in the early single ring.[28] Thus, though the current image is certainly

[24] E.g., cf. Roger Greene, "Who Says The 'Big Top' Is Coming Down? Not The Circus' Jack Mills," *Tampa Tribune* (Tampa, Fla.), July 9, 1956.
[25] The one exception would appear to be in the technical proficiency of many individual performers. Many "record breaking" feats have been performed in recent years. This is probably owing, to some extent, to a process of selectivity with regard to who can afford to remain in this institution.

[26] E.g., cf. Bill Ballantine, "How They Loused Up the Circus," *Saga*, XXIV (May, 1962), pp. 42f.; Ward Cannel, "Will Circus Become Chorus Line?" *Sarasota Journal* (Sarasota, Fla.), April 9, 1957.
[27] Cf., May, *Rome to Ringling*, p. 124.
[28] Cf. Fred D. Pfening, Jr., "Circus Songsters," *The Bandwagon*, VII (November-December, 1963), pp. 10–12.

contrary to the middle-period of American Circus history, much of these "new" elements is actually a return to the past and is therefore an unlikely contributor to the demise of the circus.

The importance of television, the most frequently cited cause of decline,[29] is certainly an important contributing factor—as are all competing media from movies to ice shows—but is probably much overestimated in its damage. The decline of the circus was well underway prior to the advent of nationwide television. Besides, the circus depends—unlike the movies which were hurt by television—upon its live presence.[30] Much of the circus' attraction has been in things like feeding the elephants, pink lemonade and cotton candy, and the immediate situational pleasures of the crowd. Television has certainly kept some people at home through its competitive attractions; but why should this affect the circus any more than it affects theatre and other live attractions, many of which are doing booming business?

Before one can understand the causes of decline, it is necessary to examine the unique nature of the American Circus and its sources of audience appeal. As we have noted in our brief historical survey, the American Circus had in 1881 initiated the now traditional three-ring form with its concentration upon spectacle and quantity. This change brought about consequences for the internal structure of the circus as well as for its relation to its audience.

Once the intimate performance was extinguished, the traditional criteria for values of excellence had to change. The performer no longer worked for rewards based on criteria set by other performers and a knowledgeable audience but for those of an anonymous mass who appreciated only the more superficial displays and the eye-staggering quantity of visual activity. Since the audience was the primary source of rewards (through their applause and attendance), the shift brought about internal changes in the circus hierarchy. In addition to the increase in work crews needed to put up and tear down the giant tents (the Big Top seated up to 20,000 persons), there were important shifts in performers' statuses. Most notable was the decline of the circus clown (now no longer vocal due to the immense arena) who at one time was at the top of the hierarchy of performers (e.g., the great talking clown Dan Rice earned $1,000 per week in the late 1860's, was made a honorary Colonel and aide to President Zachary Taylor, and ran for the Pennsylvania Senate) but soon became today's largely untalented actor at the bottom of the rank order.[31] It should be noted that the European circuses, which did not undergo this movement towards the spectacular, have largely maintained their old relation to their audience. And the clown still maintains an elite position in the European Circus.

What then have been the causes of shrinkage and decline? It is the argument of this paper that the death of the American Circus—like that of the dinosaur—has stemmed from the incompatability of its size with the mod-

---

[29] E.g., cf. "Clyde Beatty Says TV Hits Circus Badly," *Tampa Tribune* (Tampa, Fla.), June 13, 1956.

[30] This is highlighted by the reviews of the circus when it has been presented on television, e.g., John Crosby, "Simple Size of Circus Lost on Television Screen," *Tampa Morning Tribune*, August 3, 1956.

[31] An important exception was the rise to stardom of Emmett Kelly, the clown who brought status with him from areas outside the circus.

ernizing industrial world. This argument can best be presented through an examination of the effects upon the main elements of circus appeal and their respective symbols. The American Circus centered its reputation (especially as represented in its advertising and press coverage) around three major themes:

1. *the romantic mystique of the traveling community*, symbolized by the giant Big Top and also by the circus train;
2. *the panoramic spectacle*, symbolized by the circus parade; and
3. *the exotic and mysterious*, symbolized by the wild animals and the sideshow freaks.

### THE DEATH OF THE BIG TOP AND THE CIRCUS TRAIN

Since the Second World War, two conditions have forced the extinction of the circus Big Top, one socioeconomic and the other ecological: the rise of the labor union and the lack of large lots near the center of the city.

The status of the workingman in the American Circus was always exceedingly low. In addition to very low salaries (sometimes only five dollars a week plus room and board in the period after 1945) and very poor living conditions (sometimes two to a berth), interaction with performers was highly limited, and definite forms of segregation were maintained. For example, a canvas partition was maintained between artists-and-management and the workingmen in the cookhouse. These conditions attracted essentially a derelict variety of persons who were heavily exploited, especially through organized and routinized gambling which kept them poor but hopeful—a picture very contrary to the romantic image of the circus.

The attempted organization of the circus roustabout by the Teamsters Union, the subsequent picketing in 1956, the organization of a competitive union circus, and further difficulties with the performers' union (the American Guild of Variety Artists) all added to increasing costs and overhead and eventually led to the Ringling Show's abandonment of the Big Top in 1957.[32]

Even prior to this, the urbanization of American cities was having an effect. Interviews with management figures reveal that routing of circuses had itself become a major problem since World War II.[33] The problem was two-fold:

1. to obtain a lot large enough to locate many tents, equipment, and customers' automobiles; and
2. to be located in such a manner as to make crowd attendance optimal through maximum audience comforts such as toilets and water.

Both of these conditions are swiftly becoming impossible.

The decline of the Railway Circus has occurred for several related reasons:

1. the declining condition of the railways themselves,
2. the development of highway systems which have made transport by truck cheaper, and
3. the lack of massive equipment in the contemporary circus, which previously

---

[32] Although our reference here is to the Ringling Show, the same problems were and are vexing other circuses, e.g., Murray Powers, "Circuses Return in '57—Under New Conditions," *Sarasota Herald Tribune* (Sarasota, Fla.), September 15, 1957, p. 33; and Chindahl, *History of the Circus*, pp. 224–28.

[33] A study of circus route patterns and changes is currently being undertaken. For a concise statement on this problem, cf. Henry Ringling North and Alden Hatch, *The Circus Kings* (New York: Dell Publishing Co., Inc., 1964), p. 304.

depended upon railway transportation. In 1965 there was not a single full train being used by a circus in America.

## THE DEMISE OF THE CIRCUS PARADE

The Golden Age of the Circus Parade was roughly from 1888 to 1904. These massive spectacles were discontinued by Barnum and Bailey in 1905, and by the end of World War I, they were evident only with some very minor tented establishments. Historians have generally attributed the end of the parade to the rise of the automobile:

Automobiles began to clog our city streets. They brought more show customers from greater distances than had horses and buggies or railroad excursions but they also interfered with circus teams, made progress slower between trains and lot, cut into and broke up the street parade.[34]

And:

By the early 1920's the big circuses had found street parades impracticable. As the number of motor cars increased, and urban centers grew more crowded, to move through the traffic of any city became more and more difficult. Performers resented the tiresome trek along the streets, especially if they were about to take part in two shows, in which they often risked their lives, in stunts made infinitely more dangerous by fatigue. When a train was late, preparations were delayed and possibly the parade itself was late getting under way.[35]

An additional related element was the use of license fees required by the cities (largely justified by the necessities of traffic control), which finally grew exorbitant.

[34] May, *Rome to Ringling*, p. 234.
[35] Murray, *Circus!*, p. 257.

## THE DISAPPEARANCE OF THE EXOTIC

With the advent of modern mass education and the opening of the space age, Americans no longer can see the once "Blood Sweating Behemoth" as anything more than a hippopotamus. The emergence of many city zoos, and the advent of mass communications no longer allow us the same sense of the novel which thrilled our grandfathers. In addition to greater sophistication, we have also found ourselves amidst a host of competitive technological miracles which often dwarf a mere elephant or gorilla. The cornerstone of the American Circus audience—the rube —has largely disappeared. And as for the sideshow freak, not only has he no longer the attraction of the mysterious for today's entertainment seeker, but such unfortunate persons are largely becoming obsolete through the skills of medical science.[36]

Thus we see that the American Circus, in rejecting its European model with its stress upon the individual performance as an art to be appreciated by an audience attuned to its nature, invested its resources instead upon a grand spectacle which though it thrilled its audience, soon found itself outgrown. The continuing success of the European—and especially the Soviet—Circus, both through visits to this country and through television viewing has demonstrated that the American public still enjoys this form of entertainment. If these successes can be taken as indicators, it seems possible that the American Circus may revive once more but under a format more reminiscent of its early origins.

[36] Cf. John Lentz, "Passing of the Side Show," *Today's Health*, XLII (March, 1964), pp. 48–51.

# PART X

# Terminating Processes

The following two processes deal with the social significance of what we have, for want of a better term, called the *terminating processes;* for they inevitably must follow the close of one's days, and of one's life. These two universal facts of man's biological existence have important, and somewhat neglected (especially in the case of sleep) consequences for man's social order. Whereas sleep constitutes a temporary withdrawal from social interaction, death constitutes a permanent one. And yet, these two processes are somewhat alike in their implications for man's social organization; for in both instances, societies must make adjustments for the systematic cessation of activities by some of its members while others continue. The maintenance of the social system must be considered; and, although the specific functional methods of adaptation might be varied, the organizational problems are similar. Awareness of this similarity—in addition to the obvious fact of unconsciousness of the actors—is reflected in man's many comments on death and sleep. Two great poets have captured the point:

> How wonderful is Death,
> Death and his brother Sleep!
> One pale as yonder wan and hornèd moon,
> With lips of lurid blue,
> The other glowing like the vital morn,
> When throned on ocean's wave
> It breathes over the world:
> Yet both so passing strange and wonderful!
> —Percy Bysshe Shelley
> *The Daemon of the World*

All life death does end and each day dies with sleep.

> —Gerard Manley Hopkins
> *No Worst, There is None*

# 28

# Sleep: A Sociological Interpretation *†

*Vilhelm Aubert* and *Harrison White*

"Night, having Sleep, the brother of Death. From whose eyelids also as they gazed dropped love." This beautiful cryptic passage in Hesiod[1] seems full of unexplored meanings, some of which must concern even a sociologist. To face "the brother of Death" once a day is certainly not a trivial task, nor one which the individual can manage alone, without social support, no more than he can face death itself alone, without funeral ceremonies, rituals of bereavement, or philosophies of the passing away. The social nothingness of sleep, implied by the comparison with death, points to a universal, recurrent absence of interaction. Sleep represents the most common case of social isolation, thereby providing us with a continuous experimental situation organized around the theme night and day. Hesiod, however, did not restrict

his perspective to the nothingness of sleep. He connected the state with love, just as our own vernacular does.

Let us be clear about the starting point: Sleep is a physiological state, a biological necessity. So are sex, reproduction, illness, eating, aging and physical pain. The physiological nature of these other states, however, has not prevented scientists from demonstrating that the manner in which they are enacted, and the ways in which they impinge upon society are legitimate sociological concerns. Such is our task with sleep, to demonstrate that it is *more* than a straightforward biological activity.[2] The

* Reprinted from *Acta Sociologica*, IV, No. 2 (1959), 46–54, and IV, No. 3 (1959), 1–16, by permission of the publisher. Footnotes renumbered.

† While this paper was being prepared for publication, Kaspar Naegele sent us a draft on sleep in a sociological perspective. Like our paper, it originated at the Center for Advanced Study in the Behavioral Sciences, Stanford, Calif.

[1] *The Theogony*. Line 910. This and most of the following literary references are from Bartlett, *Familiar Quotations*. Cf. also Richard Broxton Onians, *The Origins of European Thought. About the Body, the Mind, the Soul, the World, Time and Fate* (Cambridge: 1954), p. 422.

[2] The need for doing so becomes clear when, for example, in *Time Budgets of Human Behavior* (Cambridge: Harvard University Press, 1939), P. Sorokin and C. Berger dismiss the portion of time spent on sleep as of only physiological significance. In their statistical tables on pages 192–97 in which the number of hours of participation in each given activity is broken down according to types of motivation, to sizes of participating group, and to types of social interaction involved, the entries opposite the sleep heading are left blank. We find the same blindness to the significance of sleep as a core activity of the family in the empirical monograph, *Housing Needs of Western Farm Families*, U.S. Department of Agriculture (Washington, D.C., 1952): Sleep is not even given a heading as a Household Activity. Herbert Spencer, however, did include "Ideas of Sleep and Dreams" among his "Data of Sociology," in *The Principles of Sociology* (New York, 1893), I, 132–42.

thesis of this paper is that human sleep is an important social event.

If we return to the literary tradition for a moment, it seems that the great poets and writers have been much concerned with sleep, and have adopted philosophical and social viewpoints relative to the state. Hesiod was only one among the first, known writer to clothe his worry about "the brother of Death" in poetical language.[3]

Cervantes developed another theme, the democratic nature of sleep: "Now blessings light on him that first invented this same sleep! It covers a man all over, thoughts and all, like a cloak; 'tis meat for the hungry, drink for the thirsty, heat for the cold, and cold for the hot. 'Tis the current coin that purchases all the pleasures of the world cheap; and the balance that sets the king and the shepherd, the fool and the wise man even." [4]

But sleep has also been viewed as reward for deserving conduct. The Psalmist put it this way: "He giveth his beloved sleep." [5] The aspect of social sanction is also fairly clear when the Ecclesiastes says: "The sleep of a labouring man is sweet. . . . But the abundance of the rich will not suffer him to sleep." [6] A very forceful expression of the idea that lack of sleep is a punishment for evil is given in Macbeth.[7]

The literary tradition suggests that to fall asleep is—in part at least—a motivated act, and that the idea of

sleep has been bestowed with moral, that is social, connotations. The normal state of sleep means to occupy a culturally determined role which includes the behavior in the transitional periods before and after physiological sleep. The right to enter the state with full privileges furthermore is assumed to depend upon achievements in the state of wakefulness.

Sometimes an individual may fall asleep as an autonomic reaction to great exhaustion. Usually, however, falling asleep is not the fulfilling of an immediate biological need, but a result of activities bearing many overt symptoms of role-playing. Sarbin's characterization of the hypnotic process applies well to falling asleep: "In the hypnotic experiment the subject tries to take the role of the hypnotized person; the success of his striving is a function of favorable motivation, role perception, and role-taking aptitude." [8] As concerns role perception, it is rather more than less likely to be adequate in the case of the sleeper than in the case of the hypnotized person.

Going to sleep means going through a number of culturally defined motions, such as dressing in a certain way, modifying light and sound conditions, assuming one of a limited number of postures, closing one's eyes even in darkness, expressing certain emotions and attitudes towards others, and so on. These motions, together with the perceptions of the actual state of sleep, and motions associated with awakening constitute the role

[3] Cf., in Bartlett, quotations from Homer, Sophocles, Plutarch, Leonardo da Vinci, Bartholomew Griffin, Shelley, Aristophanes, Swinburne, Shakespeare, Tennyson, John Donne, Philip Freneau, Byron.

[4] Don Quixote, Part II, Book IV, Chapter 68, p. 898.

[5] The Bible: Psalms, 127:2.

[6] The Bible: Ecclesiastes, 3:12.

[7] Shakespeare, Macbeth, Act II, Sc. 2, lines 36 ff.

[8] Theodore R. Sarbin, "Contributions to Role-Taking Theory: I. Hypnotic Behavior," Psychological Review, LVII (1950), 255–70. Cf. also R. W. White, "A Preface to the Theory of Hypnotism," Journal of Abnormal and Social Psychology, XXVI (1941), 477–505; André M. Weitzenhoffer, Hypnotism. An Objective Study in Suggestibility (New York and London, 1953), pp. 91 ff.

of the sleeper. Since childhood most people have been trained to take this role, often with great difficulty. The training of children shows beyond any doubt that sleep at the proper place and time is not a process which is being left to be determined by biological needs alone.

The concept of role-playing is usually based upon the notion that incumbents of positions respond with consciousness to expectations from the social environment. This notion applies to peripheral sleep activities, but apparently not to the content of deep sleep. Dreams are the most significant events occurring during deep sleep. To what extent are they socially meaningful events, in the sense that they constitute a response to preceding social interaction, or become meaningful in subsequent social reality?

The existence of dreams presents man with several large philosophical issues. The most important one is the settlement of the reality of dreams. Which one is the real world, against which to measure the other one, that which we experience when awake or that which we experience when asleep? [9] It needs no elaboration that the way in which this problem is settled has wide social ramifications. What may be less obvious is that the way in which the problem is settled is—partly—determined by culture, by socially shared norms and beliefs. Our culture gives a rather definite answer to the question: The world we experience and manipulate in our waking life is the real world; and the world of the dreams is unreal and irrational. Several non-literate cultures, however, give a different answer. "Thus the Ashanti assume that, if a

man dreams of having sexual intercourse with another man's wife, he will be fined the usual adultery fee, for his soul and hers have had sexual intercourse." [10] Here the assumption of reality is closely connected with the idea of responsibility for the content of dreams. This contrasts sharply with a much used phrase within Western culture: "The one who sleeps does not sin." Other non-literate cultures deal with the world of dreams in philosophical terms analogous to those of the Ashanti. Still others have interpreted dreams as having a meaning, not in relation to everyday, profane, reality, but as events taking place in the realm of a supernatural reality, toward which man is supposed to respond actively also in everyday waking life. In other words, the assumption that waking life is real while life in dreams is unreal seems to be culturally determined to some extent, and not a necessary derivation from the inherent physiological properties of the states of sleep and wakefulness. [11]

We propose that the validity, reality, and responsibility associated by a culture with the supernatural sleep world of dreams are in part a reflection of the contemporary social structure. We mean by validity the degree to which events in the sleep world are perceived as a true guide to the waking world; by reality the extent to which the sleep world is perceived as cut of the same cloth as the waking world; and by responsibility the extent to which individuals are rewarded and sanctioned for events in

[9] For a classic statement of the problem, cf. Blaise Pascal, *Gedanken* (Stuttgart: Reclam, 1956), pp. 121–22.

[10] Ralph L. Woods, ed., *The World of Dreams. An Anthology* (New York: 1947).

[11] Cf. Sigmund Freud, *The Interpretation of Dreams* (London and New York: 1932); and Erich Fromm, *The Forgotten Language. An Introduction to the Understanding of Dreams, Fairy Tales and Myths* (New York: 1951).

the sleep world. These three general attributes vary strikingly from culture to culture: among the Ojibwa, children are encouraged to develop pleasant dreams which may foretell reality,[12] while we have lost belief in the direct validity of dreams; the Tikopia sleep in sex-avoidant positions in the buildings of female deities [13] and the Rwala assert the danger of being made an idiot by a full night's exposure to the sleep world,[14] but the Woleaians attribute no reality to dreams;[15] the Ashanti have reputedly killed men for what occurred in their dreams [16] while the Tikopia do not punish even killing by a man awakened from sleep by visions.[17] Furthermore, these three attributes apparently can vary independently, and in particular, reality and responsibility do not necessarily go together as we can see from the Tikopia. Certainly the general nature attributed to the sleep world is tied to religion and other elements in contemporary culture. But we assert that often this nature directly reflects the social structure. In our society we deny the validity, reality, and responsibility of sleep life. And in our society the achievement norm ranks high. According to this pattern, the justification of social actions is to be made by reference to intersubjectively test-

able performances or experiences by the actor, not by reference to inherent personal qualities or cues from the divinities. Since dreams are exempt from intersubjective testability they form a poor basis for social actions of modern men, and tend to be classified as invalid, unreal events for which the actor is not accountable.

The raw material for dreams is in part taken from waking social life, the "day-rest" of Freud. Stresses inherent in the statuses of individuals will be expressed in dreams and, since the sleeper is relatively blameless, he may experience unacceptable and original solutions to waking conflicts. The degree to which this may provide a guidance carried into social interaction depends upon other aspects of the philosophical definitions of dreams and the role of the sleeper. It may do so by making the actor aware of his own motives relative to others or by making him directly mention the dream as a mild social sanction of others.

Even if dreams are interpreted as invalid descriptions of outer reality, they may be conceived of as reliable experiences of the inner world of the sleeper, providing insights possibly denied the person when awake. This raises the question of the value assessment of the dream content. Are dreams expressions of man's irrational and evil aspects or do they represent what is good and insightful? Both points of view have been maintained among philosophers and psychologists, probably corresponding to a parallel duality in folk theories.[18]

Both the expectation that sleep brings out the best and that it brings out the worst in men, present social problems, in the first case mainly associated with falling asleep, in the

[12] F. Densmore, *Chippewa Customs*, Bulletin No. 86, Bureau of American Ethnology (Washington, D.C.: 1929), p. 60.

[13] R. Firth, *The Work of the Gods in Tikopia* (London: London School of Economics, 1940), p. 65.

[14] A. Musil, "The Manners and Customs of the Rwala Bedouins," *Oriental Explorations and Studies*, No. 6, p. 412 (New York: American Geographical Society, 1928).

[15] L. Wyman, *American Anthropologist*, XXXVIII (1936), 651.

[16] Woods, *op. cit.*

[17] E. E. Evans Pritchard, ed., *Essays Presented to C. G. Seligman* (London: Paul, Trench, Trubner & Co., 1934), p. 67.

[18] Cf. Freud, *Interpretation of Dreams;* and Fromm, *Forgotten Language.*

latter case mainly associated with awakening. ". . . in all of us, even in good men, there is a lawless wild-beast nature, which peers out in sleep," said Plato. This may obviously cause—or support—conflicts about falling asleep, just as theories of the sinfulness of sex cause—or support—sexual conflicts. In the fear of the lawless wild beast may lie one of the roots of insomnia, a deviance from the normal sleep pattern, usually interpreted as a disease subject to medical treatment.[19]

If the optimistic theory of dream contents is accepted, it may in our society present conflicts over leaving the role of the sleeper, moving from good to worse. If dreams have given new self-insights, which demand action, how is one to find grounds on which to act, since dreams do not furnish legitimation in socially shared experiences? The new psychological theories of dreams, with a positive colouring, may derive support from the increased emphasis upon perception of the self as a significant element of any actor's social reality.

The transitions to and from the physiological state of sleep are perceived as hazardous, in part due to the cultural definition of the role of the sleeper. The possible fears can crudely be classified as: fear of death or not awakening; fear of separation from the everyday world and loneliness; fear of helplessness and passivity; fear of unacceptable inner impulses; fear of insomnia. These fears are in part assuaged by the social structures surrounding sleep, to which we shall return later; and by soothing cultural patterns, like lullabies for children and night-prayer. The Chagga of Tanganyika sleep with their heads pointed to Mt. Kibo,[20] and the Tikopia sleep on the graves of their ancestors,[21] examples of semi-religious practices thought to ensure safe sleep. The artifacts of sleep such as night clothes and bedding, and approved postures of sleep may be reviewed as reassuring ritual patterns, called forth by the latent fears which may be aroused by the imminency of sleep.

From the point of view of the sleeper the culturally established kinship with death is a disturbing one. From the point of view "memento mori", it is a soothing and clarifying notion. Assuming that death requires social structuring and learning in order to be accepted, we may view the bed as a training ground for dying; in the words of Browne:

Sleep is a death; oh make me try
By sleeping, what it is to die,
And as quietly lay my head
On my grave, as now my bed! [22]

A quiet death, and the dying person's resignation to his inevitable fate, appear to be highly valued in our culture by the bereaved ones.

The notion of sleep as a model of death, the new awakening, and immortality, may possibly be carried one step further. The diurnal cycle, with sleep as a focal point, furnishes a miniature model of the life-cycle, of being born, maturing, aging and dying. Such an over-all perspective on life, anchored in more concrete experiences, seems necessary in relation to man's long-term activities and social co-ordination in terms of roles appropriate to various stages in the life cycle.

[19] Cf. papers by Conn, Gilman, Karpman, and London in *Journal of Clinical Psychopathology*, XI, No. 2 (1950).

[20] O. Raum, *Chagga Childhood* (London: Oxford University Press, 1940).

[21] R. Firth, *We, The Tikopia* (London: George Allen & Unwin, 1936), pp, 77, 90.

[22] Sir Thomas Browne, *Religio Medici*, Part 2, Sect. XII.

These considerations evoke a different problem, the phenomenology of time spent awake and asleep. All societies have some concept of time and apply it to phenomena viewed consciously. This subjective perception of time, however, seems to break down in the state of sleep. There seems to be in our culture a fundamental ambiguity in the perception of time from the point of view of the sleeper. A night may appear like an eternity; but it may also appear as no more than a moment's unconsciousness. For other cultures in which the homogenous time of the clock and Newton is not so much or at all imbedded, the contrast between the perception of time when awake and asleep may not be so great.

Sleep and wakefulness, night and day, may be perceived differently—even from the outside—as scenes for the unfolding of time as a historical process. Daytime is in some sense cumulative. The perception of self and others as growing, developing or, at least, aging, seems to refer to daytime, or time spent awake, and ignores, by and large, time spent in sleep. Sleep-time is predominantly non-cumulative, almost withdrawn from the process of growth and aging. It is, we surmise, perceived in static terms, as a scene of life to which one returns "in the same place" over and over again. Comparing the two images of time, the irreversibly vanishing stream and the monotonously recurring pointer enclosed by the circle of the clock,[23] the former image appears more associated with daytime, the latter image more with sleep-time—the wasted time. By this cultural definition, sleep-time becomes a redeemer from the fears associated with the inevitable passing of time and the definitive loss of the past, "le temps perdu." In more than one sense sleep represents an encounter with the past, a recurrent regression,[24] whereas daytime impresses upon actors the necessity to decide on what to leave behind as parts of an incontrovertible past.

The qualitative break in time concepts between night and day places a formidable social barrier between two successive days and the social activities they encompass. The proper way to approach this cyclical aspect of social systems may be in terms of Parson's "latency phase".[25] We need a notion of this kind to explain that social relationships are different after a period of no interaction from what they would have been without this passed time, apparently void of social content. Phenomenologically this is expressed in most cultures in the idea that to awaken from sleep is to begin afresh, to start a new segment of activity with the past partially cancelled. Since sleep is in a different kind of time, each day's events tend to have their own origin and significance, something more than merely filling in a section in an endless stream of events.

We may possibly view sleep as a communion rite in which minor sins and cares are washed away. Among

[23] Cf. Alfred Schuetz, "On Multiple Realities," *Philosophy and Phenomenological Research*, V (1944–45), 533–76, especially 540; Hubert Griggs Alexander, *Time as Dimension and History* (Albuquerque: The University of New Mexico Press, 1945), pp. 6–7; Pierre Auger, "Two Times, Three Movements," *Diogenes*, No. 19 (1957), 1–17.

[24] Cf. Freud's theory of sleep as a narcissistic regression to the mother's womb. B. D. Lewin, "Sleep, Narcissistic Neurosis, and the Analytic Situation," *Psychoanalytic Quarterly*, XXIII (1954), 487–510.

[25] T. Parsons, R. Bales, and E. Shils, *Working Papers in the Theory of Action* (New York: The Free Press, 1953), p. 185.

the Aleuts there is sometimes ceremonial bathing upon awakening.[26] There are an abundance of adages pointing in a similar direction: "Tomorrow is another day"; "He got out of the wrong side of the bed this morning." The social function of this cultural theme is probably to introduce greater flexibility into behavior, and providing a mechanism for reducing both guilt and need of self-defence. Without a loss of status, an actor may start on a new sequence of behavior, even if it violates the norms which he seemed to support on the previous day when interaction went into the latency phase. He "has slept on it" and started "a new day".

With sleep goes irresponsibility for perception and action, in our culture. This gives sleep and night-time a specific function in relation to innovation and creativity. Many artists, and some scientists, claim to have made important creative strides during sleep or in the peripheral zones of sleep.[27] No doubt this is related to the physiological process of relaxation. However, cultural definitions play their part, too. It appears, namely, that creative workers have shown an unusually high preference for night as the proper time for work, that is, for activities in full consciousness. If we assume that the relationship between this choice and the creative productions is more than incidental, it may be by virtue of a definition of night-time, bestowing upon it a social atmosphere in which demands for conformity and protection of status are greatly lowered.

Sleep is, also in a different sense, defined as the proper time for creativity, namely with respect to sex. The association of sexual life with night-time, although deeply rooted in our culture, is not a universal one. Ford and Beach have discovered, on the basis of cross-cultural material, great variations between different societies in this respect.[28] The material suggests that practical considerations, connected with conditions of privacy, determine in part the preference for night or day as the proper time for love-making. We doubt, however, that narrow practical considerations alone can account for the fairly universal association, in our culture, between sex, the bed, sleep and night-time.

We shall approach this cultural link from two sides. Let us start with a consideration of the surreptitious, "deviant" nature of sexual life. By this, we mean something more than that sexual life to so many people, under a variety of "illicit" circumstances has come to be defined as a sin. We make the wider claim that, for even more general and profound reasons, sexual union is surreptitious in the sense that it is surrounded by an unusual amount of secrecy, in the form of modesty, and circumlocutions in references, etc. The secret aspect of sex tends to associate it with the night, for some people to the extent that they depend upon darkness as a condition of performing intercourse.[29] More generally, the night with its rigid and predictable patterns of contact and isolation (a point to which we shall return later) provides the proper social structure for the per-

[26] I. Venamionov, *Notes on the Islands of the Unalaska District* (St. Petersburg: Russian-American Company, 1840), pp. 109–10.

[27] B. Ghiselin, ed., *The Creative Process* (New York: Mentor Books, 1955), pp. 36, 44, 64, 82, 85, 124; J. Maritain, *Creative Intuition in Art and Poetry* (New York: Meridian, 1955), pp. 88–89.

[28] C. S. Ford and F. A. Beach, *Patterns of Sexual Behavior* (New York: Harper & Brothers, 1951).

[29] Cf. A. C. Kinsey, *et al.*, *Sexual Behavior in the Human Male* (Philadelphia: 1948), pp. 664–65.

formance of any activity to which norms of secrecy are attached. Another concept, of sleep-time as an institutionally protected time reservoir, gives additional weight to the established association. For most adult persons the day is crowded with expected activities. Any expenditure of time that would interfere with work, household chores, expected sociability, or participation in public affairs, demands explicit legitimation. Now, although love is a central value in our culture, love-making is still too private, too secret, even in marriage, to furnish ready-made legitimation. The very private nature of sexual contacts makes them poor competitors with the more robustly social activities of modern man. Here, the association with sleep-time affords a legitimation, since sleep is an activity which is readily legitimated even under conditions far from physical exhaustion, and a state which is highly protected.

The latter point needs some elaboration. Evidence from many cultures suggests that sleep is institutionalized as a state or a role with high priority, given fulfilment of the proper conditions of time and place. The form of interaction with those in sleep is defined as avoidant [30] and takes high precedence over other social relationships. It means that usually the sleeper is not awakened in order to assume a different role in interaction. The Navaho believe that evil is brought by even stepping over a sleeping person.[31] Among the Bedouin Rwala "a culprit while asleep cannot be killed

by an avenger since this would bring vengeance on the latter's own head." [32] Parents usually have tender feelings toward their sleeping children, while also respecting the inviolability of the sleep state.[33]

Let us now return to the association between sleep and sex, and mention a second type of consideration which may help to explain the phenomenon. The component of a person's status known as residence, which identifies the person with a definite spatial location, is given by the normal sleeping location. A person "lives" where he sleeps. This seems to apply to Western society and to the primitive societies we have surveyed,[34] where adequate information was available. One exception is typified by the temporary factory laborers in large Indian cities who consider themselves as "living" in the villages from which they came, and not in their frequently changing sleep locations, sometimes in the streets.[35]

[30] Avoidant relationships "de-emphasize direct contacts and . . . conduct such as exist on a relatively formal basis." M. Levy, *The Structure of Society* (Princeton, N.J.: Princeton University Press, 1952), p. 353.

[31] C. Kluckhohn and D. Leighton, *The Navaho* (Cambridge: Harvard University Press, 1946), p. 47.

[32] A. Musil, "Rwala Bedouins," p. 496.

[33] Cf. Ibsen's play *"Kongsemnerne,"* where the duke, Skule, watching—alone—the cradle of his daughter's son, the prince, who is an obstacle to his own royal ambitions, exclaims: "There is protection in sleep" (*Det er vern i søvnen*).

[34] The societies we took up, in the Yale Human Relations Area File, are in Asia the Khasi, Lolo, Miao and Toda; in Africa the Chagga, Mbundu, Thonga, Twi, Tiv and Azande; in the Middle East the Rwala; in North America the Navaho, Aleut, Copper Eskimo, Iroquois, Southeast Salish and Ojibwa; in Oceania the Pukapuka, Samoa, Tikopia and Woleai; in Russia the Samoyed, Yakut, Chukchee, Kamchadal, Koryak; and in South America the Siriono, the Cuna, the Jivaro and the Tupinamba. We refer to the original monographs in the footnotes to specific items used in the body of this paper; only those which received an evaluation of "excellent" from the File Analyst were used for references.

[35] K. Davies, *The Population of India and Pakistan* (Princeton, N.J.: Princeton University Press, 1948).

Now, the nuclear family is in most societies organized around the criterion of residence. An important, actually one of the most stable, functions of the family is the provision of a common sleeping group for its members. On the other hand, the communal sleeping is doubtless one of its great cohesive forces; in the modern suburban families, living in sleep-towns, it may become the single remaining task around which the family members order themselves in interaction. From these considerations it follows that sexual unions will tend to be restricted to the family group, that is to husband and wife.

The close association between sleeping arrangements and family structure tends to support the taboo which, for different reasons, exists against extramarital sexual relations, against "sleeping with" somebody outside the family. Also in this respect, the cultural structuring of sleep tends to protect the family from sources of friction. The proverbial sexual exploits of men who sleep outside their family, like seamen and traveling salesmen, illustrate the thesis.

We have been dealing with the night as the proper time for surreptitious activities, whether they consist in sexual activity or cultural innovation. But night-time is even more massively defined as the time for evil and crime. From the division of forces by the Essenes in the Sons of Darkness and the Sons of Light [36] to the tremendously popular thriller about Dr. Jekyll and Mr. Hyde, this notion is so deep-rooted, that it may appear completely trivial that the day should have positive moral connotations and the night negative ones.[37] Linked to

this are, however, more concrete and less trivial associations both of criminal and of police activities with the night. In many societies the police actually developed from the paid night-watchman. It is also apparent that night and day make for different relations between the citizen and the agents of the Law. For the police to accost a person in daytime a specific, explicit legitimation is required. At night the burden of proof shifts. The usual presumption of innocence lacking overt evidence of crime seems often to be reversed by the police to the presumption of suspicious intentions on the part of people up and about in the middle of the usual sleep period. Curfews are linked to the same institutional complex.

It has already been mentioned that the state of sleep has very often been given a religious significance. In most cultures the sleep role is conceived as one in which interaction with the supernatural world is expected, both through dreams and otherwise. There are exceptions such as the Woleaian culture of Micronesia,[38] but the anthropological reports on most of the societies we surveyed indicate a variety of such beliefs about sleep, which are also present in early Western society in similar form. We can recog-

---

[36] A. Powell Davies, *The Meaning of the Dead Sea Scrolls* (New York: Signet Books, 1956), pp. 21–22.

[37] There are, however, strains in our culture which support the notion that the night may be the scene for enactment of what is "real" and "moral" while the day time scene presents us with the unreal or only apparently real, and with the immoral or distorted. Thus some Norwegian fairytales describe princes who are themselves during the night, but are doomed to appear as polar bears or other animals in the daytime. Cf. in P. C. Asbjörnsen and J. Moe, *Folke og Huldreeventyr*, I (Oslo, 1928), pp. 164–72, the tale "Östenfor sol og vestenfor måne"; this in contrast to stories of humans who are werewolves during the night.

[38] M. Spiro, *Ifaluk: A South Sea Culture* (Pacific Science Board, National Research Council, 1949), p. 96.

nize two major types of interaction with an invisible world in sleep. There is communication through dreams, of which the sleeper is aware at the time and which he may remember specifically after awakening. Second, there is interaction of which the sleeper is not aware but which he is taught to infer from general knowledge and the course of events. For example, among the Navaho during the long magic rite for illness the patient can't sleep or bad spirits would "win back the chant." [39] Sleep may also be viewed as a medium through which interaction with other people takes place, as for example when one attempts to induce sickness or nightmares through sleep spirits in another person.[40]

In order to assess the religious function of dreams we shall take as a given that all known cultures (except possibly the emerging communist civilizations) reckon with a supernatural world as a vital sphere of existence. It raises serious "technical" problems, however, to communicate with this world, especially to receive messages about which one may feel reasonably secure that they do not originate in everyday profane existence. All intermediaries, priests, medicine men, shamans, magicians, are under suspicion of polluting messages with profane motives or interpretation. It appears to us that there are only two means of communication which have a logical structure that distinguishes them clearly from profane messages: chance devices [41] and dreams. By the very physiological

nature of sleep and even more by virtue of its social structuring, sleep experiences, dreams, appear to be experiences of a different order from daytime secular life. Dreams give, as it were, the raw material for construction of elaborate theories of supernatural communication, culminating in dream books or dream codes [42] which determine how dream messages are to be translated as guidance to secular activities.

Dreams, as a kind of divination or contact with gods and spirits of the ancestors, are doubtless the most important factor bestowing positive value upon sleep. From this assumption derives the emphasis upon training and preparation for sleep and dreams. From anthropological reports it is known that people in many cultures go through elaborate preparations in order to secure dreams of a prescribed content, as a requirement for an initiation rite or as a means of divination connected with illness, crimes or witchcraft. Especially the candidate for the role of shaman may "work" very hard in order to induce the proper dreams at the appropriate time and place.[43] The relative success of these exertions indicate that dreams should properly be viewed as a learned activity, and not only in the very indirect, hard to trace, fashion suggested by orthodox Freudian dream theory.

If the learning approach applies to specific dream contents, it should do so even more to the formal structure of dreams. One should think that the validity and reality attributed to

---

[39] L. Wyman, in *American Anthropologist*, XXXVIII (1936), 650.

[40] E.g., see R. East, ed., *Akiga's Story* (London: Oxford University Press, 1939), p. 118.

[41] Cf. V. Aubert, "Change in Social Affairs," *Inquiry*, II (1959), 1–24.

[42] For an example cf. T. A. Sebeok and F. J. Ingeman, *Studies in Cheremis: The Supernatural* (New York, 1956), pp. 269–79.

[43] G. Devereux, "Dream learning and individual ritual differences in Mohave shamanism," *American Anthropologist*, LIX (1957), 1036–45.

dreams contribute to determine the amount of detail, precision and orderliness experienced in dreams. It seems possible that the blurred, distorted, illogical nature of the dreams of Western man is linked to the social uselessness of his dreams, in contrast to the practical usefulness of dreams in most primitive societies. If this is a sound way of reasoning one might also guess that modern dreams spring from even deeper, more infantile and irrational layers of the personality than those of primitive men. Or, to put it differently, it seems likely that the dreams of primitive men are more exposed to the ordinary processes of social control than are those of modern men. The dreams of Western man are relatively unsocialized events in contrast to the heavy socialization of primitive man in his role as sleeper.

It is time to indicate in more general sociological terms what we have been doing in the, admittedly highly impressionistic, considerations advanced above. We have taken a certain human state, sleep, and enumerated some of the more obviously social meanings associated with it. Certain conditions that regularly have to be fulfilled in order to enter the state (over and above fatigue) have been indicated. The compatibility and incompatibility of the sleep state or night-time with certain other roles has been discussed. Rights and duties of the sleeping person, or the person close to sleep, have been analyzed. In general we have treated sleep as an object of perception, and attempted to describe phenomenologically its properties, the conditions required for proper learning of adjustment to the object, and the social consequences flowing from this adjustment.

It will be noted that so far relatively little has been said about the actual (behavioristic) structuring of

sleep in time and space. Neither have we discussed the question of to what extent this structuring is physiologically, respectively socially determined. The time has come to approach these problems with the preceding phenomenological analysis as a background.

Sleep is a physiological function of the human organism, and before we can state how sleep is structured by social systems we must seek to establish the biological limits within which sleep may vary.[44]

From the point of view both of the evolution of species which has led to man and of the evolution of individual men with age, it is not sleep that needs to be explained but wakefulness. The normal state of lower forms of animal life and of the human infant is sleep; wakefulness occurs when some specific physiological need is aroused which requires conscious activity for its satisfaction. The wakefulness of choice found in adult man is a new biological development, which, however, is apparently still governed by the specific wakefulness center in the central nervous system. This wakefulness center under cortical stimulation prolongs the wakefulness of necessity after the physiological needs have been met. Sleep results either when neuromuscular fatigue cuts down cortical excitation or when for physiological reasons still not fully understood both the cortex and the wakefulness center become inactive after a period of two days or more. It is known that interest in the environment can for some time maintain the activity of the center, but continuous physical activity is the

[44] Concerning the physiology of sleep we rely very heavily upon the standard work by Nathaniel Kleitman, *Sleep and Wakefulness* (Chicago: University of Chicago Press, 1939).

only stimulant effective with the wakefulness center as long as a few days.[45]

There is no specific physiological mechanism connecting human sleep with darkness or the astronomical cycle of day and night. Apparently there is no inherited cyclical aspect of the physiological nature of sleep. Infants are trained to conform to the accepted pattern of human sleep in their society, and gradually they develop a physiological rhythm appropriate to this pattern. When the pattern is changed, as during military duty or on shift work, the physiological rhythm shifts to conform, with a lag of some weeks or months.[46] The patterns of human sleep can, therefore, not be explained primarily on the basis of physiology.

The minimum amount of sleep physiologically necessary, and the physiological value of additional sleep, depend on the pattern of sleep under consideration. Even taking as a given a single period of continuous sleep during each night, these questions cannot be positively answered. The best opinion at present is that at least seven hours sleep on the average (with a variation of at least two hours between different individuals) is the necessary period for adult human beings, over a long period of time. If broken down by age, this average minimum period decreases with age.[47]

Sleep is not a physiologically uniform period of existence. Electroencephalographs, motion-recording mechanical devices, and other instru-

ments have been applied to the measurement of sleep intensity during entire sleeping periods. At least in our culture, the general pattern is a rather rapid fall to deep sleep once consciousness is lost, followed by a continuation of rather deep sleep for several hours, with the remainder of the night a succession of light and moderately deep periods of sleep, and a rather lingering process of returning to consciousness in the morning.[48]

Recent work by Kleitman and Dement has led to a better identification of the duration and timing of dreams. Dreams seem rarely to last longer than fifteen minutes in duration. The latter half of sleep of a conventional night's duration is the location of the great majority of dreams. Motor activity, especially of the eyeballs, seems to occur frequently and to be associated with the content of the dreams.[49]

The conclusion of central importance to us is that a very wide range of sleep behavior is physiologically possible.

Let us now for a moment consider sleep among animals in relation to their social systems, in the hope that the admittedly crude analogies we may draw with sleep in human society may be suggestive.

Most of the information on primate behavior has been obtained under zoo or laboratory conditions in which we do not really see a separate society but rather a meld of human and animal societies. However, recent unpublished work by Washburn on troops of baboons rather free of interaction with human society gives us

---

[45] *Ibid.*, Chapter 36.

[46] *Ibid.*, p. 269; N. Kleitman and D. Jackson, *Journal of Applied Physiology*, III (1950), 309; ——— and T. Engelmann, *Journal of Applied Physiology*, VI (1953), 269.

[47] Kleitman, *Sleep*, Chapter 13.

[48] *Ibid.*, pp. 123, 151. Depth of sleep actually has too many facets to be so simply treated.

[49] W. Dement and N. Kleitman, Article to appear in *The Journal of Experimental Psychology*.

preliminary data.[50] Two basic points are made about sleep: a) The best single definition of membership in a troop of baboons is given by sleeping location in the tree(s) occupied at night by the group; b) there is a rather definite arrangement of sleeping positions of different baboons in the tree with respect to one another. Family groups have not emerged at all clearly in the baboon troops; rather the troop constitutes a large primary group with social structure based on the relative strengths of the adult males, who dominate the adolescents and the mother-infant pairs. This social hierarchy is reflected, according to the partial observations, in the gradient of positions in the tree. The most dominant males sleep in the lower branches, where they are in a position to (and will in fact) fight attackers, and generally baboons of higher status have the more desirable locations. Moreover, there is a connection between the arrangement in the tree and the manner of getting down from the tree with dawn and forming a functioning group.

From the point of view of ecology the many species of animals in, for example, a forest constitute a community because of their many significant interrelationships.[51] A given species usually has a period of simultaneous sleep spent in a sheltered habitat. The habitat is usually common to a number of individuals, who in fact carry on the same migration to the substratum of the forest floor from the upper regions at the beginning of their sleep period. Part of the

safety of the sleep habitat is usually due to the parasocial relations between individuals. More important, the social relationships between species can be analyzed fruitfully in terms of their relative sleep habits as to timing and habitat. Usually the activity of the community as a whole is rather constant over time, as a result of what can be considered as a shift-work principle of utilization of time by the nocturnal and diurnal species. As with human societies, the twenty-four hour cycles in such important environmental factors as light, temperature, and relative humidity are important constraints. But most species show an ability to work out a wide range of adjustment to these constraints, and in any case the community as a whole functions relatively independently of these constraints.[52]

Nothing seems to be known about the need of individual insects for the equivalent of our sleep. Some of the insect societies seem to be diurnal or nocturnal like other species of animals, with no activity during the quiescent period. It is well established, however, that in a number of insect societies activity goes on at a constant rate throughout the twenty-four hours; this apparently is the case with the more highly evolved societies, e.g., the ants.[53]

In the case of the primates we see direct and clear analogies with the organization and significance of human sleep. Even when we turn to species which are biologically unlike man and which have little social organization we see some parallel with human sleep when we take an ecological perspective of the community of the species taken together; here too the analysis of sleep patterns and re-

[50] S. Washburn, Lectures at Center for Advanced Study in the Behavioral Sciences, Stanford, California, 1957.

[51] W. Allee, A. Emerson, O. Park, T. Park, and K. Schmidt, *Principles of Animal Ecology* (Philadelphia: W. B. Saunders Co., 1950), p. 9.

[52] *Ibid.*, pp. 544–60.
[53] O. Park, *Ecology*, XXII, 1941, 165.

lationships is a valuable tool for investigation of the community. Finally, among the social insect societies we find a development parallel to that which human society seems to be undergoing: a complex social organization both requires and makes possible the elimination of sleep periodicity in the community as a whole.

Let us now specify the basic characteristics of the timing and ecological distribution of human sleep.

Most adult humans sleep uninterruptedly for about 7–8 hours every night. A few societies show significant deviations from this periodic pattern. In several societies, among them modern industrial society, the holders of certain occupations may for very long periods show an entirely different sleep pattern. Naps may occur regularly among adults outside the central sleep period. Children and young people sleep longer than older people. At least in modern industrial society, the sleep periods are somewhat differently located for different social strata. Sleep patterns vary somewhat with larger calendar cycles, weekly and yearly.

Most humans sleep regularly in the same physical location, although deviations exist in certain nomadic peoples, and in certain types of modern occupations. Even if physical locations shift it is normal for a person to have his place of sleep rigidly defined in relation to groups of others. It is a fairly universal arrangement for the nuclear family to sleep "under the same roof." Significant exceptions exist, however, e.g., for students of boarding schools or college dormitories and members of a Kibbutz. Within the nuclear family there usually exist rigid arrangements of sleep places, dependent upon family roles. These arrangements do vary a great deal between different cultures.

Above are mentioned both some universals and some variables in human sleep arrangements. The variations indicate very directly that some of the aspects of sleep normally taken for granted as physiological necessities are socially determined. But what about the universals, or near universals? Do they spring from biological factors alone, or are they codetermined by social requirements, the functional prerequisites of any society?

The habit to sleep regularly for long periods every night in total societies appears to be the only "natural" response to the interplay between physiological needs and environmental constraints. Night is the time when visual isolation and "quiet" are easily obtainable, and when temperature induces a need to be indoors and under the same kind of protection from climate which sleep demands anyway. During the night man's poor ability to see in darkness makes work, gathering, hunting, fishing and agriculture, inconvenient. We shall not deny that these factors may be sufficient to account for the basic fact in the timing of sleep. This, however, does not preclude the possibility that social functions may work in the same direction. And whether they do or don't is not without significance. For we have seen lately that the technical development has changed the inhabited surface of the world, especially in cities, so much as to do away with the physical constraints for a great deal. This has for instance led to a great expansion in shift-work operations and a concomitant and widespread deviation from the normal sleep patterns.[54] We may put the question of what the conse-

54 Cf. J. B. Knox, The Sociology of Industrial Relations (New York, 1955), pp. 216–17.

quences will be for social systems where a growing percentage of the population will deviate from the habit of sleeping during the night.

Even if we should find, however, that the normal sleep-timing is entirely determined by the interplay between physiological needs and physical constraints, this regularity may be of fundamental significance to sociology. The interplay between nutritional needs and environmental opportunities is generally considered as a basic non-sociological fact accounting for social structures. Similarly with sex. That the need for sleep should have had wide repercussions on social structure, e.g., on family organization, does not seem to have impressed social scientists very much. To us it seems blatantly obvious, but still far from trivial, that the necessity of providing for satisfactory sleep for its members has presented all existing social structures with a formidable problem. The problem is such that it cannot be solved except by a very widely defined ordering of social arrangements. In order to sleep one must not only be near a gratifying goal; one must find oneself in a certain "place" within a total social structure.

Sleep is, for physiological reasons, an insecure and exposed state. Consider two gold-diggers playing poker, isolated in deep snow in the interior of Yukon. The one has won the total stock of gold from his comrade, and hatred has sprung up between the two. They are armed. Fatigue is becoming unbearable. What are they to do, however? Agreement to go to sleep at the same time appears to be the only conscious solution which would serve the minimal interests of both; in other words, to be defenseless at the same time. Whatever the motives are, most communities oper-

ate on the same principle, and thus solve the problem inherent in the enormous difference in power between people awake and asleep.

To withdraw to one's own domicile at any time of the day affords protection against climate and animals. In this sense, reasons of security do not demand a specific sleep-timing, only a specific sleep location. If we consider the possibility of social enemies and competitors, however, it seems that adherence to the social norm of nightly sleep must be enforced in order to ensure mutually protected rest. It is easy to visualize the need for a mutual "agreement" of this kind in societies where incumbency of privileged roles was often closely linked to the possession of movable physical objects, to adornments or concrete spatial location (e.g., on a throne, in a men's house). In modern society there are few opportunities for a competitor to "steal" incumbency of the waking status of a sleeping person. Modern law provides fairly adequate protection on this point. Most status criteria are thus defined that they cannot be invalidated by simple physical manipulations of the kind which the power differential between awake and sleeping persons permits. There are exceptions, however. The night editor may influence a newspaper in a way which ricochets upon the status of the responsible editor. By inadequate maneuvering the mate may seriously damage the status of his captain. The ship offers a clear-cut differentiation between positions with a 24 hour responsibility for role-performance (captain and chief engineer) and positions with definite time limitations of responsibility, omitting normal sleep periods from possible blame. We believe this to be a generalizable phenomenon of considerable significance for the study of social status. It should be mentioned here that the withdrawal from authority positions in periods of sleep offers a training ground for aspiring incumbents.

There is a different sense, also, in which a person needs protection during his sleep. Considering the behavioral facts of the sleep state, a sleeping person will deviate heavily from the expectations that apply to him in his awake role. To sleep may constitute a challenge to his right to occupy the roles appertaining to the daytime personae. Now, this possible conflict with its threatening discontinuity, is settled by various mechanisms. Simultaneity of sleep is one of them, excluding, by and large, social control and observation of sleeping persons. Secondly it is settled by the lower status of the sleep-role, thus permitting abandoning of waking roles. This is, of course, associated with the irresponsibility of the sleeper. Another norm of timing, which may serve the same function, is the habit of older people to sleep less than young people, especially of parents to go to bed after their children, and in general, for people of higher rank to sleep later than people of lower rank. Finally the location of sleep within the family implies that only individuals, whose relationships depend heavily upon immutable biological criteria, observe each other asleep.

We have given some social reasons why sleep specifically must be coordinated on a regular basis of simultaneity and why modern industrial societies are exempt from some of these reasons and give adequate status protection also to people whose sleep follows different patterns. There exist social reasons, also of a different kind, springing from the general need for coordinated timing of activities within collaborating groups. Even from this general viewpoint, however, it seems that a deviation from sleep simultaneity is the one possibility with the widest ramifications.

The stress on family solidarity induced by the irregular sleep pattern of the railroader has been described by Cottrell.[55] On the other hand, the positive consequences for union democracy of deviant sleep-timing among printers has been claimed by Lipset et al.[56] When shift-work makes interaction between status equals difficult, however, it may have a disruptive tendency also beyond the family group and possibly create alienation from society.[57]

Simultaneity of sleep prevents conflicts and certain kinds of competition. It is closely related to simultaneity of other activities, eating, leisure-time activities, etc., and therefore, significant for solidarity in groups. But simultaneity of sleep within the family, or in other intimate groups, may in itself be a token of solidarity and trust, thereby strengthening the bonds within the sleep group.

All societies surveyed showed regular and continuous sleep during the night. This holds, however, only if "sleep" includes activities such as urinating, spasmodic chatting, smoking and other intermittent behavior considered part of the cultural pattern of sleep. Thus even though peoples like the Siriono and the Ituri

[55] F. Cottrell, *The Railroader* (Stanford: Stanford University Press), 1940.

[56] S. M. Lipset, M. Trow, and J. Coleman, *Union Democracy* (New York: The Free Press, 1956), p. 135.

[57] Cf. P. Pigors and F. Pigors, *Human Aspects of Multiple Shift Operations*, M.I.T. Department of Economics and Social Science, Series 2, No. 13 (Cambridge: Massachusetts Institute of Technology.)

Pygmies are reported to engage in a good deal of such activity throughout the night we consider them as sleeping simultaneously.[58] As for the physical causes of the details of sleep-timing we can mention that while the Jivaro[59] and Siriono[60] retire before nine and arise far before dawn, other societies in very similar conditions rise at dawn. Also, arctic cities in the permanent daylight of the summer follow fairly conventional sleep patterns.[61] In crisis situations, such as the presence of deep sea fish at Tikopia, sleep may be foregone by some people for many days.[62] Similar deviations from the regular sleep patterns are known from many cultures, but give us little significant information except to emphasize the plasticity of the physiological need for sleep.

The length of the period usually set aside for sleep by most social structures seems according to the best physiological estimates to be somewhat longer than required by biological needs. Kleitman tends to explain this by boredom.[63] Sleep serves as a way of doing nothing, of passing time. Considering the importance of this need for the prisoner, it is in good accordance with this claim when prisons allocate such long time periods for sleep or activities in a room with no other significant furniture than a bed.[64]

If socially instituted sleep periods are longer than physiological needs require, it provides a constant supply of surplus time. The night contains a time-reservoir which can be drawn upon both for emergency actions, ceremonies and for the completion of unfulfilled tasks. The significance and dramatic value of New Year's eve, e.g., in the United States, and the yearly festival among the Navahos both rest in large part on their taking place in a period which usually is a quiescent period both in fact and in normative belief. Nor could the celebrants of the ceremonial be numerous enough to convey a sense of universal solidarity if in fact shift work in factory or with animal herds systematically kept large blocs busy. Similarly the efficiency of collective emergency actions may depend upon the availability of people simultaneously though not always immediately. There is a further kind of latent community emergency in a complex social system: on any day many individuals do not fulfill their tasks because of the impossibility of perfect coordination and planning. With a common and in part biologically superfluous sleep phase, these chronic gaps can be met through the omission of sleep without further disrupting the coordination of activities; in a shift-work social or economic structure the new shift is disrupted by any late activity of the old. An important advantage of the sleep phase when it comes to holding ceremonies and to emergency action of either kind can be the lack of interaction among

[58] C. Coon, A Reader in General Anthropology (New York: Henry Holt and Company, 1947), p. 334.

[59] A. Holmberg, Nomads of the Long Bow, Institute of Social Anthropology Publication No. 10 (Washington, D.C.: The Smithsonian Institution, 1950), p. 40.

[60] R. Karsten, The Head-Hunters of Western Amazonas (Helsingfors: Centraltryckeriet, 1935), p. 243.

[61] N. Kleitman and H. Kleitman, "The Sleep-Wakefulness Pattern in the Arctic," Scientific Monthly, Vol. LXXVI (1953).

[62] R. Firth, Primitive Polynesian Economy (London: Routledge & Kegan Paul, Ltd., 1939), p. 156.

[63] Kleitman and Kleitman, op. cit.

[64] Cf. Johan Galtung, Fengselssamfunnet [The Prison Community] (Oslo: Oslo University Press, 1959).

sleepers, since awake organizations have their own ends and patterns of activity often in conflict with the needs in an emergency or ceremony.

While gross simultaneity of sleep seems to be a characteristic of all societies, minor differentiations appear with regularity, a regularity associated with status differentials. They seem to symbolize, and probably support, social stratification along a prestige dimension. The Lynds, for example, report that higher prestige in Middletown is associated with later retiring and awakening times.[65] The same pattern is reported in the fiction of the last few centuries and for the Roman and Greek states. Available studies of people's time budgets indicate similar differences when statistics are broken down by occupational groups.[66] Now, this is probably related to a privileged position in work, permitting shorter hours for higher status groups. Traffic statistics for Oslo indicate three waves of high frequency traffic in the morning, one when manual workers go to their jobs, a later one when white-collar workers fill the streetcars, and a third even later one, when the bosses go. Still, it seems that the differences in sleep-timing have taken on normative character to the extent that late hours are "normal" even for high-status people with long working-hours. It may be that staying up late at night is associated with a notion of conspicuous waste of working time, and of time assumed to be needed for recuperation in sleep before next day's labor. On the other hand, Weber pointed out that Calvinist ethics frowned upon sleep beyond what appeared to be necessary, as a waste of the supremely scarce commodity: time.[67]

Differences in sleep-timing, especially within the family, differentiate between roles in terms of rank or authority. The young must go to bed before the older ones, thereby eliminating members of a solidary group according to a definite ranking system. The permission to stay up longer and longer with increasing age, and also as rewards for meritorious behavior, links bed-timing to prestige. For children there is a "career-line" within the family; and one of the most significant rewards in this career-line is the promotion to a later sleep-time. This is, of course, also one of the main reasons why parents' decisions on what is the proper bed-time often are so hotly contested by the children, usually with references to playmates, enjoying a more privileged position in this respect. These conflicts may, by the way, serve to impress upon children the scarcity and value of time, almost like ice-cream.

Just as there is a determinate succession of phases of activity in the 24 hour period, there will be phases in other periods of time which constitute the units of a basic cycle of social activity. We would expect that a shift in the sleeping period of a given day would correspond to the latency phase of a calendar period. The most obvious example is the custom of late sleep on Sunday in Western society.[68] This may be regarded as the latency phase marking

[65] R. Lynd and H. Lynd, *Middletown* (New York: Harcourt, Brace & World, Inc., 1929), p. 53.

[66] As shown for example in the time budgets emerging from Norwegian surveys of Radio Listening. Cf. also, Robert Macnish, *The Philosophy of Sleep* (Glasgow: 1854), pp. 316–17.

[67] Max Weber, *The Protestant Ethic and the Spirit of Capitalism* (New York and London: 1930), pp. 157–58.

[68] G. Lundberg, M. Komarovsky, and M. McInerny, *Leisure* (New York: Columbia University Press, 1934), p. 94 footnote.

the weekly cycle of activity, preceded by an integrative phase on Saturday and followed by the instrumental phase on Monday. Prolonged sleep during yearly vacations may be another example. In a country with the geographical position of Norway, it is possible to view the winter (the "Winter night") as one extended latency phase, marked by long nights and, in rural areas at least, extended sleep periods. Spring is proverbially the new awakening, an experience hard to imagine for those located closer to the equator. The diurnal cycle is very clearly perceived as a miniature model of the yearly cycle.[69]

Cases of nonsimultaneous and irregular sleep occur frequently, although usually in limited quantities. In addition to the physiological needs they serve, they may also achieve social ends. It is above all a way to legitimize withdrawal and isolation. Even if physiological sleep does not take place, retiring to a bedroom or lying down on a couch justifies refusal to participate in interaction with close alters at certain times of the day. The "afternoon nap" is an institution which may serve such functions. Assuming sleep-like postures, closing one's eyes, justifies abstention from interaction with passengers in a public carrier, even if there is no physiological sleep.

The component of status known as residence, which identifies a person with a definite spatial location and hence a community, is usually given by the normal sleeping location. Some concomitants of this phenomenon, affecting the family, have been mentioned above. What needs to be emphasized here is that a very rigid system of social control operates to

[69] J. Storaker, *Tiden i den norske folketro* [*Time in Norwegian folklore*] (Kristiania: 1921).

enforce the norms of sleep location. It is dramatically demonstrated when the question of "alibi" is being put, and the suspect fails to show that he slept at the proper time at the proper place. Viewed from an entirely different angle: for a youngster to stay out overnight without parental approval of alternative sleeping place, is a kind of deviance which may lead to extensive control measures. These are intimately related to other norms against sexual activities and against gang delinquency. But whatever the motives behind the invoked sanctions are, they function so as to emphasize the strict normative rules governing sleep location. They may be viewed as a countermeasure against a threat to family solidarity, an attempt to eliminate a disturbance of its most sacred ritual.

The rigid identification of a person with "his own good bed" may have an important psychological function. During sleep and its peripheral zones the identity problem becomes more acute than is otherwise the case. In a very literal sense, the person does not know who he is when asleep; even in dreams the experience of self is often blurred and uncertain. It seems reasonable that such inner uncertainty should call forth rigid external frames. It is no accident that the great Danish-Norwegian playwright Holberg let his peasant Jeppe wake up in the baron's bed, and there, in the bed, was exposed to a playfully vicious scheme to confuse his identity so as to make him believe he was the baron. It may be related to the subjective identity problem, as well as to the social one, when soldiers' one stable location in a barrack is their bunk.

Also the social identity—that is, relative to the agents of society—is in many ways dubious during sleep. The person will not on his own respond actively to external stimuli unless they aim directly at him in his bed. To meet emergencies, especially, it is of great importance that others—police, watchmen, guards etc.—should know where a person is located at a time when he is immune to more generally aimed messages. Or one could put it this way, that "society" must know, from its registers, who and where a person is, when he is incapable of knowing it himself. When people sleep, some of the responsibility they have for taking care of their own and society's interests is transferred to others. Watchmen and guards who stay awake when others sleep symbolize this transfer of protective functions.

It has been pointed out earlier that the night is the time for police activities par excellence, for raids, arrests and mere patrolling. The rigidity of public controls during the sleep period is probably related to the breakdown of informal controls. When interaction ceases, there are no other sanctions left than official threats or physical manipulation. During the night the legal structure of society is laid bare, stripped of the complex system of informal social controls that are the meat and blood around the skeleton of law in daytime. Above all, rigidly defined spatial positions seem to take the place of explicit interaction in continuous confirmation of the relative statuses in the group.

Simultaneity and propinquity of sleep are a major cause, consequence and recognized criterion of the interaction of a small number of people in certain types of groups, of which the family is the outstanding example. But if our reasoning is sound concerning the function of sleep in the family, it should also throw important light upon

other sleep groups. One interesting type is the British public schools. Under this educational system the boy was torn out of his family and placed in a peer group, the most private, family-like scene of which was the dormitory. It can hardly be doubted that this, quite apart from more personal repercussions, must have lowered the degree of identification with the nuclear family and the geographical home community, while intensifying peer-group identification. Is the relation between this educational system, of which peer-group sleep is only one particularly salient trait, and the highly efficient "aristocratic democracy" in Britain, a purely incidental one? Many prominent British politicians have thought not. When Baldwin became a premier, one of his first thoughts was reportedly that his should be a Cabinet of which Harrow would not be ashamed.[70] And the extensive reliance upon informal social contacts and control in British politics, compared with American politics,[71] seems related both to the identification with contemporaries, crossing family, party and geographical—but not class—lines, and to the relative absence of parental control. Since sleep in peer groups has been a social privilege, it gives to the upper classes (and to males) an advantage in organizational adjustment, and may thus have served not only effective political leadership, but also the preservation of a class society. The existence of reformatories and children's homes is, in this context, a mark of degradation for the pupils, and serves to up-

[70] W. L. Guttsman, "Aristocracy and the Middle Class in the British Political Elite 1886–1916," *The British Journal of Sociology*, V (1954), 17.

[71] Cf. E. Shils, *The Torment of Secrecy* (New York: The Free Press, 1957).

hold a quasi-community of the alienated at the bottom of the social ladder.

Location of sleep within or outside the nuclear family is indicative of more pervasive traits of society at large. Even more markedly, however, the ecological distribution of sleepers within the family is indicative of the family structure.

In almost every society surveyed for which relevant information was available, there is a definite mutual arrangement of the sleeping locations of the family members, possibly different for various major groupings within the society. An extreme example is the Yakut of Siberia: there is a uniform assignment of different roles in the family to the eight sleeping alcoves of the standard hut, with a recognized prestige value for each alcove.[72] Moreover there is usually a definite pattern of responsibility for taking care of various contingencies arising during sleep for the group. This pattern is correlated with both the relative accessibility of the different locations of sleep, and with the waking pattern of responsibility in the family group. Such a pattern is reported in detail, for example, for the Copper Eskimo of North Canada.[73]

In recent unpublished work, John

M. Whiting[74] has found a strong correlation between sleeping arrangements of mother, father, and infant and the structure of authority and affection in the family: for example, where the mother sleeps in a single bed with the infant and thus the father is not near the infant, formal initiation rites for boys are found significantly more often than for a double bed arrangement, possibly because forceful action is required to move a son from a mother-centered to an agnatic system of solidarity and authority. A number of other variables such as post-partum sex taboos and residence patterns are also correlated with initiation, and so the pattern is a complex one. Our point here is that the sleeping arrangements reflect and determine numerous other important characteristics of kinship structure; and this is a fruitful field for empirical study in primitive societies. In our own society, the rights of children under various conditions to sleep with their parents is a clue to the general pattern of change of parent-child relations with age, and to the status of different children in a given family. One convenient and objective tool for investigating the troublesome question of the exact nature, development, and strength of incest taboos is the determination of the sleeping rights of the parties with respect to one another.

---

[72] W. Jochelson, *The Yakut* (New York: American Museum of Natural History, 1933), pp. 135–36.

[73] D. Jennes, *The Life of the Copper Eskimos* (Ottawa: Acland, 1922), p. 85.

[74] J. M. Whiting, R. Kluckhohn, and A. Anthony, "The Function of Male Initiation Ceremonies at Puberty," unpublished manuscript, p. 17.

29

# Death and Social Structure *

*Robert Blauner*

Death is a biological and existential fact of life that affects every human society. Since mortality tends to disrupt the ongoing life of social groups and relationships, all societies must develop some forms of containing its impact. Mortuary institutions are addressed to the specific problems of the disposal of the dead and the rituals of transition from life to death. In addition, fertility practices, family and kinship systems, and religion take their shape partly in response to the pressure of mortality and serve to limit death's disorienting possibilities. In this paper I shall be concerned with the social arrangements by which the impact of mortality is contained, and with the ways in which these arrangements are related to the demographic characteristics of a society. In particular, I hope to throw some light on the social and cultural consequences of modern society's organization of death. Because of the abstractness of these questions and the inadequacy of the empirical data on which I draw, many of my statements should be read as speculative hypotheses rather than as established facts.

Mortality and its impact are not constants. In general, the demographic

structure of preindustrial societies results in an exposure to death that appears enormous by the standards of modern Western life. Malinowski, writing of the Trobriand Islanders and other natives of Eastern New Guinea, states that "death . . . causes a great and permanent disturbance in the equilibrium of tribal life." [1] The great impact of mortality and the vividness of death as a theme in life emerge clearly from Goody's account of the LoDagaa of West Africa.[2] Jules Henry's study of the Kaingang "Jungle People" of the Brazil highlands depicts a tribe whose members are in daily contact with death and greatly obsessed with it.[3] Kingsley Davis speculates that many characteristics of Indian life, such as the high birth rate, the stress on kinship and joint households, and the religious emphasis, may be attributed to the nearness to death that follows from the condi-

* Reprinted by special permission of the William Alanson White Foundation, Inc., and that of the author from *Psychiatry*, XXIX (1966), 378–94.

[1] Bronislaw Malinowski, *Argonauts of the Western Pacific* (London: Routledge & Kegan Paul, Ltd., 1922), p. 490; cited in Lucien Levy-Bruhl, *The "Soul" of the Primitive* (London: George Allen & Unwin, 1928), p. 226.

[2] Jack Goody, *Death, Property and the Ancestors* (Stanford: Stanford University Press, 1962). This is the most thorough investigation in the literature of the relations between the mortuary institutions of a society and its social structure; I am indebted to Goody for many ideas and insights.

[3] Jules Henry, *Jungle People* (Richmond, Va.: William Byrd Press, 1941).

tions of that subcontinent.[4] The relatively small scale of communities in most preindustrial societies compounds death's impact. Its regular occurrence—especially through the not infrequent catastrophes of war, famine, and epidemics—involves more serious losses to a society of small scale, a point that has been made forcibly by Krzywicki:

Let us take, for instance, one of the average Australian tribes (usually numbering 300–600 members). The simultaneous loss of 10 persons is there an event which quantitatively considered, would have the same significance as the simultaneous death of from 630,000 to 850,000 inhabitants in the present Polish state. And such catastrophes, diminishing an Australian tribe by some 10 persons, might, of course, occur not infrequently. An unfortunate war-expedition, a victorious night attack by an enemy, a sudden flood, or any of a host of other events might easily cause the death of such a number of tribesmen: in addition, there were famines, such as that which forced the Birria, for instance, to devour all their children, or the epidemics which probably occurred from time to time even in primitive communities. And, what is most important, conditions of primitive life sometimes created such situations that there was a simultaneous loss of about a dozen or a score of persons of the same sex and approximately the same age. Then such a misfortune affecting a community assumed the dimensions of a tribal disaster.[5]

[4] Kingsley Davis, *The Population of India and Pakistan* (Princeton, N.J.: Princeton University Press, 1951), p. 64.

[5] Ludwik Krzywicki, *Primitive Society and Its Vital Statistics* (London: Macmillan & Co., Ltd., 1934), p. 292. The very scale of modern societies is thus an important element of their control of mortality; unlike the situation in a remote village of India or the jungle highlands of Brazil, it would require the ultimate in catastrophic mortality, all-out nuclear war, for death to threaten societal survival.

This is not to suggest that a continuous encounter with mortality is equally prevalent in all preindustrial societies. Variations among primitive and peasant societies are as impressive as common patterns; I simply want to make the point that *many* nonmodern societies must organize themselves around death's recurrent presence. Modern societies, on the other hand, have largely succeeded in containing mortality and its social disruptiveness. Yet the impact of mortality on a society is not a simple matter of such demographic considerations as death rates and the size of the group. Also central is the manner in which a society is organized, the way it manages the death crisis, and how its death practices and mortuary institutions are linked to the social structure.

## Life-Expectancy, Engagement, and the Social Relevance of the Dead

Death disrupts the dynamic equilibrium of social life because a number of its actual or potential consequences create problems for a society. One of these potential consequences is a social vacuum. A member of society and its constituent groups and relationships is lost; and some kind of gap in institutional functioning results. The extent of this vacuum depends on how deeply engaged the deceased has been in the life of the society and its groups. The system is more disrupted by the death of a leader than by that of a common man; families and work groups are typically more affected by the loss of those in middle years than by the death of children or old people. Thus a key determinant of the impact of mortality is the age and social situation of those who die, since death will be more disruptive when it frequently strikes those who are most relevant for the functional activities and the moral outlook of the social order.

In modern Western societies, mortality statistics are more and more made up of the very old. The causes are obvious: the virtual elimination of infant and child mortality and the increasing control over the diseases of youth and middle life. Almost one million American males died in 1960. Eight per cent were younger than 15 years. Fifty-five per cent were 65 or older (29 per cent were past 75), and another 18 per cent were between 55 and 64. The middle years, between 15 and 54, claimed the remaining 19 per cent of the deaths.[6] As death in modern society becomes increasingly a phenomenon of the old, who are usually retired from work and finished with their parental responsibilities, mortality in modern society rarely interrupts the business of life. Death is uncommon during the highly engaged middle years, and the elderly are more and more segregated into communities and institutions for their age group.

Although accurate vital statistics for contemporary preindustrial societies are rare, the available data indicate that the primary concentration

of death is at the opposite end of the life-span, in the years of infancy and childhood. For example, among the Sakai of the Malay Peninsula, approximately 50 per cent of the babies born die before the age of three; among the Kurnai tribe of Australia 40 to 50 per cent die before the age of 10.[7] Fifty-nine per cent of the 1956 male deaths in Nigeria among the "indigenous" blacks were children who had not reached their fifth birthday. Thirty-five per cent of an Indian male cohort born in the 1940's died before the age of 10.[8] The same concentration of mortality in the early years was apparently also true of historical preindustrial societies.

Aside from this high infant and child mortality, there is no common pattern in the age composition of death in preindustrial societies. In some, there appears to be a secondary concentration in old age, suggesting that when mortality in the early years is very high, the majority of those who survive may be hardy enough to withstand the perils of middle life and reach old age. This seems to be

[6] United Nations, *Demographic Yearbook, 1961*, 13th ed. (New York: Department of Economic and Social Affairs, 1961), see Table 15. A very similar age distribution results when a cohort of 100,000 born in 1929 is tabulated in terms of the proportions who die in each age period. See Louis I. Dublin and Alfred J. Lotka, *Length of Life* (New York: The Ronald Press Company, 1936), p. 12. The outlook for the future is suggested by a more recent life-table for females in Canada. Of 100,000 babies born in the late 1950's, only 15 per cent will die before age sixty. Seventy per cent will be 70 years old or more at death; 42 per cent will die past eighty. See United Nations, *Demographic Yearbook*, pp. 622–76.

[7] See Krzywicki, *Primitive Society*, pp. 148, 271. A more recent demographic study of the Cocos-Keeling Islands in the Malay Peninsula found that 59 per cent die before age five. See T. E. Smith, "The Cocos-Keeling Islands: A Demographic Laboratory," *Population Studies*, XIV (1960), 94–130. Among 89 deaths recorded in 1952–1953 among the Tikopia, 39 per cent were of infants and children below age eight. See W. D. Borrie, Raymond Firth, and James Spillius, "The Population of Tikopia, 1929 and 1952," *Population Studies*, X (1957), 229–53. The Rungus Dusun, "a primitive, pagan agricultural" village community in North Borneo, lose 20 per cent of their females in the first year of life, and another 50 per cent die between the first birthday and motherhood. See P. J. Koblenzer and N. H. Carrier, "The Fertility, Mortality and Nuptiality of the Rungus Dusun," *Population Studies*, XIII (1960), 266–77.

[8] See United Nations, *Demographic Yearbook*, pp. 622–76.

the situation with the Tikopia, according to the limited demographic data. Thirty-six per cent of the deaths in one period studied were those of people over 58, almost equaling the proportion who died in the first seven years.[9]

In other societies and historical periods, conditions are such that mor-

TABLE 1. NUMBER OF DEATHS DURING SPECIFIED YEAR OF AGE PER 1,000 MALES ALIVE AT BEGINNING OF AGE PERIOD *

| Country | Age | | | | |
|---|---|---|---|---|---|
| | 20-25 | 25-30 | 30-35 | 35-40 | 40-45 |
| Congo, 1950–52 | 54 | 49 | 68 | 82 | 96 |
| Mexico, 1940 | 46 | 53 | 62 | 71 | 84 |
| U.S.A., 1959 | 9 | 9 | 10 | 14 | 23 |
| Canada, 1950–52 | 2 | 2 | 2 | 2 | 3 |

* From United Nations, *Demographic Yearbook*, 13th ed. (New York: Department of Economic and Social Affairs, 1961), p. 360. Decimals have been rounded off to the nearest integer.

tality remains heavy in the middle years; and few people reach the end of a normal lifespan. Thus calculations of age at death taken from gravestones erected during the early Roman empire (this method is notoriously unreliable, but the figures are suggestive) typically find that 30 to 40 per cent of the deceased were in their twenties and thirties; the proportion who died past the age of 50 was only about 20 per cent.[10] The life table of the primitive Cocos also illustrates this pattern. Only 16 per cent of the deaths are in the old-age

[9] See Borrie, Firth, and Spillius, *op. cit.*, p. 238.
[10] Calculated from tables in J. C. Russell, "Late Ancient and Medieval Population," *Transactions of the American Philosophical Society*, XLVIII, part 3, 25–29.

group (past 55 years), since mortality continues high for that minority of the population which survives childhood.[11] The contrast in death frequency during the middle years is suggested by the data shown in Table 1 on mortality rates for specific age periods for four countries.

The demographic pattern where mortality is high in the middle years probably results in the most disruption of ongoing life. Procedures for the reallocation of the socially necessary roles, rights, and responsibilities of the deceased must be institutionalized. This is most essential when the roles and responsibilities are deemed important and when there is a tight integration of the society's groups and institutions. Such is the situation among the LoDagaa of West Africa, where many men die who are young and middle aged. Since the kinship structure is highly elaborated, these deaths implicate the whole community, particularly the kinship group of the bereaved spouses. The future rights to these now unattached women, still sexually active and capable of child bearing, emerge as an issue that must be worked out in the funeral ceremonies through a transfer to new husbands.[12] In contrast, in

[11] See Smith, "Cocos-Keeling Islands." In Nigeria during 1956, only 13 per cent of male deaths recorded were of men older than 55 years. Twenty-eight per cent occurred among males between 5 and 54. Similarly, in Algeria during the same year, 30 per cent of all male deaths among the Moslem population took people during the middle years of life (between 15 and 49). Only 13 per cent were old men past 60. See United Nations, *Demographic Yearbook*, Table 15.
[12] See Goody, *Death, Property, Ancestors*, pp. 30, 73 ff. In some high-mortality societies, such as traditional India, remarriage is not prescribed for the affected widows. Perhaps this difference may be related to the much greater population density of India as compared to West Africa.

modern Western societies, the death of a husband typically involves only the fragmented conjugal family; from the point of view of the social order as a whole, it makes little difference whether a widow replaces her deceased husband, because of the loose integration of the nuclear family into wider kinship, economic, and political spheres.

Another way of containing the impact of mortality is to reduce the real or ideal importance of those who die. Primitive societies, hard hit by infant and child mortality, characteristically do not recognize infants and children as people; until a certain age they are considered as still belonging to the spirit world from which they came, and therefore their death is often not accorded ritual recognition—no funeral is held.[13] Aries has noted that French children were neither valued nor recognized in terms of their individuality during the long period of high infant mortality:

No one thought of keeping a picture of a child if that child had . . . died in infancy . . . it was thought that the little thing which had disappeared so soon in life was not worthy of remembrance. . . . Nobody thought, as we ordinarily think today, that every child already contained a man's personality. Too many of them died.[14]

One of the consequences of the devaluation of the old in modern society is the minimization of the disruption and moral shock death ordinarily brings about.

[13] Robert Hertz, "The Collective Representation of Death," in Hertz, Death and the Right Hand, trans. Rodney and Claudia Needham (Aberdeen: Cohen and West, 1960), pp. 84–86. See also Goody, op. cit., pp. 208 ff.

[14] Phillipe Aries, Centuries of Childhood: A Social History of Family Life, trans. Robert Baldick (New York: Alfred A. Knopf, Inc., 1962), pp. 38 ff.

But when people die who are engaged in the vital functions of society —socializing the young, producing sustenance, and maintaining ceremonies and rituals—their importance cannot be easily reduced. Dying before they have done their full complement of work and before they have seen their children off toward adulthood and their own parenthood, they die with unfinished business. I suggest that the almost universal belief in ghosts in preindustrial societies [15] can be understood as an effect of this demographic pattern on systems of interpersonal interaction, and not simply as a function of naïve, magical, and other "unsophisticated" world views. Ghosts are reifications of this unfinished business, and belief in their existence may permit some continuation of relationships broken off before their natural terminus. Perhaps the primitive Manus have constructed the most elaborate belief system which illustrates this point:

Each man worships a spirit who is called the Sir-Ghost, usually the spirit of his father, though sometimes it may be the son, or brother, or one who stood in the mother's brother-sister's relationship. The concrete manifestation of this Sir-Ghost is the dead person's skull which is placed in a bowl above the inside of the front entry of the house. Any male can

[15] After studying 71 tribes from the human area files, Leo Simmons generalizes that the belief in ghosts is "about as universal in primitive societies as any trait could be." See Simmons, The Role of the Aged in Primitive Society (New Haven: Yale University Press, 1945), pp. 223 ff. Another student of death customs reports that "The fear of a malignant ghost governs much of the activity of primitive tribes." See Norman L. Egger, "Contrasting Attitudes Toward Death Among Veterans With and Without Battle Experience and Non-Veterans" (Master's thesis, Department of Psychology, University of California, Berkeley, 1948), p. 33.

speak to his Sir-Ghost and receive communications from him. The Sir-Ghost acts as a ward, protecting his son from accidents, supervising his morals, and hopefully bringing him wealth. The relationship between the Sir-Ghost and his ward is a close parallel to that between father and son. With some changed emphases, it continues the relationship that existed in life and was broken by death. Since Manus die early, the tenure of a Sir-Ghost is typically only one generation. When the ward, the son, dies, this is seen as proof of the ghost's ineffectiveness, and the son's son casts him out, installing his own newly deceased father as Sir-Ghost. The same spirit, however, is not a Sir-Ghost to other families, but only a regular ghost and as such thought to be malicious.[16]

More common in primitive societies is an ambivalent attitude toward the ghost. Fear exists because of the belief that the dead man, frustrated in his exclusion from a life in which he was recently involved, wants back in, and, failing this, may attempt to restore his former personal ties by taking others along with him on his journey to the spirit world. The elaborate, ritually appropriate funeral is believed to keep the spirit of the dead away from the haunts of the living,[17]

[16] Adapted from William Goode, *Religion Among the Primitives* (New York: The Free Press, 1951), pp. 64 ff., 194 ff. The former Sir-Ghost, neglected after his forced retirement, is thought to wander on the sea between the villages, endangering sea voyages. Eventually he becomes a sea-slug. A similar phenomenon is reported with respect to the shades of ancient Rome; a deceased husband began as a shade with a distinct personality, but was degraded to the rank of the undifferentiated shades that haunt the world of the dead after time passed and the widow remarried. Thus the unfinished business had been completed by someone else. See James H. Leuba, *The Belief in God and Immortality* (Boston: Sherman, French, 1916), pp. 95–96.

[17] The most complete materials on ambivalence toward ghosts are found in James G.

and the feasts and gifts given for the dead are attempts to appease them through partial inclusion in their life. It would appear that the dead who were most engaged in the life of society have the strongest motives for restoring their ties; and the most feared ghosts tend to be those whose business has been the least completed. Ghosts of the murdered, the suicide, and others who have met a violent end are especially feared because they have generally died young with considerable strength and energy remaining. Ghosts of women dying in childbirth and of the unmarried and childless are considered particularly malignant

Frazer, *The Fear of the Dead in Primitive Religion*, 3 vols. (London: Macmillan & Co., Ltd., 1933, 1934, and 1936). Volume II is devoted to various methods of keeping dead spirits away.

The connection between the ambivalent attitude toward the ghost and the neomort's uncompleted working out of his obligations on earth is clear in Henry's description of the Kaingang: "The ghost-soul loves and pities the living whom it has deserted, but the latter fear and abhor the ghost-soul. The ghost-soul longs for those it has left behind, but they remain cold to its longings. 'One pities one's children, and therefore goes with them (that is, takes them when one dies). One loves (literally, lives in) one's children, and dies and goes with one's children, and one (the child) dies.' The dead pity those they have left alone with no one to care for them. They have left behind parts of themselves, for their children are those 'in whom they live.' But to the pity, love and longing of the ghost-soul, the children return a cry of 'Mother, leave me and go!' as she lies on the funeral pyre. The Kaingang oscillate between a feeling of attachment for the dead and a desire never to see them again." See Henry, *Jungle People*, p. 67.

Eissler suggests that an envy of the living who continue on is one of the universal pains of dying. Such an attitude would be understandably stronger for those who die in middle life. See Kurt R. Eissler, *The Psychiatrist and the Dying Patient* (New York: International Universities Press, Inc., 1955), pp. 149–50.

because these souls have been robbed of life's major purpose; at the funeral the unmarried are often given mock marriages to other dead souls. Ghosts of dead husbands or wives are dangerous to their spouses, especially when the latter have remarried.[18] The spirit of the grandparent who has seen his children grow up and procreate is, on the other hand, the least feared; among the LoDagaa only the grandparent's death is conceded to be a natural rather than a magical or malignant event, and in many societies there is only a perfunctory funeral for grandparents, since their spirits are not considered to be in conflict with the living.[19]

The relative absence of ghosts in modern society is not simply a result of the routing of superstition by science and rational thought, but also reflects the disengaged social situation of the majority of the deceased. In a society where the young and middle aged have largely liberated themselves from the authority of and emotional dependence upon old people by the time of the latters' death, there is little social-psychological need for a vivid community of the dead. Whereas in high-mortality societies, the person who dies often literally abandons children, spouses, and other relatives to whom he is owing affection and care, the deceased in advanced societies has typically completed his obligations to the living; he does not owe anything. Rather, the death is more likely to remind survivors of the social and psychological debts they have incurred toward him —debts that they may have been intending to pay in the coins of atten-

tion, affection, care, appreciation, or achievement. In modern societies, the living use the funeral and sometimes a memorial to attempt to "make up for" some of these debts that can no longer be paid in terms of the ordinary give and take of social life.

The disengagement of the aged in modern societies enhances the continuous functioning of social institutions and is a corollary of social structure and mortality patterns. Disengagement, the transition period between the end of institutional functioning and death, permits the changeover of personnel in a planned and careful manner, without the inevitably disruptive crises of disorganization and succession that would occur if people worked to the end and died on the job. The unsettling character of the Kennedy assassination for our nation suggests the chaos that would exist if a bureaucratic social structure were combined with high mortality in the middle years.[20]

For the older person, disengagement may bring on great psychological stress if his ties to work and family are severed more abruptly and completely than he desires. Yet it may also have positive consequences. As Robert Butler has described, isolation and unoccupied time during the later years permit reviewing one's past

---

[18] See Frazer, Fear of the Dead, III, 103–260.

[19] See Goody, Death, Property, Ancestors, pp. 208–9; Levy-Bruhl, "Soul" of the Primitive, p. 219; and Hertz, Death and the Right Hand, p. 84.

[20] See Elaine Cumming and William E. Henry, Growing Old (New York: Basic Books, Inc., Publishers, 1961) for a theoretical discussion and empirical data on the disengagement of the old in American society. In a more recent statement, Cumming notes that disengagement "frees the old to die without disrupting vital affairs," and that "the depth and breadth of a man's engagement can be measured by the degree of potential disruption that would follow his sudden death." See "New Thoughts on the Theory of Disengagement," in New Thoughts on Old Age, ed. Robert Kastenbaum (New York: Springer Publishing Co., Inc., 1964), pp. 4, 11.

life.[21] There is at least the potential (not always realized) to better integrate the manifold achievements and disappointments of a lifetime, and doing so, to die better. Under favorable circumstances, disengagement can permit a person to complete his unfinished business before death: to right old wrongs, to reconcile long-standing hostile relations with relatives or former friends; to take the trip, write the play, or paint the picture that he was always planning. Of course, often the finances and health of the aged do not permit such a course, and it is also possible that the general status of the aged in a secular, youth-and-life oriented society is a basic obstacle to a firm sense of identity and self-worth during the terminal years.

## Bureaucratization of Modern Death Control

Since there is no death without a body—except in mystery thrillers—the corpse is another consequence of mortality that contributes to its disruptiveness, tending to produce fear, generalized anxiety, and disgust.[22] Since families and work groups must eventually return to some kind of normal life, the time they are exposed to

corpses must be limited. Some form of disposal (earth or sea burial, cremation, exposure to the elements) is the core of mortuary institutions everywhere. A disaster that brings about massive and unregulated exposure to the dead, such as that experienced by the survivors of Hiroshima and also at various times by survivors of great plagues, famines, and death-camps, appears to produce a profound identification with the dead and a consequent depressive state.[23]

The disruptive impact of a death is greater to the extent that its consequences spill over onto the larger social territory and affect large numbers of people. This depends not only on the frequency and massiveness of mortality, but also on the physical and social settings of death. These vary in different societies, as does also the specialization of responsibility for the care of the dying and the preparation of the body for disposal. In premodern societies, many deaths take place amid the hubbub of life, in the central social territory of the tribe, clan, or other familial group. In mod-

---

[21] Robert N. Butler, "The Life Review: An Interpretation of Reminiscence in the Aged," Psychiatry, XXVI (1963), 65–76; see p. 67.

[22] Many early anthropologists, including Malinowski, attributed human funerary customs to an alleged instinctive aversion to the corpse. Although there is no evidence for such an instinct, aversion to the corpse remains a widespread, if not universal, human reaction. See the extended discussion of the early theories in Goody, Death, Property, Ancestors, pp. 20–30; and for some exceptions to the general rule, Robert W. Habenstein, "The Social Organization of Death," International Encyclopedia of the Social Sciences, (forthcoming).

[23] Robert J. Lifton, "Psychological Effects of the Atomic Bomb in Hiroshima: The Theme of Death," Daedalus, XCII (1963), 462–97. Among other things, the dead body is too stark a reminder of man's mortal condition. Although man is the one species that knows he will eventually die, most people in most societies cannot live too successfully when constantly reminded of this truth. On the other hand, the exposure to the corpse has positive consequences for psychic functioning, as it contributes to the acceptance of the reality of a death on the part of the survivors. A study of deaths in military action during World War II found that the bereaved kin had particularly great difficulty in believing in and accepting the reality of their loss because they did not see the body and witness its disposal. T. D. Eliot, "Of the Shadow of Death," Annals of the American Academy of Political and Social Science, CCXXIX (1943), 87–99.

ern societies, where the majority of deaths are now predictably in the older age brackets, disengagement from family and economic function has permitted the segregation of death settings from the more workaday social territory. Probably in small towns and rural communities, more people die at home than do so in urban areas. But the proportion of people who die at home, on the job, and in public places must have declined consistently over the past generations with the growing importance of specialized dying institutions—hospitals, old people's homes, and nursing homes.[24]

Modern societies control death through bureaucratization, our characteristic form of social structure. Max Weber has described how bureaucratization in the West proceeded by removing social functions from the family and the household and implanting them in specialized institutions autonomous of kinship considerations. Early manufacturing and entrepreneurship took place in or close to the home; modern industry and corporate bureaucracies are based on the separation of the workplace

from the household.[25] Similarly, only a few generations ago most people in the United States either died at home, or were brought into the home if they had died elsewhere. It was the responsibility of the family to lay out the corpse—that is, to prepare the body for the funeral.[26] Today, of course, the hospital cares for the terminally ill and manages the crisis of dying; the mortuary industry (whose establishments are usually called "homes" in deference to past tradition) prepares the body for burial and makes many of the funeral arrangements. A study in Philadelphia found that about ninety per cent of funerals started out from the funeral parlor, rather than from the home, as was customary in the past.[27] This separation of the handling of illness and death from the family minimizes the average person's exposure to death and death's disruption of the social process. When the dying are segregated among specialists for whom contact with death has become routine and even somewhat impersonal, neither their presence while alive nor as corpses interferes greatly with the mainstream of life.

Another principle of bureaucracy is the ordering of regularly occurring as well as extraordinary events into

[24] Statistics on the settings of death are not readily available. Robert Fulton reports that 53 per cent of all deaths in the United States take place in hospitals, but he does not give any source for this figure. See Fulton, *Death and Identity* (New York: John Wiley & Sons, Inc., 1965), pp. 81–82. Two recent English studies are also suggestive. In the case of the deaths of 72 working-class husbands, primarily in the middle years, 46 died in the hospital; 22 at home; and 4 at work or in the street. See Peter Marris, *Widows and Their Families* (London: Routledge & Kegan Paul, Ltd., 1958), p. 146. Of 359 Britishers who had experienced a recent bereavement, 50 per cent report that the death took place in a hospital; 44 per cent at home; and 6 per cent elsewhere. See Geoffrey Gorer, *Death, Grief, and Mourning* (London: The Cresset Press, Ltd., 1965), p. 149.

[25] Max Weber, *Essays in Sociology,* trans. and ed., H. H. Gerth and C. Wright Mills (New York: Oxford University Press, 1953), pp. 196–98. See also, ————, *General Economic History,* trans. Frank H. Knight (New York: The Free Press, 1950).

[26] Leroy Bowman reports that aversion to the corpse made this preparation an unpleasant task. Although sometimes farmed out to experienced relatives or neighbors, the task was still considered the family's responsibility. See Bowman, *The American Funeral: A Study in Guilt, Extravagance and Sublimity* (Washington, D.C.: Public Affairs Press, 1959), p. 71.

[27] William K. Kephart, "Status After Death," *The American Sociological Review,* XV (1950), 635–43.

predictable and routinized procedures. In addition to treating the ill and isolating them from the rest of society, the modern hospital as an organization is committed to the routinization of the handling of death. Its distinctive competence is to contain through isolation, and reduce through orderly procedures, the disturbance and disruption that are associated with the death crisis. The decline in the authority of religion as well as shifts in the functions of the family underlies this fact. With the growth of the secular and rational outlook, hegemony in the affairs of death has been transferred from the church to science and its representatives, the medical profession and the rationally organized hospital.

Death in the modern hospital has been the subject of two recent sociological studies: Sudnow has focused on the handling of death and the dead in a county hospital catering to charity patients; and Glaser and Strauss have concentrated on the dying situation in a number of hospitals of varying status.[28] The county hospital well illustrates various trends in modern death. Three quarters of its patients are over 60 years old. Of the 250 deaths Sudnow observed, only a handful involved people younger than 40.[29] This hospital is a setting

for the concentration of death. There are 1,000 deaths a year; thus approximately three die daily, of the 330 patients typically in residence. But death is even more concentrated in the four wards of the critically ill; here roughly 75 per cent of all mortality occurs, and one in 25 persons will die each day.[30]

Hospitals are organized to hide the facts of dying and death from patients as well as visitors. Sudnow quotes a major text in hospital administration:

"The hospital morgue is best located on the ground floor and placed in an area inaccessible to the general public. It is important that the unit have a suitable exit leading onto a private loading platform which is concealed from hospital patients and the public." [31]

Personnel in the high-mortality wards use a number of techniques to render death invisible. To protect relatives, bodies are not to be removed during visiting hours. To protect other inmates, the patient is moved to a private room when the end is foreseen. But some deaths are unexpected and may be noticed by roommates before the hospital staff is aware of them. These are considered troublesome because elaborate procedures are required to remove the corpse without offending the living.

The rationalization of death in the hospital takes place through standard procedures of covering the corpse, removing the body, identifying the deceased, informing relatives, and

---

[28] David N. Sudnow, "Passing On: The Social Organization of Dying in the County Hospital" (Doctoral thesis, University of California, Berkeley, 1965). Sudnow also includes comparative materials from a more well-to-do Jewish-sponsored hospital where he did additional field work; but most of his statements are based on the county institution. Barney G. Glaser and Anselm L. Strauss, *Awareness of Dying* (Chicago: Aldine Publishing Company, 1965).

[29] See Sudnow, *op. cit.*, pp. 107, 109. This is even fewer than would be expected by the age-composition of mortality, because children's and teaching hospitals in the city were likely to care for many terminally ill children and younger adults.

[30] *Ibid.*, pp. 49, 50.

[31] J. K. Owen, *Modern Concepts of Hospital Administration* (Philadelphia: W. B. Saunders Co., 1962), p. 304; cited in Sudnow, *op. cit.*, p. 80. Such practice attests to the accuracy of Edgar Morin's rather melodramatic statement: "Man hides his death as he hides his sex, as he hides his excrements." See E. Morin, *L'Homme et La Mort dans L'Histoire* (Paris: Correa, 1951), p. 331.

completing the death certificate and autopsy permit. Within the value hierarchy of the hospital, handling the corpse is "dirty work"; and when possible attendants will leave a body to be processed by the next work shift. As with so many of the unpleasant jobs in our society, hospital morgue attendants and orderlies are often Negroes. Personnel become routinized to death and are easily able to pass from mention of the daily toll to other topics; new staff members stop counting after the first half-dozen deaths witnessed.[32]

Standard operating procedures have even routinized the most charismatic and personal of relations, that between the priest and the dying patient. It is not that the church neglects charity patients. The chaplain at the county hospital daily goes through a file of the critically ill for the names of all known Catholic patients, then enters their rooms and administers extreme unction. After completing his round on each ward, he stamps the index card of the patient with a rubber stamp which reads: "Last Rites Administered. Date _____ Clergyman _____." Each day he consults the files to see if new patients have been admitted or put on the critical list. As Sudnow notes, this rubber stamp prevents him from performing the rites twice on the same patient.[33] This example highlights the trend toward the depersonalization of modern death, and is certainly the antithesis of the historic Catholic notion of "the good death."

In the hospitals studied by Glaser and Strauss, depersonalization is less advanced. Fewer of the dying are comatose; and as paying patients with higher social status they are in a better position to negotiate certain as-

pects of their terminal situation. Yet nurses and doctors view death as an inconvenience, and manage interaction so as to minimize emotional reactions and fuss. They attempt to avoid announcing unexpected deaths because relatives break down too emotionally; they prefer to let the family members know that the patient has taken "a turn for the worse," so that they will be able to modulate their response in keeping with the hospital's need for order.[34] And drugs are sometimes administered to a dying patient to minimize the disruptiveness of his passing—even when there is no reason for this in terms of treatment or the reduction of pain.

The dying patient in the hospital is subject to the kinds of alienation experienced by persons in other situations in bureaucratic organizations. Because doctors avoid the terminally ill, and nurses and relatives are rarely able to talk about death, he suffers psychic isolation.[35] He experiences a sense of meaninglessness because he is typically kept unaware of the course of his disease and his impending fate, and is not in a position to understand the medical and other routines carried out in his behalf.[36] He is power-

[32] See Sudnow, *op. cit.,* pp. 20–40, 49–50.
[33] See Sudnow, "Passing On," p. 114.

[34] See Glaser and Strauss, *Awareness of Dying,* pp. 142–43, 151–52.
[35] On the doctor's attitudes toward death and the dying, see August M. Kasper, "The Doctor and Death," in *The Meaning of Death,* ed. Herman Feifel (New York: McGraw-Hill Book Company, Inc., 1959), pp. 259–70. Many writers have commented on the tendency of relatives to avoid the subject of death with the terminally ill; see, for example, Herman Feifel's "Attitudes toward Death in Some Normal and Mentally Ill Populations," *Meaning of Death,* pp. 114–32.
[36] The most favorable situation for reducing isolation and meaninglessness would seem to be "where personnel and patient both are aware that he is dying, and where they act on this awareness relatively openly." This atmosphere, which Glaser and Strauss term an "open awareness context," did not

less in that the medical staff and the hospital organization tend to program his death in keeping with their organizational and professional needs; control over one's death seems to be even more difficult to achieve than control over one's life in our society.[37] Thus the modern hospital, devoted to the preservation of life and the reduction of pain, tends to become a "mass reduction" system, undermining the subjecthood of its dying patients.

The rationalization of modern death control cannot be fully achieved, however, because of an inevitable tension between death—as an event, a crisis, an experience laden with great emotionality—and bureaucracy, which must deal with routines rather than

events and is committed to the smoothing out of affect and emotion. Although there was almost no interaction between dying patients and the staff in the county hospital studied by Sudnow, many nurses in the other hospitals became personally involved with their patients and experienced grief when they died. Despite these limits to the general trend, our society has gone far in containing the disruptive possibilities of mortality through its bureaucratized death control.

## The Decline of the Funeral in Modern Society

Death creates a further problem because of the contradiction between society's need to push the dead away, and its need "to keep the dead alive.[38] The social distance between the living and the dead must be increased after death, so that the group first, and the most affected grievers later, can reestablish their normal activity without a paralyzing attachment to the corpse. Yet the deceased cannot simply be buried as a dead body: The prospect of total exclusion from the social world would be too anxiety-laden for the living, aware of their own eventual fate. The need to keep the dead alive directs societies to construct rituals that celebrate and insure a transition to a new social status, that of spirit, a being now believed to participate in a different realm.[39] Thus, a funeral that com-

---

typically predominate in the hospitals they studied. More common were one of three other awareness contexts they distinguished: "The situation where the patient does not recognize his impending death even though everyone else does" (closed awareness); "The situation where the patient suspects what the others know and therefore attempts to confirm or invalidate his suspicion" (suspected awareness); and "The situation where each party defines the patient as dying, but each pretends that the other has not done so" (mutual pretense awareness). See Glaser and Strauss, *Awareness of Dying*, p. 11.

[37] See *Ibid.*, p. 129. Some patients, however, put up a struggle to control the pace and style of their dying; and some prefer to leave the hospital and end their days at home for this reason (see Glaser and Strauss, *op. cit.*, pp. 95, 181–83). For a classic and moving account of a cancer victim who struggled to achieve control over the conditions of his death, see Lael T. Wertenbaker, *Death of a Man* (New York: Random House, Inc., 1957).

For discussions of isolation, meaninglessness, and powerlessness as dimensions of alienation, see Melvin Seeman, "On the Meaning of Alienation," *The American Sociological Review*, XXIV (1959), 783–91; and Robert Blauner, *Alienation and Freedom: The Factory Worker and His Industry* (Chicago: University of Chicago Press, 1964).

[38] Franz Borkenau, "The Concept of Death," *The Twentieth Century*, CLVII (1955), 313–29, reprinted in Fulton, *Death and Identity*, pp. 42–56.

[39] The need to redefine the status of the departed is intensified because of tendencies to act toward him as if he were alive. There is a status discongruity inherent in the often abrupt change from a more or less respon-

bines this status transformation with the act of physical disposal is universal to all societies, and has justly been considered one of the crucial *rites de passage*.[40]

Because the funeral has been typically employed to handle death's manifold disruptions, its character, importance, and frequency may be viewed as indicators of the place of mortality in society. The contrasting impact of death in primitive and modern societies, and the diversity in their modes of control, are suggested by the striking difference in the centrality of mortuary ceremonies in the collective life. Because death is so disruptive in simple societies, much "work" must be done to restore the social system's functioning. Funerals are not "mere rituals," but significant adaptive structures, as can be seen by considering the tasks that make up the funeral work among the LoDagaa of

West Africa. The dead body must be buried with the appropriate ritual so as to give the dead man a new status that separates him from the living; he must be given the material goods and symbolic invocations that will help guarantee his safe journey to the final destination and at the same time protect the survivors against his potentially dangerous intervention in their affairs (such as appearing in dreams, "walking," or attempting to drag others with him); his qualities, lifework, and accomplishments must be summed up and given appropriate recognition; his property, roles, rights, and privileges must be distributed so that social and economic life can continue; and, finally the social units—family, clan, and community as a whole—whose very existence and functioning his death has threatened, must have a chance to vigorously reaffirm their identity and solidarity through participation in ritual ceremony.[41]

Such complicated readjustments take time; and therefore the death of a mature person in many primitive societies is followed by not one, but a series of funerals (usually two or three) that may take place over a period ranging from a few months to two years, and in which the entire society, rather than just relatives and friends, participates.[42] The duration of the funeral and the fine elaboration

---

sive person to an inactive, nonresponding one. This confusion makes it difficult for the living to shift their mode of interaction toward the neomort. Glaser and Strauss report that relatives in the hospital often speak to the newly deceased and caress him as if he were alive; they act as if he knows what they are saying and doing. Nurses who had become emotionally involved with the patient sometimes back away from postmortem care because of a "mystic illusion" that the deceased is still sentient. See Glaser and Strauss, *Awareness of Dying*, pp. 113–14. We are all familiar with the expression of "doing the right thing" *for the deceased*, probably the most common conscious motivation underlying the bereaved's funeral preparations. This whole situation is sensitively depicted in Jules Romains's novel, *The Death of a Nobody* (New York: Alfred A. Knopf, Inc., 1944).

[40] Arnold Van Gennep, *The Rites of Passage* (London: Routledge & Kegan Paul, Ltd., 1960 [first published in 1909]). See also, W. L. Warner, *The Living and the Dead* (New Haven: Yale University Press, 1959), especially Chapter 9; and Habenstein, "Social Organization," for a discussion of funerals as "dramas of disposal."

[41] See Goody, *Death, Property, Ancestors*, for the specific material on the LoDagaa. For the general theoretical treatment, see Hertz, *Death and the Right Hand*, and also Émile Durkheim, *The Elementary Forms of the Religious Life* (New York: The Free Press, 1947), especially p. 447.

[42] Hertz, *op. cit.*, took the multiple funerals of primitive societies as the strategic starting point for his analysis of mortality and social structure. See Goody *op. cit.*, for a discussion of Hertz (pp. 26–27), and the entire book for an investigation of multiple funerals among the LoDagaa.

of its ceremonies suggest the great destructive possibilities of death in these societies. Mortuary institutions loom large in the daily life of the community; and the frequent occurrence of funerals may be no small element in maintaining societal continuity under the precarious conditions of high mortality.[43]

In Western antiquity and the middle ages, funerals were important events in the life of city-states and rural communities.[44] Though not so central as in high-mortality and sacred primitive cultures (reductions in mortality rates and secularism both antedate the industrial revolution in the West), they were still frequent

and meaningful ceremonies in the life of small-town, agrarian America several generations ago. But in the modern context they have become relatively unimportant events for the life of the larger society. Formal mortuary observances are completed in a short time. Because of the segregation and disengagement of the aged and the gap between generations, much of the social distance to which funerals generally contribute has already been created before death. The deceased rarely have important roles or rights that the society must be concerned about allocating; and the transfer of property has become the responsibliity of individuals, in cooperation with legal functionaries. With the weakening of beliefs in the existence and malignancy of ghosts, the absence of "realistic" concern about the dead man's trials in his initiation to spirithood, and the lowered intensity of conventional beliefs in an afterlife, there is less demand for both magical precautions and religious ritual. In a society where disbelief or doubt is more common than a firm acceptance of the reality of a life after death,[45] the funeral's classic function of status transformation becomes attenuated.

The recent attacks on modern funeral practices by social critics focus

---

[43] I have been unable to locate precise statistics on the comparative frequency of funerals. The following data are suggestive. In a year and a half, Goody attended 30 among the LoDagaa, a people numbering some 4000 (see *op. cit.*). Of the Barra people, a Roman Catholic peasant folk culture in the Scottish Outer Hebrides, it is reported that "Most men and women participate in some ten to fifteen funerals in their neighborhood every year." See D. Mandelbaum, "Social Uses of Funeral Rites," in *The Meaning of Death*, p. 206. Considering the life expectancy in our society today, it is probable that only a minority of people would attend one funeral or more per year. Probably most people during the first 40 (or even 50) years of life attend only one or two funerals a decade. In old age, the deaths of the spouse, collateral relations, and friends become more common; thus funeral attendance in modern societies tends to become more age-specific. For a discussion of the loss of intimates in later years, see J. Moreno, "The Social Atom and Death," in *The Sociometry Reader*, ed. J. Moreno (New York: The Free Press, 1960), pp. 62–66.

[44] For a discussion of funerals among the Romans and early Christians, see Alfred C. Rush, *Death and Burial in Christian Antiquity* (Washington, D.C.: Catholic University of America Press, 1941), especially Part III, pp. 187–273. On funerals in the medieval and preindustrial West, see Bertram S. Puckle, *Funeral Customs* (London: T. Werner Laurie, Ltd., 1926).

[45] See Eissler, *Psychiatrist*, p. 144: "The religious dogma is, with relatively rare exceptions, not an essential help to the psychiatrist since the belief in the immortality of the soul, although deeply rooted in man's unconscious, is only rarely encountered nowadays as a well-integrated idea from which the ego could draw strength." On the basis of a sociological survey, Gorer confirms the psychiatrist's judgment: ". . . how small a role dogmatic Christian beliefs play . . ." (see Gorer, *Death, Grief, Mourning*, p. 39). Forty-nine per cent of his sample affirmed a belief in an afterlife; twenty-five per cent disbelieved; twenty-six per cent were uncertain or would not answer (*Ibid.*, p. 166).

on alleged commercial exploitation by the mortuary industry and the vulgar ostentatiousness of its service. But at bottom this criticism reflects this crisis in the function of the funeral as a social institution. On the one hand, the religious and ritual meanings of the ceremony have lost significance for many people. But the crisis is not only due to the erosion of the sacred spirit by rational, scientific world views.[46] The social substructure of the funeral is weakened when those who die tend to be irrelevant for the ongoing social life of the community, and when the disruptive potentials of death are already controlled by compartmentalization into isolated spheres where bureaucratic routinization is the rule. Thus participation and interest in funerals are restricted to family members and friends rather than involving the larger community, unless an important leader has died.[47] Since only individuals and families

are affected, adaptation and bereavement have become their private responsibility, and there is little need for a transition period to permit society as a whole to adjust to the fact of a single death. Karl Marx was proved wrong about "the withering away of the state," but with the near disappearance of death as a public event in modern society, the withering away of the funeral may become a reality.

In modern societies, the bereaved person suffers from a paucity of ritualistic conventions in the mourning period. He experiences grief less frequently, but more intensely, since his emotional involvements are not diffused over an entire community, but are usually concentrated on one or a few people.[48] Since mourning and a sense of loss are not widely shared, as in premodern communities, the individualization and deritualization of bereavement make for serious problems in adjustment. There are many who never fully recover and "get back to normal," in contrast to the frequently observed capacity of the bereaved in primitive societies to smile, laugh, and go about their ordinary pursuits the moment the official mourning period is ended.[49] The lack

[46] The problem of sacred institutions in an essentially secular society has been well analyzed by Robert Fulton. See Fulton and Gilbert Geis, "Death and Social Values," pp. 67–75, and Fulton, "The Sacred and the Secular," pp. 89–105, in *Death and Identity*.

[47] LeRoy Bowman interprets the decline of the American funeral primarily in terms of urbanization. When communities were made up of closely knit, geographically isolated groups of families, the death of an individual was a deprivation of the customary social give and take, a distinctly felt diminution of the total community. It made sense for the community as a whole to participate in a funeral. But in cities, individual families are in a much more limited relationship to other families; and the population loses its unity of social and religious ideals. For ethical and religious reasons, Bowman is unwilling to accept "a bitter deduction from this line of thought . . . that the death of one person is not so important as once it would have been, at least to the community in which he has lived." But that is the logical implication of his perceptive sociological analysis. See Bowman, *American Funeral*, pp. 9, 113–15, 126–28.

[48] Edmund Volkart, "Bereavement and Mental Health," in *Explorations in Social Psychiatry*, Alexander H. Leighton, John A. Clausen, and Robert N. Wilson, eds. (New York: Basic Books, Inc., Publishers, 1957), pp. 281–307. Volkart suggests that bereavement is a greater crisis in modern American society than in similar cultures because our family system develops selves in which people relate to others as persons rather than in terms of roles (see pp. 293–95).

[49] In a study of bereavement reactions in England, Geoffrey Gorer found that 30 of a group of 80 persons who had lost a close relative were mourning in a style he characterized as *unlimited*. He attributes the inability to get over one's grief "to the absence of any ritual, either individual or so-

of conventionalized stages in the mourning process results in an ambiguity as to when the bereaved person has grieved enough and thus can legitimately and guiltlessly feel free for new attachments and interests.[50] Thus at the same time that death becomes less disruptive to the society, its prospects and consequences become more serious for the bereaved individual.

## Some Consequences of Modern Death Control

I shall now consider some larger consequences that appear to follow from the demographic, organizational, and cultural trends in modern society that have diminished the presence of death in public life and have reduced most persons' experience of mortality to a minimum through the middle years.[51]

### THE PLACE OF THE DEAD IN MODERN SOCIETY

With the diminished visibility of death, the perceived reality and the effective status and power of the dead have also declined in modern societies. A central factor here is the rise of science: Eissler suggests that "the intensity of service to the dead and the proneness for scientific discovery

are in reverse proportion." [52] But the weakening of religious imagery is not the sole cause; there is again a functional sociological basis. When those who die are not important to the life of society, the dead as a collective category will not be of major significance in the concerns of the living.

Compare the situation in high-mortality primitive and peasant societies. The living have not liberated themselves emotionally from many of the recently deceased and therefore need to maintain symbolic interpersonal relations with them. This can take place only when the life of the spirits and their world is conceived in well-structured form, and so, as Goode has phrased it, "practically every primitive religious system imputes both power and interest to the dead." [53]

Their spheres of influence in preindustrial societies are many: Spirits watch over and guide economic activities, and may determine the fate of trading exchanges, hunting and fishing expeditions, and harvests. Their most important realm of authority is probably that of social control: They are concerned with the general morality of society and the specific actions of individuals (usually kin or clansmen) under their jurisdiction. It is generally believed that the dead have the power to bring about both economic and personal misfortunes (including illness and death) to serve their own interests, to express their general capriciousness, or to specifically punish the sins and errors of the living. The fact that a man as spirit often receives more deference from, and exerts greater power over, people than while living

---

cial, lay or religious, to guide them and the people they come in contact with." The study also attests to the virtual disappearance of traditional mourning conventions. See Gorer, *Death, Grief, Mourning*, pp. 78–83.

[50] See Marris, *Widows*, pp. 39–40.

[51] Irwin W. Goffman suggests that "A decline in the significance of death has occurred in our recent history." See "Suicide Motives and Categorization of the Living and the Dead in the United States" (Syracuse, N.Y.: Mental Health Research Unit, February, 1966), p. 140.

[52] See Eissler, *op. cit.*, p. 44.

[53] See Goode, *Religion*, p. 185. Perhaps the fullest treatment is by Frazer; see *Fear of the Dead*, especially Vol. I.

may explain the apparent absence of the fear of death that has been observed in some primitive and ancestor-worship societies.[54]

In modern societies the influence of the dead is indirect and is rarely experienced in personified form. Every cultural heritage is in the main the contribution of dead generations to the present society,[55] and the living are confronted with problems that come from the sins of the past (for example, our heritage of Negro slavery). There are people who extend their control over others after death through wills, trust funds, and other arrangements. Certain exceptional figures such as John Kennedy and Malcolm X become legendary or almost sainted and retain influence as national symbols or role models. But, for the most part, the dead have little status or power in modern society, and the living tend to be liberated from their direct, personified influence.[56] We do not attribute to the dead the range of material and ideal interests that adheres to their symbolic existence in other so-

cieties, such as property and possessions, the desire to recreate networks of close personal relationships, the concern for tradition and the morality of the society. Our concept of the inner life of spirits is most shadowy. In primitive societies a full range of attitudes and feelings is imputed to them, whereas a scientific culture has emptied out specific mental and emotional contents from its vague image of spirit life.[57]

## Generational Continuity and The Status of the Aged

The decline in the authority of the dead, and the widening social distance between them and the living, are both conditions and consequences of the youthful orientation, receptivity to innovation, and dynamic social change that characterize modern society. In most preindustrial societies,

[54] See Simmons, *Aged,* pp. 223–24. See also, Effie Bendann, *Death Customs* (New York: Alfred A. Knopf, Inc., 1930), p. 180. However, there are primitive societies, such as the Hopi, that attribute little power and authority to dead spirits; in some cultures, the period of the dead man's influence is relatively limited; and in other cases only a minority of ghosts are reported to be the object of deference and awe. The general point holds despite these reservations.

[55] See Warner, *The Living and the Dead,* pp. 4–5.

[56] The novel, *Death of a Nobody,* by Romains, is a sensitive treatment of how its protagonist, Jacques Godard, affects people after his death; his influence is extremely short-lived; and his memory in the minds of the living vanishes after a brief period. Goffman suggests that "Parents are much less likely today to tell stories of the dead, of their qualities, hardships, accomplishments and adventures than was true a hundred years ago." See "Suicide Motives," p. 30.

[57] In an interesting treatment of the problem from a different theoretical framework, Goffman (*Ibid.*) has concluded that the sense of contrast between what is living and what is dead in modern society has become attenuated, in large part because of the decline in exposure to death. He has assembled evidence on social differences within our society: For example, women, lower-class people, and Catholics tend to have closer and more frequent contact with death or images of the dead than men, middle-class persons, and Protestants.

The question of what is the representative American imagery of afterlife existence would be a fruitful one for research. Clear and well-developed imageries are probably typical only among Catholics, fundamentalists, and certain ethnic groups. The dominant attitude (if there is one) is likely quite nebulous. For some, the dead may be remembered as an "absent presence," never to be seen again; for others as "a loved one with whom I expect (or hope) to be reunited in some form someday." Yet the background of afterlife existence is only vaguely sketched, and expectation and belief probably alternate with hope, doubt, and fear in a striking ambiguity about the prospect and context of reunion.

symbolic contacts with the spirits and ghosts of the dead were frequent, intimate, and often long-lasting. Such communion in modern society is associated with spiritualism and other deviant belief-systems; "normal" relations with the dead seem to have come under increasing discipline and control. Except for observing Catholics perhaps, contact is limited to very specific spatial boundaries, primarily cemeteries, and is restricted to a brief time period following a death and possibly a periodic memorial.[58] Otherwise the dead and their concerns are simply not relevant to the living in a society that feels liberated from the authority of the past and orients its energies toward immediate preoccupations and future possibilities.

Perhaps it is the irrelevance of the dead that is the clue to the status of old people in modern industrial societies. In a low-mortality society, most deaths occur in old age, and since the aged predominate among those who die, the association between old age and death is intensified.[59] Industrial societies value people in terms of their present functions and their future prospects; the aged have not only become disengaged from significant family, economic, and community responsibilities in the present, but their future status (politely never referred to in our humane culture) is among the company of the powerless, anonymous, and virtually ignored dead.[60] In societies where the dead

[58] In primitive societies, ghosts and spirits of the dead range over the entire social territory or occupy central areas of the group's social space. In ancestor-worship civilizations such as Rome and China, spirits dwell in shrines that are located in the homes or family burial plots. In these preindustrial societies symbolic contact with the dead may be a daily occurrence.

Likewise, in the Middle Ages, cemeteries were not on the periphery of the societal terrain but were central institutions in the community; regularly visited, they were even the sites for feasts and other celebrations, since it was believed that the dead were gladdened by sounds of merry-making. (See Puckle, *Funeral Customs*, pp. 145–46.) The most trenchant analysis of the cemetery as a spatial territory marking the social boundaries between the "sacred dead and the secular world of the profane living" in a small modern community is found in Warner, *The Living and the Dead*, Chapter 9. Yet Warner also notes that people tend to disregard cemeteries as a "collective representation" in rapidly changing and growing communities, in contrast to the situation in small, stable communities. Goffman ("Suicide Motives," p. 29) notes that "increasingly the remains of the dead are to be found in huge distant cemeteries that are not passed or frequented as part of everyday routines . . . [or] in cities in which our very mobile population *used* to live."

[59] Feifel has suggested that American society's rejection of (and even revulsion to) the old may be because they remind us unconsciously of death. See "Attitudes toward Death," p. 122.

[60] According to Kastenbaum, the tendency of psychiatrists to eschew psychotherapy with the aged and to treat them, if at all, with supportive (rather than more prestigious depth) techniques may be a reflection of our society's future orientation, that results in an implicit devaluing of old people because of their limited time prospects. See Kastenbaum, "The Reluctant Therapist," in *New Thoughts on Old Age*, pp. 139–45. The research of Butler, a psychiatrist who presents evidence for significant personality change in old age despite the common contrary assumption, would seem to support Kastenbaum's view. (See Butler, "Life Review.")

Sudnow contributes additional evidence of the devaluation of old people. Ambulance drivers bringing critical or "dead-on-arrival" cases to the county hospital's emergency entrance blow their horns more furiously and act more frantic when the patient is young than when he is old. A certain proportion of "dead-on-arrival" cases can be saved through mouth-to-mouth resuscitation, heart massages, or other unusual efforts. These measures were attempted with children and young people but not with the old; one intern admitted being repulsed by the idea of such close contact with them. See Sudnow, "Passing On," pp. 160–63.

continue to play an influential role in the community of the living, there is no period of the lifespan that marks the end of a person's connection to society; and the aged before death begin to receive some of the awe and authority that is conferred on the spirit world.

The social costs of these developments fall most heavily on our old people, but they also affect the integrity of the larger culture and the interests of the young and middle-aged. The traditional values that the dead and older generations represent lose significance, and the result is a fragmentation of each generation from a sense of belonging to and identity with a lineal stream of kinship and community. In modern societies where mobility and social change have eliminated the age-old sense of closeness to "roots," this alienation from the past—expressed in the distance between living and dead generations— may be an important source of tenuous personal identities.

These tendencies help to produce another contradiction. The very society that has so greatly controlled death has made it more difficult to die with dignity. The irrelevance of the dead, as well as other social and cultural trends, brings about a crisis in our sense of what is an appropriate death. Most societies, including our own past, have a notion of the ideal conditions under which the good man leaves the life of this world: For some primitives it is the influential grandfather; for classical antiquity, the hero's death in battle; in the middle ages, the Catholic idea of "holy dying." There is a clear relationship between the notion of appropriate death and the basic value emphases of the society, whether familial, warlike, or religious. I sug-

gest that American culture is faced with a crisis of death because the changed demographic and structural conditions do not fit the traditional concepts of appropriate death, and no new ideal has arisen to take their place. Our nineteenth-century ideal was that of the patriarch, dying in his own home in ripe old age but in the full possession of his faculties, surrounded by family, heirs, and material symbols of a life of hard work and acquisition. Death was additionally appropriate because of the power of religious belief, which did not regard the event as a final ending. Today people characteristically die at an age when their physical, social, and mental powers are at an ebb, or even absent, typically in the hospital, and often separated from family and other meaningful surroundings. Thus "dying alone" is not only a symbolic theme of existential philosophers; it more and more epitomizes the inappropriateness of how people die under modern conditions.

I have said little about another modern prototype of mortality, mass violence. Despite its statistical infrequency in "normal times," violent death cannot be dismissed as an unimportant theme, since it looms so large in our recent past and in our anxieties about the future. The major forms, prosaic and bizarre, in which violent death occurs, or has occurred, in the present period are:

1. Automobile and airplane accidents;
2. The concentration camp; and
3. Nuclear disaster.

All these expressions of modern violence result in a most inappropriate way of dying. In a brilliant treatment of the preponderance of death by violence in modern literature, Frederick Hoffman points out its inherent ambiguities. The fact that many people die at once, in most of these situations, makes it impossible to mitigate the effects on the survivors through ceremonies of respect. While these deaths are caused by human agents, the impersonality of the assailant, and the distance between him and his victim, make it impossible to assign responsibility to understandable causes. Because of the suddenness of impact, the death that is died cannot be fitted into the life that has been lived. And finally, society experiences a crisis of meaning when the threat of death pervades the atmosphere, yet cannot be incorporated into a religious or philosophical context.[61]

[61] Frederick J. Hoffman, *The Mortal No: Death and the Modern Imagination* (Princeton, N.J.: Princeton University Press, 1964), see especially Part II. In a second paper on Hiroshima, Robert J. Lifton also notes the tendency for the threat of mass death to undermine the meaning systems of society, and the absence of a clear sense of appropriate death in modern cultures. See "On Death and Death Symbolism: The Hiroshima Disaster," *Psychiatry*, XXVII (1964), 191–210. Gorer has argued that our culture's repression of death as a natural event is the cause of the obsessive focus on fantasies of violence that are so prominent in the mass media. See Geoffrey Gorer, "The Pornography of Death," in *Identity and Anxiety*, Maurice Stein and Arthur Vidich, eds. (New York: The Free Press, 1960), pp. 402–7; also reprinted in Gorer's *Death, Grief, Mourning.*
The inappropriateness inherent in the automobile accident, in which a man dies outside a communal and religious setting, is poignantly captured in the verse and chorus of the country and western song, "Wreck on the Highway," popularized by Roy Acuff:
"Who did you say it was, brother?/Who was it fell by the way?/When whiskey and blood run together,/Did you hear anyone pray?"
*Chorus:* "I didn't hear nobody pray, dear brother/I didn't hear nobody pray./I heard the crash on the highway,/But I didn't hear nobody pray."

## A FINAL THEORETICAL NOTE: DEATH AND SOCIAL INSTITUTIONS

Mortality implies that population is in a constant (though usually a gradual) state of turnover. Society's groups are fractured by the deaths of their members and must therefore maintain their identities through symbols that are external to, and that outlast individual persons. The social roles through which the functions of major societal institutions are carried out cannot be limited to particular individuals and their unique interpretations of the needs of social action; they must partake of general and transferable prescriptions and expectations. The order and stability required by a social system are threatened by the eventual deaths of members of small units such as families, as well as political, religious, and economic leaders. There is, therefore, a need for more permanent institutions embedding "impersonal" social roles, universal norms, and transcendent values.

The frequent presence of death in high-mortality societies is important in shaping their characteristic institutional structure. To the extent that death imperils the continuity of a society, its major institutions will be occupied with providing that sense of identity and integrity made precarious by its severity. In societies with high death rates the kinship system and religion tend to be the major social institutions.

Kinship systems organized around the clan or the extended family are well suited to high-mortality societies because they provide a relative permanence and stability lacking in the smaller nuclear group. Both the totem of the clan and the extended family's ties to the past and the future are institutionalized representations of continuity. Thus the differential impact of mortality on social structure explains the apparent paradox that the smaller the scale of a community the larger in general is its ideal family unit.[62] The very size of these kinship units provides a protection against the disintegrating potential of mortality making possible within the family the varied resources in relational ties, age-statuses, and cultural experience that guarantee the socialization of all its young, even if their natural parents should die before they have become adults.

In primitive and peasant societies, the centrality of magic and religion is related to the dominant presence of death. If the extended family provides for the society's physical survival, magic and counter-magic are weapons used by individuals to protect themselves from death's uncontrolled and erratic occurrence. And religion makes possible the moral survival of the society and the individual in an environment fraught with fear, anxiety, and uncertainty. As Malinowski and others have shown, religion owes its persistence and power (if not necessarily its origin) to its unique capacity to solve the societal and personal problems that death calls forth.[63] Its rituals and beliefs impart to the funeral ceremonies those qualities of

the sacred and the serious that help the stricken group reestablish and reintegrate itself through the collective reaffirmation of shared cultural assumptions. In all known societies, it serves to reassure the individual against possible anxieties concerning destruction, nonbeing, and finitude by providing beliefs that make death meaningful, afterlife plausible, and the miseries and injustices of earthly existence endurable.

In complex modern societies there is a proliferation and differentiation of social institutions that have become autonomous in relationship to kinship and religion, as Durkheim pointed out.[64] In a sense these institutions take on a permanence and autonomy that makes them effectively independent of the individuals who carry out the roles within them. The economic corporation is the prototype of a modern institution. Sociologically it is a bureaucracy and therefore relatively unconnected to family and kinship; constitutionally it has been graced with the legal fiction of immortality. Thus the major agencies that organize productive work (as well as other activities) are relatively invulnerable to the depletion of their personnel by death, for their offices and functions are impersonal and transferable from one role-incumbent to another. The situation is very different in traditional societies. There family ties and kinship groups tend to be the basis of economic, religious, and other activities; social institutions interpenetrate one another around the kinship core. Deaths that strike the family therefore reverberate through the entire social structure. This type of social integration (which Durkheim termed "mechani-

[62] The important distinction between ideal family structures and actual patterns of size of household, kinship composition, and authority relations has been stressed recently by William Goode, *World Revolution and Family Patterns* (New York: The Free Press, 1963); and by Marion Levy, "Aspects of the Analysis of Family Structure," in A. J. Coale and Marion Levy, *Aspects of the Analysis of Family Structure* (Princeton, N.J.: Princeton University Press, 1965), pp. 1–63.

[63] Bronislaw Malinowski, *Magic, Science and Religion* (Garden City, N.Y.: Doubleday Anchor Books, 1955), see pp. 47–53.

[64] Émile Durkheim, *Division of Labor* (New York: The Free Press, 1949).

cal solidarity") makes premodern societies additionally vulnerable to death's disruptive potential—regardless of its quantitative frequency and age distribution.

On the broadest level, the relationship between death and society is a dialectic one. Mortality threatens the continuity of society and in so doing contributes to the strengthening of social structure and the development of culture. Death weakens the social group and calls forth personal anxieties; in response, members of a society cling closer together. Specific deaths disrupt the functioning of the social system and thereby encourage responses in the group that restore social equilibrium and become customary practices that strengthen the social fabric. Death's sword in time cuts down each individual; but with respect to the social order it is double-edged. The very sharpness of its disintegrating potential demands adaptations that can bring higher levels of cohesion and continuity. In the developmental course of an individual life, death always conquers; but, as I have attempted to demonstrate throughout this essay, the social system seems to have greatly contained mortality in the broad span of societal and historical development.

# APPENDIX

## A Selective Bibliography for the Interested Student

(The following constitutes a selected bibliography of materials dealing both with everyday life and with somewhat offbeat areas. It is far from exhaustive, and numerous other such studies can be found in the footnotes scattered throughout this volume.)

Alexander, Robert, "Premarital Intercourse: A Socio-Psychological Analysis." Doctoral dissertation, University of Wisconsin, 1953.

Allen, Phillip M., "The Sociology of Art in America." Doctoral dissertation, Emory University, 1956.

Baker, G. H., "Glue Sniffers," *Sociology and Social Research*, XLVII (1963), 298–310.

Becker, Howard S., *Outsiders: Studies in the Sociology of Deviance*. New York: The Free Press, 1963.

Blazer, John A., "Married Virgins—A Study of Unconsummated Marriages," *Journal of Marriage and the Family*, XXVI (1964), 213–14.

Brown, Roger, and Marguerite Ford, "Address in American English," *Journal of Abnormal and Social Psychology*, LXII (1961), 375–85.

Bowman, Le Roy E., "Funerals and Funeral Directors in the United States, a Sociological Analysis." Doctoral dissertation, Columbia University, 1954.

Broyles, John Allen, "The John Birch Society as a Movement of Social Protest of the Radical Right." Doctoral dissertation, Boston University, 1963.

Bryan, James H., "Occupational Ideologies and Individual Attitudes of Call Girls," *Social Problems*, XIII (1966), 441–50.

Cameron, William B., "Sociological Notes on the Jam Session," *Social Forces*, XXXIII (1954), 177–82.

Cavan, Sherri, *Liquor License: an Ethnography of Bar Behavior*. Chicago: Aldine Publishing Company, 1966.

Christ, Edwin C., "The Adult Stamp Collector." Doctoral dissertation, University of Missouri, 1958.

Churchill, Lindsey, "Notes and Everyday Quantitative Practices," Paper read at the Annual Meeting of the American Sociological Association, Miami, Fla., 1966.

Conrad, Jack R., "The Bullfight: The Cultural History of an Institution." Doctoral dissertation, Duke University, 1954.

Crespi, Irving, "A Functional Analysis of Social Card Playing as a Leisure Time Activity." Doctoral dissertation, The New School for Social Research, 1955.

Cumming, Elaine, "The Naming of Infants: A Study of Role Differentiation," Paper read at the Annual Meeting of the American Sociological Association, Miami, Fla., 1966.

Daniels, A. K., and R. D. Daniels, "The Social Functions of the Career Fool," *Psychiatry*, XXVII (1964), 219–29.

Davis, Fred, "The Cabdriver and His Fare," *The American Journal of Sociology*, LXV (1959), 158–65.

Davis, Kingsley, "The Sociology of Parent-Youth Conflict," *The American Sociological Review*, V (1940), 523-35.

———, "The Sociology of Prostitution," *The American Sociological Review*, II (1937), 744–55.

Devereux, Edward C., "Gambling and Social Structure: A Sociological Study of Lotteries and Horseracing in Contemporary America." Doctoral dissertation, Harvard University, 1950.

———, "Gambling in Psychological and Sociological Perspective," *International*

*Encyclopedia of the Social Sciences,* in press.

Doob, Leonard W., "Goebbel's Principles of Propaganda," *Public Opinion Quarterly,* XIV (1950), 419–42.

Dressler, David, "Burlesque as a Cultural Phenomenon." Doctoral dissertation, New York University, 1937.

Elkin, F., and W. A. Westley, "The Myth of Adolescent Culture," *The American Sociological Review,* XX (1955), 680–84.

Etzkorn, K. P., "Musical and Social Patterns of Song Writers." Doctoral dissertation, Princeton University, 1960.

Felton, Gary S., "Psychosocial Implications of the Coffee-Break," *Journal of Human Relations,* XIV (1966), 434–49.

Finestone, H., "Cats, Kicks, and Color," *Social Problems,* V (1957), 3–13.

Garfinkel, Harold, "Studies of the Routine Grounds of Everyday Activity," *Social Problems,* XI (1964), 225–50.

——, "The Rational Properties of Scientific and Common Sense Values," in *Decisions, Values and Groups,* ed. Norman F. Washburne. Pergamon Press, Inc., 1962, pp. 304–24.

——, "Conditions of Successful Degradation Ceremonies," *The American Journal of Sociology,* LXI (1956), 420–24.

——, "Common-Sense Knowledge of Social Structure: The Documentary Method of Interpretation," in *Theories of the Mind,* ed. Jordan M. Scher. New York: The Free Press, 1962, pp. 689–712.

——, "Aspects of the Problem of Common-Sense Knowledge of Social Structures," *Transactions of the Fourth World Congress of Sociology,* IV, Milan and Stressa, September 8–15, 1959.

——, "Remarks on Ethnomethodology," Paper presented at the Annual Meeting of the American Sociological Society, 1965.

Gasser, Robert L., "The Confidence World as a Criminal Behavior System." Doctoral dissertation, American University, 1955.

Goffman, Erving, "Embarrassment and Social Organization," *The American Journal of Sociology,* LXII (1956), 264–71.

——, "The Nature of Deference and Demeanor," *American Anthropologist,* LVIII (1957), 473–502.

——, "On Cooling the Mark Out," *Psychiatry,* XV (1952), 451–63.

——, "On Face Work: An Analysis of Ritual Elements in Social Interaction," *Psychiatry,* XVIII (1955), 213–31.

——, *The Presentation of Self in Everyday Life.* Garden City, N.Y.: Doubleday Anchor Books, 1959.

——, *Asylums.* Garden City, N.Y.: Doubleday Anchor Books, 1961.

——, *Encounters.* Indianapolis, Ind.: The Bobbs-Merrill Co., Inc., 1961.

——, *Stigma.* Englewood Cliffs, N.J.: Prentice-Hall, Inc., 1963.

——, *Behavior in Public Places.* New York: The Free Press, 1963.

Gluckman, Max, "Gossip and Scandal," *Current Anthropology,* IV (1963), 307–16.

Goldman, Irwin J., "The Willingness of Music and Visual Art Students to Admit to Socially Undesirable and Psychopathological Characteristics." Doctoral dissertation, Columbia University, 1962.

Habenstein, Robert W., "The American Funeral Director: A Study in the Sociology of Work." Doctoral dissertation, University of Chicago, 1955.

Hasselkorn, Harry, "The Vocational Interests of a Group of Homosexuals." Doctoral dissertation, New York University, 1953.

Hirschi, Travis, "The Professional Prostitute," *Berkeley Journal of Sociology,* VII (1962), 33–49.

Ichheiser, Gustav, "Misunderstandings in Human Relations," Supplement to *The American Journal of Sociology,* LX (1949).

Jahoda, Mari, "The Consumer's Attitude to Furniture," *Sociological Review,* XXXVIII (1946), 205–46.

Kaplan, Arlene E., "A Study of Folksinging in a Mass Society," *Sociologus*, V (1955), 14–27.

Karen, Robert L., "Some Factors Affecting Tipping Behavior," *Sociology and Social Research*, XLVII (1962), 68–74.

Klapp, Orrin E., *Heroes, Villains, and Fools*. Englewood Cliffs, N.J.: Prentice-Hall, Inc., 1962.

——, *Symbolic Leaders*. Chicago: Aldine Publishing Co., 1964.

Klietsch, Ronald G., "Clothesline Patterns and Covert Behavior," *Journal of Marriage and the Family*, XXVII (1965), 78–80.

Levitin, T. E., "Role Performance and Role Distance in a Low-Status Occupation: The Puller," *Sociological Quarterly*, V (1964), 251–60.

Lewin, H. S., "A Comparative Study of the Principles and Practices of the Adolph Hitler Youth and the Boy Scouts of America." Doctoral dissertation, The New School for Social Research, 1950.

Lowe, Harold E., "A Study of Sports Preferences." Doctoral dissertation, New York University, 1949.

Luchterhand, Elmer, "Prisoner Behavior and Social System in Nazi Concentration Camps." Doctoral dissertation, University of Wisconsin, 1953.

McCall, George, "Symbiosis: The Case of Hoodoo and the Numbers Racket," *Social Problems*, X (1963), 361–71.

—— and J. L. Simmons, *Identities and Interactions*, New York: The Free Press, 1966.

McClelland, W. G., "The Supermarket and Society," *Sociological Review*, New Series X (1962), 133–44.

Miller, Stephen J., "The Social Base of Sales Behavior," *Social Problems*, XII (1964), 15–24.

Miner, H., "Body Ritual among the Nacirema," *American Anthropologist*, LVIII (1956), 503–7.

Mussbaum, Martin, "Sociological Symbolism of the Adult Western," *Social Forces*, XXXIX (1960), 25–28.

Riesman, David, Robert J. Potter, and Jeanne Watson, "The Vanishing Host,"

*Human Organization*, XIV (1960), 17–27.

Polsky, Ned, *Hustlers, Beats, and Others*. Chicago: Aldine Publishing Co., 1966.

Roberts, John M., and Brian Sutton Smith, "Child Training and Game Involvement," *Ethnology*, I (1962), 166–85.

Roberts, John M., "Pattern and Competence: A Consideration of Tick Tack Toe," *El Palacio* (Autumn, 1965), pp. 17–30.

——, "Cross-Cultural Correlates of Games of Chance," *Behavior Science Notes*, I (1966), 131–44.

——, and Wayne E. Thompson, "Expressive Self-Testing in Driving," *Human Organization*, XXV (1966), 54–63.

Rush, G. B., "Toward a Definition of the Extreme Right," *Pacific Sociological Review*, VI (1963), 64–72.

Schettler, Clarence, "Does Your Name Identity You?" *Social Forces*, XXI (1943), 172–76.

Schutz, Alfred, "Making Music Together: A Study in Social Relationship," *Social Research*, XVIII (1951), 76–97.

Scodel, Alvin, "Changes in Song Lyrics and Some Speculations on National Character," *Merrill-Palmer Quarterly*, VII (1961), 39–47.

Sommer, Robert, *Expertland*. Garden City, N.Y.: Doubleday & Company, Inc., 1963.

Spivak, Sidney, "Religious Attitudes of Physicians and Dissemination of Contraceptive Advice." Doctoral dissertation, Columbia University, 1960.

Stoller, B. J., H. Garfinkel, and A. C. Rosen, "Passing and the Maintenance of Sexual Identification in an Intersexed Patient," *A.M.A. Archives of General Psychiatry*, II (1960), 379–84.

Strauss, Anselm L., *Mirrors and Masks: The Search for Identity*. New York: The Free Press, 1959.

Sutton Smith, Brian, and John M. Roberts, "Game Involvement in Adults," *Journal of Social Psychology*, LX (1963), 15–30.